D1044902

JLBrower
London,
Autumn 1998

Rebirth of a Nation

Rebirth of a Nation

An Anatomy of Russia

John Lloyd

MICHAEL JOSEPH

LONDON

MICHAEL JOSEPH LTD
Published by the Penguin Group
27 Wrights Lane, London w8 5tz
Penguin Putnam Inc., 375 Hudson Street, New York, New York 10014, USA
Penguin Books Australia Ltd, Ringwood, Victoria, Australia
Penguin Books Canada Ltd, 10 Alcorn Avenue, Toronto, Ontario, Canada m4v 3b2
Penguin Books (NZ) Ltd, 182–190 Wairau Road, Auckland 10, New Zealand

Penguin Books Ltd, Registered Offices: Harmondsworth, Middlesex, England

First published in Great Britain 1998

Copyright © John Lloyd, 1998
3 5 7 9 10 8 6 4 2
All rights reserved.
Without limiting the rights under copyright
reserved above, no part of this publication may be
reproduced, stored in or introduced into a retrieval system,
or transmitted, in any form or by any means (electronic, mechanical,
photocopying, recording or otherwise) without the prior
written permission of both the copyright owner and
the above publisher of this book

Set in 11.75/14 pt Monotype Bembo
Typeset by Rowland Phototypesetting Ltd,
Bury St Edmunds, Suffolk
Printed in England by Clays Ltd, St Ives plc

A CIP catalogue record for this book is available from the British Library

ISBN 0 7181 3862 7

The moral right of the author has been asserted

for
Marcia Levy
Natasha Dmitrievna Starkova
and to the memory of Joan Adam Todd Skowronski

Contents

Acknowledgements ix
Introduction xiii

PART ONE: *Power*

1   '*Almost too Russian*'   1
2   '*The most important thing now is reform*'   18
3   '*This disastrous, vicious circle*'   34
4   '*What is the alternative?*'   51
5   '*Tsar Boris*'   71

PART TWO: *State*

6   '*The law as a tool of dominance*'   95
7   '*The Russian army is past reforming*'   111
8   '*A real underground empire*'   131
9   '*Eaten by corruption from top to bottom*'   142
10   '*They labour in vain that build it*'   157
11   '*You are the masters of the country*'   172
12   '*Chechnya is just an excuse*'   191

PART THREE: *Economy*

13   '*Releasing the human factor*'   205
14   '*The very edge of the precipice*'   212
15   '*Reforms, but not at the people's expense*'   231
16   '*The creation of a bourgeoisie*'   240
17   '*A creative period of transition*'   259
18   '*White Nights*'   270

CONTENTS

19 'Money'   282
20 'The most vigorous and progressive section'   296
21 'Who cares anyway?'   311

PART FOUR: *Near and Far*

22 'The Russian state will never be an empire'   329
23 'A state which only says yes'   352
24 'Do no harm'   369

PART FIVE: *Culture*

25 'An attempt to be optimistic which failed'   379
26 'The sweet aura of the forbidden'   387
27 'Is it a Russian playing?'   400
28 'Everything will be OK'   421
29 'The restoration of Russia – that's what art is for'   442

Notes on Sources   451
Index   459

Acknowledgements

Writing a book about the first years of the New Russia is to operate in a territory between journalism, political analysis and what used to be called sovietology. It is also to try to excerpt some six years of a ceaseless flow of events from what came before and what may come after it ended. Finally, it is to impose an order on that flow which it did not have: here, as in all of the countries thrown into a cauldron by the break-up of the Soviet Union, improvisation was the necessary order of the day, and the formal business of elections, law-making and inter-governmental agreements and disputes was, much more often than in the settled democracies of the West, a mask of manoeuvres which had little to do with the formalities.

Improvisation is a major – perhaps the major – theme of this book. None of the institutions which were set in place, or which were revived or reformed, were set on solid ground. They could not be. Some – like the military, the security services and the public service infrastructures – were taken over by the New Russian power and reform was attempted in conditions of ceaseless crisis. Some, like the parliament, the presidency, the regional and local governments and the constitution, which was supposed to hold these and other institutions in a stable relationship with each other, were designed on mainly Western models but did not, in the period covered by the book, succeed in developing such a relationship. Power remained in the Kremlin – though there was and is at least the potential for its slow diffusion through a society grappling with the possibilities and responsibilities of a democratic habit.

The book, like all such books, thus depends hugely on those who assisted me in trying to perceive the meaning of the contradictory movements in this turbulent society. My first debt – it is very large – is to Arkady Ostrovsky, a young critic and writer who worked with me so closely on part five of the book – Culture – that he is the joint author. His contribution did not end with that: he was a constant sounding board for much that I learned and thought about Russia, and remains one still. His family, one of the flowers of the Soviet scientific intelligentsia, were frequent hosts.

Of the many people in public life who gave me time, both as a correspondent for the *Financial Times* and as author of this book, I will pick out only those to whom I returned time and again – though, like any journalist, I trespassed a great deal on the time and patience of men and women whose lives were extraordinarily harried and who usually responded with patience, or at least with phlegm. Yegor Gaidar, acting prime minister in 1992, later deputy prime minister for the economy and now head of the Institute for the Study of the Economy in Transition, was unfailingly friendly and courteous, as was his chief aide, Vladimir Mau. Three early guides to the group of reformers who came to power in 1992 were Boris Fyodorov, deputy prime minister for finance 1993–4; Alexander Shokhin, who held a number of posts including deputy prime minister for the economy, 1993–4; Konstantin Kagolovsky, who was a minister, the representative for Russia on the IMF and then a senior banker from 1994; and Andrei Ilarionov, economic adviser to the prime minister 1993–4, then head of his own economic think tank.

Of the business people – the real New Russians – I owe most to Kakha Bendukidze, chairman of the Nipek Corporation, who frequently and with good nature pointed out my naïvety; and to Vladimir Gusinsky of Most, proprietor of the newspaper *Sevodnya* and of NTV.

In the rich field of Russian journalism, I benefited from the help of, among many others, Sasha Bekker, Mikhail Berger, Oleg Golembyovsky and Yevgeny Kiselyev.

There were many foreign advisers: I relied a great deal on Jeff Sachs, Stanley Fischer, Richard Layard, Anders Aslund, Jean Foglizzo and Thomas Wolfe of the International Monetary Fund, Ardy Stoujesdijk and Charles Blitzer of the World Bank, Roger Gale and Tony Doran of the International Finance Corporation. When researching this book, I visited the HQs of these organizations in Washington several times, and was given lengthy interviews by almost all of the many executives and economists working on Russia.

Arkady Ostrovsky and I spent the summer of 1995 seeing what seemed like nearly everyone in the world of Russian culture in

Moscow: our special thanks go to Anatoly Smelyansky and Inna Solovyeva.

I could not have worked at all without a series of networks of colleagues and friends. First, at the *Financial Times* office in Moscow, Quentin Peel, my predecessor as Moscow correspondent and now the *FT* foreign editor, Leyla Boulton and John Thornhill, colleagues with me in Moscow, Chrystia Freeland, my successor, Steve Levene, who covered Central Asia and the Caucasus and was wounded in Chechnya, dear Natasha Belova, the *FT* office manager, Nina Golovyatenko, Dmitri Volkov, Misha Kuyazev, Olga and Katya. Two editors at the *FT* – Sir Geoffrey Owen and Richard Lambert – were tremendously supportive, as were David Palmer, Juerk Martin and Robert Thomson. The *FT* was and remains a great institution, in which a journalism of care and detachment survived.

I learned a good deal from my colleagues in Moscow – among whom I would mention Peter Schulze of the Friedrich Ebert Stiftung, Jonathon Steele and David Hearst of the *Guardian*, John Kampfner and Alan Phelps of the *Telegraph*, Bruce Clarke then of *The Times* and now of the *FT*, Angus Roxburgh of the BBC, Michael Dobbs of the *Washington Post*, Michael Specter and Alexandra Stanley of the *New York Times* and Sergo Rossi of *24 Ore*. I was fortunate to know two outstanding UK ambassadors – Sir Roderick Braithwaite and Sir Brian Fall – who with Francis Richards, the senior minister, and their colleagues extended to me and to many others knowledge and hospitality.

Two institutions above all others provided temporary homes during the writing of this book. At Harvard, I owe a huge amount to Professor Graham Allison and Liz Sherwood of the project on Democratic Institutions, both of whom served in the Pentagon during the first Clinton term. Their colleagues at Harvard, especially Fiona Hill, were generous with time, information and friendship.

Immediately after my return to the UK, I was granted the status of Senior Associate Member – which I still have – at St Anthony's College, in Oxford. Lord Ralph Dahrendorf was warden then; he and his wife Ellen – herself deeply attached to Russia – were welcoming. Professor Archie Brown sponsored my membership, and provided – with Dr Alex Pravda, Dr Harry Shukman and others – constant warm support and encouragement.

Finally, I had and retain a connection with the Institute of East West

Studies in New York. Founded and directed by John Mroz, the IEWS is a powerhouse of thought and action in Central and Eastern Europe, which has done much to show me what can be done with dedication to the task of deepening democratic structures.

At Michael Joseph, Susan Watt, the editorial director, was a great supporter from the inception of the project, which my agent, Anne McDermid, then of Curis Brown, proposed.

I had many Russian friends. I will pick out two – Lena Naumirovskaya and Yury Senokossov – as special. Lena, with her husband Yury's help, started the Moscow School of Political Studies, which remains a medium for the open and passionate discussion of the wrenching changes in their country. They had many vicissitudes – a minor one of which was my inflicting my Russian on them in long nights of talk. They gave what Russia is rich in – the gift of friendship which was demanding, frank and engaged.

Introduction

Russia is free, as freedom is now reckoned in the world.

It has all the formal features of a democratic state, from a constitution to local council elections. For the first sustained period in its history, it has no overarching ideology which sustains its rulers in office without reference to the popular will, periodically expressed in elections. For the past five years, it has been struggling to become what its reformers' ambitions were to make it: a 'normal' country.

It is worth beginning a book on its first years with such statements of fact, for they have been rendered – at times – apparently meaningless or hollow by the shocks from which the society still suffers. Russians have been forced, again and again in the nineties, the decade of their freedom, to count its price. They continue to cleave to it, and to vote for its continuation – if often ambiguously. But much of what follows is about the various prices that they have had to pay, and are paying yet.

Becoming 'normal' was conceived as constructing a civil society – by which was meant both introducing the institutions of a democratic order, and allowing citizens to come to their own settlements and decisions on their lives, under a rule of more or less objective law. The long decades of the effort to declare a fully socialist society continuously overrode what might have been people's plans for their own lives: freedom from communism was seen as an end to such a project, and the beginning of true private lives lived within a society where relations were uncoerced.

But the freedom which Russians – and others – received when the Soviet Union and the Communist Party collapsed at the end of 1991 was only a necessary, and not a sufficient, condition for the realization of the reformers' ideal. Liberation from communism had to be followed by a series of parallel and terribly hard processes of constructing the elements of a functioning and free state.

This is what should have happened in the first years of Russia, which were presided over by Boris Yeltsin, Russia's first elected president. Some of it *did* happen. But much which could have been achieved, or at least attempted, was not. It has not been a wasted period; but it has been a period in which the dangers within Russia, and the dangers Russia poses to the world, have not been cancelled. It continues to be a turbulent area of great uncertainty, where decisions are often made arbitrarily and mysteriously or not made at all; where corruption explains as much as the workings of democratic rule; where the decay of the Soviet-era institutions still pollutes the atmosphere, hanging like a sickly vapour over the task of construction.

It was, at the end of the Yeltsin period, a country still in waiting – for itself. This book is about the efforts of its first new élites to refound Russia on a transformed basis – efforts which were often herculean and courageous, but which did not and could not succeed in the time limits they set themselves. The transformations set in train were at times halted, always disputed, sometimes partially reversed.

The restructuring of the former communist Central European economies of the Czech Republic, Hungary and Poland was, by the second half of the mid-nineties, clearly a success: growth rates were rising strongly, and all the main political forces had broadly agreed that markets and democracy were the cornerstones of the state. Russia was not like that: the constituencies in society for whom radical change was an outrage were too strong to allow reform to be driven through, and attain its own, self-sustaining dynamic. A stasis had settled over the political arena: reaction could not win, reform could not continue. Thus policy zigzagged this way and that: a reform to make more liberal the workings of the financial markets, for example, would be followed by a thunderous denunciation of the West and a threat to rearm.

The institutions of a democratic polity were, with difficulty and through bloodshed, erected. There is a constitution; a parliament with an upper and lower house; regional and local assemblies; a formally independent judiciary with a hierarchy of courts; media with freedom constitutionally guaranteed. But they are afflicted with two problems.

First, the constitution is strongly presidential. In purely formal terms, it is not so much more so than either the US or the French systems (it was modelled on the latter in particular), but the hyper-centralist traditions of the country, and the historical irrelevance and very brief existence of elected assemblies, mean that the centuries-old power of the centre has been reaffirmed, and countervailing powers given narrow bases from which to develop their authority.

Second, the informal networks of politics – the way the political system actually works – remains highly personalized and opaque. In any system, the formal rules are filled out, and to a degree circumvented, by a thick web of informal behaviour: but when the informal behaviour goes further than commonsense circumvention and subverts the formal rules by consistently unconstitutional, illegal and corrupt acts, these rules become emptied of authority for all.

This is what is happening in Russia. The last year and a half of Boris Yeltsin's first term of office – to June 1996 – was a period in which the ailing president was sustained by a constant and transparent deceit that he was fully able to govern, while the mechanisms which could replace him constitutionally by an elected figure who could govern were blocked. In these circumstances, cabal politics prevail – especially after Yeltsin, artificially reinvigorated through drugs, contested and won the 1996 presidential election. The strategic reforms which the country required, especially in its internal political arrangements, in the restructuring of industry and in the direction of its foreign policy, were not taken. The sustaining of a power which had no vitality meant constant backstairs dealing with the powerful figures in finance and the regions. The privileges and concessions they received then came to constitute the real, but hidden, constitution of the country, one in which the ordinary citizen has little share. Yeltsin submitted to long-delayed heart surgery after his re-election and – in the most astonishing of his many acts of political survival – lived on to resume a little of his old élan. But the country remained shorn of vigorous leadership, run by a liberally inclined government with a narrow base, shrinking finances, a reputation for massive corruption of some of its leading members and afflicted with the galloping decay of the armed forces, health and social provision and its educational and cultural capital.

The very large achievement in economic terms has been the maintenance of a relatively tight monetary policy from 1994 onwards – a policy which brought inflation down from over 30 per cent a month to as low as 1 per cent in some months in 1996–97. The International

Monetary Fund signed a three-year agreement with Russia worth $10.3 billion in March 1996 – thoughtfully placed a little before the presidential elections – and claimed that the observance of the basic monetary parameters by the Central Bank and the Finance Ministry was good.

But it was at a huge price, which is increasingly visible and increasingly worrisome to the IMF and the main Western – Group of Seven – governments which seek to guide Russia's transition. Since tax collection consistently falls below targets – by as much as 20 per cent – deep cuts in the already exiguous budgets must be made to maintain monetary discipline. In May 1997, the prime minister, Victor Chernomyrdin, came before a hostile parliament (or Duma) to beg it to approve Rbs108,000 (nearly £12 billion) of cuts in expenditure because tax revenues had fallen short by one-third.

The most pervasive manifestation of this is unpaid salaries, the backlog of which grew rapidly in 1996–97; less obvious, but more serious in the long run, is the slashing of investment in education, health, transport and other infrastructure. With the partial exceptions of Moscow and St Petersburg, the services and health and supply systems of the cities and towns of Russia are becoming dangerously overstretched. Like any systems, these require maintenance – and it is maintenance budgets which are being slashed. Sooner or later, major accidents or epidemics will happen; already, all but forgotten diseases have reappeared. On the same day – 22 May – on which Chernomyrdin asked for the £12 billion cuts, a report was aired on the BBC showing mental patients at a hospital north of Moscow dying of starvation.

While public infrastructure is not being renewed, private enterprise is not being restructured. The placing of the major part of Russian industry and services in private hands, effected at breakneck speed from 1992 onwards, has been represented as a triumph of reform: and indeed, there was no available alternative but to do so, since the state could not support the largely loss-making enterprises which emerged from the Soviet period. But the banks and finance houses which were the major beneficiaries of privatization – especially of the most valuable assets – have barely begun the colossal job of restructuring. They have become accustomed to making short-term profits from small loans on minor – often trading – projects; their shares in the large enterprises, even where these shares are themselves large, are largely dormant, as the new owners baulk at the height of the obstacles they would have to overcome to turn the companies into profit-making, competitive, modern enterprises.

We shall see why later in the book. The enterprises are not only – too often – monstrously inefficient, they are also deeply hostile to the financial yardsticks which the banks seek to apply. Their managers, usually co-owners, have been trained to produce – not to make a return to shareholders, or to win customers, or to compete, or to sack workers. The local and regional authorities tend to make common cause with the managers against the representatives of Moscow capital – as do workers who cling to companies which provide flats, health care, social services and holidays as well as wages (which they frequently do *not* provide). Restructuring a Russian company has no model in the business school textbooks. The methods must be invented; the would-be inventors, understandably, quail before a job which would be seen as a declaration of war on communities.

Many, Russians and foreigners, who have dedicated large energies to the economic transformation of Russia in its first years, argue that it will be the miracle growth economy of the last years of the millennium, or at the latest the first years of the next. It should be. It has a large and relatively well-educated population, avid to consume more; an unparalleled wealth of natural resources; an unfunded, basic but still very extensive transport infrastructure; and an exceptionally tough and often creative entrepreneurial class, now growing in sophistication and technical skill very rapidly. These elements should and very possibly will combine to force the 'breakthrough' to an economic surge which will run through the enormous country and begin to bring to large numbers of its citizens something of the wealth they have glimpsed, but not yet tasted.

But there is nothing inevitable about it. The lessons of Russia's first years include the harsh realization that the absence of communist economics is not enough, that capitalist economics requires institution-building and institutional networks, the lack of which enmires development in uncompleted transformation. In this state, the market is anathematized for present failure while socialism is idealized for past security. This in turn freezes the political forces into immobility – unable either to resurrect a functioning command economics, which they realize is impossible, or to clear the tubes of the detritus which impedes market operations, which they know will be harsh for years to come.

The successful resistance to grand-scale restructuring might have pointed to a society which has produced autonomous citizens and workers groups, which, even if obstructing necessary change, still testify to a developing civil sense, and a working and a professional class with traditions and vigour. But it does not. The resistance to change, even if popular, is generally mounted not by self-created and self-led trade unions or citizens groups, but by 'masses' led by, or allegedly represented by, enterprise directors, politicians opposed to reform because they would suffer from it. Years after a 'revolution' which was to break the power of Party and state bosses, the same bosses, in different or in the same guise, continue to manipulate their workers or their constituents with promises of unsustainable better times so that they will oppose change which has a chance of saving something from a ruin.

Organizations and societies have been created for the Soviet people, not by them: the lack of civil expertise and confidence is a deep one of long duration, and the first years of Russia actually saw a drop in the levels of public participation which marked the later Gorbachev years. Then, institutions like Memorial were started to exhume the buried histories of, and pay belated honour to, the victims of the camps and the purges; hundreds of democratic political clubs were begun; new organizations of artists of various kinds were formed. Many of these have since withered, while the pastimes organized by the state, or more often by the enterprises, for sporting and leisure pursuits, which millions enjoyed, have suffered widespread closures for lack of funds or custom. Foreign travel, on the other hand, has risen hugely, and Russian has joined the babel of foreign tongues in the tourist centres of the world.

The largest change which affected Russian society through the nineties was an adaptation to new ways of getting by. Bit by bit, it was made plain to people that the state or the enterprise could not provide for a decent living standard – but that their own efforts could supplement the miserable wages they received. This was patchy and, like so much in the new Russia, desperately unequal. Teachers, on starvation wages or none at all, gave private lessons; car owners turned their cars into taxis; people with flats in Moscow, St Petersburg or other desirable centres rented them out, and squeezed in with relatives; millions obtained private plots of land, and grew vegetables and potatoes; thousands flew to and fro from such low-cost markets as Turkey or India with goods for resale on the streets and markets of the cities. Workers who were paid in kind by their enterprises became, perforce, merchants for the products they made. Military officers turned their hands to freelance car mechanics.

The secure indolence of much of Soviet life gave way – for those who had the opportunities and the energy – to a fragmented worklife made up of what people could get. Many in previously high-status jobs felt the keen humiliation of doing a service job which they would have previously scorned; but the process was one of a very rough sorting-out of what was, and what was not, marketable – a process the rougher for being centuries overdue. The insecurity and pressure it caused was said to be a large component of the disastrously low average mortality age for men: 57–58 in the mid-nineties. The women, the drudges of Soviet society, seemed to bear it better, and lasted, on average, to their early seventies.

For all Soviet citizens, the experience of the nineties has been one of national humiliation. At the global level, Russia shrank from being the core of a Soviet empire and hegemonic power in East-Central Europe with dependencies throughout the world, to being at best a regional power whose authority was constantly an issue with its neighbours and decisively rejected by many – like the former Soviet Baltic states and, to a less emphatic degree, Ukraine. The Soviet Union's pretensions may have been mocked by its more internationally aware citizens in the past, but its power, its claimed (and conceded) co-equality with the US, its global reach, the nervous respect it commanded and the awesomeness of the military force it was assumed that it could deploy really were the source of pride for all but the most dissident or cynical.

All of this is gone (though not forgotten). Russia plays only relatively minor roles in any theatre of international diplomacy outside of the Commonwealth of Independent States, which is what the Soviet states, minus the Baltics, have become, and none at all in many where it had been active or even decisive before. It has very largely withdrawn from Latin America, Africa and South-east Asia. It retains some influence in the Middle East – but it is as an arms or nuclear energy supplier to those states which cannot get either from the West, activities which earn it the suspicion of those Western countries on whose financial and other aid it relies. It plays a part – through the provision of troops – in the Bosnian peace-keeping operations, but under US command; its diplomacy was not decisive.

The early years of independence were marked with an exaggeratedly pro-Western – especially pro-American – posture which brought it severe disappointment. Though some of its inflated expectations were encouraged irresponsibly by Western politicians bidding for the mantle of the saviour of Russia, the inflation was largely done by Russian politicians and the lack of reality was certainly a Russian phenomenon. The disappointment and bitterness were as exaggerated as the early idealism: by the latter half of the nineties, the plans of Nato to expand to take in the Central European, former communist, states were being represented by centrist and former liberal officials and policy-makers as tantamount to a re-declaration of the Cold War.

But Nato expansion – unwise though the project was in itself – was a proxy for an unresolved debate within Russia. The communist and nationalist forces, who dominated the legislature from the mid-nineties, saw Nato simply as a hostile force which had won the Cold War and was taking advantage of Russian weakness to move closer to its frontiers. They thus saw only one possible reaction: to re-form what kind of opposing alliance Russia could muster. They were not so foolish as to believe it could restore the Warsaw Pact, but they did think it could draw the former Soviet states about it, supplemented by the radical Arabian countries of Iraq, Libya and Syria, with former allies such as Cuba and those African, Latin American and South-east Asian countries doing badly out of globalization. The communist-nationalists were also often 'Eurasians', that is, they believed that Russia was only partly a European power. That which made it distinctively a separate civiliz-ation was its vast bulk hunched over Central Asia and out into the Far East.

This strategy, so disastrous for Russia's long-term interests, neverthe-less commanded substantial support in the foreign policy community and in the political class – if only because they thought, or told the West they thought, that they would be forced to bow to communist-nationalist pressure. Victor Chernomyrdin, the Russian prime minister, said in February 1997 that Nato expansion would, all but automatically, cause a rearming of Russia. 'The military production facilities are there, in mint condition, ready, waiting. This is how the unemployment problem will be solved. The tanks and the planes will roll out again. Do we need this?'

Clearly not – it would further reduce a largely bankrupt country. Russia's future, on any rational calculation, lies in a close relationship with Europe, not in a recoil from it. But the habit of greatness, and the intolerability of a further slight to greatness, was too deeply ingrained to be challenged – even by a politician like Chernomyrdin, who had bought in to much of the Western agenda. The country, he claimed, was at the limit of the compromises it could make with an expansionist West. Not only had it failed to find a role, it had failed to find a place large enough for its self-image (while being modest enough for its resources). The Soviet legacy was nowhere as lasting and as tenacious as here.

That legacy is a terrible one; it lies behind – and not far behind – all of the events described in this book, the constant companion of the efforts of all the reformers to change their country. Nothing has become so clear in the years since the collapse of the USSR as the revelation that Russia's past constrains and cramps the efforts of those who struggle to renew its present and build its future. A revelation? Yes, it seemed, to those who assumed the leadership of the state, since their pronouncements both before and after the collapse spoke of a leap out of totalitarianism into modern, democratic, liberal-capitalist statehood. But they both exaggerated the nature of late Soviet rule – Gorbachev was no totalitarian – and grossly overestimated the ability of Russian (or any) society to make a great leap forward, unweighted by the past. The malignity of that past, and the grip it exercises, is causing a new book to be written on the modernization of states.

Soviet rule was itself the inheritor of tsarist, absolutist traditions which the early Bolsheviks also believed could be wholly transcended and which the man who was the highest expression of their essential murderous utopianism – Joseph Stalin – selectively renewed and hugely strengthened. Stalin was no aberration, he was of a piece with his party. Nikolai Berdyayev, the religious philosopher, said of the 1917 revolution that the past was repeating itself, only behind masks; and while the remark missed the revolutionary elements of the Bolsheviks' theory and practice (their most horrifying part, as it would turn out), it did catch their complete lack of attachment to any kind of reform which would widen popular power and choice.

Communism, which was forged into an instrument of national and then of world domination in Russia, was the most complete system for moulding and remoulding states, institutions and individuals the world has seen. Communism posed an end – a classless, strife-free society of plenty and ease – and insisted that the means was a communist party practically free, at least in the initial, revolutionary period, of all restraint to pursue that end. In the seven Soviet decades, the rule of the Communist Party was never allowed to be questioned. Only its leaders could say what its 'mistakes' had been, and they said so largely to increase their own power to make their own mistakes. Its monopoly on political life was total. In economic life the Party strove with a very large degree of success to enforce the rules of state production, distribution and exchange. In social life it entered, during Stalin's time, into the most intimate relations of the family and of individuals in a way which has no parallel elsewhere in Europe in the twentieth century.

One figure above all others haunted this uniquely diabolic period: it is that of Pavel Morozov. The boy who informed on his father for assisting 'kulaks', or rich peasants, during the period (early thirties) when *kolkhozes* (collective farms) were being imposed on the protesting peasantry was the archetypical Stalinist hero and icon. The poet Valentin Borovin, one of the many hacks of the thirties, put this verse in the young Morozov's mouth:

> . . . as a Pioneer, I proclaim:
> My father is a traitor to October.
> So that all the kulak threats
> Never cause us to fear,
> I demand strict justice for my father,
> For the traitor of the kolkhoz.

Morozov became – in the myth which was created on the basis of what was in reality a miserable peasant family revenge tragedy – a figure who defined a critical moment of class struggle. He had transferred his primary loyalty from the family to the state. He had brought his father to judgement for what in other contexts would have been seen as acts of common humanity. Morozov was the hero for Pioneers until the eighties. His statue, placed in a central Moscow park, was pulled down in August 1991 in the wake of the unsuccessful coup, at the same time as the statue of the first Soviet secret police chief Felix Dzerzhinsky was winched off its pedestal outside of the KGB's Lubyanka headquarters.

The lesson Pavel Morozov taught was that the Party and the state were higher on the moral scale than families. This was driven deep into the Soviet psyche. It failed to destroy family life, but it rendered a morality based on family loyalty difficult to sustain except in private, even furtively.

After Stalin, the state's ambitions to remould the individual and his or her affiliations shrank: both Party and state retreated to hold a ring outside of which a private life was possible. All social relations beyond the family circle had to conform loosely to Party-led structures, organizations and rules, but these could be and were subtly subverted, to bring them down to closer to the scale of human vices and virtues. The legacy, however, of an order which strove to create a new man while destroying or compromising the old meant that the transition from a rural to an urban society was accompanied by the deliberate and energetic inculcation of suspicion, fear and the lesson that self-betterment came through betrayal.

The fusion of the Party and the state which characterized later Soviet society transmuted itself into a clannish structure. All of work and social life fell into formal and informal groupings which were commanded to relate vertically, up towards the apex. Horizontal relationships were both proscribed and shunned. The 'us' and 'them' were absolute categories in the Soviet system, and remained so afterwards. The struggle for resources and preferment was fought out between the various institutions competing for central favour. Thus the enterprises, the branches of the military, the regional and ethnic-national authorities, the cultural and social institutions, the Party organizations all vied with each other pitilessly for the premium share. It left a society in which the only possible message of social life was that it was a game with a loser and a winner – and that the winner took all, and held the losers at bay.

Hence the arrogance and ruthlessness of the New Russian rich, who emerged in the first half of the nineties once the struggle for control of Soviet resources got fully under way. Foreigners from societies which had been capitalist for centuries were horrified and puzzled by the behaviour, since they had been socialized into a system in which wealth and power had had its no–holds–barred days and had been checked and balanced. Not so in Russia: the Soviet lesson was to grab and hold; the post-Soviet experience was that flaunting wealth could be done with impunity, as long as you bought or created protection from behind which to do so.

The economy which these new rich milked so well in the first years had worked in a way unlike any other. It was tightly centralized: the Leninist model of the economy had been a giant factory and, in so far as such a thing was possible, it was so organized. Enterprise above the most trivial level was forbidden; even as late as Gorbachev's period, cold frames in which peasants were growing cucumbers for the market were smashed and the produce destroyed. The state, as far as possible, monopolized production, trade, finance, transport. Innovation, the lifeblood of late-twentieth-century capitalism, was cumbersome, suspected, contested through a myriad of committees and, where adopted, increasingly imitative. The early twentieth-century model of a factory, organized like Henry Ford's basic model plant, was by the eighties an industrial mastodon. That defined the entire Soviet economy.

The façade of Soviet society was egalitarian; the inequalities were hidden. The ideology's need to proclaim the triumph of socialism meant that the privileges accorded to Party workers, or KGB operatives, or government officials were enclosed behind high walls and officially denied, or brusquely justified as being the necessities of tireless labour.

Yet at the same time, it *was* a society much more equal than others by conventional standards. The differences that mattered were between communal apartments and one-room flats, or one-room flats and two-room flats. Those who had more than that were few. Only power could legitimize access to luxury goods – such as good food and clothes, reasonable medical services, large flats and country *dachas*, foreign trips and relatively good cars. Wealth without power, or the protection of power, did not exist, because private property without the sanction of power did not exist.

The ethic was egalitarian. Most leaders of the Communist Party had poor, or very poor, youths. Lenin was the only leader of the Communist Party who was not the son of a worker or a peasant. The public presentation of the toils and troubles of their childhood were at least as important as a log cabin for a US president: in both cases, it sanctified a national ideology. But in the Soviet case, it was the triumph not just of an individual (which was the covert message) but of a class.

Emerging into an era when rewards could officially be allowed to be disproportionate, Russian society became the field for a long and continuing struggle. The struggle is between, on the one hand, an egalitarianism which was as much a result of pre-communist communal village life as it was the socialist ideology which had sanctioned and enforced it, and which is still clung to or appealed to by millions, and on the other, a Darwinian hierarchy in which the new rich and powerful are contemptuous, overtly and covertly, of those who fail to see how the world is changing, and cannot even adapt, let alone master it.

Civil society could hardly exist under Stalinism: the society was too fragmented, ground into atoms by the weight of terror. But it did emerge after the terror period: in a recognition of individual and mass suffering in the three decades of Stalinism; in the celebration by a new generation of writers and artists of spontaneous – if unthreatening – emotion; in the realization that a contract of sorts was possible between the Party and the people, under which the first would not return to Stalinist extremes and the second would observe the rituals demanded of them by the Party.

It was of course not really civil, since the authorities always held the reins of any activity and could and did jerk them in. But it meant that dissident artists could paint and write and compose – and that the natural scientists, secure in their indispensability to the state, could use their institutes to stage readings or exhibitions of those denied a state-sponsored venue. It meant that there existed two levels of intellectual and creative people – those who from idealism or from ambition or both worked well within the system, and maintained it; and those who paid the minimum dues necessary to receive their wages and be left alone. It meant that some power passed to workers, since they could take a variety of actions short of the forbidden strikes which would force extra payments, or more leisure, or both – activities which, coupled with the generally low, ill-trained and increasingly technically backward level of Soviet management, meant that productivity fell to disastrously low levels and the growth of the gross national product was near to negative before Gorbachev came on the scene.

Civil society, in the distorted form in which it existed, had developed habits and practices which were at least implicitly hostile to the system.

It gave rise to a state of mind in the intelligentsia which was deeply cynical about the Party and state authorities, deeply utopian about the West and the possibilities for change based on Western practice.

The irony was that the last Soviet ruler was as close to an idealist as the system could produce, and much *more* of an idealist than the system could, in the end, bear. Mikhail Gorbachev was a leader who embodied and tried to contain impossible contradictions: one who embarked on the impossible transformation of one system into another while trying to ensure that each coexisted with the other. He wanted to make a country democratic in habits and authoritarian in form; an economy which was a market one in its operations but with socialist outcomes; a society civil in its core but guided by the Party in all of its important moments.

A convinced Marxist-Leninist – he kept Lenin on his desk, and constantly referred to him, seeking canonical backing for his 'new thinking' – he destroyed the Communist Party by removing its ideological props. He thought that the preservation of the Soviet Union was a 'sacred task', and made sure it could not survive, since he allowed the resurgent nationalist forces in the Soviet republics to gather strength and to hollow out the institutions of Soviet and Party rule.

Almost everyone around him – contemporaries, aides, commentators, enemies – agreed that he did not know what he was doing. The commentator Andranik Migranyan put it well when he said: 'He could never decide whether to be Luther, or the Pope'; that is, he was unable to make either a coherent defence of the system or a coherent attack on it, often claiming to be doing one while actually doing the other.

He had taken on four vast tasks, which no one could have achieved in their entirety. These were: to effect fundamental change in Soviet foreign policy orientation; sweeping economic reform; political liberalization and *glasnost*, or openness; and the renewal of relations between the centre and the republics and localities. He had poor advice about all of these, with the partial exception of foreign policy, and his own ideas were – compared to the scale of the tasks – primitive.

But, most importantly, he had never seemed to grasp – as previous general secretaries most assuredly had – that once he started to prise away such foundation stones of his rule as the threat of the use of terror, the untouchability of the Party, the iron unity of the Union, he could do nothing to stop the resulting avalanche once it had been allowed to gather momentum. He did not seem conscious that, in deliberately encouraging autonomous action, free expression and initiative from below, he was tilting not just at the communist legacy but at the Russian one. Gorbachev was truly heroic – and like many heroes, no great shakes as a thinker.

Successful rulers can be inconsistent; Gorbachev's predecessors certainly were. One of them, the Empress Catherine, was another bold reformer who sincerely sought to inculcate a civic spirit in Russia, yet also believed – and acted on the belief – that Russia had to be governed as an autocracy. But hers was an age of imperial autocrats, in which a tilt to French-inspired radicalism could be overlooked as an act of eccentricity. Gorbachev lived in an age of democratic nation-states. Catherine could rely on the temper of the times to save her from democratic excess; Gorbachev lived in a time when the measured decompression of an authoritarian empire was seen, inside and outside of it, as an evasion of fundamental reform.

Yet he never seriously prepared for or tried a phased reform, in part because he fell in too much with a Western-imposed rhythm of rapid change. Alexander Yakovlev, Gorbachev's longtime and most consistently liberal aide, told me once in an interview that he believed that Western politicians and journalists 'spoiled him' by hooking him on the praise and assistance of the West – his most enthusiastic and most faithful constituency.

Raised in Soviet certainties, his 'new thinking' proved to be mostly a mish-mash of Western liberalism bolted on to Soviet realities. To read his *Perestroika*, written during a vacation in 1987, is to enter a miasma of contradictions. For example, the Soviet Union is represented as having irrevocably made its 'socialist choice', at the same time as Gorbachev appeals for criticism and reappraisal to be radical. At the very apex of a system moulded by totalitarian power and never fundamentally changed, Gorbachev proclaimed his belief in the coming of a humanistic socialism.

The chaos in society, the catastrophic collapse of state finances and the steady retreat of the Soviet Union from nearly all of its positions of advantage in the world finally stirred a group of conspirators to act against him. The immediate cause of the coup of August 1991 was the imminent signing of a treaty between Gorbachev as Soviet president and the heads of most of the Soviet republics. The treaty was allegedly designed to usher in a loose confederation of states; in fact, the powers of the centre and of the states were so ill-defined, especially in the critical issue of taxation that, as the putschists accurately observed, it was less of a solution to the vexed problem of the Union as an invitation to its further dissolution.

The members of this group were men close to Gorbachev – including the head of the KGB, Vladimir Kryuchkov, the defence minister, Dmitri Yazov and the prime minister, Valentin Pavlov – whom he had placed in their posts to serve his constantly changing will. They were, as they almost certainly knew from their own intelligence services, under threat of dismissal under the terms of a secret agreement Gorbachev had made with the presidents of Russia and Kazakhstan – Boris Yeltsin and Nursultan Nazarbayev – during the negotiations on the treaty. The balancing act between stability of the system and change which threatened it, the brilliance of which had dazzled the world for six years, had ceased to work.

Gorbachev was right to see that the Soviet Union could not continue as it had been, but could find no new foundation on which to retain its existence in any coherent reform. The putschists were right to see that his actions were destroying the Union, but had neither the will nor the support to haul it back into the structures which had once maintained it. 'Our multinational people has for centuries lived filled with pride for their homeland, and we were never ashamed of our [Soviet] patriotic feelings,' they proclaimed in the appeal they promulgated on the first day of the coup, on 19 August. That was, in fact, a reflection of the feelings of millions of men and women – not just Russians – throughout the Soviet Union, as the subsequent years were to show. But it was not the tide of the times, which flowed with the democrats in Russia and the nationalists in the republics, then in ecstatic alliance. It was too hollow to provide the requisite spine-stiffening for the conspirators who – in spite of the urging of Kryuchkov and of some senior officers who supported them – could not will the violent means to suppress the opposition to their actions which had gathered round Boris Yeltsin and his supporters in their citadel of the White House, the Russian parliament.

The coup collapsed in two days. It did something which the putschists may or may not have meant to do – they were unclear on everything

– it destroyed Gorbachev. But the beneficiaries were not the putschists, who were jailed for short periods, but Boris Yeltsin and the leaderships of the Soviet republics, who found themselves in one bound free, whether they had wished or prepared for freedom or not. Gorbachev, humiliated by Yeltsin at a session of the Russian Supreme Soviet on his return, struggled to reassert some rags of authority, with no hope of success.

Thus Boris Yeltsin inherited the unchallenged leadership of Russia. He represented this as a triumph – a triumph of the forces of democracy and freedom over a crumbling authoritarianism. He, and the democrats who supported him, had seen the Soviet Union and its system as *the* problem, the removal of which made everything possible. But, as the Soviet flag came down over the Kremlin on 25 December 1991 and Gorbachev made his last, dignified speech as Soviet president, the revolution caused by the unleashing of popular expectation and power was not over. It had merely emerged from infancy.

PART ONE

Power

'It [communism] had feelings and gestures, but remained empty and Godless within . . . for in the end the era turned its coat and betrayed its religious spirit, and it has paid dearly for its rationalist heritage, swearing allegiance to it only because it failed to understand itself. Rationalist scepticism has been eating away at Christianity for two centuries now. Eating away, without destroying it. But communist theory, its own creation, it will destroy within a few decades.'

Milan Kundera, *The Joke*, 1965

CHAPTER ONE

'Almost too Russian'

Boris Yeltsin came to power in 1991, a vigorous, extrovert, handsome man, exuding a charisma and a taste for the populist gesture: these had been the qualities assisting his ascent to power through the unfamiliar – to Russia – route of a popular vote. By the end of his first term in office in 1996 he had been reduced to occasional and brief set-piece appearances, walking slowly and stiffly, his face pallid, his hands wrinkled and trembling. The presser of flesh and stump orator, who had loved the touch and the feel of the crowd, ended his rule as immured from the people as Mikhail Gorbachev, whom he had despised for being so. His recovery in the second part of 1996 was extraordinary but partial; he never again dominated by his presence, though he continued to do so by the fact of his occupation of the Kremlin, by the continued loyalty of the security forces and the support of the West.

The leader who came to office with a florid apology that three young men had died in his parliament's defence (which was not his fault) closed his first term lying – through his aides – about the deaths of thousands in the republic of Chechnya, the invasion of which he had ordered. The reformer who promised the market would bring wealth saw that brought to only a few – many of whom were rich through his patronage. The Westernizing democrat became a grudging, resentful autocrat, surrounded by a court.

He can appear a tragic figure within a comic or melodramatic exterior; but he was also a deeply manipulative politician who drew deeply on the black arts he had learned as a regional first secretary – while professing the aspect of a bluff, even simple man from the Russian provinces. He captured the 'democrats', and held most of them with him through all of an office in which the violations of constitutionality and the broadest winking (at the least) at criminality were frequent.

He professed himself the saviour of the new business class, and held

3

the support of many of *them* because they had nowhere else to go, even as his governments extorted tax from those it could make pay. He made himself the 'candidate' of the main foreign powers, who stuck with him through his volatilities and disappearances and swings of policy both because they feared something worse, and because they were quickly drawn in too far to shift easily to another candidate. Though his sense of when to act and how far he could go was blunted over the years, it was for most of his political career a very finely tuned instrument indeed.

A measure of his success was that, after five years in which the economy crashed, crime soared, he had appeared visibly drunk while representing his country abroad and finally ceased actively to govern at all, he won re-election to the presidency. The quality of his competitors, the subservience of the media, the support of the richest businessmen and the traditional obeisance to power all helped. But he himself had been decisive in ensuring that the power around him was capable of resisting even his own inactivity and unpopularity. Mikhail Gorbachev was a living, and resentful, testament to what happens when that is not ensured.

A large, strong and courageous character, he nevertheless created nothing which might be called Yeltsin-ism. He came to power as a liberal, seeming to accept the need to build the institutions of democracy and of the market. His closest aide in the ascent to power and first year of exercising it, Gennady Burbulis, a former lecturer in Marxism-Leninism in Sverdlovsk turned extreme neo-liberal, drafted or vetted the key speeches. Yet his executive style was patched together from crony-ism, an assumption that his authority was supreme and a preference for personal deals over the observance of rules.

Famously at his best when under attack or pressure, as famously slack when more routine duties of ruling were called for, he brushed against great ideologies rather than embracing any. His initial professions of market and political liberalism were undercut by his later practice – though he never wholly abandoned these beliefs, and kept about him to the end aides from the democratic or liberal camp (who themselves changed under the pressure of government into pragmatic men of power). His nationalism could often seem no more than a guarding of his flanks against those more extreme than he – yet he learned something of the need to project an image of Russian greatness, and after his successful squashing of the parliamentary revolt against his authority had more strongly nationalist themes injected into his rhetoric. His religious observance was self-confessedly an affair of state rather than of the heart or mind, but he appeared to have too much respect for it to use it as a personal prop – unlike such ambitious figures about him as General Alexander Rutskoi, his first and only vice-president, or Yuri Luzhkov, the mayor of Moscow.

At the end of his first term, Russia's transformations were at best incomplete. For this he was criticized from every quarter – because he appeared to occupy, then desert, every quarter. Yet in his defence must be entered this very large consideration: that he governed a country which had embarked on a series of vast changes, and he governed it without the aid of an autocratic or totalitarian rationale, and he never once proposed that one be exhumed to support his régime.

The very fact of keeping power, and keeping it for a government which remained formally wedded to the ideals which motivated Yeltsin's run for the presidency, was a large achievement. It must always be a touchstone when considering Yeltsin's career: he was frequently very bad, but the possibility of someone worse was never simply an invention to keep him in office, or to retain Western support.

He spanned Russian politics, shamelessly stealing clothes from opponents when they seemed to be attractive to the electorate. He cobbled together his successive cabinets from a galaxy of radicals and former nomenclaturists, who represented quite inimical traditions and styles, but it answered the need to broaden their base from one dominated in the beginning by radical liberals, and it also allowed him to shunt his senior officials round continually, allowing none of them the reflection that they were indispensable.

He damaged economic reform by making (and keeping) promises to those who screamed loudest and nearest to him for continued state support or privileges; yet at the same time he was its backstop, and could usually be prevailed upon by visiting Western statesmen, or the heads of the international financial institutions, to continue on the path they thought would bring his country to prosperity, in the end. He never formed a presidential party to sustain him, or be sustained by him. It meant that there was never, in his period in office, a real challenge to the still formidable organization of the Communist Party, though it also meant he was above politics, free to switch about dizzily across an ideological spectrum which was itself in a constant flux. He did not, after the collapse of the Union and the Communist Party, move rapidly to set in place constitutional and parliamentary institutions which, coupled with fresh elections for the parliament, might have filled some of the gulf left by the disappearance of these former pillars of the Soviet state. Yet it meant that, when confrontation came with the parliament in 1993, he could argue that it was an illegitimate body.

Boris Yeltsin was governing in a space devoid of the criteria on which definite judgements could be made: he had to make it up as he went along, as any ruler of Russia would have had to do. It was as likely or unlikely that a chaotic and arbitrary governing style would win through to stated goals as a defined, costed programme to which he rigorously adhered – if such a thing would have been possible. It was not – nor could it be – that he was a one-eyed king in a country of the blind; rather it was a country in which people of tunnel vision were engaged in a thousand differing stratagems of survival, enrichment and enlargement of power. Short of the iron fist – a strategy which he never seemed to seriously consider outside of Chechnya – one way of keeping the show on the road could be as good as any other.

He was always and perhaps will always be compared with Gorbachev because the two were rivals and appeared, at least at times, really to hate each other. Yet they also treated each other, by their country's standards, not too indecently. Gorbachev, when he purged Yeltsin from the Politbureau in 1987, fatally left him enough rope to hang, not himself, but the last general secretary of the CPSU. Yeltsin in his turn allowed Gorbachev to keep an institute and a position in public life from which he launched decreasingly effective salvoes against his usurper.

They were complementary figures. The Russian president took over from the Soviet one when the Soviet Union itself was exhausted, a state of affairs which the former assisted in bringing about but did not invent. They could, in theory, have done much better than they did had they been more generous and more far-sighted men: had Gorbachev played the role of a de Klerk to Yeltsin's Mandela, the transfer of power from the Soviet Union to Russia would have been smoother and above all the wounds caused by the ending of the Soviet Union might have been easier to heal. But Gorbachev went out, though peacefully, in bitterness; and he did so in part because Yeltsin, lacking any conception of what he wanted to do, gave Gorbachev no vision with which he could, as his last act of power, identify and which he could adopt as his own. Unlike de Klerk, Gorbachev never came to the conclusion that the regime over which he presided was finished: he thought and continued to think that it could be renewed.

They had similarities. Both had forebears who were repressed for being independent peasants, and survived. Both were outgoing, not in the dour mould which so many fellow communist leaders were. Both were at crucial parts of their careers Westernizers, liberal in instinct, persuaded to harshness only in extremis. But the differences were more evident: Gorbachev was at once more cosmopolitan, more self-disciplined and more proper than the Siberian who, in Alexander Solzhenitsyn's phrase, was 'almost too Russian' to make the impression on world élite opinion which the last Soviet leader did.

Above all, Yeltsin was less attached to the Party than was Gorbachev. Raised in great poverty in Sverdlovsk (now Ekaterinburg), he graduated as a construction engineer in an institute where he met and married his wife, Naina, and from which he moved on to a series of jobs in the construction industry. He was brought into full-time Party work only in his early thirties as head of the regional Party's construction section, and thence – jumping over at least one superior – to the high post of first secretary of the Sverdlovsk region in November 1976. His version of the period is that he accepted the Party post 'with reluctance', took on the first secretary job on the mandate that 'we should above all be concerned with people and their welfare, since if you treat people well they will respond with improved performance', and that he ran Sverdlovsk in this spirit, driving himself and others hard for ten years, pushing through large projects like the building of a length of new highway and housing the hundreds of families who still, when he was appointed, lived in makeshift huts like the one in which he himself had been born. His known shame – about which he comments only briefly in his first volume of memoirs, *Against the Grain* – was to carry through a secret Politbureau order to bulldoze the Ipatiev house, in whose cellars Tsar Nicholas II and his family were gunned to death in 1918. The order, he writes curtly, 'was impossible to disobey . . . I can well imagine that sooner or later we shall be ashamed of this piece of barbarism'.

He was brought to Moscow by Gorbachev – with whom he was friendly – in June 1985, to head the Central Committee's construction section, and thence, when Gorbachev was ready for the move in his early rapid game of personnel chess, to succeed Victor Grishin as head of the Moscow Party, a post which carried with it candidate membership status in the Politbureau, in December 1985. There, at the summit, Boris Yeltsin had the intuition of his life. He sensed that the Party was weak, and he decided – it was a decision which matured over years – to pit himself against it.

Two, quite contrary, views are held of Yeltsin in this period. One tends to see him as a super-perestroikist, elevated so rapidly by Gorbachev because he simply fitted with the mood the general secretary wished to create, inhibited even by the generous bounds which Gorbachev set, breaking them then sweeping on to lead the democrats to victory against the system. He acquired through this version the generally accepted status of a victim, 'one of us' who were being kicked about by 'them' – an important attribute for a populist politician in Russia to possess. He was the only one of the democratic leaders, apart from Andrei Sakharov, the former dissident physicist, to have acquired it. The other view sees him as both more impulsive and opportunist, a man too headstrong to submit to anyone's authority but his own, possessing at least some of the 'inordinate personal ambitions' with which Nikolai Ryzhkov, the Soviet prime minister, credited him. He was certainly no Sakharov, and was not really a victim of the system. Both were men of courage, but Sakharov's nature was that of the intellectual with a backbone, who, having argued himself into a position of principle, rests on it. Yeltsin also had backbone, but it sustained a personal drive for power through a system whose failure he felt rather than understood to a goal which he guessed existed, not one for which he had prepared himself or which he even desired.

As Moscow secretary, he drove himself crazily, adopting a regime of work which left him at the end of the day unable to alight from his car. He launched himself against the corruption of the Grishin apparat – though it was one of the frustrations of his life that he could not rout it. He developed, and quickly became famous for, his personal appearances – staying at the ZIL truck and engineering plant round the clock to see the shifts change, rising at five to ride into work with dozing labourers from the dormitory towns, standing in queues in shops, publicly denouncing instances of corruption, urging citizens at public meetings to demand even faster progress than the general secretary was prepared for. As a result, 'a certain alienation was making itself felt'. He clashed increasingly frequently with Yegor Ligachev, then second in seniority in the Politbureau and ironically the man who had suggested to a sceptical Gorbachev that he come to Moscow in the first place. Finally, he measured up to Gorbachev himself.

By his own admission, and by the testimony of many of his colleagues, Yeltsin at that period was an imperious man, jealously protective of his autonomy, with a dislike of authority over him (he writes in his memoirs almost affectionately, if also contemptuously, of Brezhnev's later years, when there was no control from the centre on the part of the general secretary). Ligachev, an active disciplinarian, wanted to intervene directly in the Moscow organization; they clashed frequently in the Politbureau. Still, it was a surprise to all when, at the full meeting (plenum) of the Central Committee in October 1987, after Gorbachev had introduced the themes of his keynote speech to be made in November at the revolution's anniversary (the seventieth, and hence more than usually important), Yeltsin attacked Gorbachev for encouraging a culture of 'adulation' in the Politbureau, said that 'nothing substantive' had come from *perestroika* to date, and asked to be allowed to resign from the Politbureau.

It was a request for a martyrdom, which was accepted. Yeltsin was given a roasting by the Central Committee, and then a more serious one when, while under sedation in hospital for severe chest pains, he was ordered to appear at a plenum of the Moscow City Party Committee and was 'murdered with words' by the assembled members. Wrung out – Gorbachev bizarrely comforted him after the roasting he had arranged – he went back to hospital, then took a job as first deputy chairman of the State Construction Committee. From then on, he was set on a course wholly antagonistic to Gorbachev's.

His plenum attack on Gorbachev contained the themes which drove him in opposition, and which were of a piece with what he saw as his governing purpose. He was, by instinct, simply a different kind of politician from his colleagues, one who had developed a form of populism under the shell of Party leadership. He sensed, early, the growing unpopularity of both Gorbachev and *perestroika*, saw the disillusion and the contempt. Others were beginning to sense the same groundswell – but most of them tried to haul the project back within the bounds of a slightly modified orthodoxy; he had the instinct and guts to call for it to be pushed further. Here was another, the crucial, difference between him and Sakharov, and indeed between him and many of the leaders of the democratic groups with whom he would work and who helped raise him to power. Intellectuals in the main, they pursued certain causes – of economic reform, of destalinization, of human and civil rights. He adopted these slogans and made some of them his own, but his strength lay in his natural ability to sniff the popular mood, to represent it, and to represent himself as, like the people, a victim of the system. The popularity of the victim in Russia is well attested: Yeltsin became the victim-leader, the man who waxed in popularity the more the Party leaders excoriated him. Populism was not unknown in Russia before Yeltsin; indeed, a certain kind of populism – confirmation of economic privileges and subsidies for fear of sparking revolts if basic prices were raised – was a common feature of the Brezhnev years, and contributed greatly to the economic collapse of the system. But it is a measure of his nerve that he was the first leader to go to the people and to promise personally that he would make things better. The respect he won, grudgingly, from Western leaders was based on that above all: their recognition as fellow politicians of the magnitude of the leap he made, from Politbureau consensus to personal responsibility.

He gradually gathered back his strength. One can readily surmise that revenge was a large part of the fuel for his renewed energy in the public arena: but so too was a feeling that he was in a unique position to be a popular tribune, working in the very space which Gorbachev's reforms was opening for him. He worked the system to get a delegate's card to the Nineteenth Party Conference in June 1988, a conference which marked the high-water mark of *perestroika* and *glasnost*, but which also saw Yeltsin both repeat many of the accusations he had made at the plenum and ask for political rehabilitation – a request which was received with another flood of condemnation, especially from Ligachev, who was almost inarticulate with rage. It spoiled, as he noted later with satisfaction, the Party script; and though it was a minor diversion for an admiring foreign audience, it caught the imagination of many in the country – for here was *glasnost*'s first dissident from within. At first, he later wrote, he again felt beaten: 'I did not want to do any more fighting, any more explaining. I just wanted to forget everything.' But then, suddenly, 'a fantastic demonstration of popular support': letters and telegrams flooded into his office, expressing the fiercest, most passionate support. 'I did of course understand exactly where these burningly sincere emotions were coming from: our long-suffering people simply could not stand by calmly and watch dispassionately as a man was being pilloried . . . I was able to lean on them to get on my feet again. And to go forward once more.'

He went forward very rapidly. In March 1989, he stood for the Moscow seat of the newly created Congress of Peoples' Deputies. His opponent, Yevgeny Brakov, who was the general director of ZIL, was humiliated – Yeltsin took 90 per cent of an 84 per cent turnout – and with him the 'old-style' Communist Party (Yeltsin was then still a Party member). Kept out of the full-time Supreme Soviet – the inner chamber of the Congress – a fellow democrat called Alexei Kazannik bequeathed him his seat. Kazannik was later to be named by Yeltsin as procurator general after the siege of parliament in October 1993, only to resign in February of the next year after writing that it was 'another kind of crime' that Yeltsin's administration had not tried serious negotiations with the parliamentary leaders before the tanks attacked the parliament.

But that was ahead; Yeltsin went on to be elected a deputy of the Russian Supreme Soviet in the spring of 1990, and was made its chairman in May of that year. In July he left the Communist Party, and began preparing for his election to the presidency of Russia – a new post approved in a referendum in March 1991. He won easily in June 1991, over the official Party candidate Nikolai Ryzhkov (who had resigned from the premiership some months earlier) and, in third place, the new boy on the national scene, Vladimir Zhirinovsky, leader of a new party called the Liberal Democrats. There were setbacks: a visit to the US in 1989 was described by an article in the Italian daily *Repubblica* as a drunken crawl, an article instantly reprinted by *Pravda* and denounced as a lie by Yeltsin. Soon after he returned he fell into the river while visiting an old friend in the village of Uspenskoye, just outside Moscow – suggesting in his memoirs, if elliptically, that it was a KGB job. The word went round that he liked a drink, but it damaged him little. The intelligentsia, initially distrustful, first co-operated with and then embraced him. Some five years later, most were to reject him.

Though he became a member, and a leader, of the Interregional Group of deputies in the Supreme Soviet – a collection of democrats and liberals from all over the Soviet Union whose many divisions were at first masked by a deep distrust of the Communist Party and, increasingly, of Gorbachev himself – he never was fully one of them. He had his own group – most of them men from Sverdlovsk, such as Gennady Burbulis, Oleg Lobov and Victor Ilyushin – who had known him for years or, like Burbulis, had attached themselves to him as he began to rise. These people were quite different from the democrats in many ways – but Yeltsin never seemed to discriminate between them.

As long as he continued to project the image of 'the man being pilloried', he was able to reach out beyond the circles of democrats in the cities to the masses in the country – in particular, to the miners who, from 1989, began themselves to push at the weakening limits of the Soviet state in order to present at first economic, then political demands. The first strike recorded was in July 1989 at a West Siberian pit where the miners found there was no soap available when they came off shift; two years later, as Yeltsin barnstormed the country, they had won the end of the Communist Party's right to political monopoly with the abrogation of Clause Six of the Soviet Constitution, and with Yeltsin's encouragement were calling for the resignation of Gorbachev (which they also 'won', though neither in the way nor with the consequences they expected). These rallies were, for Soviet occasions, spectacular events: there was great admiration and some adulation of Yeltsin, but there was also a quite evident accent on the independence of the new miners' movement and an insistence on pit-by-pit or even group-by-group decision-making and debate. This was in conscious reaction to the voicelessness and passivity which the old official unions had encouraged – but meant, too, that the strikes were disjointed and uncoordinated, and that a new nationally organized union was never able to replace the old, nor to establish itself as a political power at the centre in distinction to a political protest from the regions. The miners did not get, nor did they seriously try to get, much support from workers in trades ancillary to their own – such as steel-making, electricity generation or railways. Yeltsin, touring the country with his little entourage, could see for himself that the new forces were novel, proud, powerful – and inchoate.

Nineteen ninety-one was Yeltsin's year, and his finest. Revived, vigorous (at sixty, on 1 February) and applauded, he benefited hugely from the lurch Gorbachev had felt constrained to make towards an authoritarianism which violated both his nature and his preferences and towards a suppression which he could never admit, and yet in truth never disavow. When fourteen Lithuanians were killed by Soviet special forces when the latter attacked a demonstration round the Vilnius TV tower on the night of 12/13 January, Yeltsin instantly issued an appeal to Russian soldiers not to shed blood, and flew to Lithuania himself. In February, he used a TV broadcast to demand the Soviet president's resignation – 'Gorbachev does not want to undergo *perestroika* in reality, but merely wants to preserve the system, preserve the harshly centralized government, not give independence to the republics, Russia above all . . .' Other republican leaders, more circumspect in their manoeuvres away from Moscow, tut-tutted over the speech. On a subsequent trip to Strasbourg to meet European MPs, Yeltsin was sharply criticized by the leader of the socialist group, Jean-Pierre Cot, for betraying Gorbachev. But in spite of winning a referendum which seemed to signal popular support for the unity of the Soviet Union, Gorbachev's time was slipping away and his powers fading rapidly.

Yeltsin was by a long way the *primus inter pares* of the rising new powers – the republican leaders – with whom Gorbachev was constrained to negotiate. Through the spring and summer of 1991, at the government *dacha* of Novo-Ogarevo just outside of Moscow, Gorbachev and the men whom he and previous general secretaries had been accustomed to treat as subordinates thrashed through a mish-mash of a document which in the end proposed a racketty federation in which critical issues like tax powers were simply fudged and which was capable of widely differing interpretations according to who wished to emphasize powers or freedoms. Just before Gorbachev left for a three-week break at the end of July, Yeltsin and Nursultan Nazarbayev, the leader of Kazakhstan and the most responsible of the leaders there, demanded of Gorbachev that he fire his security and military chiefs, his prime minister and the head of state television. According to Yeltsin, Gorbachev agreed. The conversation was taped, and the transcript given to the plotters of the August putsch. Yeltsin reasonably enough speculates that it may have pushed them into it.

The coup, launched on 19 August, was not defeated only, or arguably largely, by Yeltsin. The putschists were laughably disorganized, many were drunk throughout it and none had the drive to take over and command that blood be shed to ensure its immediate success. Weakened by an inner fear that the Union they were preserving was slipping away irrespective of the compromises made by Gorbachev, faced with a democratic opposition large enough to give them pause, torn between incompatible accounts of the putsch being sanctioned by, but in opposition to, Gorbachev and unable to secure from him any sign that he approved, they were a sorry lot.

Yeltsin's superb rising to the occasion gave the resistance to the coup its symbol and its core. He went straight to the White House – the unit sent to his *dacha* to arrest him had, or said they had, no clear orders – and within hours of reaching it had the brilliant impulse to give an impromptu speech from the turret of one of the tanks which surrounded it, and which had come over to the 'Russian' side. It was no great speech, and the audience was not large, but it was picked up and relayed on TV – that very night, showing how lax the control was over the media – and thus became a national and international symbol of courage and defiance. He was not foolhardy – he agreed to an escape plan via the nearby US embassy, and at one stage went down into the White House basement for safety – but soon mounted again and stayed in his office through the night of 20/21 August, when an attack on the parliament was most likely and indeed had been planned.

The sweetness of his revenge on Gorbachev was savoured cold two days after the coup's ending, when Gorbachev belatedly appeared before the Russian deputies and was forced to acquiesce in Yeltsin's flamboyant signing of the Communist Party of the Soviet Union into oblivion. Gorbachev did not seem to know what was happening (nor, perhaps, did anyone, though Yeltsin sensed it clearly enough). He struggled through the autumn and early winter to re-ignite the Novo-Ogarevo process, only to see the republics peel off from it and proclaim complete independence. Ukraine's declaration after a referendum on 1 December was the end of what had become farcical: a week later, Yeltsin, with the presidents of Belarus and Ukraine, agreed at a hunting lodge outside of Minsk on the construction of a Commonwealth of Independent States – which all other states but the Baltics ultimately joined – and in doing so ended the life of the Soviet Union.

Thus began the rule of Boris Yeltsin of Russia, one which was to cover the first years of its independence and which he, fitful and capricious ruler though he was, undoubtedly dominated, and did so in part because of the *élan* and vigour with which he took office.

Once the Union collapsed, the only possible camp from which a leader could be drawn was the democratic – for the Soviet leaders were discredited, the new nationalists were still emerging from the democratic consensus and the new communists had not yet been born. Within this camp, Yeltsin was unchallenged: the rest of the leaders were largely intellectuals who – though some evolved into strong leaders, like Anatoly Sobchak, the mayor of St Petersburg – were generally incapable of the organization and the projection of power which leadership required. Yeltsin had these: he had created, as he later wrote, the image of a 'wilful, determined strong politician', round whom a variety of differing forces gathered and competed for attention. His three decades of service in the Communist Party, a large part of that near or at the top, had given him a knowledge of how power was retained and displayed, a knowledge which remained essential in the post-Soviet era. He had acquired, immediately after he was stripped of his Politbureau rank, a shadow in the form of Alexander Korzhakov, the former KGB official who became and remained until the spring of 1996 chief of his security and his closest confidant and friend, a man whose influence was unmatched and who more than any other kept the Yeltsin wagon rolling, even as its motor lost momentum. He lost close associates – such as Yuri Skokov, whom he had been close to naming as prime minister immediately after the coup – but he never made the mistake of Gorbachev in allowing potential traitors into his inner circle, nor of keeping cronies there on whose absolute loyalty he could not count.

He never followed a clear line, and never formed a party, because it would have meant forming a policy. He preferred to stay unconstrained, and thus capable of manoeuvre. He began his office as a liberal Westernizer, with a sincere admiration of American plenitude and ease; moved to a more centrist economic stance and adopted a nationalist rhetoric; faced a showdown with his enemies in parliament and strengthened his presidential authority through appointment and the adoption of a super-presidential constitution; and finally put on the mantle of war in order to attempt, and fail, to quell the Chechen revolt in the Russian North Caucasus. He never once stood at the head of a particular current of opposition to the Soviet system; instead, he epitomized a general resistance to the wrongs, inefficiencies and humiliations, his own contrary and stubborn nature providing a field within which were gathered more precise and deeply felt oppositions, such as the demand for political and civil rights articulated by the democrats, the demand for national independence of the Baltic and other republics, including Russia; and the strategy for radical economic reform. He absorbed rather than espoused these, speaking – sometimes very well – in favour of each, but never being wholly owned by any and thus able to dilute or even desert them without apparent difficulty. Though his style, certainly in the first half of his rule, allowed him to be flexible, it also stopped him from institutionalizing his rule and left in doubt the basis of his successor's.

His vigour left him for increasingly large periods of time. He suffered heart-attacks and fits of debilitating depression for weeks, he fell back more and more on a reliance on Soviet-era figures with whose com-mandist instincts he felt more in tune. Nikolai Travkin, whom he was to woo into his camp from leadership of the Democratic Party, said well of him in 1994 that 'The president has not been running the country, he has been passively reigning over it,' and this before he disappeared almost wholly from public view. His early populism trans-muted into a style which emphasized the direct relationship between the president (and the state) and the people, without intervening institutions – as it was bound to do, the more so since the parliament of the first two years quickly joined a battle for supreme power which could be nothing other than deadly.

But these tendencies were never monolithic. He twice commanded blood to be shed: in the attack on the White House in October 1993, at the climax of his confrontation with parliament; and much more murderously, in giving the go-ahead to an invasion of Chechnya in December 1994. Though his mistakes contributed to the first, he could not after a certain time avoid it; he could certainly have avoided the second, though only by exerting a slow, patient squeeze on the Chechen leadership of which his military was not capable. These two events aside, he was permissive in a way rulers in Russia have rarely been: the raucous development of the market was delayed and distorted, but never attacked; the freedom of speech and publication was never fundamentally threatened; parliament, though weak, was not after 1993 in danger and tended to wax in power; the vastly increased intercourse between Russians and foreigners was not halted; the surrounding states, though never sure of Russia and some cases suffering its more or less overt intervention, were free to attempt to strengthen their individual statehoods and their links with third countries, and most did.

He was very far from an ideal ruler of a post-communist Russia. He shamed his country in public on several occasions, appearing to be drunk, certainly incapable. Real economic radicals, such as Yegor Gaidar, and real civil libertarians, such as Sergei Kovalev, both broke with him – in both cases over Chechnya, though Gaidar came back, *faute de mieux*. Long-serving aides, such as Sergei Filatov, resigned in despair towards the end of his first presidency – and also came back to help fight the election; others stayed on without a break, deeming it worth the effort to fight for what was left of reform. And with Yeltsin, there always *was* something left of reform, for he never dropped the rhetoric and never quashed the results of it. In an interview with *Le Figaro* in February 1996, the Czech President Vaclav Havel said of Yeltsin: 'I think, despite his tendency to a very authoritarian style of government, [he] really does aspire to reform Russia. It seems to me he does want to lead his country down the irreversible road of democracy and market economics. I believe that at present these are his genuine convictions.'

But if he did retain an attachment to democratic values, and if he was indeed 'almost too Russian', he was never quite enough post-Soviet. In his late fifties, when he began a serious run for power, he dragged with him the lumber of Soviet beliefs unthinkingly absorbed and Soviet command practices naturally used as a crutch. He could not properly create a new society because, while he had some notions of what he wanted it to be, he had little idea of how to get there. He did put challenges in front of his country, but he was also carried along by its reactions and accommodated himself to forces wholly antipathetic to his founding ideals in order to survive. But in his survival, much else grew – unruly, but also unforced.

CHAPTER TWO

'The most important thing now is reform'

The first two years of the Yeltsin presidency, from mid-1991 to October 1993, were consumed with a deepening and increasingly bitter struggle for supremacy between the president and parliament.

It was a period of continuous political crisis, which came to a head in 1993. The crisis showed that, though the end of the Soviet Union had wholly changed the landscape, the sheer inertia of the forces which had held ranking positions within its structures possessed a very large power to frustrate the efforts of the democrats to fulfil a mandate they felt they had been given by the election of Yeltsin to the presidency. Indeed, it was during this period that the nature of the 'mandate' itself changed radically: when it became clear, at least in retrospect, that Russia was not going to submit to a period of rapid economic and democratic transition – as other former communist states were doing when Yeltsin took power.

Yeltsin came to office as a Westernizing democrat; in his rhetoric, he was much more purely and uninhibitedly one than Mikhail Gorbachev. But from the beginning, his policies were never all of a piece; specifically, they were never uniformly liberal. He combined a series of responses to the crises he faced, which were terribly contradictory – and which were possible only because few cared about the inconsistency, because there had been no period of democratic consistency against which to measure them. Few could sort out what a coherent programme was.

He was liberal – indeed, initially neo-liberal – on the economy, the subject of Part 3. He addressed it by taking the advice of his aide, Burbulis, to appoint the radical young economist Yegor Gaidar to lead the reform team within the cabinet and drive pell-mell for a breakthrough to market capitalism – a decision which he described, perhaps rightly, as 'the most important of my life'. The cabinet was led by him as chief executive, with Burbulis as first deputy prime minister – though within a few months, he had ceded the first place to Burbulis, and then to Gaidar in an 'acting' capacity which was never to be confirmed.

A speech to the Duma on 28 October 1991 set the guidelines for the reform, and promised the country – absurdly, in retrospect – an improvement in plunging living standards in one year's time. It marked a break, even before the formal collapse, with both the Soviet Union and the rest of the Soviet republics. Russia was putting itself first, as Yeltsin backed Gaidar's view – which he took in probably intuitively rather than after careful study – that Russia could prosper only by sloughing off the yoke of dependants (the other republics), who were anyway clamouring, in defiance of economic rationality, for independence.

In that first year – 1992 – Yeltsin gave strong support to Gaidar, even where his public rhetoric revealed unease or incomprehension over reform's progress. From the beginning, however, the politics were a different matter. These he did understand, knowing better than the democrats whose company he had kept in recent years that there would be a raw struggle for power and its fruits. From the beginning, he defined the presidency's role as one responsible for security, foreign policy and the integrity of the state, and he increasingly rejected the intrusion into the political sphere of other significant actors. His model of the state's supreme role was as an office which was both charismatic and absorptive: holding out the ideal of a new statehood and the wealth possible through the development of a new economy, while at the same time taking into himself and then reflecting many (not all) of the quite differing political currents which began to develop.

He soon decided not to hold the early elections which had become a commonplace throughout the other former communist states, and which had cleaned out the dummy legislatures of Hungary, Czechoslovakia and Poland of most of the hacks of the previous era. His case was, to be sure, very different from those of the Central European leaders: he had been elected as head of the Russian Congress of Peoples' Deputies – the Soviet-era republican parliament – in 1990, after elections to it had brought in a number of reformers and anti-communists. He did not believe either the Congress or its standing council, the Supreme Soviet, would be 'obstructive' – and indeed, it backed his economic reform plan in October of 1991. Many of its deputies had stood with him as they rebuffed the putschists in August. Its communists were discredited (and the Party banned), its nationalists mainly still operating under the umbrella of the Democratic Russia group to which Yeltsin himself belonged and which had not evolved into the root and branch critic of the system which it was later to become. As a parliamentarian himself in both the USSR and the Russian Supreme Soviets, he had experienced the heady release of energy which was the mark of the first sessions, and appeared to believe it would continue to serve as a 'national forum', supporting him in his (and their) programme to modernize and liberalize, or at least allowing him to get on with the job. There was a reasonable case to be made that there was no need to go into elections when economic reform had to be undertaken rapidly.

Two other considerations undoubtedly weighed on him. His primary struggle had not been to establish democratic institutions but to remove Gorbachev. Once that was achieved, he appeared more interested in substituting his rule for that of the former leader than in establishing new relationships and divisions of power. Parliament – unreformed, rather racketty, divided and avid for privileges – probably suited him well enough. Second, immediately after the coup he wearied of the political scene, and disappeared to a *dacha* in the Black Sea resort of Sochi, where he was reported to be drinking heavily and doing little work. He did not even receive key members of his staff. It was the first public example of what was to become a pattern, especially after a burst of activity.

It was during that time that the Congress began to demonstrate that it would cause him trouble. It would not debate a new constitution, instead using the Soviet-era constitution, full of ambiguities and contradictions, as its rationale for extending its power deep into the areas which Yeltsin wanted to arrogate to himself. It pressed ahead with the election of provincial governors, though Yeltsin wanted more time to ensure that they were his men.

The Russian president was just as much as Mikhail Gorbachev a split personality – though split on different, actually less publicly visible, lines. Put starkly, where Gorbachev's rhetoric was frequently Soviet, his instincts were often democratic; and where Yeltsin's rhetoric was, after he was thrown out of the Politbureau in 1987 (and even before), often democratic, his practice was often autocratic. In fact, in neither case could one say that one tendency or the other was the 'real man': both operated in a constant state of tension between the two. But Yeltsin was a doer, and had always prized the cavalry charge above the tactical campaign. His heroes, as he told the film director Eldar Ryazanov before the 1993 elections, were Peter the Great and Margaret Thatcher, whose very different reputations depended on the exercise of power rather than the balances of consensus. In October 1991, he called in a speech for 'action, action and more action. Now we are going to have fewer political debates . . . the most important thing now is reform and the drafting of the relevant laws and decrees connected with reform and the implementation of reform. There must be responsibility for implementation from top to bottom, because this vertical line of executive authority is now being reconstructed . . . it will now be fully built up.'

Lacking new elections and constitutional reform of any systematic kind, Russia began its life with a Soviet-era assembly whose most prominent members were democrats, but which had a large share of deputies elected on the communist ticket; with a constitution inherited from the Soviet era in which the ritual phrases spelling out rights and freedoms were designed, in their complete lack of specificity, to mask the reality of Party rule; and a political field in which parties were both held in low esteem and had no elections round which to organize. The president, who had been elected with a substantial majority on a popular vote, had come to power on a ticket not so much pro-democratic as anti-totalitarian. He was seen, and saw himself, as the focus and guarantor of democratic reform.

However, the forces which had come through with him, while also anti-totalitarian, displayed perhaps the most diverse panorama of political views available anywhere in the world at the time. The radicals among the democrats were high-minded intellectuals who had Andrei Sakharov as their political mentor and for whom the newly liberalized field of politics was one in which their beliefs and credentials, often recently acquired, were deployed for rhetorical, not purposeful, effect. It was a field without apparent boundaries: for the democrats, any proposal, any rearrangement of powers, could be presented as a complete solution, and was.

Galina Starovoitova was one example – a frequently quoted one, because her sex, intelligence and fluent command of English appealed to Western media, while the same attributes also attracted Russian media attention, though of a steadily less appreciative kind. An ethnographer by training and profession, never a communist, though from a family whose head was a leading defence industrialist, she expressed, in 1988, sympathy with the then burgeoning Armenian campaign to win back the Armenian-dominated Nagorno-Karabakh district in Azerbaijan, and attracted so much devotion (from Armenians) for taking their side that she was elected as a deputy from the country to the first Congress of Peoples' Deputies in 1989.

Her beliefs were strongly expressed, sharply varied and were pushed without compromise, a typical stance for a democrat of the time. She believed, for example, that the Soviet period had destroyed the best of the Russian character and gene pool; that a constitutional monarchy would be the best régime for the new Russia; that self-determination of any group of peoples should always take priority over the interests of the larger state in which they might find themselves members; and that the Western desire for stability and fear of too close engagement betrayed Russia and its democrats at the critical period after the putsch. Bold and clever, she was a fundamentalist by nature and by conviction, seeing democracy (particularly the British version) as a moral system, not a governing process. She became an aide to Yeltsin for ethnic questions – but was soon sidelined because of her insistence that all ethnic demands be met, and because of her tendency to travel constantly to the West to attend conferences and other set-piece occasions. It was a habit which afflicted many in the democratic camp, and gave their enemies – and more poisonously, their less fortunate friends – ammunition with which to gun them down when the West became less automatically popular. She left the administration in late 1992. Her beliefs were principled things, untested by governance, developed in opposition to a Soviet culture in which it was assumed they would never be deployed as the foundations for practice. She was typical of many democrats, and this trait explained much of why so few of them made good politicians, even when they made excellent companions.

With the radicals were a spectrum of other forces, apparently agreeing on basic principles at first, but quite quickly revealing deep and irreconcilable differences. There were Christian Democrats, whose largest grouping was led by Victor Aksyuchits; the rather anomalous but initially very pro-Western Democratic Party, led by Nikolai Travkin; and the Communists for Democracy, led by Colonel (later General) Alexander Rutskoi, who was chosen by Yeltsin to be his vice-presidential running mate.

All of these groups had begun life as the most ardent espousers of democratic and usually also market values. Aksyuchits saw his party as in the mainstream of European Christian democracy, citing especially the post-war German party as a model; Rutskoi's party led the charge against the Communist Party conservatives, vigorously protesting against limitations on political freedom; while the Democratic Party, which brought into politics some of the most radical democrats – such as Father Gleb Yakunin, a former dissident and camp inmate and Arkady Murashev, a leading campaigner for civil rights – was in the late eighties and early nineties dismissive of any model of development which did not accord with the most ideal-type of Western democratic practice.

Many of these – not all – moved towards one or other version of authoritarianism and of nationalism, if at different speeds. Aksyuchits emerged as a leader of the nationalist bloc in the Russian parliament in 1992, while Travkin's party, founded before the Christian Democratic Movement, metamorphosed into a party still with some diversity, but bitterly hostile to the break-up of the USSR. From 1993 it was dominated by the brooding presence of Stanislav Govorukhin, an actor and director of apocalyptic films portraying the degradation of the new Russia, and later by Sergei Glaziev, a former associate of Gaidar who left his cabinet to become the most prominent economist in the opposition. Travkin left the opposition to Yeltsin in 1993, as a result both of cajoling by presidential aides and his own dislike of the company he was keeping there – and lived an attenuated political life as a minister without portfolio, and a politician without a cause.

These did not stay with Yeltsin for a variety of reasons – some principled, some less so. In the first category was the opposition of deputies, many of whom would call themselves socialist, to a form of 'shock therapy' which had already been instituted in the Central European states and was at the trough of its early stage, with unemployment (especially in Poland) rising and output falling sharply. The opposition deputies were, after all, representatives; they could see the effects economic reform would have on their constituents, and once most prices were liberalized in January 1992, their opposition increased dramatically.

Less principled, if as human, was their feeling of being scorned by the Yeltsin administration. Burbulis was a man of effortless arrogance who insulted deputies he did not like and patronized those he thought might be useful. Gaidar, and the young economists he brought in with him – such as Anatoly Chubais, Pyotr Aven and Konstantin Kagalovsky – came from the Moscow intellectual élite, never highly rated outside of the beltway. The government was surrounded by foreign advisers, who were given time when deputies were not. It would have been a strange assembly which did not feel they were ruled by a group who neither understood them, nor wished to. Hence the ranks of the democrats dwindled – and many of those who remained loyal did so with misgivings.

This decline of the democratic movement was encouraged by the pull of the political forces outside of it. The years of decay of the Soviet Union were marked by the growth of all forms of overt political activity – including fascist, neo-Stalinist and extreme nationalist. Pamyat, a fissiparous group whose largest section was led by a former photographer and actor Dmitri Vasilyev, began public life in 1987 as protectors and restorers of Russian monuments, especially the churches – which were allowed to revive from that time. By the early nineties, Vasilyev had come out as a fascist, though he carefully, even indignantly, distinguished his beliefs from Nazism. He turned his most concentrated fire on the Jews, detecting their evil behind both the democrats (who were indiscriminately described as Jews: Gavril Popov, the first democratic mayor of Moscow, attracted a disproportionate share, although – or because – his ancestry was Greek) and the communists. In the republics, especially in the Baltics, 'Interfronts' were set up to defend the rights of the Russians and others who did not belong to the ethnic majority. These attracted the vocal support of the new patriotic organizations in Moscow. The cultural figures who had done well from the Soviet Union, or – as in the case of the 'village' writers – had begun to articulate a Russian traditionalist or nationalist case in a veiled way during Soviet times, formed a range of quickly changing groups and fronts, and supplied the rhetorical support for the new nationalist politicians.

Some of the nationalists, like the writer Igor Shafarevich, initially accepted the break-up of the Soviet Union gladly, seeing in a delineation of the new Russian borders a liberation from the burdens of the Soviet past. But most did not; they saw the collapse of the Union, the scramble for independence of the fourteen non-Russian states and the shrivelling of Russia to borders more constrained than at any time since Peter the Great as a tremendous loss, a source of humiliation, and identified, as the wreakers of that humiliation, the West, and above all the United States. This feeling of humiliation was at the core of a union which was consummated soon after the formal collapse of the Union – a union of formal opposites, Russian nationalism and the inheritors of Soviet communism.

Russian nationalism had had its promoters within the Communist Party since the sixties, who pressed it into service as a defender of the (socialist) motherland and, in particular, as a well of venom to be discharged at the 'Zionists' whose reactionary designs on Russia coupled with their control of international finance capital and media repeated traditional, if updated, anti-Semitic themes. The Party was, of course, always in control: it permitted and marked the limits of this nationalist discourse. In the rapidly developing conditions of freedom under Gorbachev, nationalism both of a restorative, cultural and broadly democratic variety associated with the intellectual figures of Dmitri Likachev and Sergei Averintsev as well as of a harsher, more resentful and vengeful kind, were both in evidence. Pamyat was one such version of the latter: but the 'extreme' nationalist movements were much richer than Vasiliev's ranting.

They drew on nineteenth-century themes developed by Nikolai Berdyayev, the religious philosopher, and by Fyodor Dostoyevsky, as well as, older than these, themes inscribed in Russian Orthodoxy. These were woven into a cloak whose primary colours were unity of the people, centrality of the state, and rejection, or contempt, for the West (Shafarevich once memorably described Western-style freedoms as having as much strength 'as a spoonful of sugar stirred in a cup of tea'). Once the form of the new Yeltsin government became clear, once the media and the new establishment made obvious their pro-Western orientation and frequent dislike of Russian traditionalism, and more especially once the first economic reforms sent their shock waves through society, the nationalist networks, old and new, were mobilized.

They quickly discovered they had more in common with the communists – legalized once again, after the Constitutional Court in a judgement early in 1992 had reversed Yeltsin's ban on the Party – than they had thought. Nationalist propagandists began to re-cast the once-hated Marxism as expressive of something elementally Russian. Alexander Dugin, one such figure, proclaimed at the end of 1991 that Marxism was in a sense Russian in origin: 'Our people is too great, too spiritual and too organic to have identified with a provocative, anti-national foreign doctrine.' The West was seen as soft, secular and liable to collapse under the weight of its own consumerism; the poverty and trials of the Soviet era, used by the liberals as a major reason for constructing a new system as rapidly as possible, were in the new nationalist discourse regarded as cleansing processes productive of unity and comradeship.

This accorded well with the views of all but the most dogmatic of the communists. After two nationalist bodies – the Russian All Peoples' Union under Sergei Baburin in December 1991 and the Russian Peoples' Assembly in February 1992 with Aksyuchits in the leadership – a third, the most extreme, was the medium through which organized communism fused publicly with organized nationalism. This was the Russian National Council, which had a collective leadership including the writer Valentin Rasputin, former K G B General Alexander Sterligov and the leader of the Russian Communist Party, Gennady Zyuganov. The latter's entry had been prepared for him by aides and advisers who purported to find in Leninism a fount of traditional Christian ideals; he himself, in a later (spring 1993) speech, said in a piece of breathtaking bravado: 'Jesus Christ, who defended the best moral values of humanity, was crucified for his beliefs in a fundamental social justice. We have our own roots in the most important moral values of the Russian Orthodox Church and for that reason we must give full credence to our origins and the long-standing tradition of collectivism.'

After that union, there were others: Zyuganov was also a leader of the National Salvation Front created later in 1992 (it was banned, and the ban lifted by the Constitutional Court early the next year). He stood on platforms with anti-Semites and fascists, men like Alexander Barkashov, formerly of Pamyat, who openly espoused racial cleansing, and whose fascist platoons would form the backbone of the defence of the Russian White House (the then parliament building) against Yeltsin's tanks in October 1993. As the opposition to the effects of reforms grew both within the élite and in the population at large, the effective identity of view on most issues gave the nationalists and communists – the 'red-brown' alliance – a new *élan* and purpose. Though the personalities were jealous and deceitful, consumed with rhetoric and indifferent to organization, they were kept together by their deepening dislike of Yeltsin and his government. And in the Russian Unity bloc in Congress, founded in April 1992, they possessed a vehicle for harrying, shouting down and ultimately voting down the first reform government.

These groups were the most vivid opposition to Yeltsin, but they were not initially the most successful. The second sphere of opposition was made up of *soi-disant* centrists, a group of parties and movements which could be described as led by those who had done well out of the Soviet system and wished to do well out of the post-Soviet system. They were bedevilled by the dilemma of defining what 'centrism' was in a polity whose left and right were not yet formed – but their philosophic baseline was a belief in a strong and guiding state, a vision of Russia as looking both west and east (as does the two-headed eagle, its crest), and a scepticism amounting to hostility (never expressed, or felt, as strongly as that of the patriotic groups) to Western economic liberalism. Sergei Stankevich, the former deputy mayor of Moscow who swung from a liberal to a centrist-nationalist position while an adviser to Yeltsin, wrote in March 1992 that Russia was a Eurasian power, pulled eastwards as much as westwards, that it had been doomed through history to split into warring camps, and then again to unite, and that it was 'pointless to complain about the nature of this historical destiny. It is simply important for everyone who wants to speak on Russia's behalf to listen closely to the voice of her essence.' This had overtones of the mystic invocations beloved of the red patriots; but it was much less enclosed and neurotic, suffered less from alternating complexes of superiority and abasement. This line of thought made strong links with Gorbachev, and the institute he had founded after his resignation. One of the scholars in it, Alexander Tsipko, was among the earliest to identify the loss of the Soviet Union as an act of massive criminality for the people in it – and to see, in the extreme cosmopolitanism of the radicals in the cabinet, the seeds of their rapid downfall.

The guiding spirit (and bankroller) of the centrists was Arkady Volsky, a clever, humorous man who had served successive CPSU general secretaries as an adviser, done various jobs for Mikhail Gorbachev, including, in the late eighties, being his representative in the contested Armenian enclave of Nagorno-Karabakh in Azerbaijan, not an easy billet. As the Soviet Union faded, he set up a body called the Russian Union of Industrialists and Entrepreneurs, modelled on the West European employers' associations – especially the Italian Confindustria, with which he had close links.

Volsky had a Machiavellian style and indeed had the aspect of a Florentine noble, with a handsome fleshy face and a cap of slicked black hair. But he also had some battle honours. He had organized to save Gorbachev from possible defeat at the hands of a reactionary Central Committee late in his presidency; he was the man to whom Gorbachev talked when he managed to get a phone call out from captivity during the August 1991 putsch; and he had, with only a slight hesitation, strongly backed Yeltsin during the putsch, collecting money for his members to buy supplies for the White House in the event of a long siege. He was keen on foreigners investing in Russia – as long as they touched base with his association first – and he set himself up as their main port of call.

But, as with all who called themselves centrists, he was opposed to the break-up of the Soviet Union and he was a believer in a strong state. His last task for Gorbachev had been to try, in concert with the young economist Grigory Yavlinsky, to keep at least an economic union going. His favoured mode of development was the Chinese: he saw in that country's policies the virtues of order, growth and high investment, all of which were lacking in his own country. He used his members with some skill to pressurize the government and to attempt to isolate it from the president. Cut out of a cabinet he had hoped to head, spurned by Gaidar and his followers in government as a state industry boss with a begging bowl, Volsky formed a group called the Civic Union which drew in some political parties: the Democratic Party; a paper party led by his associate Alexander Vladislavlev, called Resurrection; and most importantly the Peoples' Party of Free Russia, which is what Alexander Rutskoi's Democratic Communists had metamorphosed into. He quickly concluded an alliance with the Federation of Independent Trade Unions, the former official trade union centre – whose weakness amounting to irrelevance was well demonstrated by their progressively greater reliance on Volsky and the industrialists, who gave them political presence and even funded a daily paper, *Workers' Tribune*, which reflected their views.

In the inchoate atmosphere which persisted through 1992 and 1993, the edges between these two broad camps blurred and merged. The centrists, who were quick to claim democratic credentials and reformist spirits, were most to blame for this: they rarely made clear their distance from politicians whose views were close to fascist. The position of two commanding individuals who called themselves centrists illuminates the problem and shows the difficulty Yeltsin would have had – even had he tried much harder than he did – to win over the centrists to his side. These two had been, or were thought to have been, close to Yeltsin, had stood with him during the attempted putsch of 1991 – and yet turned against him, in the end, almost to the death.

Alexander Rutskoi was an air force colonel, a hero of the Afghan war, when he formed the Communists for Democracy group in the Russian parliament, and thus found himself chosen as Yeltsin's running mate for the 1991 presidential ticket. Dashing, in his mid-forties, jovial and impatient by turns, emotionally raw, he famously and early dismissed the young economists whom Gaidar had brought into government as 'the boys in pink pants', and was soon being wooed by the media to give interviews and make TV declarations which were wildly disloyal to his president – to whom, as Yeltsin later bitterly noted, he was simultaneously pledging eternal loyalty. In a series of articles written for various newspapers at the beginning of 1992, he lamented, in a fluently and passionately elegiac style, the passing of Russian traditions and culture, and the 'McDonaldization' of the Russian consumer – not the first, nor probably the last, politician in the world to use that image as a proxy for national loss.

He had entered the public stage as a Russian, or perhaps a Soviet, nationalist (he mixed elements of both). He founded, in 1989, a club called 'Fatherland', which united nationalist and communist military officers, and which was explicitly anti-*perestroika* in tone: he was not at that time (and after it) far from the ideas and practice of the then better-known military officers who sat in the Supreme Soviet and called for the resignation of Gorbachev because he was selling out the empire. The main theme of an unsuccessful campaign for a Moscow seat in the Congress of Peoples' Deputies in 1989 was bombastic nationalism. His successful 1990 election race for a seat in the Russian parliament mixed calls for a renewed love of the Motherland with demands for complete economic freedom. He dropped and picked up platforms and beliefs tremendously quickly, even by the standards of the time: in choosing to support Yeltsin, he stowed away his nationalist rhetoric to become a super democrat – only to return to nationalism a few months later.

In the first year of parliament he remained more or less in the centrist camp. His party had a social democratic tinge, it was part of the Civic Union and his appearance at a nationalist rally in early 1992 made him the target of Pamyat and evoked from him a limp condemnation of excesses. He was never given anything decent to do. Yeltsin once publicly insulted him by contemptuously and publicly commanding him to look into the reform of agriculture – traditionally, in the Soviet system, a graveyard job. Had he had some meaning in his official life, he might have stayed loyal: his ideas were very half-baked, his vanity very large. But that is doubtful. He was too loose a cannon, and he was also a Soviet officer with a distinguished record; the rapid collapse of the institutions he had served would probably have persuaded him to oppose sooner or later.

Ruslan Khasbulatov, with whom he was forced into a closer and closer union, was very different; but Khasbulatov was very different from everyone else. His dominance of the Congress was a tribute to his public skill, wit, organizing abilities and use of patronage – but he was no one's comrade, he neither formed nor joined any party and had allies but no political friends.

In part, this was because he was a Chechen, a race unpopular in Russia because of their contumacious refusal to accept or forget repression, and their disproportionate presence in organized crime. He was deported with most of his people to Kazakhstan in 1944 when they began to rise against the Soviets during the advance of the Nazis. He was raised on a collective farm in (as he tells it in his memoirs) great poverty; however, his father became chairman and he was bright enough and/or favoured enough to be sent, like that other country boy Gorbachev, to Moscow State University. After two years' full-time work in the Komsomol, he became an academic, rising to a professorship at the Plekhanov Institute in Moscow. A democratic publicist in the *perestroika* time, he was elected to the Russian parliament from the Chechen capital of Grozny in 1990, with the help of the Republican Party first secretary, Doku Zavgayev, and with some adroitly phrased rhetorical bones thrown to the rising nationalism of his people. He became deputy chairman in the Russian Supreme Soviet to Yeltsin and then, after the August 1991 putsch, was confirmed as chairman.

From that position, and once Yeltsin had formed a government and launched economic reform, Khasbulatov pitted himself ferociously against the reformers, and thus against Yeltsin himself. More than any other single politician of the time, Khasbulatov operated on sheer arrogance – expanding the role of parliamentary chairman from an arbiter of debate into the supreme position of a rival power to the presidency – an act made possible by the extreme fragmentation of the parties in the Congress. He created a large number of posts in an expanded bureaucracy, took direct command of the 5,000-strong parliamentary guard and deployed them on a mission to close down the daily *Izvestiya*, which Khasbulatov claimed as parliamentary property, and manipulated votes, committees and procedures. He saw parliament, he said, as the superior of the institution of the presidency because of its greater representativeness and propensity to stabilize the country. 'The authority of the state', he wrote in 1992, 'depends on the constitution and the law, which are the embodiment of parliament.' In fact, the constitution which his parliament constantly amended was a Soviet creation, the law was woefully incomplete and the parliament full of fluid, incoherent groupings. It was a forum in which only demagoguery could succeed.

In spring of 1991, the forces ranging against Yeltsin and his governments had not cohered. Some hated each other more than they did the government. Neither Khasbulatov nor Rutskoi, though at times violent in their rhetoric against economic reform, were ready for full confrontation. The Yeltsin camp in the Supreme Soviet were still capable of mustering a majority on some votes. When the opposition did get a majority for the sacking of four of the economic radicals from the cabinet, Gaidar – in a *tour de force* before the Congress – could frighten enough of those voting for the motion to consent to a compromise in which a resolution demanding inflationary spending policies was balanced by another resolution expressing general support for the current policies. Yeltsin tried again to get agreement to introduce a new draft constitution; it was again thrown out. The Congress ended in a show of amity; but once it was over, the Congress leadership on one hand and Yeltsin and the government on the other turned to their supporters in the country, and sought their support for what all felt would be an inevitable clash.

But between April and December, the struggle turned against Yeltsin, and against Gaidar, who had by then become, by presidential decree, acting prime minister. Yeltsin began to shift in advance of a Congress in December he knew would be hostile, bringing into the cabinet centrist figures, including Victor Chernomyrdin and Vladimir Shumeiko, to placate Volsky. The control of spending was loosened. Gaidar, in his own efforts to move into the centre, chose to present Victor Gerashchenko to be confirmed by the Supreme Soviet as chairman of the Central Bank: Gerashchenko had been president of the USSR State Bank, and had been fired after he used the coup to attempt to whip the republican state banks into line with the centre.

The atmosphere turned sour, then tense. Less than a year after the coup against Gorbachev which confirmed Yeltsin in power, coups against Yeltsin became the stuff of constant rumours. These were fed by an article in the daily *Izvestiya* by Andrei Kozyrev, the foreign minister, who pointed to elements in the KGB and the military supporting separatists in former Soviet republics (as they were) and warned that there was a rising camp within the bureaucracy and the secret services which wanted an anti-Western foreign policy (as there was). He ended by prophesying a coup – which earned him a rebuke from Yeltsin, who gave a confident performance of control in a July press conference – a prophecy made the more convincing by his first extended public critique of the West, for imposing too tough economic conditions on the provision of aid to Russia.

When the seventh Congress came, it quickly developed into a seething cauldron, in which both Gaidar and Yeltsin were greeted with jeering and calumny. A stumbling presidential opening speech again asking for constitutional reform was refused, and democratic and opposition deputies struck each other on the floor of the house.

Yeltsin offered concessions – that the Supreme Soviet would have the right of veto over the ministers of foreign affairs, security, home affairs and defence – in return for confirmation of Gaidar as prime minister. Khasbulatov, with the sleight of hand he mistook for statesmanship, took the concessions and rigged a vote against Gaidar. Yeltsin, having spent part of the night locked in his steam bath and having to be dragged out forcibly by Korzhakov, his bodyguard, mustered the spirit for defiance. He returned to the Congress the next day, accused it and its chairman of duplicity, and attempted to lead out his supporters to deprive the parliament of a quorum. But too few left; parliament carried on and Yeltsin was forced to do a deal, part of which was, though it was never stated, that he sack his deeply unpopular chief aide, Burbulis, in return for being allowed to hold a referendum the following spring on a new constitution. The Congress also moved to an immediate vote on the post of prime minister, from which process emerged Victor Chernomyrdin, not as the man with the highest vote, but as the one acceptable to both sides. Gaidar conceded with grace, but in private was bitter, believing that Yeltsin could have made more of a fight for him. Yeltsin himself, anxious to compromise, was also torn between his admiration for Gaidar's radicalism and his sense that it could not be sustained.

Yeltsin said afterwards that he smelled blood in the air at that Congress; and rumours of coups, declarations of states of emergencies and interventions were the common currency of the media and the corridor gossip. Naturally, for in its first year, the parliament had shown itself first unwilling to settle on a constitutional order with the president, then adamantly opposed to it. It had a good enough case, at least in theory, that parliamentary government would be more representative and more stable than a presidential system. But its chief representatives did not seek to advance it in a rational spirit, to agree a constitutional debate in which such issues could have been aired. The Congress's first instinct and last thought was to attack, to weaken, and to destroy. In this way ended Yeltsin's first full year of power.

CHAPTER THREE

'This disastrous, vicious circle'

Three events made 1993 the critical one of Russia's first five years.

In that year, Yeltsin banned, and then besieged, a rebel parliament and established a presidential constitution – a harsh, shocking manoeuvre forced upon him both by his own miscalculations and mistakes, but much more decisively by a Congress determined to destroy him. It also saw the election of a new parliament which reverted to the old, pre-Revolution name of the Duma, whose composition reflected popular dislike both of the economic policies of the government and the siege of the White House. Yet neither the violent confrontation nor the peaceful election of extreme nationalists and communists in large numbers to the new parliament brought an immediate end to reform, nor a violent change in policy, nor an assertion of authoritarianism – all of which were widely forecast by a foreboding Russian political class, and by domestic and foreign commentators.

Yeltsin entered the year deprived of Yegor Gaidar, the man who had written himself into the earliest pages of post-Soviet Russia as the creator of its capitalism. He had attracted the hatred of the dispossessed – especially those most dispossessed of most power – and the allegiance of the thinning bands of Westernizers and their allies abroad. In his place was put Victor Chernomyrdin, boss of a Soviet gas industry which possessed some half of the world's known reserves, who had already, in mid-1992, replaced a Gaidar ally in becoming deputy prime minister for energy. Chernomyrdin was uncommunicative, careful and apparently averse to the 'bazaar' which he saw about him in the streets of central Moscow, as what seemed to be half the capital's population sold their belongings to the other half.

Yet there was no reversal of policy. The radical Boris Fyodorov, who had been a minister in the first Russian government Yeltsin formed in 1990, left a soft billet as a senior, if semi-detached, executive in the

34

European Bank for Reconstruction and Development in London to come into the cabinet as deputy prime minister for finance. With the privatization minister Anatoly Chubais, he began to bear down on the inflationary creation of credit which he privately blamed Gaidar for allowing. Chernomyrdin, who had come into power talking of a price freeze, was taken aside by Fyodorov and Chubais and told the facts of economic life; the price freeze was dropped before it could take any effect. Within a few months, Chernomyrdin was demonstrating his loyalty to Yeltsin, and letting it be known that he was no Soviet reactionary: he spoke in the Supreme Soviet in support of 'a strong presidential power that is a guarantor of reform'. Those who – like the Civic Union – had hoped for a change of course were disillusioned: in a meeting with Yeltsin, they lectured him (he thought) like a schoolboy on his and his government's inability to grasp the crisis to which reform had brought Russian industry.

In his fairly steady support for economic reform, Yeltsin aggravated relations with the Supreme Soviet and continued to provide them with fuel for their denunciations. But economic change had ceased to be the key issue. The two institutions, Supreme Soviet and presidency, were locked in a struggle for victory which one or other had to win. Khasbulatov relentlessly wound the spring tighter: he argued that the referendum should be scrapped, and found an ally in the Constitutional Court chairman Valery Zorkin, an overpromoted and politically con-fused official, who – though he had guaranteed the agreement of which the referendum was part – now began to say that it threatened the constitution itself. 'Double power', and the fear of anarchy it had brought to Russia in centuries past and appeared to be bringing now, was a reality awaiting a dénouement.

It came, if slowly. In March, two successive Congresses (the eighth and ninth) were held, in a febrile confusion. The first saw the deputies renege on their agreement to hold the referendum; they also voted to strip the president of his powers to issue decrees, claim control over the media and order investigations of the work of the foreign and privatization ministers. The second of the two Congresses – held, according to Sergei Shakhrai, 'a hair's breadth away from civil war' – came immediately after Yeltsin issued a decree introducing 'special rule', a decree rescinded since neither Vice-President Rutskoi, nor the then head of the Security Council, Yuri Skokov, would sign it.

The ninth Congress almost impeached the president: 617 deputies voted for the motion, seventy-two short of the two-thirds required. In the wake of its failure, the Congress conceded that a referendum would be held – but stipulated that the first two questions on support for Yeltsin, and for his economic policies, would require an impossible 50 per cent support from all eligible voters (later reduced, by the Constitutional Court, to 50 per cent of those participating). Throughout these manoeuvrings, Khasbulatov played an opaque, zigzagging role – now screaming at the government and the president for their betrayal of the people, now making compromises with Yeltsin's aides which he could not persuade the Congress – which had grown suspicious and critical of him – to accept.

The referendum, on 25 April, was won by Yeltsin, against all received wisdom. He received 58 and 53 per cent respectively for support for himself and his economic programme; 67 per cent called for elections to a new parliament – reflecting a deep dislike of the Supreme Soviet evident in public opinion polls; while less than 50 per cent voted for early presidential elections. The pro-Soviet, opposition forces were momentarily disoriented. The president, in a TV address of some moderation, said parliamentary elections should come in autumn, and that a new constitution should be drawn up and itself submitted to a referendum. He then, as had become his custom, retired from the public view for some weeks to rest, to sink into black wells of depression – and to drink.

In that hiatus, the confrontation went to the streets. May 1 saw a crowd of hard-line anti-Yeltsinites launch themselves on the police during a demonstration at the foot of Yeltsin's statue in Moscow's October Square, and kill a militia sergeant. Khasbulatov called a commission to investigate why the demonstrators had been attacked.

Rutskoi moved on a different tack from Khasbulatov. He took the issue which was beginning to obsess political circles and the media – corruption at the top – and made it his theme, proposing himself as the honest soldier among a nest of shysters. He accused members of Yeltsin's circle, in particular Mikhail Poltaranin and Vladimir Shumeiko – the two ministers closest to the president – of massive diversion of state funds. Yeltsin's aides responded with allegations of corruption against Rutskoi. These allegations, all involving the sale of state property and the placing of the proceeds in foreign bank accounts, were interwoven with claims from two *émigré* businessmen, Boris Birshtein of the Swiss-based Seabeco and his former business partner Dmitri Yakobovsky. These two were part used by both sides, part used them, in a web of intrigue and corruption centred mainly on the illegal sale of Soviet military property in East Germany as the troops withdrew. Both were also involved in the career, and firing, of Victor Barannikov, the security minister and heir to the KGB empire. Yakobovsky was almost confirmed as co-ordinator for security in the cabinet at the age of twenty-nine, having been promoted from militia captain to general in order to better execute his duties. In Yeltsin's account, Yuri Skokov – who was head of the national security committee – discovered the ploy and brought the case to the president to abort.

This web, chronicled day by day by an avid and uninhibited press, was for much of the public both wholly confusing and wholly revolting. The corruption was fabulous, shameless and at the highest levels: it was the confirmation of the suspicions which hard-pressed men and women harboured as they saw the Mercedes swish by, the boss in the back attended by crew-cut thugs. It was proof that the new power was absolutely corrupted, their dirt besmirching all, even to the presidency itself. Though Yeltsin, most thought, was clean, his circle was not: his patronage had given protection to men and women whose desire for wealth, long pent-up, flowed out unassuageably, too strong for serious disguise. Few of these cases came to court; none was properly investigated. Birshtein of Seabeco was a fabulously omnipresent figure, deeply involved not just with the Russian government, but with the administrations of the Ukraine, Moldova and Kirgizia. In each of these states, he was accused of buying the permission from ministers for trading concessions worth millions of dollars. That corruption was taking off strongly in this period is beyond doubt: it was to become and remain a deep stain across the new Russian political class. But it could not be said that it was the preserve of one side or the other: though the presidential side had more opportunities, the parliamentary side did its best.

By mid-year, little else counted except the struggle for power. The presidency and the legislature were locked into a confrontation from which all hope of compromise had vanished – though these were still tried. Only government, constitutionally torn between president and parliament on their first loyalty, but siding strongly with the president, continued to work to anything like a routine.

Rutskoi's ambitions were now very large: his advisers openly briefed journalists to expect a coup by the summer. The vice-president, unrestrainedly against his president since the turn of the year, smarting from his exclusion from all participation in government, had reverted to his shallow political roots. He appeared on the national stage as a patriot and as a moral avenger of the corruption inspired by the president. It was a role for which his heavily handsome appearance was well suited. His stance split the Civil Union, persuaded such centrist figures as Nikolai Travkin to move over to the presidential camp and put Rutskoi wholly in the hands – ultimately in the titular leadership – of the 'red-brown', communist-nationalist opposition.

Khasbulatov, more sinuously, moved with him. The weakness of his base in the Supreme Soviet had been demonstrated at the eighth Congress, when he was himself almost forced to resign for attempting to broker a compromise with Yeltsin. He did not wish to make the same tactical mistake again, and thus committed a strategic one: he chose not to join Yeltsin in constructing a new constitution (he would have had, to be sure, no secure place in a new parliament, but could have bargained for one) and instead began to denounce Yeltsin the more fiercely for destroying the Soviet Union, a move he had at the time supported, and for transforming Russia into 'a colonial enclave' by means of economic reforms which he had spent the earlier part of his rise to power recommending.

At the same time, he prepared a series of massive salvoes for the next Congress. A budget was passed with a Rbs22 trillion deficit; the State Privatization Committee, headed by Chubais, was neutered; and constitutional amendments were readied which would remove the president from chairmanship of the Security Council, and deprive him of the right to sign international treaties.

In this unforgiving, grinding confrontation was moulded the tragic paradox which was to run on through Russia's first term of freedom, and to tighten its politics into a series of knots which will present later generations of politicians with a legacy of cynicism and disillusionment. The president retained the support of the democrats and the reformers, for they had nowhere else to go. Yet he increasingly disappointed them, making queasy their untested political stomachs through a series of manoeuvres they had to support because his enemies were theirs. He had taken power after a populist campaign; he had been unable or unwilling to reform the political structures which had brought him to power; he demanded support through referenda which mobilized the masses against the representative institution of the parliament, failing to support or to develop a party system which could mediate between himself and the people. He was, however, still to be counted on for broad support for economic change; he was enfolded into the club of major world statesmen, to whose pressure he would often bow in the matter of retaining liberal ministers or passing pro-market legislation; and though he allowed his military to indulge in adventures in the Caucasus, in Moldova and in Central Asia – precisely those areas where Andrei Kozyrev had claimed they were out of democratic control – he steadily refused to act (though he did pose) as a neo-imperialist, contenting himself with invocations of greatness. The democrats thus remained with him, but it ceased to be anything like a coalition of equals, and took on the aspect of individuals huddling miserably round the feet of a doubtful saviour.

The Congress of Peoples' Deputies, though elected under communist auspices, could have been a great civic lesson for the people – as was its Soviet equivalent during the last three years of Gorbachev's power. Many of its deputies were new to politics, and were at least initially committed to democratic procedure and norms. Khasbulatov was an ardent exponent of the superiority of parliamentary over presidential government for a new democracy – a view in which he enjoyed the support of many foreign political scientists. 'The defining symbol', wrote Khasbulatov, 'of a democratic state is its representative power, the parliament. It is this which guarantees legislative and supervisory functions in all spheres, and its effectiveness signifies stability within the state.' There were many foreign, as well as Russian, observers who saw the speaker as he presented himself – a man struggling with an arrogant and overweening executive to retain the powers of a popular assembly.

But he, with the support of what came to be a majority, ensured that the legislature destroyed itself. Having agreed to economic reform soon after the coup, the deputies then turned on those charged to carry out reform as soon as the hard pounding from its effects began – or even before. The Congress assented to the notion that there should be a clear division of power, but instead of taking advantage of Yeltsin's early pliability to work out what that division might reasonably be, it sought to take all effective power away from the presidency through a constitution which – hopelessly compromised by its origins in the communist period – could never serve as the founding document of a new state. Constantly confronted with its own unpopularity, the Congress clung like a limpet to office. Created in the period of Soviet collapse and greatly assisting that collapse, the legislature quickly sought to recoup the loss of empire and, through its decisions and threats, alarmed the shaky sovereignty of its neighbours. In all it did, from the election of Yeltsin as president in the summer of 1991 to its destruction in October 1993, it sought to achieve power and to slough off responsibility for the exercise of power. The Congress held before the Russian people the spectacle of an institution claiming the highest mandate, while degrading its own potential.

In this sense, those who claim that Yeltsin simply swept aside an institution which he could not bend to his will are wrong: he did not provoke, but stumbled into, armed confrontation with the opposition deputies. He had tried compromises – foolish and inconsistent, but nevertheless largely initiated by him. He acted unconstitutionally, but he was president of a country nominally owing allegiance to a constitution which could be (and was being) changed at will by the Supreme Soviet, and which had been written under Leonid Brezhnev. He should have abolished the Congress when he had the wind behind him and Russia at his feet, after the coup, but that act (which would also have been unconstitutional) could have stimulated an earlier confrontation and derailed economic measures he regarded, with some justice, as more urgent. The deputies were offered more than one exit from the impasse, but it would have meant their submission to a new election, and to an attempt to create a constitution in which their constitutionally unlimited power would have been greatly reduced. They chose to gamble all, and thus had the largest responsibility for the confrontation and a very large responsibility for the subsequent closing of the political space.

The Khasbulatov programme for the next Congress loomed over Yeltsin: the talks on the new constitution which he had convened soon deadlocked hopelessly, as the regional and republican leaders, playing parliament and presidency off against each other, demanded incompatible privileges. Yeltsin convened a gathering of the regional leaders in a body he called the Federation Council, but it was attended by only a few. The main foreign states which had agreed to put up a $44 billion package of aid, debt relief and tied loans in mid-1993 began to say that none of it could come to a country with such a stasis at the heart of its policy-making.

But Yeltsin promised that September would be a hot month and he made it so. On 10 September, he told Khasbulatov he would not sign the inflationary budget. On 15 September, he reappointed Yegor Gaidar to the cabinet as first deputy prime minister in charge of the economy. He spent some high-profile time with army divisions around Moscow. Then, on 21 September, he made a speech on television. If his decision to institute radical economic reform was his most important decision, this was the most fateful speech of his career, one which had both immediate and much more long-term consequences. 'Parliament', he said, 'has been seized by a group of persons who have turned it into the staff of the irreconcilable opposition . . . my duty as president is to state that the current deputies' corps has lost its right to be in control of crucial levers of state power. The security of Russia and its peoples is more important than formal obedience to contradictory norms created by the legislature.' Announcing a decree – number 1,400 – to ban the Supreme Soviet in perpetuity and calling elections to a new parliament in December, Yeltsin went on: 'The measures to which I had to resort were the only way to defend democracy and freedom in Russia . . . the only way to overcome the paralysis of state power is to fundamentally renovate it on the basis of the rule of the people and constitutionality. The current constitution doesn't allow that – neither does it allow for the passage of a new constitution. Being the guarantor of security of the state, I must offer a way out of the stalemate, to break this disastrous, vicious circle.'

Yeltsin had finally recognized that the post-Soviet impasse in which he had allowed himself to be trapped had to be broken, and could only be broken by going beyond the bounds of pseudo-constitutionality, within which he had himself risen to power. He had to betray a network of commitments and pledges in order to serve a higher purpose: to put Russia on a constitutional footing which could provide a basis for normal political development, free from a power crisis which could never be peacefully resolved. In doing so, however, he had to take all responsibility on himself: he did indeed become 'the guarantor of the security of the state'. But in becoming so, he had to elevate his already awesome burden of responsibility to a point where he and only he set the rules – a position which enjoined the most extraordinary discipline, wisdom and self-restraint. He chose, as ever, boldly; it was the consequences of his choice which, as ever, found him unprepared.

But that was to come. Decree 1,400 had immediate effect and evoked an immediate response. Khasbulatov called on all security forces to disobey the president. Rutskoi called the announcement a 'state coup', and claimed the presidency, in which he was later confirmed by the Supreme Soviet at a midnight session. 'This', he said, standing erect on the platform, 'is an assault on the citizens of Russia, on their children and grandchildren. Each of you stands before a choice: to defend, or not to defend, your rights, your statehood, your future.' A Congress was called, and deputies (not all) arrived at the White House, whose services were one by one switched off. Yeltsin issued a further order – for the dissolution of the parliamentary guard, and the paramilitaries who had been drafted in as the White House defenders under the command of Alexander Barkashov, the most active of the fascist leaders and the only one to have, in Russian National Unity, a convincing private army. The order was ignored.

The shock, however, appeared to work. Deputies who wished to leave were allowed to do so without hindrance, and many did: Yeltsin's people claimed their numbers fell from more than 600 to under 200 in a week. Victor Barannikov, sacked by Yeltsin because he was implicated in a scandal with Boris Birshtein, was elected by the Congress as its security minister – but sought a meeting with Chernomyrdin to tell him he had 'always been loyal' to Yeltsin. Khasbulatov and Rutskoi, cooped up in the dark, their ambitions to lead Russia limited to the confines of the parliament and its nervy defenders, fell out, Rutskoi reacting in a towering rage to a Khasbulatov remark to the deputies that he would 'tell the acting president to see to it'.

No compromise – whether brokered by the reform politician Grigory Yavlinsky, or the head of the Constitutional Court Valery Zorkin or even, at the last moment, the Orthodox patriarch – were of any use. The parliament refused to obey the order to hand over its arms, repudiating two negotiators who had agreed to it. On Sunday 3 October, Alexei II, patriarch of Moscow and All the Russias, went to the

Uspensky cathedral with the country's most sacred icon, the Smolensk Madonna, to pray for peace. The previous evening, the Metropolitan Kyrill of Smolensk had pronounced anathema, in a TV broadcast, against all who shed blood. At around the same time as the patriarch moved through the packed church, the censers swinging behind him, the first of a group of demonstrators began to gather at October Square. The group swelled to some ten thousand.

What happened next appeared to be revolution. The crowd held a brief rally, then began streaming off down the inner ring road in the direction of the White House some 3 kilometres away. The militia put up some resistance – with clubs and fire hoses – but were beaten back. As the crowd surged around the ring, the militia stood back in side streets, their riot shields up and their helmets on. There was no serious attempt to stop the crowd. At the White House, fusillades of shots rang out – but they came from troops firing in the air, who then pulled back. The crowd surged in, milling round the main entrances. Out came Rutskoi, two guards holding a flak jacket before him. Addressing the seething crowd, he cried: 'Form up into detachments, arm yourselves, we attack the mayory and Ostankino [TV station].'

Barkashov's men did attack the mayoral building which stood a hundred yards from the parliament. There was a brief firefight, a lorry was rammed through the doors, and the militia stationed inside were allowed to escape, ignominiously, through a shattered window. Then, led by General Albert Makashov and the nationalist deputy Ilya Konstantinov, the crowd set off for the Ostankino TV centre.

There, they met the first real resistance, from a few score of well-armed Vityaz special troops who had been deployed at the centre for the past ten days, backed up by armoured personnel carriers sent there when it was learned that the centre was to be attacked. A firefight broke out in the mid-evening, and went on all night; in the course of it, there were several deaths, including reporters caught in a crossfire. At different times throughout the night, the parliament forces took the ITAR TASS news service building, the Customs Committee headquarters and a radio station; they attacked some military installations, including the military counter-intelligence centre, from which they sought to broadcast appeals for support to military units in the country.

Early the next day, after Yeltsin had spent part of the night persuading a reluctant military to intervene, armoured personnel carriers and tanks rolled up to the White House and bombarded it into submission – a spectacle as shocking as it was engrossing, watched by thousands of Muscovites mingling with reporters within easy range of stray bullets. By the end of the afternoon, surrender. After vainly demanding, through the medium of two Italian reporters summoned inside the bombarded White House, for a meeting with the European Union states' ambassadors, Rutskoi, Khasbulatov and their lieutenants came out under armed guard, to be taken to the Lefortovo Prison.

The circumstances of the events gave rise to the theory that the whole incident was an elaborate presidential plot. It was argued that the ease with which the demonstrators were allowed access to the White House, the melting away of the Interior Ministry troops from the cordon they had maintained and the fate which awaited the rebels once they had launched an attack gave rise to the view that the insurrectionists had been 'pulled on to the punch'. Why was there no police or special forces resistance to the mob breaking into the parliament? Why did the Interior Ministry troops melt away so rapidly? Would not the authorities have known of the parliament forces' plans through monitoring phones (which had not been cut off). An anonymous security expert, writing in the weekly *Moscow News* immediately after the events, said that Yeltsin (or his security chiefs) 'had set a trap for Rutskoi and Khasbulatov [and] they swallowed it hook line and sinker'.

This version of the events would render Yeltsin's actions much more bloody and calculating than the account he himself gives. His narrative is of an administration taken off guard, with the interior forces on orders not to use excessive force against the demonstrators and the fate of the capital and the country hanging in the balance throughout the long night of 3/4 October. It is a version not without its gaps and inconsistencies; but to be credible, the conspiratorial account must explain how the authorities knew that the demonstrators would storm the White House, how they could be certain that the parliament side would not raise sufficient support from the army, why they had to plead through the night for army support if they had planned the day's events. Nor does it address the conclusions of a report by Sergei Parkhomenko, one of the sharpest journalists in Moscow and then political writer on the daily *Sevodnya*, who wrote, in a report suppressed by the censorship operating immediately after the coup, that the reaction within the Kremlin (where Parkhomenko was stationed) to the demonstrators' break-in to the White House was one of irresolute panic. Yegor Gaidar, sitting in the Council of Ministers building in Old Square, was so concerned with the lack of support and the immunity with which the parliament's forces were roving the streets that he broadcast an appeal for the democrats to arm themselves (as some did). Late on Sunday, the government demanded delivery of a large cash fund from the Central Bank to pay and feed troops, and, according to Boris Fyodorov, was faced with delaying tactics on the part of the Bank chairman, Victor Gerashchenko. No memoir written since the event, some of which are highly critical of Yeltsin, has exposed a conspiracy within the presidential entourage, a conspiracy which would have had to be entrusted to a large circle of people responsible for giving orders to the troops and others.

It is, however, certain that the immediate results of the suppression of the rebellion were tremendously satisfactory to Yeltsin, and to the democrats who supported him. Dual power was removed. The opposition press – such as *Pravda*, and the ultra-nationalist *Den* ('Day') were suppressed – later to be legalized once more. A range of parties were banned, of which most were also later legalized. All of the major foreign states supported Yeltsin – indeed, congratulated him on his victory over the parliament. The Constitutional Court was dissolved, and a new constitutional commission appointed to thrash out a draft which, it early became clear, would usher in a 'super-presidential' state. Negotiations were opened with the IMF over the rapid payment of a second tranche of the systemic transformation facility. The regions, which had been recalcitrant to – in some cases – the point of rebellion, came rapidly into line, most agreeing to dissolve their own Supreme Soviets and hold elections to new regional bodies, to be called *dumas* in imitation of the federal parliament, in December. Boris Fyodorov, ever a man who relished the exercise of power, said that 'after the tanks, the regions became positively co-operative'. Yeltsin withdrew an earlier promise to hold presidential elections in 1994 but kept to his insistence that the new Duma be elected in December – though with deputies serving only two years before new elections.

There was tremendous confidence that the democrats would win the kind of decisive majority in parliament they had never had since elections began. Russia's Choice, the grouping Yegor Gaidar had built up in his months out of office between January and September, was seen quite simply as the vehicle for reformist power – uniting within it many of the older, late-Soviet-era democrats and the new economic reformers. It was confidently predicted that it would take 40 per cent of the new parliament. Its leading members, ministers in the government, busied themselves with plans to stabilize the economy early in 1994, to widen and deepen privatization and to drive ahead with land and agricultural reform.

But beyond the preparations in the government offices and the sobering effects of the demonstration of presidential power, Russian society continued to reflect and to respond to the same themes which had moved the deputies in the Supreme Soviet – insecurity, fall in living standards, shame at the loss of the Soviet Union, hatred of the new rich class. Even if they had degraded their mandate and betrayed their trust, the Congress deputies had represented real fears and frustrations. Yeltsin's popularity increased in the wake of the October events, but the democrats, after an early surge in the polls, began to fall back as polling day, 11 December, neared.

The democrats were undermined, though they did not notice it at the time, by three things. First, they had not produced what had been promised: rapid economic reform leading to rapid improvement of living standards. Yeltsin had said life would get better by the end of 1992; it was still getting worse, for most, by the end of 1993. Inflation was around 20 per cent a month for much of the pre-election period – a legacy of high Central Bank crediting earlier in the year. The all-but exclusive focus on the technicalities and modalities of economic reform meant that ministers or their spokesmen would casually say such shocking things as that unemployment was too low, or that the cities within the Arctic Circle, in which hundreds of thousands were maintained by massive state subsidies, should be closed down. When, in late November, Gaidar went on a campaign trip to one such city – Vorkuta, a settlement created as the headquarters of a system of concentration camps – he was greeted with stony silence when he invoked the region's savage past and was later blockaded in his room by miners' leaders and local officials demanding payment of wages. His and the other democrat leaders' exposure to the realities of the cities and the countryside on their campaign trips – insofar as they undertook them, which was rarely

– revealed a populace more traumatized by reform than enthused by it, more resentful of those within the Moscow inner ring road than looking to them for leadership. Gaidar was an honest and clever man, but he had almost nothing of Yeltsin's flair for the grand gesture or the intimate anecdote. Yeltsin himself again ignored pleas by aides – above all Gennady Burbulis – to found his own party or get solidly behind Gaidar's. Instead, he put what energies he expended on the campaign into calling for the draft constitution to be ratified in the referendum which had accompanied the parliamentary vote.

The democrat camp was not monolithic: two other parties, Grigory Yavlinsky's Yabloko and the Party of Russian Unity and Accord, led by Sergei Shakhrai and Alexander Shokhin, competed for reformist votes, but in doing so offered a harsh and informed critique of government – democrat – economic policies. All parties, in greater or lesser measure, called for a strengthening of the state and many – especially the communists and Zhirinovsky's Liberal Democrats – called for a re-assembly of the Soviet Union, with agreement or without (Zhirinovsky consistently took the latter position, though not so consistently that he could not deny it when pressed).

Second, the democrats were allied to the rising class of 'New Russians' – bankers, entrepreneurs, traders – who had made clear their fear of parliament's victory because of what they believed with some justice would be at least curbs on their business activities, perhaps arrest for corruption or worse. Vladimir Gusinsky, the chairman of the rising Most finance and media group, believed that a showdown had come, and had mobilized his small private army for use against the parliamentary forces. The business people contributed generously to the expenses of the democrats on their electoral campaigns and their party building: but they were seen in much of the country as alarming and often shady characters whose fortunes had come from speculation, not honest labour. The claims and counter-claims of corruption at the top, which had been such a feature of the spring hostilities, had received wide coverage and gone deep; there seemed a general acceptance that those in power were venal.

Finally, the democrats had made a bargain with Yeltsin and had to live with its consequences. The most bitter of these was the feeling of revulsion, which gathered as the year waned, against the violence with which he crushed the parliamentary revolt. Parliament itself freed the leaders of the parliamentary revolt a few months after they were imprisoned: once free, they began to organize against Yeltsin with added venom. The spectacle of the shellfire-blackened parliament building, though refurbished in record time by gangs of Turkish construction workers, was for months a standing reproach to the presidency, which had initiated the attack on it. Vitaly Tretyakov, acid editor of the *Nezavisimaya Gazeta*, wrote of it that 'Yeltsin's action has historical parallels with those of Nicholas II and Lenin, both of whom destroyed elected assemblies and moved towards authoritarianism and repression'.

In fact, Yeltsin did not move towards either. Most of his most intransigent and irreconcilable enemies stood on one ticket or another in the elections. The notable exception was Sergei Baburin's Russian National Union, which remained banned; but this did not stop Baburin standing (and winning) in his native Omsk as an independent. The media were freed from all curbs — though government subsidies to papers probably did buy some support, and the two main TV channels were unmistakably, if not slavishly, pro-government. Calls by the excitable Vladimir Shumeiko, a first deputy premier, for the banning of the Communist Party and for the disqualification of candidates who propagandized against the constitution were ignored. The first wholly free elections for a Russian parliament in three-quarters of a century could be and were criticized for much: Gaidar's Russia's Choice was continually displayed in news bulletins and was far better funded than the other parties; the time granted for party organization and campaigning was short; the presentation of politicians and platforms dull. In the round, though, the elections were free.

With this freedom, the people chose to punish their new rulers. Mastering a complex, mixed system of voting in which half of the new Duma's 450 seats went to candidates on party lists according to their national showing (with a cut-off below 5 per cent) and the other 225 seats to single-constituency candidates, the voters gave only 15.5 per cent to Russia's Choice in the party lists, though elected 30 of them, twice as many as any other party, for the single mandates. Yabloko received 7.9 per cent and the Party of Unity and Accord 6.8 per cent, bringing the combined (though they did not combine) democrat vote to under 30 per cent, or 78 in the party seats, with a mere 34 in the single mandates, 112 in all.

The Communist Party, reviving under Gennady Zyuganov's dog-gedly opportunistic leadership, took 12.4 per cent in the party seats and 16 seats in the single mandates, a total of 38; with the Agrarians' 33 and the Women of Russia's 23 (both reckoned as their allies) they had 94 seats. The Democratic Party crept in with 5.5 per cent of the party seats (and one single mandate). All others, including the once proud Civic Union (which took a mere 1.9 per cent of the party vote) were excluded.

All others, but one. Vladimir Zhirinovsky had run a storm of a campaign, alone in doing so. Proclaiming that no publicity was bad, he had held rallies in the streets, filled halls, harangued opponents on television. He had promised to restore Russia's greatness and to humble the surrounding states which presumed to disagree with him. 'We will bring them to their knees!' he would cry. 'Why should we suffer? We should make others suffer!' A documentary aired on the first TV channel which aimed to show him in a sinister light appeared to attract more to him. He would speak as though in a stream of consciousness – promising instant betterment of the economy, free vodka, respect for the country through renewed imperial expansion, vast profits from expanded arms sales. His staccato, often funny, sometimes scabrous delivery was wholly unmatched. He never varied his pitch: he was the same from Brest to Vladivostok, and he really did campaign from one to the other.

He won 23 per cent of the party vote, nearly 8 per cent more than Gaidar, though his party did badly in the single mandates (where the Zhirinovsky effect was not felt so strongly). He was the party, though he kept himself elusive, with an image of at once a soaring leader and a trampled victim. His memoir *Last Push to the South*, published just before the elections, shows him in the victim role – a victim of poverty, of a distracted mother and uncaring stepfather, of an indifferent school, of the Kazakh élite in his native Alma Ata, who received all of the privileges while the Russians did the work. Yet on the public platform, and in his party, he commanded absolutely, leaving space for no one else – a trait which would push out many of his lieutenants, including the talented and horrifying author Eduard Limonov and the mass hypnotist Kashpirovsky.

His elevation, and with it the strong showing of a Communist Party which ran on a platform of opposition to a 'global, cosmopolitan

49

dictatorship', poleaxed the democrats. The horror of the new establishment was displayed for all to see by the main TV channel Ostankino, which had put an all-night post-polling party on air on the explicit assumption that it would be a victory celebration of Russia's Choice (for which the then Director General of Ostankino had been a candidate). As the first results came in from the Far East, and it became clear that there was no victory, the thin patina of sophisticated revelry fell away. The announcers ceased to talk for long periods, the camera panning aimlessly around the floor of the Kremlin hall in which it had been staged, showing a cheerful table of Liberal Democrats, a jolly collection of Women of Russia, and, all but alone with his wife, a grim, curt Anatoly Chubais, surrounded by empty chairs which should have been occupied by victorious comrades. The year of living dangerously ended on that image, with a tinselly comeuppance for democratic arrogance.

CHAPTER FOUR

'What is the alternative?'

Boris Yeltsin won a great prize from the elections of December 1993: the approval of his constitution. It was much less noticed than the results of the elections of the Duma, which took place at the same time, but it meant that the president was the true winner of elections in which he had not stood. In the next two years, he threw away that victory in great, careless handfuls, and managed to win back power in 1996 only with great, indeed almost fatal, effort – because his opponents were weaker and less trusted than he.

The pact between Yeltsin and the economic liberals finally unravelled – though economic reform continued, jerkily, in different hands. In the immediate aftermath of the elections, Gaidar and Fyodorov, the leading reformers, demanded of the president that their control of economic policy be confirmed. This was refused, and they went, leaving only Anatoly Chubais of the original Gaidar Group, still battling on at privatization.

Yeltsin had not, in fact, deserted the cause of economic reform, but he had deserted the individuals who espoused it most militantly (he was persuaded to keep Chubais largely through pressure from President Clinton, who came to Moscow in January 1994 for a demonstration that the partnership between America and Russia was still in vigorous health). In the clannish, personalized world of Russian politics, personal sacrifices had to be made and new figures cut into the action at the centre. In Yeltsin's calculations, the results of the elections, which were a defeat for the inflated expectations of the democrats and for the lackadaisical, arrogant campaign which they ran, had to receive a public rebuke. His concern was for stability and balance, since he did not believe he had the luxury to be uncompromising.

He repositioned himself, strengthened themes he had raised before, but in a more muted form than he now did. His keynote speech to the

51

new Duma stole some Zhirinovsky clothing, calling for an increase in arms sales abroad to pay for public spending at home, and for a new war on crime (there had been, and were to be, many such declarations). He increased the volume of his concern for the Russians living in the former Soviet states outside of Russia, absurdly vowing to punish breaches of their civil rights, or discrimination against them (which was widespread and continuous) with 'deeds not words'. He warned the West that Nato expansion, then beginning to be seriously mooted, was a 'path towards new threats for Europe and the world'. Yet still, he claimed fidelity to economic reform, in particular to low inflation and to production for the market.

But the larger and more noticed difference was his carelessness over his ruling style. It seemed as though he had concluded that he had attained security for his regime, and that he could behave as he liked – the very opposite of what this raw period of a new constitutional order and a fractious legislature demanded from an executive president. He had always withdrawn for large stretches of time – most notably immediately after the August 1991 coup, when he was being urged to ride the wave of popular acclaim. But these absences grew almost as large as his presences. In early 1994, he was away from Moscow for much of the first two months. He withdrew again in March, again for a long period in summer and for shorter periods later in the year. He was a man often in pain from back and other injuries, and he required drugs and treatment to continue working – which, some days, he did only fleetingly. He was also prone to numbing, all-enveloping depressions – periods when he would sit staring at the wall, unable to move, to read, to receive. Never a consistent ruler, he became a very sporadic one, and thus, though he always held the reins in the last analysis, his power naturally tended to be taken by, or was given to, others.

Sometimes worse than his absences were his appearances. He appeared to be – and almost everyone believed he was – often drunk, in public. He had seemed to be so at some summits of CIS leaders – in particular in Tashkent in 1993, where he had had to be helped off his plane, had been called a drunkard by nationalist deputies the next day, and reacted to the criticism at the press conference by a long, rambling monologue, in the course of which he ridiculed Mikhail Gorbachev, then on a speaking tour of the United States, for still thinking he was president of the Soviet Union. At the end of March 1993, he had made a speech to the Supreme Soviet which was slurred, disjointed and absurdly sentimental in such a hostile forum. In September, Khasbulatov signified his contempt by referring to Yeltsin while flicking his finger against his neck, the Russian's non-verbal euphemism for a drunkard.

These incidents could be explained, or explained away. But the two occasions later in 1994 which could not happened on foreign soil, and were a permanent disaster because they played so brutally into his citizens' feeling of humiliation. In September, he went to Berlin to take part in a ceremony marking the final withdrawal of Russian troops – a difficult occasion, requiring poker-backed solemnity and much verbiage. Instead, he was shown seizing the baton from the conductor of a military band, conducting the band in a jerky, excited fashion and singing loudly the words of the song they played. In October, on a trip to the US for talks with Clinton, he staged a press conference at which he harangued the reporters, gestured wildly and talked incessantly. On the brief stopover visit to Ireland returning from the US trip, he rendered the visit farcical when his plane stopped in Shannon, taxied up to the red carpet beside which stood the Irish president, prime minister and cabinet, the door opened – and no one appeared. Finally, Oleg Soskovets, the first deputy prime minister, ran down the steps, apologized profusely, but said that the president was not well and could not visit. When he returned to Moscow, Yeltsin said his security guard had not woken him, that he had been furious, but that he was fine. It was an insult to a sovereign nation which the Irish took without fuss – but it was also without precedent.

That flurry of occasions was a low point. He was never so bad in public again, and on a number of set occasions – such as the visit of Queen Elizabeth II towards the end of 1994 and the celebrations marking the seventeenth anniversary of the Great Patriotic (Second) War in March 1995, he conducted himself with the massive dignity he could muster quite naturally, and which had contributed to his leadership aura. But for the Russian head of state to so abase himself among foreigners, for Russia to be so represented, brought a flood of real pain.

Who ran the country? For many, after 1993, it was General Alexander Korzhakov, a stout, active man in his late forties who had been the KGB officer assigned to Yeltsin while the latter was in the Politbureau, and who left with him to provide him with protection as outcast, candidate and president. His initial sacrifice of position and money was hugely well rewarded – less (initially) in money as in the power to which Yeltsin gave his aide access, and the full trust he reposed in him. Little of moment was done in the presidential suite over which Korzhakov could not have an influence. A measure of how extraordinary that influence was could be seen when letters he had written in November 1994 to Chernomyrdin were leaked: the letters showed him 'proposing' to Chernomyrdin that the latter 'review' decisions to liberalize oil exports because the decision, pressed upon the government by the IMF and the World Bank, 'is wholly inadmissible both for the political and economic consequences of this country'.

In December, officers of the presidential guard commanded by Korzhakov seized members of the bodyguard of Vladimir Gusinsky, chairman of Most Bank and a man close to Yuri Luzhkov, the Moscow mayor, at that time a rival of Yeltsin's and a possible contender for the presidency. The ostensible excuse was that they had been in possession of weapons on the route taken to and from the Kremlin by Yeltsin; indeed they had, and had been for some time, since the route was substantially the same as that taken by Gusinsky to and from his office. The Moscow KGB, summoned by Gusinsky, backed away from a confrontation. Gusinsky left the country for a long period immediately afterwards. Korzhakov was said to have remarked with satisfaction that his favourite sport was 'goose-hunting' (a pun on Gus-insky, the Russian word being the same as the English).

What was publicly known, and what was rumoured, about General Korzhakov pointed to a relationship between him and Yeltsin of great trust, continual closeness and astonishing licence. The use of his men to arrest Gusinsky's guards – a simple act of humiliation – was wholly unpunished, his role as arbiter of Russia's economic policy neither explained nor denied. But, like much else in Russian public life, it was alarming in its implications, less so in its apparent and immediate effects. Gusinsky returned to Moscow, and continued to thrive. The government did, not long after Korzhakov wrote the letter, liberalize oil exports. Yeltsin insisted, angrily and publicly, that Korzhakov was no more than his chief security man, and that government policy was decided at the meetings he held with Victor Chernomyrdin.

Such an assurance – like that of any head of state and government who insists that the cabinet is where policy is made – was both true and false, though in Russia there was rather more falsity in the balance. The government did govern, in the economic sphere, but its decisions were second-guessed, delayed or blocked by the president's swollen staff, or by powerful industrialists and lobbies who captured the president's ear, or by the crises of the moment, which, in many cases, the president himself had either caused or exacerbated. Yeltsin adopted the style, in his last two years of rule, of blaming his ministers for mistakes or omissions, and typically accused them of 'lack of co-ordination' of policies – a state of affairs he made much worse by his random interventions.

Many who attempted to explain the byzantine workings of the presidential-government machine used the analogy of a clan society, in which groups founded largely on common economic interests competed, through their representatives within government, for influence, power and money or access to making it. On this model, the government was composed of a 'security clan' headed by Yeltsin himself, with Korzhakov and General Mikhail Barsukov, who became head of the Federal Counter-intelligence Service (former KGB) in 1995, as its lead members; an 'energy clan' headed by Chernomyrdin; a 'military-industrial clan' headed by Oleg Soskovets, the first deputy prime minister; a 'Western clan' headed in government by Anatoly Chubais, who remained a first deputy premier until January 1996; a 'Moscow clan' headed by Yuri Luzhkov, the powerful mayor of the capital, and various other clans or sub-clans representing this or that interest – such as agriculture, large regions like the Urals, or valuable resources like gold and diamonds. These groups all pursued their own interests ruthlessly and continually, but did so peacefully (save for the occasional assassination) and with a common and overriding interest in stability. Thomas Graham, a smart diplomat at the US Embassy in the mid-nineties, provoked a stiff protest when he allowed to be published (in *Nezavisimaya Gazeta*, 23 November 1995) an article which stated flatly that the government *was* the clan system, that it had ensured stability, but that it had its limits which were growing ever tighter. Graham wrote:

There are very few committed supporters of democracy in any of the clans. Democratic procedures, including elections, are mostly seen as weapons in the struggle for power. All of the clans speak of the necessity to introduce 'order' and achieve stability; in current Russian conditions, that would

inevitably lead to a limiting of democratic freedoms. In economic policy
. . . the fault line lies not between the supporters and opponents of economic
reform, but between the free traders and the protectionists – those who
want to integrate Russia into the world economy now and those who
believe it can only be done after a period behind protective walls. In foreign
policy . . . a steadily hardening line in pursuing Russian national interests
has everyone's support. This applies to European security and the extension
of Nato, as well as over the war in former Yugoslavia.

This explained much, and accorded well with the ingrained pattern of
Russian public life, in which networks and groups reward and promote
their own while excluding or punishing outsiders in a vigorous and
routine way. In this it was often compared to Italy. But the Russian
game was played for much higher stakes and was more ruthless; nor
was there on the horizon any reform movement of the kind which
appeared in Italy in the early nineties. The clan analysis explained the
large gap between reform rhetoric and actual stasis, the vast tax and
other privileges given by a cabinet desperate for public revenue to
energy and other companies, the continuing stream of subsidies to
unreforming enterprises and institutions, the importance of balancing
the government with various apparently incompatible people there less
for their skills or experience than for their representative capacity.

It did not explain, however, why both reform, and a certain liberality,
remained on the agenda. If much remained unreformed or even
untouchable – as agriculture appeared to be throughout the first five
years – still, the government nerved itself to withstand the temptations
of money-printing, of nationalist or neo-imperialist rhetoric, of suppression of the media and of supine despair – all of which had been
the constant policies, or had been deployed at different times by the
communist regimes which went before them. There was, besides the
networks of clans and the semi-legal or illegal acts they constantly
committed in pursuit of power and gain, a separate dynamic which was
an active recognition of the need for reform.

Yeltsin, who preserved many decencies even as he committed many
indecencies, was in part responsible for this. Chernomyrdin was another
large factor. Victor Chernomyrdin was a close, careful man of sharp
intelligence and shrewd judgement who spent his first year in office
learning how to operate the levers he had at his command, and educating
himself on the realities which confronted him. Brought in to placate

the Supreme Soviet, he early disappointed, then infuriated, its deputies by unequivocally pronouncing himself the president's man. In the 1993 confrontation with the parliament, Chernomyrdin's unambiguous support for Yeltsin and his accompaniment of the president to the Defence Ministry before dawn on 4 October 1993 to persuade the defence chiefs to assault the parliament were extreme tests of his loyalty which he passed, and which made him, for a time, unassailable.

He held himself aloof from the 1993 election campaign, seeking medical treatment abroad and taking a holiday just before it. He was thus untouched by the collapse of the democrats' hopes, and with the resignations of Gaidar and Fyodorov lost the two men who were the main conduits for Western advice and aid – thus allowing him to become that himself. Even as the official figures showed a production drop of 25 per cent over the previous year, as debts of the enterprises rose to over Rbs30 trillion, as oil production continued to decline sharply, Chernomyrdin turned, not to the money-printing press or to the world of command economics he had known, but to the West.

He found himself a go-between in this crucial dialogue. This was a man named Peter Castenfeld, a discreet, courteous Swedish-born financier who had been on the board of a number of blue chip companies and who had a range of contacts across the financial world and at the top of the international financial institutions – including Michel Camdessus, the managing director of the IMF. Castenfeld carried a message to Camdessus: in sum, it was that Chernomyrdin was serious about reform, and could deliver. Chernomyrdin was aware that negotiations between the IMF and his own officials on the budget were going badly, and that the IMF team had little faith in the government's ability or determination. He wanted a summit with Camdessus, in which his own determination to break out of the impasse could be expressed.

In face of deep scepticism on the part of the IMF officials, who had gone grey in the pursuit of consistent reform in Russia, Chernomyrdin got agreement. He took Camdessus to the hunting lodge at Zavidovo where Brezhnev had talked to Nixon and Kissinger. Together, the two men appeared to reach an understanding which bridged Chernomyrdin's suspicions of IMF intent and the Fund director's fears that the money might disappear down the black hole of a budget which had a gap between income and expenditure of $36 billion, then worth 9 per cent of Russian GNP. Camdessus promised to pay the second half of a $3 billion fund named the 'systemic transformation facility' – a way of getting money into Russia while ignoring many of the IMF's own criteria – whose first part had been disbursed the previous June. Chernomyrdin said he would reduce inflation of 7 per cent a month by the year end, and raise new taxes.

Camdessus, under pressure from the Group of Seven nations to do something for Russia, gambled on Chernomyrdin; he had little choice. In doing so, he cleared the way for the Russian premier to be seen both as a reformer, and as a more reliable partner than the erratic, often absent Yeltsin. Chernomyrdin seemed to enjoy the role, writing a remarkable article in the *Financial Times* in May 1994 which revelled in the transformation (in truth, in its very early stages) of cities with their Soviet-era 'dejected, sombre queues' into places with 'smart advertising hoardings and attractive, lively goods'.

The gamble failed in the short term, but appeared to succeed in the longer. The government and the Central Bank did boost the supply of money, breaking the IMF guidelines – and failed to bring in adequate tax revenues to cover the gap. By the end of the year, inflation was over 10 per cent a month – higher than at the time of the IMF deal – output was still falling and the Central Bank was intervening continually to cushion the fall in the rouble. In October, the rouble crashed by 20 per cent in one day: it recovered the next, but the consequences were a presidential witch hunt for the 'guilty men' led by the security chiefs, and the firing of Victor Gerashchenko, the Central Bank chairman, Sergei Dubynin, the acting finance minister and a little later Alexander Shokhin, the economic minister. A few days later, a vote of no confidence in the government was narrowly survived after a tough speech by Chernomyrdin to a noisy Duma.

The struggle over economic policy over which Chernomyrdin presided was a murky one – hard to follow, even by insiders, bitterly contested by the lobbies, ever open to presidential, and other, interference. Yet by the end of 1995 one thing was plain: Chernomyrdin had accepted that the basics of a market economy must be set in place in Russia, and in the broadest of terms he was supported by Yeltsin. Anatoly Chubais, reflecting on his long (by contemporary Russian standards) period in office soon after being forced from it by Yeltsin early in 1996, said of Yeltsin:

He has made more mistakes than one can count, fundamental ones. But we kept reform going for over four years and he was president all of this time. You always had to ask – what is the alternative? That was the basic question for any minister in the Yeltsin governments.

Chernomyrdin's importance was not confined to the economic sphere. As Yegor Gaidar observed in 1994, he had changed the definition of centrism – from being a fundamental if disguised objection to a policy of tight money and rapid privatization to one of accepting both of these while manoeuvring to soften their effects, or at least polish their image. The previous quintessential figure of the centre had been Arkady Volsky, a man from the same background and roughly of the same age as Chernomyrdin – in fact, in the Gorbachev period, with rather more lustrous reformist credentials. He had used centrism as a moral/political bludgeon to preserve privileges and slow or halt change, even while preaching the need to dismantle the command system. But the result of that was to produce stasis – as Chernomyrdin, though from the same mould, had seen. He thus redefined centrism as dogged persistence with hard reforms, on the grounds that, to use the old British Labour Party slogan, 'you know it makes sense'. This shift within the ranks of the Soviet technocracy was an important one: it effectively destroyed the old 'centre', propelling some of them into the presidential camp, others into a more overtly oppositionist stance increasingly identified with the Russian Communist Party.

Chernomyrdin's view increasingly became that of the Westernizers. He owed that in some measure to the education he got from his younger, liberal colleagues – and from the fact that his 'clan', the energy clan, was not a protectionist one (always assuming that foreigners would not own Russian oil companies, or any major part of them). Thus, though he failed to stabilize the currency in 1994 – a Black Tuesday in which the rouble crashed by 25 per cent was an expression of that failure – he was able to recover from it, to work with a cabinet in which Chubais had been appointed first deputy premier in charge of the economy and finance, and with a new Central Bank governor, Tatyana Paramanova, who took her cue from Chubais in a way Gerashchenko never had done.

As the Russian army committed itself to the quagmire of Chechnya in December 1995, a parallel series of discussions were under way between the IMF and the government, on the lending of $8.3 billion over the following year. The international institutions accepted that they could do business with Chernomyrdin, and though admiration of him was not universal in their circles because of his determined exemption of 'his' Gazprom corporation from rational levels of taxation and any surveillance, he was seen as tough enough and convinced enough to hold a tight budget.

All through 1995 and into 1996, he did – bolstered by a speech from Yeltsin early in 1995 which promised his support to a 'third attempt at stabilization – because the international financial institutions expect it of us'. 1995 was, for the reformers and the international financial institutions, the most successful year of their co-operation with Russia. The IMF put people in the Central Bank and the Finance Ministry, monitoring the adhesion of the government to money supply and credit targets, disbursing the money in monthly tranches once they had satisfied themselves that the indicators were on track. The rouble, held within a 'corridor' of upper and lower exchange rates with the dollar, strengthened considerably. Inflation sank to 3 per cent a month by the end of 1995. The fall in industrial production slowed; in a (very) few sectors, it even began to stabilize, or rise slightly.

For the Russians, the effect of the policy of reducing the budget deficit and keeping the money supply tight was very bad. Real wages, halved by the Gaidar shock in January 1992, had recovered a little in the next four years; in 1995, they sank below the January 1992 level, and stayed there, recovering to match it only in December. Consumption also fell sharply to early 1992 levels – though it recovered more strongly to reach near the previous year's levels by the autumn. What Chernomyrdin and his cabinet knew made sense did not accord with what the population knew. The government went into the 1995 Duma elections having delivered, quite consciously, a 'feelbad' factor to most of their potential voters.

These parliamentary elections, the second and last of the first presidential term, were conducted on a political landscape which was said by many Russian analysts to have 'normalized' – by which they meant that it was not, as the 1993 election had been, under the shadow of a blackened White House, nor was it fought on the prior assumption that one 'party of power' would emerge victorious. It was to be a real struggle. It *was* a real struggle – perhaps the most real Russia had ever seen – but it was normal only in a Russian context.

The democrats had fallen apart politically in the two years since Russia's Choice had failed to take power. In order to create Russia's Choice before the 1993 elections, its organizers – who included Gennady Burbulis – sought to unite the Gorbachev-era democrats and the new Russian élites which had thrown their lot in with Yeltsin, and expected the fruits of power. Gaidar, however, was at once too principled and too diffident to lead a coalition of such a kind; and after its failure, its strongest personalities shot off in different directions, at different times, creating and merging with new parties in the Duma to further their ambitions.

In a conversation recalling the travails of Russia's Choice, Sergei Golovkov, one of its main organizers, reflected in 1995 that its leading personalities would not be told what to do, and would sometimes do nothing at all.

They were mainly ungovernable. Many of them were or had been ministers, and they wished to be treated like that within the party. All had different ideas on what the campaign should be, all had different platforms on which they wanted it to fight.

By the 1995 elections, the remains of Russia's Choice and Democratic Russia were in half a dozen parties, or in none. Gaidar's group, renamed Russia's Democratic Choice, competed with Boris Fyodorov's Forward Russia, Irene Khakamada's Common Cause, Sergei Shakhrai's Party of Russian Unity and Accord, Svyatoslav Fyodorov's Party of Svyatoslav Fyodorov, Ella Pamfilova's Bloc Pamfilova and Anatoly Sobchak's Russian Movement for Democratic Reforms. These parties competed futilely against each other, none – including Gaidar's – scoring above the 5 per cent minimum required to put deputies into the party list section of the Duma. Since, for the most part, the party leaders headed their lists, they lost or did not gain a seat. Some, like Boris Fyodorov, stood in single mandate districts and were elected: it showed a certain lack of faith in one's own party, but it was canny.

That which personal ambition and their failure to secure a Duma majority in 1993 had not destroyed of the democrats' unity was completed by the war in Chechnya (the subject of chapter 12). Indeed, it would be true to say that the first casualty of Chechnya was not democracy, as many liberals claimed, but the democrats. Oleg Boiko of Rossisky Credit Bank, Gaidar's main funder and a leading member of the Russia's Choice executive, split with Gaidar over the latter's passionate opposition to the war (and thus to Yeltsin) and transferred his allegiance to the centre parties which Yeltsin's aides were forming in 1995 to act as a support for the president. It was a telling moment: Boiko had been an apparently sincere democrat and free marketeer – as well as something of an Anglophile, using a large black Daimler for his business trips round Moscow. He realized, however, that his bank, a major one on the Moscow scene but overextended and dependent on government backing, needed political support. That came at a price: by 1994, it was clear what price the businessmen would have to pay to ensure they did not find themselves out in the cold.

Andrei Kozyrev, the foreign minister, increasingly tied to Yeltsin, also left Gaidar. The thread, constantly fraying, which attached Kozyrev to power was wholly in the president's hands. Boris Fyodorov, ever a strong-state man, came out in support of the war – though it did not seem to much help his vote, which was below 2 per cent. Gennady Burbulis also left Gaidar, in part because of his opposition to the anti-war policy, but did not align himself strongly to any party thereafter, and stood successfully as an independent in his native Sverdlovsk region. On the other hand, both Gleb Yakunin and Lev Ponomaryev, veteran liberals who had joined the Russia's Choice faction in the Duma, also left because they thought Gaidar was too *soft* on Yeltsin by offering him co-operation if he would start negotiations with the Chechen leadership.

The one group which did worse than the democrats – though they had never done well at the polls – were the old centrists, who comprised a variety of small groups of which the most noted was the Party of Unions and Industrialists, with Arkady Volsky at its head. Joining them in defeat were the Women of Russia, who had broken through in 1993 but made little mark on the Duma or on political life. They, like Volsky's various groups, had preferred platitudes to policies, and though much less sinister than many who did much better, they were clearly seen as a throwback to some of the more pious hopes of the Gorbachev era.

Where Chernomyrdin defined one kind of centrism, Grigory Yavlinsky defined another. His Yabloko Party was formed before the 1993 elections with the then ambassador to the US Vladimir Lukin and the anti-corruption campaigner Yuri Boldyrev (who dropped out of the party before the 1995 elections) in the collective leadership. Yavlinsky had emerged as an impressive if never quite clearly focused politician – for reform, but not Gaidar's (or post-Gaidar) reforms. He had always been against the break-up of the Soviet Union; had been for privatization before price liberalization; had always supported regional initiatives. He was the clean democrat, but his party's voting record in the Duma was more anti-Yeltsin than Zhirinovsky's, and Yavlinsky was violently opposed to the shelling of the White House (he tried to mediate between Rutskoi and Yeltsin). After the Chechen war broke out, he found some common cause with Gaidar in condemning it, but went further, calling for Yeltsin's impeachment – testimony that his main concern was for the presidency. His programme and propaganda explicitly endorsed relatively high inflation – up to 5 per cent a month – as a lesser evil than continued industrial decline and cutting of already meagre social and investment programmes. He claimed the mantle of the leader of the democrats, and since his was the only party which could claim such a name, which also passed the 5 per cent barrier in the 1995 elections, he appeared to have a strong position in the more important presidential race. But his party vote was down, to 7 per cent from its 1993 level of 8 per cent (though he took 10 per cent of the Duma seats), and Gaidar and Chubais were deeply reluctant to trust him – the more since, soon after the elections, he began serious talks with Zyuganov's Communist Party on co-operation.

Where Russia's Choice had been the 'party of government' in 1993, a new one – a centrist one – had appeared for the 1995 elections. As the democrats fractured and the communists strengthened their position, presidential aides led by Sergei Shakhrai and Georgy Satarov began to put together the bases of a support mechanism within the Duma – their efforts taking extra urgency after the beginning of the Chechen war, when it became clear only Zhirinovsky's Liberal Democrats would support Yeltsin. Three factions – Duma 96, Stability and Russia – appeared, attracting deputies away from existing groups, each espousing vague left- or right-of-centre loyalties with support for the authorities and the war. In April 1995, Chernomyrdin said he would put himself at the head of a new bloc – and scooped most of the members of these three into it.

The idea, very much one incubated in the offices of the Kremlin advisers, was that Chernomyrdin would found a party, which was named 'Our Home is Russia' as a right-of-centre grouping, while a left-of-centre party would be led by Ivan Rybkin, the Duma speaker. These were not parties in what had come to be the West European meaning of the word – mass, or once-mass organizations mobilized to sustain representatives in parliaments. They were centres round which national and regional élites were supposed to rally; and their ideological positions were pre-determined to express the permissible limits of debate.

Rybkin's 'party' failed, but Chernomyrdin's took into it most of his fellow ministers (Chubais was a notable exception), most of the regional leaders and a number of public personalities, of whom the most outstanding was the nationally venerated actor and film director Nikita Mikhalkov, who was put second on the party list after the prime minister. Its programme was composed of slogans: it was running on a claim of competence, a continuation of the reforms, stability.

'Our Home is Russia' had formidable resources behind it, attracted some of the most experienced organizers and had most of the governing names attached. But an anti-establishment mood was running; the regional leaders, closer to public opinion, scented the party's low popularity and many peeled away as the election approached. Yeltsin, as before, stayed aloof, especially after Chernomyrdin gathered a surge of popularity when he talked down the hostage crisis in Budennovsk in a conversation with the leader of the Chechen hostage-takers which was shown on TV. The prime minister added campaigning to his other burdens, and did it with obvious effort. The message of 'steady as she goes' was not a winner, for most people had not experienced the motion as a steady one. Still, relative enrichment in the large cities saved them from débâcle, and the party took just over 10 per cent of the party list places, with over 12 per cent of the Duma seats.

The winners were said to be the communists and the nationalists – and this was true, though it needed to be qualified. All of the nationalist parties bar one did poorly. In particular, the one that had been talked up to be the breakthrough nationalist party of the elections performed very poorly indeed. This was the Congress of Russian Communities, led by a troika of the former secretary of the National Security Council Yuri Skokov, the former trade minister Sergei Glaziev, and – the group's star – General Alexander Lebed, the commander of the Russian Fourteenth Army in the Slav area of Transdnestr, in Moldova.

It appeared a well-balanced leadership: Skokov, once an intimate of Yeltsin's, had broken with him early enough to be a credible oppositionist; Glaziev, once a radical reformer, had broken with the reformers over the direction of economic reform and had become the only oppositionist able to argue with his former colleagues on their own terms; while Lebed, an Afghan hero, protector of the Russians in a former Soviet republic and uncompromising opponent of the war in Chechnya, appeared to give the ticket its backbone and glamour.

The Congress of Russian Communities appeared made for the general. It was based on the Russian communities in former Soviet and Russian ethnic republics who felt themselves threatened by the rise of ethnic nationalism – precisely the people Lebed had defended (while expressing a soldierly contempt for the quality of their civilian leaders, whom he saw as corrupt and self-serving) in Transdnestr. He made his coming-out speech at the Congress's assembly in April 1995, and – delivered in his harsh, deep voice to a rapt hall – it was a considerable rhetorical achievement.

We live in hard and anxious times: a time of war in Chechnya, of misery, of economic catastrophe, of limitless criminality. Times when powerless politicians, who have plunged our country into chaos and transformed the inheritors of a great Russian culture into a herd of resigned beasts, do not dare tell the people the truth. In Chechnya, the military leadership uses aircraft and artillery to re-establish constitutional order: they have shelled a city where tens of thousands of innocents are buried in cellars. Our leaders, their brains addled with alcohol, decorate their friends for such actions. How can they look at themselves in the mirror? . . . If the army survives, Russia survives because, like the country, it is founded on eternal principles: national pride and religion . . . In all our debates on the rights of man, on democracy, on reforms, we have lost the Russian man. A boy who from childhood is used to trafficking in drugs, to filling his head with pornographic and violent rubbish will never become a citizen or a soldier of his country. A girl who is surrounded by vicious men who promise to make her into a model but who are in fact intent on making her into a whore will never become a citizen and a mother. It is the moral decomposition of our country which is the most horrible thing of all.

And on his opponent in the nationalist camp:

Zhirinovsky makes a fanfare before the cameras, surrounded by whores, promotes criminal ideas while extolling the superiority of the Russian people and poisoning our relations with other nations.

Whether or not he wrote the speech himself, it supported the image he wished to project. Yet neither his sentiments nor he himself caught on in that campaign; immensely popular in polls, especially among his fellow officers, he could not raise his party above Skokov's dourness or Glaziev's rather abstract discourses on the economy. For all Lebed's scorn of him, it was to Zhirinovsky the nationalist electorate turned in larger numbers – enough to make the Liberal Democrats comfortably the second largest party to the Communists, though its vote in the party lists had halved since 1993 – perhaps because of Zhirinovsky's pirouetting to the cameras from Paris to Tokyo.

In his two years in parliament, Zhirinovsky had played a curious, schizophrenic game. No one was as loud and outrageous as he in denouncing the government and at times the president. Yet in all of the crucial moments he had supported Yeltsin – in the siege of the White House before entering the Duma, in the adoption of the constitution as a prelude to elections, in the invasion of Chechnya in December 1994, and in the hostage crises in 1995 and 1996 at Budennovsk in Southern Russia and at Pervomaisk in Dagestan. In each of these he was – as he frequently explained – concerned to support the strengthening of the executive power, as antechambers to the dictatorship he believed essential and was ready to install.

At the same time he was relatively moderate in deed. In spite of a little black-shirted guard called 'Zhirinovsky's Falcons', deployed on occasion, no storm troops toured the streets (as Cossacks did in some of the southern Russian cities) and the Liberal Democrat deputies – their leader apart – were no more outrageous than any other group. Indeed, by the 1995 election, the party began to acquire a modest number of candidates drawn from the upper reaches of the regional and federal administrations, including the deputy mayor of the city of Yakutsk, Yuri Posdnyakov, and – more bizarrely for an overtly anti-Semitic party – Vasily Kazko, the deputy head of the Cultural Ministry from Bizhorbijan, the Autonomous Jewish Region (who may or may not have been Jewish: the Jewish autonomous republic's population had only 5 per cent of its titular nationality).

But Zhirinovsky was above all a stream of injured consciousness, a never-ending, sometimes vicious, sometimes witty, always personal commentary on a world turned upside down – yet at the same time hanging his thoughts on the bones of opinions one could hear every-where. At a press conference given a few days before the December elections, he gave some of his thoughts, typical of the man:

Lenin was right when he said that capitalism was decaying. It would have decayed without us. This parasitical capitalism. It is our sweat and our money that keeps the West afloat. It is not a dying capitalism because we are bailing it out. Were it not for Russia the West would have long fallen under the onslaught of the Turkish forces, the Tatars and the Mongols, as well as North Africa. Those invaders more than once laid siege to Budapest and Vienna. Negroes are marching on Washington. Half of Paris is groaning under the Algerians. Millions of Turks are keeping Germany in fear. German right-wingers are burning Turks alive in houses on the territory of Germany. That is democracy and everyone keeps silent. That is why the LDPR, like Russia, does not have allies . . .

This was the essence of the Zhirinovsky style, of the kind he had been peddling for five years. It was a kind of tabloid political history, relentlessly pushing buttons of fear and hate with the shrewdest sense of which buttons to push. Zhirinovsky appealed to prejudice, he produced fantasies to excite a politically rootless people – and he also told the truth, at times, in a way few others did.

We want only those who genuinely profess communist ideas to call them-selves communists. When some communist parties are such only by name and have long retreated from communist slogans, have forgotten about internationalism, but turn out to be nationalists, patriots, champions of private ownership, what sort of communists are they? . . . we are for state power, the Russian idea, but what has the name Communist Party got to do with it? . . . all must have slogans that correspond to their views and correspond to reality. Let us not kid ourselves and each other. So if Mr Zyuganov [the Communist Party leader] has become a permanent fixture in the American embassy and is talking tenderly to American businessmen, how can you speak about a state [-owned] economy? Americans are not interested in a state-owned economy . . . we are against hypocrisy. We are against Gennady Andreyevich [Zyuganov] trotting over to the American embassy for breakfast, to the British one for lunch, to the French one for cocktails and still calling himself a communist . . .

This tirade was composed of pique that *he* was not called to talk tenderly to the American Chamber of Commerce, as Zyuganov famously had in December 1995, and of a bid to attract disaffected communists to the LDPR. But it was also right. The Communist Party, the winner of the 1995 Duma elections, had been positioned by Zyuganov in a space even more ambiguous than that which it occupied under Mikhail Gorbachev.

It had been a long march for Gennady Zyuganov. As the Soviet Party began to break up into factions in 1990, those members who wished to remain loyal to Leninism founded the United Workers' Front – the core for later groups, especially Victor Anpilov's Russian Communist Workers' Party – and, later, the Russian Communist Party. In a legal limbo once the Soviet Party of which it was nominally a part was banned following the August 1991 putsch, it rehabilitated itself with a successful defence of the CPSU during its trial in late 1992, winning a judgement which allowed the Russian Party to organize. Zyuganov was elected its leader in March 1993 – only to have it banned again after that year's 'October events'.

Released from its ban weeks before the December 1993 election, the party did surprisingly well, with 12 per cent of the vote, particularly in Central and Southern Russia. The CPSU had had some 18 million members on paper when it was banned; the Russian Communist Party claimed 500,000 once it was able to mobilize them. But that was hundreds of thousands more than any other party; and in many towns and collective farms, the habits of meeting and talking and organizing continued. Many of these members were elderly, but the elderly voted more heavily than other groups. Close to the Agrarian Party and moderately so to the Women of Russia, the RCP built up a reputation for discipline and relative cleanness – in a sharp contradiction of the antics of many on the 'democratic' and the nationalist sides.

Zyuganov adopted – and perfected – the tactic already familiar to many democrats, and to many nationalists, and increasingly to the president himself: he refused to stick to a clear line, but merely added new positions to old ones, whether or not they contradicted each other. His party programme allowed that private property should have the same rights as state and co-operative property; and it explicitly committed the RCP to pluralism. But at the same time it proclaimed that privatizations would be reversed and RCP leaders – especially the most senior regional figure in the party, Aman Tuleyev, head of the Kuzbass administration – often referred to their aim of re-establishing it as a vanguard party, the first among (non-) equals.

Two months before the Duma elections, Zyuganov gave his speech to the American Chamber of Commerce monthly lunch. Only the restless, nervous mobility of his bruiser's face and powerful body marked him out from the business people: he was as soberly suited and tied as they, as were the officials he brought with him. He told them:

We know what prevents you from making investments. Many things: first of all, the absence of sophisticated legislation, taxes, the high level of corruption, absence of guarantees of personal safety. We have already drafted documents that would allow business people to safely invest their capital here in the hope of reaping profits, without having to fear for their personal safety. In my conversations with Clinton, Christopher, Gore, Sam Nunn and a number of other senators I said directly that elections are the only guarantee of the democratic process, including a good business relationship . . . over the past years when I have been a peoples' deputy I have studied the experience of many other countries . . . our party is striving to absorb all that is best in the experience of the world . . . I preach good neighbourliness and co-operation.

I heard Zyuganov give a stump speech in Orel, his home city, a few weeks before the 1995 elections. I had interviewed him a few days before, and had found him relatively jovial and self-controlled. I asked him if he thought of himself still as a Marxist. He smiled, and said: 'You know, they say Jesus Christ was the first Marxist.' A colleague then asked if he were a religious man. 'You know, Christianity is very close to socialism in many ways.'

Nothing of this in Orel. The hectoring, dogmatic speaker he had been when he appeared on the national scene in the early nineties was still visible, but had been augmented by the tricks of a stump speaker's trade, which meant that he now brought the semblance of passion and some wit into a performance of caustic denunciation of casino capitalism and its effects on the population.

The power which has been over you since the Soviet Union was destroyed has cheated you of your savings, your inheritance, your wealth. We had a common right to the wealth we had, and now we see it sold to criminals and to foreigners. We had a country which was great in the world, and now we see it treated with contempt by America and robbed. We lived in peace with people of all nationalities and now we have national leaders who sow hatred of Russians and threaten them. This is the state to which the democrats have reduced you . . .

With such a portmanteau approach, with many – especially the elderly – flocking to him to try to secure the old virtues he implicitly held out as rediscoverable, with some business people quietly funding his party and telling each other that the communists were now tame, with the IMF privately giving assurances (it could do no other) that it would work with any régime, including a communist one, as long as it could approve its policies, Zyuganov took over 22 per cent of the party list vote and, with the single mandate seats, 35 per cent of the seats in the Duma. The other leftist parties all failed to clear the 5 per cent hurdle, but all – especially the Agrarians – had single mandate members, which pushed the left vote up to over 42 per cent. In January 1996, the party had its nominees win the chairmanship of the Duma, and of the Federation Council, or upper house; it also took the chairmanship of most of the important Duma committees. It saw Anatoly Chubais, most hateful to it because of his resolute anti-communism, lose his post as head of the government's economic strategy, to be replaced by Victor Kadannikov, general director of the Avtovaz car plant, a much more emollient figure.

Zyuganov was confirmed in April as his party's nominee for the presidency – with no one being any the wiser as to what he really believed in. For Chubais it was plain: he was the unreformed inheritor to a murderous party, dangerous both because of the programme, but more because of his ignorance of what Russia had become and his desire for vengeance on those who had made it so. Out of office, Chubais went round his friends in the finance houses and raised money to fund a centre which put out an anti-communist message in the run-up to the presidential elections. He was unusual; most others, at home and abroad, had tried to convince themselves there was no need to worry.

CHAPTER FIVE

'Tsar Boris'

In January 1996, the public opinion polls showed Boris Yeltsin scoring around 5–6 per cent. Not only was he behind Gennady Zyuganov, the leader of the Russian Communist Party, but he was behind every other declared contender for the presidential elections scheduled to be held later that year – Vladimir Zhirinovsky, Alexander Lebed, Grigory Yavlinsky, even Svyatoslav Fyodorov, the eye surgeon who was only a semi-serious political figure. Many of his aides and advisers thought he could not win. The majority of members of the presidential council, a group of public figures and intellectuals with whom Yeltsin occasionally discussed ideas and strategies, advised him against standing. Some liberals, led by Yegor Gaidar, were not even sure they wanted him to win because of their opposition to his war in Chechnya. They began to put out feelers to Boris Nemtsov, the governor of Nizhny Novgorod and more seriously to Victor Chernomyrdin, the prime minister, to try to persuade them to stand.

The atmosphere was dismal. Yeltsin had retired once more behind a screen of official evasions about his health and assurances that he was handling a normal workload from the seclusion of his *dacha*. He appeared rarely, and looked ill when he did. The victory of the communists in the Duma elections, though followed by a period of relative restraint, nevertheless gave the party a stature in society which was reflected in growing nervousness in the business community and a growing confidence in the communist-inclined regions and institutions. A spate of rumours began running, to the effect that the elections would be cancelled on some pretext in order to prolong the life of an administration which dare not test its standing against an electorate apparently wholly disillusioned with the man they had acclaimed five years before. These rumours had a real basis; indeed, they came close to being fact.

In January, at that low point, the president's then rudimentary election team began to do some focus group work on how Yeltsin was viewed. It was the first time such groups – composed of a nominally socially balanced selection of citizens and commonly used by political parties and companies in the West to test their strategies and products – had been used so intensively, and the aides who took part in them or studied their results found little to encourage them. Yeltsin was seen as distant, uncaring, incompetent; he had failed to fulfil his promises to the people to bring them a better life, had failed to safeguard Russia's position in the world and had led the country into a bloody and draining conflict in Chechnya, while the people suffered and only criminals, rampant throughout society, prospered. Such were typical responses.

There was only one finding which ran against the trend. The majority of those questioned, even though they professed dislike for Yeltsin and his policies, thought he was a *leader*. They thought he was able to shoulder the burden of power. They thought that of no one else. And this finding accorded with an even more curious one thrown up by the conventional polls: even as he scored in single figures when people were asked their voting intentions, he scored highest when people were asked who they thought the next president would be.

The communists did not use focus groups. They did not appear to need them. Dominant in the Duma, they had also retained a membership claimed to be 500,000 who were energized, organized and which had substantial funds put at their disposal by pro-communist business groups as well as the money the Party had managed to squirrel away before its outlawing in August 1991. Zyuganov had emerged as, if not a charismatic, at any rate a competent, performer and a man capable of articulating the complaints of a dispossessed population. The communists were strong in many of the urban centres of European Russia, with the exception of Moscow, in the countryside, and in Siberia. They had sympathetic national newspapers in *Pravda* and *Sovetskaya Rossiya*, and many of the regional and local papers in the red bases.

Above all, they had a cause. The upturn promised in 1996 was not emerging; production had ceased to tumble, but it was still falling – officially, it had sunk to less than half of its 1991 levels. The government, bent on observing the IMF guidelines, continued a monetary policy which starved enterprises and the public sector of investment and which deprived large groups of workers of regular pay. Decent, ordinary people could see no hope in the future. Interviewed in the *Commersant* newspaper in July, Lydia Samokhvala explained why she was a communist voter: 'I have higher technical qualifications. I'm forty-five. I work for a branch of the Ministry of Energy, and I just got paid for April. I can't find another job. Neither can my husband, who's a retired colonel.'

It appeared to many in Russia that a weakened, internally divided unpopular presidency was meeting the resurgence of a force it had wounded but not slain, one which had nursed itself back to vigour as the administration, snouts in the trough, had ignored it. The fusion effected by Zyuganov of communism and nationalism was formalized in the creation of an electoral bloc, the National Patriotic Front, which took into it a number of – small – even tiny – nationalist groupings led by such figures as Alexander Rutskoi, Nikolai Ryzhkov and Sergei Baburin, as well as the more substantial neo-Stalinist Working Russia Party of Victor Anpilov. Zyuganov's astute capitalization on the widespread sense of shame before Russia's demeaned state appeared to have created a political force capable of resurrecting the past – not, as in Poland, Lithuania and Hungary, one which had been thoroughly democratized and captured by Western consensus economic policies, but one dedicated to virtues and institutions at once Russian and socialist.

Yet at the heart of the communist surge lay a weakness, almost an inertia. Victory appeared, if not assured, certainly within its grasp; but at the same time it did not appear to want to win. Pavel Voshchanov, formerly Yeltsin's press secretary, writing presciently in the *Komsomolskaya Pravda* daily as early as January, said that the communists did not really want to be in power because 'they would have to take over responsibility for events which they cannot manage'. If they won, and failed in government, 'it would be the second exit of the communists from power, perhaps for ever'. Alexander Batanov, a political consultant for Mayor Luzhkov, said soon after he joined Yeltsin's campaign in the spring that 'it is not in Zyuganov's psychology to want to win. He was a middle-ranking official in the Party apparat and remains one in his spirit.' Better to be in opposition to wait for events. Better, in one strategy mooted by the party, to push for the post of prime minister, and wait for Yeltsin's death when, under the constitution, the premier would take over as acting president and call elections in a post-Yeltsin environment. Then, perhaps, constitutional changes could be put through to downgrade the role of the presidency from an executive to a figurehead one – a central constitutional plank of the communists' bloc, though not one which was emphasized during the election campaign.

Their economic programme, which they kept under wraps (because they could not agree on it) until June, was, when it appeared, a mish–mash, easy meat for the hostile commentators and communists. It was developed by Yuri Maslyukov, a communist deputy who headed the Duma's economic committee and had been, in Gorbachev's time, the head of Gosplan. Maslyukov was a well-padded figure who looked the part of the senior Soviet bureaucrat; he was far from unreconstructed, and had taken time to visit Germany at the invitation of the social democratic Friedrich Ebert Foundation shortly before he presented his programme, a trip which gave him a fund of little comments about the appositeness of the German model to the Russian economy – in contrast to the 'Chicago School' of neo-liberalism, which he claimed still provided the inspiration for the current government.

His was, indeed, one of the social democratic faces of the Communist Party, but it was a wholly unconvincing one. The mantra chanted by Maslyukov and on occasion by Zyuganov was that the communists wished to see a mixed economy – but what kind of mix was never unequivocally stated. As Alexander Livshits, Yeltsin's economic adviser, observed during the campaign, 'a mixed economy covers everything from the US model to the Stalinist one. After all, as Stalin used to say, his was a mixed economy – there was state property, and collective property.' In fact, though the communists could not have re-introduced a Stalinist system, they had no consensus on what kind of system they would introduce and less idea of how to run the one they would inherit. The party's own programme, published in January of 1995, called for extensive renationalization: much of this survived in the electoral programme of the bloc, though it was never made clear on what basis the renationalization would be made.

The party made a series of blunders. On 15 March, it proposed and carried in the Duma a resolution declaring that the agreement of December 1991 to create the Commonwealth of Independent States – and thus to dismantle the Soviet Union – was illegal. The move, playing to the gallery of Russians who resented the loss of international prestige, was promptly denounced by the leaders of all of the independent states save Belarus: and in April, Yeltsin concluded a pact with Alexander Lukashenko, the erratic Belorussian president, for a union between the two countries which deprived the communists of even that argument. Yeltsin was thus able to appear as the man most able to conclude a real coming together of the former Union, on terms acceptable to them and without the conflict – and expense – of a new imperial adventure.

In June it held a pre-election conference which produced not the open acclamation of their candidate which the circumstances required, but a closed-door session in which – from the reports which were leaked to the press – there was a quarrelsome display of discontent from the large fundamentalist section of the activists over the too-conciliatory position of Zyuganov, his deputy Valentin Kuptsov and others of the 'social democratic tendency' who had floated the possibility of coalition and shared power. The government, it was said, was at all levels full of non-Russians, non-patriots and Zionists (Jews). General Valentin Varennikov, a communist deputy in the Duma and prominent among the August 1991 putschists, was widely quoted as saying that 'we [communists] have a minimum programme, and a maximum programme which is not published. First let's take power and then we'll talk about the programme.' He was regarded as an embarrassment by the 'social democrats', but never disowned because they were not strong enough to do so. Anatoly Chernayev, Gorbachev's former foreign policy aide, commented to Jack Matlock, the former US ambassador, then on a visit to Moscow, 'You can be sure his party won't let Zyuganov be a normal democratic politician – even in the unlikely event that that is what he wanted.'

Is that what he wanted? It was not entirely unlikely, but Zyuganov never clarified the issue. He had re-made himself from a middle-ranking apparatchik into a national leader; from a Brezhnevite communist into a Russian nationalist who loved the Church; the last transformation, into a convincing social democrat was beyond him, because it was anathema to too much of his party and to his partners in the bloc. In his book *I Believe in Russia*, published just a few months before the election, he had lauded Stalin, saying that the dictator 'understood the urgent necessity of harnessing the special destiny of the country'. Had he lived on, 'he would have saved the country from cosmopolitanism' (the Jews). On the evidence of his book and of many stump speeches away from the cosmopolitans of Moscow, he really did seem to believe in a vast conspiracy composed of the Trilateral Commission, the US

Council on Foreign Relations, Harvard University, the IMF, the World Bank, the European Bank for Reconstruction and Development and others plotting to choke the life out of Russia. He proclaimed 'our right to follow our own path in accordance with our own traditions and conditions' – the old Slavophile demand, ironically best answered by Stalin, which had doomed the country to backwardness and poverty. He saw Yeltsin and his governments as a fifth column, traitors to Russia who had prostituted themselves before the foreigners in return for corrupt spoils. Yet he proposed alliances with them.

Gennady Zyuganov was, for all his manifest limitations, a politician of considerable cunning and mental strength. He had built up the party from destruction. He had kept it out of the débâcle of the White House in October 1993, refusing to respond to Ruslan Khasbulatov's call for a national uprising. He had done turns before businessmen, Western reporters and, in early 1996, had been under siege in Davos at the World Economic Forum by foreign business people and politicians asking, for the most part courteously, what his plans were if he became president of Russia. To keep one's feet when being able to enthuse rallies made up largely of neo-fascists and Stalinists on one day and to reassure conferences of multinational managers on another took nerve and skill, as well as a very high degree of dissimulation. The writer Victor Astafev once remarked that Zyuganov had the face of a Chichikov, the opportunistic hero of Gogol's *Dead Souls*; there *was* something of the fictional character's blinkered energy about Zyuganov, yet the real character was much more inventive in his own self-creation and re-creation.

But he could never solve the basic dilemma: that he needed the party organizationally while being burdened with it ideologically. He lacked the time, base and perhaps the desire to change its ideology; and his partners in the bloc were generally more extreme than he, none more so than Anpilov of Working Russia, who used the leverage of his near 5 per cent vote in the Duma elections to claim the implicit right to be Zyuganov's communist conscience, ever calling for more extreme measures, ever requiring to be weakly disowned at press conferences. The party learned, in the heat of campaign, that a kind of rough accountability had come to Russia: that statements were taken to mean something, and were expected to be either confirmed or denied. This was wholly unfamiliar territory.

The communists' base was impressive: the Duma elections of 1995 had shown it was more than one-third of the electorate, and that it was solid, loyal and active. Though it could not be taken for granted – in a system with so many other candidates, it had other places to go – it could be built on. To try to do so, Zyuganov flogged himself around the country, spending proportionately more time in those areas where the communists had less support than in the red bases. He tended, however, to give his audiences – mainly enthusiasts, wherever he was – what they wanted rhetorically; and what they wanted fed the fears of what turned out to be the majority.

It was not all his fault. Besides the hostile media, Zyuganov had a hostile establishment with which to contend. In most regions, the Yeltsin-appointed governors refused to meet him, sending their deputies instead to do discreet honours. Only three governors held talks with him – Boris Nemtsov of Nizhny, Mikhail Prusak of Novgorod and Eduard Rossel of Sverdlovsk. All of these had been elected, and thus regarded themselves as independent political figures, not beholden to Yeltsin's favour. But all three were in the Yeltsin camp, even if sceptically; all said, after they had met Zyuganov, that they were unimpressed. He held no more such meetings.

Interviewed in *Commersant* in July, just after the second and final vote, Anatoly Chindyshev, a worker, was quoted as saying: 'I voted for Yeltsin. I have children and grandchildren and I want a future for them. To vote for Zyuganov was to vote for a previous era.' He could not shake the Soviet snow off his boots. The previous era, for which the party leader and many others felt a genuine affection, was not so regarded by the majority. Even those suffering from the present did not, generally, want the return of the past.

The immediate, as opposed to the idealized, past was also represented in the presidential race. Mikhail Gorbachev, against the advice of most of his well-wishers and the mockery of the large majority who wished him ill or merely to mock him, had put himself in the lists. His was an admirable campaign, a tribute to the courage and the stoicism of a man who, though never apparently fully aware of what he was doing when he was doing it, still never reneged on the substance of it. He subjected himself to humiliations his fellow retired world leaders – Ronald Reagan (by then increasingly disabled with Alzheimer's Disease), George Bush, Margaret Thatcher and the still-ruling Helmut Kohl – would never have dreamed of doing. He squeezed himself – and often his wife – into the exiguous seats of Aeroflot's zany internal flights; was accorded no honours, or the very minimum of honours, at airports; went to halls which, when full, were fuller of those who wished to berate than support him; stayed in the flyblown local hotels and ate the indigestible food.

Why? He had a book of memoirs coming out in translation in Western Europe and the US, and the publicity his trip received from foreign papers naturally helped (though the US and UK launches, scheduled for the spring, were delayed). Many thought this a complete explanation of his venture, but it was not. He was vain enough to think he might break through to a support for him, for a socialism with a human face and for a reassembly of the Union which he believed lay beneath the surface. As the last years of his presidency showed, he was more capable than most of self-delusion. But if vanity fuelled his determination to run, its effect was to show those few Russians who cared to observe him the fundamental decency of this extraordinary figure – and to show to *him*, if he could grasp it, the mood of Russians, and the epoch which had passed since he resigned his office. In the interviews he gave as the election results came in, he would repeat a prepared phrase: that he hoped for three things from the election – that they would be held, that they would be democratic, and that he would win. 'Two out of three is not bad' was the punchline, one designed to show him to be a man of humour and pluck. And that, indeed, is what he seemed to have become.

The more poignant figure of the campaign was not Gorbachev, but Grigory Yavlinsky. The youngest of the candidates at forty-three, he was also the one with the best democratic credentials. His Yabloko group had secured – if not increased – its place in the Duma, from which Yegor Gaidar's Democratic Choice and other liberal-inclined groups had been ejected. He was – he argued – the sole possible receptacle for democratic votes: he opposed the war in Chechnya, was staunch against corruption, had always been associated with the principles and practice of the free market and of a liberal democracy. This position appeared to be underscored when, two months before the election, five leading liberal figures – including the human rights campaigner Sergei Kovalev, the former social security minister Ella Pamfilova and the radical historian Yuri Afanasiev – came out for him, saying it was impossible to support one stepped so far into the blood of Russians and Chechens as Boris Yeltsin.

Their adherence to him, however, was less evidence of a wave of support than testimony of marginalization. The high-profile liberals – Yegor Gaidar, Anatoly Chubais, Boris Fyodorov, with others in the business world – had long concluded, first, that they did not trust Yavlinsky; second, that they did not think he would ever get anywhere; and third, that Yeltsin was the centre of power in Russia until he willingly relinquished it or died. Gaidar had campaigned vigorously against Yeltsin's Chechen war. He tried to persuade Chernomyrdin to stand. In the end, he fell back, not to Yavlinsky, but to Yeltsin. Anatoly Chubais, who had been fired from his post as first deputy prime minister in early 1996, came back into his camp to help run his campaign, fuelled with funds put up by the pro-administration businessmen.

Yavlinsky's conduct in the election campaign appeared to bear out the liberals' scepticism. He could not make up his mind. He demanded liberal support, and talked to Gaidar about an agreement; it came to nothing. He tried to woo Lebed to be a vice-presidential candidate, then joined in discussions about the creation of a 'third force' composed of liberal, centrist and moderate nationalist groups which would agree on a single candidate to oppose both Yeltsin and Zyuganov – which were also wrecked on competing ambitions for the presidential nomination. He talked to the communists, though neither side would give precise details about what. He talked to Yeltsin, yet treated the talks less as an exploration of possibilities as a media opportunity to present a series of demands – that Yeltsin fire his prime minister together with his defence, security and internal affairs chiefs, withdraw from Chechnya and change his economic course – the kind of demands which could not be entertained, let alone discussed. Yavlinsky, the flagship of the liberals, in the end got little visible liberal support. He felt entitled to a reward for being the consistent and best-represented democrat; it was denied him.

The larger loser, however, was Vladimir Zhirinovsky. His retention of a solid, if diminished base in the Duma after the 1995 elections and his ability to beat into third place (after his Liberal Democrats and the communists) the official 'Our Home is Russia' party of Victor Chernomyrdin, disguised the erosion in his vote. But by the time the presidential elections came – a much more serious struggle for power than the Duma elections – he found that the ground he had claimed as his own had narrowed. The man who had articulated a nationalism aggressive to the point of absurdity for six years, who had counterpointed his own demotic lifestyle to that, first, of the nomenclatura and then to the self-enriching democrats, who had at times brilliantly exposed the hypocrisies of his opponents and who could, on occasion, produce as trenchant if paranoid an account of Russia's geo-political and domestic positions as any, who had explicitly endorsed the view that Russia was meant to be ruled autocratically from the centre if the well-being and pride of its people were to be served, had fallen victim to the theft of his themes, to his own vainglory and to the indifference of others. In the presidential campaign, attention focused on his record, and he suffered mockery in both the pro-communist and pro-Yeltsin media. He had been too high-profile in too many foreign fleshpots; he had failed to break out of the politics of outrageousness; he had failed – and his colleagues in the Liberal Democratic Party had failed – to produce anything from their rhetoric; he had made huge mistakes, such as his support in 1994 for Sergei Mavrodi, the boss of the MMM pyramid-selling organization, which had left in its wake hundreds of thousands of cheated Russians. He no longer held the nation in his thrall; the act, which had been astounding in its nerve and energy, was simply wearing thin, and had too few sources of renewal.

His main themes remained the old themes. He promised to return Russia to greatness, indeed, to a greatness even more lustrous than before – though he no longer claimed suzerainty over Finland and Alaska, and indeed denied he ever had. He put the fight against crime at the centre of his concerns, and said he would press the Federal Security Service into service against crime gangs, and order the shooting on sight of leading mafia figures. He fulminated against any concessions to or talks with the 'Chechen bandits'. He singled out Caucasians as the main instigators of Russia's woes, especially in the increase in crime. He used – rather more than before, it seemed – the threat of a Zionist plot to dominate Russia, apparently wholly unfazed by the revelations in 1995 in both Russian and foreign media that he had, as had long been thought, a Jewish father.

His recently acquired obsessions were obscure. He revealed an increasing fondness for Germany: he went so far as to criticize Stalin – who had, he said, a Caucasian's lack of a strategic vision – for seeing in Germany not a friend, but an enemy (not, in fact, something for which Stalin could be blamed: he had, after all, tried friendship). In Zhirinovsky's view, proposed during the election campaign, Russia and Germany as civilized northern countries should come to an agreement to dominate the uncivilized southern states – a kind of recrudescence of the nineteenth-century 'white man's burden' argument, which would give Russia the moral right to invade India.

On the economy, he was simply populist. He said that the fall in inflation had been caused by the withholding of wages – yet agreed that inflation should be lowered. He inveighed against the communists' demand for renationalizations, yet proposed a system of state control. He called for modernization of the economy, but blamed the 'Western bandits' for enriching themselves at Russia's expense. In speech after speech he warned the New Russians that they must 'understand that it is better to be representatives of a rich and powerful country than rich representatives of a banana republic. The Russian bourgeoisie must either become nationalist, or disappear.'

His electorate had heard this before and was pulled in differing directions – most of all by the communists. The message had been hollowed out by imitation. The communists had taken the theme of reconstruction of the Soviet Union, without the threat of war with which Zhirinovsky accompanied it. Yeltsin had himself learned too much from both 1993 and 1995 to leave his nationalist flank uncovered: he balanced the image of a world statesman on a par with the most powerful of his fellow presidents and premiers, and that of the simple Russian patriot come to power from poverty to save and raise the nation.

Above all, perhaps, Zhirinovsky lost the oxygen of attention, and wilted. He had, in his biographical *Last Push to the South*, presented himself as a man deprived of love and attention – his father dead, his mother harried by a huge family, his teachers cold or abusive. The message seemed clear enough: for the rest of his life he craved and sought attention, and succeeded on a global scale. But this time there were new claimants. Indeed, in Vladimir Bryntsalov, a New Russian millionaire, the media even found a rival figure of farce and outrage, who presented his younger and beautiful wife to the cameras with the comment 'She's my latest wife – so far', and who said he would ensure a $1,000-a-month minimum wage for all – about ten times the median.

The communists probably did most to dislodge Zhirinovsky's vote, but Lebed did most to freeze him out of the people's tribune slot. The success of Lebed – after his failure to break through in the Duma elections – was a key element of the campaign.

The constraints of the Duma campaign when he was deputy leader of the Congress of Russian Communities were lifted: Lebed could become, not himself, but a construct based loosely upon those realities of his character and career which would appeal. General Lebed, viewed widely as the most genuine of candidates – a bluff, plain-speaking officer, seeing simple solutions to the problems of crime, poverty and war – was in fact the greatest creation of the campaign.

He was assisted in this, from midway through the campaign, by funds and advisers seconded from Yeltsin's team. They polished the presentation, assisted in the production of dramatic TV commercials – one showed a dress-uniformed Lebed watching a volcano (of crime) erupt, followed by his earnest pledge that it would be stopped – and helped in the selection of themes. His own programme, on which the liberal economist Vitaly Naishul had worked, was a mixture of calls for a state limited to defence, foreign affairs, the provision of law and order and of basic social services; tax-cutting to stimulate industry and investment with a greater burden to be borne by property and energy-production; withdrawal from Chechnya; and a reconstruction of the military into a smaller, professional force.

All of this was comprehensible and even modern – far from the mish-mash of state control and reluctant free-market ideas both of the platform of the Congress of Russian Communities and of his own autobiography, *An Offence to Power*, in which he did little more than present himself as a man always able to surmount large obstacles. In contrast to the autobiography's threatening tone, his emphasis during the presidential campaign on law and order was judicious – dramatically presented certainly, but rarely, despite the pastiches of it, going beyond what a democratic state would consider faced with a Russian-scale rise in crime and corruption. As he put it in an interview to the magazine *Der Spiegel* in June:

For me, order means that people can enrich themselves at the same time as their country and not at its expense; order is a state which can assume protection and assistance to all citizens and not just to the super-rich; order à la Lebed is the guarantee of freedom for honest business. Here, crime controls all of the country; access to the market is forbidden to the great majority of people; there is fraud and corruption everywhere. This vicious circle must be broken.

Lebed gave himself a narrative. He told his voters that he had been born, in 1950, in the city of Novocherkassk. When he was twelve, he remembered the KGB, sent to quell workers' riots by Khrushchev, gunning down the rioters. This had given him, he said, a lifelong hatred of the KGB. That he had played leading roles in superficially similar actions in Tblisi and Vilnius thus had its antidote.

He presented Chechnya as a vast racket. In this narrative, 'Colonel' Dudayev had been promoted to major-general by the rising Russian power in 1991, sent to Chechnya to be a 'pocket president', encouraged to milk the republic for his own and for his Moscow sponsors' enrichment through trade in drugs, weapons and oil, then turned too radical, and had finally to be dealt with.

He was schizophrenic about the West. In his programme, he briefly mooted the possibility of partnership with the US, and with Western Europe, and he expressed himself indifferent as to whether or not Nato was enlarged to take in the Central European states. Yet in statements and interviews, he sometimes resorted to seeing the West as interested in keeping Russia weak through encouraging the disarray of its armed forces. He usually used the *Rossiyaniye* word for Russians, meaning all inhabitants of Russia, rather than the ethnically selective *Russky*, and he talked of bringing together all ethnic and religious traditions. But after the first round of the elections, with a large vote behind him, he reverted to the style of his autobiography, slurred Jews, warned of the threat to Russia from foreign religions (especially, for some reason, the Mormons) and said that his approach to crime-prevention was 'he who shoots first laughs last'. By that time, however, he was inside the Yeltsin tent: the president had, once again, faced all challenges to him – including Lebed's – and surmounted them. He had shown, indeed, that he might renounce power, or might die in office, but power could not be taken from him.

Yeltsin ran a campaign in a country more changed than probably he and his team knew, at least at the beginning of the campaign. It seemed to have become accustomed to democracy, at the same time as many in it hated what democracy appeared to have brought with it and said they needed a strong figure at the top, even if that meant losing the democratic niceties. It had certainly become a country in which there existed a substantial entrepreneurial class, who were anxious to have their wealth protected. They had become powerful as well as rich.

In February of 1996, many of the New Russian business élite had returned from the Davos World Economic Forum, where they had seen Zyuganov strut his hour upon the world stage. They were concerned: they saw he had made an impression, and believed it was a false one. They believed that the communists would cause chaos, even if they did not grab back everything which had been grabbed from them. The new business figures had spent time and vast sums of money winning over the new political élite to their side; they did not want to do it again with the communists, and some even feared they could not. Their businesses had grown, but none was of world status: their roots were shallow, the scope of their operations restricted.

They contacted Anatoly Chubais, who for the first time in four years had no job to do, following his firing by Yeltsin in January in a move designed to placate the rising new power of communism. They told him of their fears, and said that Yeltsin's election team, led by Oleg Soskovets, the first deputy prime minister, was passive. They made it clear they would back Chubais with money and support, if he were to take over. In March, Soskovets was shunted to one side – but typically for Yeltsin, not entirely out – of the campaign team. Chubais was elevated to a leading position within it, a position he shared with another highly influential aide, Tatyana Dyachenko, Yeltsin's daughter.

Of all the leading political figures, Chubais was the most anti-communist. He had relished taunting the communists in the Supreme Soviet and (after December 1993) the Duma with his privatization programme; he saw that programme as much as an instrument for depriving them of their economic base as a means for founding the private sector in Russia. His campaign tactics thus emphasized the threat of communism; the tone of it was well expressed in the weekly newspaper which was printed by the Yeltsin campaign and delivered everywhere across Russia. God Forbid (Ne Dai Bog) was filled with memories of an oppressive past and warnings of a chaotic future: lurid by Western standards it succeeded – as negative campaigning always appears to do – in implanting a feeling of threat. The campaign chimed in with what was coming through from the focus groups and polls –

that while the electorate had no huge feeling for Yeltsin, they did have a substantial dislike of communism. They also, the group work showed, greatly feared civil war – and tended to associate a communist victory with its possibility.

Chubais had come far since he had arrived in Moscow from St Petersburg at the end of 1991 to be privatization minister – and had to room with friends because the Gaidar group would not use their influence to acquire flats. The security police's dossier on him claimed he had a house in Denmark; true or not, his lifestyle had, inevitably, become that of a Russian man of power. He had above all become adept in power's use: as the only senior survivor of the cabinet liberals, he had learned the value of networks of supporters in high places, of rewarding friends and punishing enemies, of making alliances through favours and deals. Though he and Chernomyrdin were not personally close, both understood the qualities and strengths of the other. In dislodging Soskovets – whom Chernomyrdin had long seen as a danger-ous rival for his close connection with Korzhakov and Barsukov, the security chiefs – Chubais was reconfiguring the power relations within the Kremlin which had been more or less settled for the past three years.

The Yeltsin team, gearing up only in late winter, had the covert assistance of a group of US political consultants. These included Joe Shumate, George Gorton and Richard Dresner – most of them associ-ated with the brief run for the Republican presidential nomination in 1995 of Pete Wilson, the governor of California. Opinions vary greatly on the influence of this group, whose existence was only fully reported by *Time* magazine in July, after the second round of voting. But it is likely that they contributed a sharper analytical edge to the data coming in, and seem to have encouraged the Yeltsin team to push as hard as they could on the button marked 'fear of communism'. Further, in a culture still not accustomed to paying attention to the opinions of the masses, they forced the messages from the ground level into memos to the president, even when they were unpleasant. They encouraged Yeltsin to be active, demotic and understanding of the people's prob-lems, even to the point of admitting he had caused them. They advised him to flatter and even woo both Yavlinsky and Lebed, then signalling that they were considering creating the 'third force' – arguing that the inflation of ego would cancel out the unlikely eventuality of the two men agreeing on one to be the candidate. They even pushed Yeltsin to crack down on the state-owned TV networks, which in March were still critical of Yeltsin (an intriguing insight into US political advice); by April, the networks were brought into line, and were fully supportive.

The Americans, and Chubais with Dyachenko's assistance, were convinced that Yeltsin could only survive politically if he repeated some of his 1991 tactic of barnstorming the country. Unfortunately, this strategy for political survival was at odds with his failing health. Yeltsin – it had been clear since mid-1995 – needed a heart-bypass to avoid a further stroke, which would be fatal. The decision had been postponed until after the election; but his chances of survival, not high, would be made much worse by hectic electoral activity.

The media were biased, by objective standards grossly. Most of the national dailies were for Yeltsin, including *Izvestiya*, the most prestigious, and *Komsomolskaya Pravda*, the most popular. The regional papers were more mixed, but *God Forbid* circulated in them every week and most were at least constrained because of their dependence on regional budgets for subsidies. Reporters were routinely paid to write boosting copy by presidential aides. Much of what Zyuganov did went uncovered.

The TV was worse. In the first round, out of all appearances on the three main TV channels – Russian Public TV, Russian TV and Independent TV – Yeltsin took 53 per cent of the time devoted to all candidates, Zyuganov had 18 per cent, Lebed 7 per cent, Yavlinsky 6 per cent, Zhirinovsky 5 per cent and the other candidates 11 per cent. The effect was strengthened by the fact that much of the comment which attended Zyuganov was critical or downbeat. Bend-Peter Lange, the head of the European Institute for the Media, which had monitored the media during the election, said after it was over that 'Russian media coverage . . . marred the fairness of the democratic process'.

Marred, but not ruined. This was a different world: a monopoly of view was no longer possible. There were pro-communist, pro-Zhirinovsky, pro-Lebed, pro-Zyuganov and pro-Yavlinsky national and regional papers, and some regional TV stations supported rival candidates to Yeltsin. National TV itself changed before the second round. In the first week of the last stages of the campaign, Yeltsin's appearances to Zyuganov's were running at a ratio of between two and three to one. In the last week, they were one to one – on Independent TV, the ratio was slightly in Zyuganov's favour.

The Chechen war, which was on very shaky hold because of a ceasefire, had received less attention during the campaign, but far from none. TV continued to show the horrors, even if it also emphasized the government's plans to stop them. The candidates' statutory appearances were guaranteed; they could, and did, buy extra time for themselves.

Finally, most of the leading journalists believed in what they were writing or broadcasting, at least in large part. They did think that a communist victory would be bad for Russia and – as they had been reminded in a meeting with Mayor Luzhkov of Moscow as far back as January – it would certainly be bad for them. Yevgeny Kiselyev, the nation's most prestigious anchorman, announced on his *Itogi* programme in April that he was suspending objectivity because the stakes were too high for the luxury of retaining it, and that normal service would be resumed after the elections. Others did not make it so open, but did the same.

The message which Yeltsin himself gave was as much with the body and the purse as with the mouth. Astonishingly active for a man with such a history of heart trouble, he acquiesced in an energetic schedule, pressed flesh and cracked one-liners in city after city, did the twist in Red Square and peasant dances everywhere. Like his 'Friend Bill' (Clinton), he was clearly at his best campaigning, and drew obvious energy from it. He acted the benign tsar, demanding on one occasion that the head of a company in Ekaterinburg be fired for non-payment of wages – the issue had been identified by the US consultants as a matter of deep resentment, and thus much attention was given to ostentatious back payment. The elderly consistently showed in the polls as hostile to Yeltsin, for the communism which had provided the context for their lives; Rbs2.2 trillion were paid to the pension fund to raise the pensions, and extra funds were promised to the war veterans. The IMF, whose strategy had been fashioned to underpin Yeltsin and whose future existence in Russia was in question without his victory, watched the promises roll out, drew their breath and sat it out. Their officials were more concerned with the lack of income from a tax revenue as much as 40 per cent below target than with the promises of spending – since experience showed that such promises were routinely broken once the Finance Ministry and the Central Bank had protested they could not pay.

The campaign was relatively sophisticated: a little industry of political and public relations consulting had grown up in the past five years, staffed by Russians who had learned and developed these skills as quickly as they absorbed everything else. Naturally, the industry was anti-communist, it was at Yeltsin's disposal. His TV spots were made by a Russian company named Video International. They were directed by Mikhail Margolev, who had worked for five years at US advertising agencies and had been both a Soviet Communist Party propaganda expert and an undercover agent – posing as a TASS journalist – for the KGB. They eschewed the old-fashioned hard-sell approach of most of his competitors, and showed average Russians coming to an often grudging realization that Yeltsin was the best of the bunch on offer. Almost English in its self-deprecation, it went down well.

The tactic which caused most comment was that of sending out messages, 'personally' addressed to each voter by name and 'signed' by Yeltsin, which sought to address their concerns – women's issues, youth issues, wages. The flyer to the pensioners and the veterans made a point of stressing patriotism and gratitude for their courage and stoicism during the Great Patriotic War. By contrast, the communists' use of war imagery was to reproduce – in anonymous leaflets – the hackneyed language of the Brezhnev period, urging voters to 'come to the elec-toral front'. In a culture so heavily respectful of the written word and with a tradition of petitions to the leader, a message from him with his signature automatically reproduced on the bottom was a treasured event.

He adopted, with greater success, the essence of a slogan used in 1996 by the British Conservative Party: 'Yes it hurt. Yes it worked.' In fact, he had used that line in various permutations for much of the past five years – and it, at least, still seemed to work. By late April/early May, the distance between the two candidates had narrowed to very little, and Yeltsin's own private polls showed him pulling ahead.

At around this time, there developed a covert split in the Yeltsin camp – between those who believed he could win, and those who believed he might not. Yeltsin's daughter, Tatyana, Chubais and the liberal aides who had most access to (and most believed) the evidence of the private polling and the focus groups were in the first camp.

Indeed, by mid-May they were warning each other not to be too confident, and even talking of victory in the first round – an outcome in which Yeltsin himself came to believe. On the other side were those who had been shunted to one side of the campaign – Soskovets, Korzhakov and Barsukov, the so-called 'party of war' (because of their support for intervention in Chechnya), who did not believe he would win, or, in the suspicion of Yegor Gaidar, voiced in an interview at the time, did not want him to win democratically because a fresh mandate would loosen their hold over him.

In early May, Korzhakov, interviewed on the campaign trail by the *Observer*, blurted out that he thought the elections should be postponed. Yeltsin quickly repudiated him, but a window into the Kremlin battles had been opened. Korzhakov was thought by many to be speaking for Yeltsin; he was not, but he was speaking for more than the security services. At the end of April, a group of leading Russian business figures led by the Avtovaz chairman Boris Berezovsky wrote an open letter to Yeltsin asking for a compromise with the communists and proposing a pre-electoral pact which would logically rule out the need for elections at all. These men, now propertied, rich and therefore vulnerable, were increasingly nervous that the last heave by Yeltsin might prove insufficient. They wanted a compromise brokered, rather than the possibility of hazarding all. The theme had been a constant one in the business community: Kakha Bendukidze, head of the Nipek Corporation, had run it before the Duma elections. There was nothing of sympathy for the communists in this: Berezovsky and Bendukidze were both vocally anti-communist. Instead, there was fear – and its reverse, a confidence that if a deal could be offered, they could make it sweet enough for the communists that they would not be inclined to make more than cosmetic changes to the business environment.

The feeling of nervousness went beyond business. At a private seminar for Duma deputies in late May, Georgy Satarov, a liberal and long-serving (and long-suffering) aide to Yeltsin, confessed his state of mind: 'If, on the morning after a victory for Zyuganov, the president were to ask my advice, I would have an option: to tell him to hand over power, or to tell him not to. I honestly do not know now which I would advise.' Postponement and cancellation theories were circulating thickly right up to the first round of voting, on 17 June: with them went the confident prediction that Yeltsin would get the vote he wanted by falsification – as it was likely he had during the referendum on the constitution in December 1993.

Yeltsin himself was probably ambiguous about the issue. In March – according to the anchorman Yevgeny Kiselyev and the foreign policy analyst Sergei Karaganov, speaking on separate occasions – he had prepared decrees to dissolve the Duma and declare a state of emergency. He made a speech in June in which he said of the communists coming to power: 'This must not be allowed to happen', which could be interpreted as a warning that he would overturn a vote for the Communist Party. The cancellation option was in the air about him, and he breathed it.

But it did not happen. The elections went ahead in an orderly fashion. The communists had observers in every polling station, the other parties where they could. The communists also made their own analysis of the polling results. The results – 35 per cent for Yeltsin, 32 per cent for Zyuganov, 15 per cent for Lebed, 7 per cent for Yavlinsky and 6 per cent for Zhirinovsky, with the others under 1 per cent and the numbers of votes 'against all' (a stated option) or spoiled under 3 per cent. The turnout was over 70 per cent. It was a model outcome.

Both before and after the vote, Zyuganov and Yavlinsky were manoeuvring – Zyuganov to form a government of national unity, Yavlinsky to get changes in the cabinet in exchange for a declaration of support. Yeltsin played them along, but gave nothing; Yavlinsky, in pique, refused to endorse Yeltsin in the second round, only to see the overwhelming part of his supporters vote for Yeltsin anyway. In fact, the Kremlin had already written both of them out: the significant player was Alexander Lebed, whose 15 per cent of the vote brought him into the Kremlin after the first round as national security adviser, bringing (most of) his vote with him. It meant that Yeltsin won the second round with 54 per cent of the vote, to Zyuganov's 40 per cent. It was among the most dramatic – and important – political comebacks of the century.

Besides bringing in Lebed, Yeltsin also fired the 'war party' – Korzhakov, Barsukov, the head of the Federal Security Service and Soskovets, the hardline first deputy premier. Tatyana Dyachenko later said that the sacking of Korzhakov had been draining on her father, since he was 'one of the family'. The war party had, apart from instigating and boosting the war itself, waged relentless war on the liberals within the Kremlin, forcing the firing of those who had, over a year before, written a memorandum pleading for an end to hostilities. They had fed the suspicious, apparatchik-like tendencies in Yeltsin. Oleg Poptsov, once a close friend of the president whom the latter had named as the first head of Russian TV in 1991, wrote in his book *A Chronicle of the Times of Tsar Boris* in 1996 that Yeltsin was bound to fall prisoner of the worst elements of the old apparat, and that his capture by the war party from 1994 onwards was 'the triumph of those with whom the leader goes to the bathhouse, or celebrates around the dinner table, or swims, or hunts, or goes fishing'.

The 'war party' did not go, however, simply because it had distrusted the will of the people; a much more decisive reason was that they lost out in an internal power struggle with Chubais and Dyachenko. Korzhakov and Barsukov had long sought to compromise Chernomyrdin, believing him to have salted away many millions of dollars in secret Swiss bank accounts. A few weeks before the election, they arrested one of his aides and an aide of Chubais who had collected $500,000 from Chernomyrdin's office for election expenses – in breach of a rule which laid down that no significant amounts of cash must be carried in the grounds of the White House. The aides, who were being interrogated by Korzhakov's men to obtain compromising material on Chernomyrdin, were released due to Tatyana Dyachenko's personal intervention, an intervention prompted by Chubais, who warned that Western support would be lost and that the liberals would desert the campaign. They pressed for the resignations of the war party – Chernomyrdin was delighted to add the name of Soskovets to those of the two security chiefs, since he had long resented his rival source of power – and got them.

Yet in the end, Yeltsin appeared to know that he had no choice but to trust himself to the vagaries of an election. He owed his position to the ballot box: to attempt to re-position himself through a constitutional coup was to lose the one prop he had, uncertain as it was. The implicit advice of the war party had been to rely on their control of the security forces. But to end a leadership which promised liberation to the Russians with a régime which owed its survival to secret policemen was in the end unacceptable. He could not trust the armed forces to come to his aid again; as if in recognition of this fact, the faithful but unpopular Grachev was also fired from his post as minister of defence, and replaced by General Igor Rodionov, passed over by Grachev, with a reputation for ruthlessness, but also for hostility to corruption and for opposition to the Chechen war.

The communists played an unsung but extremely important role in securing a democratic result. They participated – thus giving legitimacy to a constitution which they had ritually denounced as illegitimate. They vouched for the probity of the elections themselves. And Zyuganov conceded defeat as gracefully as any Western democrat. 'I congratulate you on your success at the polls,' he said on 4 July, as the results made it clear he could not win. 'I hope that the common efforts of all of society's social and political forces will lift Russia out of its current crisis, and guarantee her people the best, most dignified, freest, happiest and richest of futures.' It was a tall order, and his phrase 'common efforts' was a shadowy repetition of his plea that the communists be brought into the government – but it was an overt acceptance of the rules of the game by the leader of a party which had been ambiguous about playing by them. His sourest note was reserved for a media which had 'manipulated people instead of informing them' – a deserved reproach to many of those to whom it was addressed.

Alexander Solzhenitsyn, by then a Cassandra, had written before the election that 'a shattered society was emerging from under the rubble of totalitarianism' and that 'under the nascent, savage, non-productive capitalism, ugly new ulcers have surfaced from years of torment, ushering in such repulsive forms of behaviour and such plunder as the West has not known. This, in turn, has gone so far as to bring an unprepared and unprotected population to a nostalgia for the "equality of poverty" of the past.'

He was, as usual in his new Russian manifestation, too apocalyptic. Equality of poverty was no longer the desire of the majority. Savage, non-productive and ulcerous Russia's course under Yeltsin certainly was, but the 1996 presidential elections appeared to show that the population, prepared or not, feared to leave the ship on which they had clambered five years before.

PART TWO

State

'I do not believe that Russians were fashioned for the whip.'

Boris Yeltsin, August 1995

CHAPTER SIX

'The law as a tool of dominance'

At the centre of the hopes and ideals of the democrats who came out of their protective shells during the Gorbachev period was the demand for a 'law-governed state'. Gorbachev could not deliver it; Yeltsin did, but not in the way they wished.

Paradoxically, the Soviet state *had* been buttressed by a panoply of laws, and different versions of a constitution, which were formally as supportive of democratic institutions as any in the world. But they were a hollow sham, a device to fool foreigners, and to provide propaganda matter for the Soviet and foreign communist parties. Alexander Yakovlev, the legal scholar who helped shape the present Russian constitution, says of the Soviet precursors that the omnipresence of the Party meant that it constituted the hidden and real constitutional order, operating beneath the formal constitution: 'This was the essence of the two-fold structure of power – one side of it was "external", legal and unreal; the other "internal", political and real.'

The passion for a state of law derived mainly from those who began to speak freely for the first time in the late eighties, and who had a period of influence in Yeltsin's early years of power. The dissidents, especially those who stayed in the Soviet Union, were men and women who had experienced with painful immediacy the tension between the 'real' and 'unreal' constitution; it was their experience, mediated above all through the august figure of Andrei Sakharov, which provided the moral boost to the search for a constitutional order in which the distance between the real and the unreal would be narrowed to a 'normal' distance.

In so far as there was a successor to Sakharov in Russia, it was to be found in the figure of Sergei Kovalev, a frail man who exhausted and nearly killed himself in expressing a principled opposition to the war in Chechnya and who sometimes seemed to bear the entire agony of that conflict on his shoulders. These shoulders were as stooped as Sakharov's, and Kovalev entered into his most testing political struggles in his mid-sixties, as Sakharov had. But his determination and courage were also great – as was his placing of the moral question before every practical one. The remark of the nineteenth-century philosopher Pyotr Chaadayev – 'I cannot love my native land with my eyes closed' – could have been framed for Kovalev; he kept his eyes painfully wide open, and suffered for doing so.

He had got used to suffering. A biologist and mathematician, he had dedicated his life in his thirties to a dissidence that he knew would bring him harsh punishment, and which was directed at forcing the authorities to observe the laws they themselves had framed and advertised as the most progressive in the world. He was an editor of the *Chronicle of Current Events*, the samizdat newspaper which circulated in grubby typewritten copies to remind those who would read it that their rights were abused and that their state and its ruling party were the abusers. He was arrested in 1974, and served six years in the camp for 'politicals' in Perm (Perm Six), one in prison at Chistopolsk and three in exile in Magadan. He returned to Moscow in 1987, and was elected to the Russian Supreme Soviet in 1989.

His record was of the kind that made him the natural choice for the chairman of the committee which Yeltsin created that summer on human rights. He talked a good deal to Yeltsin at that period: he later recalled that Sakharov had said of Yeltsin that 'anyone who had risen as far in the Party as Boris Nikolayevich had had to make a pact with the devil' – but that only someone who had done so could know the rules of the Soviet game and could thus play them to good effect, precisely one of Yeltsin's many paradoxes. When he talked to Yeltsin, Kovalev felt the former Party boss *wanted* to understand about human rights and the rule of law, and how to protect and further them. He saw the Russian leader walk behind Sakharov's coffin all the way to the cemetery, spurning his proffered limousine in the deep cold of December 1989; and he thought Yeltsin's trip to the Baltic states in January 1991, after protestors had been attacked and killed in Lithuania and Latvia, was 'a brave, an extraordinary step'. After the August 1991 putsch, Yeltsin called him to his office and showed him a list of names: twenty-two people were on the list – the names of those the putschists had deemed necessary to be shot. It began with Yeltsin and ended with Kovalev.

For Kovalev and those like him, Yeltsin's embrace of market economics was taken on trust: of a piece with his commitment – as they believed – to a human rights agenda. They accepted – and accept – the equation of human rights and a free economy: Kovalev thought Yeltsin typically bold in appointing Gaidar, and was anyway too preoccupied with human rights causes to pay much mind to what else was happening.

In the deepening struggle between Yeltsin and the parliament, he took Yeltsin's side with reservations; but he did so above all because he saw that the patched-up Russian constitution on which the parliament rested its case for supremacy was one which tied the country up into a knot which there was no untying. His experience of the real workings of the unreal Soviet constitution kept him steady in his opposition to those who would reinstitute some version of Soviet rule. Thus he accepted that Decree 1,400 – the 21 September 1993 order under which Yeltsin discharged the Supreme Soviet – was right in purpose, even if bloody in its effects. Later, after he had himself been comprehensively bloodied by Chechnya, Kovalev reflected: 'I had been thinking in straight lines. I could not see that dissolution of parliament led to Chechnya.' There was, in fact, no such inevitability, but Kovalev had more right to the illusion than most.

Kovalev, like Sakharov, had a passion for human and civil rights. The experience of both, and especially of Kovalev, had confronted them in the starkest way with the fundamental lawlessness of the Soviet state, for when challenged to respect rights to which it subscribed in its Stalin- and Brezhnev-era constitutions and in its international declarations – masterpieces of civil libertarian rhetoric – it not only continued to deny them, but imprisoned those who demanded that respect. Kovalev was arrested soon after a press conference he gave, with other *Chronicle* editors, in Sakharov's flat in May 1974. In a statement given to the Western correspondents then, he said: 'We believe it is essential that truthful information about violations of basic human rights in the Soviet Union should be available to all who are interested in them.' At the centre of their concern was the need for a state in which the laws should both be promulgated and upheld, in which institutions would be constructed to bear the weight of civic demands.

This dissident tradition was one stream which fed and nourished the search for constitutional order: the other was the reformist one, in which the legal scholar Alexander Yakovlev – a quite separate figure from the Gorbachev aide who bore the same name – played a large part. Yakovlev was prominent among the academic lawyers who had nursed hopes of constitutional and legal reform in institutes and university departments – especially in the Academy of Sciences' Institute of State and Law, which produced a number of reformist figures in the late eighties. Yakovlev and his colleagues were students of international law, and saw how foreign constitutions – or lack of a constitution, as in the UK – accorded more closely with real freedoms. He was fond of comparing the 'unreal' Soviet constitution, which vested all power in the Congress of Peoples' Deputies (actually, the Communist Party) with the US and French constitutions, in which a separation of powers is clearly spelled out. Without a separation of powers, Yakovlev taught, there could be no civil liberties or 'real' rights.

He had a concept of a 'genetic code' within the law – which owed its origin to the way in which civil rights and the constitution of any given state were first adopted and given protection. He saw one such genetic code in the covenant which the (adult, male) passengers in the *Mayflower* drew up in 1620, under whose terms they agreed to bind themselves to all laws agreed by them in their new settlement, a code which ran through the US constitution and was able to provide the nucleus of a vigorous democracy. He saw no such moment in Russian history; instead, he believed that all attempts to usher in a constitution in his own country had foundered on the ability of the rulers, tsars or commissars, to see that law was a compromise between a series of demands. 'They understood the law', he wrote, 'as a tool of dominance.'

Yakovlev had been a USSR Supreme Soviet deputy and had seen and tried to assist Gorbachev's efforts to introduce a law-governed state. The Soviet President did go some way towards it – he persuaded the Congress of Peoples' Deputies to abolish the article in the constitution which guaranteed the primacy of the Communist Party – but he could not overcome the irreconcilable contradictions of trying to institute civic freedoms while retaining a communist system and a command economy. Gorbachev had not given up on this: in the last substantial piece he wrote as president of the Soviet Union – it was composed a few days before the August coup, while he was on holiday on the Black

Sea – he wrote of his dedication to pluralism and of his 'determination to achieve it by constitutional means'; said that 'we have to make ourselves understand more quickly that any society or state can only develop normally if there exists a strong executive authority based on popular support'; and claimed he saw a 'growth in society of the civic spirit, the Soviet people's growing awareness of their rights and their readiness to defend those rights'.

The coup cut short any effort to increase further the civic awareness of the *Soviet* people; from then on, the states of the Soviet Union each faced the task of building – or shirking the building of – a constitutional order on its own. All came to independent status unconstitutionally. It could not be otherwise: since the Soviet constitution was a façade, real change had to happen outside of it. The republics which had been negotiating with Gorbachev on a new federation before the coup had been in varying degrees committed to it; the coup made it clear to all of them that a centre which could not organize a proper effort to preserve its power could scarcely recover that power after it. Thus the leaders of the three Slav republics of Belarus, Russia and Ukraine came together on 8 December to declare the Soviet Union dead and the Commonwealth of Independent States born. Not only had they no constitutional basis for doing so, they had no democratic mandate of any kind either. The Russian parliament ratified it after the event, and some four years and four months later, in March 1996, rescinded it. Thus was a major subject of international law wound up: Gorbachev resigned on 25 December, and the USSR Supreme Soviet dissolved itself the next day. Fifteen states became subjects of international law, with hollow shells as constitutions, only academic knowledge of what constituted a living constitution and in most cases – the Baltic republics were the exception – no 'genetic code' which could be discovered and elaborated to assist them.

Yeltsin had never shown much interest in institutional and constitutional change. Thus he did not call elections in the autumn of 1991. Thus he was slow – till pushed by his aides, especially Sergei Shakhrai, a lawyer – to focus on the need for a replacement of the Constitution of the Russian Soviet Federative Socialist Republic, which had been a decorative part of the façade of Soviet life. Since its provisions were known by all to be meaningless, they were extensive. The result was that the new state's parliament was ushered into existence on the basis of a range of rights for which it had not struggled nor was ready to match with responsibilities – but which it did not wish to lose. It thus naturally retained the constitution and the articles which gave it powers. In its early days it amended those articles considered to be too offensively communist in tone, while in its latter days it amended those which could be interpreted as giving the presidency larger or even equal powers.

The Supreme Soviet preferred to keep on reworking the constitution to suit its purposes of the moment – a constitution well described as 'a patchwork of democratic reforms stretched over a totalitarian frame'. Ruslan Khasbulatov, the speaker, nevertheless recognized that this looked bad, and thus a process of thrashing out a new constitution was continued. The key figure in the committee charged with this was a young political scientist named Oleg Rumyantsev. He had been secretary of the constitutional commission since its inception in 1990, when he was twenty-nine. Rumyantsev was an early leader of one of the Moscow pro-*perestroika* political clubs, founded the Social Democratic Party which he defined as more interested in creating democracy than in socialism, and threw himself into the labour of elaborating a modern, democratic constitution on a committee chaired by Yeltsin himself.

Rumyantsev changed; indeed, he almost wrote the textbook for post-Soviet change. From being as pro-Western a democrat as any other in the late eighties, he turned sharply towards national-statism, splitting the small party he led (in which the social democratic parties of Western Europe had invested great hopes, and significant funds) into three parts, throwing in his lot with the communists and the nationalists who dominated the Russian Supreme Soviet, reshaping the constitution to accord with their wish to make the parliament supreme and the presidency a figurehead. By spring of 1993, with a state of full hostility declared between the Supreme Soviet on the one hand and Yeltsin and his government on the other, the Rumyantsev draft reflected the interests of the latter: a nominally democratic parliamentary system, in which such old institutions as collective (state) property were accorded a privileged place and ethnic and civil rights were limited. A presidential draft produced in April by a commission chaired by Sergei Shakhrai was long on individual rights, with at its apex a powerful presidency envisaged as both head of state and chief executive. A third draft, written by leading members of the Communist Party – regrouping rapidly in the Supreme Soviet – was a frankly reactionary document.

The two main drafts pointed up a debate which had begun as the communist bloc broke up, driven by the experiences of the post-communist states. The debate was and is on the structure of the polity which can best sustain the nation through a transition from a totalitarian to a democratic state: whether a presidential or a parliamentary system would best serve to both make the break with the past, and to sustain democratic institutions in the early, difficult years. The early evidence – not just from the post-communist world – favoured parliamentary systems; indeed, the most successful of the post-communist states were and are, with the partial exception of Poland, all parliamentary systems – the Czech Republic, Hungary, Estonia, Latvia. Poland, where the president is more than a figurehead but less than a pivotal figure, was in the early nineties dominated by the ambitions and then the presidency of Lech Walesa, whose period in office was fraught and awkward and whose ceding of it to the former communist Alexander Kwasniewski ungracious and foreboding.

In the former Soviet Union, every state save the Baltics developed a presidential over a parliamentary system. In none, including Russia, were democratic institutions working well by the latter half of the nineties – though these cover a vast gamut from the frankly authoritarian personality-cult regime of Turkmenistan to the much more open system of presidential-parliamentary trade-offs of a Ukraine or a Moldova. In nearly all, the president took or struggled to take power over all of the areas of national life which the former first secretary (often, the president *had been* the first secretary) had enjoyed; as a rough rule of thumb, where the civil society was more inert or inward-looking, the more success he had in the endeavour.

One could expect this accretion of power to corrupt. As presidents extended their grasp, the parliaments and opposition parties grew shriller and more uncompromising in their efforts to retain areas where they held sway. Since all were unused to a political culture where compromise was accepted, these confrontations were often violent – at least verbally, sometimes physically, at times murderously. The presidents, who had taken care to secure the loyalty of the armed and security forces, always won. The losers appeared to be the political system and the society. The parties which had flourished after the communists' fall typically ranged across a spectrum of political philosophies, ethnic and even religious affiliations and regional interests; that such a vigorous flowering should be crushed or at least ignored appeared to be a reversion to a modified authoritarianism.

But the parliamentary argument was attractive only speciously. In none of the former Soviet states, including Russia, did the parliament produce a majority party, or a working coalition of minority parties, from which a leadership could emerge and be sure of stable support. In Czechoslovakia (before the split), Hungary and Poland they did – in each case, the majority party or coalition being composed largely of those groups which had effected or helped effect the liberation of the country from communism. In Russia, the coalition of pro-democratic groups which assisted Boris Yeltsin to power were an apparent parallel to the Central European movements; but, as Yeltsin knew better than most of his democrat-comrades, they had much shallower roots in, and much less respect from, society. In the Central European states, the new forces were anti-communists, and because communism was widely seen as a foreign imposition, these forces could take on the mantle of patriotism as well as of democracy and reform. In Russia, the democrats were largely a part of the Communist Party which had allied with, then split from, Gorbachev. They were too liberal and distrustful of the nationalists to be proper Russian patriots, and were certainly not Soviet patriots. Reform was all they had. They could not have dominated parliament: without a strong figure with an elective mandate of his own, government would have been at the mercy of a legislature which would have shifted wildly about the political spectrum, and which may have been unable to produce coherent government at all.

This was one – good – reason why Yeltsin saw himself as best placed to appear to be above politics, a line pushed by his more conservative aides, in contrast to Sergei Shakhrai and Gennady Burbulis, then close to him, who advised him to build a party – indeed, Burbulis twice announced himself commissioned to be his agent in doing so. His support in the Supreme Soviet drained away – rapidly, as the harsher effects of the economic policy came through – and the presidential party was reduced to a minority. The democrats thus became even more dependent on the will and strength of the president, and even less inclined to grant more powers to a parliament they experienced as hostile, fractious and wholly irresponsible.

It was in this mood that Yeltsin's constitution was framed, and in this mood that he fought and won the April 1993 referendum on his popularity and policies. Once he regained activity following his customary period of retreat following a major event, he then confronted a Supreme Soviet ever more bent on impeaching him, and on 21 September, issued his fateful Decree 1,400, overthrowing the present constitutional order for the sake of the future security of the country. That was illegal, but in doing so, and in securing the grudging backing of the army general staff to use that part of its force it could persuade to fight in Moscow, he took to himself all state power and thus effectively choked off the avenues which the parliamentary forces were desperately exploring to find a basis for a civil conflict they thought they might win.

In the aftermath of victory over the parliamentary rebels, Yeltsin's team produced a constitution which reflected the fact of victory. Sergei Shakhrai, who took a large part in its preparation, said it had to be adopted quickly in order to give legal backing to a political space filled only – after the shelling of the parliament – by presidential power. An alternative proposed by many democrats, to pass a provisional constitutional act to operate in place of a constitution for a year or two while a constitutional assembly drafted and passed a properly agreed constitution, was brushed aside.

It was, however, the first constitution of an avowedly democratic Russian state. It had many faults, of which presidential triumphalism was one. But the greater danger lay, and would lie for some years, in the threats to it rather than the dangers it itself possessed.

'A constitution', wrote Samuel Finer, 'resembles a sharp pencil of light which brightly illuminates a limited area of a country's political life before fading into a penumbra where the features are obscured – even if that surrounding darkness may conceal what are the most potent and significant elements of the political process.' It is the second part of Finer's simile which is, rightly, of most concern to Russians when they assess the efficacy of their new constitution. But the first – the 'sharp pencil of light' which is the Russian constitution itself – *does* illuminate something: in that pool of light lies a significant part of Russia's hope for the future.

The Russian constitution lacks the grand sweep of the French, the libertarian brevity of the American, the exactness of the German. It commits itself to the provision of a range of rights in the home, at work and as a citizen which only a super-state could provide, and which raises fears that a hyper-bureaucracy would use the commitments as a rationale for its expansion and intrusion. It is vague and contradictory on the provisions of federalism and multi-nationalism, expressly committing itself to a respect for both, but indeterminate as to how they are to be managed. It retains the same administrative-territorial divisions of the Soviet times, and with them, the differing statuses of republics, territories (*krai*) and regions (*oblast*). Unlike the union republics in the Soviet constitution, these areas have no right of secession – a fact which was to be crucial in the case of Chechnya.

The presidency is naturally the dominant institution: the president is head of state, commander-in-chief of the armed forces and head of a security council which, though sketchily defined, itself has purview over all the armed services and security forces. He appoints the prime minister and can dismiss him and the government. The parliament must ratify these and other appointments – such as the chairman of the Central Bank, and the senior members of the judiciary – but if it fails to ratify three times the president can dissolve it and hold fresh elections. Parliament appears to have at best ambiguous rights to ratify international treaties or to intervene in international negotiations; it has a say in the declaration of a state of emergency or martial law, but only retrospectively.

More ominously, Article 90 states flatly that 'the president of the Russian Federation issues edicts and decrees . . . [which are] mandatory throughout the territory of the Russian Federation.' The one condition upon these edicts and decrees is that they be in conformity with the constitution and the law: they have no need to be submitted at any stage to parliament, or to the people. That clause alone makes the Russian president a potential dictator, albeit a 'constitutional' one – one of the largest reasons why Vladimir Zhirinovsky, the frank dictator-to-be among the presidential candidates, always solidly supported the constitution.

Zhirinovsky's endorsement was not its only taint. The document was not submitted to either the federal or the state legislatures – which themselves had been dissolved following the October events; instead, it was published, and submitted to a Yes/No referendum to be approved on 12 December, as the population elected the new state Duma – provisions for which were laid out in the as-yet unadopted constitution.

The constitution had to be approved by a simple majority, but of at least 50 per cent of the population; and it was unclear, and remained unclear, how many voters there were. A figure of some 107 million had been used; the Electoral Commission, however, calculated the figure before the vote at 105 million, later revising it up to 106.2 million, without explanation. After the vote, the Commission said that 55 per cent had approved the document – 31 per cent of the eligible population.

Four months later, *Izvestiya* published a report based on findings by Alexander Sobyanin, who had been appointed by Yeltsin to review the adoption of the constitution. Sobyanin had found that no fewer than 9 million votes had been falsified, which in turn meant that only 46.1 million voters had actually taken part, well short of the 50 per cent threshold required for the constitution to pass. On his account, regional authorities in rural areas had recorded quite different numbers voting than those later published by the Central Electoral Commission: further, some districts had recorded inexplicably high turnouts combined with very low numbers of invalid ballots.

The result of the report was the firing of Sobyanin. Strangely, no major political figure took up the issue of falsification – though it was widely accepted that the Sobyanin report was true.

Yeltsin hailed the adoption of the constitution as the largest victory of the election: many democrats, reeling from the shock that Zhirinovsky's LDPR had dominated the party lists and that their own stock had fallen so precipitously low, clung to the comfort that 'their' president was at least a powerful one. Kovalev was among them: the feudal nature of post-Soviet Russian politics, where powerful barons and claimants upon power captured and held positions of strength and sought to expand their powers beyond them, had enforced on the liberals and democrats the necessity of personal politics, and of seeking protection and support within the retinue of the preferred baron or – in their case – the king.

Yeltsin's guardianship of the constitution after its adoption was – as with everything he did – a mixed record. In this area as much as any other, it was very hard to make a judgement on whether he had betrayed the high ideals with which he had taken office, or was keeping alive a democratic option while making necessary compromises with quite undemocratic forces in order to gain time. In June 1994, he issued a decree on fighting crime which authorized wiretapping and summary arrest – both explicitly forbidden in the constitution. In October, he dismissed a number of ministers, and the chairman of the Central Bank, following the crash of the rouble – a task he should at least have shared with Chernomyrdin and the Duma. He did not, to be sure, attempt to stop the Duma releasing the putschists in February 1994, but he put pressure on Alexei Kazannikov, the Justice Minister, to annul the move, and caused Kazannikov to resign and denounce him by doing so.

He was constrained, less by 'his' constitution, than by the weakness of the political forces who had helped project him to power, and by his need to appeal to a new set of forces who required new deals and compromises. He assiduously courted the regional leaders; and in signing, in February 1994, a treaty with Tatarstan, he introduced a constitutional novelty (on the slim grounds that the constitution allowed him to devolve unspecified powers to the regions), which was to grant those regions and republics powerful enough to insist upon it a semi-autonomous status in which *their* constitutions defined them as independent and the Russian defined them as 'subjects of the Federation'.

The Duma, too, was constrained, in part by memories of the exercise of presidential brutality, in part because its leaders were beginning to jockey for position in the presidential elections and wanted to keep political balance while doing so. It was not until July 1995 that the deputies attempted to amend the constitution to give them more say over the nomination of the 'power' ministers – security, defence and foreign affairs. The initiative failed narrowly, and was not renewed.

The manner of Yeltsin's declaration of war on Chechnya was also challenged – in the Constitutional Court in July 1995, six months after the invasion itself. On this occasion, it was members of the upper house who argued that a military action on Russian territory demanded the declaration of a state of emergency, which had not happened; that all enactments bearing on human and civil rights (of which the declaration of war in Chechnya was one) had to be published, and this was not done; and – Kovalev himself brought forward this argument – the invasion breached international treaties, which under the constitution took precedence over Russian law where they conflicted.

The Court, a fledgling institution, ruled that the government had, essentially, no case to answer. One of its decrees had since been repealed, another was ruled to be outside the Court's jurisdiction. The overall justification for the invasion was found to be in the absence of a clause allowing secession and the duty of the president to safeguard the integrity of the Federation. In the highly charged atmosphere surround-ing the conduct of the Chechen war, it was represented as a kow-towing to the president: but in fact, only a small majority of the Court – eleven of the nineteen justices – had been fully behind its judgements, while the remaining eight had taken positions ranging from substantial agreement with the position of the Federation Council deputies to more nuanced judgements on the president's actions.

The Court had had a terribly bad start. Its first chairman, Valery Zorkin, was a man who interpreted his brief as one allowing him – indeed, enjoining him – to become a participant in the political struggles of the early part of Yeltsin's period of office. His first overt intervention was to issue a statement in June 1992 indirectly condemning Yeltsin for threatening the constitutional order by seeking a referendum, and blaming the government for instituting divisive economic policies. As the confrontation between congress and president grew deeper, Zorkin allowed himself to become more and more identified with the first of these – though never wholly as its tool.

He was a bad choice as chairman, but his decisions were not wholly capricious. The Constitutional Court's mandate in any country is to uphold and rule on the constitution: Zorkin and his fellow judges had as their basic text a document which, on any reading, gave supreme power to the congress. That this produced at best a logjam and at worst civil conflict was not, strictly speaking, the Court's business.

Nervous and excitable, Zorkin allowed himself to be caught up in the febrile politicking of the times. He spoke out, in interminable interviews, against presidential and government decisions which could never be interpreted as under his jurisdiction. But he was faced with a presidency which was trying to get rid of the constitution under which he had been appointed to work – or at best, to circumvent it.

The Court was slowly reformed after October, getting under way only in 1995 under the chairmanship of the legal scholar Vladimir Tumanov. The June 1994 law which regulates it specified a twelve-year term for its judges, without possibility of renewal, prohibited the Court from initiating cases on its own (a look over the shoulder at Zorkin's antics) and excluded it from decisions on impeachment (another over-the-shoulder measure). Tumanov interpreted his brief as narrowly as

Zorkin – who remained one of the judges – had done so widely. The Chechnya intervention was the most controversial case taken to the Court, and it was handled in a deliberately low-key fashion. The problems, as Tumanov saw them, were not in the grand clash between the written word of the constitution and the reality of Russian life, they were in smaller issues – the lack of qualified and active judges at every level of the court system, the shortage of funds to pay them and the court officials, the overloading of the system by the surge in crime.

The deeper problem, which the Yeltsin period only began to address, was the pervasive lack of trust which the citizens had in the courts. The Soviet-era tribunals worked better than their reputation at least in one area – crime; but they enforced heavy penalties against any kind of entrepreneurial activity, were under the control of the local Communist Party officials and discriminated routinely in their punishments of, or even in their involvement in, cases according to the rank of the person involved. Those in the nomenclatura – those with Party cards and Party or state positions – could not be touched without Party approval; those in the upper reaches could only be toppled if it was politically possible or necessary that they be so. Since everyone understood this, it meant that the system of justice had no status as an objective system of law.

Reforms were undertaken during the late Gorbachev period – when the courts were placed under the exclusive control of the local councils, and removed from party tutelage (at least formally). But that simply meant that the local councils told the judges what to do – a situation which continued after the Soviet collapse.

In the civil law, the judicial system was deluged from the beginning of 1992 with a flood of new commercial and financial law which many judges did not understand, which was often badly drafted and which usually conflicted with existing law which had not been repealed, or repealed only partially. Ownership rights in particular were vague and varied according to the type of business. Details were often lacking, or referred to local administrations – which, in turn, were often hostile to business and intent on using the law to hamper it. A civil code which would provide the principles against which financial legislation would be tested was contested and slow in coming. The incapacity of the courts to deal with the rapidly growing number of disputes between businesses, or between companies and the local administrations, meant that the new enterprises frequently resorted to private agencies to enforce contract, collect debt or scare off creditors. These agencies leached away the more active police officers, since they paid much higher wages. This in turn weakened further an already weakened police force, and made it more open to a corruption which was very widespread.

There were signs of change. Arbitration courts in Moscow and St Petersburg were reported to be working better by 1994–95, and enterprising lawyers in the capital set up private arbitration agencies – such as the 'Justice and Law' agency – which reported success in settling disputes. But the larger the company, the more it was assumed – rightly – that it would resort to force or the threat of it if it wanted something badly and could not get sanction through the courts for it.

Criminal law had been better, and it was more quickly improved by the removal from its lists of crimes such activities as buying, selling and lending. The death penalty was retained, but the offences attracting it were reduced to aggravated murder, rape and terrorism. Rights of criminals were more clearly specified – though their treatment in the terrible prisons did not improve – and the accusatorial bias which had been a feature of Soviet law toned down.

But here, as in the criminal code, the field of struggle – which grew more intense as the initial influence of the legal reformers waned towards the middle of the decade – was occupied increasingly by officials and politicians who sought an antidote to the leaping crime figures in a reversion to old norms and habits. The right of suspects not to be detained for more than forty-eight hours was bitterly contested by the procurators, who had been accustomed to extensive powers – as was the giving to the courts the right to decide who should be detained, and for how long.

In June 1994, Yeltsin issued a decree – 'On Urgent Measures for the Defence of the Population against Banditry and Other Manifestations of Organized Crime' – which dramatically curtailed rights granted in previous laws, and rights stipulated in the constitution. Suspicion of involvement in mafia activities was sufficient to allow police to search and seize any kind of document or data, and to detain for up to thirty days without charge – on the word of the procurator, not of the court. The decree was angrily justified as essential if the state and the people were to be preserved from a wave of criminal anarchy – which the authorities themselves stressed was an epidemic. But it meant a huge breach in the commitment to abide by constitutional legal norms, and was instantly used by the procurators and the police to riffle through the files of a host of businesses regarded by all as those which had not been able to buy immunity.

The reformist activities in the judicial system – such as the introduction of trial by jury in certain areas – continued even as the pendulum swung back to more powers to the procuracy and the police. Indeed, jury trials were reckoned a success, and were recommended for extension to other areas – a move which was curbed on, it was claimed, financial grounds. The judges on the Constitutional Court are serious, avid to learn from international practice and resolute in their professed independence from the state and the politicians.

The system remains embryonic. It is still mired in habits of thought and action which privilege the accusers and mystify the accused. Its contradictions and lapses encourage evasion and corruption. And the actions of high state officials, including those of the president, do nothing to diminish the pervasive cynicism of a public whose at least passive trust is essential for the sustainment of an efficient system.

Yet the cornerstone of the law – the constitution – may remain one of Yeltsin's great achievements, in spite of the way in which it was approved, in spite of the fact that, inevitably, its 'genetic code' had to be inserted from the top, rather than seeping up slowly from the society over centuries and in spite of the way in which the law developed – with one step forward and two back – in the years of his rule. In this area, as in all others, Russia had to invent a 'code' quickly, creating itself as a constitutional state in imitation of others who had had the luxury to arrive there by stages. The constitution was an ideal, but it was an ideal which was embedded in the law of the state, and remains as a benchmark to which the society, and above all its rulers, still have to match themselves.

CHAPTER SEVEN

'The Russian army is past reforming'

The Russian military has suffered a greater loss of prestige, support, funds, esteem, fighting capacity, strategic capability and *raison d'être* than any significant force in peacetime in this century. The scale of the disaster which has overtaken the Russian armed forces is such that, when it is grasped, the wonder is that they have not staged a revolt or a coup more successful than the botched affair in which their leader – Dmitri Yazov, the defence minister – was involved in August 1991, or the parliamentary rebellion of 1993, which was co-led by General Alexander Rutskoi, the vice-president, and with which other officers were associated and many more felt in sympathy.

It has been pulled back thousands of miles from its advance bases in the very centre of Europe – the largest retreat of any army since the war. It has lost any semblance of parity with Nato or US forces. Its grand global – and virtually casualtyless – role has been replaced with a clutch of bloody internal or border wars which earn it odium. Its draft of conscripts fell to dramatically low levels, yet the state could not afford the expense of turning it into a professional army. Its officer corps was hardly paid and wretchedly housed, performed tasks usually the preserve of private soldiers or NCOs and grew steadily more demoralized. It was, according to General Pavel Grachev, the defence minister, speaking in 1995, 'hungry, barefoot and underfinanced'. A year later, General Alexander Lebed said it did not have enough money to save it from collapse.

Gorbachev, not Yeltsin, had been responsible for beginning this vast demoralization. It became clear that the loss of an enemy – which Gorbachev-era officials would joke was the worst thing they had done to the West – was a much worse thing to happen to the Russian armed services.

The Soviet military's combat-readiness and discipline had been exaggerated in the West – but it was still, in the mid-eighties, a vast and fearsome force, under firm Party control. The ideology which had given cohesion to the army had been Marxism-Leninism, shaped to present the West as an unassuageable aggressor, bent on a destruction of a socialist way of life which was prevented only by constant military vigilance in association with the ideological vigilance of the Communist Party. This ideology served the Soviet army well. From the mid-fifties onwards, the Soviet general staff was able to respond to the technically and numerically superior armies of the Nato alliance by developing nuclear and conventional strategies which achieved parity with the West by the early seventies and kept it until the eighties. The navy and air force were vastly extended, a nuclear force built up, the army modernized. The forces of the Central European communist states were developed by, subordinated to and integrated with Soviet command from the creation of the Warsaw Pact in 1955. Soviet military advisers served in such successful theatres as Vietnam and Ethiopia, Mozambique and Nicaragua. The military's prestige was unquestioned – it had been the saviour of the country. Its loyalty was secured, bound as it was with hoops of steel to the Party.

Gorbachev did not at first seek to weaken these: his changes at the top soon after taking power were the replacement of often very elderly senior commanders with his own men, the natural desire of a new leader to have his own people in command. But as his policies weakened and then destroyed the structure of the Soviet Union, the commanders he had appointed – such as General Dmitri Yazov, the defence minister, and Marshal Sergei Akhromeyev, chief of general staff and then military adviser to Gorbachev – turned against him because they saw him betraying the cause they had sworn to defend. Yazov was a coup conspirator; Akhromeyev committed suicide after it, leaving behind a letter saying that since 1990, everything in which he had believed was destroyed. One could hardly admire these men for providing the defence for an empire as oppressive as the Soviet one, but their devotion and faith were probably as genuine as that of any military staff, and their patriotism probably stronger.

The agreements with the West, the pell-mell withdrawal from Central Europe and then from the Baltic states, the loss of bases and *matériel* in the former Soviet republics meant that the military was, from 1989 onwards, overwhelmed with administering a full-scale retreat on insufficient funds. It lost to other republics half of its combat aircraft and most of its armoured vehicle repair facilities (which meant that, by 1994, the tanks it used in Chechnya constantly broke down). At the same time, the élite units were drawn in to aid the militia control nationalist revolts in hot spots from the Baltics to the Caucasus.

In the latter theatre, riots in Tblisi in 1989 brought in two commanders, General Igor Rodionov and General Alexander Lebed, to oversee an operation which had troops use sharpened shovels on demonstrators. In the summer of 1996, the first was made defence minister of Russia and the second was the president's national security adviser after achieving 15 per cent in the elections for the presidency. Thus suppression of nationalist riot and protection of Russians would become – as it had been in the nineteenth century – a route for advancement in the new Russian army.

A habit of insubordination was born in Gorbachev's times. In the winter of 1990, one could talk to officers in the bases of the Baltic states who – while usually not giving their names – would rail to foreign reporters about the stupidity and weakness of their commander-in-chief, Gorbachev, and Shevardnadze, their foreign minister. The commanders in these imperial garrisons had been cast adrift, huddling with leaders of the Russian communities in ultimately futile plots to restore order or seek to compromise with the new nationalist powers. It was on an Estonian air force base, in 1991, that Colonel – later General – Dzhokar Dudayev, who became president of Chechnya, allowed an Estonian flag to be flown.

Thus when Gorbachev returned to Moscow from his temporary imprisonment at Foros during the 1991 coup, his veiled appeal to the military to come to the aid of the crumbling Union fell on ears as deaf as all others he addressed in the last four months of the Soviet Union. The old guard, who had been his top commanders and who ultimately sought his removal or at least his being brought to heel, were in prison or in disgrace, keeping their heads low. The new men were those who had done well out of the coup by refusing to obey orders to mobilize their men to attack the Russian parliament. Boris Yeltsin – who addressed the top military in December 1991 to promise them higher pay – inherited the Soviet military.

It was in very poor shape, and was to get worse. The coup was followed by a brief interregnum during which the Soviet military was transferred to the notional command of the Commonwealth of Independent States under Marshal Yevgeny Shaposhnikov, an air force general. In the spring of 1992, a separate Russian military was formed and General Pavel Grachev – a paratroop commander who had distinguished himself by disobedience the previous August – was appointed defence minister, with General Mikhail Kolesnikov as chief of the general staff. Dr Andrei Kokoshin, formerly deputy director of the USA-Canada Institute of the Academy of Sciences and an expert in disarmament and defence conversion, moved into the white Defence Ministry on the Arbat as the first civilian to take such a high rank since the early Bolshevik period.

These men and their senior colleagues confronted chaos – and, in the main, they deepened it.

The military was divided: though it was largely passive during the coup and key commanders did refuse orders to attack, there were more generals than Yazov who agreed with the spirit of the coup – though all, including Yazov, were disgusted by the shambles its execution turned out to be. General Valentin Varennikov, for example, flew to Kiev to exhort the Ukrainian leadership to support the coup. The Ukrainians wavered until they saw the project would fail, then issued a ringing declaration of support for Boris Yeltsin.

The commanders' decision to go with Yeltsin was one of *faute de mieux*. He was all there was. He had won the struggle for power with Gorbachev. He held out some hope of stability, perhaps of preserving the Union under another name. Yet even in March 1992, a poll showed that only 17 per cent approved his reform policies – by then, under the direction of Yegor Gaidar, wreaking havoc with military orders – while 56 per cent opposed them and the rest abstained from an opinion. By December 1993, a majority of officers were prepared to vote for Zhirinovsky; and in December 1995, for the Communists. But – and this was always the weightiest response – 90 per cent of the respondents in the March 1992 poll thought politics best left to politicians. Better to keep one's hands clean.

Keeping one's hands clean politically did not extend to other spheres. The military rapidly became among the most corrupt and corrupted institutions of the Soviet state. The generals began looting the Central European bases from which they were ordered to withdraw from 1989, as soon as they knew the imperial days were over; weaponry, including tanks and artillery, was bartered for cars and electronics. A series of scandals, including the selling of military property in East Berlin, were publicized but neither proved nor – as far as could be told – properly pursued. As the new private *dachas* or *kottedzhi* (cottages) began to rise round Moscow and St Petersburg, many among them were built by young army recruits using material trucked in on army transport and erected under the direction of burly men in their fifties – the generals who were converting their acquired wealth into property. General Lev Rokhlin, a politicized general who became a senior member of the 'Our Home in Russia' party, told the Russian parliament in 1996 that one of his former colleagues kept a 'serf battalion' of conscripts to build *dachas* for senior officers outside of Moscow; at the same time, he accused three other generals of embezzling, between them, $30 million from army funds.

This scale of criminality compensated for the loss of Party control, and helped keep the military out of direct intervention in politics. They were busy exploring the possibilities of being an organized, relatively well-equipped and armed horde in the midst of a society in which controls were light, spasmodic or non-existent. For such a horde, or at least for the best-placed members of it, the prospects of plunder were golden – and were conducted with virtual impunity.

There was, in Yeltsin's first term, no high-profile trial of corrupt officers. At best, a figure round whom corruption allegations swirled most obstinately might be removed. In February 1995, General Matvei Burlakov, the former head of Soviet forces in East Germany and briefly deputy defence minister, and General Nikolai Seliverstov, first deputy commander of the Soviet air force based in Germany, were removed from office. Seliverstov was found guilty of embezzling nearly DM 65,000 and receiving bribes worth a further DM 20,000; Burlakov was dismissed (though no further action was taken against him) 'in connection' with investigations into the murder of the young journalist Dmitri Kholodov, who had been assassinated by a briefcase bomb while investigating corruption in the Western group.

There is no doubt about the criminality of this group. German police using undercover methods learned that weapons from automatics to MIG 29s were being sold. The military prosecutor, Grigory Nosov, presented Grachev with a report of a large number of officers using their positions and premises to conduct businesses. The weekly *Moscow*

News (*Moskovskiye Novosti*) discovered that an Austrian company was providing foodstuffs to the Western group despite the food being in many cases inedible – and showed links between the company and Burlakov. As early as November 1992, Yuri Boldyrev, a young reformer appointed chief state inspector, gave a report on the Western group's corruption to Yeltsin, showing how five generals had embezzled millions of roubles through false contracts – but Yeltsin did nothing with it.

The vast quantity of military *matériel* which was sold to governments or rebels or both in the newly independent states and in the Russian Caucasus was never the subject of proper investigation – though its sale, or rent, was open enough. In the summer of 1992, I sat in the office of an official of the Azeri government of Baku as two senior officers of the Russian army discussed, with no apparent inhibition, the leasing of tanks to the forces struggling (unsuccessfully) to contain the Armenian advance in and beyond the Armenian-dominated region of Nagorno-Karabakh in the north-west of Azerbaijan. The fighting in Chechnya was conducted with Russian (Soviet) weapons on both sides: Russian soldiers selling the weapons to their enemies as the fighting went on.

Yeltsin reportedly did confront Grachev with evidence that the Ministry of Defence had a secret account in Germany, opened in the autumn of 1992 and filled with millions of dollars from the sale of Soviet equipment. Later newspaper reports claimed that Grachev had misappropriated funds from a bank account containing $20.6 million, also in Germany. Yet he hung on until June 1996, too loyal or too knowing to be fired – while the leadership of the military grew ever more venal.

The late Soviet experience of the military at all levels had been that it was unwise to follow orders. The special troops who had killed demonstrators in Baku, Tblisi, Vilnius and Riga in 1990–91 were regarded by the new political powers as murderers, not defenders. Their commanders were – at the time – vilified by the democratic parliamentarians and by the nationalists who were soon to form the governments of the countries in which they had operated. This message was very strongly reinforced by the experience of the 1991 August coup: the growing bifurcation in the power structures and the difficulty of knowing which orders would be backed by an authority which would protect those who followed the orders in the longer term produced a recoiling from any hint of involvement in political decisions and the great difficulty Yeltsin had to persuade any forces to come to his aid in the struggle with parliament in 1993.

The military became a consensual organization, in which major orders could no longer be given but were replaced by a bargaining or on occasion a voting process. This process achieved its apogee in 1994, when Grachev, stuck with an invasion of Chechnya which he had boasted would be over in days, yet which he probably did not want, bargained with his regional generals for troops and air support. Chechnya was itself the prime lesson in the rewards of disobeying orders. After the 1996 presidential election, Yeltsin sacked the faithful but hated Grachev and promoted to defence minister General Igor Rodionov, who had opposed the war – while General Alexander Lebed, one of the war's most astringent critics, became national security chief after attracting a sizeable vote in the presidential elections.

Lebed's career highlights the fact that the traditional non-involvement of Russian and Soviet officers in politics had ended – at least for a period. Not only were they involved, they were also ambitious. Alexander Rutskoi, a colonel made general by Yeltsin, chafed at being sidelined when vice-president, broke with Yeltsin, was a leader of the parliamentary revolt and after being freed from prison founded his own party, Derzhava, or State Power. General Boris Gromov was the vice-presidential candidate to Nikolai Ryzhkov in 1991 when Yeltsin carried all before him in the Russian presidential elections; he later became deputy defence minister, was moved to the Foreign Ministry after criticizing the Chechen war and formed his own movement, My Fatherland. Lebed, the most successful, was also in many ways the least extreme. Indeed, in wooing many thousands of officers away from Vladimir Zhirinovsky, he brought them back to the centre of Russian politics.

The military rapidly became poor, and undermanned. Defence budgets were cut dramatically: by 1994, after only half of the already skeletal military budget had been released, Grachev testified that the army 'will simply collapse'. Much of this fell on the defence industries, which lost huge capacity, but it also produced real suffering in the military. The returning officers had no flats: as late as 1995, nearly 200,000 were living in makeshift accommodation, including tents.

Exercises were cut to far below levels previously thought to be minimal, as was maintenance – leaving a military which was barely operational.

A draft of servicemen could scarcely be maintained: in some areas it was under 10 per cent of target. Medical certificates attesting to the incapacity of the holder for service could be bought, in 1996, for $500. This meant that an establishment officially set at 2 million was, by 1996, around 1.2 million: the number of operational divisions stood at 22, as against an established figure of 48. Officers fled the service if they could: a planned cut of 71,500 officers between May 1992 and July 1994 was exceeded by over 100 per cent – 157,400 officers left the service, of whom over half were under thirty – many of these swelling the ranks of the private security firms.

The Soviet army had struggled to re-orient itself to change in both its social and military environment – but was still struggling when collapse overtook the Union. Gorbachev had in the late eighties sought to professionalize the army (while retaining its conscript character): troops were no longer to be used for harvesting, or for construction work. But this was reversed from 1991; indeed, harvesting became only one of the ways in which the military sought to keep itself alive, and a 1992 Ministry of Defence order allowed troops to be hired out to various employers. They built some of Moscow's prestige office buildings, their negligible wages greatly contributing to the profits of the Russian and foreign owners of the businesses which 'employed' them.

The army remained, deep into the nineties, very largely locked into a structure in which the officers – proportionately much more numerous than in other armies – maintained a wide gulf between themselves and the recruits. The enlisted men were given little training and no motivation – an approach which the increasingly well-educated young men from the large cities would not tolerate as the peasant lads of the pre- and immediately post-war armies had. Observers from foreign armies were surprised at how bad the training was when they were allowed to look inside the barracks after 1990. One Pentagon general, a lifetime Soviet military watcher, said in an interview in 1995: 'We saw a very low level of technical skills among the soldiers, except for a few specialists. Everything was done by the officers. The non-commissioned officers were pretty useless – they were essentially Komsomol types, there to keep people in line and nothing else.'

Conscript life was a mixture of the tedious, humiliating and dangerous – with the danger coming from older recruits who treated the entrants abominably. Estimates made in the Russian army of this 'hazing' pointed to four out of five recruits suffering physical brutality, of whom one in three had to be hospitalized and one in twenty was the victim of homosexual rape. Food, accommodation and medical care was so bad that one in five left the army chronically ill.

These figures, even if more indicative than precise, nevertheless point to a military establishment unable to mobilize itself, or even to keep itself at a minimally efficient level. Indeed, General Lebed made this a central theme of his presidential bid in 1996. In an interview a few weeks before the election, he told me: 'The army is now in a state of crisis more acute than during the Great Patriotic [Second World] War. Then it was in a military crisis from which it had to be saved by firm leadership – which was available. Now it is in a moral crisis, and the leadership is not there. The Russian army is past reforming. It must be saved.'

The military-industrial complex had seemed, in the early nineties, almost past saving. It was a monster, overproducing artillery, tanks and small arms on a heroic scale and thus a victim as much of the end of the Cold War as of the savage cuts it suffered in 1992.

As with so much of the Soviet way of life, its nemesis was Mikhail Gorbachev, not Boris Yeltsin. He broke the rule, established under Brezhnev, that the military-industrial establishment asked for, and was given, whatever it wanted – without significant oversight by the government or even by the Party. The decoupling of plan from need, yawning everywhere, was most evident here by the late eighties: huge numbers of inter-continental ballistic missiles were delivered to the strategic rocket forces – and stacked in warehouses, since they could not be deployed. Dozens of Blackjack bombers were built and delivered – of which, according to Russian analysts, *none* worked well enough to be operational. Yet some 90 per cent of research and development carried out in 220 research centres was fully or partly militarized; 80 per cent of engineering in 1,100 plants, mostly large, was mainly producing weaponry or weapon systems; some 12 million workers, including the most highly skilled and highly qualified, worked directly on military production; and 20 per cent of all consumer goods were produced in military plants. Military output accounted for between 20 and 25 per cent of Soviet GNP in the late eighties. As a comparison, both the US and the UK, relatively high spenders among the wealthier states, spent (in 1993) 5 per cent and 3.7 per cent of GDP on the military as a whole, France spent 3.4, Italy 2.1, Germany 2 and Spain 1.5 per cent. The Soviet Union had the profile of a very poor Third World country whose rulers spent their meagre earnings on weaponry, both to deter their enemies and cow their subjects.

Gorbachev took some peace dividend in the late eighties, cutting the military procurement budget from Rbs32.6 billion in 1989 to Rbs24.8 billion in 1991, while military research was cut from Rbs15.3 billion to Rbs10.2 billion. But neither then nor later was military industry restructured – though, of course, plans were produced for doing so – and thus the plants, the institutes and the intellectual store of knowledge was allowed to rot rather than be redeployed. An example: where in the early-mid-eighties the air force would normally have taken delivery of 450 fighter aircraft a year, it received 23 in 1993–94. Russian pilots flew some 25 hours a year, compared to Western norms of around 200. Conversion, a Gorbachevian talisman, had a few successes, and these were ambiguous: the Saratov aircraft plant reduced military output from over 50 per cent in the eighties to under 10 per cent by the early nineties – but its main product, the small YAK 40 and 42 jets, were an ageing design, noisy and hard to sell outside of the previously captive markets.

Conversion was largely hated by the convertors. They called it 'degenerate conversion', a desperate search for commodities to make to keep the workforce employed and some income flowing. The Irkutsk jet-fighter plant, for example, turned its hand to tents, toys and dishes. An aviation plant in Moscow made barbecue sets – from titanium. I had a coffee grinder made by the same Moscow plant, cleverly set in a painted wooden doll, unwearyingly efficient but with a motor which sounded like a jet engine and a top so tightly fitting it needed two people to open it. The funds allocated for conversion were often used to pay wages, in an effort to staunch the leaking-away of the best workers to the co-operative and private sector.

Foreign joint ventures with military plants were in nearly all cases a minor part of the overall production. Typically, the foreign company would form an association which used a line in one part of the plant separated from the rest of it, paying its workers higher wages – the focus of jealousy and envy of the rest of the workforce. St Petersburg, where 1 million workers depended on the military sector, had several of these – like the Gillette razor blade joint venture with the mighty Leninetz plant. They worked well enough, but they did not and could not save the companies from the crisis in which they found themselves, nor were their techniques quickly copied.

As conversion (contraction) did not work, the planners and politicians swung back, from 1992, to expansion through foreign sales. The Soviet Union had been a major – often, the major – supplier of weapons to foreign countries – to its partners in the Warsaw Pact and Comecon, to Middle Eastern, African and South-east Asian states. These sales gave it something around 40 per cent of the world arms market in the late eighties – a share which had shrunk to under 10 per cent in 1993–94.

The opening of the Soviet-dominated or -influenced world was a disaster for the arms industry. It released captive markets to shop around; it allowed the Central and East European former satellite states to transfer allegiances from the Warsaw Pact (which collapsed) to Nato (which did not) – and thus to Nato's weaponry. It exposed cruelly the relatively low technical quality of many of the Soviet weapons – a technological gap vividly demonstrated during the Gulf War, in which the Iraqis struggled with Soviet armour and weapons systems and the US and its allies deployed (and tested) the latest from their rather smaller but more advanced military-industrial complex. The Soviet industry had believed itself to be a repository of unique, world-level or above-world-level skills and products. It was not. It – with the space sector – was the best the Soviet Union could do. It was not competitive, except for individual items like the most advanced MIGs, or when priced very low. However, low pricing was a norm in the world arms markets – since it was very far from being a simple market.

States had a stronger vested interest in selling weapons than any other good. Thus military orders were highly political, were accompanied by arm-twisting, diplomatic cajolery, very large open inducements and often larger hidden inducements. In all democratic states, they were the most common source of government scandal – as government ministers sought private profit from deals with foreign rulers, or heads of governments ordered covert supplies of weapons to régimes or movements of which they approved but their legislatures did not, or as governments connived to break, or studiously avoided noticing others' breaking, sanctions against arms supplies. Russia, which as the Soviet Union had had a more or less straightforwardly coercive relationship with most of its customers, was a novice in this world.

The state began to fight back from 1993, with the founding of the Rosvoruzhenie corporation at the end of that year. It employed some high-profile managers – Konstantin Borovoy, the mercurial founder of the Moscow Commodities Exchange and of the Economic Freedom Party, went as deputy chairman – and it quickly established offices in some forty countries, concentrating on former allies and the Middle East. It had some strengths: it could usually undercut Western prices, and it had a very large installed base – worth an estimated $200 billion – on which it could build and which it could service (though servicing had never been Soviet industry's strong point: in late 1996, Aeroflot refused to buy jets with engines made in the Perm jet engine factory, instancing the inability to rely on post-installation service; it bought Rolls Royce instead). China, Iran and India continued to offer large markets, though Iran was a poor payer and India began looking west for purchases of arms, as other goods.

The market itself continues to shrink. The world's arms industry, downsizing quite rapidly in most of the advanced countries, is thus the more competitive. In Europe, the traditional insistence that each country had its own – often state-owned – industry has given way to largely private businesses which are interlinking across national boundaries and are beginning to evolve into a few large centres of production in which companies either merge parts of their operations or co-operate closely on given projects – such as the Eurofighter. At the lower, small arms, end of the market, India, China and the former Czechoslovakia are tough competitors. Russia thus confronts competitors who are themselves driven, well-financed and with extensive networks of political influence and military leverage. It will sell more weapons than it did in the early years of the nineties, but to regard arms production as a major pillar of the economy – as some Russian politicians, including Vladimir Zhirinovsky, claimed to do – is to court disappointment.

To discover that the technical heights of the country's industry were not, in the main, competitive in the world was one more of many blows that the Russian élite had to swallow. The chiefs of the military-industrial complex had been the lords of the Soviet universe: they guaranteed the country's defence, and provided the means by which it exported its most precious commodity – revolution. With the collapse, they had perforce to give way to those who earned the country money by exporting oil and gas, and even to the despised clerks who shunted money about. Corruption was – for many – a poor substitute for past glory, and they continued to be the most nostalgic and reactionary of the new Russian élite.

The hardliners in the military were, however, not wholly without compensations. As the Yeltsin period wore on, and as he and his advisers became more seized with the need to project at least the semblance of Russian greatness, the generals' ideas received some attention at the top. This did not mean that Yeltsin again posited the Leninist enemy– imperialism (of the West) – as once more the threat against which Russia had to be defended. But by the beginning of his second term, his aides were speaking in tones reminiscent of Cold War rhetoric: in January of 1997, for example, Prime Minister Chernomyrdin spoke of the 'inevitability' of a new arms race if Nato went ahead with plans to expand eastwards. Well before that, however, Russian military doctrine became itself explicitly imperial, even if relatively modestly so.

Gorbachev had, from the fireside chat with President Reagan in 1987 at which the two men mooted total nuclear disarmament, destroyed the image of the one enemy. The elimination of the intermediate-range nuclear weapons, the cuts in the conventional forces, the agreements on chemical warfare, the Strategic Arms Reduction Treaty (START I) had been international high points in his leadership, winning him the Nobel Peace Prize in 1990 – though no longer any plaudits at home. The military doctrine which he had decreed into force in 1990 was a pacific one, with talk of 'reasonable sufficiency' in weaponry and 'human values' in relationships, excising the imperialist threat from the rhetoric.

The military had not liked it, and saw themselves as justified in their dislike by the collapse of the Soviet Union before precisely these forces of imperialism which it had been their duty to keep at bay. The creation of Russian forces from the spring of 1992 demanded a new military doctrine, but the rush of events – the retreat of the divisions from the west and the north, the flaring of wars in the Caucasus, the unplanned reduction in military strength, the huge cuts in the military budget – disoriented the general staff. It cobbled together a doctrine in 1992 which reverted in many features to the pre-Gorbachevian Soviet verities, but it was squashed by a parliament still sufficiently liberal to object to a reassertion of military priorities. The limbo thus continued.

It was broken by the attack on parliament in October 1993. Yeltsin called on the military's aid. Their price for a very half-hearted assent was his acquiescence in a military doctrine which, though remoulded, was a licence for intervention in the former Soviet Union. More than any other single document, the doctrine asserts unambiguous Russian hegemony over the 'near abroad' – a hegemony which is justified by the need to defend the Russians who remain outside of Russia.

The largest 'concession' to the changed international environment was the recognition that the threat of a nuclear attack on Russia was much reduced, and that the main threat to security had altered from a superpower confrontation to a multiplicity of smaller-scale attacks on the borders or near to them. The 'imperialist threat' remained in a warning against any expansion of a 'military bloc' – meaning Nato. At the same time, the old Soviet prohibition against the first use of nuclear weapons disappeared (it was, in any case, meaningless), to be replaced by the determination to use nuclear weapons if Russia were attacked by a state possessing nuclear weapons or an ally of such a state. The old doctrine of military parity also went, to be replaced by the need to maintain forces at the level required to inflict the 'desired damage' on an enemy.

The most radical parts of the document were those privileging Russian interests in other sovereign states – the former Soviet republics. The army was charged with the defence of Russians and Russian interests in these countries, and though it stated that operations would be conducted beyond Russian borders by agreement, it also appeared to sanction unilateral actions. The main zone of instability was seen – naturally – as being in the south, both because of the Caucasian wars and because powers like Turkey, Iran and Afghanistan were seen as expansionary and potentially hostile.

Military force was also sanctioned *in Russia* on a variety of grounds, from combating organized crime to a threat to overthrow the state, or of secession. In including this, the military gave themselves (and Yeltsin) retrospective justification for their part in subduing the parliament – an affair which continued to divide Russian society long after it had occurred.

The doctrine also legitimized – and may have foreseen – the intervention in Chechnya. It gave the necessary cover to the (barely) covert operations in the Caucasus, particularly in Georgia, where the Soviet army took the side of the Abkhazian rebels to put pressure on the government of Eduard Shevardnadze to concede bases in his country and thus access to the Black Sea, and to the operations on the Tajik-Afghan border, where Russian troops attempted to stem the incursion of mujahedin into Tajikistan, a state preserved by Russian arms.

It was advertised as being a provisional doctrine, like most things in Russia's first five years. It held a line, but it also did more than that. It established new ones, beyond the border. The first period of Russian power did not make it clear how deep these lines would prove to be.

Nor did it become clear how far Russia was prepared to relinquish its view of itself as a beleaguered citadel. Russian – and foreign – commentators would delight in pointing out the long tradition of embattled distrust of an outside world which constantly invaded (Genghis Khan, Napoleon, Hitler) across the long flat steppes, thus creating the imperative national need for protection through a buffer of surrounding states. The new doctrine, implicitly, continued that self-serving tradition – a tradition which ignored the fact that Russia has invaded and conquered more often than it has been invaded (and has never, since the Khan, been conquered).

Yet, immediately after the Soviet fall, the Russians could be excused for feeling beleaguered. Their buffers to the south, west and especially the north had turned into independent states – in many cases hostile (though only rhetorically), at best neutral. Under the Lisbon agreement of 1992 the three other Soviet republics which had nuclear weapons stationed on their territories – Belarus, Kazakhstan and Ukraine – were recognized as nuclear powers. All three promised to return them and ultimately did between 1992 and 1997 – though Russia continued to base SS25s in Belarus, by agreement. But there was a period in which Ukraine debated keeping its missiles (over whose guidance systems it had no control) and Russia was named as their target in some over-heated nationalist rhetoric. The US, disturbed by the fact that Ukraine's 1,800 missiles were still pointing at its territory, worked hard and ultimately successfully at convincing Ukraine – with the aid of several hundred million dollars for dismantling, transport and storage of the missiles – to despatch the rockets to Russia, a decision which allowed Ukraine to accede to the nuclear non-proliferation treaty and for the START 1 treaty to enter into force.

But this successful concentration of the missiles on its territory could not increase Russia's sense of security. Its missiles, and its nuclear complex as a whole, fell into a dreadful state, a greater danger to the world than when they had been under the command of the Soviets. The morale in the Strategic Rocket Forces was – as elsewhere – low: shooting incidents were reported on some bases and the rockets were said to be improperly maintained. The nuclear-armed submarines patrolled very little because of the expense. Early warning systems went out of operation.

The deterioration of the nuclear forces was a danger most of all because they had ceased to be secure. The huge size and primitive storage practices of the Soviet nuclear archipelago meant that it was probably inadequately accounted for before 1991. The collapse, the commitments to dismantle imposed by treaties and the return of the rockets from the east and south all imposed further strains on a system already in some disarray.

There was no unified command. The some 1,200 tonnes of weapons-grade fissile material was split between the Ministry of Defence, the Ministry of Atomic Energy and numerous institutes and research centres. The dismantling of the warheads – at the rate of some 2,000 a year, so that the 45,000-strong arsenal of 1986 had come down to around 25,000 by 1996 – meant that vast pipelines of fissile material were flowing to and fro across Russia, in trains and trucks, guarded lightly or sometimes not at all.

The problem was, in part, a bureaucratic war. The Ministry of Atomic Energy had won control of the nuclear material – which meant that it passed out of secure military bunkers to insecure warehousing. At the Korchatov Nuclear Institute in Moscow, at Ust Kamengorsk (CHK) in Kazakhstan, at the closed city of Chelyabinsk 65, highly enriched uranium was found stored in ordinary, unguarded warehouses.

Hundreds of cases of nuclear smuggling have been reported; six are known certainties, one has been admitted by the Russian authorities. In one case (not the one admitted) Captain Alexei Tikhomirov of the Russian navy walked into the Sevmorput shipyard near Murmansk in the Arctic, entered a building in which unused submarine fuel was kept, took three pieces of the reactor core with about 10 pounds of highly enriched uranium and walked out. Eight months later, when Tikhomirov tried to sell the material (for $50,000), he was arrested. Of the other four, three smugglers were caught in Germany and one in Prague. It is a reasonable guess that others evaded detection, especially if they went south through the Caucasus or Central Asia through borders which were virtually open – or could be opened for a bribe. Nuclear smuggling is certain to be an established practice now: the fissile material is relatively easily made into a detonative device. The fear that a terrorist group would, sooner or later, threaten to use such a device is perfectly rational. Those who thought about such things in the West – not many – felt a more urgent fear than the background, routinized fear of the Cold War days.

But Russia had a quite different fear, a remnant of the Cold War. It was of the expansion eastwards of its old enemy, Nato. The issue, the most fraught between the West and Russia and one on which debate within the West was intense, crept up on both sides. In mid-1993, Warren Christopher, the US Secretary of State, said, 'Nato expansion was not on the agenda.' A few months later, it was, and a few months further on, it was a pledge. By early 1994, Nato was set to expand, a move which in every respect rubbed salt in the wounds of Russian weakness. It could do nothing, as its erstwhile allies in Central Europe demanded the protection of Nato against it. That they should regard it as a potential menace was gall to the democrats and liberals, who had tried (and failed) to ensure that all that was seen as ended. That it should be unable to strike fear in the hearts of these turncoat allies was bitter to the nationalists and conservatives, who regretted the loss of hegemony.

The enlargement of Nato was preceded by a period – after 1991 – in which the former communist states were 'united' in the North Atlantic Co-operation Council. That was replaced by Partnership for Peace, a kind of Nato infinite waiting room in which the former communist states (including the post-Soviet ones) could reach a relationship with Nato of differential strengths within an overall framework. But heavy lobbying by the Central European diaspora in the US, and by the Polish and Czech governments – especially by the then president of Poland, Lech Walesa – produced a promise from President Clinton in January 1994 that it was 'no longer whether Nato will take on new members, but when and how'. Yeltsin's first reaction to the idea, on a visit to Poland in August 1993, was insouciant: the communiqué from his meeting with President Lech Walesa referred to the 'understanding from President B. N. Yeltsin' of Poland's intention to join Nato as consistent in the long term with 'interests of Russia'.

The when and how then waited for clarification, and the Russian position, after a fierce campaign by the diplomatic and foreign policy establishment against Yeltsin's response, turned to hostility. The states between the Central European applicants and Russia would be squeezed, the Baltics would be left out indefinitely and the whole exercise would be fearsomely expensive – somewhere between $50 billion and $100 billion, of which most would have to be borne by the Western states. Nato expansion hung in a limbo, irritating everyone.

It hung because the two arguments were so finely balanced. The Central Europeans should have the right to choose their own security alliances – an argument the region's leaders spiced by adroit reminders of Western indifference to their fates before both dictatorships in the pre- and post-war periods. Yet to provoke Russia was to increase the strength of the nationalists' hands, and that at a time when Russia was manifestly unable to threaten anyone.

Russian leaders made inflammatory statements, especially in the run-up to the 1995 Duma elections and the 1996 presidential elections. General Grachev threatened to make 'new alliances in the east' – presumably China, or perhaps Iran. President Yeltsin said that the enlargement would 'fan the flames of war'. The Western states tried hard to placate Russia, while retaining the intention to expand. Military-to-military ties were instituted by all the Western states, especially between the armed forces of Russia and America: in June 1994, Russians and Americans did joint amphibious training at Vladivostok, and in September of the same year held infantry exercises at Totskoye in the heart of Russia (after the second of these, General Fyodor Ladygin, head of Russian Military Intelligence, said in an interview that one-third of the 250 US troops involved at Totskoye were spies). The Conventional Forces in Europe treaty, which specified lower concentrations of armour than the Russians wished – and, indeed, deployed – in the Caucasus, was relaxed to meet Russian demands. It was made clear that expansion would not include the Baltics or Ukraine, and that neither nuclear weaponry nor Nato troops would be moved eastwards into the new member countries. Russia, however, was unconvinced: Sergei

Karaganov, the leading foreign policy analyst of the Yeltsin period, said at a conference in Moscow in January 1997 that the West was 'spitting in the face' of Russia.

At root was the old problem: could the Russians believe that Nato – in the words of Senator Richard Lugar, one of the architects (with Senator Sam Nunn) of the assistance package which achieved the consolidation of the missiles in Russia – was an alliance 'which guarantees stability in Central Europe, a stability which is just as much in Russia's interest as our own'? There were some signs it might: General Lebed, hawkish in many respects, said in July 1996 that he was indifferent to Nato expansion; however, he said two months later that it would not be tolerated, and added that 'our missiles may be rusting, but they are still missiles'.

His flip-flops were not merely personal indecisiveness, they represented a profound and bitter debate within the Russian political classes on how to react to what was seen as a humiliation and a threat. However, the sharper minds understood that to react with threats was to court a further, deeper humiliation when these threats proved empty. Karsten Voigt, the long-serving foreign policy spokesman for the German Social Democrats and a close Russia watcher, replied to Karaganov's 'spitting in the face' outburst by observing, at the same Moscow gathering, that 'the one thing you could be sure of, if you reacted by trying to create a military alliance in opposition to Nato once more, [is] that half of your partners in the CIS would immediately apply to join Nato – led by Ukraine'.

Vaclav Havel, writing in June 1995, said: 'As long as the broadening of Nato membership to include countries who feel culturally and politically a part of the region the alliance was created to defend is seen by Russia as an anti-Russia undertaking, it will be a sign that Russia has not yet understood the challenge of this era.' That was true, but Russia had to swallow the hard truth that it inspired fear across that part of Europe which knew it best, and that Nato's expansion was restrained not by the strength of its military, but by the weakness of its liberals.

Yeltsin, revived after his operation, got down to hard bargaining and produced by May 1997 a deal signed in Paris which included a charter between Russia and Nato guaranteeing the former's consultation on all matters of importance, and a permanent Russian presence at Nato headquarters and the solemn assurance that the Alliance had no reason, intention nor plans to move men or missiles into the Central European states it had brought under its aegis. The charter gave the Russians no veto, though Yeltsin suggested it had. It left a number of states, especially the three Baltic republics, outside of Nato and unlikely to be invited to join, though they were most at threat from an expansionist Russia. Nato expansion was achieved, but it would take years to tell if it was the beginning of a new relationship or a colossal mistake.

The new treaty did not rise to the 'challenge of the era', though whatever Nato did, it was Russia which had most to do to rise to this challenge. Its military would have to enter into a period of deep reform, which it had delayed since the creation of Russia. Much of that first five years had seen the continuation of the Soviet military, by other means, in other guises; reform had been neither demanded from outside, nor seriously considered from within. The military remained, substantially, a caste apart; oversight by the parliament was weak to non-existent; and the power of the Russian state was so limited that vast corruption could flourish unpunished, while each command was less an order than an invitation to bargain.

In its weakness, and its humiliation in Chechnya, lay one hope of renewal. The other was the continuing passivity of the officers. Indeed, there was some evidence, from a survey conducted in mid-1995, that the majority (however they voted) were committed to the 'basic tenets' of democracy, did not support the *forcible* re-creation of the Soviet Union and wished democratic reform to continue. This was an apparent paradox – but only if one assumed that the officers would blame democracy for their ills. They did not seem, on this evidence, to be doing so.

By the end of the first period of Russian power, the military had little other direction to go but up. The challenge to it was a choice: would it seek to refashion itself as an imperial force? Or to act as the eastern pillar of a new European security system, the protector and guarantor of a democratic order?

CHAPTER EIGHT

'A real underground empire'

In no area of Russian society was there more need for change than in that of the security services – the area dominated by the organization which acquired fame and odium as the KGB, the Russian acronym for the Committee of State Security. In none has change been so ambiguous.

In April 1992, a few months after Russia had embarked on a process which its leaders continually advertised as a complete rupture with the Soviet past, General Vadim Kirpichenko gave a speech at a conference in Sofia on 'The Proper Role of an Intelligence Agency in a Democracy'. General Kirpichenko was head of the Intelligence Group of the Russian Foreign Intelligence Service, itself a new creation, having been separated from the main body of the KGB at the end of 1991, but being very largely the KGB's first directorate, responsible for spying and counter-intelligence.

General Kirpichenko was a famous figure within the KGB. First recruited in Stalin's times, Kirpichenko was – like the man who had just become the Service's first head, Yevgeny Primakov – an Arabist. A former KGB resident in Egypt (who correctly warned Moscow that President Anwar Sadat was about to expel all Soviet military advisers in July of 1972), he had been elevated to the head of the 'S' Directorate, which prepared 'illegals' who would infiltrate themselves into target societies and which included in its duties the 'V' department for direct action, or assassinations and support for terrorist organizations.

In Sofia, the general declared that the intelligence services must 'reject the old idea of the services as an instrument for political confrontation or subversive activities. Such ideas have been cultivated for decades on both sides of the iron curtain.' Now, he said, a 'reasonable openness' must instead be offered to the public in the democratizing societies.

And then he added: 'Obviously, intelligence agencies cannot be more democratic than the society they serve and cannot go beyond the goals that society sets for itself.' In this phrase, almost lost as yet another truism in the stream of mush he read out (such as 'We believe that an intelligence officer who completes his tasks with dignity deserves the respect of society'), is contained the crucial question: How 'democratic' has the new Russia allowed the successors to the KGB to be? How far do its successors remain – as it was since the beginning of the régime – the 'sword and shield', not now of the Party, but of the presidency?

First, the assumption of equivalence ('cultivated . . . on both sides of the iron curtain') which Kirpichenko inserted as a matter of course into his talk – and which is often assumed in Western commentary as much as Russian – has to be severely qualified. The main Western intelligence services owe their origins to the needs of war and danger of subversion by foreign countries. The KGB (only one of its acronyms, the best-known to the post-war generation, now superseded by others) owes its foundation to the danger of subversion of the Communist Party by the population it ruled.

The first manifestation of the Bolshevik secret services, the Extraordinary Commission, or Cheka in its Russian initials, was founded on Lenin's order and charged with instituting the red terror: Felix Dzerzhinsky, its founding chairman, was given complete freedom to wage war against Bolshevik enemies, who included anyone of the wrong class (neither poor peasant nor working class). 'We represent in ourselves organized terror,' Dzerzhinsky told an interviewee in 1918.

The KGB was reined in from its orgies of terror in the pre- and post-war periods; Lavrenti Beria, the last and most powerful head of the Stalinist organization, was shot soon after the leader died. It became more restrained and less sadistic, the sphere of what it could deem to be punishable subversion contracted sharply. In human terms – the numbers of people executed, or sent to camps – this was a large and benign change.

But the traditions remained unchanged. Throughout the Khrushchev and Brezhnev years, and in the brief interregnums of Andropov (who had headed the KGB) and Chernenko, it continued to infiltrate, disrupt and monitor every organization of any importance – and to harass and arrest individuals who went outside the prescribed limits of dissent. Gorbachev, who was a protégé of Andropov and may have considered a KGB career (his university degree, in law, was a popular topic for the Chekists), was certainly the organization's choice to succeed Chernenko, because of their view that he was a younger and fitter Andropov and his belief that the KGB's unsentimental critique of Soviet backwardness had to be addressed with vigour.

An organization such as the KGB is wholly indispensable to the ruler of a dictatorship, no matter how benign: the signals of a society with free institutions are not available, and thus intelligence work must substitute. Mikhail Gorbachev naturally used KGB intelligence data and wiretaps – and did so to the end of his period of rule. He placed the chairmen of the organization in the Politbureau, ensured that when Viktor Chebrikov was retired in 1988 he was, for a time, employed in a powerful and influential post, and did not attempt any reform. When the new Soviet parliament formed a Defence and Security Committee, it had little effective oversight of the KGB and contained a number of members with close links to it. When the law on state security organs was passed in 1991, it turned out to offer no challenge to the prevailing practices and ethos, its most radical provisions being to decentralize some functions to the republics. It remained in possession of powers to investigate everything and everyone; to enter homes and offices, wiretap and open mail without special permission; to define who and who should not travel abroad.

The KGB ended the Soviet period unreformed and – with the democrats at least – unpopular. Yeltsin had suffered at the hands of the Chekists when, after his expulsion from the Politbureau, they engaged in the usual black propaganda about him. With other reformers in the Soviet parliament, he attacked the organization and, in a debate in May 1989, called for a 'radical restructuring of the KGB' of the kind at which Gorbachev had always baulked, said that the body should be split into a domestic and foreign service and demanded that it provide details of its terror over the past seven decades. The 1991 coup was largely controlled – in so far as it *was* controlled – by the KGB chief, Vladimir Kryuchkov. The KGB chairman bugged and followed the main targets of the coup, convened meetings of what became the State Committee for the Extraordinary Situation in a KGB safe house, alerted and briefed his senior officers just before the coup's announcement, cut the presidential and other phone lines once the coup was under way, blockaded Gorbachev in his *dacha* on the Crimea, had the Moscow head of the KGB, General Nikolai Kalinin, appointed

Moscow governor, prepared its Alpha division to arrest Yeltsin and later to storm the White House – and, uniquely, stayed sober throughout the affair.

That the KGB should be a major target of Yeltsin's reforming zeal seemed obvious. The democratic movement, of which he was the political expression, was fiercely opposed to the KGB. It contained within its ranks those who had suffered at its hands, like the dissident priest Gleb Yakunin, and it accepted the definition of the organization given in the May 1989 debate by Yuri Vlasov, the former Soviet champion weightlifter, that it was 'not a service but a real underground empire that has still not yielded its secrets, except for the graves that have been discovered'. The most famous target of the victorious crowds who roamed Moscow the day the coup collapsed was the statue of 'Iron' Felix Dzerzhinsky in front of the Lubyanka, the building from which 'orders for the persecution or annihilation of millions of people were issued', as Vlasov had put it. It took all afternoon and much of the night to shift the vast statue, and it went at last with the help of oxy-acetylene torches and a giant crane. It was one of the most joyful public moments I have ever witnessed: the crowd, at once determined and disciplined, the Lubyanka behind, with the occasional twitch of a curtain revealing the watchers within, the apparently sure instinct of the crowd in singling out Dzerzhinsky for their particular care to remove.

There was immediate action after the coup. Kryuchkov was of course removed and jailed with the other main putschists. After a brief interim, Yeltsin and Gorbachev together appointed Vadim Bakatin, a liberal-minded former interior minister fired by Gorbachev to make way for the hardline Latvian Boris Pugo (who shot himself and his wife after the putsch). He was appointed two days after the coup failed; in his account, he has talked of his nomination being an 'impulsive' one by Yeltsin and Gorbachev, the first driving the second to relinquish his instruments of power, ordering the Soviet president to write on the decree appointing Bakatin that his task was to liquidate the KGB. Andrei Grachev, Yeltsin's last presidential press secretary, recalls that the decision – taken at a meeting of the State Council (all the republican presidents with Gorbachev) – was a perfunctory one, even though the resolution of the meeting read 'to eliminate the KGB of the USSR'.

It was of course not eliminated, except in the formal sense that as the USSR ceased to exist, so did its KGB. Bakatin believed deeply that a disease ran through Soviet society, and that no one was immune from it. Thus a complete purge would be useless. He told an interviewer from the *Literaturnaya Gazeta*: 'We are, after all, from the same world, from the same society, from the same system . . . so what should we do, then? Remove all of those people and bring in some new ones? Where would we find them? Who would undertake to be the judges?' When asked, a few days after his appointment, if he intended to open the millions of files (as had been done in East Germany and in Czechoslovakia, with mixed results), he replied: 'I am convinced that opening the files would not only be inexpedient, but highly dangerous. It is not people who are to blame, but the system, which brought people up in such a spirit that they often turned, willingly or unwillingly, into informers.' With this view, he was gentle with the Chekists whom he had been sent to 'liquidate'. He was anyway given little help from outside. A state commission to investigate the activity of the security organs contained a solid phalanx of serving KGB officers, and was chaired by Sergei Stepashin, a colonel in the Interior Ministry who, though a Yeltsin supporter and chairman of the Russian Supreme Soviet's Committee on Defence and Security, was in line for a senior appointment in the KGB. Liberals on the commission, who included Yevgenia Albats, a *Moscow News* journalist who had done more than any other to expose KGB evils, were soon taken off it. No fewer than four other committees were created to investigate the KGB and/or its role in the putsch; none came to any firm conclusions and the only results came from a brief internal inquest which resulted in a few of the most compromised senior officials being fired.

The organizational problem – that commissions were at some point either taken over or neutralized by the KGB – was a reflection of the underlying moral and political one. There was no victorious anti-communist power, nor was there an occupying force. Occupation had forced a public penitence on post-war Germany, and oversaw the development of a politics – it took over a decade to embed itself – which continued to promote a political and moral atmosphere wherein anti-Nazism was an obligatory and often active element. In Russia, by contrast, the fact that communism crumbled from within and that the main agent of the eventual collapse of the Soviet Union was a former regional first secretary and a member of the Politbureau meant that it was impossible to expect a cleansing – as to a degree happened in Czechoslovakia, when the security police files were opened and collaborators with the organization were barred from political life or public service (though not from business – one of the largest companies in the Czech Republic, which began buying newspapers in 1996, was headed by a former security agent).

There was no 'clean' class available to rule, and thus none in the position to judge. The 'clean' people were the handful of dissidents, many *émigrés*, who were largely members of the intelligentsia – or they were the majority who never joined the Party, lived more or less decently within the system but had no interest in running it or any other. Bakatin's plaintive question – where would we find the new people? – was the critical one, and would remain so until a new generation appeared, able to judge for itself without taint.

Thus monsters were allowed to go free. Indeed, fewer were called to account than were during Khrushchev's purges of Beria's organization. Albats herself pursued and exposed the former NKVD (KGB's former acronym) investigator and torturer Vladimir Boyarsky, living under the peaceful and respected cover of a professor of the history of mining at a Moscow Academy of Sciences institute. She reckoned he had either tortured to death, had shot or sent to death in labour camps 117 people while working as chief of the NKVD in the North Caucasian republic of North Ossetia. Her revelations forced an investigation, and though he lost his awards and titles, he was not brought to trial. Boyarsky and people like him were – when unmasked – despised and shunned by most. But even in the late eighties, when the destalinization drive was at its height, there was no mechanism or will to go beyond publicity. By 1991, the energy had gone out of even that.

Thus Bakatin had been given a job reforming the KGB (the 'liquidation' notion had been rapidly dropped, by him as well, as a piece of rhetorical utopianism) for which there was no effective backing. Further, he had been given the job of reforming the *Soviet* KGB, at a time when the Soviet Union was being wound up. He was thus doubly handicapped, and bound to fail.

He did succeed in decentralizing the organization to the Union republics – though in many cases, they were ahead of him in 'nationalizing' what they could of the local KGB offices. He effected the split into foreign and domestic agencies, and appointed Primakov, his fellow aide to Gorbachev, as the former's head. He took the Border Guards, numbering between 200,000 and 240,000, out of KGB control; the Ninth Directorate, responsible for guarding the president and other high officials, was also spun off, augmented by the anti-terrorist Alpha unit and made directly answerable to the Soviet, and later to the Russian, president.

Though these moves were structurally important and were to last, the two main currents flowing fast below the surface were the gathering of Russian power and its ambitions to inherit as much of the old Soviet structure as possible; and the regrouping of the KGB and its desire to maintain as much of its structure and privileges as before. A Russian KGB had not existed before 1991; Yeltsin had persuaded Kryuchkov to create one, but it was a tiny force of a little over twenty officers, headed by Major General Victor Ivanenko. But from September 1991, more and more of the Soviet KGB was transferred to Russia. In November, with most of its assets transferred, Yeltsin signed a decree bringing into being the Federal Security Agency. An inter-republican security service, set up by Bakatin to co-ordinate the republican KGBs, never led more than a ghostly life and was wound up in December.

The next three to four years saw a replacement of Party control of the KGB with that of presidential control. In that the presidency was an elective office, it was argued that the security services of Russia had for the first time ever been made accountable to the people who paid for them and whose security they were meant to protect. However, the first years of Russian power have not closed that argument.

Bakatin was removed. What should have been his strength – that he was not part of the KGB and thus could reform it – was a weakness where he had no outside (or inside) support. He infuriated his colleagues by turning over to the US ambassador, Robert Strauss, diagrams of the bugs in the office block within the US embassy compound built a decade before but never completed or used because of the presence of vast numbers of hidden microphones. Most of all, he was not Yeltsin's man – he had actually run against him in the Russian presidential campaign – and thus he gave way to one who was, Victor Barannikov.

Barannikov, a close friend of Yeltsin's and head of the Interior Ministry, came in with a strategy to merge his own ministry with the new service – a plan which got the backing of Yeltsin because he saw it as a way of controlling the more dangerous agency. The merger, signed by Yeltsin as he left the country to meet foreign leaders in December and unknown to all of his main aides, was a very large piece of empire-building by Barannikov – ostensibly to serve Yeltsin's demand that an agency be quickly created which could counter reactionary efforts to destabilize him.

The structure, hated by the security officers, did not last – though it lasted long enough, according to contemporary reports, for MVD officials to find and destroy KGB files detailing their participation in organized crime rings. Parliament voted against the measure – and the Constitutional Court, newly formed, ruled it unconstitutional, perhaps swayed by KGB pressure to do so, since it was unclear on what grounds the decision was taken.

The two, barely brought together, were thus separated once more. The Interior Ministry resumed its previous title, and beside it was created a Security Ministry, which Barannikov continued to head. He rapidly assumed the coloration of the establishment: told to cut staff to about 140,000, he delayed and (as far as can be judged by estimates, since no figures are produced) probably retained at least twice that number. General Nikolai Golushko, who had headed the Ukrainian KGB, was brought in as Barannikov's first deputy – a hardline, and very pro-Soviet, appointment. Then and later, former persecutors of dissidents – like Golushko – were given high appointments. A new image was created for the Ministry of Security – that of crime-fighter, targeted towards the organized crime gangs, the drugs traffickers and the arms traders.

Barannikov did not reign long. In May 1993, he 'hijacked' Yeltsin away from a ribbon-cutting ceremony of a new Western hotel in Moscow, persuaded him to come back to his *dacha*, and introduced him to Boris Birshtein of Seabeco – a meeting arranged, as it later appeared, to pay back a debt to Birshtein. A few weeks after the meeting – as Yeltsin relates the story in his memoirs – he received evidence via Yakubovsky that the wives of Barannikov and another senior Interior Ministry official had been treated by Seabeco to a Swiss shopping spree worth $350,000. Having secured a confession that it was true from Barannikov during a painful interview, Yeltsin fired him and replaced him with Golushko.

The 'deep disappointment' Yeltsin said he felt over the treachery of Barannikov – who openly sided with the parliament during the October 1993 events, becoming its nominee as 'minister of security' – was translated into a drive to integrate the security services ever more closely into his personal retinue. After the 1993 elections, in an announcement which stressed that the Ministry of Security had performed only cosmetic restructuring and could again become a political/thought police, he abolished the ministry and created the Federal Counter-intelligence Service, first under Golushko and then under Sergei Stepashin. Yet again – as far as could be told – no real cuts were made, and the rearrangements of departments were no more than bureaucratic moves.

Increasingly, the main figures in security became not counter-intelligence or interior ministers or officials, but the two generals physically and personally closest to Yeltsin – Mikhail Barsukov, head of the Main Guard Directorate, which had been transferred to the presidency, and Alexander Korzhakov, head of the president's guard. In June 1995, Stepashin was fired as part of a move to head off a Duma vote of no confidence, and replaced by Barsukov, thus sealing for a time the connection between the president and counter-intelligence.

The Foreign Intelligence Service managed to stabilize itself under Primakov, whose skills recommended him so much to Yeltsin that he was made foreign minister in January 1996 in succession to Andrei Kozyrev. Though he led a depleted service – he cut back sharply on residences in African and other countries not central to Russian interests – he managed to concentrate his service's attention on rooting out technological and other information of use to Russian industry and enterprises. Russian diplomats, journalists and others continued to be expelled routinely from Western countries: in March 1996, the British parliament's security select committee reported that it believed about as many Russian spies were active in the country as in Soviet days.

In addition, Primakov's skills as a former ideologist – he had been a *Pravda* journalist – were reflected in a series of publications which cast the West in an increasingly hostile light. In mid-1994, he took a rare press conference to launch a pamphlet called 'Russia–CIS: Does the West's Position Need Correcting?' It accused the West of seeking to prevent the re-integration of the former Soviet countries in order to keep Russia weak. Early in 1995, he issued a much harsher report, accusing a range of institutions – including the RAND Corporation, the Carnegie Peace Centre, the Ford Foundation, the Soros Foundation, Harvard University, the Peace Corps and others – of being fronts for

US intelligence with the mission of draining off the best Russian brains abroad, gathering information and recruiting agents. In fact, all of these organizations did have offices in Russia and all worked with Russian researchers; some had done opinion polls, usually with Russian polling centres; all were active in trying to further this or that aspect of Russian reform − no doubt, at times, in a manner which bruised the egos of leading officials in their host country. All of their activities were interpreted in a sinister light.

None of the laws adopted in this period was aimed at changing or did change the basic KGB wiring of the renamed institutions. The Duma had no effective oversight of the staffing and budget of the intelligence services, and no details were volunteered (formally, this was until recently the same position as that in the UK; the Russians were formally better in that the chiefs of the services were named, public figures). Former dissidents − such as Sergei Grigoryants in Moscow and Boris Pudsintsev in St Petersburg − were harried or, in the latter's case, beaten up by unknown assailants, events he ascribed to the security services of which he had such experience in the past.

Two major elements must be set beside these negative tendencies. First, the intelligence services no longer commanded unlimited resources, and their pay was no longer substantially higher than the norm. Thus an increasingly large flow of officers, including senior officers, left for private business: one estimate reckoned that 80 per cent of joint ventures with foreigners had a KGB officer on its staff. General Leonid Shebarshin, a former head of the first (counter-intelligence) directorate, set up his own consultancy providing security services for banks, and gave interviews to foreign journalists. Some pointed to this as the suborning of business; it could also be seen as the commercialization of the KGB, and its dissolution into society.

Second, the old structures and habits of mind remained but the old actions were not − as far as is known − undertaken. The assumption of a general immunity from redress could no longer so confidently be made − since, whatever their limits, there was a free press, there was a multi-party parliament and even if one's friend was the president, there were limits. There was a constitution, which, though breached − as we have seen − by the president himself most of all, was still an inhibition, since it was no longer understood by all to be there for merely decorative purposes.

Indeed, the intelligence services could be no more democratic than the society they served. Yet Kirpichenko's warning was disingenuous in one important regard: services like the former KGB do not merely take their cue from society, they influence it directly and in their case very substantially. The secrecy, suspicion and furthering of paranoia which these services encourage and promote survived deep into the new Russia, and coloured all of its politics and many members of its political class.

CHAPTER NINE

'Eaten by corruption
from top to bottom'

Foreigners, especially Americans, who got to know Russia in the Yeltsin years were drawn irresistibly to compare it to what they had read of America in the later part of the nineteenth century. Bob Strauss, the US ambassador to Russia who took up his brief appointment as the 1991 August putsch ended the hopes his country had for a continued Gorbachev presidency, said of the Moscow he came to know that 'it's like an old Texan boom town, a constant parade of con men, promoters and shady customers; the greatest collection of sleaze bags in the world'. Wilfrid Thalwitz, the World Bank vice-president who oversaw the teams working in Eastern Europe and the former Soviet Union, could think on his retirement in 1995 of no better explanatory text on Russia than Robert Altman's film *McCabe and Mrs Miller*, the story of a gambler (McCabe – Warren Beatty) and a madame (Mrs Miller – Julie Christie). Set in a dark and cold northern mining town, the film shows McCabe and Mrs Miller trying to corner the supply of booze, gambling and prostitution to the new settlement – only to find that a big mining company is prepared to (and does) murder McCabe to take the prize for itself.

There were similarities indeed, but the parallel was rather too comforting. It had an implicit happy ending: once the fever to grab and to hold had subsided, the law could advance and gradually the demands of the market and of mass democracy would wash away the enclaves of lawlessness to the point where crime was, if not marginal, at least not the defining characteristic of most of business life. But in Russia, no such happy ending could be assumed. Indeed, by the end of the first Yeltsin presidency in mid-1996, Russians appeared to believe that crime and corruption were the endemic, omnipresent and eternal companions of their lives. Hardly surprising – their president had, in

February 1993, described his country as 'a mafia state on a world scale', 'eaten by corruption from top to bottom' and so in the grip of organized crime that it 'posed a direct threat to . . . strategic interests and national security'.

Whether or not crime would corrupt the new state absolutely was, at the end of the first five years, one of the many open questions, and one of the most wrenching. Those who looked on the bright side were relatively insouciant about the long run – even, in a few cases, about the short run. Edward Luttwak, the American writer on international affairs, claimed that the local organized crime groups 'resist the excessive concentrations of economic power brought about by government corruption . . . they are, in effect, competitors which use physical force, usefully, to offset monopolistic market power in a still lawless economy'. However, most agreed that the situation in the latter half of the nineties was bleaker than that vision of competitive criminal gangs, but thought that a division of the property, the need on the part of the new owners for state protection for their possessions, the presence of clear property rights, the development of a judicial system capable of enforcing rights and the law, would greatly diminish crime and allow for the deployment of effective policing.

The pessimistic view was well summed up in another question, put by an Italian writer, Federico Varese: is Sicily the future of the Russian state? In this view, the need of an emerging commercial class for protection from each other – and from the state – gave birth to an organized criminality which, once entrenched, not only refused to budge but developed vast and expanding criminal activities in narcotics, international prostitution, arms trading and even nuclear smuggling. Indeed, even if the lawlessness were to diminish, it would, on this view, leave behind a significant number of gangs capable of national and international operations which would pose a threat not just to Russian national interests, but to those of other states as well. The growth in international crime would have been ratcheted up another notch.

Private property came late to Russia. Until almost the nineteenth century, there was no effective distinction made, in law or in the public mind, between the property of the tsar and the state; the tsar effectively commanded and could dispose of both. The private citizen, even the aristocrat, in theory, had no land of 'his own'. Distinctions were made *de facto* in the nineteenth century (though land in theory was all owned by the tsar), and property and its rights and revenues were generally respected by the state. No mafia – in the sense of gangs offering protection – seemed to have been called for. If there was a specifically Russian form of pre-revolutionary crime, it was to be found in the increasing identification of criminal gangs with political protest: by their very strong corporate ethic and rituals, entailing obedience to a strong master and relative egalitarianism within the gang, and by their tendency to put as much space as possible between themselves and normal society – to create a 'thieves' world'. The brigand-like quality of Russian criminals, their capacity to become popular heroes, was more powerful than in other societies. The revolutionaries of the nineteenth and early twentieth centuries found a tradition of violence and robbery used for political ends in which they operated very readily (Stalin was a leading organizer of robberies and other criminal acts in the Caucasus).

Some of these traditions survived through the early Soviet decades. The harshness of communist rule did produce a society freer than the capitalist states of many of the common types of urban crime. It also accentuated the enclosed, state-rejecting world of the criminals, dominated by the figures of the 'thieves in law' (*vory v zakone*) – gang bosses, often elected to the post in prison or camps, who controlled their followers from their cells. If their own testimonies are to be believed, they followed a relatively ascetic life of criminality which observed certain rules towards women and children, and – according to the stories of the Soviet policemen who dealt with them – had a natural authority at times larger than the formal power of a local Party boss, at times spiced with some learning and a display of wisdom.

The economic base of this world changed under Brezhnev – a shift which was as large as, though much less obvious than, the shift which occurred under Gorbachev and Yeltsin. Terror was lifted; belief at all levels faltered, disappeared, turned to cynicism; a subterranean passion for consumption grew among those who learned something of the explosion in living standards in the advanced capitalist countries; the needs of production grew more diverse and were badly met; the example set by the highest in the land was increasingly – and increasingly brazenly – corrupt.

The result was a society in which crime was, to Western eyes, a curious mélange of commercial activities which were forbidden and often punished with rigour, including the death penalty; of pervasive corruption in which bureaucrats, medical personnel, teachers, shop and restaurant workers had to be bribed to produce or deliver what they were supposed to; of corners being cut by managers who needed to keep production going and who thus hijacked or bartered for goods which they required; of an escalating habit of removing property from the workplace and using it for private purposes; of large-scale networks engaged in scams worth millions of dollars; and of underground crime empires which included factories, distribution chains, protection agencies and even punishment systems, complete with prisons and executions.

Much of this was considered to be crime because the Soviet definition was explicitly anti-market. One who would be a relatively honest, busy shopkeeper in the West had to become in that system, perforce, a thug who corrupted others in order to get at his market. Alexander Gurov, a senior Soviet policeman who assisted in the creation of the first organized crime unit, told a Western reporter: 'In the West, the mafia rose out of purely criminal activities like extortion or bootlegging; but with us even normal activities, like making profits, creating associations without having to ask permission from the state, were illegal. That's why crime organizations have been part of our Soviet society from the beginning.'

These crime organizations *were* big. When Vasily Mjavanadze was deposed as first secretary of the Georgian Communist Party by Eduard Shevardnadze in 1972, he commanded a very large network which, among other things, fed him and his family a stream of tribute including diamonds, furs and large *dachas*. Pyotr Shelest, the Ukrainian Party first secretary at around the same time, was a byword for corrupt practices stretching through every level of the administration of a country as populous as Italy. The Communist Party leadership in the resort town of Sochi, on the Crimea, had in the seventies organized the main activities of the town into a gigantic slush fund for themselves and their associates, all under the protection of the regional Party boss, Sergei Medunov. The most famed of all the Party crime lords was Sharaf Rashidov, first secretary of Uzbekistan from 1959 till his death in 1983. In his period, he had milked the state of billions of roubles through false accounting processes, degraded the governing and intellectual élite by corrupting the higher education system, run the republic through nepotistic and clan networks and promoted the existence of a mafia which offered both protection and punishment and assassination services. A similar level of corruption in the neighbouring republic of Kazakhstan under the secretaryship of Dinmukhamed Kunayev resulted in the appointment of a Russian first secretary – and the earliest ethnic explosion of resistance to Russian rule in 1986. Yuri Churbanov, Brezhnev's son-in-law and a deputy interior minister, was closely linked to both the Uzbek and the Sochi networks.

Soviet society got to know a limited amount about these figures because Yuri Andropov, the KGB chairman who succeeded Brezhnev in 1982, was willing and at first able to take action against some of them, and because Gorbachev, who was Andropov's protégé, continued his attack. That it was limited, linked to political objectives and could not reach, or even call into question, some of those at the very top of the pyramid went without question: the legal and journalistic exposés were valuable, but in the end controlled. Nevertheless, real abuses were opened up to the public gaze and real criminals sentenced.

Even if we assume very great underestimation in the Soviet crime figures, the anecdotal evidence cannot be ignored. Russian cities passed rapidly from being relatively safe to relatively dangerous. Very large parts of the economy became criminalized. The public officials – civil servants, local authority bureaucrats, customs officials and the police – became corrupt. The reasons lie in the way in which the Soviet economy went private, in the way in which the society struggled to become a civil one and in the way in which the state lost, and sought to regain, its monopoly of violence, punishment and adjudication of crime.

Russia's descent into crime was rapid, and the effects of it shocking. Few societies, without a war or its aftermath, have gone through such a process. As soon as the Gorbachev decrees on state enterprises and on co-operatives were promulgated, and managers and others realized that what had been criminal was now shakily legal (or what was still illegal could more easily be undertaken), there was a burst of entrepreneurial activity, and with that went a demand for and the supply of protection. The sources of the funds for the new businesses were in many cases from capital accrued in the black economy – thus by definition illegal. The other main source was from the state, and often illegal, because the uses to which it was put were not those which had been declared. Thus the early business people were operating in an environment criminalized from the start. In the same way as those laws in force in a number of countries permit possession of drugs but not their peddling, or permit the act of prostitution but not the necessary advertising or soliciting, so Russian capitalism permitted enterprise without legalizing capital. In operating outside of the law, the new business people needed to provide, or buy, their own security – since the state not only would not do it, but could arrest the businessmen for precisely these activities which required protection.

So the world was instantly sleazy. The Russian Union of Industrialists and Entrepreneurs did a survey in 1990, and claimed its results showed that 49 per cent of the co-operatives' capital was 'black' and that over a quarter of the co-operators had criminal records when they entered the movement. These figures tended to become more and more dramatic: by the early nineties, the Interior Ministry was claiming that half of the top twenty-five banks were controlled by, or involved with, organized crime – a claim made plausible by the evidence of Vyacheslav Zakharov, the vice-president of the Association of Russian Banks, who said in 1995 that mafia leaders gave banks a simple choice: launder their dirty money, or be shot.

In 1985 (according to the Interior Ministry), ten crimes involving explosives were committed in Russia; in 1995 there were nearly 600. Business had become the main target of criminals, but the main victims were passers-by, or office workers. In the latter year, the head of a company in Vladivostok delivered a bomb to the factory of another, with whom he was feuding. The bomb was packed with screws, and killed three workers, hideously injuring a dozen more.

Most victims, if they survived, refused to testify. The Governor of Ekaterinburg, Vladimir Mashkov, wrote a letter to his president in 1993; it said that 'our country is now constructing a state the world has never seen before: one run by organized crime'. He did so as polls in the city showed that the citizens feared the mafia twice as much as anything else, including sickness or the loss of a job – not surprisingly, since Ekaterinburg had, like Moscow, spent much of 1992 and 1993 in the grip of a bloody battle for power between old and new criminal gangs, one so comprehensive that none of the many mafia bosses who commanded slices of city territory in 1991 was alive in 1993. Journalists who wrote about it were killed or beaten; so were policemen who attempted to be zealous.

The Ekaterinburg model was followed elsewhere: throughout Russia's cities and regions, the old *vory*, or crime bosses, were giving way to new men – harsher, richer and with fewer scruples and longer purses than they. The old *vory* and the police – according to both, no doubt with rose-coloured retrospect – had a wary respect for each other; the new bosses, usually called *avtoritety* (authorities), simply bought off the militia, or murdered them. The stakes had become very large: the Ministry of Finance estimated in 1994 that something like Rbs3–10 trillion of credits were being misappropriated, much of that made up the $1–2 billion a month, which was illegally being exported from Russia, to be lodged in foreign bank accounts. The long absence of a law on copyright (and the virtual absence of policing of the one which appeared) meant that in the first half of the nineties, an estimated 90 per cent of foreign books were pirated, while 95 per cent of computer software available was bootleg. When a Moscow publisher bought the rights to publish *Scarlett*, Alexandra Ripley's sequel to *Gone with the Wind*, he discovered that ten other bootleg copies were already being sold, and none could legally be stopped. He gave up, as many others who tried to do business the legal way also did.

The shock of crime was not merely the numbers of murdered (up from a few hundred in 1985 to 32,000 in 1994 – more than twice the US rate, five times that of France and Germany, fifteen times that of the UK and twenty-two times that of Japan). It lay in the arrogance and the impunity of a criminality so clearly in the service of rapid acquisition. By 1992, the price of inner-Moscow flats had risen to levels comparable to New York. Property developers hired thugs to winkle out the tenants in flats which were often communal homes to a number of families, and where they would not go for a few hundred dollars, they went on the threat, or delivery, of violence. Cases of pensioners being killed were publicized by the militia. In mid-1995, the new tenant of a basement flat in Moscow found a corpse decomposing in a cupboard; the incident had lost any capacity to be remarkable.

In February 1996, John Hayden, a British lawyer, was killed by a stray bullet as he waited for a client in a hotel in St Petersburg. He had had the bad fortune to be a bystander at a mafia shooting. In June 1995, Andrei Orekhov, a leading broker, saw his young daughter gunned down in crossfire as he took her to her primary school, in a firefight between his bodyguards and assassins out to shoot him. In the central Moscow street of Staraya Basmanya, one day in May 1995, three headless corpses were found in rubbish bins one morning; the local militia, whether in jest or not was unclear, said they had not paid their rent. In the corner of the same street three months later, a bomb exploded in a truck. These are random incidents over an eighteen-month period, united only by the fact that I saw them, or knew well the victims, or the main person involved in the discovery of the victims. A journalist living in central Moscow may live a more eventful life than the majority of Russians; but in my experience, many were directly touched by this huge change. A weekend spent with friends of friends in the small city of Yaroslavl in July 1995 revealed that, in their dingy little block of flats in a suburb of the town, they had gone out one morning to see, hanging in the lift shaft, the body of a local Chechen gangster – his face near black, his tongue lolling below his chin. It had become the central fear of their lives: they spent much of their meagre savings on a steel door.

The movement from state control to free-for-all was extremely rapid: from the first tentative flirtings with 'the market' under Gorbachev in 1987 to the 'big bang' of 1992. The crime which rose in apparent perfect harmony with the increase of economic freedom was seen to be the latter's consequence, and that was right, for the reforms threw open to the powerful and the ruthless the opportunity to take and to own which they had been denied for decades. But it gave rise to an illusion, pushed by the politicians who were in opposition to the reformers – who, by mid-decade, appeared to include, at times, Yeltsin himself. The illusion was that crime could be curbed by controls and tougher policing. In fact, crime could only be dealt with by continuing market reforms, particularly by constructing a working market infrastructure of commercial law, financial institutions and bank regulation. Only then could the kind of behaviour the market societies define as rational – taking out loans, acquiring capital, issuing shares, observing contracts – be prised loose from its connections with crime.

This argument – between control of the market and rendering it more transparent and institutionally secure – swayed to and fro, the controllers securing more and more support, the reformers never quite relinquishing a hold on power and influence. Both sides accused the other of benefiting from the corruption, and both sides were right in general (though the particular was notoriously elusive to prove). But even had they both been pure in heart, they could have done little to regulate the scramble for property which communism's fall unleashed.

Two main phases distinguish the scramble for property. First, there was the scramble to possess, and secure, state and Communist Party property and funds, a struggle whose life and death quality could be seen in the 'suicides' of three leading Party financial officials – Nikolai Kruchina, the Party treasurer, his predecessor Georgy Pavlov and a Central Committee official in charge of funding foreign communist parties, Dmitri Lissovilik – soon after the August putsch was aborted. From reports – which were never confirmed, and which an inquiry ordered by the Russian government by the US detective agency Kroll Associates was unable to verify – up to 2,000 tonnes of Soviet gold was shipped out to the West. Up to Rbs200 billion of Party funds (at an exchange rate then of 18:1) were, according to the TV journalist Vladimir Pozner, exchanged and put in foreign bank accounts by the early nineties (Vladimir Kryuchkov, the KGB chairman to 1991, put the figure at Rbs12 billion). Thousands of *dachas*, flats and other buildings were sold or leased through front companies to the new powers – the banks, the property developers, the traders.

The longer-lasting movement was that which was called privatization. Its first phase saw the sale of shops and workshops. Capital acquired in the black market was laundered through the purchase of these, and by 1993, the Moscow police believed that over 30 per cent of the shops were owned by organized criminal groups. The second phase was mass privatization, in which the beneficiaries were largely the workers and managers, with others taking a share of companies through the exchange of vouchers; in this phase, too, black market capital was said by numerous police and other reports to be extensively involved. The third was post-voucher privatization, in which a group of finance companies and banks were given insider deals on large shares of some of the most attractive Russian companies. At each stage, the transfer of property was accompanied by bribes, coercion, the use of black market or criminal capital, and the collusion of state officials with business people to secure the latter monopolistic positions in this or that marketplace.

It was in the lasting and powerful grip of the state on private

transactions that crime flourished. The privatization of Moscow's property – the hottest part of the process, and one conducted by Moscow's
government in defiance of efforts by the central authorities to control
it – offered a classic case, where the senior officials, the property
developers and the banks created a seamless but very powerful web of
mutual self-enrichment. Here flourished such figures as Andrei Stroyev,
who 'privatized' the state building corporation Mosinzhstroi in the late
eighties, and formed a joint venture with a US company in Atlanta to
create a firm called Perestroika, which quickly became the dominant
supplier of luxury offices and homes for the foreign business community.
The link man with the Moscow government was Andrei Resoin, who
sat on the Mosinzhstroi board and was also head of urban development
in Moscow.

Moscow was the richest, and probably the most corrupt city, not
just because of the quality of the pickings, but because its mayor from
1992, Yuri Luzhkov, had decreed that land could not be bought and
sold freely, leaving all final decisions as to allocation of property to the
city hall, a fantastic source of kickbacks. The normal method of operation
was for a developer to strike up an alliance with a senior official, for
the official to sell to his ally an apartment building at a low price, for
the developer to renovate and sell at up to one hundred times the
purchase price, and for the two – and the others involved in the deal
– to split the very large profits.

All of this needed protecting, and that protection has been very
largely private. The failure of the police to bring the new commercial
activities under their authority has been almost total. They early gave
away authority when, in the late eighties, they began to charge the first
of the co-operators for extra protection (which meant that those not
paying would get less protection – a state of affairs in which no serious
police force could acquiesce, let alone propose). Even had they not
done so, however, their demoralization, loss of authority, lack of
technology (including, initially, fast cars), miserable salaries and thus
openness to (as well as a tradition of) bribery would all have ensured
that the new business environment had to have recourse to private
protection – a major source of the new criminality, and the largest parallel
with the mafia-dominated societies of Sicily, some Latin American states
and some US inner cities.

The new businesses, by the middle of the decade, had at the respectable end taken security very seriously. Sergei Rodionov, chairman of the important Imperial bank, reckoned 60 per cent of his staff costs were paid to security personnel. Vladimir Gusinsky, chairman of Most, hired a former KGB general to head his 2,500-strong security force – which had its own training school and firing range. Alexander Smolensky, chairman of the Stolichny Bank, employed members of the KGB's Alpha squad – the élite of an élite – to be his guards and intelligence service. Some 80 per cent of the banks – disproportionately the smaller ones who could not afford Rodionov's or Gusinsky's private armies – paid protection money, which could be 20–25 per cent of their profits.

The line between security services and 'protection' was thin and wavy. General Valery Velichko, former head of the KGB's Ninth Directorate, set up with two senior ex-KGB colleagues a company called Commercial Structures Protection Bureau, which did well and was presumably relatively straight. But a company called Top, which was (according to the Moscow police) involved in criminal deals, hired two groups of security guards which both protected their employers and went into business for themselves, extorting money from shops in Moscow suburbs.

At the blackest end were the monotonously regular murders of businessmen and bankers – which provoked, in 1995, the Association of Russian Bankers to take to the streets to demand the protection which they had connived in ensuring that the state could not offer them. In 1995, the Interior Ministry reported the going rate for assassinations: $7,000 for killing a man without a bodyguard; $12,000 for killing a man with a bodyguard; and $180,000 for killing the president of Russia. Most of the assassinations were by high-powered rifle, but explosives were sometime preferred and poison was used to kill Ivan Kivlidi, head of Rosbiznesbank and a founder of the Russian Business Round Table, in August 1995.

The growing horror of Russians that their state might have exchanged a merely ideological criminality for an overt one was matched by that of foreign countries, who became aware in the first half of the nineties that the Russians had arrived. One of the first to voice the fear – which was not to be dissipated by events – was Giovanni Falcone, the anti-mafia judge murdered by Sicilian mafiosi in May 1992, as he was being driven from Palermo airport to the Sicilian capital. In his book *Men of Honour*, published posthumously, he writes:

The current situation, in which criminal organizations from a few countries agree limited and local pacts, is one thing: quite another is the eventual evolution of organized crime towards a federation of vast dimensions. The extremely dangerous prospect of a homogenized model of criminal organization . . . would create a kind of global Mafia, and I ask myself how it could possibly be opposed.

Others who concerned themselves with organized crime – including senior police officers – saw the emergence of the Russian mafia as the link which would forge a girdle of mafia organizations round the earth: the Sicilian and Neapolitan families, the Colombian drug lords, the US gangs, the Japanese Yakuza, the Hong Kong and Taiwanese Triads – and now the Russians. Louis Freeh, head of the FBI, set up an office in Moscow to try to assist the militia in controlling the epidemic and has described the Russian networks as 'a new transnational enemy'. David Veness, an assistant commissioner of London's police force, said that Russians might control much of British inner-city crime by the end of the century.

A world controlled by crime bosses who have managed to put aside their enmities and expand their limited visions and intellectual resources seems unlikely. But there are a number of indications that the Russians' emergence on the scene has made a bad situation worse, and that it will continue to do so.

Russian crime emigrated with Russians. This happened years before the collapse of communism. The Russian-Jewish outflow in the seventies created substantial communities in Tel Aviv, in New York (Brighton Beach) and in Antwerp. Some became active in crime circles in their countries, and some of these provided 'financial' and other services for the criminals, black marketeers and Party money launderers of the Soviet period. One such figure was Rachmiel Brandwain, who had emigrated in the seventies as a boy and who set himself up in Antwerp, selling Western goods to Soviet sailors, graduating to assisting Soviet officers in Germany bank the proceeds from their looting of the military inventory in the second half of the eighties.

However, the uninhibited flooding out of people and money from the late eighties signalled a change in quantity and quality. The old godfathers of Brighton Beach were displaced by new men sent from Russia, much in the way in which the former *vory* had been shouldered aside – or gunned down – by the *avtoritety*. Vyacheslav Ivankov – or

STATE

Japonchik, the 'little Japanese' – had been reportedly named in 1991 by a convocation of Russian crime leaders to take over Brighton Beach; he succeeded in doing so, though was arrested in the summer of 1995 in the Beach's Little Odessa area and charged with extortion. His contacts ran through Israel, Antwerp – but also to Latin America and Berlin.

The new commodities in the post-Soviet criminal trading networks were hugely profitable. There was protection for Russian merchants and business people overseas – protection which, as in Russia itself, began as battening on the Russians abroad and flourished to fasten on commerce in the host country, especially in Central and Eastern Europe. There was the drugs trade, fed by the huge growth of marijuana and cocaine in Central Asia and the Caucasus, taking advantage of what was in the eighties a relatively under-narcotized domestic population (the estimated 130,000 Russian addicts in 1990 is predicted to grow to 7.5 million by the end of the century) and spilling out into Europe and beyond, augmented by new synthetic wonder drugs like 3MF; and the arms trade, a speciality of the Soviet military and of the Chechen and other Caucasian crime groups. Nuclear smuggling (see chapter 7) presented a much greater nightmare.

Western secret services were, in the mid-nineties, paying particularly close attention to a man named Grigory Loutchansky, a Jewish-Ukrainian who grew up in the Latvian capital of Riga. Loutchansky, a former economics professor at the Latvian state university, went into trading agricultural fertilizers in the late eighties, then – showing a talent for the task – was encouraged by the Communist Party to found a company named Nordex. Nordex was officially a medium through which joint ventures could be concluded with foreign companies to assist the modernization of Russian industry; in fact, these ventures were conduits for funds being taken out of the country and placed in foreign bank accounts for the later use of senior Party and state officials.

From these beginnings, Nordex grew into a trading and financial company officially turning over (in 1993) $600 million a year, with headquarters in a palace in Vienna and links all over the former Soviet Union. Many of its deals have been the trading of commodities – metals, oil, gold – from the former Soviet Union to the West, at times in transactions which were relieved of export duties. In one such

154

deal, 30,000 tonnes of copper was exported from Russia, allegedly to build statues of Christopher Columbus (which were never built); Prime Minister Victor Chernomyrdin intervened to waive export taxes after a request to do so from the Moscow mayor, Yuri Luzhkov. The Moscow city agency Glavsnab, set up to build a brewery, transferred $13 million in an interest-free loan to Nordex — evidence, a Nordex spokesman said, of 'a long continuing relationship of trust and confidence'.

Working through presidents and the prime ministers, Nordex — like Boris Birshtein's Geneva-based Seabeco — organized huge trade deals with the more resource-rich parts of the former Soviet Union. In 1993, Nordex's *annus mirabilis*, it was lauded in Ukraine for having 'saved' the country by bartering Russian oil for fertilizer and sunflower seed after Russia had refused to supply oil to Ukraine. Later, the company was accused of undervaluing the commodities and Loutchansky took a suit against the government for non-payment of $100 million in debts. Through Russian first deputy premier Oleg Soskovets, Nordex took an interest in the vast steel mill at Karnets, in Kazakhstan's Karaganda area; Soskovets, the target in Russia of various corruption allegations, had been a steel mill manager, then deputy prime minister, in Kazakhstan.

The most alarming allegations, and those which made Loutchansky — in the words of *Time* magazine, which published a July 1996 dossier on him — 'the most investigated man in the world', was evidence that he was smuggling Scud missiles to radical Middle Eastern states, and that he was exporting nuclear bomb-making components to Iran and North Korea. These were never proved; when evidence was put to Loutchansky, he denied it. Nordex's income shrank in the mid-nineties, as foreign governments denied him a visa and cracked down on deals he tried to broker with their companies. He blames both former Soviet and Western intelligence agencies for the rumours — 'disinformation' — and says they are pursuing him to justify their existence.

Corruption of officials, from the top to the minor, made these kinds of operations possible, easy and largely immune from detection or punishment. Corruption, frequently practised in the communist period, became pervasive: the Interior Ministry estimated in 1995 (though on what evidence was not revealed) that bribes assisted 30 per cent of major transactions in 1985, and more than 50 per cent ten years later.

But this understates the case – for where venal officials posed the greatest danger to the state, there they were most venal.

Anatoly Kulikov took over as interior minister in the summer of 1995. His predecessor, Victor Yerin, had been fired after his troops had botched the handling of the hostage-taking in the southern Russian town of Budennovsk organized by Shamil Basayev, most daring of the Chechen commanders. Kulikov followed recent Russian tradition by presenting the worst possible face on his country's crime problem – claiming in January 1997 that criminal dealings accounted for 40 per cent of all economic activity. Other – Western – estimates point to some 5,000 major mafia gangs operating in Russia, controlling 40,000 businesses, including over 400 banks.

The pessimistic view of the problem points to the growing control of the crime cartels over key sectors, their sophisticated organization, assisted by the presence in the gangs of former KGB and police officials, the ruthlessness of their punishment squads, the strong links with high officials and important politicians, the evidence of nuclear trafficking, the alliances with longer established mafias – all of these, it is argued, could lead to the world's first 'criminal superpower'. The situation is rendered impervious to cure, it is argued, because of the fate which awaits anyone who really tries to take on the crime bosses: contract killings are estimated (in 1996) to have reached 500 a year.

Against this, the sunnier vision that the problem will 'wash out' as capitalism becomes more transparent has been struggling to convince. The American parallel assumes a society in which an honest business ethic, drawing on both religious and secular codes, has a strong foundation in government, law-enforcement, in the media and elsewhere. In Russia, such an ethic was and remains weak. The old morality had been discredited, a new one was struggling feebly with a tide of greed, fear and cynicism.

CHAPTER TEN

'They labour in vain that build it'

The services of the Orthodox Church strike the foreigner as rituals of abasement and of transcendence. The abasement is physical: the congregation, often a sparse scattering of elderly women, descend to their knees before the icon, or the priest; in certain places, as in the church of the Holy Trinity and St Sergius at Sergeiv Posad, north of Moscow, they will prostrate themselves before blessed remains of St Sergius, or bow to kiss the container which holds them. They cross themselves – forehead to stomach, right to left shoulder – constantly and vigorously. 'Christ has risen!' call the priests, again and again, during the Easter services, in one of the few comprehensible parts of any service. 'In truth he has risen!' fervently calls back the congregation, usually swollen to capacity for the celebration. The priests alternately gabble and intone their way through the services; the choirs chant, hauntingly. The acolytes swing the censers to and fro as if their future in the church depended on it, thick aromatic smoke left trailing in their wake.

The services are in Old Church Slavonic, which Russians do not understand. It is rare for a priest to address the congregation directly, as in a sermon. When one of the congregation approaches him before or after the service, it is timidly, with respect and deference. The priest may be kindly, but even if he is he will tend to be reserved, shy, distracted – as though he would rather not be approached. The Orthodox Church is one dominated by monks, for whom the episcopal and higher roles are exclusively reserved. Tough as it was to create the other-worldliness and retreat from mundane pursuits in the few pressurized, harried monasteries of the communist period, still a distance from the world was cultivated as far as possible and is again being more vigorously pursued with the restoration of the monasteries, convents and seminaries of the post-communist Church.

Religious observance, before the communists waged a murderous campaign upon it from the twenties, was devout. The peasantry prostrated themselves in their millions before icons – a few old women and young devotees still do – they kept the holy days, obeyed the priests and infused the religion with all kinds of pre-Christian superstition which gave it more of a medieval than a modern character. The Orthodox Church, inheritor of Byzantine Christianity after the Turks broke up the Byzantine empire in the mid-fifteenth century, was essentially a national religion, unlike Protestantism and Catholicism, which were and are world religions with national traditions. This has assisted in giving to the Russian Church much more the character of a state Church than any other in modern times. Orthodoxy disliked Catholicism and Protestantism, a dislike which has transmitted itself into national culture, and which supported and supports the Slavophile, anti-Western movements and traditions. It also explains the latent correspondence between communism and Orthodoxy, even as the first sought to stamp out the second: both were anti-Western. Thus when the communists sought to revive themselves after the collapse of the Soviet Union, they turned to the Church – or at least to the more nationalist-inclined clerics – in the expectation that they could exorcise the mutual antagonisms of the past by an agreement on a common hate in the present.

Distance from the West and from the world is only part of the contemporary story. Easter 1996 was celebrated in Moscow in an occasion which harshly underscored the presence the Church must now maintain at the very heart of the modern Russian state. Held in the part-completed cathedral of Christ the Saviour, presided over by Patriarch Alexei II and with the attendance of President Yeltsin, the gorgeous occasion illuminated the embrace into which the secular and the spiritual powers have locked themselves at the top levels of the governance of both Church and state. It is one in which each implicitly absolves the other of the need to examine its respective past, in which both can attempt to exist in a present as partially reconstructed as the cathedral itself then was.

The dilemmas facing the patriarch and the president – and at least the former gave them some thought – were and would remain grave and elusive. It was not clear, for all the pomp of the occasion and the intertwining of Church and state symbology implicit in the reconstruction of the great imperial Christ the Saviour cathedral itself, how far the Church would become part of the state, and whether it was likely to remain so. It was not clear whether it could succeed, even partially, in becoming the instrument of spiritual and civic renewal it had set itself to be. It was not clear whether it could take and keep a place in the society which would give it some kind of moral voice – hegemony was too tall an order – to which the citizens could refer. And above all it was not clear in what tone that voice would speak.

The Church had been almost destroyed, and emerged into the new Russia terribly compromised. For some within it, destruction of the old Church would have been better than the continued existence of a compromised one. The shifts and evasions it had to make to survive in any form meant that, in the freedom which the nineties brought to it, when it should have been engaged wholly in re-establishing its physical presence and its moral capital, it was consumed by a series of splits and controversies which went to the deepest recesses of its past and its practice.

It had always been a Church forced to bend low before the state's will. Its autonomy and co-equal power with the tsar – a *symphonia* of the spiritual and the political realms in which the Church retained a large power – was very much weakened by Peter I (the Great); it became part of his totalizing vision of a society bent to his own driving ambition to modernize it. Its self-government through the patriarchate, including the election of the patriarch himself, was replaced by a state council overseen by an official of cabinet rank; and though the letter of the Church's subordination to the state never went so far as that of the Church of England, which recognized the sovereign as 'the only supreme governor of the realm ... as well as in all spiritual and ecclesiastical things', still it effectively rendered to the tsar a practical overlordship. The Church played its own part in the general ferment of the first two decades of the twentieth century: it agitated for separation of Church and state and a restoration of the symphonic ideal – achieving it, ironically, in 1917, when the Bolsheviks took power and its council elected, for the first time in two hundred years, a patriarch, Tikhon.

Lenin was formally correct in his pre-revolutionary intentions towards the Church: he wrote that it must be opposed ideologically, and only ideologically. But the venom with which he and his associates viewed a body they saw as tsarism in a more hypocritical guise was given a release at the time of the famine which accompanied the civil war: the Church, on Lenin's orders, was looted for its wealth (though the evidence does not seem to show that the money went in the main to famine-relief), priests were executed or imprisoned and Tikhon was himself imprisoned – released a little before his death on the signing of a statement which repented of crimes against the state order and dissociating himself from the Whites.

The Church became what the historian Dmitri Volkogonov called 'a decorative embellishment' on the state. Preserved – only just, in the thirties – at the top, it was hollowed out below. Most churches, monasteries, convents and seminaries were closed: they became warehouses, animal sheds, museums of atheism. Priests and the religious were swept into the maw of the gulags and the prisons; those who clung to the outward shows of devotion were persecuted, unless they were too old and feeble to be bothered with. By 1937, some 80,000 of the religious had been killed; there were a mere 2–3,000 churches still offering some sort of service in the entire Soviet Union, where there had been 80,000 before the revolution.

Ironically, it was the German invasion which brought relief, for two reasons. The Germans allowed – even encouraged – the re-establishment of churches in the areas they occupied; and the need to mobilize patriotic sentiment meant that the régime was forced to draw on every sort of tradition and collective memory. Stalin met the patriarch and his colleagues in the Kremlin, and there was some restoration of churches. Three years after the war, repression was resumed, but not at full intensity. The opening of the camps in 1956, three years after Stalin's death, meant thousands of former priests and believers returned into society. Khrushchev revived an anti-Church campaign in the late fifties and early sixties, which saw a wave of closures once more. These slowed after Khrushchev's going, and the Brezhnev years were marked by a corrupting accommodation between the régime and the patriarchy – with a growing Christian dissident movement calling into question the nature of that accommodation.

Accommodation had had a long history. In 1927, Sergei, the successor to Tikhon, had on his release from imprisonment signed a document which accepted 'the Soviet Union as our civil motherland whose joys and successes are our joys and successes and whose misfortunes are our misfortunes'. This document has tolled down the decades. At the time, it was condemned by the many bishops imprisoned in the early camps, and by the Russian Orthodox Church Abroad, which had been founded in Serbia in 1922 – the latter disowning Sergei's (and subsequent patriarchs') authority. The dissidents of the sixties and later – including the priests Gleb Yakunin and Nikolai Elishman, whose appeal for a separation of the Church from the state went back to the pre-revolutionary agitation – acted in the name of a Church which they saw as impelled to bear witness against the actions of the regime. After some shadow boxing to and fro in the seventies, many of the religious were arrested at the end of the decade, at around the same time as Andrei Sakharov – who spoke for them, but was not one of them – was sent to exile.

It was Gorbachev who gave the Church its most recent lease of life. He took the side of those in the Communist Party who wished to see the Church celebrate the millennium of its existence in 1988 in grand style: he received the aged patriarch, Pimen – once more, in the Kremlin – and the five other metropolitans who were members of the Holy Synod. He had already allowed the restoration of a number of monasteries, including the Danilov in Moscow. Pimen asked for many more, and in a relatively short time got them. Priests were restored to their parishes, monks to their cloisters, teachers to the seminaries.

Alexei II took the patriarch's office in 1990, after Pimen's death, in freer circumstances than any of his predecessors for over two and a half centuries. The law on freedom of conscience was passed that same year. There were still some features irksome to the Church in it, but it did give a legal basis for the practice of the faith and for institutional rebuilding. When, in July 1991, Alexei conferred the presidency of Russia on Boris Yeltsin in the Palace of Congresses in the Kremlin, he was able to say in the presence of the general secretary of the Communist Party of the Soviet Union (who was still the state's president):

Our communist rulers believed that it was only the imperial rule of Russia which was bad and that on the assumption of power they would construct a new society from – as they put it – human material. We see now what tragedies all of this brought. Seven decades of destroying our spiritual health and internal unity were accompanied by the strengthening of the heavy chains of repressive statehood.

Alexei II, sixty-one when elected patriarch against a candidate seen as more liberal than he, was judged by some in his country and abroad as unfit to pronounce such words. In his person and career he contained much of the dilemma of a Church emerging from communism. He had risen extremely fast, becoming bishop of his native Estonia at thirty-two, the earliest age he could do so, a fact which attested not merely to his spirituality and his intelligence, but to close links with the KGB. Like others in the hierarchy, Alexei was given a code name ('Drozdov') by the KGB. His file, details of which were published, seems to reveal him as complaisant and trusted by the agents who ran the Church Council. In a phrase that would haunt him, they spoke of him as one who showed a commendable 'lack of interest' in strengthening the Orthodox faith.

The revelations of the KGB *compromat*, revealed early in 1992 by a commission of investigators who included the former dissident Gleb Yakunin, had almost no obvious effect: the compromised bishops and metropolitans kept their posts except in one instance – and his dismissal was probably for other reasons. It did, however, give a basis for those in the laity – and the few radicals in the priesthood – for distrusting the older two generations of hierarchs and priests, for it was clear that compromise and collaboration was a general habit. Sergei Averintsev, the Byzantine scholar and writer, said of this period that 'the laity believes that men of weak character have been elevated to the priesthood'.

Consciousness of what he had (as he saw it) had to do gave an extra passion to Alexei's claim, in an interview in *Izvestiya* in June 1991, that the original pact with the state and communism by Sergei had been because he

wanted to save the Church. I know that many people, hearing these words, protest that it is Christ that saves the Church, and not the people. This is true. But it is also true that, without human efforts, God's help does not save . . . where is the celebrated Church of Carthage? Are there Orthodox believers today in Kaledoniya, in Asia Minor, where Gregory the Illuminator and Basil the Great earned their renown? Before our eyes the Church in Albania was destroyed . . . and in Russia there were powers wishing to do the same thing.

Alexei and his colleagues were in a familiar enough position – especially familiar in the twentieth century: bargaining and acquiescence could win small gains or stop large damages to the Church, head-on confrontation on moral or religious grounds earned spells in prison or the camps. As members of the hierarchy, they had larger responsibilities than their own freedom or comfort (and the life of a member of the patriarchy could, in Brezhnev times, be quite comfortable by any standards). Alexei's own sense of history, evident in the *Izvestiya* interview, was a tragic one – not at all a simple belief that God would save his faithful in the end if they acted always in his name. But had martyrdom been the chosen route of the patriarchy, would they have galvanized the believers and perhaps others into a resistance which the Church could have led and from which it could, after the fall of communism, have reaped great moral dividends? The experience, after all, of the generation before Alexei's and even of his own (he was a little older than Mikhail Gorbachev) was of a power which was ruthless – fanatically so in his early years, dully but inexorably so in his later ones.

The result, however, was to produce a patriarchy which was inevitably transitional and which has been disinclined to take a strong moral stand on anything. Pruned of men who were remarkable, it passed into freedom led by men who, in most cases, were probably ashamed to be compromised but could and did live with it. Further, the patriarchy showed a tendency to react more vigorously against dissenters from the liberal than from the conservative side. Yakunin was defrocked and threatened with excommunication for continuing to engage in active politics (he was a member of the USSR Supreme Soviet and of successive Russian parliaments). Metropolitan Ioann of Leningrad was an overt and very active anti-Semite, who published his views in newspapers of the far and fascist right, and who endorsed the veracity of the old slander, the Protocols of the Elders of Zion, the alleged Jewish conspiracy to murder Christians first forged by the Okrana, or tsarist secret police, in the nineteenth century. He died in 1995, unchided, at least publicly, by the patriarch. Priests and their seniors have been associated with other far-right groups – especially since these groups have often been active in rebuilding churches and monasteries, and in assisting the Church in its campaign against the infiltration of foreign sects into Russia.

Alexei's defenders – who include the London-based Metropolitan Anthony Bloom and the American scholar and Librarian of Congress

James Billington – portray him as, in Billington's words, a 'parish priest' (though, given his rapid elevation, there is much less of the priest in his background than with most in the patriarchy). He has been extremely active in opening churches, cathedrals and monasteries; but any patriarch would, in a time of rapid revival under the aegis of a benign state, have had a similar good fortune. A more substantial defence lies in his apparent weakness: lacking a strong sense of mission, he has been able to keep in one Church conservative and liberal figures, deflecting the wrath of the former from the latter and disapproving of the latter's 'excesses' without dividing them from the Church. In combining that with a concern for the revival of parish life, he has given the Church an opportunity to re-establish itself, again in Billington's words, as 'the leaven in a new life of prayer, hard work and Christian education that will renew local communities in which private property and individual rights will be respected'.

Three large dangers confront the Church in seeking to attain this, or some similar, condition: splits within it, indifference all about it and the design of the state to suffocate by embracing it. All of these dangers afflicted it at once, as soon as its renewed position in society was secured. Like much else in the new Russia, it emerged into freedom weighed down with chains at best half struck off.

The splits were ferociously deep, and went back in most cases to Patriarch Sergei's accommodation. The Russian Orthodox Church Abroad energetically set about organizing once it was free to do so: by the mid-nineties, it was credited with some 100 parishes, two bishops and Archbishop Lazar of Tambov. Its most concentrated presence appeared to be in the old religious centre of Suzdal, one of Russia's best-preserved and most lovely towns, where Bishop Valentin had taken most of the parishes with him in his defection.

The Church Abroad had not softened in exile. It had a series of demands, including the canonization of Tsar Nicholas II; the breaking of the Church's links with the World Council of Churches and an end to ecumenicism; the repudiation of Sergei's protestation of loyalty to the Soviet state; and repentance for past sins of collaboration. None of this was forthcoming; indeed, it was one of Alexei's quiet achievements that the Council moved more in the very gently reformist direction he seemed to wish it to take, when in late 1994 it reaffirmed by a large majority its support for ecumenical dialogue, proposed the translation of a number of services into Russian to assist comprehension and affirmed the need for different points of view (as long as these 'did not break the bounds of love' – perhaps the most tender ambiguity available). All of these positions were distasteful to the Church Abroad, and indeed to conservatives within the Orthodox Church itself.

But this was not the most serious split – that lay to the west. Ukraine was the most religious – at least in formal terms – of the regions of the Russian Orthodox Church. Parishes had been founded there during the Nazi occupation, and remained in being afterwards. It thus had more churches than the rest of Russian Orthodoxy. Further, it had a large (and suppressed) minority, concentrated in western Ukraine, of Uniates, or Orthodox Catholics – Catholics who accepted the eastern rite.

The Ukrainian independence movement and the faltering of Soviet imperialism thus had a much greater and more immediate effect on believers there than elsewhere in the Soviet Union. The Uniates, encouraged by Gorbachev's entente with the Pope in 1989, were given leave to form parishes and began an acrimonious campaign to win back their former churches from the state or – much more acrimonious – from the Orthodox Church. In 1991, Filaret, metropolitan of Kiev and one of the members of the patriarchy most compromised by the revelations of Yakunin and his colleagues in 1992, put himself at the head of a movement in the Ukrainian Church which paralleled the country's declaration of independence with a call for autocephaly, or the right to elect its own head. Called to a Moscow convocation in April of 1992 to be condemned for this, Filaret repented, promised to resign his post as head of the Ukrainian Church – then, on return to Kiev, recanted his repentance and took his Church through a long and continuing travail of religious and political schism – schism which included splits within the independent Ukrainian Church itself and within the Church loyal to Moscow.

It was at times violent: priests fought each other for the physical possession of churches, involving or being involved by members of their congregations. The extreme (and fascist-tinged) Ukrainian Nationalist Self-defence Guard occupied churches loyal to Moscow and handed them over to Filaret, took possession of St Vladimir's cathedral in Kiev and attacked the ancient Monastery of the Caves. Leonid Kravchuk, the Ukrainian president, supported Filaret throughout. The result was

STATE

an embittered religious landscape, charged with grievance on every side, with the religious loyalties closely paralleling the divisions in the country between a fervently nationalist west and a pro-Russian east.

The Church split further: the Estonian Church, the former see of the patriarch himself, declared itself autocephalous in 1996; the Latvian Church remained within the Russian patriarchy, but attached by the most slender of threads. The demands of nationhood, the view that Russian Orthodoxy – like the Catholic Church in England before the eighteenth century – was an intruder, possibly a fifth column, from an at least potentially hostile power, deeply penetrated the Church and sent the hierarchy, the priests and the believers this way and that.

The believers themselves were a mixture. In parish after parish, the faithful who turned out to the old or more often the newly established Church were those who had kept the flame lit for decades – augmented by a few young believers, often young men who were testing their vocation for the priesthood. The churches were – with exceptions, but they *were* exceptions – indifferent to or repellent of outsiders; the concept of 'outreach' was as incomprehensible to them as their chanting was to others. At the Tolgsky Convent outside of Yaroslavl, I stood with Russians in the finely restored church, its icons returned from local museums, a choir of nuns chanting delicately while a priest officiated at the service. We were the only people there who were not of the convent and – though the church was open to all – we were made to feel intruders.

Numerically, Alexei had by the mid-nineties done more than any patriarch since the Church followed the expansion of the old empire. He restored 32 dioceses, bringing the number up to 114, created 8,000 new parishes, re-opened 293 monasteries and convents, 12 seminaries and 2 religious academies. He had taken the Church into the military – still a redoubt of a sour Leninism – and had published a prayer book for Orthodox soldiers. Priests blessed the Russian troops in Chechnya and sprinkled holy water on the new MIG-AT before it took off for its test flight. In 1994, a poll showed that some 30 per cent of the under-25s had converted to Orthodoxy – which should mean a healthy Church for decades. Yet other polls showed that few – less than 10 per cent – believed; the post-Soviet generations of all ages seemed too bewildered and too intent on coping with the avalanche of novelty

166

which had descended upon them to care much about the faith. Thus all the figures were contradictory: there was a strong revival of the felt need for faith, a much weaker expression of faith as evidenced in attendance at church. There was a very remarkable fashion for celebrating the main rituals of life in church – especially marriage – and for wearing crosses. But most confined it to that.

There was no outburst of suppressed faith. That seemed to have largely gone: the big cities were inhabited by a secularized people, most a generation or two off the land, with every possible good reason for avoiding religion and, even with the Church's energetic restoration programme, often with far to go to get to church. This was true of faiths other than Orthodoxy: the Jews continued to leave in large numbers, though those who remained tried – with difficulty – to set up synagogues and schools in the cities in which there were communities. The Moslems, though their leadership split, were luckier, because they were more concentrated in certain areas – such as Tatarstan, Bashkortostan and the Caucasian republics. The majority, coming together in the Union of Russian Moslems, were ostentatiously loyal to Yeltsin; the minority, which looked towards Chechnya and abroad, were at best sceptical. Alexei sought and found at least formally good relations with these old-established faiths. And though the relationship with the Jews could never be easy (the Orthodox greatly preferred Islam to Judaism, and indeed to Catholicism and Protestantism), it was not marred by any officially sanctioned anti-Semitism.

Yet the conservatives within the Church, spurred by the inroads the other Christian faiths made in the Orthodox areas, were able to scotch any real rapprochement with them. Pope John Paul II, who had identified an intensified dialogue with the Orthodox Church as one of the last great challenges of his papacy, suffered a cruel rebuff in September 1996: a scheduled meeting with Alexei at the Hungarian monastery of Pannonhalma, at the crossroads of Catholicism and Orthodoxy, was cancelled by the patriarch because – as the Hungarian ambassador to Moscow tartly commented – of divisions within the Church: these had seen the conservatives accuse Alexei of indifference in face of the Catholic inroads into their territory. John Paul had himself gone far to meet Orthodox objections, by issuing an encyclical in June 1995 on unity between the two faiths (called 'Light of the East') and by agreeing to discuss – at some unspecified point – the issue of papal authority, the largest formal division between the two Churches. But, faced with a hierarchy angered by the rapid re-establishment of Catholic parishes and bishoprics in Ukraine and Belarus, both prelates drew back, with no further meeting envisaged.

It had been Pushkin's view that Russia, through her martyrdom to the Mongols, had saved Catholic Europe to develop in peace. To see the Catholics swarming back over the still inert, again martyred body of Russia, was deeply distasteful to many priests and to many of the faithful. A people who in the majority had – until the nineteenth century – responded to the question 'Who are you?' by saying 'I am Orthodox' rather than 'I am a Russian' found it hard, even in the declining years of the twentieth century, to admit religious competition within Slav borders.

The most enthusiastic of the new Orthodox priests tended to live at the extremes. That part of Orthodoxy which allied itself to the patriotic cause was a significant, though not under Alexei II dominant, part of the Church, much wider than the fulminations of Metropolitan Ioann of Leningrad. They formed, or became part of, military-patriotic clubs; joined in the far right's demonstrations; pronounced public benedictions on the far right's leaders; and attacked the Jews and the West. Their followers were enthusiastic: they were in some places the backbone of the restoration movements.

The liberals were very far from them – much further, it seemed, than the 'bounds of love' would stretch. They were, in the main, in the tradition of Father Alexander Men, a man whose (in Orthodox terms) extraordinarily open ministry in a parish outside of Moscow was made the more remarkable by his having been a converted Jew, and was converted into a martyrdom by his murder in September 1990 at dawn near his home, in circumstances which pointed suspicion at the KGB, or a patriotic extremist. Men did not take a political position, as did Yakunin or on the other side Ioann, but his ecumenicism, his inclusiveness, his belief that – as he put it in a sermon on the Sunday of the Holy Fathers – 'God loves the human race – each individual soul and all of us together' – marked a gulf between him and the inward-turning or reactionary prelates with whom the KGB were more comfortable.

His followers regard him with a veneration which derives from their contemplation of a life which was packed with scholarship (he wrote a seven-volume history of religion and beliefs over some twenty years, together with many other essays and countless talks), with a ministry largely conducted at the parish of Novaya Derevnaya, to the north-west of Moscow, with an evangelism rare among the intelligentsia, and with a faith at once fundamentalist and ecumenical. One of these claimed, in a volume of memoirs published in 1992, two years after his murder, that he would come to be seen as standing in relation to Russian Orthodoxy as Pushkin stood in relation to Russian literature – creating a language (a spiritual language, in Men's case) for the future. Certainly, not much of it was current in the years immediately after his death as the Church's language of the present, though Men's tradition still did represent a pole which the theological 'centrists' in the patriarchy had to and did recognize.

In his last lecture, given on the eve of his murder (which begins with the words 'And so together we have reached the end of our journey', strengthening the belief among his followers that this was a foreseen martyrdom), he at once asserts the primacy of Christianity – 'the summit . . . that sparkling mountain spring wherein the sun is reflected' – and its inclusiveness – 'The strongest impulse in Christian spirituality is not to deny, but to affirm, to include and to complete.' This was an aspiration for Orthodoxy, not a description of its practice in the first period of its liberation.

A handful of priests in the Men tradition were prominent: Fathers Alexei Borisov and Georgy Kochetkov both ministered to Moscow parishes, though the latter was moved to a distant charge and both were the target of constant attacks by the conservatives, especially for displaying literature of other faiths in their churches' bookstalls. Alexander Ogorodnikov, a believer and a veteran like Yakunin of the camps, struggled for a year to keep open a soup kitchen serving Moscow's destitute, and a refuge for the floods of young prostitutes. His rent was raised tenfold by the city council, humanitarian aid addressed to him was confiscated and he was threatened with closure on 'health' grounds. He received support from Christian groups in the West – but that support was seen by his enemies inside and outside the Church he served all of his life as proof of his corruption.

The largest temptation of the Church was that of the state, and it was large because the leadership of both state and Church were so uncertain of themselves, and were thus driven to support and praise each other in order to feel both more authentic and secure. The largest symbol of this joint insecurity was the cathedral of Christ the Saviour, in which Church and state joined to celebrate Easter, and which rose steadily in the middle of the decade to loom over the Moscow River by the Stone Bridge next to the Kremlin.

The cathedral had been conceived to celebrate the 1812 victory over the French, but was completed only seventy years later. It was given out that it had been built through subscription; in fact, practically all of the money came from state coffers. It was fantastically grandiose: the cupola was covered in gold; rare stone was sought around the world; a mass of 100,000 laboured year after year to build it; the most prominent artists and sculptors made its decoration the centrepiece of their lives' work. It was finished, in 1883, in the reign of Alexander III.

In 1931, after being stripped of its wealth (Eleanor Roosevelt bought the gold iconostasis, and gave it to the Vatican), it was blown up. A Palace of Soviets was to have been built on the site, the tallest building in the world, with a 70-metre statue of Lenin planned for the summit, but the marshy ground would not bear it, and it was turned into a swimming pool in the fifties.

In 1992, the idea arose to rebuild the cathedral. It came from, or was immediately endorsed by, Mayor Luzhkov of Moscow, who said he was 'consumed' by the idea. The cost was variously estimated between $150 million and $300 million. Gold was again ordered for the dome – but underground parking and conference halls and American lifts to the cupola were part of the package.

The intelligentsia and the liberals hated it. They recalled that it was built to the eternal glory of the Russian army – and was rebuilt as its modern successor was sucked into the humiliation of Chechnya. It commemorated a victory over the French, as the Russian state petitioned to be allowed to join France in the Group of Seven. Most of all, it took resources which could have built hundreds of parish churches, or preserved some of the 2,000 architecturally valuable buildings which crumble in Russia each year because of lack of money.

But it could not be stopped. The state appeared to need it, even if – as the priest Mikhail Ardov quoted in *Izvestiya*, 'except that the Lord build the house, they labour in vain that build it' (Psalms 127: 1). There was nothing of the late-twentieth-century modesty or ambiguity which conceived the monument in Washington to the Vietnam veterans as an inconspicuous wall of polished metal; instead, there was a desire which knew no financial check to impress with size and dominate with reconstructed grandeur.

Alexei reflected none of the oppositionist currents; he appeared to accept his role as leader of a revived Church, as he had accepted his role as a hierarch in a K G B-supervised simulacrum of a Church. Yeltsin, who had begun his presidency by disclaiming any faith, increasingly lent himself to portrayal as a church-going tsar, perhaps because his main rival for the presidency in 1996, Gennady Zyuganov, put aside his malleable communism to don religious robes as the election came closer.

What more could Alexei II do? He was not a Solzhenitsyn nor a Sakharov; his Church had no precedent of leaders who opposed their will and the Church's power to that of the state — and even had he wished to do so, he could not be sure that the Church had the power to counterpose. He could carry on, with a careful, studied reserve, until a time when the Church produced a stirring within it which would answer the open questions about its direction, its vigour and its mission in Russia and the world. And that would probably not be in the lifetime of one born in 1929 — if ever.

CHAPTER ELEVEN

'You are the masters of the country'

In the late summer of 1990, Boris Yeltsin, then leader of the Russian Supreme Soviet, did a speaking tour through three of Russia's twenty-one 'ethnic' republics – Tatarstan and Bashkortostan on the Volga, and Komi in the north. In the course of a trip undertaken to show his face around areas where he was not known and where the regional powers were already showing signs of profiting by the weakening of central authority, he uttered a phrase, in his then ebullient and unbuttoned style, which was to be quoted back to him until he choked on it. 'Take all the authority you can swallow,' he told the regional leaders. It has haunted Russian politics ever since.

His comments were not the result of a considered strategy of federal reform; there were no such strategies in his mind then. He was, as ever, concentrating on the immediate issue of power, and how to wrest it from Gorbachev. For him, the weakening of the Soviet Union, and thus of the Soviet presidency, was the prize; the regional leaders' restiveness, with public expressions of discontent levelled at the Soviet not the Russian power centre, was grist to that mill. The Russian Supreme Soviet had already claimed suzerainty over its territory, and had issued a declaration on the need to 'broaden substantially' the rights of all the republics and regions in that land. Yeltsin had accepted, without much thought, the ideas of the constitutional radicals like Andrei Sakharov and Galina Starovoitova, leading figures in the Inter-regional Group of Soviet deputies which he had made his power base, that sovereignty should be built from the ground up, rising in a surge of popular pressure from the villages to the cities to the republican and regional centres and thence to Moscow – a reversal of the flow of centuries of Russian history in a moment.

From the thirties, there had been constructed in the Soviet Union a system of regional and local government of huge complexity. The fifteen union republics were divided into *oblasts*, or regions; these were then subdivided into *raions*, or counties; a simple enough order, common in many countries. However, there were also – largely in Russia, by many times the largest – a number of republics, designated by the name of the dominant, or more often once-dominant, ethnic group: thus Tatarstan, the home of the Tatars, or Bashkortostan, the region of the Bashkirs, and so on. These were supplemented by *krais*, or territories, which were a mixture of a region and a republic, whose distinguishing feature was the presence of several small ethnic groups organized in autonomous *okrugs/oblasts*, or districts. The twenty republics – which became twenty-one when Chechen-Ingushetia separated into its two named parts – had more rights than *oblasts*, though they were usually smaller in terms of population. They generally had a member of the titular ethnic group as head of the republican Supreme Soviet, or as first secretary of the Communist Party – even where, as was the case in all but four of the republics, the ethnic group was in the minority.

This complexity had two main features. First, it was an attempt to deal with the nationalities problem inherent in an empire which had created itself by continual centrifugal expansion. It had its advantages: it meant that, whether they were ruled by Russians or Soviets, the native peoples were allowed to stay in their ancestral homelands and to maintain, because of that, a certain autonomy. But it meant both a *de jure* and *de facto* inequality. *De jure*, the rights of the ethnic republics were greater than those of the regions, and were made more so in the Brezhnev period, as the regime sought to buttress itself by drawing the leaders of the ethnicities into the web of power and spoils. *De facto*, the Russians – or Soviets – were dominant, and the hidden (or not so hidden) wiring of the real constitution reflected it. Russians were usually the second secretary of the regional or republican Party Committees, or head of the local KGB, or both. Thus both 'sides' – Russian and ethnic – had grounds for grudge: the ethnic side having a historic wrong to right, the Russians experiencing, once the republics began to swallow more power, the feeling of discrimination and even threat.

In the Soviet period, this complexity and asymmetry was made to work in the way everything else was made to work: through the real hidden wiring of the system, the dominance of the Communist Party and its centralized command structure. The Party held the system together, as it did all else – supplemented by the KGB, the Interior

Ministry troops, the military, the regional network of Gosbank and Gosplan and the large enterprises which had independent relations with Moscow through their ministries or, if very large and/or strategically important, through the Central Committee. The centralization of planning meant that housing was identical and was increasingly superimposed upon pre-revolutionary diversity; the retail outlets, cinemas and restaurants, hoardings, services, wedding palaces and funeral halls – all were the same in Tula, Kazan and Vladivostok – a reminder for the few who travelled that, though the system was devolved in form, it was regimented in content.

Yet the vast majority of people did not travel far. The regions, far more than in genuinely federal states, bounded their lives. They were organized centripetally, with a republican or *oblast* capital usually much larger and better provided for than any other town, hogging the big enterprises and cultural and academic centres, with the roads running to and from it as in a spider's web. In turn, these republican capitals were linked to Moscow: there were few horizontal links between the regions, few cross-regional border contacts.

The regional élites – the first secretaries, Supreme Soviet chairmen, big enterprise directors and others – grew stronger as communism 'matured' from the sixties. 'You are the masters of the country,' the wheezing Konstantin Chernenko told a meeting of regional and republican first secretaries immediately after he was elected for a brief term as general secretary in 1983; it was not too much of a hyperbole. The Communist Party apparatus had made accommodation in the republics with the still-existing ethnic clan structures; had fused with the enterprises and the institutes; had become skilled in lobbying and fiddling the figures; had played up local grievances and needs in the battle for hand-outs. These were local politics; but there was no policy discussion, and of course no overt political debate.

The *oblasts* were essentially a mock-federal arrangement in which the devolution was more apparent than real. It was in the ethnic republics where the most tortuous deceptions were practised. At one extreme, these were ancestral homelands: Chechnya – as the world has come to know – was where the Chechens lived (and from where they had been deported), though Russians made up over 30 per cent of the population and dominated, as was the case elsewhere, the regional capital. At another extreme, the oil-saturated Khanty-Mansi autonomous region, within the *oblast* of Tyumen, had 0.7 per cent of its population made up of Khants and 0.4 made up of Mansi. Russians were in the majority in nearly half of the republics: in others, particularly the fantastically diverse republics of the Russian North Caucasus, the majority were non-Russians but split into a myriad of small, often antagonistic groups. The 'ethnicity' of these areas was thus often a sham; where it was not, it was defined by the state and the Party, given shape by official ethnography (which was, however, often knowledgeable and could be concerned to preserve identity and languages) and kept from unauthorized expression by the KGB. Some of these cultures had noble histories; others, like the Chukchi – the butt of many sophisticated Muscovite jokes – had been pre-literate. To be sure they had not, like the native American cultures, been destroyed and their remnants rendered into tourist attractions, but they had been suppressed, subjected to terror, cramped into a mould and denied free exploration of their pasts and expression of their present dissatisfactions or despairs.

The 'masters of the country' as Chernenko called them were indeed the Soviet élite – and remained a large part of the Russian one. Yeltsin was one such master, regional secretary of Sverdlovsk when listening to Chernenko's address. Gorbachev, then waiting with impatience for Chernenko's short travail in power to end in order to advance from second to first position in the Politbureau, had been another. Both of these men had been exceptional, and were thus noticed at the centre for their energy and ability. But they had relied on patronage and local networks for their rise (in Gorbachev's case) or brought to Moscow an entourage of trusted allies who had proved loyalty in the region (in Yeltsin's). The patronage and clan networks of the region were, for the boss, decisive in defining the scope of his power. It was more marked in ethnic republics, where the leaders of the dominant ethnic group(s) would rise to head of the Party or the Soviet as much through his clan and family ties as through the Party – particularly in the north Caucasian republics, where a subterranean ethnic competition was the arena of effective politics.

The slackening of central control from the sixties and the planned and unplanned devolution to the regional structures of Party and executive power allowed local networks to extend their reach and to reorganize the vast authority they wielded in ways which were more comfortable to themselves. In all areas, these were a mix generally composed of the Party apparat, the clan leaders, the plant directors, and heads of the local security police, interior police and military, the heads of the regional ministry branches and institutions. From the latter part of the eighties, as the Gorbachev reform began, this mélange of interests and powers was augmented by the first fruits of what became the private sector – the bolder and more far-sighted of the nomenclatura, with a few relative outsiders, usually young, who grasped the new opportunities, began to form co-operatives and trading ventures, or put their plants on a self-financing model, or made contact with foreign companies, all of which gave those managers and officials who had the foresight to engage in these activities much stronger virtual ownership rights over the project.

The nature of the system dictated co-operation – indeed, dictated the kind of insider relationships which would prove to be so resistant to change, or innovation from the outside. To get the necessary permissions, supplies, clearances and finance through Moscow a network had to be drawn into, and rewarded by, the venture; and since there were no autonomous providers of business services, no independent suppliers, no custom of observance of contract and no dominance of law and provision of sanctions for breach of faith, the first businesses *had* to depend on personal trust – or, if not trust, at least the complicit bonding of those who knew what the others were up to and could turn that knowledge into a functioning partnership – at least for a time.

These new entrants into the regional élite circles were thus testing their new powers as Boris Yeltsin was testing his. Andrei Klimov was a good example of the new provincial man: in his early thirties when the Gorbachev reforms began to accelerate in the late eighties, he used his knowledge of English gained at the language institute in his native Perm, in the Urals, plus his contacts with the local leadership circles made when he was prominent in Komsomol circles, to set up associations aimed at attracting foreign business to his industrial city. His hard work and persistence won interest and some consultancy contracts. In 1991, he put together a Perm Business Club with himself as organizing secretary and the local 'business' leaders – who included the director of the state mint, the chairman of the local Soviet and the managers of the biggest enterprises, many of them defence plants. He did not attract much foreign business to Perm, but did, in 1994, find himself in a position to set up a bank with some other young and ambitious men, all having proved themselves worthy of inclusion in an establishment which they had been instrumental in redefining.

Boris Yeltsin and the regional leaders stepped into the future, or into the void, together. As the former was grinding down Mikhail Gorbachev in the *dacha* of Novo-Ogarevo in the summer of 1991 during the talks on the federation treaty, Mintimer Shamiev, the president of Tatarstan and the republic's first secretary, was testing the limits of his new power by demanding to join the talks as an equal participant. Gorbachev, sensing an ally where there had before been opposition, was encouraging. But Yeltsin could see the threat as well as the Soviet president, and a compromise was worked out under which Tatarstan and the other Russian republics signed the federation treaty, but as subjects of the Russian Federation.

The hare of separatism was running, however. Shamiev, deliberately flirting with Muslim separatist elements in the republic while balancing the interests of the Russians – only a few thousand less numerous than the Tatars in the 5-million-strong republic on the Volga – refused to attach a question on the creation of a Russian presidency on the March 1991 referendum on the preservation of the Soviet Union, and later made no official facilities available for the June 1991 presidential election (though over 35 per cent of the population did vote). Others following suit were the Caucasian republics of North Ossetia, Chechen-Ingushetia (as it then was) and the Siberian republic of Tuva (or Tyva).

Each of these had a specific case to make. The Tatars were an old nation; the Tuvans had had an independent state (Tannu-Tuva) until forced into the Soviet Union in 1944; the North Ossetians were calling for union with the South Ossetians in Georgia; the Chechens wanted their own state. What united them, and gave them a common cause with the other ethnic republics at least, was that the mask of the Soviet Union had been stripped away, and they were left face to face with what they feared would be Russian imperial domination once more. While the Russians were nominally one member of the multi-ethnic state which was the Soviet Union, the fact of their hegemony could be avoided and was anyway diluted in an official Sovietism which was not merely Russianism by a different name. Once, however, a Russian ruler was again in the Kremlin and a debate under way on the nature of the Russian state, peoples with strong national memories or ambitions of their own were bound to feel restless and to seek some separate identity.

The Soviet Union had suppressed 'nationalism' in the name of an internationalist ethic which depended formally on a free decision by the Soviet people to associate and to build socialism together, and informally on a complex skein of deals involving ethnicity, clan balance, power and later revenue-sharing and finally on the threat of force. These informal arrangements, the real constitution of the Soviet Union, were seen by the leaders of the ethnic republics as in danger of being swept away by a resurgent Russian power impatient of the old hypo-crisies. This was the political and ideological impetus behind the declar-ations of sovereignty which appeared from the earliest days of Russia's independence. But it was not the only reason.

The vacuum of power left by the Soviet and Party collapses was a complex phenomenon, which worked at all levels. Soviet power ebbed rapidly from the Russian regions; Russian power was very slow to seep back, since in the ensuing period it had been picked up by the people on the spot, and barriers erected around it. From the earliest months of the new Russian state, the regional leaders actively sought to weaken it by a series of strategies, designed to bolster their power, protect their bases and enrich themselves. The very substantial success of these efforts has been one of the largest factors in ensuring that, while Russia's constitution gives its president more power than most other elected heads of state or government, the practical power wielded has been limited in the extreme, subject to continual bargaining and concessions. It also helps to 'explain' the invasion of Chechnya at the end of 1994: the system had so little of a normative base, depended so much on personal and political bartering, that when a personal relationship was denied as the Chechen leadership denied it to its Russian counterparts, the only recourse was either to cede independence or intervention with force.

The regional élites, reshaping themselves rapidly in the new environ-ment, used a range of tools — new and old, or old in a new guise — to milk the centre for funds. The last years of Gorbachev had been a relatively carefree period for the enterprise directors, since they could pass on costs and keep income. Economic reform presented them with the challenge of an adaptation and restructuring in hard times with little assistance; it also gave the regional leaders the unloved task of passing on price rises and coping with discontent and complaint. The big enterprise directors and the local politicians, already closely linked, thus renewed and updated their alliances and lobbied the central government unmercifully for subsidies. By late spring of 1991, they had worn down much of the resistance of the Gaidar government, which began pumping money through the system once more to relieve the enterprises of their worst pressures. At the same time, a number of regions and republics – Tatarstan among them – continued to subsidize basic foods through their own budgets.

From this time, there began a syndrome which became one of the main machines for compromising and slowing consistent economic reform. The regional and republican budgets, approved centrally, were meant to act as constraints both on their spending and on state subventions to them. But they were never treated as more than opening shots in the battle. A large part of politics at the centre was lobbying for increased resources; and the lines which the finance ministers tried to draw could be and were usually undercut by the president, or by other members of the government, promising and delivering subsidies or tax breaks in return for a political favour. Boris Fyodorov estimated that, in 1993 when he was an unusually tough finance minister, all eighty-nine republics and regions and territories had their budget limits more or less substantially softened in negotiations.

The regions naturally sought to protect their economies. Since the central allocation system no longer worked, and since the market was also in the earliest stages of being created, the regional authorities tried to secure supply by blocking exports. This was done for everything – farm produce, industrial goods, food products, even money. There soon emerged within the territory of the Russian Federation tariff and other barriers on the free movement of goods; while, as a corollary, the regional or republican authorities began to conclude 'treaties' or agreements with each other, and with the former Soviet republics, for the supply of essential commodities, often on a barter basis. This replacement of the allocative system by one-off agreements staved off want, but also crowded out market mechanisms and substantially slowed their development.

The move towards a kind of mild economic autarchy was accelerated by the extension of the control of the local authorities over the forces of law and order. The Interior Ministry forces began to pass under effective regional control from 1992, while regional and republican militias and private security agencies mushroomed. Only the security services, and to an extent the military, kept a federal structure.

The extension of control did not stop there. The regional authorities sought to have more autonomy devolved to the regional offices of the Russian Central Bank, so that it could finance local initiatives (and local debt). They created 'off-budget funds' to finance their own projects; in St Petersburg, a rare example of an authority which declared it, the off-budget fund amounted to 15 per cent of its revenue.

The opportunities offered by privatization were both seized and rejected by the local leaderships – in many cases, rejected at first then seized afterwards. The local enterprise directors, co-operative owners and bankers bought in heavily to the small scale privatizations, which were organized at regional and local levels. They also were the main beneficiaries of the privatization of the larger plants, since the most favoured method of privatization put into their hands the largest part of the assets which they managed. In the cases of Tatarstan, the neighbouring Bashkortostan and other republics, the actual rules of privatization were decided locally.

This has meant that a process designed to introduce a uniform capitalist market was adapted to become a series of local semi-marketized fiefdoms. The strategies adopted, more or less spontaneously, to protect and to enrich in the period of reform created regional élites which were a mixture of industrial bosses, financiers, administrators and traders. Their interests were generally limited to the city or region in which they worked; they thus had a very large interest in keeping the assets in their hands, away from the possession of the much more powerful banks and finance houses in Moscow and St Petersburg and to a lesser degree the large Urals cities like Ekaterinburg and Perm.

The claims for 'independence' or 'sovereignty' were thus intimately linked to the local élites' view of how far that would serve their power and ability for self-enrichment. In the extreme case of Chechnya, the old ideal of independence from the Russians was crossed with a desire to control the flow of oil and to base the state, more or less explicitly, on the proceeds of organized crime. In the less extreme cases of Tatarstan, Bashkortostan, Komi and Sakha (formerly Yakutia), oil or gold or diamonds provide the base of the local regimes' power. The negotiations with the centre since 1992 were aimed primarily at extending regional control over these resources, whether privatized or still in state hands.

The weakness of the centre, the power of the local authorities – especially when they could use the rhetoric of sovereignty, and stir the always latent popular feeling against Moscow – and the ability of the old-new nomenclatura to bribe and cajole their employees and citizens into acquiescence, enforced a process of bargaining, always from a position of weakness at federal level when the region or republic was a 'donor' – that is, it put more into the budget than it took out. It meant that the efforts at finding a constitutional settlement – which were at very best only partially successful in the Yeltsin period – were wholly dependent on the balance of power between the centre and the localities – a balance which changed dramatically in the Yeltsin years.

Part of the power of Boris Yeltsin's appeal to the Russians on his ascent to power was a complaint that Russia had been – paradoxically, in a Russian-dominated empire – uniquely disadvantaged. It had no institutions – even sham institutions – of statehood, and though its republics and regions were formally subordinate to Moscow, there was no treaty nor any constitutional protection for regional or republican rights and duties. Rightly, by Soviet logic, for once the formal or declaratory powers were claimed by the new leaderships as real powers, the edifice revealed its craziness.

Because it was so crazy, many of the reformers – as well as reactionaries, like Zhirinovsky – favoured a complete restructuring of the regional system, replacing the quilt of titular 'ethnicities' with an administrative structure which paid no heed to ethnicity in the boundaries of the regions and treated all as citizens. Emil Pain, an adviser to Yeltsin who was to struggle unavailingly to halt the Chechen war, pointed out from the earliest days of the administration the absurdity of a hierarchy of regions offering a hierarchy of rights according to ethnic divisions which often barely existed.

But politics could tolerate absurdity for the sake of maintenance of power. Yeltsin, increasingly besieged by the parliamentarians, turned to the regional leaders for support; they were willing to bargain. The result, signed by all but two of the republics, by the regions or *oblasts* and by the *krais* or territories, was a Federation Treaty negotiated in the first half of 1993 which gave a legal basis to the Federation – while leaving open or vague everything of contention between the centre and the regions. The republics were described as sovereign, but their rights were not made explicit and there was no right to secede. The republics and regions were held to 'own' the land they occupied, but since private ownership of land was illegal and since the patched-up Soviet constitution gave the right of land 'ownership' to the centre, the formula did not help. The division of tax and export revenues and the control of natural resources were all similarly vague. The formula allowed for a continuation of the power struggle within a more regulated environment, which was all that could be expected at the time.

The politics of the centre played into the regional leaders' desire to be left alone to extend their powers and enrich themselves. Since both parliament and president wanted supporters, neither proposed anything but more of what the regional leaders wanted. In turn, the regional and republican leaders grew arrogant and careless of central authority; withheld tax revenues; banned export of goods; controlled prices; stopped privatizations; dealt direct with other republics and with foreign companies. After winning a referendum vote in support of himself and his policies in April 1993 – a vote which many republics, however, boycotted – Yeltsin set out to draw up a constitution for the state. The regional leaderships withheld support for either the presidential or the parliamentary drafts, and were cool to Yeltsin's idea – outlined in a speech in Petrozavodsk in August – to create a Federation Council with (as ever) vaguely defined powers but a presumption that it would be the upper house or senate of a new parliament and that it would pass the constitution.

Though they had failed to agree to anything, the republics and to a lesser extent the regions had wrung concession after concession out of Yeltsin – even while criticizing him publicly for 'Bonapartism'. The resource-rich areas were allowed to keep large percentages of the proceeds of the sale of their resources: Yakutia-Sakha, for example, won the right to keep 25 per cent of the revenue from its diamonds (and, unusually, the president of the republic, Mikhail Nikolayev, returned the favour by overt support for Yeltsin). Four republics – Chechnya, Tatarstan, Bashkortostan and Yakutia – stopped paying taxes but continued to receive subsidies, that is, the regions still paying were heavily penalized. The ethnic areas were given, in the draft constitution, twice the number of seats per size of population as the regions and territories. It was calculated to inflame the revolt of the ethnic Russians, and leaders on the nationalist side added fuel to these flames. But the politics of the times dictated that the parliamentary side, no less than the presidential side, competed for the favours of the ethnic leaders, at the same time as their followers denounced the favours doled out to these leaders.

When the parliamentary crisis broke in September, Valery Zorkin, the chairman of the constitutional court, organized a gathering of the republican leaders – given the name of the Council of the Subjects of the Federation – in opposition to Yeltsin's disbandment of parliament. The most prominent role was played by Kirsan Iliumzhinov, president of Kalmykia, who had come to power earlier that year on a fantastic programme of instant enrichment of his impoverished republic's population coupled with the abolition of most of the republic's institutions (none of it was even attempted). Claiming to be neutral, the Council effectively supported parliament, giving it the illusion of a mass base of support.

Yeltsin's victory over the parliamentary forces had the immediate and highly gratifying (to him) result of bringing the republican and regional leaders into line. Those heads of the administrations and the regional legislatures who had opposed him were fired or dissolved; the president appointed his own heads of administration; elections were decreed for the regions by the following spring; and the republics warned that non-payment of tax revenues would be penalized by loss of subsidies and concessions.

The draft constitution reflected the new access of presidential power. Drafted without attempting to reach a consensus which was never available before October (and would not have been available after, either) it ended the privileged status of the ethnic republics. The move was made to address the complaints of the regions, and their determination both to have equal status and to squash the separatist rhetoric in which the ethnic leaders loved to indulge – a drive which resulted in secession being explicitly ruled out in the constitution.

It was not, however, a return to a unitary and centralized state. Yeltsin had neither the will nor the inclination to disband the Soviet-era boundaries and designations: his need for the present and future support of those who had come to power in these regions was far too large to permit a rational federal settlement to be even publicly examined. Thus the eighty-nine republics, regions and territories remained unreformed, within their existing boundaries. They were given powers of independent taxation and legislation; responsibility for human and ethnic minority rights; co-ownership with the federal authorities of land and mineral resources; and an equal say in foreign ventures on their territories. The federal government had the duties of defence, foreign affairs, macro-economic policy and general social and cultural policies; it controlled air space, rail traffic, pipelines and power grids, the security police and the Interior Ministry forces. All else not specifically assigned to the centre was deemed to be under the jurisdiction of the regions.

The problem was not centralization but vagueness in wording and incoherence in implementation. After the constitutional settlement, the processes of bargaining and concessions continued, even if the implicit or explicit threats of secession were replaced by a public rhetoric of retaining the country's integrity. The power of the resource-rich and of determined political leadership could still prevail against a centre in which the 'democratic coup' of October was not followed by a consistent pressure for reform – the less so after the December 1993 elections returned Zhirinovsky's Liberal Democrats in force and showed a strong revival in the communists' vote, and the subsequent manoeuvring forced the second resignation of Yegor Gaidar and the first of Boris Fyodorov.

The republic which prevailed the most, and which set a model for the late Yeltsin years, was Tatarstan. Four hundred years after Ivan the Terrible defeated the Volga Tatars and began the planned (but never completed) Russianization of their culture and extirpation of their Sunni Muslim religion, the Tatars were able to hold out for a form of bilateral treaty with Russia which pointed to (but did not establish generally throughout Russia) a form of federalism of a uniquely loose and ill-defined kind. It stimulated other republics – the neighbouring Bashkortostan, Tyva, Komi and Yakutia (Sakha) in the north – to push to obtain similar concessions; and it was able to do so despite the new Russian constitution which expressly prohibited many of the arrangements arrived at.

The root achievement was to have the Tatar and the Russian constitutions treated equally, and to make Russian legislation subordinate to the Tatar on the latter's territory. In the bargaining which went on for two years between Tatarstan's refusal to sign the 1992 Federative Treaty and the signing of a bilateral treaty in February 1994, the republic's leaders dropped their demand that they have an independent foreign policy and replaced the desired 'associated' to Russia with 'united with'. After a tax strike in 1993, Moscow was able to collect 60 per cent of the corporate profits tax – the largest – and to insist that trade barriers were eliminated and that the rouble circulated without competition.

But the republic devised its own privatization programme; set its own minimum wage (double, in 1995, that in the rest of Russia); controlled prices; owned the controlling interest in Tatneft, the republican oil company. It was pumping 100 million tonnes a year in the seventies, down to nearer 20 million by the mid-nineties; but that still accounted for the bulk of a hard currency export of $1.3 billion a year, $500 million more than imports. With that surplus, the pains of transition could be eased (though at the cost, often, of any perceptible transition at all). Its major plants – the helicopter factory, which makes the Mi7 –Mi8 helicopters, aviation (Tupolev) fabrication and motor plants, the Kamaz truck facility – were all subsidized by the republic and their life prolonged (possibly uselessly) beyond that of their equivalents elsewhere. Tatarstan retains, uniquely, its own security police – which are active, and follow the foreign visitor closely.

Mintimer Shamiev, the president who transformed himself in 1990 into a Tatar patriot from being first secretary of the republic's Communist Party – rather in the mould of Leonid Kravchuk in Ukraine, but with much more success – was a tribute to the skills learned at the top of the Party. Low-key, reserved but apparently effortlessly absorptive of pressure, he steered between the outburst of nationalism of the late eighties/early nineties and the anxieties of a Russian population not much smaller than the Tatar one. At the same time as pressing for sovereignty, he suppressed amateurish efforts to arm a nationalist militia with ostentatious vigour. He used Vasily Likhachev, a locally-born Russian international law expert, as his vice-president, to reassure the Russians, later placing him as speaker of the State Council, or parliament. Kazan had been birthplace or alma mater to a disproportionate number of great names – Tolstoy, Lenin, Nureyev, Nikolai Lobachevsky, the nineteenth-century mathematician, and Sultan Galiev, whose ideas on national communism went around the Third World, and who was executed in 1937. All were promoted as native sons, irrespective of ethnicity.

The Tatarstan agreement was a compromise, a mark of the power of a strong republic and of a weak state. Boosted as a system by Shamiev's main adviser, Rafael Khakimov, under the title of 'global federalism' – which envisaged a second UN chamber composed of representatives of peoples rather than states – it was much less a theoretical construct than a response to conditions on the ground by a determined leader with a competent entourage and above all an independent resource base. Its drawback was clear: when it stood out for and obtained such an extreme version of devolution, no rational federal structure was possible. Its advantage was its peacefulness, and the fact that its very existence enforced a plurality in a state inclined to the crushing of dissent and difference. It was both an outstanding example of the irresponsible populism and self-aggrandizement of the local élites and a case of a people attempting to regain something of a culture which had been Russified, then Sovietized, almost out of a distinctive existence. In most of the centre–periphery struggles in Russia, something of both of these could be found.

Dissent and difference, indeed, became the rule and remained so in the Yeltsin years. Regions, republics and cities were no longer linked to Moscow by Party and sometimes only marginally by money; when the distance from Moscow was very far, the breakdown in these relations was exacerbated by the concomitant drop in inter-regional trade, largely a result of the steep railway tariffs.

The furthest region from Moscow was also the most extreme in its *de facto* enjoyment of an autarchy which mixed criminality with a debased national-patriotism. The far eastern territory of Primorsky Krai, an area close to the size of the UK with a population of a little over 2 million, became in the middle period of Yeltsin's rule a region in which the federal writ barely ran at all. Of all of Russia, it was the one where conditions most nearly approximating to those of the anarchic Wild West were found – a Wild West town from which the federal marshal had been driven out and the citizens' action committees silenced.

In April 1993, a coalition of business and old Party interests got a vote of no confidence in the local Supreme Soviet against Vladimir Kuznetsov, a liberal reformist whom Yeltsin had appointed governor.

The coalition proposed a mining enterprise manager named Yevgeny Nazdratenko as his replacement; he was accepted. Starting either before his appointment or soon after it, Nazdratenko seems to have created within Yeltsin's administration and close entourage a range of supporters who were prepared to back him, speak for him and protect him; these have been reported as including the former presidential chief of staff Victor Ilyushin, the former first deputy premier Oleg Soskovets and the head of the Federation Council Vladimir Shumeiko. Allegations of bribery have been frequently made.

As soon as he came to office, Nazdratenko took effective charge of the privatization process, creating a joint stock company PAKT whose leading members were also the top officials of his regional administration. This company became a vehicle to obtain nearly a quarter of a million shares in the privatized companies for low prices at auctions from which significant competition was excluded; at the same time the executives received interest-free loans from the regional budget.

The links between PAKT and the burgeoning local crime gangs were barely disguised. The gangs were used to harass and intimidate local journalists, politicians and others who protested or sought to publicize PAKT's activities. When a local commercial TV channel broadcast a programme damaging to Nazdratenko because it showed him embracing the disgraced former vice-president Alexander Rutskoi, the producer of the programme suffered an apparent assassination attempt; other reporters were beaten up. Vladimir Cherepkov, the reformist mayor of Vladivostok, the largest city and the seat of the regional government, was forcibly removed from his office by OMON militia in March 1994 on Nazdratenko's orders, after a series of disputes between the two; Cherepkov's son was jailed for seven years for the alleged theft of a computer from his school.

The regional organs of justice, of law–enforcement, of economic reform and the heads of the military and border guards were all suborned to the governors' office. The Pacific Fleet, rapidly disintegrating, was protected by Nazdratenko as its commanders used their ships for illegal exports and even sold them abroad. The local Soviet was reduced to a rubber stamp body. The Vladivostok stock exchange, an early private venture, was controlled by a securities commission set up to supervise it.

Nazdratenko appeared invulnerable. The presidential representative in the region, Valery Butov, reported regularly and at length on the little totalitarian state in the making: Nazdratenko pressed for his dismissal, and secured it in January 1994, replacing him with an ally, Vladimir Ignatenko. A report on the area's gross corruption and abuses was published by the main liberal parties in the federal Duma – a rare example of co-operation which showed the depth of the crisis. It stimulated parliamentary hearings and investigations, none of which came to anything. Nazdratenko accompanied Yeltsin on a visit to Japan and secured large credits from Prime Minister Chernomyrdin to subsidize the energy sector.

Nowhere was the conjoined power of the new business with the new freedom for regional authorities to go their own way more evident. Those who continued to testify on the rule of the Primorsky governor – such as Cherepkov – were rewarded with indifference on the part of the federal authorities and threats or worse by the local administration.

Why did he get away with it? He used the territory's geographical position well. He fulminated constantly against the Chinese filtering across the border – a number estimated as anywhere between 100,000 and 1 million remained in the area after their permitted term of stay expired – and called for closing the border. He demanded that the Kurile Islands be placed under his jurisdiction in order to protect them from a supposed Japanese invasion. He threatened regional separatism, and was rewarded with more subsidies. The fear of the central authorities that the area, the eastern populated edge of Russia, securing thousands of miles of Siberian waste between it and the Urals, would secede or come under the control of the Chinese gave Nazdratenko a leverage – while the inchoateness of the federal settlement and his friends at the Kremlin court gave him the means for achieving and holding a thoroughly corrupted power.

Where, in Tatarstan and others of the republics, there was real competence shown by the leaderships who sought a distance from Moscow and a real resonance in their claims to re-establish a link with their buried histories, the rhetoric employed by Nazdratenko and his cronies in justifying their calls for autonomy were studiedly cynical. Their carving-up of the local wealth left plants idle and workers unpaid; the energy utilities regularly ceased to provide heat and light, and Vladivostok was a city in which independent initiative or protest would be met with suppression. It was the indictment of the system, or rather the lack of a system.

The frailty of central power encouraged authoritarian regional bosses – even at the centre itself. When Yuri Luzhkov succeeded Gavril Popov in mid-1992 after the latter's resignation, Moscow discovered what it was to have a city boss whose power was not even subject to the scrutiny of the colleagues in the Politbureau, where the Soviet-era first secretaries of the capital had sat. Luzhkov, who called his immediate subordinates ministers and tightly centralized all business in his office, had none of the intellectual and liberal inhibitions of his predecessor. He insisted on preserving his own privatization system – just like Tatarstan and Primorsky Krai – and in a showdown with Anatoly Chubais, then privatization minister, won the backing of Yeltsin. Moscow was not – could not be – the closed regional dictatorship Primorsky Krai (formerly a closed city, after all) became. But it did become a personal fiefdom of Luzhkov, whose milking of business and whose adroit populism won him a huge vote when re-elected mayor in mid-1996 and gave him ambitions to think of himself as a future president of Russia.

Like other bosses, he boosted his own office's power at the expense of the city council. The latter was not a rubber stamp body, but could offer little effective opposition. Its problem, like that of many of the post-Soviet legislatures, was that when it did have power it frittered it away in endless talk, personal posturing and opposition for its own sake. It unwittingly conspired in the creation of an autocratic leader by making the public disillusioned with the process of a democratic legislature.

The failure of the federal authorities was not complete: they had managed to decentralize some services and taxes and had begun the huge work of transferring social and other services from the large enterprises to local authorities. Separatism, the panic of 1993, was off the agenda everywhere but in Chechnya – a fact which showed the hollowness of one of the main reasons given for the intervention there, that of 'stopping the rot' of republican secession. Here and there, reformist governors were attempting to turn their regions into properly functioning units.

But if the leaders of the Russian Federation had safeguarded the integrity of Russia, they had not succeeded in making it into a federation.

The emptiness where a local civic culture should have been, coupled with the anarchy and invitation to corrupt enrichment which the post-Soviet era brought, meant that the best-meaning attempts were undercut and partial – pointers to a future, not foundation stones of a present order.

CHAPTER TWELVE

'Chechnya is just an excuse'

In an interview given in his hideout in the mountains of Chechnya in a frozen mid-February of 1995, the republic's president, General Dzhokar Dudayev, said (in response to a question on what the West could do about the Chechen issue):

The whole world must understand that Chechnya is just an excuse. The problem is that the government of Russia, the Russian state and all three branches of power do not have any real basis or any real legitimacy . . . without these very important foundations, both the army and the special services remain without direction and control . . . there is no control over the law and its implementation. There is no working body of executive power . . . because of the illegitimacy of the different branches of power, this chaos is leading Russia into an uncontrollable situation.

It was an excellent summary of the crisis in the Russian state – albeit from the mouth of a man who had presided over a régime much less legitimate and much more unpleasant than the Russian one. Chechnya harshly exposed the dark, at times nightmarish, elements which were below the surface of Russian power. It strengthened these elements, gave them their head, allowed them to blow back their fumes into the country's polity and society. All wars do this to a greater or lesser extent, but this one was and remained particularly corrosive because of the slapdash, hole-in-the-corner way in which it was conceived and executed, in the huge gap between its reality and the pronouncements of Yeltsin and other spokesmen for his administration and in the shame it visited on the military and on the population who witnessed their soldiers fail so badly.

It showed the arbitrariness of power at the top, the lack of respect for law and lawful procedure; that decisions, on life and death, were taken on whims, or on the outcomes of inter-departmental feudings;

that government simply did not work in a sustained and inter-connected fashion; that the military was no longer capable of properly planning and sustaining major campaigns and that its senior officers could no longer be counted on to obey orders, even (perhaps particularly) those from their commander-in-chief.

Chechnya is the hardest part of a hard region. The North Caucasus, split up in Soviet times into half a dozen 'autonomous republics' largely within Russia, was the nineteenth-century empire's wild frontier, the setting for Lermontov's *Hero of Our Time* and several of Tolstoy's stories – including 'The Woodfelling', which described how the Russian imperial army chopped down forests to deprive the Chechens of their necessary cover. For forty years, as they consolidated their hold on the Caspian and Black Seas, Russian armies froze and sweated and died in the gorges of the Caucasus hills, as they struggled to subdue the tribes of the region, at the core of which were the Chechen warriors, the most unyielding of all. Their struggle did not end in 1865, with regional pacification: the partisan movement of the late nineteenth and early twentieth centuries, the emirate of Uzun-Kadzh during the Russian Civil War, the anti-Soviet revolts of the thirties and forties, the partisan wars of the later forties – all were a unique and violent testament to the tenacity of Chechen rejection of oppression.

But they were repressed, most of all in the mass deportation of Chechens (with others, as the neighbouring Ingush, the Crimean Tatars and the region's Greek communities) to Kazakhstan in 1944, moves designed to pre-empt pro-Nazi risings as the German columns swept south and east. Both of the native Chechen-Soviets who came to fame in the nineties spent their early years in exile – and both came to fame as opponents of the new Russian tsar, Yeltsin. These were Ruslan Khasbulatov and Dzhokar Dudayev.

Both had seemed to be leading the lives of successful, assimilated Soviet men. Indeed, had the Soviet Union survived, they would probably have died so. Dudayev had joined the air force, and had risen through fast-track military academies in Tambov and Moscow. In 1990, he commanded a strategic bomber base near Tartu, Estonia's university town, where he was said to be tolerant of the increasingly militant displays of Estonian nationalism, including the flying of the national (pre-Soviet) flag at the base. Returning to the Chechen capital of Grozny in November of that year with his Estonian wife, he attended, and was elected chairman of, the first All-National Congress of the Chechen People, a body which, in the days of a visibly failing communist and Soviet power, attracted support from many of the clan elders, from the black marketeers and from the Muslim clergy.

The Chechen administration under Doku Zavgayev tried, as others elsewhere, to contain the challenge by absorbing it: the Supreme Soviet passed a declaration of sovereignty immediately after the Congress had met, but baulked at secession. Dudayev seized the initiative and declared the Soviet illegitimate. When, after the August putsch, the Supreme Soviet temporized about whether or not to obey the orders of the putschists, Dudayev's Congress guards seized the TV and radio stations (though no open conflict resulted).

The new Russian authorities were initially friendly, welcoming the apparent support from Dudayev, believing him to be a rising power but one which could be contained within the Russian Federation. They were wrong: in early September, the Chechen Congress forces seized the Supreme Soviet, forced Zavgayev to sign a resignation letter and get out, and took over the government. Yeltsin decreed that government could only be changed in accordance with the constitution; and at first, through the interventions of Khasbulatov (whose Supreme Soviet seat was in Grozny) and later Vice-President Rutskoi, it seemed as though elections would be held in an orderly way. They were not: the KGB and Council of Ministers building were taken over early in October, and the provisional Soviet, which exercised interim power, fled. Yeltsin demanded that all weapons be handed in; Dudayev called that 'a virtual declaration of war'. At the end of the month, presidential elections were held against the express command of the Russian government. Dudayev claimed to have won with 85 per cent of the vote on a 77 per cent turnout.

Yeltsin declared a state of emergency; 2,500 Interior Ministry troops were ordered to Grozny. The first 600 airlifted in were soon surrounded in the Chechen Interior Ministry building in the capital. The Russian parliament then revoked Yeltsin's decree of intervention, and the troops were allowed to leave, between jubilant Chechen warriors shooting volleys in the air, in tourist buses. It was the first humbling of the new Russian power.

In the three years until the invasion, Russia tried for one year to negotiate with Dudayev and for two years to overthrow him. In 1992, the Russian government appeared to make real efforts: Chechnya and Tatarstan both refused to sign the Federal Treaty, and both were wooed and talked to at length, in Moscow and elsewhere. In Chechnya's case, the rapidly worsening economy was subsidized heavily – Rbs7.5 billion in 1992.

By 1993, the opposition to Dudayev within Chechnya was strong both in his government and in the parliament. The Chechen president refused compromises, strengthened his position through a new constitution, abolished the parliament and dismissed the Constitutional Court. Fighting broke out by mid-year, and in June various factions of the opposition withdrew to those regions they controlled. Minor clashes continued thereafter. These factions were hopelessly mutually jealous and disunited, and were badly, where not eccentrically, led. I once interviewed Uvar Avurkhanov, one of the leaders of the opposition and the administrator of the Nadterechny district, while his wife, dressed in a short tight skirt and cowgirl outfit played Jim Reeves numbers on a vast sound system. Yet they became the focus of intense interest on the part of the Russian counter-intelligence service, and politicians.

That interest finally flowered into full-scale assistance in late 1994: the Russian counter-intelligence service provided the opposition with tanks, helicopters and regular army officer-volunteers, which were launched against Grozny – fighting their way to the central Freedom Square before being repulsed.

With the capture of some of the Russian officers and revelations in *Izvestiya* on their recruitment, the Russian hand was blown and Dudayev's strengthened. The general commanding the Kantemirov Guards' division from which the officers were recruited, Major General Polyakov, resigned in protest over the issue, not having been consulted. It was then, at the end of November and the beginning of December 1994, that the fateful decisions were taken, and Yeltsin committed Russia to a Chechen war from which it could not extricate itself before he had again to face an electorate whose distrust in him, in his mendacity and in his failure to improve the economy was rising steadily.

The nature of the decision-taking on the war was fatally cast in the mould of the byzantine court Yeltsin had created, or allowed to be created, around him – and in this case, no liberal voices were allowed to penetrate. Defence Minister Grachev, delighted by the failure of the rival security service, proposed that he could take Grozny with a paratroop battalion in a few hours. Grachev needed a diversion: his deputy, General Matvei Burlakov, had been dismissed with dishonour the previous month because of allegations of corruption in the Western group of armed forces (based in Germany), which had been under his command until September; the head of the Duma Defence Committee, Sergei Yushenkov, had demanded that the defence minister go too, to 'help the moral cleansing of the army'. Grachev, it was said later by insiders, did not really want to go to war. Though desperately unpopular and relatively inexperienced, he was enough of a soldier to realize the problems. But he was trapped in a particularly hard place; and he volunteered his men in much the same spirit as a Stalin-era tractor plant director might have pledged to double output.

The crucial decisions were taken without reference to parliament – and that body was not asked to legalize them retrospectively. The decision was based on the 1993 Russian military doctrine, which permits troops to be used within the Federation to put down rebellion. The intervention was aimed at emphasizing to the world community that Russia was prepared to act resolutely and would brook no hindrance in doing so within its own sphere of influence, still less within its own borders. At a meeting earlier in December in Budapest of the Organization for Co-operation and Security in Europe, Yeltsin had insisted on this right, demanded an increase in the amount of armour deployed in the Caucasus under the Conventional Forces in Europe agreement and issued a warning against the expansion of Nato. The Chechen decision, taken in the aftermath of these *démarches*, was of a piece with them and designed to reinforce them.

It was also a statement of resolution to the Russian electorate and to the republics and regions which were still grasping after more power from the centre than the latter wanted to give. Yeltsin had, after the 1993 elections, deliberately refashioned himself in the image of a nationalist president – stealing some of Zhirinovsky's thunder. He remained attached to market reform – indeed, he repeated that commitment soon after the invasion, in order to secure a deal with the IMF, but needed something more hot-blooded for the people. All the signs are that he thought it would be a 'nice little war', and popular – as the US operation in Haiti (which had taken place in September 1994, securing nearly all of its objectives) had been, in spite of dire warnings.

However, though the fateful decisions were made and carried

through, they demonstrated that even within a narrowed circle of military officers and presidential advisers, there was no unanimity of view as to what should be done. Nikolai Yegorov, from the Krasnodar region's leadership, most hostile to the Chechens and other Caucasians because of the refugee crisis swamping their region's economy, was made nationalities minister by Yeltsin on the eve of the invasion and was the most vocal of the 'war party'. Chernomyrdin, a member of the Security Council, was not, nor were many of Yeltsin's advisers – in particular Emil Pain, deputy head of the analytical department in the presidential administration and a nationalities specialist. Valery Tishkov, a previous (liberal) nationalities minister, said on leaving the job in 1994:

Every political leader of any prominence has his own nationalities policy. Russian policy in that complex region (of the North Caucasus) is eclectic, springing from different power centres and thus not thought through. In all conflicts coming out of the break-up of the Soviet Union, the Soviet and then the Russian governments played passive roles, merely reacting to events after they had happened.

Yeltsin had decided that he who dares, wins. But he who dares must also prepare; and the lack of strategic, tactical and logistical preparedness was, for those of us who witnessed it, a revelation.

The decision to invade horrified a substantial number of senior military commanders – including Deputy Defence Minister General Boris Gromov, the last commander of the Soviet forces in Afghanistan; General Eduard Vorobyev, deputy commander of land forces, who chose to resign rather than take charge of the operation; and General Alexander Lebed, then still commanding the Fourteenth Army in Moldova, who blasted the government for sending 'untrained kids' into a holocaust, and said that 'step by step, we are repeating our Afghan experience'. In the field itself, General Ivan Babichev, commanding a column approaching Grozny from due west, halted his tanks some 30 kilometres from the city and told the aged women who surrounded them that he did not have the moral right to move on. 'When I look into your faces,' he said, 'I see the face of my own mother.' There were indeed soon to be Russian mothers about (if not his), come to pull their boys back from a war they thought they should not be fighting, or to ask after a son gone missing and unaccounted for.

General Babichev's halt was the most obvious, but not the worst, feature of the early campaign. It soon emerged that the soldiers were – as Lebed had said – raw recruits, scraped together from units all over Russia and hurled into the maw of a war which became, as they painfully slowly closed in on Grozny, ever more bloody. Oleg Blotsky, an Afghan veteran who reported for *Literaturnaya Gazeta*, wrote that the Chechen war made his own grim experiences seem tame, because the level of professionalism, of training and of supply was so much lower in the later war. Kabul, after all, *had* been taken, by parachutists and others, in a matter of a day.

Blotsky wrote that he had seen companies, even entire battalions, come under fire and be in danger of being overrun a mere 2 or 3 kilometres from large Russian forces who did nothing to assist, because they had finished their day's mission and it was not their job. When, after weeks of irresolution, the Russians did enter Grozny, they did so encased in armour, because the soldiers refused to provide cover, preferring the apparent security of the tanks or the armoured personnel-carriers, allowing the Chechens to drop or launch armour-piercing grenades with impunity. The low morale was evident to all who visited – evident, because inquiries of soldiers often evoked a response explosive with contempt for the politicians in Moscow, for the general staff and for the conduct of the war. Arms, petrol and supplies were routinely and with minimal disguise sold to Chechen middlemen, who sold them on to the guerrillas. The Russian soldiers, especially those assigned to combing the countryside once Grozny had finally been taken in April, appeared to eat little but kasha (buckwheat porridge) and bread; they often slept on the ground without the benefit of sleeping bags. Yet at the same time there was a huge inflation of medal-giving; some 100 generals were assigned to the campaign; and official mendacity on the nature and success of the campaign became ingrained after, in January, Yeltsin announced an end to the bombardment of Grozny while it continued for two days after he spoke.

The Chechen soldiers, by contrast, fought magnificently. They operated in an environment which was totally supportive, and armed to the teeth: Chechens, as they will cheerfully admit, love weapons dearly. Anatole Lieven, one of the best and bravest of the many correspondents who covered the war, wrote:

Their success stems from a perhaps unique combination of 'primitive' and 'modern' military qualities. Primitive in that most Chechen units have been formed spontaneously on the basis of familial and neighbourhood links, and the individual Chechen soldier has been motivated and disciplined primarily by considerations of personal and familial honour and shame; modern in the sense that the Chechens have used with great success relatively large-scale military units and sophisticated weapon systems.

The country could not be pacified. A Russian-backed Chechen government was installed late in 1995 under Doku Zavgayev – the same man General Dudayev had chased out of Grozny in 1991. Elections – widely boycotted – were held at the same time as in the rest of Russia in December 1995. But guerrilla bands continued to operate relatively freely, not just in Chechnya but beyond: in June 1995, a band of fighters under Shamil Basayev – the most daring of the Chechen commanders – stormed into the town of Budennovsk in Russia's Stavropol region and holed up with hostages in the hospital, leaving behind a hostage screen after negotiations conducted by Chernomyrdin (in Yeltsin's absence at a G7 summit in Canada). In January 1996, an even bloodier raid was made on the village of Pervomaiskoe in Dagestan, the neighbouring republic to the east of Chechnya. That ended with a storming of the town by Russian special forces and heavy – but disputed – numbers of casualties among the hostages, guerrillas and troops.

Taking the capital had not ended the resistance. Grozny had been established (in 1818) as a Russian garrison town, and had remained largely Russian right up to the seventies. The Chechens lived in the country, and in the towns and villages outside of a capital which they only began to dominate numerically in the seventies and eighties. Their symbol was not the seventies central administration building-cum-presidential palace, which the Russians struggled to take; if they had a symbol, it was the hills and the villages, where the tribal elders lived and to which Grozny's Chechens fled in late 1994/early 1995, leaving the Russians – many pensioners – to bear the brunt of the bombardment, and to die under it.

The damage Chechnya wreaked on Russian politics in the last period of Yeltsin's power was immense, most of all in the direct destruction of lives and of economies (not just the Chechen) already tottering on the verge of subsistence. Its secondary targets were the trustworthiness and reputations of the leading politicians (also already tottering), the effectiveness of the military, and the ability of the political class to think through a coherent response to a crisis.

Pre-war Chechnya *did* present the Russian state with a very serious challenge. Dudayev had rapidly and dramatically upped the ante, basing himself increasingly on the most irreconcilable and criminal elements in the republic. Though a good deal of Chechen crime was stimulated by the blockade which was (ineffectively) imposed upon the republic and the need of the Chechen armed forces to acquire weapons, still 'independent' Chechnya was from its inception a haven for gangs who were above all concerned with weapon trading. Stephen Handelman writes in *Comrade Criminal*:

Whether or not the Dudayev government directly profited from the illicit arms trade, it made little effort to stop the business. In Moscow, police traced the Chechen's swift rise to power in the post-Soviet crime world to their profits from the sale of drugs and weapons. Within two years of Dudayev's appearance as president, the Chechens were the premier arms dealers of post-communist society. They owned more than 500 flats in the capital, as well as an estimated 140 businesses and joint ventures, and half a dozen hotels. While no one could come up with a conclusive link between the syndicates and the government in Grozny, there was circumstantial proof of their mutual dependence. The timing of the Chechen gangs' transformation from small bands involved in petty extortion and stolen car rackets into sophisticated crime conglomerates trading in guns and drugs coincided with the rise of Chechnya as a financial and political force.

Yeltsin had, for about a year, probably tried to negotiate in good faith. He succeeded in signing a treaty with Tatarstan, which had seemed to be as formally obdurate as Chechnya, and later with Bashkortostan. For three years, the republic had been outside of any effective federal law or control – during which its own parliamentary and judicial systems were destroyed, armed clashes became routine and the non-Chechen population either fled or were routinely threatened.

Further, Chechnya was a vital link in an oil chain. Though its own reserves were dwindling, the main pipeline from the Caspian came through Grozny en route to Novorossisk on the Black Sea. This line, always important, gained in significance in the early nineties as Russia sought to exert a grip on the supplies coming out of Kazakhstan and the Azeri fields off Baku. Just as the Russian military referred to the

US intervention in Haiti as a model and rationale for restoring order in Chechnya, so they could point to the allied action in the Gulf as evidence that the West did not brook a threatened interruption to its oil supplies.

There is no question that Chechnya was a sore to which any state would have to devote time, and possibly force, to cauterize. But the Russian moves revealed neither logic nor competence, desire to limit casualties nor a consideration of the endgame. Haste, hope for a quick fix, rivalries within the élite, prejudice and a wish to bolster the presidential position emerged too clearly as the guiding principles.

The affair also revealed the inability of the main Western states to influence Yeltsin when he did not wish to be influenced. Yeltsin's newfound 'partners' in the G7 (or 'political G8', as it had then become, marking Russian's accession to the political dialogue, though not fully to the economic one) were not consulted and barely kept informed; the insistence from the Russian side was, simply, that this was an internal affair. They accepted that – more and more grudgingly as time went on, but without imposing significant sanctions (the European Union delayed ratification of a trade agreement). Soon after the intervention, the IMF signed an agreement for its largest loan ever; a year later, Russia was accepted into the membership of the Court of Human Rights.

If one can speak of one 'good' outcome of the war, it was that the politicians, especially those on the democrat side, were forced to (and were free to) testify to their moral abhorrence of the war – positions taken by Yegor Gaidar, Grigory Yavlinsky and others, with Sergei Kovalev as their moral mentor. Kovalev (see chapter 6), a member of the presidential Council and formally an adviser on human rights, spent weeks under bombardment in Grozny, negotiated the release of Russian prisoners, was roundly abused by the Duma and by Defence Minister Grachev, and finally, in January 1996, resigned. Chechnya was, for Kovalev, the final agony of the Yeltsin presidency. His resignation letter read:

In this conflict we have seen in full measure contempt for the law, flouting of the constitution, demoralization and disintegration of the army, outrageous incompetence on the part of the security services, inept careerism on the part of the chiefs of the power ministries, and awkward and cynical lies orchestrated by the first persons of the state. But what is particularly horrifying is another aspect of the régime you've created, which has been revealed by this crisis: utter contempt for human life . . . I certainly don't put all the blame on you. The totalitarian order, which was dealt a serious but possibly not fatal blow, is defending itself by typical means: manufacturing a crisis, misleading the people, and subverting civic values. Your personal guilt lies in encouraging these tendencies instead of checking them. It's sad for me that you have lost your soul, that you are unable to evolve from a Communist Party secretary into a human being. You could have done so . . .

This must have been satisfying, and Kovalev had cause for his bitterness and bile. But it could not be the last word. In the affair of Chechnya, as in others less dramatic and bloody, Yeltsin and the other main players revealed themselves as confused as much as brutal, contradictory – indeed, all too human – as much as determined. The impulse to go in was at best ill-judged; thereafter, Yeltsin revealed himself as a man swaying between two worlds – that in which an assertion of Russian might over its unruly subjects was the way to settle the matter, and one in which conflicts like that of Chechnya were ring-fenced, played long and sooner or later internationalized to a greater or lesser degree. Throughout the period of conflict, members of his staff – notably Emil Pain – continued to propose exits based on a recognition of Chechen sovereignty. Even in Chechnya, the harshest test and the largest failure of his presidency, could be glimpsed a response which drew, or attempted to draw, on the experience available from other states with cognate experience, or from the international bodies. The dominant voice was that of old Russia (or old Soviet Union); but some newer strains were heard, *sotto voce*.

'We lost Chechnya in the moment we conquered it' was the bitter reflection of Alexei Salmin, a member of the presidential advisory council, at a seminar he gave on the constitution to Russian parliamentarians in May of 1995, when the republic had been formally 'taken'. This was not just the recognition that the Chechen nation would not accept Russian rule, it was also the understanding that Russia was no longer capable of imposing that rule, not just because it lacked the military force but because it lacked the will.

In the end, the inevitable: Russia withdrew. General Alexander Lebed, who had opposed the war from the first, negotiated a deal in August 1996 which took out the Russian armies in return for a five-year moratorium on the republic's status. Presidential elections were held in January of the following year, and gave a convincing win to Aslan Maskhadov, who had been a colonel in the Soviet army and had been the Chechen forces' chief of staff throughout most of the campaign. As he took office, he pledged to strengthen the Muslim religion, to bring the different armed clans under control and to stop crime – tall orders in each case. 'Now it's the duty of each and every one of us', he said, standing on the stage of a dingy, bullet-riddled assembly hall in the ruined capital, 'to realize the expectations of our ancestors, our heroes fallen in the holy war, of the right to live freely and independently. For hundreds of years our nation was not allowed to live freely, to be master of its country. Killed when they (the Russians) wanted to kill, burned when they felt like burning, labelled bandits when they felt like it, deported when they felt like it.'

In the audience sat Alexander Lebed, who had negotiated the deal, but not President Dzhokar Dudayev, who had been killed in a Russian air strike on his headquarters the previous year. He had begun it, had pressed it to a confrontation, and victory had been his, in death (though many of his followers believed he still lived – certainly no body was ever produced). Chechnya – desolate, shattered and free – seemed unlikely ever to submit to Russia again. Even as a formal end was declared – typically, with the question of ultimate sovereignty left hanging with different interpretations on each side –Yeltsin's greatest mistake had only begun to work its effects through the political system.

PART THREE

Economy

'It was precisely the fact that capitalism was being built by the nomenclatura "for themselves" which made it possible for the country to reach it peacefully. But one must pay for everything.'

Yegor Gaidar, 1994

CHAPTER THIRTEEN

'Releasing the human factor'

The story was told by Vaclav Havel, in his dissident period, of a vegetable-shop manager in socialist Czechoslovakia who, on the high days of the socialist calendar, would put a sign in the window to say 'Workers of the World, Unite'. Of the shop manager's motives, Havel wrote: 'That poster was delivered to our greengrocer from the enterprise headquarters along with the onions and the carrots. He put them all into the window simply because it has been done that way for years, because everyone does it, and because that is the way it has to be. If he were to refuse there could be trouble.'

Havel's perception – that the sign was delivered with the vegetables – was designed to show the passive resignation which gripped the citizens of a socialist régime. But it also displays the essential nature of the socialist shop. The socialist shop was deprived of autonomy; Havel's tale points up that deprivation by revealing its role as a dispenser of ideology with the onions.

In 1993, in the city of Nizhny Novgorod (Gorky in Soviet days), which had become something of a show-house for reform, a cheese shop opened in the main shopping street in the old town. It had been a standard provisions shop with the usual miserable range: one, at most two, soapy cheeses. But it was privatized (Nizhny was the laboratory for privatization of small shops and enterprises) and taken over by its former managers. They searched about, and found a range of different cheeses produced within a tradeable range of the town; soon, they offered a selection of some ten or twelve.

They were inundated with Western interest. The managers, who developed a line of patter for visiting reporters, had a large visiting card wallet full of their cards, divided into national sections. The customers, interviewed, said they liked it too – who would not? But the problem was, they said, the cheeses were so dear. The privatization of the shop had meant the loss of subsidies; the searching for and decent presentation of the cheeses increased the costs; the raising of the wages of the staff, part of the deal by which the managers got control of the shop, had to be paid for. It survived, because enough of Nizhny's citizens got rich enough to sustain it and it came under the protection of one of the local mafias. It was a beginning; at least it no longer had to put up agitational posters. But it showed how difficult it was to begin a capitalist shop in an environment so used to the socialist kind.

The socialist shop was among the most visible of Soviet institutions, even if there were relatively few of them – less than one-third as many per head of population compared with the US, a quarter compared to France, one-eighth as many as in Japan and one-tenth of those in the world centre of stylish consumption, Italy. They were the public departments, the front offices, of an industrial system conceived by Lenin as one giant factory, a flow of production and consumption which worked all but automatically. The flow meant that nothing under the highest authority of the Party could arrest the process, and inject different criteria into it. It meant that just as shops received goods and dispensed them, so factories received raw material and processed it into the pre-assigned shapes – both with the minimum amount of knowledge and interest in their source or destination. Neither factories nor shops cared for their customers, nor wished to. The customer did not exist; there were only the masses.

Money was passive. It was assigned to construct plants and invest in them – no one calculated what rate of return it could command. In the suburbs of Bishkek, the capital of the former Soviet republic of Kirgizia, there are lines of decaying factories. One is a sugar plant, whose raw material was Cuban sugar cane, transported across oceans, mountains and deserts to be refined – and then sent to Russia. Another is an agricultural equipment plant, which had supplied markets in Eastern Europe. Both were developed to give jobs to incoming Russian workers and to create a proletariat from the Kirgiz nomads. Both closed in the early nineties, with their mission, unfortunately, partially fulfilled.

By the eighties, when the situation was finally acknowledged at the highest levels to be critical, the economy was – compared to the modern economies of the world – hopelessly out of date. Nearly 40 per cent of the Soviet workforce was employed in industry or construction and these accounted for nearly 60 per cent of value added; the US had only

20 per cent of its workforce in these sectors and they accounted for only 30 per cent of value added. By contrast, half of the US workforce was in services producing just under half of national value added; Soviet services employed less than a quarter in services, and it accounted for less than 15 per cent of value added. Tanks were plentiful – but just try to get a plumber.

Tanks were plentiful because military industry was so vast, and so favoured. Eight ministries had all or much of their production in the military sphere. It did also make substantial numbers of civil goods, but the civil sector made a substantial number of military goods. Like almost everything else, these enterprises were state-owned: in all, the Soviet state controlled more than 220,000 enterprises of various kinds. They did not compete, nor did they set their own prices. They did not trade directly with their customers, at home or abroad, did not determine their workers' pay levels, did not draw up and implement their own investment plans, were not in control of the appointment of their top managers, could not bargain with their trade unions, which anyway could not strike, could not introduce major new models of the commodities they made at their own initiative, nor discontinue old ones. They were controlled in various ways by the Party, the ministries, the KGB (not shown on flow charts) and the local authorities. They could retain or develop considerable resistance and expand their autonomy of action within that; but it was a reactive, not a proactive force.

Economic science was all science, and no economics. The economic institutes were either centres of orthodoxy or – like the Central Mathematical Institute (Tsemi) in Moscow or the Economics Department of the Novosibirsk branch of the Academy of Sciences – home to reformist economists who studied John Kenneth Galbraith and Robert Samuelson. Yevsei Liberman was the first Soviet economist of stature to propose (naturally after the death of Stalin) a decentralization of power from the ministries to the enterprises in order to make the latter more responsible and the former less overbearing – but though some experiments were run along the lines he proposed, his work was largely extinguished under Brezhnev.

The system could not accommodate change, was not supplying growth, and was certainly not permitting innovation. There were and remain arguments about the Soviet growth figures, though none that they declined steadily from the early sixties, after the stage of labour-extensive growth had been passed. Official Soviet figures are discounted; CIA figures showed growth at a very low 1.4 per cent by the end of the seventies, while those of Grigory Khanin – the only economist to publish in samizdat – showed a negative rate, of -2 per cent a year. The Politbureau and the Central Committee may – but probably did not – know the whole picture: as late as 1983, Yuri Andropov kept a massive defence budget even from Mikhail Gorbachev, whom he regarded as his successor and who was in charge of economic policy in the Central Committee. However, it was clear enough that decline had become endemic. And Mikhail Gorbachev's platform was that he was the man – with the vigour, the conviction and the will – to reverse it.

There were three stages to Gorbachev's efforts to reform the Soviet economy. The first was probably hopeless, the second was certainly hopeless, and the third was desperate. All were abandoned.

The first was a continuation of what Andropov had set in train. This had some sense to it, since it seems that the former KGB chairman had reversed the decline of the Brezhnev years, and pushed growth up by about 1.8 per cent, according to Khanin's figures. Gorbachev announced that he wanted 'acceleration' – a Stalin-era slogan – mainly by increased investments in engineering. When he first used the word *perestroika*, or restructuring, it was in June 1985, three months after his election as general secretary – and he instantly linked it to the greater task of protecting the Soviet Union: 'It is necessary to persist in our efforts to strengthen the defensive power of the Motherland.' In the tradition of Andropov, disciplinarian and secret policeman, he sought to limit purchase of alcohol through closing shops, and output by ripping up vineyards and shutting vodka plants. This was a terrible thing to do to Russian men, who instantly turned to the illegal still, to floor polish, perfume and ethyl alcohol; but it did mean fewer drunks. It is an intriguing thought: if Gorbachev had retained the command economy, had kept on tightening discipline, had spurred innovation, could he have kept at least modest growth for a few more years and sought a renewed *détente* with the West from a position of apparent equality? 'Under even a reasonably good manager', says the economist Vladimir Kontorovich, 'the Soviet economy was a workable system . . . while decidedly inferior to the capitalist economies, it was compatible with modern industrial society and capable of technological change, increasing consumption and taking on the world in military hardware.'

One can see, however, why this was not Gorbachev's perception. He was in a vice. Two vigorous anti-communists, Ronald Reagan and Margaret Thatcher, led the US and the UK, and were stiffening the West's anti-communist spine and increasing arms expenditure – notably on the Strategic Defence Initiative (Star Wars). Oil exports, that solvent of Leonid Brezhnev's economic problems in his last decade, were being sold at lower prices (and production was soon to turn down, though he may not have known that). The costs of empire were rising: oil and gas were exchanged for sub-standard machinery at highly subsidized prices, as part of the unwritten social contract Moscow had with the socialist bloc. Gorbachev's dash for growth was producing too little, too slowly.

The general secretary turned to the reformist economist Abel Aganbegyan, head of the Novosibirsk Institute of the Academy of Sciences, and Tatyana Zaslavskaya, a sociologist at the same institute, to develop a method of bringing in market mechanisms without introducing the market itself. These ideas, long matured by Aganbegyan, Zaslavskaya and others were passionately held, brilliantly expounded – and wrecked the Soviet economy without being capable of replacing it with a capitalist one.

The core idea was to reconnect the worker-citizen to his work and to society, by releasing his own capabilities from the restrictions and inhibitions of previous régimes: 'releasing the human factor', was Zaslavskaya's phrase, which Gorbachev took up. Characterizing the Brezhnev years as being ones of stagnation, and lauding Khrushchev's initiatives, Gorbachev had adopted, in January 1987 and May 1988, laws on state enterprises and on co-operatives. The first allowed directors greater discretion over pricing, production and pay; the latter allowed a group of individuals to set up what amounted to a small business.

A young economic commentator of the time named Yegor Gaidar, setting out increasingly radical economic views in the pages of *Pravda* and *Kommunist*, called the enterprise law 'The Law on the Liberties of the Directors'. Another Russian commentator, reflecting on the same law's effects, writes that the workers (whom Gorbachev had believed, or said he believed, capable of a return to their early Soviet heroism) 'revealed an inclination towards collective egoism, electing comfortable and complaisant bosses, striving at all costs to raise the prices of their products – and their wages'. However, the bosses had every reason to be complaisant to their workers: many of them found, in this era, a sudden release from the dictates of plan and ministry – and an avenue for self-enrichment. Acting with a few fellow managers, a plant director could now route orders for services and materials through a co-operative – which he and they had founded and controlled. The services and products would normally be very highly priced.

Thus everyone seemed to win – the workers through higher wages, those bosses who were sharp through the fruits of 'ownership'. They did this rather than, as had been the intention, attempt to create a new wholesaling and retailing network through which 'private' (non-state) orders would be routed – these latter seen as amounting to 50 per cent within a few years. But in this the fundamental fallacy of the Gorbachev 'liberalizing' reforms was revealed: such a network only made sense if there were to be open-market relations, in which prices could be openly expressed (and profits openly made). Since there could not, the bosses stuck to public orders, and to private fiddling.

In the last two years of his rule, Gorbachev went over from a policy which tried to use greater workplace freedom as a stimulus to higher production which did not materialize to one of populistic appeasement to shore up support which steadily evaporated as the economic situation worsened. A cut in social expenditure was reversed as soon as protests gathered. Prices were untouched as subsidies soared – until Valentin Pavlov, the last Soviet prime minister, brusquely jerked them upwards in 1991, only to compensate the population for the effects through higher wages. As oil production dropped increasingly rapidly from 1988, the debt to foreign countries tripled to over $60 billion.

The economic legacy of Gorbachev was malign, much worse than the one he had inherited. By the end of 1991, the budget deficit had risen to between 15 and 20 per cent; foreign debt had grown from $20 billion to $60 billion to finance consumption; the decline in production was accelerating past 10 per cent; goods had been cleared from the shops as money wages rose and rose and production went down; the external debt had become so critical that the first serious foreign economic mission was not to give, but to get back money; inter-enterprise links were substantially disrupted, largely by the movements towards autonomy in the various Soviet republics; the general belief was that the cities would starve that winter. The European Union was convinced of it, and it sent emergency food supplies to Moscow and

St Petersburg, the distribution of which was under the command of a genial German general. The irony of a German general ensuring that St Petersburg/Leningrad had enough to eat in the winter was much commented on.

More seriously in the long run, the enterprises had experienced a kind of luxurious reform – higher wages, less work – which was the opposite of the hard work and sacrifice which would be required to re-orient and revive the economy. The managers had been let loose to become robber-barons, cynical and anti-social, buying off worker discontent and enriching themselves. The organized crime which was to be associated with free-market reform from 1991 had in fact been born in the high Soviet era of Brezhnev and come out into the semi-light during *perestroika*.

Mikhail Gorbachev destroyed the Soviet economy. To paraphrase Philip Larkin, he did not mean to but he did. As with all his other ventures, the destruction was to serve the purposes of a reconstruction, which began only after he left the stage in December 1991, in conditions for which he was immediately responsible and for which he would later blame Yeltsin and the Russian reformers.

As he did not understand what he was doing, he has since appeared not to have understood what he had done – saying that he had followed a carefully phased, social democratic strategy from the first, a strategy which was derailed by irresponsibly nationalist politicians among whom Yeltsin was the most irresponsible. Perhaps only one who was trying to do something else could have undertaken the great work of rendering the Soviet economy unsustainable. At any rate, he handed it over to Boris Yeltsin and his young reformers in a state of complete and utter collapse.

CHAPTER FOURTEEN

'The very edge of the precipice'

An immediate effect of the market reforms begun in Russia in 1992 was to make obvious what had before been hidden, or forbidden. Poverty had been high on the list of hidden things: from foreigners, from the people, from the authorities themselves. There were and are many arguments about how far absolute poverty has deepened in Russia, but none that it has become more obvious.

In a dank underpass near the office where I worked for five years in Moscow, a man of perhaps forty sat day after day on an upturned box playing the accordion, a plastic bag rolled down before him to collect what charity he could stimulate. Beside him his son of six, banging on an old tin drum with a muffled stick, in time to his father's unskilful playing. Above them, Kutuzovsky Prospect, the road Napoleon took out of Moscow – now, in the mid-nineties, showing signs of bright commercialization, its shops displaying imported goods in window displays. From time to time, the man would allow his son to go up to look in the windows of the Malysh toy shop at the toys he could not buy.

Such images were regularly used by Russian oppositionists and foreign TV companies to display, respectively, the essence and the dark side of the ending of a socialism which never tolerated such a public display of misery. A decade before, that kind of tableau would have been the propaganda representation on state TV of capitalist ruthlessness. In the nineties it was still so employed, but at home.

The accordion player had been a primary school teacher, and said he might return to his trade; however, the pay, always wretched, had become impossible. On a pitch like Kutuzovsky Prospect, a relatively élite quarter, with many rich Russians and foreigners living in its square flat blocks, he usually received between Rbs20–30,000 for 5–6 hours' playing. This gave him an income on a five-day week (had he worked it) of Rbs400–600,000 a month, then worth up to $130, around the average Moscow wage.

That such sights as he (and much worse, in terms of human suffering) were displayed for all to see was a shock: Soviet practice had been that these sights be walled up, as in the appalling homes for the mentally retarded, the dying poor and the abandoned children. Yet here were victims, openly displayed: obviously victims of shock therapy. Or better, victims of shock, with no therapy.

A US deputy secretary of state had coined that phrase 'shock without therapy' in an interview with *The New York Times* in 1994. Strobe Talbott, like many in his administration, must have been feeling queasy over the results of reforms which they had backed with great vigour, and that queasiness led him to inject into the debate a phrase which summed up the view of many abroad and very many in Russia – that the reform process inaugurated at the beginning of 1992 might fail. He and they were both right and wrong. There was shock, great shock, in the Russian reform, but there was also too much 'therapy', too soon, of the wrong kind.

Shock therapy is the name given to a range of measures, such as freeing prices, stabilizing the currency, cutting budget deficits. On a broad definition, shock therapy includes privatization and the rapid installation of a social safety net to cope with those who do badly out of the process. Crucially, these measures are linked and are done simultaneously or as near simultaneously as possible, since to do one only means that the unreformed parts of the economy usually become even more distorted than they were before. For example, if an enterprise is 'restructured' to make it competitive with others while prices are still controlled, then its management is receiving two strongly contradictory signals – one to compete, the other to be unable to charge customers prices which would ensure profitability. For enterprises used to a socialist economy, the natural and obvious signal to obey is the traditional one of controlled prices – which naturally brings with it state subsidies to make up the shortfall between costs and earnings.

The classic instance of shock therapy applied to a former command economy is Poland at the beginning of 1990, when the deputy prime minister for the economy, Leszek Balcerowicz, oversaw a shock therapy package and saw (though he had by then fallen victim to the cost of his own success) the zloty become real money, market relations established with startling speed and Poland attaining growth rates of 5 per cent a year by 1994. Shock therapy is also called 'big bang'; both phrases denote simultaneity, speed and depth in the effort to jolt the economic actors from one universe of values and practice into another.

Some four or five years after the post-communist transformations began – in 1990 in Central Europe – the protagonists of the big bang approach proclaimed that it had become clear: the bigger the shock, the bigger and quicker the therapy. Leaving to one side the artificially successful East Germany, the states reporting breakthroughs of various kinds – Albania, the Czech Republic, Croatia, Estonia, Latvia, Hungary, Poland, Slovenia – all in different ways adopted a range of reforms either simultaneously or in rapid succession, and after typically two years of falling national wealth and rising unemployment, began to grow, in some cases rapidly. Those states which tried to retain much of the old system and to find a third way between communist and capitalist economies initially enjoyed a less rocky ride – but quite quickly plunged deeper and stayed longer in crisis. Ukraine until 1995, Belarus beyond that, were notable examples. Russia, at the very core of the system, both led and dawdled. It had the most to be done, it had some of the hardest resistance to doing it, but it also had the most remarkable team of reformers to do it.

These reformers were themselves a shock for the Russian political class, and for the population. The men who formed the economic team within the first Russian government under Boris Yeltsin were a bunch of bright young scholars – irreverent, clever, arrogant – who had spent much of the eighties reading and discussing the works of neo-liberal Western economists. Their leader, the outstanding economist of his generation, was Yegor Gaidar, who was thirty-five in 1991. He was Soviet aristocracy, the son of a senior naval officer who was the military commentator on *Pravda*, one who, in spite of his uniform and his assignment, was a liberal man shocked by the Warsaw Pact invasion of Prague in 1968. Gaidar grew up in a (by Soviet standards) liberal, and cultured, household. He was the grandson of a civil war hero and one of the most widely read of the early Soviet children's writers (popular to this day). Grandfather Gaidar had written a famous story called 'Timur and his Gang' (his son, Gaidar's father, had been named Timur). Written during the war, the story was about a group of fearless and patriotic children who, at great risk and without revealing their actions, assisted the war effort by daring exploits, usually at night. The group of young men who became colleagues in government in 1992 inevitably were known as 'Gaidar and his Gang'. Their exploits were daring, but they were done in the glare of the day.

They *were* his gang. He had gathered them round him when he set up a think tank called the Institute of Market Reform in 1990, but most had been meeting, discussing and writing papers since the mid-eighties, holding a private conference in Leningrad in 1985. Most of them had studied at the Central Mathematical Institute, the most radical of the economic institutes in Moscow. They read the available Western texts at first, then began to probe into the stacks in the libraries which needed special permission for access. Anatoly Chubais, who was to enjoy the longest period at the top of politics of any of the Gang, recalled in 1995 the 'happiest days of my life – reading Hayek late at night' when an academic in Leningrad.

Though they followed the debates and initiatives of the reform communist economists – such as Aganbegyan, Abalkin, Petrakov and Shatalin – they did not get involved. They tried to stay a step ahead. Most of them could read and speak at least English and some had been abroad. Once the somewhat furtive (if never really dangerous) contacts became more frequent with the coming of *glasnost* after 1988, they made links with the network of like-minded spirits elsewhere – Vaclav Klaus in Czechoslovakia, Leszek Balcerowicz in Poland. Hungary was important because of its relative freedom; many of them went there for longer or shorter periods, and the Hungarian economist Janos Kornai – whose books on the failures of socialism were a rare critique from within the system – came to Moscow to give seminars to them. Pyotr Aven, who became trade minister, had spent a year in Austria working with the US-funded IASA institute. Konstantin Kagalovsky, who became minister for relations with the foreign financial institutions then Russian director of the IMF, went further: through the *émigré* Yugoslav economist Ljubo Sirc (whom he met in Budapest in 1989), he was introduced to (Lord) Ralph Harris, head of the Thatcherite Institute of Economic Affairs and formerly an inspiration to Thatcher while she was leader of the opposition. Harris gave him seed money to found his Centre for Research into Economic Transformation, with Sergei Glaziev – also to become a trade minister, then to pass from a member to a fierce critic of the Gang – as his deputy.

They were the opposite of what Russians had come to expect a government to be. They were mostly in their thirties – even Gorbachev's new bloods were in their fifties, and Soviet premiers and ministers were invariably in their sixties or seventies. Scholars were almost unheard of in government; Leonid Abalkin was an exception, who served unsuccessfully under Gorbachev as a deputy premier in charge of the economy. None had been invited into pre-Gorbachev cabinets. By contrast, the Gang was almost wholly composed of academics. Any Soviet leadership's first enemy was the West, until Gorbachev swung his country round to a posture of openness; Gaidar and his Gang were largely pro-Western to a fault from the beginning. Previous governments, especially under Brezhnev, had been careful to fund and flatter the army; they openly derided it, and cut the expenditure on military industries down to less than a quarter of its previous levels at a stroke. Money had been a residual for previous ministers; the Gaidarites' central concern was to give money a value and a meaning. In October 1991, when it became clear that President Yeltsin would support fundamental reform, Gaidar and others of the Gang signed a 100-rouble note to mark the fact that it would soon have a real value. It did soon acquire a real value. The tragedy for the Gang was that it soon lost it all over again.

The August putsch in 1991 was their turning point and their opportunity. Before it, as with all reform economists, they assumed economic change would be Soviet. After, they were the first to grasp that the Union was doomed and that Russia had to go its own way. In coming to that realization, they met the political ambitions of Boris Yeltsin, who had increasingly been frustrated in his efforts to conduct an independent Russian economic policy within a disintegrating Soviet Union, and who was casting about for a policy and a team to implement it. He had had radical economists in his cabinet while head of the Russian parliament – notably Grigory Yavlinsky and Boris Fyodorov. But both had resigned and gone separate ways.

The Gang came to power by accident. Their work was known to Sergei Golovkov, who had studied at the Central Mathematical Institute, and who in turn was economic adviser to Yeltsin's closest aide, Gennady Burbulis. Burbulis was a former lecturer in Marxism-Leninism turned liberal democrat. Like many with such a background, he looked for ideological certainty and vigour – and found it in Gaidar. Gaidar met

Yeltsin for a long talk. Afterwards, Yeltsin wrote of him that 'he had a completely unique poise . . . he would fight for his ideas to the end, precisely because they were his own . . . listening to him, you would start to see what route we had to take'. Left to himself, Yeltsin might have turned to a trusted figure to head his cabinet – such as Oleg Lobov or Yuri Skokov, both part of *his* gang from Sverdlovsk, both of whom (as time would show) had a very narrow view of economic reform. Mikhail Bocharev, a successful and early businessman, was also considered, as was Grigory Yavlinsky, who had served in and resigned from Yeltsin's first government when Russia was still within the Soviet Union. Yeltsin appeared to want a radical to head economic reform, but was doubtful if he could get one through the parliament. Burbulis, then at the peak of his influence after having crafted two successful struggles for power for Yeltsin, argued that the radicalism and depth of the reforms required Yeltsin's direct participation, and that a cabinet must be headed by the president himself, as in the US. Burbulis would take the post of first deputy prime minister – with Gaidar as deputy prime minister in charge of economic reform, and Alexander Shokhin, close to the Gaidar Gang and already minister of labour in the Russian government, as deputy premier for social affairs.

Formally appointed in November following a speech to the Russian Supreme Soviet by Yeltsin – written by Gaidar – in which the dash for the market was laid out, the Gang entered their offices like children into a formal drawing-room suddenly vacated, unsure if adult order still prevailed. They had no offices at all at first, and used phones where they could. They were assigned no cars, and all piled into Shokhin's, whose service as labour minister in the Russian government had brought him a Volga. A large number of members of the Gang – Anatoly Chubais, Sergei Vasiliev, Andrei Ilarionov, Sergei Ignatiev – came from St Petersburg, and had no flats. Gaidar called the government a 'kamikaze' one. Kagalovsky said that they might last three months, and would be lucky to escape prison. They laughed a good deal in the first weeks: the clash between the titles of deputy prime minister for this and minister for that with their just-renounced status as somewhat suspect academics was comic, and they were naturally nervous.

They were quite open about their free-market beliefs. They believed in free markets as much as it was possible to believe in anything, were scornful of anything which smacked of a 'middle way' between socialism and capitalism and had no truck with the view that Russia was 'special', at least not economically. Pyotr Aven, in a much-quoted remark, said that 'from the point of view of stabilization, all countries are the same'. Burbulis, as fervent about markets as he had been about Marxism, said that 'the aim of reform can be expressed as the creation of private property. People must live in a society where they can, freely and without fear, obtain and own any kind of private property. The experience of history teaches that nothing which better corresponds to human nature has been turned up for the last ten thousand years.' Chubais made the point popularized by his midnight study, Hayek: 'A market economy is the guarantee not just of the effective use of financial and natural resources and of capital, but is also the guarantee of a free society and of the independence of the citizen.' A few months after taking power, Gaidar invited Leszek Balcerowicz to Moscow for discussions on reform, and then presented him to the press, as if to show that he had Balcerowicz's approval. Given that his country had just ceased to dominate Poland, and their peoples tended to regard each other with more suspicion than admiration and this was before Polish reforms were showing the more obvious signs of success, the gesture was typically courageous and unwise. In a later press conference, when a questioner introduced himself as being a correspondent from the liberal-conservative *Economist* magazine, he smiled and said: 'Ah, my favourite', a confirmation of himself as a cosmopolitan intellectual who implicitly despised Russian publications, the kind of mistake the most novice of Western politicians would never make. Above all, they used and even at times quoted Western advisers, some of whom, like Jeff Sachs, had no intentions of remaining in the shadows.

A young reform economist named Sergei Alexashenko – who would later join the government to become deputy finance minister, then deputy governor of the Russian Central Bank – said of them during their first year: 'Gaidar's team behaved as if they came from Mars or Venus. They behaved as though they had no independent brains, no feelings for anyone, like robots. Quite soon they refused to discuss their plans, they were saying in effect, "We are the cleverest men in the country, we speak English very well, shut up and let us do what we want." I can't deny they were a brilliant team, the best available. But they simply said, "Follow us, we know best."'

As time would show, the Gang was not the governing spearhead of a society whose most active part was demanding a revolution. It was the economically literate (in the Western sense), paper-thin layer of a 'democratic' movement which got assent on the basis that it could quickly improve living standards and usher in something approaching a Western lifestyle. Though all of the communist countries which went through a reform in the early nineties were divided and quarrelsome places, Russia's divisions were deeper, its quarrels more rancorous and above all the supporters and clients of its socialist system more numerous and powerful than anywhere else. The Gang had no roots in a civil movement, as the governments of post-communist Central Europe had. They were there at the pleasure of the president.

They did not at first regard themselves as politicians, but merely as free-market technocrats hired by the president to do the self-immolating task of revolutionizing the economy. They at first despised politicians, since their experience of the breed was of senior communist function-aries. They had no greater stock of political skills when they came to office than any other group, and they tended, like any other group in Russia, to regard their programmes as non-negotiable. They learned rapidly, however, the need for compromise and concession; indeed, many in the Gaidar camp saw and see their leader as over-willing to compromise, certainly after the first few months.

Many overcame their professed contempt for politics to stay in it: Gaidar himself, Sergei Vasilyev, Andrei Ignatiev and most successfully of all, Anatoly Chubais, who by mid-1996 was said to be running the country. Aven and Kagalovsky left, to become rich bankers and to use their knowledge of the corridors of power to make their banks and themselves even richer. Ilarionov founded an economic think tank. Shokhin, never a full member of the Gang, co-founded a centrist party, left it, became rector of a market economy institute, lost his government job, then – unable to stay out of it – joined the Our Home is Russia party created by Victor Chernomyrdin, the then prime minister, and became, in 1996, deputy speaker of the Duma. In November 1995, Gaidar hosted a five-years-on celebration for his Gang and those close to it; it was to take the form of a friendly retrospective seminar, then a dinner party. Almost no one came to the seminar (though they did to the dinner). Mikhail Berger, the economic commentator on *Izvestiya* and closest to the group of all journalists, wrote: 'So what was there to discuss? Nothing, they evidently decided.' Gaidar's party, Russia's Choice, was then facing heavy defeat in the parliamentary elections. He had lost many of his colleagues and his largest paymaster, Oleg Boyko. He had, it seemed, indeed been a kamikaze; it had merely taken longer than he had thought to crash.

The task they faced in 1991 demanded people of brazen confidence, as well as a certain ignorance of the nature of the cauldron into which they were lowering themselves. At the end of 1991, the Soviet economy was collapsing. Abel Aganbegyan, who had been Gorbachev's early mentor in reformist economics and who had – in spite of the manifest failure of his advice – remained in or near the advisory circles of the Kremlin, saw that the world he had tried to construct was coming to an end. Sitting in his Kremlin office, he read the uniformly bad news as it came in. Among other elements of the hectic crisis was the fact that chickens were dying in their batteries; this was because the producers of feed were withholding grain since the farmers had not paid their bills. This appeared to be a huge crisis of production and distribution. The countryside, it seemed, was starving the cities just as it had done in the post-revolutionary times. The massive queues and empty shelves became clichés of both Soviet and Western television. Hunger was widely and confidently forecast.

The crisis was in fact not one of production, nor of distribution, but of exchange. By the end of the communist period, subsidies had risen hugely in order to keep prices low. At the same time, real wages had also been rising. The result was a crisis known as 'rouble overhang' – that is, a huge quantity of roubles chasing goods whose quantity was already falling fast. What in free-market economies would have been inflation was in the Soviet Union long, freezing lines for everything, or indeed anything.

If there was one easily encapsulable belief among the members of the Gang, it was that money was the source of all economic good. Their radicalism lay in recognizing that where the values of commodities were not expressed in transparent prices but instead in prices set by political priorities, everything else in the economy and much else in society was judged by the criteria of capitalist societies, hopelessly distorted. In this, typically, they were more doctrinaire than nearly all practising politicians and many practising economists and bankers in the free-market economies: they did not want to see subsidies anywhere, and were at first determined to do away with them completely – until political reality intervened.

On 2 January 1995, most controls were removed from prices. This was the first fruit of the Gaidar team, and there is no question it was bitter. Prices rose, in the first month, nearly 400 per cent on average – considerably more than the 250 per cent which the Gang had forecast. Wages also rose, but by only around 50 per cent at first. Pensions and stipends, too, lagged behind the sudden jump in prices. There were no riots, no large demonstrations, no sudden appearance on the streets of the immiserated – though later, at demonstrations, signs were displayed which read 'The March of the Hungry Queues'. But there is no doubt there was and remained real hardship in millions of homes: men and women had rapidly to seek new ways of earning money and/or acquiring food, like the accordion player in the underpass. Private plots (for which there were 3.5 million demands in 1992) and *dacha* gardens became even more prized territory than they had been before. One natural reaction, it seemed, was to go back to the land, the sign of a society not so far removed from it as most societies in the West.

Though their belief in free prices was a passionate one, the Gaidarites also knew they had no choice but to free them. Alexander Shokhin said in October 1991 that while demonopolization, privatization, reduction of the budget deficit and stabilization of finances should be done before price liberalization, it could not, because 'the economy has come right to the very edge of the precipice, and at any moment might collapse'. Boris Saltykov, a member of the Gang who survived the resignation of many of his colleagues by serving in the unglamorous post of minister of higher education, recalled in a talk at a private function at the end of 1995: 'When we would get together in these first days of government, we would discuss such things as: what would we do if the bakeries stopped working? What would we do if the transport stopped running in some big cities? On whom could we rely?' This was a government which felt itself surrounded by hostile and unpredictable forces, while it balanced on a plank over a torrent.

For all its inevitability, the price-rise was revolutionary. It ripped apart the Party-state's social contract with the masses. By letting go of prices, the government had turned the masses into consumers. From now on, they would (as long and as far as they were permitted) make choices as to what they wanted, not be the recipients of what the state thought it fit or convenient to supply. The socialist shop, beginning with those in the capital, underwent a gradual transformation from a supply point to a place where choice could be exercised.

But they were poor consumers. The price-rise immediately reversed the position of the great bulk of the population: from having too much money for too few goods and thus being forced to save, they rapidly found that many goods were beyond their means and that they had to use savings to maintain their previous level of consumption, or even to survive. Money became short – a state of affairs which was to continue for some years. What saved them from further destitution was the fact that not all prices *were* released; though the reformers would regularly quote a range of 80–90 per cent of prices freed, vitally important prices were kept low, often very low by world standards. Above all, rents of flats remained very low for years after the first price-rises, typically around 5 per cent of income – where a family in a market economy might spend one-third or more of their disposable income on rent or mortgage. Gas, electricity and telephone charges were similarly low (though rising steadily); public transport was low and remained so; and in cultural life, prices for concerts, theatres and exhibitions remained very low (foreigners were charged much higher prices in some venues, like the Hermitage in St Petersburg).

The price the Gang most regretted not freeing was that of energy. The domestic price of oil in December 1991 had been a fantastic 0.4 per cent of the world level – one which made the huge waste of energy at every stage of its production, distribution and use throughout the Soviet Union a matter of indifference to all. It was raised by some five times in January, with the intention of liberalizing by the spring; but it did not happen. Quickly, the industrial lobby, which was to choke much of the life out of the Gang's initiatives, mobilized round the issue, arguing that the shock would disrupt production. The price did rise in jerks throughout the year, to around one-sixth of world prices by the year end, and the price was regulated more by the fact that a specified tonnage of oil was allowed to be exported for world prices, while the rest found its own price-level in a protected domestic market.

They were enclosed by politics. Boris Yeltsin's debt to the coalminers meant that industry continued to enjoy the high subsidies and the low prices which the miners thought, correctly, was the basis of their continued existence. The oil and gas managers also favoured the status quo; like most, they preferred subsidies to free prices, and some saw the huge profits to be made from selling subsidized oil illegally at world market prices. The strength of the lobby was shown by its ability to persuade President Yeltsin to sack energy minister Vladimir Lopukhin – a Gang member and one devoted to freeing oil prices. He became, in June 1991, the first victim of political pressure and was replaced by Victor Chernomyrdin, former Soviet minister for gas. It was to prove the most significant appointment of the year.

The other, relatively rapid, success was the freeing of trade – both international and domestic. On the same day as many prices were freed, it became legal to buy foreign currency at market prices for imports – which meant, in practice, that the rouble became convertible inside the country, and a market in money began. Imports were more or less free, but since the rouble was allowed to float freely to find its own value, it sank rapidly from the official (but grossly overvalued) price of Rbs0.6 to the dollar to over Rbs100 to the dollar – thus making imports much more expensive, at least nominally. Very quickly, however, imports began to flood in – especially of consumer goods.

These goods quickly began to appear on the streets because the Gang also freed domestic trade. The first results were instantly visible: people came out to the streets and sold things, in a rush to trade which reflected their own privations and which acquainted a large number of people with simple market behaviour more rapidly than any training course could. The sellers turned out in Moscow all the way from the Bolshoi Theatre up to the Lubyanka, six or seven deep on the pavement, standing for hours in the raw cold. It did not last: public order and corruption together prevailed, pushing them off the streets and – a few – into kiosks which became an insistent feature of Moscow architecture in that year. The kiosks sold mostly cigarettes, liquor, sweets and flowers, and all came sooner or later under the 'roof' (as the Russians put it) of one or other protection gang. Those which did not, or which annoyed one or other of the competing mafias in some way, could be seen in smoking ruins in the early morning. Bit by bit, these kiosks either became more sophisticated, or their trade moved back into the shops as the latter were privatized and grasped the new rules of the game. Bit by bit, trading began to move out of the ambience of illegality in which it had lived since the twenties; bit by bit, it ceased to be called 'speculation' and became simply buying and selling.

The base of the taxation system was changed. Instead of the profits and turnover taxes, which had been the main source of Soviet tax collection, the new government sought to raise its revenue through VAT, income and excise taxes – none of which was collected efficiently. Taxes, which had accounted for about 37 per cent of GNP in Soviet days, sank to 24 per cent of Russian GNP in the first year of reform. The tax-collection service was untrained, had too few people and very little information technology; even four years after reform, it was still running hard to catch up with a private sector which could evade many taxes – to say nothing of a non-tax-paying but large criminal sector. The new taxes made it clear – painfully clear – what the state take was: where before they had been taken off turnover at source, now they were openly operating on the population's incomes and expenditure. They moved the business of financing the state from the shadows to the light, and made the latter more potentially responsive and responsible before the people on whose labour its operations depended – a unique posture for the Russian state.

The central intellectual battle of Gaidar's first year, which he did not then win, was over the acceptance that the creation of money was the root and largest cause of inflation. The view was not a neutral one; it was a product of the neo-liberal economic debates in the West of the sixties and seventies, being accepted reluctantly by governments (such as the 1974–79 Labour administration in the UK) which had been raised to believe they could and should spend their way out of recessions. The Gang had read these debates and accepted the view – which had become dominant in the West – that 'printing money' beyond the productive capacity of the country fed through, sooner or later, into ever higher prices. Further, they also accepted the view which had always been orthodoxy in the International Monetary Fund and had largely become so at the World Bank, that inflation was the basic evil to avoid, one whose continuing presence at high levels distorted every other signal in the economy and which, if allowed to attain the level of hyperinflation (defined as more than 50 per cent a month) would destroy both the economy and democracy. Low inflation, the alpha and omega of the financial strategy of the Group of Seven advanced industrial states, had become the same for the Gang.

But not for the Central Bank of Russia. The successor of the Soviet State Bank (Gosbank) was run for the first six months of the reform period by Georgy Matiukhin, said to be a former KGB officer, who had written a number of books on banking, had advised Yeltsin on financial matters and agreed with some of what the reformers wished to do. He was, however, hopelessly tossed about by the industrialists, by the new 'commercial' banks and by the Supreme Soviet – the body to which, under the Soviet-era constitution which still ruled Russia, the Central Bank chairman reported. He was unfortunate enough to be in office when a blizzard hit him which he did not expect, which he had insufficient backing to withstand, and which he did too little to contain while doing enough to create a coalition against himself. He raised interest rates to 80 per cent – a huge leap, but one which left them still lagging behind inflation. He tried to restrict credit – which earned him the wrath of the enterprises who were screaming for it – but did not restrict it sufficiently to bring inflation down.

Matiukhin had his office throughout his brief tenure in the plain, modern down-at-heel offices of the Central Bank of Russia, with its inscription from Lenin in the hall on the need for a Central Bank as a building block of the communist economy. He wished to mark the fact that this was the Russian, not the old Soviet Gosbank, whose offices were in a fine, late-nineteenth-century building on Neglinnaya Street, built as the offices of the pre-revolutionary Central Bank. The man who took over from him once he resigned in July 1992 naturally went to Neglinnaya Street, because it was as much his home as anywhere. Victor Gerashchenko was the son of a former Gosbank chairman, and had headed the Bank in the Gorbachev period. Horrified by the collapse of his banking network and by the huge build-up of suppressed inflation, he took advantage of the brief coup in August 1991 to issue orders to the increasingly disobedient republican branches of Gosbank to obey central instructions. He was fired for that. He was back within days, ironically saved by the capitalist bankers and business people who put pressure on Yeltsin to reappoint a man who enjoyed their trust. But he could not survive the collapse of the Union which he struggled hard to preserve, and went again later in the year.

His return for a third time was a sign of deepening uncertainty in the Gang. They had survived six months in office but seemed only to have made matters worse for the largest part of the population. Though the president supported them still, he was pressing them hard for some results – and for some softening of their rigour. At the same time as

Matiukhin went, Yeltsin felt himself constrained to broaden the base of the cabinet to include two men who had been factory managers: Vladimir Shumeiko, later to become chairman of the upper house of a reformed parliament, and Georgy Khizha from St Petersburg, a former defence plant director who never reconciled himself to either the Gang, Yeltsin or politics. Gaidar, confronted with a choice between Gerashchenko and the radical Boris Fyodorov, chose Gerashchenko – a choice for which Fyodorov did not forgive him, since there was at that time and for some time subsequently nothing more dear in public life to Boris Fyodorov than the chairmanship of the Central Bank of Russia. Gaidar did so because he wanted to placate the industrialists and the deputies; because he had too little experience of politics to know that enemies such as those he had are not assuaged but only encouraged by compromise to go further; and because, it seems, he did not know what Gerashchenko would do.

It was not a secret for long. Gerashchenko believed that his duty was to support Soviet industry, even after the collapse of the Soviet Union. He thoroughly agreed with the view of the industrial managers that prices were rising some seven or eight times faster than the growth of the money supply. He held, quite sincerely, to the view that money supply was not the cause of inflation. He was deeply concerned by the explosive growth of inter-enterprise debt. He began pumping out credit to the enterprises to attempt to arrest the fall in production – an effort which had a partial and temporary success. Called – by the Harvard economist Jeffrey Sachs – the 'worst central banker in the world', he was to a degree rightly annoyed by the appellation. After all the government, too, was conspiring in the credit explosion, doling out billions of roubles to the agricultural lobby for the harvests, to the cities and settlements in the Arctic circle for the winter supplies. The slashing cuts made in the first month or two of the new government, especially to the military industries, were very substantially reversed. The expropriated were compensated, and the knell of monetary stability had sounded.

Monetary stability had another slayer: the states of the former Soviet Union, now proudly (and fearfully) calling themselves independent, ordering Mercedes for their top people – and broke. They had, besides flags and presidents, each a Central Bank, precisely those institutions which Gerashchenko had tried to whip into line when the putschists reigned for three days in August 1991. These banks began to issue credits to enterprises hit even harder than the Russian ones by reduced credit and orders, and their issuance was credited by the Central Bank in Moscow. This went on until, in June 1992, Ukraine suddenly doubled the volume of credits to its enterprises. Thereafter, the issue in the other republics was limited by set quotas of 'technical credits'. At the same time, the Russian Central Bank differentiated between the roubles issued to the various republics, and these roubles began to exchange against each other at differential rates. Inevitably, they moved – slowly – to adopt separate currencies, having helped debauch Russia's. Efforts to retain a rouble zone, backed by the IMF, were numerous, and failed badly – since none of the new independent states would cede back to Moscow the kind of governance over their affairs which the maintenance of a common currency would mean.

The economics of change were intertwined even more closely in Russia than in more stable states with the political struggles for power. Grim though it is, the narrative does nevertheless show that the Gang were able, in these few months when movement could be made at rapid speed, fundamentally to alter (though not reform) the bases of Russian economic life. The Supreme Soviet had been elected in Soviet times on an at best semi-democratic mandate, but it did reflect much of the opposition in administrative and industrial circles as well as the confused, contradictory nature of popular 'will'. It was clear from an early stage that both those who cleaved to some form of communism or socialism and those who sought to advance some form of Russian nationalism were united in seeing the reforms as a dangerous and where possible foreign imposition.

Many in the opposition believed that the essence of Russia had been preserved by communism. Alexei Sergeev, one of the few economists who sought to extend communism's life in its dying days, expressed very clearly a belief which lay beneath many of the Supreme Soviet deputies' views on economic life, when he claimed:

The communist idea was not brought into Russia from 'outside', but sprang up from within, from its intrinsic collective consciousness. Thus the Russian people are 'born' socialists, who because of their genetic characteristics include among their national ideals full employment [unemployment is unnatural, immoral]; and absence of the hungry and wretched [pity for the holy fools, charity to the wandering poor]; social care for the sick and weak;

assistance to talent which comes up 'from below'; hatred for extortionists and contempt for the very rich; hostility to the self-sufficient who cut themselves off from the people and do not understand their need for administrative support.

It was a powerful statement of the unity of an ideology and an economic system with the national soul, which was both stirring and mendacious. That type of sentiment was affronted by the take it or leave it, techno-cratic determinism of the Gang. The Russian soul – on this definition of it – soon had its revenge.

These pressures meant that those who were inside the reform circle also had to define their position. Among the most powerful of the critics of shock therapy was the Union of Industrialists and Entrepreneurs, the grouping headed by Arkady Volsky. Volsky had neither become a reactionary nor did he remain a communist: courted by foreign business circles because of his proclaimed ability to open doors, he favoured a kind of corporate capitalism which, as it turned out, was precisely the kind which developed strongly in the mid–nineties. He reflected the complaints and concerns of at least some of his membership, among whom the most powerful were the large enterprises; they wanted a change, of course, and Volsky and his associates wanted to put either themselves or their allies into the cabinet to try to get it. Yet at the same time, they employed as resident experts and advisers Yevgeny Yasin and Sergei Alexashenko, two men who would later become government ministers on the side of radical reform and who, even as Volsky's employees, sought to inculcate in his membership an understanding of the pressures the government faced and the necessity for at least some of their actions. Gaidar himself would divide the industrialists into those who benefited from inflation and those who wished to escape from it, and aligned himself with the latter. Some managers did begin from an early stage to realize the link between money-creation and inflation – and, in less elevated vein, how rich they could become through the privatization plans which the govern-ment was developing.

The criticism was not exclusively from those who had done well out of late communism. Grigory Yavlinsky was never one of the Gang and did not wish to be. He was not a Muscovite or a Leningrader; he came from Lvov, in Western Ukraine, which had since become the centre of the Ukrainian national renaissance. He had a high estimation of his own intellectual and personal powers, but he had exhausted himself in the autumn and winter of 1991 trying, as a member of a committee which acted as a kind of Soviet government, to get a renewed economic union with republics which were straining away from the centre. He blamed the Gang for what he saw as their opportunistic endorsement of a Russian-first policy, but, rediscovering his energy and spirit, he became the most articulate of their critics who remained on the side of reform. He thought they had reformed in the wrong sequence: better, he said, to have held prices stable and set about restructuring the enterprises through privatization and other means, since to expect free prices to stimulate market behaviour while the enterprises remained unreformed was to dangle a carrot before a blind horse which lacked a sense of smell and was anyway lame. He formed a consulting group-cum-think tank called Epicentre, which did work for a range of clients – most valuable, for Yavlinsky, was the work for the reforming governor of Nizhny Novgorod region – from 1996, first deputy prime minister – Boris Nemtsov.

He early announced that he would run for the presidency when the time came, and formed a party named Yabloko, the Russian word for apple. Often blamed for not uniting with Gaidar, Yavlinsky thought on the contrary that he had kept alive the hopes for liberalism by opposing him, and thus not being dragged down with the inevitable unpopularity from which Gaidar suffered; and in that he may have been right.

Gaidar and his Gang knew, indeed at first almost seemed to relish the fact, that they would be unpopular and short-lived. As it was, they lived longer than they expected and when Gaidar was forced to resign as acting prime minister in December 1991, he left behind powerful and now experienced men in key posts who would not be dislodged for some time. He himself formed a political party, Russia's Choice, which was backed by some of the industrialists whom he had earlier identified as being on 'his side', and slipped into the role of sympathetic oppositionist. He wanted to get back into the politics he had initially scorned, though – unlike Yavlinsky – he was not naturally inclined to it. Yet he had already engraved himself into the roll of those who sought to dismantle communism. He and the few dozen of his Gang and those who joined them had lodged themselves into a largely hostile, sullen environment, proclaimed the ideals and sought to establish the practices of the free market. That they had made mistakes was inevitable in such uncharted territory. What they had given to Russia was change which did not appear reversible.

CHAPTER FIFTEEN

'Reforms, but not at the people's expense'

At the end of the first year of reform, 1992, a shock had been delivered – but more to the people than to the economy. Prices and trade had been liberalized, a limited market in money established: but the central issues, the stability of the currency and of the budget, had been only gingerly approached. Gaidar had been constrained in these areas, at first because he lacked the requisite funds; further down the line, he had run into too much opposition. He could neither make the currency fully convertible, nor balance the budget. The industrial lobbies had not just closed in upon him, they had managed to place their spokesmen in the cabinet. The credit spigots were opened by mid-year, and soon money was washing about the system. The budget deficit rose to nearly 15 per cent in the third quarter and the money supply jumped up to between 25 and 30 per cent from the mid-year.

Yet at the same time industrial production kept tumbling (nearly 25 per cent down in the third quarter of the year compared with the already low level of the previous year). Much of the money pumped into the system ended up abroad, as managers converted the cheap credit into dollars and spirited it away into foreign bank accounts. The new rich had appeared, and were flaunting themselves in their German cars and Italian suits. They were enriching themselves through trade, as foreign consumer goods began to replace Russian produce in the cities; through control of oil and gas pipelines; through exports of raw materials and semi-finished goods; through the huge new opportunities for making money out of money trading; from the fledgling stock market; from joint ventures with foreign companies; from the Moscow construction boom. Much of this enrichment was in the 'grey' area between legality and illegality, or frankly corrupt. Crime of every kind was leaping upwards. Yegor Gaidar was sacked by the parliament, and Victor Chernomyrdin succeeded him.

Gaidar was a clever, subtle but relatively straightforward man. He had come to believe in a certain vision of political economy, and he sought to further it when in power. He learned to compromise and to manoeuvre (though never very well) but it was always clear what he wanted. He was brilliant – polymathic, multilingual, autodidactic and workaholic – and dedicated to a certain goal by a certain path. Chernomyrdin, by contrast, was enigmatic – in part because he had much to be enigmatic about. Yet the conversion of Victor Chernomyrdin, and of many thousands like him, was the work of the period after shock therapy had officially ended at the close of 1992, and 'step-by-step' reform officially began.

He was fifty-four when he took over as prime minister, and he had had an exemplary Soviet career: he had a higher (technical) education, began work on the shop floor, joined the Communist Party at twenty-three, rose through the ranks to become director of an oil refinery in Omsk, and spent the late seventies and eighties oscillating between work in the energy department of the Central Committee and in the gas industry, ending up (under Gorbachev) as gas industry minister, transferring in May 1992 to the cabinet as deputy prime minister in charge of energy. He spent much of his time after the Soviet collapse creating a company, Gazprom, out of the former gas ministry – a company which was (though this was not obvious immediately) the largest in the world on most counts, and the most politically powerful single enterprise in Russia. As the Western – and radical Russian – media commented on his ascension to power as prime minister (to his suppressed fury), he appeared to be an open and shut case of a man from the previous time.

His first curt pronouncement confirmed this view. In his acceptance speech in parliament, he said, 'I am for reforms, but not at the people's expense,' which was taken to mean he was not for reforms at all. He later, in an off-the-cuff remark, said he was for the market, but not for a bazaar – which was taken to mean he was against the market. In his first, bemused press conference he said he would control prices, and indeed signed a decree to that effect – but it was never implemented. He was surrounded by radicals who, though they had lost their leader, still had penetrated the apparatus thoroughly enough to have become the main source of economic information. He inherited advisers like Sergei Vasilyev and Andrei Ilarionov, who persuaded him that price controls were not the way to fight inflation. Ever a hater of the public occasion, he disappeared into the fastness of the cabinet of ministers building – which was then housed in what had been the Central Committee headquarters. The public stage on economic reform – the central element in the government's strategy – was filled by the bulky, self-confident, aggressive form of Boris Fyodorov, who had been appointed as a deputy premier for finance at the same time as Chernomyrdin had become prime minister, as a kind of consolation prize to the Gang.

Fyodorov was then thirty-four, two years younger than Gaidar. If he had not had a model Communist Party career, it had at least been a career in the Party. The son of a worker (as he would later impress upon people when running for elective office), he went to the International Finance Institute, the training ground for officials who had to deal with the world of money outside of the socialist one. He worked in the Central Bank, where he was largely unemployed, and read the *Financial Times* and the *Economist* to later good advantage; he had a spell in the Central Committee finance department; and he was an adviser to the Finance Ministry in Gorbachev's time. Briefly Russian finance minister under Yeltsin before the break-up of the Union, he was hired by the newly established European Bank for Reconstruction and Development in 1991 – 'our man in the City', as the Russian press called him. In October 1992, Gaidar asked him to go to Washington to be the Russian director of the World Bank, of which Russia had just become a member.

He had a small job but a big salary; when he came back to Russia he stayed at the Metropole Hotel, and had time to stroll through Moscow and catch up with his reading of the new and reprinted books which were still flooding on to the market. But he wished neither money nor leisure. He wanted to be part of a process which he saw, more clearly than most, was a time for writing history in large, chiselled letters. He was bitter when Gaidar chose Chernomyrdin to be Central Bank chairman over him, saying he saw no reason for him to trim in that way when there was the prize of monetary stability to win. He, like Yavlinsky (to whom he was and remained personally close), was not one of the Gang; he was, for a Russian, an extreme loner, scorning groups and savaging people close to him – a feature which would later make him a bad party leader. He came to office as though *he* were prime minister – calling press conferences to explain the dire state of the economy, holding a widely publicized meeting of experts to discuss inflation, hurling increasingly insulting imprecations at Gerashchenko in the Central Bank.

The situation he inherited at the run-down, peeling Finance Ministry (its state a visible reminder of the degraded status it held in Soviet times) was terrible. The credits which had been pumped out in the last two quarters of the year had – after a lag of a few months – resulted in inflation of over 30 per cent a month by the beginning of 1993. The deputies, whose blood was up after the victory over Gaidar, now regularly passed resolutions raising pensions, or minimum wages, or financing this or that large project, and reduced budgeting to a nonsense. Industrial contraction continued, and the tax take was still far below target.

Fyodorov adopted a new tactic towards the pressures which hemmed him in. He ignored them. When governors and heads of regional Soviets and factory directors came to his office to lobby for funds, he left them waiting in the anteroom. When parliament passed bills demanding increased expenditure, he did not obey them. When spending went above target he stopped making payments. He even 'delayed' payment on expenditure decrees signed by the president – though, naturally, this manoeuvre had its limits. As naturally, the result was a lengthening of the inter-enterprise debts – and more seriously, an increasing practice of non-payment of wages to workers in the enterprises most dependent on state hand-outs.

He continued, and intensified, the squeeze on the former Soviet republics, railing against the fact that Russia was continuing the largest foreign aid programme in the world, transferring billions of roubles in credits and in subsidized energy and other products to countries which had demanded the right to call themselves independent. From month to month, these hand-outs were decreased – to real pain in the dependent republics, including the reforming Baltic states, which suffered as severe a shock as the other republics in losing their subsidized oil and gas supplies. Efforts to tie the states into a monetary union were made throughout 1993 – but failed, since the only logical system was one in which the Central Bank of Russia controlled their expenditure, which they would not allow. The inevitable consequences of the nationalist surges and successes in the spring and summer of 1991 were made evident in the cold of the winters of 1992 and 1993 – as oil, gas and electricity supplies across the former Soviet land mass were delayed, reduced or cut off. States like Ukraine, which had proclaimed that they would not emulate the harshness of Russian reforms, were brought face to face with the poverty of their condition and their dependence on Mother Russia. The people of these states learned, the hard way, that there is no such thing as a free freedom.

But, brutal and determined as he was, Fyodorov was not the prime mover in the economic sphere from 1993; that was the retiring prime minister. Victor Chernomyrdin had grasped the rationale of reform economics as espoused by the Gang – not just because he had Gang advisers but because their ideas appealed to *his* 'gang' – the energy clan, one of the two most powerful in the country. The oil and gas producers (though not the coal industry, which early realized that the miners' demands for free-market prices would be the death of the industry and had become one of the most powerful conservative lobbies in the land) had an asset readily saleable internationally. They were very interested in owning as much of it as possible through the privatization process, and some at least had ambitions to be the new Exxons and Shells of the nineties and beyond. They were not 'Westernizers' in the main; some, like the management of the huge Surgut Oil and Gas Company, hated the West, and wanted as little to do with Westerners as was compatible with getting their money. But they did need markets and they did want capital and technology and they began to realize that the state and the oil equipment industry could provide little of this. They were thus prepared to support a strategy which gave them some of what they wanted. That which did not suit them, they believed with some justice they could kill.

The turning of Chernomyrdin took some time, and was at first partial. Not until the second half of 1994, when the rouble crashed following an earlier credit expansion, did he fully come round to the Gang's view. His conversion was paralleled by another, also partial and reluctant, undergone by the other Victor, Geraschchenko. The prime minister and the bank chairman were close – similar in ages, in instincts, even in appearance. The banker was protected by the prime minister from Fyodorov's attacks and Western advisers' rudeness. When the radicals would urge Yeltsin to fire Gerashchenko – and they thought themselves near to success at least once, after an impassioned session with Yeltsin – Chernomyrdin had enough clout to block it. But, from spring of 1993, when hyperinflation was barely contained, Fyodorov backed by Yeltsin and Chernomyrdin managed to get an agreement from Gerashchenko to hold down credit. When, in September 1993, Yeltsin brought Yegor Gaidar back into the government as first deputy prime minister, the Gang leader was back in charge of the economics ministry, and though he and Fyodorov had little liking for each other, they could work together well. Fyodorov had revived the Credit Commission and approved all Central Bank credits; it seemed the Bank had been tamed.

Thus began the second attempt at stabilization, which lasted from the latter part of 1993 to the latter part of 1994. Inflation fell, initially slowly but gathering momentum. In the period after the bloody clash between the president and the Supreme Soviet, from October to December, subsidies were cut further and new arrangements were made on tax gathering and expenditure with the regions. This period, in which the reformers assumed everything was moving their way – both economically and politically – appeared to be one in which stabilization was becoming possible.

The results of the December 1993 elections, in which the liberals' breakthrough did not happen but the Liberal Democrats, led by Vladimir Zhirinovsky, scored best in the party list section of the state Duma, initially appeared to threaten economic reform. Once again, as a year before, Chernomyrdin gave a public warning of change, this time saying that the 'period of market romanticism' was over. He reconstructed the government praesidium, or inner cabinet of senior ministers, elevating the conservative agricultural boss Alexander Zaverukha to deputy prime minister and giving Oleg Soskovets, a former metallurgical plant manager, charge of the military industry – and the enterprise debt crisis – as first deputy premier. Gaidar and Fyodorov both resigned, both prophesying disaster, followed by two of the main foreign economic advisers to the Gang, Jeffrey Sachs and the former Swedish diplomat Anders Aslund, who prophesied disaster even more loudly.

Disaster did not happen at once. Yeltsin appointed Anatoly Chubais, head of the privatization programme, to a second first deputy prime minister post, in charge of finance: Chubais, with Alexander Shokhin, became the last of the senior Gang members to survive – though they were still supported by those who stayed in junior ministerial slots and by the gently growing contingent of supporters in the bureaucracy. A version of monetary stability continued. Chernomyrdin talked, again, of wages and price controls, but did not implement them – indeed, he cut some expenditures even further than Fyodorov had, kept the Central Bank interest rates high, got a moderately tough budget through the Duma and began to see inflation fall quite fast – to below 5 per cent by the autumn. Foreign portfolio investment began to pour into the country, and Russia came – briefly and hectically – to be seen as a success story.

Then an unpredicted disaster. On 11 October, the rouble suddenly collapsed, by 27 per cent in one day. The success of Russia had largely been illusory: the low (by Russian standards) inflation rate had been a legacy of former policies, not those pursued by Chernomyrdin since spring. Harried by industrialists, he had allowed Gerashchenko to pump credit through the system once more, had let the interest rate slip into negative and given in to the lobbies – especially to his own, the energy lobby. The exchange rate started falling, and the Central Bank – which had announced it had limited funds – began to intervene to hold the rouble, then announced it would stop intervening, both announcements being large mistakes.

The crash finally removed Victor Gerashchenko from the Bank chairmanship – as it did Alexander Shokhin from his economics post and Sergei Dubynin, Fyodorov's successor, from the Finance Ministry. It unleashed the security services, headed by the president's entourage, on a hunt for the guilty bankers who had sold out Russia's interests to the foreigners – a sign that paranoia was still a major factor in the reformed KGB. Chernomyrdin himself seemed under threat, and his cabinet was re-arranged without his participation or assent by Yeltsin.

Yet even this did not kill off the Gang's influence, nor did it change Chernomyrdin fundamentally. An acting Bank chairwoman was appointed in Tatyana Paramanova, formerly one of Gerashchenko's deputies, who for over a year played the role of the Iron Lady in keeping the Bank's monetary policy as tight as it had ever been. In this posture she was encouraged – even, it was said, commanded – by Chubais and by Yevgeny Yasin, one of the Gang's father figures, an economist in his sixties who had been among the first to popularize monetarist economics in Russia and finally came, near most men's retirement age, to practise them from within government as economics minister.

This was a third attempt at monetary virtue, and it was the most convinced. With Chubais incontestably in charge of monetary and financial policy, with a close ally in the Economics Ministry and with a central banker who was obedient to government (no scope for an independent Central Bank here!), a new discipline emerged. Chubais shaped a strategy which had been mooted for the past four years – stabilization with the aid of foreign funds. He got a budget which had a deficit of only 5 per cent through parliament, secured Yeltsin's backing for financial rigour and – crucially and most painfully – got agreement from the oil lobby to lift oil quotas. The quotas had limited oil exports and thus depressed oil prices; in their place came a régime under which, incompletely and grudgingly, the oil producers and exporters lost their ability to export subsidized oil illegally at huge mark-ups (the system that had led to oil exporting and pipeline control being among the most corrupted and criminalized in the country). Once this was convincingly enough crafted, the IMF delivered, in stages, a loan of $6.8 billion. The government then went one stage further, and fixed the rouble within a band of Rbs4,300–4,900 to the dollar – a further and important stage in the stabilization process, which had eluded successive efforts.

Like much else in Russia, the early experience with macro-economic reform was conducted on several layers at once. It was a battle of the lobbies for shares in a diminishing cake. It was the struggle between the competing gangs in and about the government for political power. It was the battle by Moscow to hold power and resources in its hands, as the regions and republics of Russia sought to whittle or grab it away. And it was the recognition, by men and women deeply reluctant to admit it, that the money economy posed much tighter constraints in certain areas than central planning did – while leaving other areas, which they had been used to and wished to regulate, free. It was also, in a very large part, a struggle by those who wished for transparency in economic policy against those who wished for it to be as murky as possible, so that they could benefit politically or financially or both from a situation initially so chaotic and unfamiliar that the pickings were easy and the accounting required nugatory.

'A macro-economic stabilization cannot be drawn out for too long,'

Victor Chernomyrdin told the Duma late in October, after the crash of the rouble almost cost him his office. It was a plaintive recognition that the costs of avoiding a shock could have been higher than those of the shock which never fully happened, but which happened enough to change the economy forever.

CHAPTER SIXTEEN

'The creation of a bourgeoisie'

In the eighties, a young researcher named Vitaly Naishul working at Gosplan, the state planning agency, noticed that the theory of the Soviet economy was wholly out of kilter with reality. In theory, he and his Gosplan colleagues should have been calmly planning the workings of the economy from their perch on Marx Avenue, at the apex of a triangle in Central Moscow between the Kremlin and the Lubyanka. But it was not like that. The planning system no longer came from above, but from below. The enterprises, seen as the branches and the outposts of the plan, had bit by bit accrued more and more information, power and authority, and had captured elements of the plan itself – making it as much an aggregation of what they did produce as a strategic and binding indication of what they should produce. In doing so, the enterprise directors had taken on, since the seventies, more and more of the attributes of a particular kind of 'ownership' – able to propose and dispose, but in the end usually evading responsibility.

In the mid-eighties, Naishul wrote an essay, which he circulated in samizdat. It was called 'Another Life', and it was a lyrical account of life in the US, comparing the real standards of living of the citizens of the two superpowers. In the second part of the essay, he gave some principles for Soviet economic reform which could set the country on the path of achieving something of the same comfort as the US.

One of his core principles was that the Soviet managerial class had acquired so much information and power, so many of what amounted to property rights, that they had to be bought out. In a passage which anticipated by several years the appearance of privatization vouchers, Naishul proposed that every citizen be given 'an equal sum of specially named investment roubles' – except for the bosses, who would be given much more in accordance with their importance. As much as 20 per cent of the total property of the USSR, he reckoned, would have to be passed over to the directors in order to ensure a peaceful and a relatively efficient transition between a kind of communism to a kind of capitalism. 'Any reform which would avoid a grandiose failure must strive to keep the bosses in their place and not have a change of personnel,' he wrote.

Naishul was a member of the Gang at the time, though he did not go into government with his friends. One of the other members who read this was Anatoly Chubais, then teaching at Leningrad's Institute of Engineering Economics. His reaction was dismissive: 'complete rubbish' is Naishul's recollection of his view. Naishul was later to have the pleasure of reminding First Deputy Prime Minister Chubais of his recipe for system change – and of pointing out that, according to most estimations, the nomenclatura had indeed managed to take, by the mid-nineties, some 20 per cent of the former property of the state into their own hands. Chubais, never gracious, said gruffly: 'I'm still against it. But, you can't do what you want, but what is required.'

For Chubais, that became not a motto but a way of life. By doing what was required he remained in government long after most of the other senior members of the Gang had resigned or been fired – in Gaidar's case, first fired, second time resigned. Gaidar says that he compromised on the macro-economic stabilization in the first year in order to safeguard the jewel, the privatization programme, Chubais's preserve. Chubais, both before and after that gesture, compromised left, right and centre on the structure and implementation of the programme itself in order that something – he would say, the core – be retained. He claimed a passionate belief in the connection between private property and personal freedom, and he certainly believed that once state property was alienated from the state, the power of the communists would be broken.

His compromises in order to achieve these goals were very great. In the first wave of privatizations, he did – as Naishul had forecast – have to provide the directors and others of the old nomenclatura with a mink-lined transit from the old society to the new. In the second wave, in 1995–96, he gave a group of banks and financial companies a huge tranche of the most valuable state assets for knock-down prices, in a series of staged auctions. For this he was hated by the opposition parties, and he also aroused the alarm of his former colleagues, and foreign governments close to the reform process, who believed he might be creating a corrupt, insider-dominated business class which had shown little interest in the hard work of industrial restructuring, but much interest in garnering the easy fruits of privatization, financial transactions, trade finance and stock market speculation.

He was also the most confrontational of the Gang, when in government. When the communist-nationalist Supreme Soviet of Russia tried to derail his privatization plans in 1992–93, he would unleash a bitter flow of invective against them, linking them with Stalin and the GULAGs (which became less and less politically correct in Russia, after 1992). He was stiff and prickly, a bit awkward, even with years in the job behind him. He was initially puritanical about money, refusing privileges, commuting to St Petersburg at the weekend to see his family because he had no flat in Moscow. He was as likely to respond to a question – especially from a source he thought hostile – with a taunt or an exasperated exclamation, as with a straight answer. Yet this was the man who was able to do 'what is required' with people he – certainly at first – disliked and distrusted, who ran with the grain of sovietized Russian life, and yet who managed to implant into the Russian economy a form of ownership which is mutating into a form of capitalism, which was what he intended. 'The only way you could do this was to get insiders motivated and rewarded. You could dream up one hundred schemes which were better and purer, but this was actually the only way you could do it.'

Naishul's early insight into the nature of decaying socialism was keen. For the reformers were to find, when they came to office to transfer property to individual owners, that it already *had* individual owners. In this area, perhaps more than any other, their own preferences and strategies were stymied by their inheritance. To privatize, they had to engage the co-operation of the industrial nomenclatura, but to do that they had to make legal the *de facto* rights of ownership the latter had already seized.

Bit by bit, as the fear and the idealism had lessened in the sixties and in the seventies, the managers of the state enterprises had felt their way round an increasing area of authority, competence and power. They had customers who were invisible and trade unions which functioned as personnel departments; thus when the government began to resemble more and more people like themselves (indeed, was composed of themselves) they could concentrate on suborning it to agreement with their priorities and needs. They had some success – though even in 'stagnation' the Party remained independent and at times demanding, and the government had to follow suit.

Thus the managers' dream was to attain more freedom from their bugbears – the Party and the ministries. It was their orders, their incompetence, their lack of experience of local conditions, which made the managerial job uncomfortable. Being allowed to take their own decisions, set their own pay rates, produce at a more even tempo undisturbed by political priorities would – they argued – improve efficiency and output. Much of the debate in the seventies and early eighties was conditioned by that view; many of the reforms that were proposed, and suppressed, stemmed from it.

The other feature of state enterprises was their increasingly corrupt character. Corruption in that world was not a choice, but a necessity, for in a planned system, especially in an economy of relatively low technical competence, shortages are endemic and thus supplies can only be ensured by circumventing the distribution system – moves which in other societies would be stealing. It was too in the Soviet Union, but was not so regarded by the people in part because it was essential and in part because, since all but the most personal effects was social property and it was allocated, diverting it for different or earlier uses was merely changing the allocation. A Party-state dominance which lacked terror and in which one could usually find someone on the side of the state willing to be complicit was an open invitation to steal, the more since it erased the moral hazard by making no definite delineation of whose property was what. Naturally, since 'reallocation' was done (and done best by the best directors) for the plants, there was only a line of personal morality separating it from reallocating to oneself. Pilfering the property of the state, on large or small scales, was thus a vast part of every enterprise's life.

Gorbachev's reforms, once the spasm of tightened discipline and crackdown on alcohol consumption had passed, were pro-management reforms in the narrowest sense. The law on state enterprises, the law on co-operatives and the law on leasing, all passed in the latter part of Gorbachev's period of office, were stages in the embourgeoisement of the nomenclatura, ways in which they could complete the transfer of effective property rights to themselves. By giving them authority to set wages and prices, to determine production targets, to reduce the percentage of production done for the state plan, the laws revealed how little management or workers wanted freedom to produce and how much they wanted freedom to reward themselves more money and privileges. By then decreeing into existence means – co-operatives and leaseholdings – through which they could transfer part of the property legally to their control, Gorbachev set the seal of perfection on the system for those active and knowledgeable enough to see what was happening. 'The ideal formula for the bureaucracy was to add property to power,' wrote Gaidar of the period. 'The production remained social but the appropriation private . . . the period of . . . 1989–91 may be called 'the golden period' for the nomenclatura, when they knew no limits.'

By the end of the communist period, Russia had a mixed economy, or at least that was how a communist would define it. There were some 200,000 co-operatives, 80,000 joint stock companies, 65,000 partnerships and over 3,000 associations. All had been legally sanctioned, but the laws were declaratory and those administering them ignorant. What emerged from this was, as an associate of Gaidar's who studied the process put it, 'some kind of symbiosis of quasi-private, quasi-state structure engaged not in competition with each other but rather in pilfering the property of the state'. The managers quite soon accepted that the old system was dead, because they were entering into the discovery that the life of a capitalist without competition was better, in many cases, than what they had before.

The Gang had no illusions about any of this. Naishul's analysis, and their own observation, left no doubt that any effort to disturb the golden age of the directors would meet with resistance which, at an extreme, could be murderous. In their discussions, they had concluded that privatization was essential, and essential quickly – and that its prime aim was, as Chubais put it early in 1993, 'the creation of a bourgeoisie' – or as the privatization programme published in mid-1992 had it as the first in its list of objectives: 'to form a group of private owners contributing to the emergence of a socially oriented market economy'. Thereafter, the aims were to 'raise the efficiency of enterprises' and to 'ensure a social safety net'. The privileged place given to the new owners reflected the Gang's belief that they and reform had no chance unless a sizeable group could rapidly be convinced that it was or soon would be in its interests to see property held in private hands.

They were working in an unknown area. Privatization on this scale had never been attempted anywhere else. The decisions they took in the first half of the nineties, often hurried and *ad hoc*, would have as large an effect on the future shape of Russian society as the Bolsheviks' choice of complete state monopoly. Marek Dombrowski, the Polish economist who had worked on his own country's reform then became an early adviser to the Gang, said the post-communist reform, and especially that in Russia, was an order of magnitude harder than the transformations in Latin America or India, or the reconstruction of Germany and Japan after the war – because of the dominance of private property in these economies before they started reform and the absence of it from the Russian.

Privatization was not, of course, their concept; it was part of the common wisdom of the international financial institutions and the foreign advisers. Privatization as a movement (as opposed to the technical matter of transforming a state into a private enterprise, which had more than a century of usually corrupt antecedents from all over the world) had been born in the UK, in the first Margaret Thatcher government of 1979–83. That government viewed the state sector as an incubus, expensive because of its large losses, disruptive because of its powerful unions and ungovernable because of its over-accommodating management. The Thatcher governments' main ideological target, in a period when Britain's governability was being called into question, was the union movement. Later, when privatization could be conflated with a period of strong economic growth and rapidly rising housing values, it was successfully presented as a medium through which a popular capitalism could be distributed.

All of this was attractive to the Gang, some of whom had been nourished and encouraged by the Thatcherites, and who regarded her as a model. But, beyond the élan and the ideology, it was of little use: the Conservatives privatized some 5 per cent of the British economy, the Gang was faced with – depending on how they looked at it – an economy wholly in state hands or, worse, an economy already wrested out of the state's hands. Chubais would say that it had neither a private sector nor a public sector, and that they had to create both. They were thus, from an early stage, concerned to make of privatization a mass movement. And since the ending of the Soviet Union followed that of the régimes of the People's Democracies to its west, they turned to these for precedents.

The Hungarian was of little more use than the British: Hungary delayed privatization, and when it did it, it followed a Chinese-like route – concentrating on the start of new enterprises, leaving the state plants to find foreign partnerships or come to the market in their own time. Poland, much admired for its rapid stabilization, seemed more promising. A voucher system had been proposed there in summer 1990, and there was an original intention to move rapidly, but the matter was more sensitive than the macro-economy because of Solidarity's strength in the large plants, and movement stalled with progress. Janusz Lewandowski, one of the Polish privatization ministers, reflected that his task had been to 'sell enterprises that nobody owns and nobody wants to buy to people who cannot pay'.

Czechoslovakia was closest. There, in 1990, an economist named Dusan Trska, working with the then finance minister Vaclav Klaus, came up with a voucher scheme which gave every citizen the right to a share of state property through presentation of a voucher distributed free to all, and though the Czech system relied on investment funds and was set at a much slower pace than the Russian, it remained closest in spirit.

The Gang wanted to do it quickly. As Yeltsin told them in his programmatic speech of October 1991, in words written by Gaidar, 'for impermissibly long we have discussed whether property is necessary; in the meantime the Party-state élite has been actively engaged in their personal privatization. The scale, the enterprise and the hypocrisy are staggering. Privatization in Russia has gone on for a long time, but wildly, spontaneously, often on a criminal basis. Today it is necessary to grasp the initiative, and we are intent on doing so.' But though they wished to act in haste, they did not want to repent at leisure, and thus they did not take the most rapid way, urged on them by Larissa Piyasheva, in charge of privatization in the Moscow City Council, which was simply to hand over the lot to the workers and managers – a move which she held would be rapid, would still the demands of the enterprises and would usher in workers' control and competition at the same time.

They had read the literature on privatization. They knew the debate about 'insiders' and 'outsiders' and how they were to be treated. Insiders were managers, workers; outsiders were the rest of the society. Insiders, receiving the enterprise, would simply use their position to pressure the government for support, or tariffs, or licences or monopolies; only outsiders could enter on to a company's board and begin to change the company to make profits, since that was their primary interest in ownership. Besides, to give enterprises only to the workers would cut out the state employees who taught, cleaned up, patrolled and pushed paper. Chubais wanted the plan to cover everyone, and to produce an outcome where the companies would have at least a future potential to become efficient.

His State Privatization Committee, housed in a run-down block next to the Kremlin, was the only ministry which had no prior existence, and he was thus freer than his colleagues to appoint his own people. He had a group of young men round him – his deputy ministers Sergei Vasiliev and Dmitri Mostovoi, and his aide Maxim Boiko, who seemed to do everything. They brought in and used a number of young foreigners, mainly Americans, who were reluctantly given passes by the security services, to assist in writing the fundamental laws for the introduction of capitalism to Russia. Chubais was sensitive to the vulnerability of these people and they kept as far as possible in the shadows. But they were of course visible, and especially so to the deputies in the Supreme Soviet, who increasingly saw Chubais as a destroyer of the state and as a treacherous trader, selling Russia into foreign hands.

Chubais simply said they were all communists. Many were, or had been. But their position often did not differ too markedly from that of British Labour Party members faced with the Thatcherite privatizations; indeed, even a former Conservative prime minister, Harold Macmillan, had murmured his dissent to her selling off 'the family jewels'. The Russian deputies had not read what he and the Gang had read, and had the same prejudices against 'speculators' as had most of their constituents. They knew well enough that privatization would be a dirty, corrupt business (many became part of it), and they already knew the nature of the New Russian business class. Chubais and his colleagues were striving for an ideal; if one did not share it, and paid attention simply to the messy reality, it was easy to have doubts, at least.

In the first six months of 1992, the deputies chewed over the privatization programme – and, in June, passed it, the last piece of major legislation presented to them by the Gang which they were to approve. That they did so was a tribute to Chubais's skill in compromise, and their doing so meant that the immediate future of capitalism in Russia would be securely in the hands of those who were taking it anyway – the directors. Chubais won – by allowing them to win too.

He had originally presented a privatization programme which, for large enterprises, gave 25 per cent of the stock free to the workers; allowed them to buy a further 10 per cent at 70 per cent of the (low) book price; allowed the managers to buy 5 per cent, also at book price; while the rest of the stock – 60 per cent – went to the population in exchange for vouchers, or was initially held by the state. But the directors' lobby, organized in parliament in the form of the Civic Union and outside of it by the Union of Industrialists and Entrepreneurs, put pressure on every spot and on every deputy it could reach. Chubais and his assistants thus put up two alternative ways of privatizing: one which gave the workers and managers 51 per cent of the company either free or very cheaply, while a block was reserved for the state and only 29 per cent offered to the voucher-holding citizenry. A final version, applying to only a few middle-sized enterprises, allowed the managers over time to buy a controlling share of the company.

Overwhelmingly, Russian companies chose to come to the market by giving the workers and managers 51 per cent of the company: the insiders won out. The scheme, produced because of directors' pressure, was naturally chosen by them and by normally compliant workforces. Once the scheme was effected, the managers usually bought more shares from workers willing to sell – often promising to retain employment, or to raise wages. Yet while it was the compromise for which they had pushed, it *was* a compromise: Chubais got something too. His vouchers were distributed to every citizen of Russia through the savings bank network: possessing a face value of Rbs10,000, the vouchers were – unlike the Czech or Polish versions – essentially currency, and instantly found a street value as those who preferred consumption to investment exchanged them for goods. By the end of 1992, voucher auctions – for some of the best known companies in Russia – were being held in Moscow and in other large centres.

Over the next year and a half, the Russian privatization programme was pushed through at a rate any other country would have thought impossibly furious. From 18 in December 1992, the number of companies privatized in a month rose to over 1,000 the following December, peaking at 1,355 in June 1994, when voucher privatization ended, with almost 14,000 companies privatized. At the same time, starting in the old merchant city of Nizhny Novgorod, shops and workshops were auctioned off for cash (with, again, large privileges to insiders). In the two years of 1992 and 1993, through all of the political shocks and threats of the time, the process continued, week by week and month by month – a tribute to Chubais and his advisers, and to the power of human greed on which, as a follower of Adam Smith, he had always depended.

The desire for ownership was evident from the start – and was an impressive sight. The first auction of shops, held in Nizhny Novgorod in April 1992, was held in a Palace of Culture with a certain razzmatazz. A professional auctioneer in a dinner suit presided, while outside employees of the shops, marshalled by the communists, kept up a steady barrage of protest that the process would lead to their redundancy and put state assets in the hands of criminals. The bidding seemed to be instantly comprehensible; for some properties it was fierce, for others one bid only was put up. The latter were later said to be a bid from an organized crime interest, against whom no one dared bid.

These auctions continued throughout the year, and resulted in most of the shops – including the cheese shop we met in chapter 13 – being held in private hands. A few, like the cheese shop, improved dramatically, but most improved only a little. The difficulty of acquiring stock, the low level of demand for anything other than the staples, the sluggish, sloppy culture of the socialist shop – all of these militated against a rapid transformation. But at least the problems became evident.

The programme had done more than anything else to make the work of the Gang irreversible – which is not to say it had done enough to ensure that it was, merely enough to make reversibility very unlikely. It had made the directors' furtive affair with ownership open and basically legal in form. Just as the British, French and other state sector managers realized with a start how much they could earn in the private sector and thus became its supporters, so the Russian managers, having enjoyed many of the privileges of ownership, were able to enjoy the fruits as well. As company debts rose into the trillions of roubles because of unpaid debts to each other, as workers went without their pay for months on end, many of Russia's company bosses from St Petersburg to Vladivostok enjoyed a period in which their incomes grew enormously and in which they managed to keep control of the company, effectively, in their hands.

In Nizhny – where the character of the local administration seems to have encouraged the go-ahead younger executives to be more active than elsewhere – a team of managers took over a plant, starkly named the Food Factory, in 1993, using the most popular privatization method to acquire 51 per cent for the employees. The management then whittled down the percentage of stock owned by the employees, bartered a quarter of future profits for foreign food-processing equipment in order to avoid high-interest loans and sold a large share to one of the major banks for a huge profit. Yet the managers retained shares, their jobs and saw their plant booming.

Though the insider-managers were generally extremely hostile to outside interests of any kind, the process did to a degree prise open what was the largest managerial closed shop in the world – enough to allow outsider interests in, both in the shape of the people through the use of their vouchers, and the institutions through their purchase (for vouchers, and later for cash) of smaller or larger stakes in the enterprises. It thus created the conditions in which outsiders could begin to grapple with the gargantuan task of creating an efficient corporate governance – one which the state wholly lacked the resources to tackle itself.

The dark side of Chubais's bargain was early obvious. By mid-1994, he was becoming more and more publicly self-confident that his programme had achieved its basic aim: the numbers of workers formally in the private sector had risen above 50 per cent, he was hailed abroad as the most radical of the post-communist architects and the signs of a new private shop culture were visible everywhere in Moscow, and in many other cities besides. But investment was falling still; foreign interest was relatively small (little Hungary was attracting more investment in absolute terms) and above all, even by 1997 most of the companies were not being effectively restructured.

Knowing that Chubais wanted speed, the larger companies made separate deals with him. The energy companies – the oil enterprises, and the Gazprom monopoly – were relieved of most of the terms of privatization, and came to the market in their own way in their own time. The car company Avtovaz cut out unwanted investors by making sure the office at which offers were received was closed early. The other big car manufacturer, Gaz, used fifteen dummy companies and 1 million vouchers to buy back its own shares at an auction it organized itself. Komi Oil, the company based in the Komi Republic, issued hundreds of thousands of extra shares to a few of the shareholders unbeknown to others after allowing the few to sell existing, highly sought-after shares before they were diluted. Surgut Oil and Gas, one of the biggest energy companies based in the oil region of Tyumen, closed the airport, cut phones and put armed guards on the doors of the building during an auction in which it, too, bought itself out at a low price. In nearly every one of the major and publicized privatizations, it was alleged that there had been a major breach of the regulations, or the law. These breaches were often blatant: in the case of Surgut Oil and Gas, its actions isolated an entire Siberian town for a day so that the managers could keep out their rivals, Rosneft, from attending the auction and bidding for its shares.

Having been privatized, it seemed all the companies were profitable: none initially went bust. None could at first, for there was no bankruptcy law or proceedings. Instead, the necessary concomitant to privatization – hard budget constraints on the companies – was not pressed, allowing companies to postpone taking efficiency measures with a supply of cheap credit. Where this was not available – and it dwindled over time – the bills were unpaid, as were the workers.

The disadvantages of throwing the companies into the privatization pot became still starker. The larger ones nearly all had a huge hinterland of social responsibilities – workers' flats, kindergartens, medical facilities, rest homes, holiday hotels, canteens, shops, sports facilities, cultural centres – which had to be built, staffed and maintained: nearly 50 per cent of municipal property in the large towns was reckoned to belong to the companies. In one-company towns, of which there were many, the company *was* the town's infrastructure. Naberezhny Chelny (formerly Brezhnev) was run by Kamaz, the enormous truck plant for which it was built, which meant that for some 120,000 people (the plant had employed 200,000 at its peak) the fortunes of Kamaz affected their lives and futures in a way as intimate as a serf might have depended on his lord in medieval times, or Dearborn depended on Ford.

Kamaz continued to function both as a truck-maker and as a social service provider deep into the late nineties, subsidized both by the central government in Moscow and by the republican government of Tatarstan, within whose borders it was: the two governments jointly owned some 15 per cent of Kamaz stock. For three years after the beginning of reform, it floundered – trying to attract outside investors without success, suffering a disastrous fire in the engine plant. In 1994, the US company Kolberg Kravis and Roberts – known for its restructuring of companies like RJR Nabisco – began to assist in the truck plant's restructuring. It has promised to bring in up to $3.5 billion in investments over seven years, in return for control of the Kamaz board. Both the agreement to lose control, and the link-ups with foreign component-makers such as Cummins for diesel engines, Rockwell International for rear ends and the German company ZF for transmissions constituted an unusual recognition by Kamaz management that their lack of technology, and of skill in design, marketing and distribution meant that outsiders had to be brought in to prevent eventual collapse.

In the main, however, foreign investors remained wary both because management like that of Kamaz were rare, and because they were never properly wooed by the Russian government. Chubais choked off the first sustained effort to attract investment, when he refused to allow the Committee on Foreign Investment to offer foreign companies special deals on Russian companies they might wish to buy. Goldman Sachs, retained to assist on foreign investment early in 1992, was dismissed by the end of the year; Chubais would not endanger the shaky acceptability of his programme by giving foreigners cosy bargains, pointing out that they could buy shares in the primary or secondary markets like everyone else. They did – nearly always in the secondary market – and the desperate Western tobacco companies, avid for markets, soon dominated the cigarette sector. The foreigners' intermediate buying secured them some 10 per cent of Russian equity by 1994, though in at least some cases they appeared to be buying companies in order to shut them down and suppress competition. In only a few cases – the Swiss power engineering company ABB was the best example in the mid-nineties – did they buy in extensively.

But the skill of the insiders in keeping out the outsiders, the corruption and the violence, the fuzziness of the law and the difficulty of taking a conflict to court, the high and constantly varying taxes, the bad infrastructure, the wretched (out of Moscow and St Petersburg) accommodation and transport – all of these and more constructed a litany of disincentives for many foreign companies. Those which stayed and persevered could make fortunes, others lose fortunes.

Chubais, in public, treated this legacy as if it were the best of all possible worlds. He kept his place at the top of government. Though he resigned in January 1996, after elections to the Duma reduced the reformists' share of the parliament to no more than 15 per cent and decimated his own party, Russia's Choice, he was back two months later as an influential figure in the presidential entourage and by May he was Yeltsin's chief of staff, then again a first deputy premier. He adopted the Western ministerial custom of assuring everyone that everything was going well, while at the same time assuming full responsibility for his brief – neither feature common amongst his colleagues. His private admission to Naishul, that he hated the compromise he had been forced to make, was never given public voice. He simply plugged on, assuming more and more responsibility, as, from late 1994, effective head of the economic and financial departments of governments, proclaiming privatization a success and anticipating further success in the second stage of the programme, when government would sell much of its remaining shareholding for cash and the companies which had escaped earlier privatization – especially the energy companies – would come under the hammer.

He was partly right, and may prove to be fundamentally right (though neither he nor anyone else could, in the second half of the nineties, know). For what he had succeeded in doing was more than simply running with the grain of a corrupted managerial-government class: he had, in tempting them on to greater and greater wealth, made them dizzy with greed and betrayed them into losing control of a process they thought under their thumb.

A new apparatus had been created, which, though crude and very buccaneering, was an imitation of a financial market and began to take on more and more of the lineaments of one. Investment funds had sprung up, promising huge rewards if vouchers were invested in them. Some of these turned out to be crooked, quickly disappearing with the vouchers; some carried on issuing shares until they diluted themselves into worthlessness; some worked well enough and did produce, from time to time, a return for their investors. The question they did not initially know how to – or wish to – answer was: what was the investor getting when he exchanged a voucher for a share in the company? A real claim to ownership? Or only to a dividend?

These questions were deliberately fudged in the 1993–94 boom of the crooked investment funds, of which MMM was the flagbearer. MMM, run by an entrepreneur named Sergei Mavrodi who, with two brothers (hence the name), had accumulated a fortune in trading in computers in the late eighties, promised and for some time delivered huge returns on investment in its shares, doing so on the simple principle of pyramid selling, the new receipts funding the older dividends until the mountain crashed. Mavrodi went to jail, then successfully secured a Duma seat in the suburbs of Moscow with the support of the Liberal Democrats. Others – like Tibet and Chara Bank – suffered a similar, if lower-key, fate. MMM actually did combine under one loosely organized roof an industrial holding company, a voucher investment fund and an investment company in which shares were traded for cash. According to the company's executives, each was independent of the other and may have been – but since the law seemed unable to regulate or even to understand where the exact crime lay, there was no public test of the structure. Not until the end of 1995 was a presidential decree signed which addressed the issue, and which promised compensation for those ruined by funds' criminal activities – to be paid for out of the funds' own earnings.

Yet the main activity of the funds was what they said it was. Organizations like First Voucher Fund, Alpha Capital and MN quickly became the investors for (in the case of First Voucher) over 2 million people, avidly and increasingly expertly buying packets of shares in companies, usually as speculative investments at first. Their purchases were, by developed markets' standards, usually corrupt: as outsiders fighting to be inside, they duplicated the moves that the insiders made to keep them out. Mikhail Kharshan of First Voucher bought his way into Moscow's Cosmos Hotel by, first, paying journalists to write disparagingly of its financial position; second, having himself interviewed on TV about its poor shape; third, ensuring through various payments that the privatization auction was held only in Moscow; and fourth, paying other investment funds to stay away. The result – he took a large share in the 1,700-room hotel for $2.5 million, a much lower price than was to appear in later offerings of the remainder of the shares or the secondary markets. In a later successful bid for a share of the Solikamsk Paper Company in the Perm region, Kharshan ensured that the auction was held on the grounds of the plant and that its security guards let no one in but First Voucher employees. He secured 10 per cent and a board seat. These activities were common and at least some were not illegal – such was the state of the law, and such was the state of mind of both the government and the new capitalists, the latter determined to get rich while the good times lasted, the former believing that the good times could last if enough people got rich.

This was a game only for insiders, who had the nerve and were able rapidly to acquire the new street knowledge which let them survive. Foreigners, at least at first, were kept out, fleeced or charged much higher prices for shares on the secondary markets – though they were often happy to pay the higher prices, which could represent bargains if the country stayed stable, if the laws got better and if the company did well (investment in Russia in the early days of its capitalism was, for everyone, surrounded with more 'ifs' than in the Kipling poem). But it was not – contrary to first impressions – wholly lawless: its rules existed, worked and could be learned. By the second half of the nineties, the equity market was dominated by foreign portfolio investment, and thus highly vulnerable to foreigners' views of the general state of the Russian economy and polity. As the 1995 parliamentary and 1996 presidential elections approached, as President Yeltsin's health wavered and as the communists and nationalists prepared to strengthen their positions, the market weakened, halving its value between September 1994 and September 1995: a normal relationship between marketplace and political upset.

Restructuring of a sort began – though, with a few exceptions such as Kamaz, it was certainly not what developed capitalist economies recognized as restructuring, with high-profile firings, takeovers, mass redundancies, mergers. Where at first there were no bankruptcies, they slowly, by 1994–95, began to accumulate: in the latter year, some 500 companies had been put into bankruptcy proceedings by the agency concerned, though the emphasis was on saving the companies from being closed down. Unemployment did begin to rise, quite sharply by the middle of the decade: there were more layoffs, but for the most part the trend continued as it had been set from the beginning of reform – workers were simply not paid, the inactive took what they could, the more active went into the 'private' sector or moved to other companies. New private companies began on the premises of the larger ones, sometimes with the large company owning or part-owning the fledgling as it took over some of the functions of the larger company while employing many fewer people to do it. Chubais claimed that privatization had itself dictated a market-oriented industrial policy. He saw the formation of an electricity corporation, and of new groups in the oil industry, as proof that the process and the market combined gave rise to a rational structure.

The struggle over how to take the privatization process further after the first, voucher privatization phase ended in mid-1994 was an intense one, for the stakes were high. Since, even after re-evaluation, Russian shares were valued at around one-tenth of an equivalent company in developed capitalist economies, it was reasonably assumed there would be sharp appreciation if and when the economy began to recover. In the mid-nineties, the issue became entwined with the desire of the banks to take a more active part in industry (or at least acquire more shares): led by the Oneximbank, a consortium of banks proposed to the government a deal where they offered loans in return for shares, these shares becoming their property if the loans were not returned – a programme which began to be instituted by the end of 1995.

Here, for many, was proof, even the culmination, of a tendency clear in Russia since the beginning of reform: the tendency towards corporatism – that is, towards a series of arrangements in which the state and business intertwine, subsidize each other's activities, and conspire to keep out all but those outsiders of whom both approve. There is an argument that when corporatist arrangements are accompanied by a weak state they will hamper strong economic growth – an argument which has clear force, but which does not seem to take adequate account of the Italian experience, in which corporate arrangements were and even after the 'democratic revolution' of the early nineties still are common, yet which have not impeded extremely dynamic growth in many sectors. Italy indeed (which had a similar GNP per head to Russia before the latter's revolution) may point to a possible development: that Russia will show both stagnation and dynamism in increasingly stark differentiation from region to region as its capitalism progresses.

That that would be progress, Chubais had little doubt, nor did he express any. 'Insiders got advantages in the first round. Thereafter the secondary market has distributed the shares to outsiders, a process which happened almost immediately. That is a logic of privatization, that is what has happened,' he said in an interview. But it was not exactly what was happening. In the second round, the large banks sought to make inside deals with the government as to which parts of which companies they would acquire. Unsurprisingly, in December of 1995, a huge row broke out between (especially) Menatep Bank on the one hand and Oneximbank, Alpha Bank and Inkombank on the other over Menatep's capture of 40 per cent of the major oil company Yukos without, the other banks claimed, the company being open to competing bids. Oneximbank itself took control of Norilsk Nikel, one of the world's biggest mining companies, for a little under $180 million; in mid-1997, it gained control of the larger part of Russia's telecommunications for $1.8 billion. It was clear, from the start of the second stage, that privatization had become a game for the large corporations, and that its name was contacts, influence, inside knowledge and corruption.

Naturally, Russians wished for personal and national wealth; and there was no plausible means of achieving either, other than the system which surrounded them and which their country had vainly tried to surpass, then keep at bay, for much of the century. In giving them title to property, Chubais made them neither rich nor free, but did insert into the chaotic social process the possibility that some might attain the first and that all might feel that what the late twentieth century offers in the way of freedom could be sustained.

But it will be a hard coming. The state retains a grip on the private sector, through its shares in the major companies. The companies themselves are fearful of moving too far away from the state and its changing priorities, because they depend so much on its concessions, import and export regulations and contracts, all of which are awarded on largely personal criteria. By 1997, unpaid debt (including unpaid wages) was a staggering 35–40 per cent of gross domestic production. What had been advertised as the most popular capitalism in the world has narrowed to be concentrated in a few large corporations, which acquired their holdings in – at best – untransparent ways.

There was – in broad terms – no other way. Faced with the collapse of state finances, the reformers were forced to throw out the assets into what hands were willing to grasp them, so that a culture of ownership and responsibility could take root where it might. And it might; indeed, there are increasing signs that it is, even if these are often swallowed up in the immensity of the Russian crisis.

In December 1995, two weeks before the elections to the Duma, Gaidar – who was the leader of a major, struggling liberal party – spent an entire weekend at a conference he had arranged for his friends and colleagues in government, and for friends from abroad. Chubais gave a rather sad speech at it, all but asking for understanding from his fellow liberals that the very unliberal insider privatization over which he was presiding had been the only way to do the job. Naishul, in an extempore speech designed to cheer up the Gang, said they must remember three things: that the Gaidar reforms had passed into the culture and were accepted as facts – unlike the dozens of projects for reform through the decades which had got nowhere; that though shock therapy had not worked as it should, there had been a shock, the shock felt after a needed surgical operation; and that, in the pre-Gang days, people had come to Moscow to get goods where they now came to make money. Chubais sat, smiling wanly.

CHAPTER SEVENTEEN

'A creative period of transition'

The creation of industry in the Soviet Union was not, as it was in other countries, a product of the desire of a new middle class to make money. It was built up for the twin purposes of creating socialism through the construction of a rational industrial process and of a working class – which Marxism-Leninism had decreed as the class of the future – and to prepare Russia to compete with, or protect itself against attack from, the advanced capitalist countries.

All over the former Soviet Union, one can find museums which laud these aims. In Gori, in Georgia, a horrifyingly mendacious museum celebrates the achievements of Joseph Stalin. Though the contents are poor – mostly press photographs – their purpose is plain: to credit Stalin with the creation of a great industrial power, and of a large, disciplined and communist working class. This is not how we naturally think of Stalin, but it is how millions of Soviets experienced his rule – as one in which the tempo of modernization was pushed along at a savage pace, transforming cities, towns and wastelands with the roar of a new industrial culture.

The museum of the Uralmash corporation in Ekaterinburg – Sverdlovsk in Soviet times – is tended and preserved by a flock of reserved, middle-aged women, dusting the working models of the giant excavators and generators which the plant turned out to give power to the Soviet Union. Besides these models, photographs of the first workers' huts in the empty tundra, of the steel cathedral rising from the muck, the first products, the photos of the medal winners and the directors, the plan demands, the war production, the rebuilding, the constant, enormous difficulties and tensions – and then, as a resolution of all of these, the achievements, the range of products from power station sets through moving cranes the size of apartment blocks to diesel engines. In the Stalin museum, the aim of politics is seen as industrial power; in the Uralmash halls, the base of industry is shown to be workers' heroism organized and inspired by the Party.

Uralmash itself is the size of a town and it made almost everything it needed, from screws to doors. Like the other industrial monsters – Kamaz truck plant in Naberezhnye Chelny, Gaz car plant in Nizhny Novgorod, Leninetz electrical plant in Petersburg, ZIL engineering plant in Moscow – these plants were as far as possible self-sufficient, insulated from the vagaries of bad or no supply of components. Thus Russian industry entered an age of increased industrial specialization, and of 'just in time' systems of supply of components to assembly plants, with an industrial structure in which everything was made on the same site.

This self-sufficiency applied beyond industrial products. In 1991, the US investment fund BatteryMarch took a group of US managers of pension funds on a tour of the Soviet Union, ending in Leningrad, where they visited the great Leninetz plant, and had lunch with the general director. They asked what his largest problems were. He said it was obtaining sufficient flats for his workers in the city, and in securing the supply of foodstuffs from Ukraine, then pulling away from the Union. They did not understand him, and it had to be explained to them that as general director he was ultimately responsible not just for production, but for a range of housing, supply and welfare needs of 50,000 people. His was as much a mayoral, even a paternal, responsibility as a managerial one.

The general directors were not merely fathers to their people but sons of the Party. They would move between Party and industrial work in many cases, and would usually have as a reward of the job a seat on the Supreme Soviet, or in the Central Committee, or both. When the Supreme Soviet became elective, they were often elected – a reflection of their status within the areas in which they worked, and the power of the 'deferential' vote of workers and their families anxious that their provider retain his customary lines of influence.

In the seventies, the Uralmash system produced a man thought to be outstanding by most of his peers. Nikolai Ryzhkov was a worker's son who got an engineering degree from the Urals Polytechnic Institute, one of the great technical forcing houses of the Soviet Union. He joined Uralmash as a craftsman in the fifties, working his way up to become a chief technologist, chief engineer, factory director and then, in 1971, head of the corporation. For a decade from 1975, he occupied a series of high industrial policy posts – number two at the Heavy Engineering Ministry, number two at GosPlan, a Central Committee secretary in charge of engineering in the early eighties. In 1985, Gorbachev asked him to be prime minister, and he served for over five years, resigning at the end of 1990. He had been brought into government because, like most of his comrades, he believed that the Soviet system could be made to work if only it were given some more freedom and managers given both larger incentives themselves and allowed to give more to their workers. He tried to keep that version of reform going even after he resigned – standing against Boris Yeltsin for the presidency of Russia in the summer of 1991 as the Communist Party candidate, receiving a little over 16 per cent of the vote.

As his later memoirs make clear, he thought slow reforms had been betrayed by hastiness and bad decisions (largely those of Mikhail Gorbachev) and he hated what the man who beat him to the presidency did with Russia. In 1995, after most had written him off, he co-founded a nationalist party, 'Power to the People', to compete for power in the parliamentary elections, and did very badly.

Like Yuri Andropov, the general secretary who advanced his career, he thought reform essential but that it should, above all, preserve a steady tempo and be controlled by the Party. In his speech to the Supreme Soviet a few days before he retired, he gave what amounted to an obituary (a good one) for *perestroika*: '*Perestroika* destroyed many established structures, both Party and government. But we have not yet created acting and effective mechanisms to replace them. This directly affected the economy, which has neither a plan nor a market now.' And he warned: 'A creative period of transition is possible only if we carry out very careful and systematic reforms. The scale of the country and the whole spectrum of realities that took shape over decades do not permit us to use shock treatment.'

This was his own voice, and it was also the voice of the industrial managers whom he knew so well and whose careers were rather similar to his. They were *the* Soviet men, occupying one of the peaks of the régime, closer to the political power than the generals and stronger on the ground than the planners. The Gorbachev era – Ryzhkov himself – had been good to them, in expanding their powers and their ability to enrich themselves. But by the end of it, they were losing suppliers, customers and subsidies, seeing the radicals in the Supreme Soviet whip up nationalist discontent and demands for an economic revolution they could not hope to deliver, had they wished to. Like any businessman confronted with government incompetence, they took refuge in cynicism and contempt; but it was the contempt of the powerless, for the disintegration of the Union and the collapse of the economy were happening even as Ryzhkov resigned.

Thus they came into the post-Soviet age. Two of their leading members had opposed Yeltsin openly – Ryzhkov for the Russian presidency, Yevgeny Brakov, chairman of ZIL, for the Moscow seat in the Supreme Soviet (in 1989). Brakov had just co-authored a book on comparisons between US and Soviet industrial management and prospects for joint ventures with scholars from Harvard Business School – for him, a large step. But they were being asked not just to take large steps, but to step out of the skin they had grown and the logic they had learned. They were embedded in 'the whole spectrum of realities' about which Ryzhkov had spoken – and on them much of the weight of the changes fell. It was to keep them at work in conditions of industrial chaos that the privatization programme was crafted as it was.

Privatization might save the director, but it could not initially stop the fall. It may have made it a little worse. Soviet-Russian industry underwent the largest decline in the peacetime industrial world, as GNP shrank by nearly 50 per cent from 1991 to the middle of the decade (on official figures). Even when one accepts that the state figures cannot be believed because of enterprises' propensity to understate in order to avoid tax, and the statisticians' inability to capture the private sector – which, on OECD estimates, reduces the rate of decline by as much as 15 per cent – the fall in output was huge, and lasted from 1990 to 1997. The slashing cuts which the Gang made to military expenditure were felt throughout all of the economy, so much of it being geared to military industry; the drop in real earnings and the switch to imported foodstuffs and other goods hit light industry; investment was cut to formal levels. Large parts of an industrial culture had come close to being destroyed. Once the centralized system of taking profits and allocating investments ended, the decision on what to do with the profits passed to the new owners. Sometimes there was no profit. Sometimes it was consumed in higher wages. Sometimes it went into the pockets of the directors.

The other part of the story was that industry was being, if not rebuilt, certainly reorganized, patched up and kept going. The industrial management class did take huge advantage of legal and illegal ways to get rich, but some also did begin to work for their wealth, and if they did not modernize their plants, did at least struggle to make them pay. While full-blooded restructuring of the kind that was needed to make industries internationally competitive was slow in coming, there was a great deal of adaptation to the new conditions.

Three broad types of post-Soviet enterprise began to emerge in the studies done of them in the mid-nineties. The good had quickly learned to demand cash from their customers up front; did not borrow from banks because they distrusted them; paid their bills on time; set good wages which were also paid on time; and made an effort to innovate, expand and market. The not bad were sometimes in too weak a position to insist on pre-payment; paid somewhere between 70 and 130 per cent of the average wage, usually on time but sometimes not; delayed their bills but usually paid them. The bad had large arrears, paid wages irregularly and appeared to be heading for bankruptcy.

In 1955, two French economists, Charles Wyploscz and Gaël de Pontbriand, conducted the largest ever survey of post-Soviet industry. It revealed a picture of enormous change and disruption: of 'good' companies, 'bad' companies and others struggling to get by. In the 'good' category was a scrap metal company which was started up in 1990, mainly recycling old military equipment. Such was its trade that it expanded from an original twelve to 500 workers in 1995, exporting 95 per cent of its production and paying between $150 and $1,000 a month to its employees. It had invested in two metal companies, with a controlling interest in one of these; had begun its own small bank and had shares in another; had bought a hectare of land for office development in central Moscow and owned a subsidiary company which collected the scrap. It carried on some of the old traditions – it bought flats for its workers, built them a recreation centre and gave them interest-free loans. Turnover was in the range of $20–25 million, with high profits of at least 15 per cent on turnover.

Another of the successful companies in the survey reduced its work-force of 700 to 250 when its main business – making nuclear power stations – disappeared. It turned to the construction of houses, riding the private construction boom that appeared in 1992. The company paid between $60 and $220 a month, always on time. It paid its taxes promptly, but delayed some other bills. It borrowed, but not much. It was privatized, with the workers and managers taking the majority of the shares, but they were bought out at 209 times the price they paid by an unknown investor who then appointed a general manager, saying he would himself take over in two years. It made no investment, had a small profit (in 1994) of some $100,000.

The second category was made up of firms which were getting by. In the Wyploscz-Pontbriand survey, these included a metals castings firm established before the revolution. Its 1,100 workforce (which had fallen slightly) owned 90 per cent of its capital after privatization. It paid its workers between $85 and $340 a month (depending on sales), always on time, but it had begun to charge for the use of its kindergarten. At the time of the last survey in May 1995, it owed about $280,000 and was owed about $250,000. Its turnover in that month was over $1.3 million, but it probably (information was scanty) did not make a profit. In the same category was a Moscow oil refinery employing 3,800 workers, paying $500 a month on time, but in need of modernization, though able to invest $200 million in a new propylene plant to be built by an Italian contractor. The company was profitable, had stopped receiving state credits, but borrowed 10 per cent of a monthly turnover of $260 million.

The bad companies were a sad testament. One, still in state hands, had been created in 1929 to give employment to disabled workers, who still made up half of the staff of 180, turning out mirrors and furniture. In mid-1996, the minimum wage was $16, the highest (for the director) $160 – wages which were paid from renting out part of its building to a bank and to a Gazprom department. Most of its customers were, like it, state or municipal companies or departments, and they paid badly. The quality of its products was too low for it to attract private customers. It had a $350,000 debt with the bank, a turnover which amounted to only half of its production, and no prospects. Another, a building materials company, kept going by paying lower and lower wages. Yet another, a clothing company, reduced its staff from 1,500 to 100, delayed wages and payments on bills, tried to diversify from children's to women's clothing when sales of the latter fell badly – but remained, in mid-1995, on the verge of bankruptcy, kept alive by debt and credit.

The composite picture is of intense, sometimes desperate activity, with more layoffs than hirings (though mostly, on the testament of these companies, voluntary or natural wastage); with some adaptation to the market where possible; with evidence (though this may be overdrawn) of a continued tradition of managerial paternalism where it could be afforded. Workers' wages were, in the economists' phrase, flexible – workers would take a cut to subsistence levels or even below to stay employed, in contrast to their fellows in developed capitalist states. The picture is of a hard, demanding environment, but not a hopeless one.

Not only not hopeless. It was possible, by 1993 and after, to find real hope in the growth of the private small business sector, which was mainly concentrated in services. So quickly did it develop that services, which had been merely one-third of the economy in 1990 (compared to the US's two-thirds), passed the 50 per cent mark by mid-1994. Much of that growth was due to small (fewer than 100 workers) companies, of which there had also been very few compared to Western experience (22 per cent of late-Soviet companies were small, compared to 94 per cent in the US). They were staffed, it seemed, by the brightest and most self-improving of the managers, workers and academics who saw their jobs disappear or become meaningless, and who opted for a double risk – to become business people, a despised occupation, in services, a despised sector. They were of course in a grey area from the first. Many of them were formed by managers within the companies they managed, 'renting' themselves space and supplying the company with services. When they exported, they often did so illegally. They paid no or few taxes – thus contributing to the estimation that some 20 per cent of GDP lay, uncounted, in the shadow economy. They changed very rapidly: going into trading at first, where some large fortunes were made; diversifying into finance and business services; then picking up on boom areas like real estate in 1994 and later. They tended to pay high wages but they provided no flats, no kindergartens and no cheap food. They could be the route out of the 'spiv' economy into production: in St Petersburg, one of the main car dealers who specialized in BMWs used his profits to start lipstick production, and got a contract with Avon, which had begun calling in the city.

But the real success of the small- or medium-sized firms could not compensate for the huge structural crises which confronted Russian industry even five years after reform. These crises included desperately bad management, technological obsolescence, lack of marketing culture, low productivity. They also included enormous duplication of output, with smallish plants producing, expensively, the same products as a smallish plant relatively close by. Gigantism, though it existed, was not really the problem of Soviet industry. Even with so few small companies, the average company size was lower than in the UK. The larger problem was tiddlerism. For example, Russia had some 80 rubber plants, one in each of its regions. They could not all be efficient, or profitable – perhaps ten to twenty could.

The crises were most acute in sectors such as cars, power engineering, military and agricultural equipment and aerospace – areas where, for the most part, the Soviet engineers had some reason to be proud of their achievements, though not as much reason as they thought.

The last of these, Soviet aerospace, was developed through a history of innovation and design creativity intertwined with political intervention into being the only alternative national centre to the US of aerospace production across the entire military and civilian range. It cannot survive in that form, but even in the second half of the nineties, the lesson had not been accepted and the shell was preserved.

It boasts great figures who were, in accordance with Russian tradition, not always honoured in their homeland. One of its chief designers was Andrei Tupolev, who set up Russia's first 'Aerodynamic Airplane Construction Bureau' in 1916, designed a series of planes bearing the initials of his name, the ANT25–30 and the Tupolevs 104 and 114, and was then, in 1939, sent to the GULAG, his books taken from the shelves, his name forbidden to be mentioned. The Nazis were his salvation: he was released with several of his colleagues and, still with the official status of criminal, began once more to design planes, which he did till his death in 1972.

Artyom Mikoyan, brother of Anastas, Stalin's longtime trade minister, designed and built the MiG fighters with Mikhail Gurevich. Sergei Ilyushin established the long line of Ilyushin bombers and civilian planes in the thirties, winning himself three Hero of Socialist Labour awards in doing so. And Alexander Yakovlev established the Yak line of fighters (the Yaks 1, 3 and 7) and then the short-haul aircraft, the Yak40 and Yak42, as well as the Yak24 helicopter.

These men, all graduates of the Zhukov Military Engineering Academy in the twenties and thirties, were lauded and rewarded throughout their lives (except for Tupolev, who was however rehabilitated in 1960 and whose son followed in his footsteps to become head of the design bureau which bore his name in 1992). They not only designed planes, they founded companies, which exist still, though in rather dismembered form. Responding more to the pressures of war than to the needs of civil passengers, they were as talented as their Western counterparts and designed planes which at most times were the match of their foes and in modern times, in some respects, surpassed them, like the MiG29, and the Tupolev Blackjack and Backfire bombers. They did not have access to all of the light alloys which Westerners had, so the design of their wings and fuselage was more aerodynamic: Russian-built airliners are slimmer and more graceful than their US or European counterparts. They lagged badly in solid state electronics, using vacuum tubes long after they had become museum pieces in the West.

They had, after the war, a stable and steadily growing market in the Soviet Union, the Comecon countries and in China. The industry was split into separate areas – research and development, design, production – which were highly specialized and quite distinct from each other, linked by the ministry. The planes tended to orient themselves on one performance parameter – speed, or manoeuvrability, or the ability to lift heavy weights; low in their criteria were fuel efficiency, ease of maintenance and passenger comfort. The result was an industry which could supply planes to the largest integrated domestic network in the world and to several other countries, but which were expensive to maintain and to run, uncomfortable to ride in and thus uncompetitive in the face of the Western airlines contoured for comfort, fuel efficiency, ease of maintenance and above all safety. They were industrial products of and for the Soviet world, and when it collapsed an immediate question appeared over their right to exist. Almost no airline bought them once it ceased being obliged to. Though their lack of safety was exaggerated, their main user, Aeroflot, did have a bad safety record. Yet its most publicized disaster, in 1994, when the pilot and co-pilots left the flight deck and controls in the hands of the former's son, who managed to disengage the automatic pilot, was ironically in one of the fleet's new West-European-built Airbuses.

They tried very hard to survive, in (for Western plane-makers) unimaginably hard times. The defence budget fell from $150 billion in 1989 to at most $40 billion in 1995; within that, military procurement was $8 billion, of which aerospace was a small part (the US defence procurement was more than five times larger). In 1994, the government bought thirty-two aircraft, including helicopters. At the same time as this was happening, Aeroflot was breaking up into some 400 separate parts – many of which could barely afford to maintain their planes, let alone replace them. Fares went up, occupancy went down. In 1994, 127 civil aircraft were planned, 46 were built, and 18 were sold.

A new generation of a quieter, more efficient engine was produced at Perm's aero engine plant; but the PS90A appeared to have a design fault, and a test flight for journalists had to be cut short with an emergency landing. The Ilyushin 96 and the Tupolev 204, both long-haul aircraft which Aeroflot would be likely to buy to replace an elderly fleet, both used the PS90A. Reluctantly, they turned to co-operation with Rolls Royce and with Pratt and Whitney for engines, and to Rockwell Collins for avionics. The Yak production plant in Saratov went through, from 1991, an extensive privatization exercise designed to put control of the firm in the workers' and managers' hands – an exercise which drew on US defence conversion expertise, and which attempted to bring its 1,600 suppliers into an alliance with the company based on rewards for on-time delivery and reliability, and which initially (in 1992) saw new markets open up abroad, increased employment and wages.

In the few years spanning *perestroika* and the creation of the new Russian state, the aviation industry was more innovative in its efforts to restructure itself than at any time in its history. But in face of tumbling markets at home and abroad, success could not be expected. It had existed in its own world; yet the industry of which it was a part was a global one, in which three large players – Boeing, McDonnell Douglas (these two merged in 1997) and Airbus Industries – and a large number of smaller (but still large) corporations competed incessantly and very hard. The investments required were huge: the Russian state could not afford to fund more than a fraction of the various projects pushed by the different bureaus and corporations, nor could the new financial institutions call on either the capital or the expertise required. Aeroflot's international arm, Russian International Airlines, some of the new independent states' lines and an independent Russian operator called Transaero leased Boeings and Airbuses.

When, in May 1995, Gazprom decided to start an executive jet subsidiary for its own and customers' use, it bought, not Yaks, but two Falcon 900B jets from the French company Dassault. Even in an election year, when Gazprom was sponsoring Prime Minister Victor Chernomyrdin's party 'Our Home is Russia', the imperative to buy foreign planes was greater than any felt need to demonstrate patriotism.

As the British had found in the fifties and sixties, the ending of empire and great power status, coupled with the opening of markets and the dwindling of state subsidies, were fatal for prestige, capital-intensive industries like the aerospace one. Even captive markets – and Russia did not have captive markets – would not have been enough. The best that seemed to be available for Russian aerospace was, by the latter half of the nineties, production of a greatly reduced number of aircraft with Western technology, and the retention of niche markets, such as helicopters, or heavy transport planes, or jet fighters. But the great days were over.

CHAPTER EIGHTEEN

'White Nights'

The curse of the Russian economy is its enormous wealth of energy resources. It is one of the largest of the many paradoxes of the Russian economy, and one of the most debilitating to the new state.

The discovery and exploitation, largely since the last war, of vast gas reserves and great oil fields – added to the huge coalfields of Russia – meant that it was internally profligate with energy, ladling it out to domestic and industrial users for a fraction of its cost. It also meant that, during the Brezhnev years when modernization of the economy was most urgent, the very high revenues from the export of oil and gas supported the expenditure required to maintain superpower reach while taking away the compulsion to use ingenuity and inventiveness within an industrial structure which had been geared to late-nineteenth- and early-twentieth-century modernization.

The reforms set in train by the first Russian government had crashed against the energy complex, but had not dared to tackle it. Yegor Gaidar counted as his largest mistake that he had not liberalized the price of oil and gas in 1992. He had allowed himself to be persuaded that to do so would unleash an unsustainable wave of inflation. The coal miners, whose militancy in the last years of the Gorbachev period had given Boris Yeltsin his greatest boost in the country, were because of their political importance, and their continuing militancy, largely immune from the restructuring the industry needed for most of the Yeltsin period. And the gas industry, the most successful of all Russian energy sectors, had turned itself into an impregnable and potentially fabulously wealthy state within a state.

Russia is rich in oil, richer than it knows. Oil in probably exploitable volumes lies beneath some 40 per cent of its territory, splayed out across the Volga Basin, the Urals range, much of Siberia and the Far North, much of that still unprospected. The Volga–Urals area was being worked extensively in the thirties and was more extensively developed in the fifties. At the same time, the prospectors moved into the West Siberian fields, which were brought on stream through the sixties to produce, by the seventies and eighties, nearly three-quarters of Russia's oil. The ground in the region exudes oil, the cities smell of it and are wholly dependent on it, the men and women who live there have mostly been brought in over the past few decades to extract it. The sheer availability of it, coupled with incessant demands to increase production both for the Soviet market and for exports, meant the wells were worked to death, with a technique known as waterflooding being extensively used to increase short-term output once the free flow of oil had exhausted itself (the technique spoils the output in the long term, because as much water must be pumped as oil). At first it was easy to get (if working in the Siberian cold and in the Siberian mosquito-laden heat can be said to be easy). But in the eighties, the reserves became harder to pump, the cost of exploitation rose, just as the price of oil on the world markets was falling, and as the Gorbachev reforms were failing. New capital investment required per tonne of oil produced doubled between 1970 and 1985, and doubled again between 1985 and 1990. Some of the capital requirements were found – at the cost of diverting funds from the rest of the economy – but the rate of investment fell sharply.

The peak of Soviet oil production was in 1987, with 569 million tonnes. After that year, the fall in production was precipitous, especially in the nineties: Russian production in the mid-nineties was between 280 and 290 million tonnes, with refineries working at 50–60 per cent of capacity and hundreds of idle oil wells. The slump in production could have been reversed: reserves were large, technology was available (though most of it abroad) and the expertise was either in place or capable of being quickly trained. But much more than slump hit Russian oil production: indeed, the fall in output became simply the background to a fundamental reshaping of the politics and structure of the industry, which in turn was of great importance in giving new contours to the Russian state.

In the first years of reform, Russian oil ceased to be a lubricant for the socialist world and became more like a commodity. It had always been so in the capitalist world's markets, but had never been so in either the Comecon countries, where it was essentially an instrument of barter, nor in the Soviet Union itself, where it had been supplied at a fraction of its true cost. On the other hand, its politics, hidden before by the conventions of intra-socialist world trade and by use, became open, unstable and increasingly a matter for international power politics.

Russian oil was marketized, even if it was a very imperfect market for years. Like much in Russian reform, the principle was accepted even as the practice continued to reflect more of the old ways than the new. But that oil should be commodified was an enormous change, for it meant that Moscow's prime economic agent of influence, an agent which had sustained living standards in the Comecon bloc at artificially high levels given the nature of their production and the productivity of their workers, was now based on price and thus – as long as there were alternative sources of supply – carried no political price tag. The East and Central European states, and such dependencies as Cuba and Vietnam, were forced after only a brief pause to pay world prices; so were the Baltic states, none of which joined the Commonwealth of Independent States. The other eleven members of the CIS were for some years sold oil at subsidized prices, or were allowed to rack up large bills, or paid in some kind of kind, or – as they all did at times – went without. Sales to the former Soviet states fell from a little under 120 million tonnes when the Soviet Union died to around 30 million tonnes in the middle of the decade; sales to Central and Eastern Europe, 45 million tonnes in 1990 when Comecon ended, fell to around 21 million tonnes by mid-decade (1993 had been lower, at 18 million). By contrast, exports to capitalist countries, which had dipped from nearly 90 million tonnes in the late eighties to around 33 million tonnes in 1992, rose to 70 million tonnes in mid-decade.

Some among the thousands of oil analysts who had worked in the many institutes of Soviet times (and who left in their thousands in the early nineties, sometimes to get rich, more often not) forecast that by 1995, Russia would be a net importer of oil. It would indeed have been, had it consumed as much oil as it had in 1990–91, when the forecasts were made (as they assumed); but its use also fell greatly, from around 300 million tonnes in 1991 to under 200 million tonnes in 1995. Price had something to do with it. When Russia began independent life, oil and petrol were small fractions of the world oil price; a few years later, they were fluctuating between 35 and 50 per cent, depending on the rate of the rouble against the dollar.

But the price went up, and thus the structural crisis was postponed.

It was perhaps the largest such crisis with which Russia, and even more the other former Soviet states, had to deal. With the rise of the prices came the rise of the Russian oil companies. This was a colossal and – at least initially – largely successful effort by a relatively small group of men to take great wealth for themselves, an effort which understandably engaged much of their attention in the early years to the detriment of their tackling the theory and practice of corporate governance, matters which the international financial institutions and foreign governments sporadically and mostly unavailingly urged them to take up. Deprived of conspicuous (as opposed to inconspicuous) high consumption for decades, the oil barons and their senior retainers wanted to catch up. For some, it seemed, this was enough, and their companies were regarded as mere cash cows for their élite's enrichment. For others self-enrichment went along with efforts to improve their companies' market position, though these efforts were hampered by their sus-piciousness of rivals, of the government and above all of foreigners.

The emergence of the new Russian oil companies was in most respects the antithesis of that of the large, Anglo-American corporations which still dominated the world market. The latter had developed from the brawling, ultra-competitive conditions of domestic prospecting or imperial exploitation at the end of the nineteenth and beginning of the twentieth century, attaining great size and international political clout and only fitfully being brought under legal control after the last war – a period in which they greatly refined their marketing and public relations strategy (and indeed, substantially modified their behaviour) in order to project a sense of themselves as liberally inclined international good citizens. The Soviet industry had been domestic, largely Russian, part of a planned development which, though exploitative both of nature and the native peoples of Siberia, whose territory was where the oil happened to be (especially the Khanty-Mansinsk people of Western Siberia), was not linked to imperial overseas possession nor did it have geopolitical status. Further, since it was a Soviet-organized industry, it was vertically divided – with research, prospecting, equip-ment purchasing, production and supply functionally separated and under the control of different ministries – each of these 'assisted in their work' by the Communist Party and the security services. Both Russian and Western oil engineers liked at times to protest that they were all oil men together, and though a demanding trade and its vicissitudes did unite them, the quite different structures and imperatives also did impart a different psychology, especially to the middle and senior management. For the Westerners, the world had been and to a large degree still was their territory; for the Russians, the world which they had conquered had been the Soviet Union.

But it was these Soviet senior managers who were the main movers in the restructuring of Soviet oil, and who were certainly its beneficiaries. They, like their fellows in other industries, tended to become the *de facto* 'owners' in the late Soviet period. The law on state enterprises legalized this trend; and the state's grip further weakened when the Ministry of Oil and Gas's responsibilities were transferred to the Ros-NefteGaz concern in 1991, then in 1993 became Rosneft (for oil only), the industry being supervised by the Russian Ministry of Fuel and Energy. The tendency since then was for the state to weaken in favour of companies: from 1993, when privatization began, there emerged some dozen companies of various sizes which were, over the course of the next two years, increasingly to consolidate themselves into vertically integrated oil companies with production, refining and distribution arms and in some cases with growing chains of petrol stations. Government's stake in the companies was reduced in the second round of privatization, when the companies – often in auctions which competitors said were rigged to prevent outside participation – bought out large chunks of their own shares at very low prices, and when the large banks, which were co-operating with the government in a scheme under which they loaned the state money in exchange for shares, began to acquire sizeable shares in the oil companies.

The companies which emerged from this process were thus very largely controlled by the managers who had run them in the late Soviet period. The privatization process had simply given employees up to 25 per cent of the non-voting, non-preference shares free; together with the 38 per cent holding the parent oil companies were initially given in their subsidiaries, this meant the companies effectively controlled the majority of shares. Foreigners were restricted to 15 per cent holding; other outsiders were, at least initially, relatively minor. This was workers' control or, as it was quickly to become, multi-millionaires' control.

The Siberian oil lords, in the main, very much disliked outsiders. They had built their industry through iron-hard winters and mosquito-infested summers; had sustained the Soviet Union and its allies from the sixties to the eighties; had suffered in the Gorbachev period and after from a drop in their investment levels just when they needed them most to rise; and had seen their debts rocket and their workers unpaid in the early years of the nineties. By the mid-nineties, they also saw how to control their companies and enrich themselves. For most, the last thing they wanted was either state regulation or foreign participation of the kind that would make them go through internationally accepted audits and examinations. During a comically useless trip organized by the European Union in June of 1994 to see Surgut Oil and Gas, some fifty more or less senior European oil executives were bussed about and around Surgut seeing ageing machinery, leaky wells and failing to have a meeting of minds with a management who reluctantly appeared and when it did, told them it did not want any more from them than their markets.

The exception to this, and the main pointer to Russian oil development, was Lukoil. It was the first of the oil companies to be formed in Russia – in April 1993 – and the first to move to control all of its assets. It took over three production associations in West Siberia with output of around 42 million tonnes in 1995, of which 15 million tonnes (with 5 million tonnes of petroleum products) it exported, making it some $2 billion. Its reserves were a matter of dispute; Lukoil said they were larger than Shell's, and even a conservative estimate showed they would last forty years.

It was run by a man who was forty-three when he took over the company, and who from the first said it was his ambition to join the world class of his trade. Vagit Alekperov was an Azerbaijani from Baku, from the republic and the city whose oil industry had been the Klondyke of the turn of the century, which had made the Rothschilds' fortune and sustained Tsar Nicholas II much as Soviet oil sustained Leonid Brezhnev, which had provided the honing ground for Joseph Stalin's organizational skills among the oil workers, which had been the prize for which the German army had striven in vain to cross the Caucasus and which, after the collapse of the Union, was seeking to revive its fortunes on the back of new underwater finds in the Caspian off Baku. Alekperov took his degree in oil engineering from the Oil and Chemicals Institute, then worked his way up the enterprise ladders in Baku and in Surgut and Kogalym in West Siberia. He was made deputy oil minister in 1990, first deputy oil minister in 1991, and president of the Lukoil 'Concern' before privatization in 1992, taking over the privatized company in 1993. It was a very rapid Soviet rise, and it was a very hard-headed post-Soviet career. Alekperov benefited from a dispro-portionate share of the 5 per cent of stock given to the managers, but was said to process up to 10 per cent himself, a figure which could on some estimates of the worth of Lukoil make him a billionaire, but on which he would make no comment.

Perhaps because of his relative youth or perhaps because he was an Azerbaijani, he appeared to have no qualms about adopting the Western model of oil company structure – hiring McKinsey to tell him how to split the company into upstream and downstream operations, how to change the company's conception of itself from being a technical vehicle into being a financial one and how to attract foreign investors. In August 1995, Arco, the world's eighth-largest oil company, bought $250 million worth of its shares, which was reckoned to give it about 5 per cent of Lukoil – thus valuing it at around $4 billion, much lower than those companies with which it wished to be compared, and a reflection of the market's view of the difficulties of ensuring that oil in the ground (however much there was) would translate into stable profits.

He rose very far very quickly. Charming and self-possessed, he was also more single-minded and focused than most of his colleagues and at least as ruthless. Like theirs, his enterprise was built on the bleak Siberian oil cities where the state had been everything and now the company was. He produced 15 per cent of Russian output, his wells were (he said) more productive and his output was falling less fast than others.

But if Alekperov was the welcoming (relatively) face of post-Soviet oil, it was not enough. Foreign companies put about $2 billion into Russia between the end of 1991 and the mid-nineties – a very small amount, given the size of the country and its reserves. And though they were allowed both to export all of their production (typically, their share of a joint venture) and to repatriate the profits, they probably barely made back their investment. The taxes were variable and heavy, the law unclear, contracts often not justiciable and the conditions harsh. Nearly all the major companies and many medium-to-small came in to 'keep their foot in the door', but few did (in oil company terms) much more than that. The experience of White Nights – a joint venture between Philbro Energy and Varyeganneftegaz in Tyumen region of West Siberia – was an early warning to all. Philbro put in $110 million instead of the originally agreed $40 million, had been slapped with retroactive taxes, had had $2.8 million of its operating funds frozen in the Vneshekonombank when that once blue chip state bank collapsed, had seen pipeline fees double and then its slots on the lines reduced and had come close to bankruptcy in 1993.

Oil was one of the two great exports (gas is the other) and would remain so while the country's industrial base was reassembled. It required capital and modernization, and both had to come from the West in the short term – and the short term was when the fall in production had to be arrested and new investments made. Thus, the logic for the industry and the country pointed to the Lukoil way of doing business; it was not, however, an immediately appealing logic to the oil men.

Gas was different. Indeed, gas became, for Russia, a kind of symbol of its own, post-Soviet character – because of the nature of the corporation which monopolized its production and supply. Gazprom, on some calculations the biggest company in the world, was at once open to new linkages with the West, but hostile to any but the most controlled foreign intervention. It possessed 30 per cent of the world's gas supplies (perhaps more) and was capable of controlling a far-flung empire of production, supply pipelines, exploration sites, research stations – and yet unable to fund the minimum necessary programme of maintenance and refurbishment. It was the state's biggest hard currency earner, and ran up huge debts domestically because customers could not afford to pay for the gas it supplied at (by world standards) absurdly cheap rates. It was a 'private' corporation, run by its managers and wholly under the control of its chief executive, Rem Vyakhirev, but its largest single block of stock, 40 per cent, was in state hands and it was so tied into the state that a former director, Pyotr Rodionov, was made energy minister in late 1996, a former board member, Sergei Dubynin, was made chairman of the Central Bank in the same year, and its former boss, Victor Chernomyrdin, had been prime minister for most of the post-Soviet period.

The Soviet gas industry had been built up after the war – an 800-km pipeline fed into Moscow from Yelshansk in 1946 – but the monster fields were discovered in Western Siberia in the sixties and early seventies, and came on stream in the eighties and nineties. They were enormous: Urengoy, the largest, has 10,000 billion cubic metres of proven reserves; in all, Western Siberia accounts for about 40,000 billion cubic metres of the 50,000 billion cubic metres proven – though Gazprom has said that it reckons there are, ultimately, Russian gas reserves of nearly 212,000 billion cubic metres; that is, 50 per cent more than the world's existing proven reserves.

Gazprom was formed in 1989, out of the Soviet Ministry of Gas, remaining wholly state-owned. In June 1992, it was transferred to the ownership of the Russian state, and made into a joint stock company in November of that year. Starting from 1994, 50 per cent of the stock was divested: 15 per cent went to employees and the inhabitants of the main gas-producing region; the population of the Yamal-Nenets region, where the largest fields are or will be, were given a special tranche of over 5 per cent. The bulk of the stock was sold to domestic investors, none of which appears to have a substantial influence on the company.

Vyakhirev and his senior managers retained total control. Directed to sell off 9 per cent of the stock to foreign investors, it sold, in 1996, a mere 1.15 per cent of the shares in the form of American Depositary Receipts – at four times the price of the domestically traded shares, raising some $429 million. An attempt by a Hong Kong-based company, Regent Pacific, to buy $200 million of shares on the domestic market in 1997 caused a furious reaction by the Gazprom leadership: Vyakhirev described the purchase as a 'threat to national security', and forced the company to back off.

Far from opening out, it closed up. It enjoyed tax breaks which meant that – on World Bank estimates – it paid less than half the tax it should have done, depriving an overstretched budget of at least $1.5 billion. It retained or acquired shipping lines, an airline, farms, food-processing plants, hotels and bottling factories – many of these serving the needs of its 360,000 employees and the 6 million people who are largely dependent on it.

It continued to protect its domestic customers with low-priced gas (for which many did not pay); and it supplied gas to most of the former Soviet republics on a barter basis, or demanded settlement in the form of their gas pipelines and supply depots which had been part of the Soviet-era Gazprom. It needed some $25 billion of capital to develop the reserves in the Yamal peninsula – but it refused to provide the kind of information on its accounts which would attract substantial foreign investment. Its position as a supplier of nearly a quarter of Europe's gas supplies made it one of the most powerful institutions in Russia, but it stimulated fears in the European countries, especially in Germany, that it would not play by the rules.

It became the epitome of the closed Russian company, working through influence and power, rather than through the markets. It had its own 'social' programme of redistribution, and its own 'foreign policy' of pressure on the surrounding states. It successfully rebuffed all efforts by the economic reformers to break it up, or to increase its taxes. It did not so much bargain with the state, as integrate itself into it. By doing so, it preserved its status and its monopoly, but it turned away from a modernization which would make secure Russian gas production deep into the future, while giving substantial benefit to the population as a whole. Though there clearly was growing within it a realization that it would have to raise capital internationally, its post-Soviet leadership could not bring itself to make the changes – and tolerate the loss of absolute control – which such an exercise would bring. It had ceased to be a part of the Soviet state, and had become a Russian fiefdom.

In an area dominated by these two sectors, coal was the very poorest of relations. The miners had been the working-class vanguard of the anti-communist revolution; their industry, and their employment, owed everything to communist economics. They were to discover this irony in the years after the Soviet collapse, for while their conditions were deteriorating precipitously in the last years of Gorbachev's rule, they were to become horrendous in the freedom of Russia for which they had striven.

The pricing structure was the root of the crisis. Coal had been priced very low in Soviet times. Prices were partially freed from 1992 – one of the miners' demands – but were prevented from rising to cost-covering levels because the very low price of the competitive gas meant that major markets would be lost if they went too high. Yet, when combined with the sharply raised railway tariffs, coal did become a relatively expensive fuel. The power stations, which were the industry's biggest customers, often could not pay. Exports were constrained by the huge distances the coal areas were from export ports, thus making the delivered coal relatively high-cost, even though the labour was cheap.

Sometimes the labour was free. The government continued to subsid-ize the industry – it was one of the biggest drains on the public purse – to the tune of $2 billion in the mid-nineties, but the periodic raids on committed expenditure by the Finance Ministry meant that miners were frequently unpaid. In Vorkuta, in the polar north, they went unpaid month after month, as the wildly unprofitable pits were closed. The communities lived on continuously extended credit, barter and hand-outs from the regional government. In the Kuzbass region in Siberia – the largest single coal-producing area – the mines stopped, started and stopped again continually.

Like the other two sectors, coal had lacked even basic investment funds for a decade; in the post-Soviet period, it received hardly any. The state's inability to fund new mines to replace the old pointed – as in the oil and gas sectors – to foreign investment. There was very little investment in coal, and what there was took quick, high profits and got out, or more often suffered large losses. Faced with the impending collapse of their industry, the managers and the government delayed, preferring to beg for subsidies (which were constantly alleged in the press to be a corrupt honeypot for the officials of Rosugul, the state-owned corporation, and for the industry associations).

Production declined hugely – from nearly 400 million tonnes in 1990 to around 250 million tonnes in the middle of the nineties. Most large coal-producing countries suffered similar or larger declines in the eighties and nineties: the UK's industry shrank dramatically, especially after the 1984–85 miners' strike, whose aftermath allowed a much more radical reshaping of an industry protected by the state's fear of confronting the mineworkers. But that and similar restructurings were generally achieved with large attention being paid to the welfare of the mineworkers, to the creation of new jobs, to the salvaging – as far as possible – of the communities in which the miners lived. In Russia, in spite of continuous urging by the World Bank, little of this was done; and the task was more urgent, because the mines were providers of most of the social services, housing and often foodstuffs in the area, and were often failing to provide these goods.

The mineworkers were the most disillusioned of all the Soviet groups by the creation of an independent Russia. They were not as badly off as some – the military conscripts, for example – but they had had much higher hopes, and had contributed largely to the fall of Mikhail

Gorbachev and with him the hope for the preservation of the Soviet Union. In the new era, they had low or no wages, deteriorating living conditions and no hope for their own or – often – their children's futures.

Thus was wealth converted to poverty – by, perversely, being hugged to the breast of Mother Russia, not being opened up to the world for investment and for the exchange of expertise. As ever, there were signs of change by the latter half of the nineties. But by the time it came, the problems had become enormous, the treatment required much more drastic.

CHAPTER NINETEEN

'Money'

Privatization, the fantastic gamble of throwing the state sector into the hands of whoever would prove resourceful and ruthless enough to grasp it, gave the Russian banks and finance houses their early character, and will mark their future for ever. Because of its scale, speed and chaos, the privatization process ensured that finance would become a Darwinian arena in which the protagonists would slug it out to the death of the weakest.

Finance, like privatization, was improvised, patched together, the domain of hard-headed men and women who wanted wealth and power and were prepared to take risks – with their lives as well as their money – to get it. It was, both to foreigners used to the smoothed down and routinized world of Western finance capital and to Russians for whom banks were dingy offices in which savings were deposited, alarming, even repellent – an opaque world of suddenly rich opportunists surrounded by thuggish guards, glimpsed in the few seconds' rush between shiny new office blocks and the waiting limousines, or buttonholing clients in the new bars and restaurants of central Moscow and St Petersburg.

From the beginning, the new financial structures grasped their goal – to make money. They did this as it is done everywhere: by concentrating on investments and opportunities which promised the largest and most secure rewards. To blame the new institutions and companies for this was to deny their essence – or, potentially much worse, to attempt to change them back to something like the forms they previously had. To work well within the Russian economy, they needed a framework within which they could operate with benefit to the society as well as to themselves; it was a point long in being grasped and longer in coming.

The previous forms were no help. The Soviet finance system had been conceived and constructed as a residual, as an accounting exercise, designed to put the necessary funds at the service of industry and trade. It could not have been otherwise, for a party as observant of its ideology as the Soviet Communist Party. The ideological saints, Marx, Engels and Lenin, had demonized finance capital (as had much Russian high culture, and popular belief) and it could have none but a subordinate status. Money followed the plan; credits were automatically allocated for approved production, interest rates played none but a tiny role. The Soviet State Bank (Gosbank), the inheritor of the Russian State Bank (founded only in 1860), delegated specialized funnelling functions to sectoral banks. By the late Soviet period, these were the Agricultural Industry (Agroprom) Bank, the Foreign Trade (Vneshekonom) Bank, the Housing (Zhilsots) Bank, the Industrial and Construction (Promstroi) Bank and the Savings (Speregatalnaya or Sper) Bank.

These were technical centres, with little or no independent powers. Indeed, the State Bank itself had little of that: monetary policy was set by the Party's experts, and by the Finance Ministry. In pursuit of the ideal of the creation of a society in which money was transcended, the monetary authorities created a cashless cash, or units of account which were used to credit the enterprises; cash was used only for payment of wages and consumers' purchases. There was a large branch network – larger, in fact, in terms of banks per inhabitant, than that of Japan in the eighties – but these were overwhelmingly branches of the SperBank, in which the Soviets deposited their savings when they did not keep them below the bed (the rate of return on the latter method of saving was little worse than that of SperBank), and which were as miserable and devoid of any but their stated function – receiving money – as any other service.

There was little interface with capitalist banking – and that largely through VneshtorgBank, and the Central Bank's foreign outposts in London, Paris, Beirut, Luxembourg and Hong Kong, of which London's Moscow Narodny Bank was the oldest and largest. In so far as there was a banking ethic, it was that production must be funded. Accounting – which Lenin had complimented by designating it as the main means of control of the socialist economy – was careful to the point of pernicketiness, with bookkeepers being held personally accountable for mistakes. It was a method of controlling the plan, as well as having the subsidiary function of telling the statisticians what was happening at various stages of the production and distribution process. Its results went to the statistical committee (Goskomstat) and to the ministries controlling this or that enterprise. Enterprise accounts themselves were never published.

The status of money in Soviet society was surrounded by more than its share of the contradictions and hypocrisies which, suppressed, ate away at the successive régimes' ideological hold on the population. Ultimately dispensable according to ideology, money was nevertheless – for much of the Soviet period, especially after the Second World War – a stable unit of value, which was required to buy necessities. It could buy a range of provisions for low prices because of hidden subsidization, but it could not buy desirable objects such as cars except after very long savings periods, or through insider dealing or corruption. As a wider circle of people became more knowledgeable about foreign practice, it became generally accepted that money could buy luxury and was thus very desirable – even as it was still assumed that Soviet goods were either naturally cheap or costless. It mattered, at times greatly, to Soviet managers what credits they received for which projects; but they had no incentives to use what they got economically. The price of what Western managers had been taught to conserve – like energy – was so low as to be residual. The price of labour was also low, and employment numbers were anyway a matter only marginally at the discretion of managers. As so often, the Soviet system in this respect achieved some of its aims: Soviets were in many ways indifferent to or 'irresponsible' about money, since its purchasing potential was limited and the state supplied so much at no or very low apparent cost. This view was aided by the fact that, inevitably, the popular economy depended on barter and favours to gain access to commodities.

Victor Gerashchenko, the former Soviet State Bank chairman, became the dominant figure in the Russian Central Bank. His return to office in 1997 brought back the Soviet concern for production to the centre of economic policy. Gerashchenko was far more concerned by the rapid contraction of industrial production and by the threat of the collapse of the rouble zone within the former Soviet Union than by inflation: he thus made credits easily available both to enterprises (through the commercial banks) and to the new states' central banks. In any case, he did not believe that inflation was created by issuing credits, holding it to be a function of *lack* of money. When challenged, he would emphasize his subordination to the Supreme Soviet; but in fact he was as near independent as any Central Bank chairman of Russia or the Soviet Union has ever been. He acted according to his independently held views.

In Gerashchenko's view, the residual element in the banking equation was the individual customer. As his colleagues abroad stressed their devotion to the least of their account-holders and strove to develop ever more tailored services to woo and keep them, Gerashchenko assisted the Soviet prime minister, Valentin Pavlov, to craft and introduce a confiscatory currency reform in January of 1991. He was to do the same without the knowledge and to the fury of the then finance minister, Boris Fyodorov, in 1993. In both cases there were reasons for it – in the first, to combat organized crime, in the second, to administer a lesson to the high-spending former Soviet states still in the rouble zone. In both cases, the (necessary) secrecy of the operation and the (inevitable) botching of its administration left rouble-holders, especially the poorer and weaker, at best alarmed and grossly inconvenienced and often penalized.

The jousting between Fyodorov and Gerashchenko, which continued during the former's year of office from the beginning of 1993 to the beginning of 1994, was a minor wonder in a field of wonders. Fyodorov, who had greatly wanted the Central Bank job and in being passed over for Gerashchenko by Gaidar never forgave the latter, would rid himself of some of the tensions of office by publicly insulting the Bank chairman – the man with whom he should have been working most closely in the world. At a meeting at the New Economic School in late 1993 at which Fyodorov addressed the cream of the new young Russian economists, he slipped into a rhetorical incantation: 'Who is ruining the Russian currency? Victor Vladimirovich Gerashchenko. Who thinks inflation is caused by too little money? Victor Vladimirovich Gerashchenko. Who is the cause of the high inflation in this country? Victor Vladimirovich Gerashchenko.' Michael Bruno, the incoming economic adviser to the World Bank, who was also taking part in the seminar, thought to himself then that a country in which the finance minister abused the Bank chairman on the record was not one ready for stabilization.

Gerashchenko was as much to blame as any official for the lack of trust in banks and bankers, a view which was to persist and deepen (often with good reason) beyond the Soviet period. It was not, however, a blame he would recognize. Those he had looked to were the Party and the state: when the first disappeared, he sought to shore up the interests of the second, as he had always understood them. Neither stupid nor malign, he was the more dangerous. He retained the support, for most of his period in office, of the Supreme Soviet then of a majority in the parliament, of industrialists glad of the lifelines he threw them, of some foreign banks, who thought he was keeping the place stable (and because, curiously, he favoured at least a limited entry of foreign banks into the Russian market), and of many of the banks which appeared after, or survived, the collapse of the Union.

What emerged after the collapse was a banking system unique in the world. It had a Central Bank which was a cockpit of struggle between those in the cabinet who wanted (or said they wanted) a tighter monetary policy and the chairman, who supported a looser one – the exact opposite of the 'normal' state of affairs. It had Soviet sectoral banks which made no sense except within a socialist environment. It had banks which made no sense except as finance departments of industrial firms. It had banks which made no sense except as laundries for organized crime syndicates. It had banks which made sense, or were trying to. It was from this brew that the Russian banking system was formed.

The Soviet-era banks tried, in their differing ways, to find a place in the new world – though the Agricultural Industry Bank tried least, possibly rationally, since it remained a conduit for credits to agriculture which kept on flowing in spite of the rhetoric of the reformers. They hired the new and expensive talents which handled the arbitrage and other operations which made money, and they lobbied the government for support, along with everyone else. Their problem was that they had portfolios of terrible loans outstanding to some terrible companies. In the Soviet period they could not choose the content of their portfolios and after it they did not, or were used by the Central Banks to keep on passing over the money.

SperBank was in a different position. Though it, too, had betrayed its customers by refusing to index their savings (it was unable to do so), it did have millions of accounts and – initially – little competition from new banks uninterested in and without the facilities to handle individual depositors. A few years after reform began, however, some new banks began to develop both the interest in and the capacity to handle the accounts of the general public: the Stolichny Bank, one of Moscow's most active, was a pioneer. SperBank's monopoly was broken, and though it began an extensive programme of training its staff, sprucing up its branches and launching an advertising campaign on the theme that the state backed its deposits, it began to lose accounts very rapidly as the smart new banks offered higher returns. The measures it took to compete were themselves risky: it began lending to households, without apparently trustworthy collateral or reliable means of enforcing payment.

Among the first of the new commercial banks were the 'finance department' or 'channel' banks – banks set up by large enterprises to act as channels for state funds, and to conduct monetary operations for them. Some were no more than that. But others which were closely linked to the dynamic sectors of the economy – above all energy – had because of the sheer volume of resources behind them a different position, and in some cases early emerged among the leaders. Gazprom, the dominant company, lay behind three major banks – Imperial, Mosbiznesbank and Gazprombank. The first of these had Lukoil as its other major shareholder, and was thus extremely well placed to grow and to command in the energy sector. The 'oil' banks included Tokobank, Neftekhimbank, Zapsibkombank and Yugorsky Bank: the first of these was in the top twenty of the emerging banking houses.

At one time or another, most of the new banks were accused, often by a competitor, of being a 'mafia' bank – owned, that is, by an organized crime group and used as an adjunct to that group's activities, both to finance them and to 'wash' the proceeds of crime. Some of this must be true on a 'stands to reason' basis: crime was so prevalent, regulation so loose, misunderstanding of what constituted criminal and what commercial activity so widespread, that some banks must necessarily be deeply involved in the criminal world and many others must have been at least touched by it. The example of the Italian Banco Lavoro and Banco Ambrosiano are clear parallels. Many 'banks' were no more than money exchanges – as good a way of laundering money as any found.

The counter-argument, used by the leaders of the new banking community, was that the more they grew the less they could afford to be mired in the muck of the Russian underworld. These men lived in a febrile and nervy universe: suddenly rich and very prominent, they were also targets of assassinations and attempted assassinations by those they had slighted or betrayed. In 1994 and 1995, a score of them died at the hands of assassins. They provided themselves with small armies of security guards, which surrounded them at all times; they drove in armoured vehicles, lived in houses surrounded by spotlights and patrolling dogs, eschewed public places in favour of private rooms and other controlled spaces. Their wives and families lived with troops of bodyguards, or abroad. Their claim was that the troops of bodyguards they employed were proof of their honesty: they were forced to live like that, they said, because they were the targets, not the accomplices, of mafia groups who sought to muscle in on their legitimate businesses. When, in 1994, the head of the Most group, Vladimir Gusinsky, was accused in an article in the *Wall Street Journal* by the Harvard Russian economy specialist Marshall Goldman of having mafia connections, he took the paper to court in Britain (where libel laws are toughest), and won.

Whatever their connections, the bankers and their banks did grow rapidly rich. Young for the most part, the new banking élite had usually been either leaders of the Komsomol or *fartsovy*, under-the-counter traders in Soviet times, selling jeans or other forbidden commodities to customers in the street or in doorways. In the *perestroika* days, they had grasped at the first possibilities of legitimate trading, and sold – in the case of Gusinsky – computer equipment or – in the case of Mikhail Friedman, who founded the Alpha group – carpets. A 'second wave' followed a route more recognizable in the West: they left government and joined existing groups. Both Pyotr Aven and Konstantin Kagalovsky, members of the Gang, became bankers, in the Alpha and Menatep groups respectively; Sergei Dubynin, finance minister after Boris Fyodorov, joined Bank Imperial (and sat on the Gazprom board), until he was appointed chairman of the Central Bank at the end of 1995.

The new banks made money from money. The highly inflationary environment of Russia after 1991 made it easy, once you grasped the mechanisms. Easiest of all was to take rouble deposits, change them into dollars, then pay back the depositors in deflated roubles which, even with apparently generous interest, left a substantial gain. The explosion of trading in previously scarce or forbidden foreign commodities was among the most popular activities: trade finance was – if carefully done – a virtual guarantee of profit. When they loaned, they did so at very high rates of interest, and for three or four months at the most. Another purpose of the security armies was to ensure that repayments were made promptly and in full (a large cause of the assassinations was the failure to make such repayments).

Thus they grew and prospered in the early years of Russian capitalism. They of course consumed conspicuously. They bought Mercedes, BMWs, Jaguars and even Rolls Royces. Their headquarters were expensively reconstructed aristocratic mansions, luxuriously revamped Soviet offices or – as they grew richer – specially built and designed contemporary blocks. They lived in or used the *dachas* of former Party bosses.

Yet in fact, they were only partially integrated into the economy. Another sign of their uniqueness was that they lived, very largely, in a separate world from the productive sphere – they grew as it declined, and they were often (wrongly) blamed as one of the causes of its decline. Much of their income came from the crisis of state finances with which the government struggled (or which it exacerbated). It was only when privatization occurred – indeed, when privatization had already pitched the majority of Soviet enterprises into the melting pot of private ownership – that the banks had to face up to the responsibility which awaited them. That was to do for their capitalism what the great houses of London and New York, Frankfurt and Paris, Milan and Tokyo, had done for theirs – provide it with money. For the Russian reformers, in their haste and anxiety to set the clock so that it could not be turned back, had created capitalism without capital.

The banks did not invest because there were so many easier ways of making money – and because they did not know in what to invest, did not know how to make sure their investment was safeguarded and were not invited to invest. As privatization was roaring ahead, they remained in their corner, making money – while the managers of the enterprises remained in theirs, acquiring power and also making money. For the purposes of money-making, it was better and (relatively) safer that way: the notorious compartmentalization of every sector of Russian life exacerbated what was anyway a natural tendency to concentrate on enrichment.

Privatization, very substantially, legitimized the control of the enterprises which the managers already, from the Gorbachev period, possessed. Its achievement was that it also prised open a number of spaces through which outsiders could, with difficulty, squeeze. One of these was that the vouchers with which everyone was issued and which they could exchange for shares were transferable, and thus could be and often were sold, thus allowing voucher investment funds and banks to accrue holdings in the shares they wanted. Further, the shares which the workers acquired in their firms could be and often were sold, again to the investment funds, to banks and to foreign investors. Thus secondary markets in shares and vouchers were created before a primary stock market had properly begun. The voucher investment funds, of which First Voucher, Alfa Capital, Moscow Invest and MMM Invest were the largest, were licensed by the State Property Agency to issue shares for, or buy, vouchers. They then invested the vouchers in shares.

In 1994, the last spurt of voucher privatization reached the largest and richest companies – including Gazprom, the oil companies, the Aftovaz car plant and Norilsk Nikel. When it was complete, the bulk of industry was out of state hands, though the state retained substantial stakes in many oil companies (not Lukoil), in Gazprom, in the main telecommunications and energy utilities, and in some industrial enterprises. However, only a minority of the shares were actually traded – since the bulk of those which did not stay with the state were held by the managers and the workers (effectively under the control of the former).

Within this traded share sector grew the Russian financial markets. It was a narrow ground: only a minority of shares were able to be traded. Only the shares of some 500 of the more than 13,000 enterprises of any size which had been privatized ever came to market, and of these around thirty – mainly in energy, pulp and paper, metals and shipping – were actively traded, becoming the 'blue chip' stocks.

The broking industry formed round these from 1994. It was led by a foreign finance house, CS First Boston, part of the Crédit Suisse group, propelled to Moscow by Hans-Jorg Rudolf, who ran the CSFB operation in London and believed fervently that Russia would be the business frontier of the last part of the twentieth century. The head of the CS First Boston branch in Moscow was Boris Jordan, who became, with the economist Jeff Sachs, the most influential foreigner in Moscow.

He was actually a Russian in origin, born to aristocratic White Russian *émigrés* in New York City in 1967, which meant that he was also among the younger foreigners in Moscow. His fluent Russian, pushiness and vaulting ambition made him a country member of the Gang. He got to know the privatization crowd round Chubais and offered them lots of unpaid and highly knowledgeable advice, a refreshing difference to the non-Russian speaking foreign consultants who swarmed round the agency, hungry for contracts and pushing their own agendas.

Jordan knew that business was done in Russia not just through contacts but through close contacts: hours and days of meetings, talk, drinking, going to the baths or restaurants or clubs. He was half in, half out of the world; he could intuit the way the business world was developing as well as comprehend it. Being half in, he was the man the Russian reformers and officials turned to when they wanted some aid, or something done; being half out, his was the institution foreigners who wanted to make money on the stock market came to.

The foreigners came flooding in in 1994, as it became clear that a bull market (which Jordan did much to talk up) was under way. He – and Chubais, one of whose functions was as chief barker to the government – made a simple point. Russian companies were, at least in some cases, likely to be very valuable. They held huge stocks of oil and gas, or were enormous utilities, or sold precious metals, or had a huge share of the car or other markets. Sure, there were problems with the laws, with crime, with management – this was, indeed, a frontier. But look at the *price*!

The prices which the fledgling stock market valued the 'blue chips' at was, indeed, minuscule by world standards. The entire market capitalization of the Russian equity market in 1993, when the stocks began trading, was less than that of Austria or Turkey, one-fifth of Brazil's, one-fifteenth of Canada's. The oil and gas reserves were valued at fractions of the Western valuations. How could prices fail to rise?

At a time when the emerging market portfolios of the big Western finance houses were looking for some refreshment, this was persuasive, and the market surged, up to a peak of over 1,700 in September 1994 from an opening of 100 in December 1993. Market capitalization of the 200 largest (non-bank) firms went from $17 billion to $43 billion between July and September 1994 alone.

For a while Jordan was close to a monopolist in this, handling around 60–70 per cent of all transactions for foreign clients, working through the burgeoning network of Russian brokers, many of whom dealt from their cars or briefcases. He was challenged by new companies – such as Brunswick, a Swedish–Russian venture, Troika, a US–Russian company and the wholly Russian companies Grant and Zerich. CS First Boston became too restrictive for Jordan, who, with one of his associates, went across town to set up shop for a new house called Renaissance, funded by Oneximbank with other banks, which the Russian financial press christened CS First Boris. The circle was completed when Rudolf, who had sent Jordan to Moscow in the first place and then himself left CSFB, created the United Commercial Bank, a joint venture between his own MC Securities and the Russian Sintez Corporation, a banking and oil group.

The market fell, of course. It was buoyed by foreign investment (which certainly included some of the $60 billion of flight capital estimated to be sitting, legally and illegally, in Western banks); when the foreign investors began to get cold feet, there was no real Russian investment to take their place. It was hurt very badly by Black Tuesday – the day, 11 October 1995, when the rouble fell by almost a quarter following a slide against the dollar in September and an indication from the Central Bank that it could no longer slow its fall. The reaction of the president was to fire Victor Gerashchenko and Sergei Dubynin immediately and Alexander Shokhin, long-serving deputy premier for the economy, later, to humiliate Victor Chernomyrdin by not consulting him about changes to his own cabinet and to institute a secret service investigation of the event on the grounds that financial interests had been working with foreign governments or businesses to undermine Russia – a response which shook the international investors. The devaluation itself helped the exporters and in the longer term appeared to convince the government of the need to bring in a tight budget for 1995 and thus attract really substantial IMF support.

These tight money policies, which the government more or less adhered to through 1995 – an election year, moreover – were the death of the first fine flourish of the banks, and indeed the death of some 500 of the weaker banks in 1994 alone. When, in July 1995, the government introduced a fluctuation corridor for the rouble against the dollar (between 4,300 and 4,900) the banks' hopes that they could speculate on rising inflation in the autumn were crushed: trading volume on the Moscow foreign exchange market was cut to one-third within two weeks.

The blow came as the banks were struggling to cope with a range of tough measures brought in by Tatyana Paramanova, the successor to Gerashchenko at the head of the Central Bank. Paramanova was inevitably dubbed the iron lady, and she was indeed tough. But her appointment, and the subsequent naming of Dubynin as her successor when she resigned after failing to be confirmed by the parliament, was a sign rather of the end of Gerashchenko's 'independence' (he had become less independent towards the end of his rule) and the taking of the bank under the firm control of the government, especially of Chubais.

Paramanova kept interest rates high, raised the banks' reserves requirements to a very high (for most of the banks) level of ECU 5 million; stopped the process of direct allocation for refinancing the commercial banks in favour of auctions of credit at which the Central Bank funds were sold to the highest bidders; and revoked a number of licences following inspections. She attracted the deep dislike of many bankers; it was commonly said, though never proved, that the larger banks bribed deputies to vote against her confirmation, with apparent success.

The crisis burst upon the banks in August 1995, when trading on the rouble–dollar and interbank money markets froze up, the overnight money rate quintupled, and even trading in government bonds declined to a trickle. A number of the larger banks – including the Russian National Credit Bank, one of the top ten – were said to be in danger and were unable to get credit on the interbank market. The government stepped in with a Rbs300 billion seven-day loan, and purchases of up to Rbs1,000 billion from the most fragile banks. Here was a warning in fire. Assuming the government remained determined to keep a grip on money, the banks had nowhere to go but into industry. They simply could not continue to grow, or to survive, on the proceeds of speculation, or in financing trade.

The larger of them had seen this coming for some time. For much of 1995, the heads of the top ten banks had been holding talks with ministers about an audacious idea – that of loaning the government large sums of money in return for the government's shares in the most valuable companies, which were, naturally, the oil giants. After many hesitations on both sides, the government gave the go-ahead for the exchange of obligations, which took place, at the end of 1995, in conditions of chaos and controversy. The large banks were avid for the stakes in companies whose value might appreciate ten, twenty or more times; the government needed the money. But in auctioning the blocks of shares, the government appeared to favour certain banks – notably Menatep and Oneximbank, two of the largest – over banks such as Most, National Credit, Inkombank (the largest of the new banks) and Alfa. The latter stridently alleged insider deals between ministers and bank directors. The two favoured banks secured large shares in companies – including Norilsk Nikel and the big oil producer Yukos – in auctions which they had been allowed to manage themselves. The losing banks clearly had a prima facie point.

The struggle was both typical of the activities in the new, young market and indicative of a new feature. It was typical that energy should be expended over buying stock not for the purposes of raising capital – almost no stock issues had been for that – but for control. The battle for property raged on, four years after the start of radical reform and twice that since the managers had begun to enter into their kingdom. The few exceptions to the rule – a share issue by Red October, the confectionery plant which stands on an island opposite the Kremlin, heavily assisted by USAID and the British Know How Fund – were few indeed.

At the same time, the banks were acquiring capital in very large companies and had to face the choice: would they be real owners, or would they simply hold the shares until they could realize a profit, perhaps by selling them to high-paying foreigners? In a speech made about the time the buying spree was going on, Hans-Jorg Rudolf warned the Russians against the second course, pointing to the example of the South American economies whose shares were controlled from New York. Yet the instincts of the Russian bankers, for all that they genuflected to the need to become corporately responsible, were for the quick profit. Few had shown any appetite for following the entrepreneur Kakha Bendukidze, head of the Nipek Corporation, into the caverns of post-Soviet industry, with the agonies of firing workers, training and motivating management, re-equipping, finding and servicing markets, competing with domestic and foreign companies – all of the manoeuvres which are meant, and masked, by the word 'restructuring'.

As they hesitated, the question remained open: would Russian banks and the financial sector follow the 'Anglo-Saxon' route of arms-length relationships, profit maximization and high yields for shareholders?

Or would it follow the 'German' model of close co-operation and cross-ownership between banks and enterprises; or, probably more to the point, the 'Italian' model, with a tight group of very large corporations sharing ownership and control of a very large field of assets. Chubais had seemed to favour the first, and his deputy, Sergei Vasilyev, was an enthusiast for it. It seemed, however, that the sheer power of the insider would defeat it.

The Russian financial sector had, in a very few years of growth, become a functioning part of the economy. Yet it remained unsure of itself. Daunted, not surprisingly, by the scale of the challenge it faced if it wished to leap from its wealthy, well-stocked little pond into the oceans beyond. It was the next step for the country; none of the individuals knew if they would survive it.

CHAPTER TWENTY

'The most vigorous and progressive section'

In November 1995 a group of Russian businessmen led by Kakha Bendukidze tried to gather support for the indefinite postponement of the parliamentary elections due to take place the following month. It was not a well-mounted piece of public advocacy: the business of launching and running a campaign such as that one was rudimentary in Russia, even where the protagonists were as rich as Bendukidze and his partners.

They were both rich and vulnerable. Bendukidze, a Georgian by birth, had bought large shares in a number of major Soviet-era companies – particularly Uralmash, the heavy engineering company in Ekaterinburg which had been one of the Soviet period's most prized and favoured enterprises. The communists, running strongly ahead of all other parties for election to the Duma, might if they came to power want to unpick the privatization of that, with other, companies; few would weep for a dispossessed Georgian. Oleg Kiselyev, like Bendukidze a former academic, born to a Ukrainian Jewish family, was head of the trading group Mosexpo, which imported jewellery for the *nouveaux riches*. Tugar Kazkhalov, a Tatar, had begun a real estate business. Many Russians thought they were the scum of the earth.

They wanted to safeguard what they had built up, with extraordinary speed, over the past few years. They no longer wore scuffed shoes and ill-cut clothes – they dressed in the best. They had expensive foreign cars and retinues of bodyguards. If married, their wives no longer worked outside of the home. Their sons and daughters would inherit wealth – if their fathers could hold on to it.

There was a certain purity about their belief in capitalism which marked these three men off from their fellows. Kiselyev would cite the passage in Saint Exupéry's *Little Prince* where the hero of the tale asked the all-powerful emperor who could do everything one summer night: 'Command the dawn to break.' 'Very well,' said the emperor, 'only wait until five o'clock.' Capitalism was like the dawn, Kiselyev believed, and businessmen like him were like the emperor: robed in apparent power and wealth, but wholly dependent on their service of the objective laws of the market. Bendukidze came back from a trip to the UK at the end of 1994, full of wonder at his discovery that significant numbers of the British spent their free time going to busy train stations, standing about all day so that they could add to their lists of numbers of trains in their notebooks. Any country, he would say thereafter, in which trainspotting was a hobby was out of any danger of revolution or serious change.

Bendukidze, their leader, thought Russia was a long way from producing a trainspotting movement. He did not think much of the views of his fellow citizens (he had taken Russian citizenship). Why, he would ask, should we be ruled by the people whom those who do nothing and know nothing select to put over us? Why should an electoral timetable, produced in haste, without thought, dictate the fate of a Russia whose civil society was far too fragile to withstand the experiments of extremist politicians? Why should we allow the communists, or the fascists, to rule us once more simply because elections have been decreed? People do not feel as if the fate of the country is in their hands. They are not responsible for their actions. Recognition of this is not an attack on democracy, it is the saviour of it.

They got nowhere: the elections went ahead, and did indeed show that the communists and neo-nationalists (Zhirinovsky-ites) topped the vote for the parties. Their action revealed the fear which underlay the wealth and apparent arrogance of many of the business people, fear that all could be taken from them, but it also revealed a certain confidence, a sense that the ground was strong enough beneath their feet to allow them to campaign publicly against the rising forces of communism and extreme nationalism, and at the same time take a position which was also contrary to received wisdom in the West, and among most of the dwindling band of pro-Westerners in Russia, that democracy would be the saving of Russia.

They had much to protect. They, and thousands like them, had become dollar millionaires (only a poor Russian would not be a rouble millionaire). Yet, though they were too earnest in their protests that they were not interested in being so, it was probably true that money was not the reason for the way they lived their lives. In an extraordinarily short time, the entrepreneurial class of Russia had taken shape and taken root; not deep enough for comfort, it was large enough for warmth. At a conference of entrepreneurs organized by one of their veterans (that is, over five years in business), Ivan Khivelidi, a statement was presented which read: 'Today there are more than 10 million of us [in business] and we represent the force on which the nation will be able to develop into a mighty and prosperous country . . . the most vigorous and progressive section of the Russian middle class is coming back to life.'

Mikhail Gorbachev was their liberator. In seeking to emulate Lenin, but with a human face, he had turned up one of the first Soviet leader's last essays, 'On Co-operation', an attempt by the then ailing dictator to find a way out of the creeping bureaucratization he saw as threatening the revolution by allowing small-scale production and services to be undertaken by groups of workers voluntarily banding together, each with equal status, none being an employee. This conception, product of a specific period and dilemma, was then worked up into a law, promulgated in May 1988. It was, with Lenin's imprimatur on it, nevertheless the legal beginnings of modern Russian capitalism.

Co-operatives were from the beginning crooked, and could not have been otherwise. The view that they would calmly and soberly find niches for themselves in those cracks in the provision of goods and services – especially the latter – was the top-down view of people who had no conception of private business, nor had the imagination to prefigure what conditions the co-operators faced. Making, transporting, servicing and selling things can be relatively tough activities in any society. In the Soviet case, the toughness was compounded by pervasive scarcity, often bad working conditions and infrastructure and frequent alcoholism. In order to rent premises, organize supply chains, find customers, expand staff, hook up to utilities, the co-operators had to resort to bribery. The established state enterprises had their own form – mutual favours. But the co-operators had, at the beginning, nothing to give in the way of favours except money. They thus strengthened the cash basis of Soviet corruption, which had tended to be barter-based. The reputation they acquired – of simply being a way of robbing the state – was deserved. But such a state could not be other than robbed.

The largest contribution which the co-operatives made to capitalism was as the escape tunnels for some of the earliest and most talented entrepreneurs. Bendukidze's partner against elections, Kiselyev, who in 1986 had become deputy head of the Institute of Chemical Physics in the Academy of Sciences – a prestigious post for a 33-year-old – nevertheless quit to begin a co-operative called Alfa-Foto, which took some of his laboratory work into the commercial arena, finding its first large order in supplying the Svet corporation with photo-synthesis plant. Ivan Khivelidi, an Abkhazian whose family had been exiled to Kazakhstan between 1950 and 1957, managed to get permission to live in Moscow and moved restlessly from an oil and gas institute to Moscow University's journalism faculty to working in a sound recording studio to managing a state restaurant – opening his first (restaurant) co-operative as soon as the law was promulgated. He quickly expanded, founding the Delta co-op, which went into construction, farming, legal services and industrial consulting. Gennady Duvanov came to Moscow from Voronezh to work on the construction of stadia and housing for the 1980 Olympics, moved to the monopoly state insurance company Ingostrakh in 1979, then in 1988 created the Microanaliz co-operative as the genesis of a private insurance company. Kiselyev and Khivelidi developed into areas far removed from their original dip into commercial waters. Dubanov stayed in the insurance business, and his company – renamed ASKO – became the major private insurer in Russia.

The other early route was through joint ventures with foreign companies, one which often opened up after a co-operative had been founded with which the foreign partner could make a deal. Kiselyev founded a joint venture called Alfa-Eco with Swiss partners. Others went straight from state enterprise or institute into business with a foreigner. Lev Vainberg, who had been researching automation and statistics at the Moscow Aviation Institute, formed the first joint computing venture, Interquadro, in 1987 and went on to chair the Association of Joint Ventures. Alexander Rubtsov worked for the Trade Ministry trying to find out what Western technologies could be acquired for Soviet use, and how. In 1987, the United Nations International Development Corporation gave the ministry its Feasibility Analysis and Research system for testing the effectiveness of investment projects; he used it to found a consulting joint venture called Vneshconsult with a

Finnish company, Mekk Rastor, then merged that with Ernst and Young to form the basis of the latter's big operation in Moscow. Andrei Stroyev, who held the Red Banner for Labour (1980) for his work on the Olympic stadia and for publications on the roofing of very large buildings, went into partnership with an American company to found the construction company Perestroika while he was head of the Moscow construction division Glavmosinzhstroi. Perestroika, which used low-cost Russian labour and charged rents which rivalled those of Tokyo, was the first into the Moscow property market, and for a time dominated its most lucrative sector, renting offices and flats to the growing foreign community.

These men were the first wave, and they tended to be (not necessarily to remain) ideologues of the free market as well as beneficiaries of it. Khivelidi, typically, uses the vocabulary of a partisan when he describes the early struggles against bureaucrats, the Party and public opinion. He viewed the state officials as an opposing force of vast resourcefulness, whose strength could be worn down only by guerrilla raids and by tight organization. With Artyom Tarasov – one of the very first of the businessmen, whose activities earned him such obloquy that he sat out three years in Britain, returning to Russia in 1995 – he founded in 1988 the Union of United Co-operatives, putting Academician Tikhonov, a doughty fighter (as Khivelidi describes him) for and theorist of the free market, in the post of Union chairman. Kiselyev, who like nearly all leading businessmen acquired a portfolio of charitable causes to which he gave a part of his profits, would nevertheless turn a hard face to any would-be entrepreneur or unsanctioned cause; each must find his own way to wealth, and the hand-out – even from a private hand – merely perpetuated the psychology of demanding or begging from the state which, in these entrepreneurs' minds, had destroyed Russia.

The second wave – which might be dated from 1989, a time of deepening crisis for the state finances, growing caution on the part of Gorbachev but increasing dynamism in the private sector – contained among others the bankers. Many of them came from the state banks, which at that time were dominated by Gosbank, with 'commercial banks' devoted to funnelling credits to particular industrial sectors. Life within these institutions was, for the talented, stifling.

Victor Yakunin, who founded the TokoBank, had a spell in Gosbank's Paris subsidiary and came back a changed man, hating the paper-shuffling nature of his work at Gosbank, then at Promstroibank, where all decisions were taken by Gosplan or the ministries and all that was left to the banks was to carve up the allotted credits among the designated enterprises according to a predetermined plan. Educated at the Moscow Finance Institute, with experience abroad, he sat fulfilling orders in which each step was written down in stupefying detail, and felt his skill and energy seeping out of him.

As both the new co-operatives and companies and the old enterprises began to feel the need for capital and set up banks to channel (mainly state) funds to themselves, they headhunted the state bankers to lead them. Mosbiznesbank, founded by some of the big stores (including GUM) and plants in Moscow and the Urals, tempted Victor Bukato away from the chairmanship of the state-owned Stroibank, which he had served for nearly thirty years. When some thirty businesses in the Moscow suburb of Mytischchi decided to start a bank, they found its president in Anatoly Kashirsky, who was director of the local Stroibank branch.

Some came from outside the banking business. Alexander Smolensky, who came out of the Moscow construction industry and ran a construction co-operative, Moscow III, until 1987, founded Stolichny Bank as a co-operative that same year, concentrating on the booming foreign currency market. Vladimir Gusinsky was trained as a theatrical director after his army service and worked in theatres all over the Soviet Union through the eighties. He founded a co-operative offering consulting and property services in 1988, turning it into a Soviet–American joint venture in 1989, called Most; the foreign capital was withdrawn in 1992, after a bank had been founded in 1991.

These men were mainly in their thirties or forties when they came to their first businesses: they were 'Soviet men' in their education, in their military service, in their first careers. Many had made careers or at least their mark in the Komsomol, like the late Vladimir Listyev, the TV star and entrepreneur, Boris Zosimov, the rock entrepreneur, Yuri Agapov, the head of Credo Bank, and Alexander Rubtsov, the founder of Vneshconsult. Already, however, a new generation of business people was appearing, who were in their early to mid-twenties by the time the Soviet Union collapsed and whose teenage years were spent in the liberalizing atmosphere of Gorbachev's régime. Their formative experience had been one of increasing freedom and possibilities. They came to the business world as something which already existed, which had rules of the game.

Dmitri Elkin, born in 1969, hopped about from institute (where he found no practical guidance for the new life) to job, and landed at the age of nineteen in a bank called Cobra, where he founded a new department assisting customers with their businesses. With a group of colleagues he left Cobra to found another bank called Favorit, whose deputy president he became and where, as he put it, he and the bank grew in professionalism together.

The privatization drive, the rapid growth of the banks and the finance houses, the increasing presence of foreign companies (at least in Moscow and to a lesser extent St Petersburg) created a structure into which the new generation could enter as professionals, rather than adventurers. They no longer came, in the main, from the Academy, as so many of the prime movers had; they either trained for business in one of the new courses which had sprung up since 1992, or, like Elkin, they dismissed the whole business of education and learned on the job. Some – especially those who secured jobs with large foreign companies, or who were sharp enough to learn of and benefit from one of the many training programmes funded by foreign governments – went abroad for training, and some came back again.

By the mid-nineties, half a decade after the fall of communism, the business people of Russia had become a large, powerful group which had made great wealth for many of its members. It had acquired so much power and influence over the new political class that it was difficult to see how it could be substantially threatened – in spite of the nervousness of some of its members before the 1995 parliamentary and 1996 presidential elections. Though they were riven with feuds and though they contributed to the clan-like structure of Russian politics, there had nevertheless emerged the basis for a drawing-together of the new capitalists and bankers who came up in the late eighties with the state managers who had become, in most cases, *de facto* owners of their companies through privatization. In some cases, this coming-together would be on the terms of the old companies, in some cases, of the new – it depended on their relative power. Yet that companies which had not existed and individuals who had been obscurely and mutely obeying orders in research labs and bank departments five or so years before should talk and deal on formally equal terms with the greatest of the 'red' (former Soviet) directors was a measure of the shift which had occurred, and of its speed.

Gazprom was a case – *the* case – of the state giant remaining in control, yet adapting to the new world. It put on its board a number of young politicians and economists identified with the first wave of reform – such as Andrei Vavilov, Sergei Vasiliev and Sergei Dubynin – and richly rewarded them for their service. At the same time, it co-founded, with Lukoil, the Imperial Bank, an increasingly powerful part of the new banking world (as well as, typically, a cockpit for a struggle for power: Gazprom and Lukoil, each with a 35 per cent shareholding, fought over the chairmanship).

First formed as the retailing arm of the Volga car plant (which makes the Lada cars), Logovaz under Boris Berezovsky became the force in the Russian (mainly Moscow) market for foreign cars, especially BMWs, Mercedes and Volvos. It branched out into media ownership, taking 16 per cent of the former state-owned Ostankino first channel (renamed ORT), which gave Berezovsky a deputy chairmanship of a board chaired by President Yeltsin; he picked up the daily *Nezavisimaya Gazeta* when, in 1995, it stopped publication through lack of funding. It opened a bank, United Bank, in Luxembourg and had financial, insurance and real estate subsidiaries in Switzerland. Berezovsky, who survived an assassination attempt in 1995 (though his driver did not) was another apparently unlikely tycoon: he had spent all of his life in academia – though it was in the Institute for Problems of Management of the Academy of Sciences, a sign that Soviet management thinking had, perhaps, not been so removed from the real world as was thought.

The properties of the New Russians became increasingly interlinked. Inkombank, which by the mid-nineties was always at or near the top of the commercial banking league, had 5 per cent of Imperial, which was 55 per cent owned by Lukoil, which in turn was a holding company for a number of different oil, petrochemical and distribution enterprises. Inkombank was part-owned by Mikrodin, an industrial holdings and retail group which had begun life as a co-operative importing computers, which had large shares in the ZIL vehicles and consumer electrics plants, the Perm aviation motors plant and itself owned two relatively small banks, Resurs and RATO. Many of these cross-holdings, and of the industrial holdings the large financial groups had acquired during privatization, seemed to make no commercial sense and probably were not meant to. The scramble for property was too rapid, too ill-informed and too competitive to allow of careful strategizing; that might emerge later.

They were tough, and prided themselves upon it – even if, when asked by journalists or researchers to reflect, they were at pains to display caring sides of themselves. Ivan Ivanov, who founded the joint venture bank Dialog, would reflect that the world he was actively and successfully engaged in creating was one which was sweeping away many of the values he had held dear, such as fellowship, leisurely thoughtfulness, indifference to wealth. Yet at the same time it was a world which must prove its ability to provide a civic and culturally rich society, or it would again fall prey to demands for an equality which, though unnatural, would be preferred to the alienation and poverty the new order had brought to many. He could not find a way out of that conundrum, any more than Western politicians or intellectuals had.

But this was for their leisure moments, and most of them insisted – probably correctly – that they had none. This theme, coupled with a protestation of asceticism, was an habitual part of any interview with them, especially those from the first wave. Educated in Soviet values and often professing a conversion to Orthodoxy, these men were more devoted to what was generally thought to be the Protestant ethic of hard work and delayed gratification than a nineteenth-century Scots banker. They constantly testified to the hard grind of their lives, to their 24-hour dedication to duty, to the devotion they had to building up their companies and to the welfare of their staff. This did not seem, from observation, to be wholly false: the business leaders and their senior associates did work without cease, generally starting later in the morning than their Western and Eastern counterparts but often working to the early hours of the next day. They put no barriers between work and relaxation: constantly surrounded by associates, allies, advisers and bodyguards, the leading businessmen moved and lived in an atmosphere reminiscent more of a court than of a Western executive suite.

They were generally more family-oriented than Westerners – the extended family remained more common than not (both in spite and because of the very high Muscovite divorce rate), the inevitable strains being accommodated for the sake of enhanced child care and as an antidote to the isolation of the old. Wives were frequently partners or advisers in the companies. Few women created companies in an atmosphere which remained heavily dominated by male rituals, but the new sectors, especially the finance sector, gave some educated women positions near the top. However, there was a heavy and quite unembarrassed emphasis on female decorativeness and sexiness: some companies advertised for secretaries '*bez kompleksov*' (without complexes), which meant that if her boss asked her to have sex with him, she was expected to agree. Soviet office practice had been exceptionally badly organized: only the very top officials had anything approaching a private office which worked efficiently; most telephones were direct to the person, with no provision for leaving messages in the event of absence; few secretaries could or would help on enquiries, and cultivated a bored aspect. The exposure of the new business class to the higher office organization began to make its impact in some Moscow offices by the mid-nineties, both warring and co-existing with the immediate post-Soviet tendency to decorate the offices round that of the boss with women as untrained and unmotivated as their Soviet predecessors, but much more glamorous.

The new businessmen were, after all, newly empowered and had discovered, as Henry Kissinger famously had on his translation from Harvard to Washington, that power is a great aphrodisiac. Power, however, was not a means to sexual or any other ends, even financial ones. It was an end in itself, a commodity hotly and often ruthlessly pursued by people who knew that it, buttressed with money, could alone give some sort of security in a society which had, in Soviet times, ensured that only power counted in the end and which, in post-Soviet times, had not provided any civic counterbalance to its use.

Though Russia's was a weakened state power, it was still the inevitable focus of lobbying because the favours it could give – permissions, property rights, exemptions, protection – could be obtained nowhere else. Soviet society had been one of networks of personal connections which, when push came to shove, were mutually exclusive and worked for the benefit of their members. This, too, was a crucial inheritance, one which the new commercial society built on to give a unique aspect to the politics of business, or the business of politics.

Some five years after the collapse of the Soviet Union, the fading hegemony of the Communist Party had been replaced by a complex series of struggles, at different levels, between political, commercial, industrial and regional groupings or clans. Some of these were founded on Soviet bases: the agrarian group, which included the Agrarian Party, the Agriculture Ministry, the deputy prime minister responsible for agriculture and the leaderships of the state and collective farms successfully perpetuated themselves without much structural alteration for years after 1992. The military industrial group, the target of the first and deepest cuts made by the Gaidar Gang in 1992, were much weakened and those plants which could attempted to convert to civilian production.

The industrialists, however, found an ally in Oleg Soskovets, first deputy prime minister from 1993, a man who in the first two years of his power became ever closer to Boris Yeltsin (he substituted for him when, in 1994, the president failed to emerge from his plane on his stopover state visit to Ireland *en route* back from the US). He overreached himself, became too closely identified with the secret service world, and was fired in mid-1996.

The new business people were initially outside of the old structures, and none had much interest in getting close to the agrarians – nor, at first, the communists. The initial orientation of many was to the liberal or democratic parties which, in the first two years of Russian independence, appeared in any case to dominate. Oleg Boiko, of the Olbi Group and National Credit Bank, threw his financial weight behind Russia's Choice, the party Yegor Gaidar formed after he was forced from office in December 1992. Gusinsky's Most group funded Yavlinsky, and also funded other groups, including Gaidar's. Leonid Nevzlin, the number two man in the Menatep group, was neo-liberal in his views, supporting both Gaidar and Yavlinsky, though his chairman, Mikhail Khodorkovsky, was a supporter of a strong, centrist government and a powerful state in partnership with the financial sector. Smolensky of Stolichny was sympathetic to the liberals, and was said to have provided the initial capital for the *Commersant* daily paper, a supporter of the democrats.

Gusinsky was the most prominent in the media, beginning both the *Sevodnya* newspaper and the NTV channel in 1993. He had been strongly linked to what became known as the 'Moscow Party' – that group led by Moscow mayor Yuri Luzhkov, which grew rich on the boom – especially property boom – which Luzhkov both initiated and controlled. However, after the attack on him in 1994, in which members of the presidential guard held some of Gusinsky's own bodyguard for some hours and which drew no apparent protest from Luzhkov, Gusinsky said he was disappointed with the Moscow mayor and no longer as close as he had been. Others saw the power of the media a little later: Berezovsky of Logovaz, a friend for a while of Soskovets and for longer of Chernomyrdin, sat on the O R T board with represent-atives of the other shareholders, which included the National Credit Bank, Mikrodin and Stolichny Bank, each with 5 per cent, and Gazprom and Itar Tass with 3 per cent. Under the directorship of Sergei Blagovolin (from mid-1995) O R T supported the 'president, the government and the party of power' – whatever that happened to be.

The formation of what was to be quite overtly the Party of Power towards the end of 1995 was an attempt to draw together disparate groups, including business people, who were casting this way and that with the decline of influence of liberal politics, especially of Gaidar's Russia's Choice. It succeeded to an extent: Boiko left Gaidar and supported the new party, called 'Nash Dom Rossiya' (Russia Our Home), led by Prime Minister Chernomyrdin. Gazprom, Chernomyr-din's creation, was the largest support, while the Avtovaz car plant came out for Chernomyrdin, too. It showed the limits both of money and the press and media coverage it could buy: the communists and the Zhirinovsky nationalists came first among the parties in December 1995, neither with much support in the media, though both with powerful backers, some from the business élite, who generally preferred to keep their support discreet. Edward Zhuk, a deputy of the Zhirinov-sky party, was the son of the chairman of Neftekhimbank, one of Russia's richest; his father, however, professed political neutrality, claiming that in the early years of existence Russia had failed to develop political parties worth supporting.

That the business people should shift their alliances this way and that was an expected matter. They had the great example of the US to show that money buys influence at the top: the new business élites were hardly less anxious than the US financiers and industrialists to have an ear in their capital, and had much more to lose if they were not heard or supported. However, the political-business world had many fewer rules of the game, and was much less subject to press, parliamentary or any other kind of scrutiny than was the American equivalent. The press, because it was seen as linked with this or that interest, was also not trusted when it did exposés, even where they seemed to have a good deal of truth in them. These relationships, as all others, were both doused in scandal by a relatively unconstrained press and untouched in any serious way by it. It produced an atmosphere in which no discrimination was or could be made between criminality and cutting corners, between the mafia and corporations striving for legitimacy. The odour of the street speculator clung to them, because so many – including foreign commentators and politicians – saw them as spivs and crooks. Ironically, the most prominent among them were striving the most strenuously to rid themselves of both the image and the reality of just such a designation.

Russian business grew up with foreign business in their midst, or as their partners. The joint venture, seen as a way of attracting high technology to Russia – as well as of siphoning Communist Party and state funds out of the country – became a significant vehicle for $2 billion of foreign investment which came into Russia by the end of the Gorbachev period, especially when the initial prohibition on majority foreign ownership was lifted. The benefits were clear enough, and were constantly stressed by those in the Russian government seeking to woo in the foreigners. The market was huge, its labour cheap and well-educated, there was a demand for everything, the government was in support. In fact, foreign business and investment remained a very small part of the whole because of what was at first, in the Gorbachev days, hidden: they were not wanted, even as their products were.

The apparatus which was put into place to try to encourage foreign investment was vast. The US alone had funded – besides the financial institutions, most of which were chasing the private investor – the Overseas Private Investment Corporation, the Export-Import Bank, the Fund for Large Enterprises in Russia, the Russian American Enterprise Fund and the Eurasian Corporation. The Gore–Chernomyrdin Commission, co-chaired by the US vice-president and the Russian premier, had foreign investment as a constant and major item on its agenda, while the Russian Foreign Investment Council, chaired by Chernomyrdin, provided a forum in which the heads of major foreign businesses in Russia could grumble at ministers. Russian embassies tried (on small resources and no experience) to woo foreign business – a hard task, when they were also burdened with providing shelter to the renamed

KGB, whose operatives had been instructed to ferret out commercial secrets.

The foreign business people who were lured by the promise of the Russian market came to understand – if they stayed – that a market had to be created: like the Russians, they had to approach capitalism from its foundations. Indeed, their relatively greater skills in every stage of the production and distribution process meant that they could play a critically important educational role, consciously or not.

They spent years, however, trying to break into the market prize – the energy sector. The experience was doleful; most of their involvement was limited to (in oil industry terms) minor projects: the larger ones were freighted down with problems. The oil companies, most of which were desperately short of the kind of capital required to stop the decline of their production, were nevertheless determined not to admit foreigners into their shrinking archipelagos of wealth. The parliament, sympathetic to their view, were cajoled only with great reluctance into passing legislation which would give a basis to production-sharing, exploitation of reserves and transportation rights. The tax régime was always unfavourable, and the companies tended to work on individual concessions granted after much pleading by the federal government. Energy investment – it was repeated like a mantra in the ministerial reception rooms, in the flashy new hotels in central Moscow and in the chambers of the endless conferences on 'Investment in Russia' which were mounted everywhere – was the key to unlock a flood. But it was also a key to the door which led to a sharing of mineral resources which bitter and recent experience had taught must be guarded from, not shared with, foreigners.

The early relationships were unavoidably unequal. Few foreign business people spoke Russian, and only a few cared to try to learn, even when they stayed for years. They inevitably depended on a few Russians who spoke English and inevitably saw those outside of this circle as incomprehensible and thus mistaken in their views and actions. Some foreigners were shrewd enough to see the social agonies which were being worked through in the minds of most of their interlocutors, partners and employees; some simply saw them as untrustworthy and dishonest. Increasingly, Russian respect for foreign know-how was succeeded by resentment, hurt pride and dislike. Relationships became more difficult – though those which lasted and which overcame the deep problems on both sides were more real. One of the few industrialists to buck the trend – beyond the cigarette companies, who quickly bought over much of the Soviet cigarette industry in a desperate, driven search for a part of the world still devoted to smoking – was the Swede Percy Barnevik, who ran the power engineering and electronics company ABB, a merger of Sweden's ASEA and Switzerland's Brown Boveri in 1988. He acquired, by mid-decade, some seventeen plants in Russia with around 15,000 employees – claiming that the economies gained on low wages and other costs allowed him to cut prices by up to 50 per cent. Barnevik – who cut double the jobs in the US and Western Europe than those he created in Russia and the East – would preach a doctrine of responsible entrepreneurialism, deprecating the 'wait till the dust clears' philosophy of his fellow Westerners, insisting that only their presence could help clear the dust. In the West, especially in Germany and the US, he was seen by union and community leaders as a common downsizer; in the East, as a rare investor, not just in production facilities but in the technical, managerial and linguistic expertise of his workers. He was a sharp illustration of what a move east could mean. But he remained a rarity for a long time.

CHAPTER TWENTY-ONE

'Who cares anyway?'

The misery of many Russians in the face of the changes described in the previous eight chapters is very largely that of a society which has lost its mass character, without acquiring a society in which individuals could co-operate and associate in a different way from the past. A system had been built to protect Russians from the worst hardships: it was wholly designed *for* and not *by* them. It fell into a deep crisis from the late eighties, as its funding was repeatedly slashed back. A system which owed its design to the input of the population was to take a long time to grow, for no one knew how to do it.

The Russian state was famously vastly powerful and at the same time incompetent, hyper-institutionalized yet with mostly creaking, fragile and inefficient institutions with no or little civic support. These constantly required the infusion from the top of some 'campaign' or 'struggle' to give them a temporary energy. The shock of the introduction of a liberal ideology and practice in 1992 to replace the fragmenting official institutions and framework of the socialist state was and remained for years after a loss of both physical security and psychological support. These contributed to further twists downward in already apparent pathologies such as rising mortality, poverty and psychological disturbances. Given the collapse of the central institutions of the Soviet order, there was little the new Russian authorities could do about this. The citizens had to shift for themselves, using what mechanisms they could to buffer themselves against the extremes of loss.

Poverty became both a great problem and a great argument. Estimates for what constituted 'the poor' varied from one by the All Russian Centre for the Study of Public Opinion in 1995 that 88 per cent were in poverty, to a claim by the economist Andrei Ilarionov in 1994 that most people were better off than at any time in the past. The unreliability of statistics, very hard to collect because of the near-invisibility of the

criminal, semi-criminal and much of the private sector, was compounded by the Soviet habit of claiming poverty in order to disguise
private well-being – one of the most pervasive of communist hypocrisies.
When probed, the large majority which regularly told surveys that 'the
country cannot go on like this' turned out to have a majority within
it who believed that 'our family will survive OK'.

Yet the drop in real wages at the very start of reform, an inevitable
prelude but one even more malign to the reformers' future prospects
than Gorbachev's campaign against alcohol, was a most obvious and
deeply felt shock. Like other dying national communisms, the Soviet
one raised wages desperately the nearer to its end it came. State and
industrial wages went up (in December 1990 prices) from around
Rbs300 a month in January 1991 to near Rbs500 a year later. They
rose a little further in the succeeding year, fell back a little in 1993,
remained more or less stable in 1994, then fell again in 1995.

This was bad enough – indeed, it hardly had a peacetime precedent
– but worse was disguised within these averages. The settled order of
the Soviet system of rewards was shaken up, revealing in a cruel, crude
fashion the realities of the relationship the Russian labour market had
to that of the world about it, once the protection was stripped away.
The cities of the Far North, whose peoples had been tempted there by
high wages, early retirement and a promise of homes in the warm
south, turned into milder forms of the prison camps some of them
(like Vorkuta) had been, as the inhabitants lost much of their special
supplements and lost, too, the automatic entitlements to a southern
transfer. Wages, once paid on the nail every fortnight, were delayed
for a month, or months – especially to such formerly high-paid workers
as coal miners, whose product ceased to carry the high value it once
had when it became clear how much it was subsidized and how
expensive it became to transport.

Huge plants began to cut back production – from double to single
shifts, from five- or six-day working to three- or two-day working,
from two days to spasmodic activity with long periods of shutdown.
Production fell in huge gasps; the managements screamed for subsidies
and at first got them – especially after mid-1992, when Victor Gerashchenko at the Central Bank decided to save what he could of Soviet
industry and the government bowed to the demands of the industrial
lobbies. But, though fitful, the squeeze was inexorable: it tightened in

the first part of 1993, then loosened, tightened again in 1994, then loosened, then tightened very sharply in 1995, strengthening the rouble, pushing up interest rates, bearing down on inflation – and decimating the big plants.

Unemployment did not at first reflect this. The official figures in the early years of reform rose from 1 to 4 per cent – with widening regional variations, as the textile mills of Ivanovo became an early victim to market failure, imports and a dwindling of Central Asian cotton supplies, but also with the boards outside the plants in Moscow and Ekaterinburg still proclaiming demands for skilled workers in a wide variety of trades.

The largest explanation for this was that wage flexibility – the Holy Grail of politicians and managers in capitalist countries, whose workers usually fought hard and often successfully to keep real wage levels constant and forced the unemployed to bear the strain – was automatically adopted by the Russian labour collectives. They took wage cuts, wage delays, half pay, unpaid leave, but they kept at least a formally employed status where they could and their managers, where they could, assisted them in doing so.

Not all spent more time with their families. The rapid growth of the service sector, from a little over one-third of GDP to around 50 per cent by 1993, was fuelled in part by many of these same workers using their free time from their formal employment to make money in an informal one. Moscow became the easiest city in the world in which to find a cab, for anyone with a car would be a cabby. Physicists serviced cars and policewomen painted apartments.

But they stayed with their employers as long as they could because the Soviet productive sector had evolved into a kind of industrial feudalism, and they knew that liberation from that serfdom would be impossibly costly. Their flats, holidays, food supplies, sport and cultural facilities, medical care and nurseries, were supplied by at least the bigger plants. A typical couple, which might be an industrial worker and a clerical worker at the same plant, could still see their daughter get a holiday and meals as she had always done, even if there was little or no work for them to do. For a while at least, some of the most famous industrial names prolonged their existence less as productive institutions than as social ones. It was a striking contrast to the finality of the closing of factories in the US and Western Europe in their great depression of the thirties, with workers pacing hopelessly outside of their walls. In

Russia, as often as not, they went in as usual, and got at least some support for their plight from what remained of its social fund, or from the state subsidies paid so that the plant could continue to fulfil the social responsibilities it had inherited. These customs stopped or delayed restructuring, to be sure, but may also have stopped revolts of the entirely and suddenly hopeless.

This state of affairs could not continue. Neither the state nor the enterprise managements could carry on administering the services they had taken on under communism, even at the low levels they had achieved. Belatedly, without adequate preparation, haphazardly, they began to divest themselves of their responsibilities on to the only shoulders which were available – the regional and local administrations. The state continued to pay pensions, from a pension fund; the share of GDP pre-empted by these rose a little, from 6 per cent in 1994 to a forecast 7 per cent in 1999, by which time the fund would not be able to afford to meet the payments without borrowing. Unemployment benefits were funded from the employment fund, which was sporadically unable to meet the low level of payments (and of take-up of payments). A social insurance fund paid for maternity and other benefits. The state, or the nationally organized utilities, subsidized what were in other countries major items of expenditure; gas prices, for instance, did not rise at all through the massive inflation from mid-1993 to March 1995. But, in contrast to its Bolshevik predecessor, which spent much of its first years nationalizing what it could, the new Russian state divested itself of what it could, showering local government and individuals with responsibilities and benefits they were unready to receive and which, at least at first, they resented and undervalued.

Health care was pushed down to the regions and the districts, the overloaded and ailing hospitals and polyclinics thus receiving a new tier of political bosses while being constrained within a falling real income. The view from above is a confusing one: the share of health expenditure within national spending grew, but national spending fell. The number of doctors per 10,000 of the population grew, and so did the number of visits made, at least in the first years after Russian independence; but the system, which had been covertly paid for before because good service (and sometimes simply service) generally depended on the payment of a gift graded according to the quantity and quality of care, became overtly fee-paying.

There is no confusion that health standards declined – a part of a demographic drama which was being played out in Russia from the mid-seventies, but which became both open and worse in the nineties. Birth rates began to fall, until by the nineties they had turned negative. At the same time, infant mortality grew sharply, from 17.4 to 19.9 per 1,000 on official figures which were held by the World Health Organization to understate the issue. Death rates rose, until by the nineties the average Russian man (women were significantly longer-living) died before he was sixty.

Here was a grim paradox. It gave the best kind of rationale for the substantial nostalgia for old times among the middle-aged (in contemporary Russian terms, elderly) male cohort. Under Stalin, even with the mass purges, the forced starvations, the horrors of war, life expectancy rose from forty-four to sixty-two – to go on to sixty-nine in the late fifties, higher than the US at the time (if the figures were genuine). By the mid-seventies, it was turning down; by the mid-nineties, male life expectancy was somewhere between fifty-eight and fifty-nine.

The fault did not seem to lie either with the health service or with hunger: malnutrition was three times less common than obesity, though obesity itself, when caused by an unvarying diet of bread and potatoes, was itself an outcome of poverty, if not of the most hellish kind. The largest explanation appeared to be despair and stress: the commonest cause of death was a heart-attack or stroke, the fastest-rising causes were murder, suicide and alcoholism, all more than doubling in the first years of the nineties. Men were drinking (and smoking) themselves to death; it seemed a reasonable speculation that the sudden promotion of a new (twenty- and thirty-something) generation in politics and the new businesses after a settled period in which plodding to (or plotting for) higher office had been a lifetime affair may have contributed.

The uninhibited *glasnost* of the nineties which replaced the directed version of the mid-eighties shone lights into corners of a health and care system which had been dark for decades. The care of mental patients, orphaned or disabled children, alcoholics and drug addicts, was by developed countries' standards appallingly bad and – when seen close up – immensely saddening. A culture of shame over the disabled or abandoned had merged with the Soviet tendency to disguise what could not be presented as evidence of Soviet success. Thus physically and mentally crippled children, abandoned often without further visits

315

by their parents (who would often be poor), were left in foul wards in their own urine and faeces, the more deeply disturbed wrapped in strait-jackets, many of the more seriously ill dying in their early teens from what amounted to neglect. The numbers – especially of orphans – grew: the Education Ministry claimed in late 1995 that orphans had increased by 250 per cent since 1991, adding that the economic disruption and the privatization and sale of flats by parents who then spent or drank the proceeds and could no longer provide a home were prime causes.

The health crisis, a topic little discussed until the early nineties and then hugely crippled by the lack of good data, pushed those who could afford it into the paying health sector which had colonized the élite hospitals and sanatoria once reserved for the upper party – or, where they could, abroad to Western Europe or the US. These included the senior politicians, usually among the rich of the land, who increasingly turned to foreign doctors for their ailments. Victor Chernomyrdin, the prime minister, took treatment in Germany in 1993. Boris Yeltsin, whose most fulsome praise for the medical profession had been lavished on Spanish doctors who treated him for back injuries after an aircraft accident in Spain, felt himself unable to do the same in spite of frequent illness and two minor heart-attacks; a US offer of medical assistance in 1995 was rejected with the observation that Russian medical science was perfectly capable of coping. In fact, it was not; the president needed a heart bypass, but no facility was properly equipped nor team of doctors properly experienced.

As health was privatized and devolved, so was housing. The Soviet population lived overwhelmingly in flats. Even in the countryside, a village might be dominated by blocks of medium- or high-rise flats, built to economize both on materials and on the provision of services in a close cluster. Much more than in other countries, Soviet housing reflected its eras. There were the solid, mainly post-war Stalin-era blocks, built to last and to withstand extremes of cold. Then, a little further from the centre of the cities or built as a suburb, the jerry-built *khrushchoby* (a coinage uniting 'Khrushchev' and 'slums') of the mid-fifties to the mid-sixties, slapped up as a temporary measure to house the overflowing millions in communal flats and hostels and by the nineties already far beyond their replacement date, visibly crumbling. Then the Brezhnev period splurge of buildings, ringing all cities, tower blocks and great walls of apartments, whole city districts of unrelieved mass housing. These were greatly welcomed by those crushed into communal or in-laws' flats, comfortable and welcoming if well-tended by (inevitably) an efficient matriarch, but badly serviced unless in the élite sector, often miles from the city centre and far from even local shops, as discouraging to the development of community networks as any Western housing projects.

They were, however, cheap, so cheap that when their privatization was first made possible (this after the nomenclatura had already 'privatized' the spacious apartments their jobs had brought them, usually in the last two years of formal communism), many tenants saw no value in paying the nominal sum demanded to buy them. The rentals, after all, were themselves nominal and carried with them the promise, if less and less frequently the reality, of municipal servicing of their common areas.

But the pressure to privatize that which the authorities could no longer maintain grew. The administrations often simply withdrew from servicing entirely. The attraction of owning a saleable asset – in Moscow (depending on location) a highly priced asset – rapidly had an effect. The sale or giveaway of publicly owned flats speeded up: by 1994, over 30 per cent had taken possession of their homes, and this would rise to over 50 per cent by the latter half of the decade. Ownership worked its usual magic: in some of the blocks, tenants banded together to pay for, or to construct a rota to do, the cleaning and maintenance of the common parts. Besides the rapid proliferation of steel doors to keep the marauding out, there could in many blocks be heard the sounds of internal reconstruction and improving, and the hauling-up in the lifts of Italian furniture and Japanese appliances. As this was happening, the municipal authorities began to nudge up the rents on the apartments remaining in public ownership. It pushed more people to take possession, but also bore down hard on the poor, who had grown used to a pattern of spending some 70–80 per cent of their income on food on the assumption that rents and utilities would remain a fraction of the remainder.

Administrations got rid of what they could because they were being swamped by new responsibilities, among which the housing of refugees loomed, in some areas, largest. The Federal Migration Service officially counted some 640,000 refugees and migrants in 1994, but its own officials estimated there were 2 million, and other estimates were double that. They had come, in the late eighties, from Azerbaijan once the fighting began between that state and Armenia (with which Russia had always been much more closely linked); they came from the North Caucasus when the tribes there, especially the Chechens, began to scratch old, anti-Russian sores; they came from Central Asia as intercommunal riots flared and as the local leaderships began to respond increasingly to pressure from the Moslem interest. They crowded into towns nearest to their former homes, such as Krasnodar and Stavropol and Rostov in the Russian south; they came north to Moscow, St Petersburg and Ekaterinburg, living in the other suburbs to evade the attention of the militia demanding resident permits – and helping to fuel the far right and fascist political agitation. They had often lost everything and could often earn nothing, at least not legally.

Russians coped with these huge disasters better than more advanced societies would (at least initially) have done because they had some networks and institutions in place to cushion the hard knocks of the Soviet era. Chief among those was the family, and that tended to mean the women: the network of family and perhaps close friends could be appealed to for support over a long term by those who belonged to it and were unable to help themselves. Second, the legacy of an agricultural society was a recent one, for all the hyperurbanization of the late Soviet period. Many Russians kept a *dacha* within a few hours of their city flat, and many more had or acquired a small plot of land on which they could grow vegetables and keep hens or pigs – plots which provided for a huge proportion of consumption, including 90 per cent of all potatoes. The produce of these plots was eaten, preserved and sold on the roadside or in the markets. The plots acted both as a provider of nourishment and of useful work for the men and women whose employment had been cut down, or cut off.

For those at the bottom, there was state relief (which was badly skewed away from some of the worst cases, and paid to those who did not need it, as in other countries), and there was charity. Charity had not existed in Soviet times – except to other nations or particular struggles, when it was called solidarity. One example was the aid to the British miners during their strike of 1984–85 – a quite involuntary and ironic donation of some £1 million to families who, however hard-pressed, were in a better position probably in the short and certainly in the long term than those donating the cash. It thus began in the nineties under clouds of official and public disapproval: the officials did not like it because it proclaimed failure of the state and put initiative in the hands of unofficial actors; and the public did not like it because the objects of charity were, in many cases, those who had fallen low through their own fault or through some genetic defect which might also have been held to be their own fault or at least was better not displayed.

One of the first of the 'charities' – though it was as much a political and social movement – was Memorial, which got started in 1988 under the patronage of, among others, Andrei Sakharov. Its aim was to identify and support the victims of Stalinist repression. Branches sprang up everywhere, from the Baltics, where memories of campaigns against class enemies which had sliced off some 10 per cent of the Estonian, Latvian and Lithuanian populations were freshest and bitterest, to the former camp colony of Vorkuta, where the chairman of the local Memorial chapter would display on the wall of his office a grisly chart which showed that the camps about the town sketched out the perfect silhouette of a skull. Memorial was less an organization than an outpouring of grief and anger, permitting and encouraging a myriad of local initiatives to uncover mass graves shunned since the thirties or to point the finger at executioners and torturers rewarded by honoured retirement or eulogized deaths.

It was fading by the early nineties, riven by battles between its chapters in republics now becoming independent and the dominant Russian organization, losing activists to politics or business, running out of public interest in or sympathy for exposés and running up against a reviving admiration for the era in which the purges and mass murders happened. But it was by that time a model: in St Petersburg, the Memorial chapter turned itself into an organization called Grazhdansky Kontrol (civil control), which significantly turned its attention not to past suppressors but to present ones – in the form of the city's, and the country's, secret services.

Grazhdansky Kontrol, like Memorial in its declining days, had only a few members, tightly organized round a series of meetings and initiatives and a supply of foreign aid. Other charities were the same: in the same city, a group called Vozvrashchenie (Return), headed by a former drug addict named Dmitri Ostrovsky, worked with addicts who were trying to kick the habit – and did so in premises donated by a military base whose commander was himself a reformed addict – but confined its membership to small groups who were given intense care.

The harshness of the environment, the indifference and at first hostility of the authorities (a situation which tended to improve) and the novelty of the activity enforced a certain defensive huddling in Russian charities. But their growth, by the middle of the decade, appeared strong and was in many areas actively promoted by Orthodox and other clerics who were themselves groping for a role. The Orthodox Church had had a tradition of relief of suffering and of veneration of the poor and simple which it struggled to revive and modernize.

The position of the Russian common man or woman was revealed as an extremely disadvantaged one. In casual meetings in stations or airports or in more formal interviews, Russians would present themselves as people deeply bewildered by and distrustful of the chaos about them. Most of them grasped on to some part of the Soviet tradition. An interview in 1993 with a mother in her seventies and a daughter in her forties revealed a common tenderness for the early fifties – Stalin's last years – when their communal apartment contained fellows whose irritating habits were outweighed by their variety and kindliness, and outside of which the courtyard functioned as playground, social club, educational forum and local disciplinary body. A long talk with a truck driver on a lift from the southern Russian town of Krasnodar to a collective farm showed a man bitterly reflecting on a life which, already more than half over, would have no meaning of any kind: his wife and children had left him, his employment was barely paid, his ability to do more than drive a crumbling truck none. He drank as he drove the bad roads in the night, not from any bravado, but simply to anaesthetize himself. A young teacher in her twenties, teaching history to bored teenagers, said she barely earned enough to cover the cost of her food and transport, and had no hope of leaving her parents' two-room apartment, where she shared a room with her sister's two-year-old child. Her boyfriend had become a drug addict, and had stolen from her.

These expressions of nostalgia or despair were often no worse in material terms than in Soviet times, and similar could be found in the West. That they were told, perhaps exaggerated, to a foreigner was a large step forward. But they were told against a backdrop of loss, not just of income, but of certainty and of a framework. There had been a near-certainty that housing, once provided, was secure, and that a job was for life. That had gone, even if most people kept their apartments and their jobs. There had also been a framework of meaning: the Soviet authorities had given their society an official purpose, and a past of pride as well as a promise of a glorious future. The new Russian rulers could not provide that. The efforts to leap backwards over the Soviet period to the pre-revolutionary Russia were largely empty gestures, since the tsarist period contained little which could arouse loyalty and pride on the part of ordinary people. They were in a world in which a revolution was supposed to have been carried out against communism; yet communism contained their memories, the traditions to which they had once adhered, and some securities. These fragments of the past were clung to by men and women who did not vote communist, as well as those who did. For thinking Russians, the sense of being adrift, of lacking a spiritual or moral anchor, was as painful as greater material hardship.

Those who felt in one way or another dispossessed could not, at least not at first, develop their own defences. The labour movement, in Western states once a response to deprivation and insecurity, constructed by workers for their defence, grew weaker, not stronger, in Yeltsin's Russia.

Pre-revolutionary trade unionism had often been militant and energetic – but it flourished briefly, was often controlled by intellectuals and others more interested in political change than organization, was penetrated by the tsarist secret police and was confined to the small minority of the population which was the pre-1917 industrial proletariat. The Bolshevik conception of unions was as transmission belts, bearing directives from the political leadership to the workers. Once fully under Party control, the unions functioned as a kind of personnel department staffed in their upper reaches by the less talented Party officials – exhorting higher effort, keeping discipline, providing pensions and social security payments, running cultural activities, providing places in children's camps and sanatoria, ensuring supplies for the work collective. In more relaxed times, they did play rather more of a representative role: they were at least there in times of need, and would – many workers were to recall this with nostalgia in the harsh nineties – offer some representation. If their loyalties were always, in the end, upwards to the Party rather than downwards to the workers, they were at least associated with some of the pleasanter aspects of working life.

In the Gorbachev maelstrom, this did not seem to matter. The 'pro-labour' legislation, like the 1987 Enterprise Law, which allowed election of directors, was followed by a rapid appreciation by the most active workers that the time was right to articulate a range of grievances – and to push for higher pay, which did indeed rise sharply in the later Gorbachev years. Workers' clubs, a fragile (as it turned out) alliance of workers and intellectuals, sprang up, and local actions were undertaken, especially by bus and other drivers, for higher pay.

It was the miners' strikes beginning in 1989 which broke the mould. In all of the main fields of the Soviet Union – the Kuzbass and Vorkuta in Russia, the Donbass in Ukraine and Karaganda in Kazakhstan (less so in the last), miners ignored their officials, elected their own leaders and struck in pursuance of a rolling ride of grievances which ranged from the intimately local to the politically utopian. From an early stage, their leaders – who included professional engineers and managers, since the most 'advanced' demands were aimed at the Coal Ministry in Moscow, or at the Party – were in support of many of the themes of *perestroika*: self-management, an end to petty tutelage, a more market-oriented economy. However, they soon went beyond these, and linked to demands for better conditions and higher wages (which were frequently conceded, at least on paper) were much more radical demands, such as the cancellation of article six of the Soviet constitution, the basis of the Communist Party's political dictatorship. An independent miners' union was formed in the Kuzbass in 1990, replacing the evanescent if politically and intellectually brilliant workers' committees which preceded it; deeply suspicious of becoming bureaucratized, it never established a strong national union, being rooted in the pit committees and thus tremendously responsive and tremendously split. Yet many of the demands were won in the short term: wages were raised, some better housing was built, article six was repealed.

Nothing else came close, though later, independent unions with some strength grew to represent the airline pilots and the air traffic controllers. A rash of independent unions, of which the largest was SotsProf and which included Spravedlivost (Justice), Nezavissimost (Independence) and Rabochii (Workers), sprang up in the major cities.

SotsProf was probably numbered in tens of thousands at its peak, but the others never rose above 2,000 members and may have had as few as a hundred. The miners defined working-class protest, delighting the Moscow and St Petersburg intelligentsia, who were passing beyond support of Gorbachev to cluster round Boris Yeltsin. It was the miners whose support for Yeltsin, and demands for the resignation of Gorbachev in 1991, gave the new Russian president his largest boost. It was they whose apparent embrace of the principles of the free market in Russia blessed his choice of economic strategy, just as the Donbass miners' support for Ukrainian independence helped Leonid Kravchuk, once the secretary in charge of ideology in the Ukrainian Communist Party, to ride to power as one of the more unlikely fathers of any nation ever.

The official union leadership could do nothing but grumble – and support the attempted coup against Gorbachev in August 1991. Its failure sealed the fate of Igor Klochkov, the Union Federation's president. Yet Yeltsin's victory, the collapse of the union and the elaboration of the new economic course was – in a limited and meagre way – the saviour of the old unions.

The miners kept their independent unions, which merged with the remnants of the old. The pilots and controllers developed theirs. Both practised sporadic militancy in the period after 1992, with formal success. The new independent unions, in so far as they had any reality, lost most of it. SotsProf was close to the new liberals in government and was favoured by them, but it could not withstand the growing disillusion with their economic policies, and split into factions which warred over policy and property, while others in its ranks went into business.

The old unions spruced themselves up, and stole from their split and disorganized rivals the title of independent – the Federation of Independent Unions of Russia. They claimed to have kept most of their members. In the course of the next few years, they actually did change: old officials retired or were voted out of office, new leaders – who tended to come from the ranks – replaced the white collar apparatchiks who had run the old system. The centralized structure was devolved down to regional and city levels, with some of the SotsProf radicals taking leading positions in especially the Moscow Federation. They corresponded more to the needs of their members – advising them on redundancies and the intricacies of the privatization process. They continued, for a time, to administer social security and kept going some of their sanatoria, though they bit by bit lost or sold off their cultural and social infrastructure.

But they soon found that, in becoming more representative of their members, they reflected their growing weakness. The real revolution was a managerial one: the managers' grab for property and power, their ability to create co-operatives as a vehicle for self-enrichment, to award themselves much higher salaries, to control the privatization process and, in the private businesses, to hire and fire at will, dictated a strategy not of militancy but of rather desperate co-operation. An implicit bargain was struck in the big plants: the managers' strategies were largely tolerated in exchange for a retention of employment – even where, as it usually did, this meant that wages were cut or even unpaid for months on end. This bargain did mean that there were few mass redundancies, of the kind 'downsizing' brought in the capitalist states; instead, workers who could left for the private or other growth sectors, while those who could not tightened their belt and stayed on.

In the parliamentary elections of 1993 and 1995, the unions allied themselves formally with the main managerial parties, and did very badly, winning no seats in the party list in either case. Organized labour had virtually no representation in either house of the parliament, and had no established vehicle for pressure on government. Efforts to create tripartite bargaining forums, begun in 1992 and revived again in 1995–96, came to little. The government gave it no priority and the managers had no need of it. A system of region- or industry-wide agreements was developed – but the rates of pay specified were too low to constitute any meaningful floor, and bargaining was in essence at the plant level with the cards in the managements' hands.

Ownership was amorphous in the first years of reform. The managers and workers usually controlled the privatized companies, but few of the workers received much benefit from their shares if they retained them, and took only a one-time cash or goods benefit if they sold them (usually to the management). As co-owners, they had a stake in the success of the company, but as the macro-economic policy tightened and as the domestic market remained deeply depressed, there was little success possible even for the efficient firms.

The dynamism was in the financial and trading sectors, the money in these and in the oil and gas industries; in neither did the unions have any purchase. Ironically, as the revived Communist Party swept to the top of the party lists in the 1995 Duma, not one of its representatives came from the ranks of organized labour.

The masses did not participate in the convulsions of the new Russia, except as the object of them. Yet they were not – as they were often seen – the simple victims of a mistaken economic experiment. They were rather the victims of distant and recent history, of traditions of both care and indifference which stretched deep into the Russian past, of a collapse so comprehensive that little of what had been solid could stand four-square in the new era. But it was also the case that they were the shocked whom little therapy could – at least immediately – reach: the already wretched rendered desperate, the once supported made precarious.

PART FOUR

Near and Far

'Russia can be either an empire or a democracy, it cannot be both.'

Zbigniew Brzezinski, 1992

CHAPTER TWENTY-TWO

'The Russian state will never be an empire'

Russia has not succeeded in establishing a stable settlement with its neighbours, the former states of the Soviet Union. It is as though they are severed limbs: they are gone, but the nerves still transmit messages of their presence, giving the illusion that they remain under the control of the central nervous system. None but the Baltics dare to move too far out of its orbit, or profess a foreign policy stance which could be interpreted as hostile to Russian interests. All except the Baltics remained tied to Russia economically.

But they had become independent states, and all except Belarus wished to stay that way. They had had in some cases democratic revolutions. In other cases, their communist-era régimes had transformed themselves into nationalist governments, casting about the ruins of their national histories (where they had national histories) to invent a nation state capable of functioning in the late twentieth century. In either case, they needed distance from Russia as much as a co-operation with it — the more since Russian politicians were too apt to interpret co-operation as dependence and then a desire to come back into the Soviet, or imperial, fold. It was a question still open, in the second half of the nineties, whether or not Russia would allow relationships of more than formal independence to unfold.

Nationalism — the term is too general for the very varied series of movements which were set in train in the Soviet Union from the late eighties onwards — was released by the policies of Mikhail Gorbachev. He himself seemed to be a real Soviet man, who did not understand that others defined themselves more particularly. He thought his nation was the Soviet Union. He had Ukrainian ancestors and a part-Ukrainian wife; he lived and climbed the Party ladder in the ethnically heterogeneous North Caucasus. His close allies and aides included at different times a Georgian (Eduard Shevardnadze), a Jew (Tatyana Zaslavskaya) and two Armenians (Abel Aganbegyan and Georgy Shakhnazarov). He appeared to think that because the Soviet nomenclatura contained a diversity of nationalities, the problem had been solved. His predecessors knew better: they *proclaimed* the problem solved, but did not act as if it were. They promoted a policy of 'nativization', which meant that, in each of the union republics and often in the sub-republican territorial divisions, a member of the titular ethos was party leader, or head of the Supreme Soviet, or both and thus held titular power. But a Russian, or at any rate a Slav, was often second secretary and another the head of the KGB. Many of the big enterprise directors were Russians and Ukrainians, as were the generals in charge of the armed forces stationed in the republics. The Party leaders before Gorbachev recognized that, in the game of masks and appearances which was the Union of Soviet Socialist Republics, the mask of native leadership had to be preserved. This was, after all, a free union of sovereign states: appearances had to be kept up so that it could be plausibly argued that it was so.

The plausibility was more for internal consumption than external show. A Ukrainian could, after all, argue that he was a part of a larger entity than the Russian empire and had some grounds for doing so. When the Union collapsed and the argument could no longer be made, the Russian expansionists were greatly hampered by having no vehicle other than the archaic imperialist one through which to express their designs.

An early indication of Gorbachev's insensitivity on the issue was when he ordered, in 1986, that the corrupt Kazakh first party secretary Dinmukhamed Kunaev be forced to retire and be replaced by the Russian Gennady Kolbin. His intention was to demonstrate that the old Brezhnevite settlement – of toleration of corruption and ethnic gerrymandering in return for calm and broad obedience to Party orders – no longer operated. There were norms of communist behaviour: corruption, and promotion of native cadres into posts or university places for which they were not suited except by ethnicity, were outside of these norms. Kolbin – who was a sensitive new Soviet man, and began to learn and speak Kazakh – ran the place as if it were a part of a state whose citizens were equal, and wished to be treated equally. It was akin to abolishing, overnight, all programmes of positive discrimination: Soviet nationality policy was, on both formal and informal levels, positive discrimination none the less so for being unstated.

But the positive discrimination was applied within republics which were a pale shadow of what sovereign nations would have been, had they been truly sovereign and nations. The firm grip on all power by the Central Committee of the Communist Party in Moscow meant that the concerns normally those of states – security, relations with other countries, economic development, national consciousness, popular opinion, national culture and its promotion, relations between the centre and the regions, constitutional forms and reforms – all were absent, fake, or handled by the centre. At best, as in the culturally rebellious republics like the Baltic states and Georgia, they were contested areas where an advance there meant a genuflection here. In Georgia, for example, street protests and the pleadings of Eduard Shevardnadze, the Party secretary, had retained Georgian as a state language; but the Georgians had to cede rights of autonomy to ethnic groups like the Abkhazians and the Ossetians – an autonomy which these groups would use to retain their attachment to Russia, rather than to Georgia, when independence came.

This strong centralism reduced the economic ministries of the republics into book-keeping institutions, the social affairs ministries into flak-catchers, the foreign ministries into surveillance nests and escort agencies for foreign delegations, the national culture into kitsch and the nation itself into an abstract entity whose true content could only be found – if at all – in the past. It also meant, however, that in a range of professions and areas of life – in the military, the security services and the Party itself, in the higher reaches of science, industry and journalism, in diplomacy, foreign trade and academia – the embrace, at least at a formal level, of Soviet norms and mores was necessary. Many more non-Russians than would later admit it did so willingly, consciously and with pride.

These republics were provincial societies kept very deliberately provincial, a state of affairs particularly poignant (and later particularly damaging to its independence) in the state of Ukraine, on a par in size and population with the larger states of Western Europe. Ambitious and clever men and women would want to escape from them to more interesting work than was available in the exclusively republican sectors. Moscow took in many of them, Leningrad others, other cities throughout the Union others again. Russia was a higher culture in at least some things – why do physics at Tartu University in Estonia if you could do it in the Kurchatov Institute in Moscow? Why write for a paper in Tblisi if you could become a correspondent for *Izvestiya*? All who live in a state with a dominant metropolis – the French, say, or the British, especially the non-English British – share some of these calculations. Many of the non-Russians were as contemptuous of the little local customs of their compatriots as the Russians were: Nursultan Nazarbayev, the prime minister of the republic when Kolbin replaced Kunaev, supported the anti-corruption drive of the new first secretary and declared that the riots which followed his appointment were an outburst of destructive nationalism nurtured in the Kunaev era. The national élites had a very large stake in the Soviet Union remaining as it was, more or less.

Below the élites, however, there was ambiguity on nationalism, an ambiguity built into the founding of the Soviet state. Dwelling within territorial boundaries defined by ethnicity, speaking in their own language which may have been slowly losing out but was not suppressed, rooted to the collective farm or the city apartment/job and much less mobile than their capitalist equivalents, the Soviet people were also national peoples – and were obliged to describe themselves as such on their internal passports. The bitterness of the clashes which did occur – in Georgia, between the different ethnic groups, from 1988; in Azerbaijan, between Armenians and Azeris from 1988; in the Osh region of Kirgizia, between Kirgiz and Uzbeks, in 1990; in Moldova between the Romanian Moldovans and the Slavs of Transdnestr from 1991 – was witness to an absence of civil mechanisms for addressing the problems of multinationalism below the formal, declarative level. The Soviet state worked well for the élites; for large numbers of the ordinary people, the influx of Slavs was unwelcome, the imposition of Russian resented and the advantages discounted.

The first stirrings of the nationalism which was to swallow up the Union were manifestations of old hatreds. In the Baltic states, the national movements of the late eighties were fuelled by the Soviet massacres and deportations of the post-war era – the deliberate decapitation of these societies of their bourgeoisie and non-communist intelligentsias, well within living memory. In the Caucasus, it was the awakening of old national grievances – above all those centred round the enclave of Nagorno-Karabakh, populated largely by Armenians but situated within the borders of Azerbaijan and subordinate to the authorities in its capital of Baku. The enmity was between the Armenians and the Azeris, whom the former called Turks – emphasizing the Armenian massacres in the early part of the century at the Turks' hands.

The national hatreds were in some cases amplified by the belief that freedom from the stifling embrace of the Soviet command economy could mean a better material life. In the case of the Baltic states, this was true: their economies had been hammered into a more or less Soviet mould, but retained elements of a more efficient economic culture which consistently put them ahead in the league of wages and living standards. Once released, they took the therapeutic market medicine and, after an initial decline, began to grow strongly – very strongly, in the case of Estonia. By contrast, the economies of Central Asia and of the Transcaucasian states were mostly raised by being part of the Soviet Union, and could not benefit from 'freedom' because their comparative advantages were initially so slight.

The people at the head of the national movements, cautious and 'pro-*perestroika*' at first, increasingly openly nationalist later, were intellectuals who had either eschewed or were incapable of taking the Soviet route upwards. These included the very different figures of the musicologist Vytautas Landsbergis in Lithuania, the philologist Levan Ter-Petrosian in Armenia, the civil rights activist and American literature specialist Zviad Gamsakurdia in Georgia and the Turkic scholar Abulfaz Elchibey in Azerbaijan. All became presidents of their countries. Their professions had at once given them an intellectual status but also provided a shelter for men for whom Party or state service, or regular obeisance to the Party ideology, was against their upbringing or nature or beliefs.

None, however, was in the model of Vaclav Havel or Lech Walesa. With the exception of Zviad Gamsakurdia – who led an authoritarian and disastrously ineffective government when he came to power – none had been prominent dissidents. Landsbergis and Elchibey were awkward and shy. Only Ter-Petrosian developed into a leader of competence and ruthlessness. They were thrown up by events; the events were the surge of national feeling in these republics focused by a strong enmity.

They were also not typical. 'Nationalism' outside of the Baltics and the Caucasus was an ambiguous and variegated series of movements which were in most cases captured and led by men who had been senior in, though not at the summit of, their republican Communist Parties. This was so in the two biggest republics, Russia and Ukraine, throughout Central Asia, with the exception of tiny Kirgizia, and part true in Belarus and Moldova. The anti-communist nationalists in these areas were not strong enough to command the political system at any time. Instead, officials who had passed their lives in the Party apparat, condemning nationalism – in the case of Leonid Kravchuk, first president of an independent Ukraine, this was a large part of the job he held as ideology secretary – turned on a copek and became defenders of the spirit of their nations.

In the last two years of Gorbachev's time in office, as he steadily declined towards the nadir of his power, the 'nationalities question' gradually took over the political space. It caused him first to swing away from the democrats who had been his support to placate the forces in the military, the Communist Party and in the increasingly raucous Supreme Soviet, who saw – rightly – a threat to the Union in his policies. Unable to find a secure base as demand for change took to the streets and his new allies demanded repression, he turned from them to the republican leaders, with Boris Yeltsin at their head. At the government *dacha* at Novo-Ogarevo, outside of Moscow, they thrashed out a Union treaty whose concessions convinced the leaders of the August putsch that its signing had to be stopped if the Union was to be preserved.

The putschists were right that the treaty was a way of disguising the dissolution of the Union. Their mistake was to believe that the rot could be stopped by a mere reassertion of central power. Real force, even terror, was required; but by that time they could not be sure of the military, and they certainly could not be sure of each other.

Yeltsin had come to power by shrewdly counterposing the Russian factor to the Soviet one. He was able – with his democratic allies in and out of the Supreme Soviet – to represent Russia as a victim of empire, a necessary position if it was to avoid the blame for being the prisoner of the nations. In doing so – and the move was, for a while, accepted as genuine by the nationalists elsewhere – he displaced the blame for imperialism to the level of the Party and, above all, to Gorbachev. In a Supreme Soviet session in 1989, Valentin Rasputin, the writer, had proposed that Russia leave the Soviet Union – the implication being that such a move was absurd. By the time Russia declared sovereignty a year later – this meant something short of complete independence – the remark seemed less absurd.

Yeltsin ruthlessly laid bare one of the central contradictions of the Soviet state. Russia was merely, in formal terms, one republic among fifteen – yet it had no Communist Party, no Academy of Sciences, no KGB, no Interior Ministry. The unstated reason was that to create such Russian institutions within a Soviet context would have been to challenge the Soviet counterparts. It was a recognition of the preponderance of Russia and of Russians' dominance of the all-Union bodies; but Yeltsin had a different tale to tell.

At the same time, Russia was poorer on the measure of average income than the Baltics, the Belorussians and most of the Caucasians, while it was much richer in natural wealth. It had not been spared repression and horror; it was as polluted, badly provided for and dismally housed as anywhere else. The story of deprivation was easily enough told; it meant that the moral foundations of the New Russia were in a shared (with the other states) renunciation of an imperial past. Yeltsin declared, boldly and movingly soon after the failed coup of August, 'The Russian state has chosen democracy and freedom, and will never be an empire, nor an older or younger brother. It will be an equal among equals.'

It really did seek to become so. Yeltsin was aware of the problem of the 25 million Russians in the other Union republics from an early stage, and said in March 1991: 'It is impossible to defend people with tanks . . . it is necessary to put our relations with these (former Soviet) republics on a juridical foundation, on the basis of international rights.' It recognized the independence of all of the new states as soon as it was declared, and accredited ambassadors from them in 1991, while the Soviet Union still existed.

But – contrary to the accusations of growing opposition to Yeltsin in the Supreme Soviet – neither he nor the Foreign Ministry were unaware of the need to preserve the former Soviet Union as a unified space, and they became increasingly concerned by the position of the Russians abroad. The first draft of a foreign policy concept, presented to the Supreme Soviet in February 1992, declared that relations with the surrounding states were the 'top priority' of foreign policy and that agreements of differing kinds should be concluded with these states. When the parliamentarians criticized the document as being too vague on the protection to be offered to the Russians abroad, an explanatory note was produced two months later which stressed Russia's responsibility for their human rights – a formula which Yeltsin sharpened in April to an explicit concern for 'the defence of the rights and dignity of all Russians'. In May, the first draft of the Russian military doctrine cited the violation of human rights of Russians in the CIS as a possible source of violent conflict. Though the official direction of foreign policy was strongly towards the West, a parallel track of asserting at least a benign – and potentially less than benign – hegemony over the surrounding states was laid down.

The framework within which relationships should have been developed was that of the Commonwealth of Independent States. The CIS was created not so much in a fit of absent-mindedness as in a euphoria of post-Soviet comradeship during a night-long drinking bout in the Belorussian nature reserve of Beloveskaya Pushcha in December 1991. Hastily convened, it brought together Stanislaus Shushkevich, president of Belarus, Leonid Kravchuk, president of Ukraine, and Boris Yeltsin, president of Russia. All had recently become presidents of their respective (Slav) states, all were of the view that the Union could not last. But they did think there was a need for some kind of federation – though they had no very clear idea of what it would be.

The meeting had no prepared agenda. The driving force at the meeting was Yeltsin, anxious to rid himself of a Gorbachev who, though dependent upon him, was doing what he could to salvage something he could still call a Union, and still rule.

They drank all night, arguing as they did so that they had a right to dissolve the Soviet Union since, juridically, the states of which they were head had created it. They slept in the morning, then signed early the following afternoon. Shushkevich, as the host, had the unpleasant duty of calling Mikhail Gorbachev with the news that they had destroyed the Soviet Union – salting the wound by telling the Soviet president that Yeltsin had talked to George Bush some thirty minutes before, and that Kravchuk had talked to Yevgeny Shaposhnikov, head of the Soviet military. The next day, Gennady Burbulis and Andrei Kozyrev convened a press conference, and told the reporters: 'The Soviet Union does not exist.'

This was hardly premature; indeed, it was belated, since the Union had ceased to operate after the failure of the August putsch and had instead hung in suspended animation, waiting for a deliverance. The winding-up of the Supreme Soviet, the assumption by Russia of most of the functions of the government ministries, the dignified resignation of Gorbachev and the lowering of the Soviet flag – all of these were rituals undergone for form's sake. The Union was dead . . . long live the Commonwealth?

The Commonwealth of Independent States has survived rather than lived. In the first years of its existence, it has grown from the original three members to (in differing degrees of commitment) twelve – the three Baltic states never joined. Yet it could not find a way out of the dilemma at its root: that it was conceived as an instrument of reintegration of a group of states-in-formation, all of which at least initially wished or were forced to develop their own nationhoods, and thus to draw away from each other. If, as most believed, they had been under the tutelage of a Russian imperialism which posed as the Soviet Union, they were in practice highly suspicious of an organization which would inevitably be dominated by Russia.

They did want some things from each other – in some cases, desperately. But many of these were Soviet things, and in post-Soviet times, it became clearer month by month that they could not be had, at least not on the old terms. Russia was revealed as being the milk-cow for the entire edifice, its energy being piped to the other Soviet states at prices sometimes set at 5 per cent of world figures. This continued to happen after the Soviet collapse. Quite soon, Russia was mounting what Boris Fyodorov, who saw what was happening when he took over the Finance Ministry in January 1993, called the largest foreign aid programme in the world. At the same time, Russia realized that, desperate to shore up the fragile national sentiment in the new states, their governments were not beyond a little Russia-bashing in their home capitals.

The first two years of the CIS were largely farcical. As the non-Russian states grew more and more suspicious of Russian intentions, the foreign policy/political establishment in Moscow grew more and more vocally hostile to Yeltsin for his having 'lost' the Soviet Union.

The industrialists, who had the best case, were agonized by the disruption of supply links between plants located all over the former Union. The communists, reviving, clung to the idea of the Union – and were joined by nationalists who conceived the Russian nation as co-terminous with the USSR borders. Even liberals, such as Sergei Stankevich, the deputy mayor of Moscow who became a Yeltsin adviser, and Yevgeny Ambartsumov, the first chairman of the parliament's foreign relations committee, turned on Yeltsin and promoted a renewed sovietism. 'Russia', wrote Ambartsumov in May of 1992, 'is indisputably something greater than the Russian Federation within its present borders. Therefore its geopolitical interests must be seen much more broadly than they have been delineated on today's maps.'

Russia poured its wealth into the mouths which snapped at it. Oil and gas was one part of that stream, the other was the rouble. All of the CIS states continued to use the rouble as their currency: they all received cash roubles from Russia, where the only money printing presses were. They all ran accounts with the Russian Central Bank, which had been Gosbank, and rapidly learned that, if they issued credits to their enterprises, they would see these plants benefit but not suffer from immediate inflationary consequences. In some cases, these sovereign nations were drawing money from the Russian Central bank, while subsidizing commodities to way below the price charged in Russia – that is, assisting their poor with Russian money. The three years of Gamsakurdia's rule in Georgia saw rhetoric used about Russia of the most rabid kind; yet the state continued to function at the low level it did only because it had not been severed from the Soviet support system. On official figures, Russia exported nearly 12 per cent of its GDP to the former Soviet countries in 1992; a generous foreign aid budget of a wealthy, advanced state is generally less than 1 per cent of government spending.

In August 1992, on the anniversary of the 1991 coup, the (private) Council for Foreign and Defence Policy issued a report, 'Strategy for Russia', which remains among the most balanced attempts to define, albeit provisionally, Russian interests. It was unequivocal: Russia should follow a strategy which the authors called 'post-imperial enlightened integration' – which assumes that the former Soviet space is a legitimate sphere of Russian interest and that a network of state bodies regulating inter-CIS trade, economies, transport, energy, finance, education, employment and culture should be created. This view, in harder or softer variations, became the common wisdom among much of the political élite.

Yet the opposite continued to happen. Bit by bit, the aid programme was closed down. It took almost two years – not because the Russians were reluctant to cease to be generous, but because the system in which the republics were entwined was also the Russian system. The subsidies to Ukrainian, Kirgizian or Uzbek plants were means by which Russian suppliers could be paid or Russian customers served. The gas and oil pumped to the near abroad kept the inner core warm, too. Russian industrialists claimed that nearly half of the fall in output in 1992 was attributable to the breakdown of inter-republican trade; the Kazakh government put the figure over 60 per cent. During the Central Bank chairmanship of Victor Gerashchenko, great efforts were made to keep the system as intact as possible: it was the largest stimulus to the guerrilla warfare between the Bank and the Finance Ministry, especially when the latter was occupied by Boris Fyodorov.

Fyodorov combined in his combative, confrontational personality the contradiction of the new Russia. He was personally incredulous at, even affronted by, the notion that Ukraine, Belarus and Kazakhstan could think of themselves as separate countries. Yet he was as affronted by the thought that these countries could draw on the Russian Bank for their expenditure. He continually mocked their efforts to have it both ways, and strove to stop them.

He succeeded. In April 1993, they were stopped from issuing credits – though most continued to use the rouble. In July, Gerashchenko – perhaps trying to embarrass Fyodorov by outstripping him – shocked the CIS by announcing a new issue of banknotes, and that only Russians would be able to change the old for the new. It meant that those continuing to use the rouble would be wholly dependent on Russian monetary policy. In the months that followed, all other states save Belarus and Tajikistan created their own, usually highly unstable, currencies. By 1994, the rouble zone was over, commodities including energy had risen to or closer to world levels and Russia was living with the consequences rather better than the other states.

The withdrawal of Russia from its twin role of milk-cow and industrial planner devastated the economies of the Commonwealth. All suffered huge falls in output, all were forced to liberalize prices, to create currencies and to search for trading alternatives in a chaotic, unplanned and wholly unprepared manner. Even those, like Kirgizia, which introduced their own currency – the som, an ancient currency whose name means catfish in Russian, and thus caused many jokes of the rotting and 'neither one thing nor the other' kind on the part of the Kirgiz Russians – were faced with economic catastrophe. The Kirgiz currency, wholly backed by the IMF, at first seemed solid and reliable, then drifted downwards, then fell steeply. The realities of an economy whose industrial structure was wholly oriented to the Soviet market, whose native population accounted for only a quarter of the industrial labour force but nearly all of the peasantry, whose higher education institutions catered more for the Russians than the Kirgiz and which has had little of the trading or market culture of the neighbouring Central Asian peoples, were too strong to be countered for long by IMF grants.

However it might have been better handled, there was no alternative to the broad movement away from Russia – or, conversely, of Russia's movement away from its surrounding states. The rhetoric was – as often – wholly out of kilter with reality. When the non-Russian republics were most dependent on Russian largesse, they most excoriated Russia. When the taps were turned off, they toned down the insults and sought to present themselves as co-operative and fraternal. But by then it was too late for an artificial reunion: all had been forced to take a hard look at what comparative advantages they had which the world, not just the post-Soviet world, might want. They had come to realize, too, that to be locked into a low-technology, semi-barter economic system would do nothing for their long-term development. But long-term development was a luxury: the short-term problems of the first years took nearly all the resources of states which lacked the most basic government infrastructure.

The economic problems were deepened, often, by continued Russian meddling. From early in 1993 – Yeltsin had torn into the Foreign Ministry at the end of 1992 for pursuing 'too Western' a stance – Russia reversed her policy of neglect, and put the CIS at the centre of her concerns. A treaty of May 1993 committed the member states to increased economic integration. Defence treaties were offered, and concluded. Where funds had simply been disbursed in the old Soviet manner, they were now controlled in the new Russian manner – in part an answer to the new monetary rigour, in part as an instrument of foreign policy, tying subsidies to good behaviour. These approaches, essentially contradictory, were conducted by different arms of the Russian government.

The core group of the CIS changed. It had been, at the beginning, the three Slav states. But the conclusion of the CIS had shocked Nursultan Nazarbayev, the president of Kazakhstan. His country had a huge Slav minority of over 40 per cent of its population on independence, and he could see the danger of a Slav union tearing his country, whose northern, industrial part is largely populated by Russians and Ukrainians, into two pieces. He demanded that the CIS be open to all. And in Alma Aty, weeks after the Beloveskaya Pushcha session, it was.

It became clear immediately that the Slavs were not the core. Ukraine was too large and its population too aroused to nation-building to submit to Russian hegemony, even if that was benign in form and plastered with official statements of respect for national independence. Belarus under Stanislaus Shushkevich – who had come into top-level politics in 1990 from academia, allied to the Belorussian Popular Front and to the ecological movement – was less prickly but had committed itself to neutrality, and thus took no part in defence pacts. The Central Asian states, by contrast, had leaderships which were all (Kirgizia the exception) commanded by men who had been republican first secretaries, and who wanted to work as far as possible within Soviet forms. They, with an Armenia which had quickly remembered its isolated position next to a Turkic world it distrusted and thus its need for Russian protection, formed the group which tended to sign most agreements, push most enthusiastically for greater integration.

Thus grew up what Boris Yeltsin referred to as a 'variable geometry'. This was the most positive of all the developments in Russian foreign policy since the Soviet collapse, because it began to recognize that the surrounding states had different characteristics, interests and relationships with Russia. It was not the end of the Russian habit of seeing them as 'ours' (most vehemently so in the case of the Slav states) or as buffer zones, or as access routes to seaways, but it was the beginning of such a possible outcome.

In this calculation, Ukraine was and is central. No other state matters so much, and no other state has such hard and delicate choices to make about its geopolitical orientation. The modern state is composed of a west which was part of Poland until the last war, a centre which had been in the Russian empire since the late eighteenth century, and eastern and southern provinces which were populated by Russians rather than Ukrainians – the Donbass coal and iron fields were largely built up by Russian labour. Ukrainian nationalism in the nineteenth century was, like many others, a thing of the villages and small towns, where the Ukrainians overwhelmingly lived; the cities, occupied by Russians and Jews, were to a large extent unaware of the growing feeling in the countryside. The experience of the twentieth century was one of almost continuous catastrophe: an effort to establish an independent state aborted, famine and suppression in the late twenties and the thirties, overrun in the war and subjected to a form of occupation which was genocidal to the Jews and merely bestial to the Ukrainians; it was gradually brought back to a Soviet 'normality' in the post-war period, the country's most extended time of peace and relative tranquillity in the twentieth century.

Ukrainian nationalism was of course banned; but it grew in covert and subtle ways. It was encoded in the pride of Ukrainian resistance to the Germans (and after the war, in the east, to the Soviets), in the size of the state, in its possession of a seat at the UN and of a culture which was discreetly promoted within limits; in its rich agriculture and expanding industries. It was a communist-dominated and -tolerated nationalism. But the influence of Ukrainians on the leadership – especially on that of Nikita Khrushchev, an ethnic Russian whose youth and early career had been spent in Ukraine and who became its first secretary – allowed it to take a place in the Soviet 'family', which meant that it could see the Union as more than the Russian empire recovered.

It could never so see any system which forced it to recognize, even tacitly, Russian hegemony. This central fact was the base of the policy followed by Leonid Kravchuk, the first president of independent Ukraine and by his successor (elected June 1994), Leonid Kuchma. They had to follow a crabwise course, which Russians saw as two-faced. Wedged between East and West, a buffer for both, any leader had to juggle and balance with an internal mixture of nationalists in the west, most powerful in the cities of Lviv and Ivano-Frankivsk, and a Russian or part-Russian population in the east, which wanted to maintain close ties with Russia. The tension was at first overlaid by the impression that Ukraine's refusal to undertake any more than cosmetic economic reforms was more 'successful' than the turbulence of Russia's shock therapy. But Kravchuk's steady inability to understand what was happening in his economy soon gave way to a very rapid decline, and the growth of envy that Russia was doing relatively better.

Ukraine was dependent on Russian energy, but could not pay for it. It eventually 'solved' some of that problem by allowing Russian Gazprom to take over many of its gas pipelines and facilities – after a period in 1993–94 when it cut gas supplies running through its territory to Central Europe, or satisfied its own demands from these flows before passing on the rest. It was dependent on Russian orders and on Russian plants for its industry – and though this was a two-way street, the ability of Ukraine to adapt plants which made sense only on a Soviet scale was much less than that of the Russian state, three times larger. It erected customs barriers to stop an outflow of its agricultural produce – a self-defeating measure in a state looking for new trade. It did not privatize until 1994 and was late in creating its own currency.

The result was declines of around 15 per cent in GNP in 1992 and 1993 with inflation reaching 10,000 per cent annually in the latter year, then a collapse in the industrial economy in 1994 brought about by the late adoption of policies aimed at stabilization, but with inflation coming back to single monthly figures. Unemployment had been kept down to 1 per cent: by 1994, though the official figures still showed it low, the actual unemployment – including compulsory unpaid leave – exceeded 40 per cent in many areas. Under Kuchma, stabilization and privatization were deepened, though with backsliding. Inflation dropped to 150 per cent in 1995, trade grew again – with the West, by 40 per cent, some of which was grain, going west for the first time in six decades.

It was able to finesse, but not solve, its outstanding issues with Russia. The largest – that which saw civil war storm warnings hoisted – was the peninsula of Crimea, where an administration under Yuri Menshkov, elected in 1993, pushed for at least closer links to, and implicitly full union with, Russia. The cause was dear to many Russian hearts: the Crimea had been arbitrarily cut away from the Russian Republic in 1954 and given to Ukraine by the new general secretary Nikita Khrushchev, fresh from overlordship of Ukraine. Resented ever since, it was given prominence early in Boris Yeltsin's presidency when his spokesman, Pavel Voshchannov, apparently casually mentioned that its status should be reviewed. The Russian Supreme Soviet assisted in this, claiming in 1993 that Sevastopol, where the Black Sea Fleet was based, was a Russian city and calling for a review of the peninsula's status. Tension continued; both Kiev and Moscow backed away, the latter refusing to encourage Menshkov with real support, the former gradually reducing his powers and, in 1995, abolishing his presidency and Crimea's self-assumed republic status with no serious consequences.

But the fleet itself, round which much of the acrimony between Ukraine and Russia was expressed, and its port of Sevastopol, continued to act as a proxy for the quarrel between the two states – a quarrel whose cause was ultimately the Russian dislike of Ukraine's independence. In 1996 and 1997, as Yeltsin's physical powers declined, the ambitious mayor of Moscow, Yuri Luzhkov, made the status of Sevastopol a central part of his unofficial drive for the presidency. He demanded its return to Russia, and with it that steadily rotting asset, the strategically insignificant Black Sea Fleet. No agreement was possible on what Russia considered a strategic necessity and what Ukraine considered its right by geography.

Ukraine formed a separate military as soon as it declared independence. It obliged all officers to take an oath of loyalty to Ukraine, a hard choice for the Russians but one most complied with, even by the first defence minister, General Konstantin Morozov. It reduced its military to some 500,000 – still too large for its size, but a considerable cut from the 800,000 it inherited. Under US prompting, it concluded an agreement with Russia to send back or decommission all nuclear weapons, tactical and strategic, on its territory – a move which earned it plaudits, and increased Western support from 1993 on, when Western and particularly US perceptions switched from a Russia-first policy to one of encouraging the independence of all former Soviet states, even where the policy angered Russia.

At the end of the first five years, Ukraine and Russia had neither formed the strategic closeness which Leonid Kuchma talked of when he took office, nor had it formed more than the possible basis for a stable and co-operative relationship. Russians still saw no sense in its independence. Even those who granted it was a nation, like the Russian scholar Sergei Averintsev, objected: 'It has never been clear where

Russia ends and Ukraine begins, and so any line of demarcation will cut through living tissue.'

However, Ukrainians, even in the east, increasingly saw no prospect of anything but continued independence. Ukraine, more than Russia, remained enmired in poverty and economic backwardness. But the two states had not fought, nor had ever looked likely to do so; the causes of war between them had been reduced. Russia was too weak to mount a challenge, and too concerned to ensure that the Ukrainian-based nuclear warheads were returned to Russia to destabilize régimes with which it had an agreement for such a return. Once Ukraine has ceased to be a potentially nuclear state, and when Russia is stronger, different calculations may surface. The largest hope is that by such a time, both states will be too strongly attached to peaceful norms of behaviour, to successful state-building and to growing economies to give the other causes of war. In the transition – if transition it is to be – they remained uneasily linked in a Commonwealth which Russia had done much to sustain and Ukraine had done much to keep non-hegemonic.

War came closer in the largely Slav area of Transdnestr, the region on the east of the republic of Moldova which proclaimed independence as early as 1990. Moldova, annexed from Romania by the Soviet Union in 1940, is a state in which ethnic Romanians constitute two-thirds of the population – with Russians, Ukrainians and other small minorities the remainder. The Slavs largely live on the left bank of the River Dnestr. The Transdnestr Slavs proclaimed an independent republic soon after Moldova declared independence – a move which saw the beginnings of civil war in 1993 and peace being restored and maintained by the Russian Fourteenth Army under Alexander Lebed. The Transdnestr government was a Soviet-style one, clinging on to both the rouble and the red flag until Russia stopped issuing its currency. Its negotiations with the Moldovan authorities in Chisinau, the capital, were desultory and got nowhere. Russia chose not to put pressure on the Moldovans but, after signing a treaty with the government in 1993, on Transdnestr, the Fourteenth Army was scaled down and prepared for withdrawal. Transdnestr was left to face realities on its own. Heavily armed, with elections showing strong gains for communist candidates opposed to dialogue with Chisinau, it seemed to have chosen a continued stand-off short of civil war.

Belarus, smallest by far of the Slav troika, was treated differently; very substantially because it treated itself differently. The election to the presidency of Alexander Lukashenko in June 1994 was a triumph for that part of the population – it seemed to be the majority – which found Belarussian independence more of a burden than an opportunity.

National feeling in the area, for centuries in contention between Poland, Lithuania and Russia (and, in the twentieth century, Germany), was very weak. Like Ukrainians, Belorussians were largely peasants, but had no sense of being other than 'the locals' and were taught, if at all, in Russian or in Polish. The nobility and middle classes were generally non-Belorussian. The very brief period of independence in 1918, terminated by the Polish invasion of 1919, was more formal than real. The Orthodox Church kept them close to the Russians, the Catholic to the Poles. The nationalist intelligentsia had groomed itself, in the nineteenth century, in Wilno (Vilnius), in Lithuania.

Their post-Soviet independence was often expressed in terms of a common tragedy – the massacres at Kurapaty Wood, near Minsk, of an estimated (by Belorussian civil rights activists) 300,000 people at the hands of the KGB between 1937 and 1941; the fallout from Chernobyl in 1986, much greater over Belarus than over Ukraine. This foundation of a common purpose in martyrology was true in differing ways of all the post-Soviet states. Indeed, a keenly competitive martyrology grew up among them, played out in part for a Western audience; but in Belarus's case, there seemed little else.

Lukashenko's election put a decisive end to the shuffling on where to stand between Russia and the West. He came to power on, and more surprisingly continued strongly to pursue, a policy of union with Russia – a policy which appeared crowned with success when it was agreed in a ceremony of great pomp in May 1996 then confirmed again with further celebrations a year later. Yet the irony was that the success masked failure: Belarus, a 'failed state' (as the Russian policy-makers would smugly say), could only produce a failed union. It was as if, having been given nationhood, it could not give it up: it had a national government which was strongly authoritarian and anti-reformist, a national currency which was highly inflationary, an industrial structure which remained in state hands and was decaying and a population which had voted for a return of an old system which the dominant partner in the proposed union had given up. Even as a province of Russia – the only terms under which Russia could effectively run any union between them – it was a liability. That it could become a provincial liability remained, certainly, a possibility.

Russian concern with the near abroad was a twofold, and two-stage process. The first was a realization of the importance of ensuring security around its borders and a parallel awakening to the fact that it could no longer claim, except diplomatically, parity with the US. It was a regional power, and had to get its region in order. Second, Yeltsin became aware, by the end of 1992, that the issue of the 25 million Russians abroad, and of the contempt with which Russia was held by some of the CIS member states, was a large issue in Russian politics. Thus the more 'imperial' behaviour of Russia from 1993 was part security, part economic, part nationalist. It was not, however, in any sensible meaning of the word imperialist, and did not look like becoming so in the near future.

It was very constrained. The Russians abroad, the issue which could most easily be whipped up by opponents of Yeltsin – and of Andrei Kozyrev the foreign minister, who was regarded with particular dislike by the opposition for his handling of the former Soviet states – were offered dual citizenship. This was fiercely opposed, most of all by Nazarbayev of Kazakhstan, who pointed out it would create an enormous fifth column within his borders. In November 1993, he went further, choosing a deliberately insulting image: 'Any talk of protecting Russians in Kazakhstan is reminiscent of Hitler's times, who also began with his offer to protect the Germans of Sudetenland.'

In the Baltics, Russia retreated. Its troops were out by 1993, it concluded agreements with all three states by 1994. The very large (comparative to the populations of these tiny city-states) Russian communities in Latvia and Estonia were given no official encouragement to hope for any more than formal Russian citizenship, and if they wished, a return to Russia with no guarantees of employment or a flat. The linguistic hoops through which the Baltic Russians had to pass in order to be able to apply for Estonian or Latvian citizenship were high enough to deter some – but the barrier was psychological rather than linguistic, the renunciation of an assumption that the space contiguous to Russia could be settled by Russians, not occupied by other peoples who demanded citizenship of Russians. The participation of Russians in the profitable openings in the Baltics – the largely illicit metals trading through Estonia, the big banking sector in Latvia – dulled the pain of the loss of nationality. The economic success of, especially, Estonia also helped. Estonians and Latvians remained very wary of the Russians, as well they might: they were among the keenest of the East European states to press for membership of the European Union, and (hopelessly) Nato. They were under no immediate threat. Their best hope, as their leaders knew, was a democratic Russia and the Boris Yeltsin who had supported their independence and expressed solidarity with their struggles in 1991 remaining in power for as long as possible.

In the longer term, the Russians of Estonia and Latvia will pose a continuing problem. Nationalist politics in these states remained strongly anti-Russian, often couched in a reckless rhetoric insulting to its neighbour. The Russians of the Narva province of north-east Estonia are a compact group, who had little representation in national or local government by their own people – indeed, the state laws barred them from such representation. It was not strange that the nationalist movements in the Baltics were as bitterly anti-Russian as they were; it was self-defeating, dangerous to their own security, that they remained so.

Russia's Central Asian underbelly was at once the most secure, because these states remained the most loyal, and the least, because it was to the south where the greatest perceived threats lay. The border which Tajikistan shared with Afghanistan became, explicitly, a Russian border, as Russian soldiers were deployed to stop incursions of the mujahedin to aid the Moslem insurgents in the civil war in the country. Some 25,000 troops were on permanent duty inside the country to support the government of Imamali Rakhmanov, while Russian aid continued to be essential for the country's survival – long after most of the Russian civilians had fled.

Tajikistan was draining for Russia, but the larger issue was to its west, around the Caspian Sea. The area was vastly rich in oil and gas, most untouched: only the fields around Baku in Azerbaijan had been exploited, and even there new fields out to sea promised a second bonanza. There were vast oil and gas fields off the shore of Kazakhstan in the Tengiz and Karachaganak fields, with estimates of recoverable reserves of oil varying between 11 and 30 billion barrels, and of gas reserves at Karachaganak of 1.3 trillion cubic metres plus 2 billion barrels of gas-condensate. These reserves do not put it in the Saudi, or even the Russian, league, but make it potentially three times bigger than the UK and twice as big as Norway in energy production.

The reserves had been seen as the next move in the Soviet energy production strategy, as the Siberian fields began running down. Work had begun in proving the fields in 1979, though at a leisurely pace. In 1987, the US oil company Chevron was permitted to investigate the field. Chevron was then part of a typically grandiose, and typically futile, Soviet–US project called the American Trade Consortium, which was trying to promote US investment in food, medicine and medical equipment. Chevron broke away from the consortium, and began to negotiate with the Kazakh authorities. With the assistance of an international oil operator named John Deuss, who then led the Oman Oil Company, it got a deal with independent Kazakhstan in May 1992 for a 50 per cent stake in the Tengiz field – the other partner being a Kazakh state enterprise called Tengizneftegaz. The prospect was good (prospects always are in such projects): 700,000 barrels a day by 2010, production spanning forty years, producing up to 20 per cent of Chevron's crude oil production, bringing the company into the heart of a developing energy region.

In rough parallel, a consortium of oil companies of which the leader was British Petroleum was crawling towards an agreement to exploit the Baku offshore reserves. The agreement, worth $8 billion and covering some 10 billion recoverable barrels from three fields along the Aspheron Ridge in the Caspian Sea, came after a prolonged period of negotiations in which the consortium was expanded to include Russia's Lukoil with 10 per cent, and small shares taken by Turkish and Saudi companies.

These deals, which saw two oil majors sign very large agreements, were preceded and followed by a barrage of Russian objections which put both in doubt. The Russian Foreign Ministry said it would prohibit any developments in the Caspian on the grounds that it is an inland sea for which the agreement of all littoral states – Azerbaijan, Russia, Kazakhstan, Turkmenistan and Iran – was required before any one could begin developments. It held that Azerbaijan's claim to control its sector of this sea had been established unilaterally, and called for the establishment of a Regional Co-operation Organization to oversee all developments – in short, a Russian veto.

The second, and more effective, mechanism was Russia's control of the routes out. The existing pipeline out from Baku across Azerbaijan, southern Russia to Novorossisk was the subject of an endless wrangle: oil from Tengiz was brought into the pipeline, but the amount was kept very low while the Caspian Pipeline Consortium, which brought together Russia, Chevron, Kazakhstan and the Oman Oil Company, fought out who would gain and pay for what. The Baku group, also embroiled in negotiations with the Russians to get its oil out through Novorossisk, decided in late 1995 to pursue a twin-route strategy: to use the existing Novorossisk pipeline (which was to be upgraded) and to build a new $3 billion line through Azerbaijan and Georgia to the Georgian port of Batumi. Later, a further line would be built, taking the oil through neighbouring Turkey to its Mediterranean port of Ceyhan. The agreements were, at best, fragile, highly dependent on the area's volatile politics.

Russia's pressure on and interference in the Caucasus has been the blackest page of its 'near abroad' policy. Chechnya aside (see chapter 12), it is certain that it played a large role in the coming to power of the ex-KGB general Geydar Aliev in Azerbaijan; and it brought the Georgian government, by then under Eduard Shevardnadze, to its knees through its support for, first, the secessionist region of South Ossetia in the north of Georgia and, second, the equally secessionist region of Abkhazia, to its west. Russian commanders backed the secessionists with weapons, tanks and fighters while denying they were doing it. Russia refused to intervene to end that support until Shevardnadze agreed, in 1994, to the establishment of four Russian military bases. Shevardnadze had succeeded Gamsakurdia early in 1992 in the apparent belief that the West would aid the economic reconstruction of the ruined economy of his country, and would guarantee its integrity. He had, after all, been a close friend of James Baker, the US Secretary of State, and lauded all over the West. But he learned, the hard way, that he was in the Russian sphere of influence.

There was supposed to be no such thing. Successive Western foreign ministers and leaders said so. And indeed, after 1993, there was much more attention paid to the non-Russian republics, much less to the putatively wounded Russian sensibilities. But Georgia, above all, made the matter very clear – clearer than Chechnya, since the latter was, after all, within Russia. When Russian power – or at least a part of it – was determined to achieve a specified goal, it would do so with little regard to world opinion.

In effect, the West also applied variable geometry to the former Soviet Union. The Baltics were signposted as being untouchable by the Russians; Ukraine was only a little less so. Moldova was not seen as a problem, Belarus could go to hell in its Soviet handcart and the Caucasian and Central Asian states were important for their energy, but too far away and of too little strategic value for effective assistance to be given in any time of need.

In an 'Open Letter to an American Friend', Vitaly Tretyakov, the editor of the *Nezavisimaya Gazeta*, wrote (to Professor Graham Allison, of Harvard's Kennedy School): 'Russia stands before a dilemma: either it survives, and is restored within the borders of the former Soviet Union, or it disintegrates once and for all. There is no third choice here. And no Russian politician has any other choice, be he a super-democrat, an ultranationalist or a mediocre communist, or whoever should end up in the Kremlin.'

Tretyakov had long believed the dismemberment of the Union was a tragedy, not just for Russia, but for the Soviet peoples and even – since he was a sincere democrat – for democracy. He was not alone in that view; but he and all who thought like him stood before a dilemma. The survival of Russia, as he defined it, was predicated on the extinction of the national rights of the surrounding states. And as the years succeeded each other, they appeared increasingly attached to them.

And Russia became less and less able to do anything about that attachment. Two years after their first report calling for increased integration, the Council for Foreign and Defence Policy issued a follow-up. This time, it thought that even limited attempts to increase integration would be bad for Russia's economy and its polity. The country, it argued, 'must only be for such integration as is profitable for it. The right to a policy of "enlightened selfishness" towards our neighbours should also be recognized.'

Yet the geopolitical facts remained. If the new states failed to make transitions to growing economies and efficient, if not necessarily demo-cratic, governments, they were open to influence by Russia at best, dismemberment by it at worst. If Russia itself failed, they were in line of fire if it, once again, compensated for its own inadequacies by grasping after its neighbours.

CHAPTER TWENTY-THREE

'A state which only says yes'

In losing an empire and in its struggles to find a role, Russia tried a series of foreign policy postures, as one rich and impatient might try on and discard a pile of new clothes. These postures reflected the philosophies and strategies of the competing élites and groups active and around, or aspiring to, the leadership. Elements of them all were incorporated in active policy, as the Yeltsin administration sought to balance its needs with its increasing limitations.

The course dictated was inexorably a shrinking of the global role, the ruins of which Russia had inherited from the Soviet Union. The inflated rhetoric of the first months of Yeltsin's waxing power was replaced by disappointment, cynicism, a revival of some of the old Soviet methods and – by the end of his office – a weary, bitter resignation to powerlessness, ground into the national psyche in the mud and blood of Chechnya, inside the official borders of the Russian Federation itself.

Russia was faced, in this as in other areas, with a task at once impossible and necessary: to define a role for a suddenly reduced state which had previously acted as an imperial power. 'No such thing as Russia exists,' said Sergei Witte, the tsarist finance minister whose 1890s state-driven reforms laid the basis for the pre-revolutionary economic growth. 'There is only the Russian empire.' When there was no longer the Russian–Soviet empire, there was an empty space which demanded to be filled with a 'foreign policy concept' – while Russia felt the withered tentacles of its former power snaking back to its frontiers, as the states around it which had been held within the Union entered into their own convulsions of self-definition and as the powerful states to its west, east and south were themselves striving to discover whether history had ended, or had merely put a surprisingly sudden stop to one of its chapters.

The western states had been spoiled by Gorbachev. Since his first fateful series of decisions to modernize the Soviet society and economy through adopting quasi-democratic practices and quasi-market mechanisms, he increasingly gave away more and more of the positions on which the Soviet Union had rested. The marriage of ideology to power which was the basic wiring of Soviet foreign policy from Stalin to Chernenko had produced such huge successes after the Second World War that it was resistant to examination. However, the sober analysis of Yuri Andropov, Gorbachev's patron, in the early eighties showed a world power whose allies were ailing economically, expensive to maintain and occasionally mutinous, whose aims to destabilize Western nuclear strategy had failed and whose economy could no longer support the reach of its foreign patronage and its military force.

Gorbachev wanted to lift the pressure on the Soviet economy by decelerating the arms race. In particular, he wanted to be able to avoid the cost of countering the 'Star Wars' missile defence system which President Reagan believed was the technology to end all wars, and was prepared to fund until it worked. With Eduard Shevardnadze, the Georgian Party first secretary whom he brought in to run the Foreign Ministry, he developed 'new thinking' in foreign policy, a series of concepts which were peddled to an astonished and at first distrustful world and which, it turned out, meant to a significant extent what they said.

New foreign policy thinking held that the use of military power was outdated; that the efficiency of the economy and the responsiveness of the political system were the real tests of a great power; that co-operation and multilateralism had to be pursued everywhere, including through membership of international institutions previously shunned by the USSR; that the main industrialized countries, led by the Group of Seven (G7) were the main actors in the world, and the Soviet Union could make an accommodation with that group while at the same time distancing itself from the poor and failing régimes which passed for its friends, and that the superpower stand-off was not as immediately threatening as terrorism, religious extremism, the explosions of nationalism, weapons proliferation and environmental accidents. There were, the doctrine held, real fears which united mankind; to ascribe imperialism and militarism to one side and peace and socialism to the other was divisive, even wrong. These fears could and should be tackled jointly.

As early as 1986, Shevardnadze proclaimed in a speech to the UN that 'freedom of choice is the lynchpin of the (new) system'. In his report to the Twenty-seventh Party Congress in February of that year, Gorbachev foreshadowed his later insistence on the 'priority of human values'. The Leninist injunction and Stalinist practice of furthering proletarian power through subversion was explicitly renounced. Describing his thinking and action at the time, Shevardnadze wrote in his memoirs that 'in an atmosphere where the world is divided into blocs by the type of [countries'] socio-political systems, how can we recognize the world as it is, interconnected and integral, where the sheer necessity for human survival breaks down the walls of ideological hostility?'

The real-world correlatives of the rhetoric also began in 1986, with an agreement for on-site inspection of military facilities. In 1987, the Soviet Union ended its superiority of intermediate-range nuclear missiles. Soviet forces were taken out of Afghanistan in 1989. By 1990, the Conventional Forces in Europe treaty began the great withdrawing roar of Soviet air and ground forces from Central Europe, as the gathering pace of reform in these states met with apparently calm acquiescence and Germany was allowed to reunite. And in 1991, Gorbachev supported both the use of economic sanctions and then the use of force against its former ally – and debtor – Iraq.

The West was slow to trust Gorbachev and Shevardnadze but lavish with their praise when it did. They had transformed the climate about their country by the time they resigned their offices. They secured the friendship – though not the financial assistance – of the main Western powers; assuaged the hostility of Japan, even if the main issue of contention between the two countries, the (continuing) possession of the Kurile Islands, or Northern Territories, by the USSR/Russia, was not addressed; 'ended the past and opened the future' (as Deng Xiaoping put it) in relations with China; and readied their country for entry into the main international institutions.

The *élan* of Gorbachev's personal diplomacy, certainly enhanced by the contrast with his mastodon predecessors and by his elegant, if hectoring, wife Raisa, was still remarkable and guaranteed him world renown long after his leadership ended. He was the first flesh-pressing, charming, publicly engaged and socially poised leader of the Soviet Union, one whose performance captivated audiences about the world.

A transformed international order was by far the most positive of his legacies: he handed on to Yeltsin a world no longer automatically distrustful of the Russians, one already willing in principle to be bound in to the process of reform.

That, however, could only be a start. The collapse of the Union meant that a new entity – Russia – had to begin a process of building a nation. Until it defined what that was, a foreign policy based upon it was necessarily an *ad hoc* affair. Georgy Kunadze, a deputy foreign minister who had – like many others of the reformers come to government – passed his adult life in an academic institute (IMEMO, in his case) expressed the dilemma early in 1992: 'We [Soviets] long ignored the very concept of national interests, regarding it as a bourgeois category. Today, when we have finally put it at the basis of our foreign policy, we see how hard it is to define national interests, to specify their components.'

Andrei Kozyrev, appointed foreign minister after Yeltsin's presidential victory in mid-1991, was the man on whom the burden of this fell. Born into a diplomatic family – in Brussels – two years before Stalin's death, he was forty when appointed and was a middle-ranking official, head of the United Nations section of the Soviet foreign ministry. Small, slight and softly spoken, fluent in English and an ultra-liberal by inclination, he had been sent abroad – to Paris – during the 1991 August coup, in order to gather Western support for Yeltsin and, in extremis, to organize a government in exile should the putschists succeed. On his return, he began to adumbrate in speeches, interviews and meetings a policy which to a large degree consisted in an even more rapid reversal of the Soviet foreign policy course than that instituted by Shevardnadze and Gorbachev – proposing, in September 1991, to re-establish an embassy in Israel, to expatriate Erich Honecker, the East German Communist Party leader in exile in Moscow, to Germany and to return the Kurile Islands to Japan (the first two were early achievements).

He was – and was to remain – roughly in step with Yeltsin. He fused together internal reform – the creation of a 'normal' society – with external relations. Explicitly and constantly rejecting imperial ambitions, he argued: 'We shall continue to seek answers for the fate of Russia not by looking for a new "strong arm" but through the elimination of the inadequacy of our own lives compared with normal countries.' For his part, Yeltsin – on a round of foreign trips through the middle part of 1992 – spoke of a 'democratic zone of trust, co-operation and security . . . across the northern hemisphere.'

This was the high idealist period. Yeltsin and Kozyrev proposed not just friendship and trust, but partnership with the West and above all with the US. Both men mooted – though were not entirely explicit about – an alliance, including a military alliance, with the arch enemy of the Soviet Union, Nato. In February 1992 – when George Bush was still US president – a Camp David declaration described the two countries as a 'new alliance of partners' working together 'against the common dangers we face'. Yeltsin even included Japan – with which no post-war peace treaty had been signed, because of the unresolved Islands question – as a potential partner. Gennady Burbulis, Yeltsin's most powerful adviser in the first months of his presidency, declared that a revival of Russia 'is impossible outside of a renewed Europe'.

It was not pure idealism. Russia needed financial assistance, and needed to ensure the assistance was calibrated with its reform pro-gramme. Kozyrev spoke of the 'need to economize our policy and diplomacy'. By that, he meant that policy had to underpin the application to join the IMF and the Group of Seven industrialized countries, and to argue for an appropriately large quota of IMF funds, befitting Russia's great power status. From an early stage, it was made explicit by both Russia and the G7 that economic assistance and democratization as well as market reforms were two sides of the bargain. Yeltsin and Kozyrev both implicitly cast the West as a guarantor of democracy, a role which early caused resentment in an increasingly restive parliament.

And not only there. The West was guilty of signalling large promises and delivering small beer. The Group of Seven advanced industrial states handed over the task of overseeing financial assistance to the IMF. In so doing, these countries, who had vied among themselves in the early years to declare the most heartfelt support for Russia, distanced themselves from the process in favour of an institution which was cautious in its practice and constrained in its ability to bend rules. At the same time it was also constrained to respond, often un-willingly, to promptings by the US in particular to do more to help Russia.

By announcing in mid-1992 a package of measures priced at $24 billion (much of which was debt relief and bilateral loans pegged to specific exports) the G7 gave an impression of generosity immediately undercut by small print conditionality which meant little of that was actually delivered in hard cash. The G7 did not quickly learn: a year later, an even larger sum – $43.4 billion – was promised, which similarly made no observable difference to the average Russian.

The shift in foreign policy which was widely marked in 1993 was prepared in the second part of 1992. Kozyrev's torment, which was to last until his resignation in January 1996, began in earnest then. Unlike Gaidar, who resigned in December 1992, he continued to enjoy the protection of a president who involved himself much more in foreign than in economic policy, and who weaved a compromise course between the various pressures from parliamentarians and the foreign policy élite.

The main opposition currents to the idealist–Western policy began to clarify themselves. In the democratic camp, a line emerged which stressed Russia's imperative need to dominate the 'near abroad' as a means both of re-establishing a great power status and securing its borders. The policy downgraded relations with Washington in favour of better relations with Europe, especially with its dominant power Germany, and gave more importance to improving links with and influence on the countries of the east and south, especially with China. In the communist-nationalist camp, the emphasis on alliance with the G7 countries was downgraded or even, in the hard versions, repudiated in favour of assertion of power over the CIS states – justified by the presence of the 25 million Russians – and a revival of alliances with the radical Arab states and some of the former Soviet clients. Some versions of the latter course integrated the foreign policy dimension with the need for an ethnic and religious revival in Russia.

These views, though quite sharply different at the extremes, lay along a continuum. At the democratic end were figures like Vladimir Lukin, the first Russian ambassador to Washington and later chairman of the Foreign Affairs Committee of the Duma, who dismissed Kozyrev's policy as 'romantic masochism' and upbraided the West for demanding an impossibly rapid economic reform and an impossibly self-abnegating withdrawal from the near abroad. Another was Sergei Stankevich, in 1992 and 1993 a state counsellor to Yeltsin for political affairs, who came out strongly against an over-'Atlanticist' policy and declared: 'Let us face the West. But the East is within us.' Among the most influential was Sergei Karaganov, deputy head of the Institute of Europe and an assiduous proponent of a strong Russia at international forums, whose Foreign and Defence Policy Council produced, in August 1992, a paper called 'Strategy for Russia' which proposed that Russia should be a moderately authoritarian state for a transitional period with a foreign policy geared to securing the territorial integrity of its surrounding states. In the press Andranik Migranyan, a member of the Presidential Council and a prolific publicist, became increasingly scathing about the drift to the West and increasingly shrill about the need for Russia to impose its will on a near abroad he saw as fragmenting into dangerous, ungovernable chaos.

Yeltsin, the great absorber of pressures and influences, took these hardening views into himself. He continued to proclaim the need for Western alliances and pushed – successfully – for inclusion into the G7, so that it became by mid-1994 a 'political G8' (the economic crisis precluded full acceptance). Yet in a speech he gave at the Foreign Ministry in October 1992, he was explicit in his dissatisfaction, complaining that 'Russia is trapped by a crisis mentality. Today the West sees Russia as a state which only says yes, occasionally overlooks the fact that others fail to meet their obligations to it and tacitly bears offence and even affront ... yet Russia is a great power. Russia's difficulty is a temporary one. Russia should neither be kept always in a defensive position nor imitate the policy of other countries. Russia is not a country that can be kept waiting in the anteroom. We are grateful to the West for the support it gives us, but we have reason formally to express a certain disappointment over the attitude of some Western countries, including the US.'

His practice, and his domestic rhetoric, changed. The formation of a Security Council in mid-1992 under the chairmanship of a then close – but conservative – Yeltsin aide, Yuri Skokov, inserted into the policy process an increasingly influential alternative centre for policy, especially towards the CIS. Skokov's inclinations were far more towards the harder-edged pragmatic school than to the West. The issue of the Kurile Islands, flagged up as one on which the Russians were willing to compromise, returned to the Soviet position – no surrender. Yeltsin cancelled a trip to Japan in September 1992 at the last moment, the first of two such switches.

Kozyrev, sensitive as ever to Yeltsin's manoeuvres, executed a large one of his own. The Foreign Policy Concept document, drafted in mid-1992, underwent substantial changes for its formal presentation to the Supreme Soviet in 1993 – incorporating, if not slavishly reflecting, the critiques of Karaganov and others. The security and territorial integrity of Russia was put first in the order of priorities; defence of the human rights and dignity of the Russians came second. The third priority repeated the need to create favourable conditions for internal reform via the encouragement of external assistance; the fourth stressed the need for wholly new and mutually beneficial relations with the CIS. The fifth was itself new: it sought to 'secure the appropriate status for Russia as a great power'. Where previous formulations had tried to link great power status to democracy, suggesting that the achievement of the second conferred the quality of the first, this clause was bald and unadorned. That, together with a very large stress on Russia's role within the CIS as not just an elder brother (as in Soviet days) but an occasionally punitive father, was a very large shift.

The changing position did not, at first, attract any public Western alarm. When the new concept was discussed and adopted, the democrats, with Yeltsin still more or less unequivocally at their head, and the conservatives organized within and around the Supreme Soviet were locked in what ultimately became a bloody struggle; no time for Russians or foreigners to examine the nuances of the Yeltsin position, when he was fighting for his political life against those who wanted an alliance with Libya. But, unheralded, the basic theoretical work of change from idealist-Westernism to pragmatic power politics and a largely uncontested claim of hegemony over the neighbouring states was achieved within a year of the collapse of the Soviet Union.

The line toughened, but it brought no success. Indeed, one reason why the pro-Western line was never wholly dropped was that it, alone, delivered some goods in the form of economic assistance while the harder line brought nothing but public and embarrassing rebuffs. Russia rapidly lost influence in Central Europe. Indeed, it was fear of it and memory of the post-war occupation that propelled the Central European states towards Nato. Milan Kundera, the Czech writer, had written an essay in 1983 on 'Kidnapped Europe', rejecting the idea common at the time in some Western circles that the area had become assimilated into the Soviet Bloc. Reflecting on this in 1995, Bronislaw Geremek, one of the founders of Polish Solidarity, said that the dissidents of Central Europe had insisted on 'Central' rather than

'Eastern' as the area's designation, in order to mark the distinction between it and the Russian east. Certainly, their post-communist politics were driven westwards, whether the government was commanded by dissidents, neo-liberals or former communists. Russia had no purchase, a ruined fraction of its former trade and a huge mountain to climb before it could be accepted as a friendly neighbour by its former Comecon and Warsaw Pact partners.

After effective exclusion from Western response to the crises in the former Yugoslavia, Russia moved away from a more or less automatic endorsement of Western policy. Kozyrev presented a plan in February 1993 which proposed a tightening on the arms embargo against the Muslims and Croats (as well as the Serbs) in Bosnia and a continuation of UN economic sanctions on Croatia if it continued to attack Serbian enclaves within the republic. Russia then abstained from voting on an April 1993 resolution of the Security Council calling for an export embargo on Serbia. The Supreme Soviet called for an even tougher line, vetoing UN intervention; and Serbia became a high-profile tourist spot for leading parliamentarians, who often declared in meetings with Serbian leaders that they upheld the historic alliance between the Russians and the Serbs. Brought into the contact group of states on Bosnia, Russia was, however, often effectively sidelined by the US, Britain and France – the former driving hard for more effective action against the Serbs, whom the US saw as the main aggressors, the latter two providing the bulk of the troops on the ground and – though more sympathetic to the Russian view and on occasion using it as a counterweight to US pressure – nevertheless seeing little need for extensive consultations with a state which had neither the means nor the will to be effective in the area. The West was ambivalent, at best, about including Russia in any systematic process of decision-making. Its diplomats, military and policy planners had few contacts with their opposite numbers, and very few would routinely talk to them on issues of the day – as happened, in a dense network of contacts, among the other G7 states.

In a forlorn interview in September 1995, a little before his resignation, Kozyrev revealed something of the realities with which he was faced: 'I go to Bosnia on commercial flights with two or three aides. Richard Holbrooke (the US special envoy) comes on two planes packed with sophisticated electronics, with ethnographers, cartographers and historians, all staying in first-class hotels. That is the difference.' Russian diplomacy was simply unable, to use the phrase beloved of Douglas Hurd, the former British Foreign Secretary, when describing his own Foreign Office, to 'bat above its weight'.

The Russian Foreign Ministry went through a period of involuntary 'downsizing', which meant it was unable to retain its Soviet-era efficiency. It was terribly under-resourced, and thus lost many of its brightest and best to the much higher-paying banks, finance houses and trading companies of Moscow, which rewarded their linguistic skills and international contacts with international-level salaries. Its embassies were cut back, starved of funds and tacitly encouraged to earn money through commercial operations. Its best diplomats remained those raised under Andrei Gromyko and schooled in the élite Soviet foreign affairs institutes, which had emphasized the hostility of the West. It was undercut by the Security Council, by the Federal Counter-intelligence Service (the former KGB's First Directorate) under Yevgeny Primakov and by the presidential staff and the president himself. Above all, it operated in an international environment of rapidly shrinking resources and prestige and a domestic environment of vast disappointment and bitterness over precisely that loss – one which meant that the area was wholly politicized and polemicized, and provided the opposition parties with their most potent field of propaganda and agitation after the plunging economy.

The rising power of Vladimir Zhirinovsky – much more interested in foreign than domestic issues – and the recovery of the Russian Communist Party with its own caustic view of foreign policy, was the most visible indication of the pressures on Russian diplomacy. Zhirinovsky represented Kozyrev as a simple agent of the West, a view repeated and amplified by such organs as *Sovetskaya Rossiya* and the weekly *Den*, whose editor, Alexander Prokhanov, was for a time a quasi-spiritual adviser to Gennady Zyuganov, the Communist Party leader. These men saw foreign policy very largely through the prism of what they conceived of as Russian values; the link with the West, and the slavish apeing of its positions and rhetoric (in the early days, there was something in this charge) were regarded as the actions of Judases who were allowing foreigners to besmirch and cripple Russia in exchange for trinkets.

The surge of support for Zhirinovsky, and to a lesser extent the communists, in the 1993 Duma elections, appeared to confirm the pessimistic view that imperialism was on the return, and that the Yeltsin government, if it survived, would have to adopt substantial parts of the foreign policy of Zhirinovsky in order to do so. That stance would lack the more baroque parts of Zhirinovsky's rhetoric, such as calls to reoccupy Poland and Finland or to blow nuclear dust into Estonia, but with much of the Liberal Democrat leader's insistence on an aggressive attitude to the CIS and a dismissive attitude to the West becoming part of the stance.

It did not. Kozyrev remained in post. Russian rhetoric grew sharper, but its actions did not fundamentally change. The CIS remained its main foreign focus, and though it could be very hard on its brothers in the Commonwealth, it was not significantly harder after December 1993 than before. The agreements with Georgia to station Russian troops there, forced out of it after the débâcle of that republic's efforts to subdue the Russian-backed province of Abkhazia, were achieved before the elections, not after. Kozyrev had already warned, in a *Washington Post* article of October 1993, that Russian interests were 'different from Western interests and at times [are] even competing'. Yeltsin had anticipated the shift in the public mood before the new politicians had come to the Duma to shout it into the microphones – that mood, as evidenced in the public opinion polls, was never remotely as aggressive to the West as the opposition politicians' rhetoric – and he had moved early.

In adopting many of the positions and some of the rhetoric of the moderate oppositionists, Yeltsin and Kozyrev succeeded in detaching an important part of the foreign policy establishment from a temporary alliance with those more extreme than they. The anti-Russianness of the former Soviet states had largely disappeared by 1993 – except in the Baltics, though even there it was moderated. The real successes which flowed from the formally good relations with the West – such as membership of the 'G8', the renegotiation of the Conventional Forces in Europe treaty to allow a larger quota of armour in the southern part of Russia, near the Caucasus, the provision (at last) of substantial funds from the IMF and the network of multilateral contacts and assistance programmes which continued in being – could in some cases still be controversial and resented, but were difficult to represent as Western imperialism except by the ideologues. The Duma, many of whose members remembered the fate of the confrontational Supreme Soviet in October 1993, was a generally less hostile body than its predecessor, and even when it was hostile to a measure, it could be drawn into a collaborative enterprise to change it. Thus Nato's Partnership for Peace, which Russia with an ill grace joined in 1994, was adapted for its special circumstances through amendments suggested by the Duma.

Relations with the West were marked by touchiness and fear of condescension; they were better with the giant to the east and south. Soviet–Chinese relations had been improved by Gorbachev, but Yeltsin, who made two visits to China, in 1992 and 1996, managed to get agreement on the demarcation of the entire 4,300 km border they share, with the exception of the two disputed islands on the Wusuli and Erguna Rivers. It was the first agreed border between the two states for three centuries. It was followed by agreements allowing for a reduction of the troop and missile concentrations on the frontiers. Trade grew in 1992–93, fell back in 1994 then grew again – to $5.5 billion, above the 1990 Soviet peak of $5.4 billion – in 1995; the two sides talked of trade volumes of $20 billion annually by the end of the century. Russia recognized that Taiwan and Tibet belonged to China and China supported the Russian view that Nato belonged on the other side of the Elbe.

The largest issue between the two countries, uneasy allies still, is the penetration of the emptying east of Russia by land-hungry Chinese; the Russian media reported anything between 1 and 5 million illegal immigrants in the area (the Chinese say even the lower of these figures is ridiculous, but do not provide their own estimate). The issue is a very large one in a Russia which became increasingly concerned about its integrity and about the sense of a weak government being unable to prevent incursions in its furthest reaches – a perennial Russian neurosis. But if they are insouciant about it, the Chinese authorities do not appear to be encouraging it.

This was – the West's support apart – the largest tangible gain of Russian foreign policy in its first years. It remained 'economized' – less to secure IMF or other funds, more to win back markets for its arms, rockets and nuclear equipment, the sale of the last two of which to India and Iran provoked large-scale confrontation between it and the US, with both sides reaching grumbling compromises in 1995. It had to suffer the loss of almost all influence in Africa and Latin America – even in Cuba, where Fidel Castro kept the red flag flying to the admiration of Yeltsin's opponents – and to a large extent in the Middle East, where some frenzied diplomacy by Kozyrev produced very little. Shrunken, impoverished and contradictory, it went through a period where it was sustained as a great power by the assumption that it was, then by a Western collusion that it still could be, and finally by a mutual recognition that though it was not and would not be again in the foreseeable future, the fact would never be brought up.

The idealism of Russia's early foreign policy days was matched on the rhetorical level by the pronouncements of Western leaders. George Bush was slow to trust Gorbachev but, when converted, worked hard to try to stop the break-up of the Soviet Union in its last year. He made a speech in Ukraine's capital of Kiev in 1990 which pointedly called its audience 'Soviet citizens' and said that 'independence is not the same thing as freedom'. He nevertheless recognized the inevitable collapse and both received and praised the new leader. Bush, and his fellow Western heads of government, had not expected the collapse of the Union, mourned the passing of Gorbachev and held generally low opinions of Yeltsin, in part because of the high opinions they had of his rival and also because of his erratic – not only drunken – behaviour. That impression was to change, as he revealed himself to be such a shrewd politician; and it did not appear to affect the strategic assessment made by Bill Clinton that the relationship with Russia was his first foreign policy priority.

'Russia first' – as the policy came to be known, largely pejoratively – was the creation initially of Strobe Talbott, the assistant (later deputy) US Secretary of State who had been a friend of Clinton's at Oxford, had translated Khrushchev's memoirs and had spent most of his working life as a reporter then a columnist for *Time* magazine. He was an admirer of Gorbachev – *Time* made the Soviet leader Man of the Year in 1990, the nadir of his domestic reputation – and a believer in enfolding the new state in an active embrace. The US assigned a very high priority to aid to Russia – it periodically badgered the IMF to be less pernickety about shovelling in the cash – and it went to some lengths to protect Russia's view of itself as a great power.

Clinton adopted the sunniest of public optimisms about the progress of reform. During 1992 and 1993, he constantly referred to Yeltsin as a fine statesman, a fighter for democracy and as a friend. After Yeltsin had shelled the parliamentary forces into submission in October 1993, Talbott publicly and fulsomely commended the victory. Clinton praised the Russian constitution, adopted later that year, and dismissed the successes of Zhirinovsky and the communists and their allies in the Duma elections. In January 1994, during a summit in Moscow, Clinton repeatedly stressed his optimism for reforms and belief in Yeltsin's leadership – though Yeltsin was, at the same time, manoeuvring to sack the pro-Western reformers in his cabinet. At the same summit, he appeared to underpin Yeltsin's proclaimed intention to intervene militarily where he judged it necessary in the CIS states, saying: 'You will be more likely to be involved in some of those areas near you, just like the United States has been involved in the last several years in Panama and Grenada near our area.' Grenada, a Reagan-era initiative, was an invasion and a deposing of the government, a precedent which, if taken to heart, would give Yeltsin *carte blanche*.

Clinton first came under attack from all sides. The twin figures of Zbigniew Brzezinski and Henry Kissinger (especially the former) were adamant that he had gone too far in making Russia the centre of attention and in ignoring the claims of the other former Soviet nations. Kissinger lamented that foreign policy should be achieved through psychotherapy for one's former adversaries; Brzezinski called for 'geo-political pluralism', which meant increased attention and aid to the other former Soviet states, way above all Ukraine, and enlargement of Nato while offering Russia a special agreement with the Alliance, irrespective of whether or not it remained democratic. Implicit or explicit in these critiques was the view that the close linkage of aid to democracy was an illusion. James Schlesinger, a former CIA director and defence secretary, objected that the promotion of human rights and the support of democracy were bad guides to the protection of American interests, since they were often in conflict with these interests. It was the objection of *realpolitik* to foreign policy enthusiasms.

It had an effect, as much because Russia began to disappoint Clinton and the West as because of the eminence of the critics. By 1994, the rhetoric did change and became more coolly sceptical. Ukraine was promoted, by the US, Germany and the UK, as a suitable case for assistance, especially after Leonid Kuchma became president in mid-1994 and instituted reforms which attracted an IMF programme.

Uzbekistan, certainly not a democratizing state, nevertheless was the target of tender concern, especially on the military side; a joint US–Uzbek staff academy was instituted. Alarmed by the dismal prospects of getting oil out of the Caspian Sea and the equally dismal prospects for the US oil company Chevron if the Russians continued to block the routes, US officials made clear that the issue was one of strategic importance to the US, even though it was in an area which Russia claimed as its own. Presidents Kuchma of Ukraine, Aliev of Azerbaijan, Karimov of Uzbekistan as well as the three Baltic leaders were pointedly received with all due respects in the major Western capitals.

The Western states were uncertain in their touch and at a loss as to what the architecture of a post-Cold War settlement should be. Margaret Thatcher and George Bush, both closely interested in and knowledge-able about the Soviet Union, had passed from the scene a little before or a little after it did. Clinton was a confessed novice; the Japanese stood aloof; only Helmut Kohl could and did engage closely with Yeltsin, becoming his closest foreign buddy – though he, too, could not cajole German business to invest in Russia and he was persuaded by his country's revulsion to become more distant after the Chechen invasion.

The advance of Nato to the former Soviet borders was the only substantial institutional response to the ending of the Cold War – a fact which the Russian political classes said they hugely resented. Yeltsin's efforts to extend the remit and build on the status of the Organization for Security and Co-operation in Europe were batted aside by the Western states, who thought of the OSCE as too amorphous and too split to play any but a formal role. It was held as axiomatic that Russia could join neither Nato nor the European Union: it was too big, too poor, too unstable – on certain accounts, not civilized enough.

The debates eschewed grand plans; there was and could be no Yalta or Tehran conferences to redraw maps, no Bretton Woods to establish grand new institutions, no Marshall plan to lift nations from poverty to developed status. There was no mood for such ventures. If the former Soviet Union was in a fluid situation, the West was not: it had secured prosperity and the largest concern of its leaders was to continue – or in the case of the US, to rediscover – its increase. The integration of Western Europe consumed the energies of the bulk of the G7 states. America led on Russian policy as on much else, but to encourage and assist, not to reshape. Russia's place in the world was assumed to be that of a large regional power which could work out for itself how to live between an integrating West and Central Europe and an enriching East.

After five years of gritting their teeth over Yeltsin, the main Western states gritted them once more and proclaimed that it was important that Russian reform continue under his presidency for a second term. Chechnya was put to one side. Germany and France gave large bilateral support. The IMF renewed its programme and said nothing about its worries. His victory was a relief: Zyuganov was too unknowable for the view – that he would be too constrained to change policy radically – to be a certain one.

But there was no rejoicing. Yeltsin had made it clear that Russia had interests, and that they were not synonymous with those of the US and its allies. He had made it clear that the concept of partnership was, in Brzezinski's phrase, 'premature'. But nothing else was clear. Russia was too weak to exercise more than a sporadic intervention in the near abroad, far too weak to do anything effective beyond that. Would it become fully democratic – and thus, it was assumed, respectful of international norms – before it became strong enough to behave badly again?

The second Russian foreign minister of the post-communist era was Yevgeny Primakov. He was sixty-seven when appointed after the 1995 elections gave the communists a Duma victory, a quarter of a century older than Kozyrev when he took the job. He was a man of a different era: schooled in Asiatic and Arab culture and languages, he had served in the state radio and in *Pravda*, where he had been a Middle Eastern correspondent and head of the paper's Afro-Asiatic department. He went into academic life, becoming deputy head of IMEMO in 1970, then its director in 1985 when Gorbachev took over. He had been close to Gorbachev: he had pressed on the rising young Politbureau member his belief that the export of world revolution was choking the life out of the Soviet Union, and that some rapprochement had to be made with the US in order to relieve the pressure on the economy. It became a cornerstone of Gorbachev's belief. He was a senior adviser to Gorbachev throughout his leadership. He was a candidate member of the Politbureau in 1989, yet he proved acceptable to Boris Yeltsin to be named head of the Foreign Counter-intelligence Service in the interregnum period between the putsch and the ending of the Union. He reshaped the former KGB agency in more modest times into a body concentrating on economic and industrial espionage. He also thrust it into the foreign policy arena, issuing reports on the penetration of Russia by the CIA and other secret services under the guise of bodies offering assistance, and warning that the Western states were deliberately trying to weaken Russia by boosting the former Soviet states around it.

A survivor – indeed, the most notable survivor of the Gorbachev period, the only one who stayed with him to the end to have found a high post under Yeltsin. He did not radically change the course Kozyrev had come to administer, though he emphasized the distance from his predecessor by making the surrounding states the objects of his first official visits. He had already contributed to the changes through which that course had passed. Where Kozyrev had been all idealism, Primakov was all realism, even cynicism: his appointment signalled that a man of power was again in the Foreign Ministry, and that business – even with a weakened state – would be conducted on the old principles of balances of strengths and weaknesses. The little party was long over. Russia would find a place in the world by degrees, not by a sudden leap.

CHAPTER TWENTY-FOUR

'Do no harm'

No one needed Russia. Much of the rest of the world feared and distrusted it, seeing it as unstable, irresponsible, demanding and potentially tyrannous. Its one export which had become essential, to Western European countries, was gas. It had a vast internal market but, in the first years, a poor one. The rest of the world worried that it remained such a major nuclear weapons power – not because it would use the threat of them to back up global pretensions it had ceased to have, but because there was a much larger risk of one going off accidentally, or a nuclear power station blowing up, or a major threat of the leakage of nuclear materials. Its politics became increasingly byzantine, its economy refused to take off, its foreign policy veered this way and that, its contribution to world problems, positive or negative, sank to negligible levels.

When Boris Yeltsin began his rule, Russia was routinely lauded as a state emerging into the light through the heroism of its leaders and the yearnings for freedom of its people. By the end of his first term, it was seen as a very large problem. In relation to its size, and compared with its recent (Soviet) past, it punched very far below its weight in the world. This was because the world, which had not expected it would have to receive it, had nowhere to put it. It had had its own world; when that collapsed, the more developed or entrepreneurial members of it – the Central Europeans, the Baltics, Vietnam – rapidly severed their links and set about forging new ones, both economic and where possible political and security. What was it without its empire? No one knew, and thus no one knew how to treat it. Since it did not know either, it did not know where to put itself.

If the mystery and the dogma had been reduced, it remained an enigma. It appeared to want to integrate with the developed world – it did seem as if it had no choice – and yet it drew back from doing so. For the world into which it emerged was not as welcoming as its Westernizing reformers had expected or wished: while the world outside was easily caricaturable as, if not an aggressive, at least an unsympathetic and even antipathetic and repellent environment for a bruised and fallen state.

Dostoyevsky, in *Winter Notes*, his diatribe against the principles of the French Revolution, wrote:

The Westerner speaks of fraternity as a great moving force of mankind, and does not understand that it is impossible to obtain fraternity if it does not exist in reality . . . in occidental nature in general, it is not present; you find there instead a principle of individualism, a principle of isolation, of intense self-preservation, of personal gain, of the self-determination of *I*, of opposing this *I* to all nature and the rest of mankind as an independent autonomous principle entirely equal and equivalent to all that exists outside itself.

This view of the outside world, especially of the wealthy states, as egocentric, self-obsessed and predatory became increasingly popular in Yeltsin's time in office. Often represented in Dostoyevskyan terms, the feeling drew strength from the reaction to the fervour with which the opposite view had been embraced, both officially and to an extent popularly, during Gorbachev's period and immediately afterwards.

Gorbachev had, in cloudy terms to be sure, represented the opening of the Soviet Union as the completion of Europe – the 'common home', 'from Atlantic to the Urals'. In 'burying the Cold War at the bottom of the Mediterranean' (as the Foreign Ministry spokesman Gennady Gerasimov put it after the stormy Malta shipboard summit in 1989), and in agreeing to the unification of Germany in 1990, the Soviet president had taken an axe through the post-war decades of institutionalized hostility. But he had not fundamentally changed the Western institutions.

Nato remained in being; indeed, it fought some hot rather than cold wars, its forces being engaged in the Gulf against Iraq, and deployed in Bosnia. Though it had been created as an anti-Soviet alliance, it had acquired secondary functions. Chief among these was to keep the US tied into the security of Europe, a function no European state was willing to see ended, for all the talk – which got little further than talk – of the Europeans providing their own security. Its declared intention to expand to take in the former communist Central European states was a leftover of its past, one about which many in the West felt uncomfortable. But from 1994, it grinded inexorably on in spite of Russian protests, because the demand of the Central Europeans to determine their own security could not be denied. No Western leader felt any imperative to challenge this consensus by proposing an altern-ative form of European security in which Russia might play a part. All that was offered – and sullenly accepted – was an enhanced participation in the Partnership for Peace, a series of treaties between Nato and non-Nato states which provided for joint exercises and exchanges.

The European Union also had ambitions to expand to the East – though it became, in the mid-nineties, increasingly preoccupied with the issue of monetary union and arguments over sovereignty, the latter largely posed by a sceptical British government. Those states committed to monetary union, led by Germany and France and followed by Italy and Spain, were experiencing high unemployment and threats of a more extensive social unrest than they had experienced since the sixties. Britain's long Conservative period was ebbing in favour of a centrist Labour Party with domestic priorities. None of these countries' leaders, save Helmut Kohl, had much interest in Russia so long as it seemed to be harmless to their interests – and Kohl's interest had subsided to occasional worried forays. There was no question of the European Union expanding to take in Russia; even the Baltics were seen as a leap far too far before deep into the next millennium.

Thus Gorbachev's rhetoric could not be given substance. Russia could not – was not required to – complete Europe; it had to face the task of working out a relationship with it. On one argument, its interests would be best served by a failure of the European Union – for then Germany, less heavily committed to its west, might explore more forcefully the relationship to its east. But that was not Germany's first choice, and was definitely not any other European country's desire.

In the east, Russia had secured a better relationship with China and could look forward to increasing trade; but the larger country could offer it little in the way of investment or modernization, since it was importing these so massively itself. Japan, which could have done both, remained distant. South Korea, with a large debt to it outstanding and no hope of recovering it, was also slow to engage.

Russia had to accustom itself to US hegemony. The fact that it was not even a junior partner with America became increasingly obvious in the mid-nineties. There were efforts to involve Russia in the former Yugoslavia through the contact group, and in the Middle East, but little else of a major rather than routine, kind. When, in September 1996, a crisis in Palestine threatened the stalled Israeli–Palestine peace process, both the Palestinian chairman Yassir Arafat and the new Israeli Premier Binyamin Netanyahu headed for Washington; no one appeared concerned what Russia's view was.

It was in the US, and with its traditional allies, that the debates on world issues were held. There was no area in the world, outside of some of the former Soviet states, which would welcome a Russian contribution to a crisis. If, as Joe Nye, an assistant defence secretary in the first Clinton administration put it, US foreign policy philosophy could be described in terms of the Hippocratic oath – 'Do no harm' – this also meant it would do little good that was expensive or ambitious, to Russia or anyone else. It was the only military superpower; but economically, it shared leadership with Japan and the European Union (or Germany).

Russia remained the second nuclear superpower; and General Alexander Lebed, in October 1996, warned the Nato expanders that 'even if our missiles are rusty, they are still missiles' – an absurd piece of rocket-rattling from a man somewhat destabilized by his ambition to succeed the dying president he was then nominally serving. But it faced developing nuclear powers on its doorstep – China, India, Pakistan, Iran – about which it could do nothing (nor could anyone else). The nuclear deterrent was even more useless than before; but it clung to it because it had nothing else with which to deter.

The world economy presented the most taxing challenge. Russia entered a world in which the market had won. This was not because the bastion of world socialism had collapsed: it had happened before that event, and had indeed contributed to it. Free-market ideas had taken over the political and economic establishments. Governments – by the mid-nineties – had become or were becoming convinced that they must withdraw as far as possible from economic management and the provision of welfare and other services. This was a crisis of Keynesian demand-management and the social policies associated with it since the war.

For Russia, it meant that the economic orthodoxy, and the patterns of investment and institutional aid, were dominated by the global capital markets and the need to adapt to them. In so far as there was a new world order, it was provided as much by the markets as by governments. In 1946, when the Bretton Woods conference began to set in place the institutions on which an economic system could be based, it was assumed that governments should undertake the task and that they were competent to do so. In the nineties, there had been no such assumption for a decade. In its place was a broad intellectual consensus that the market allocated more efficiently than the state at every level, local to global. Already by the seventies the developing countries were establishing stock markets; by the eighties, it was clear that investments in all states, developed and developing, would be on terms dictated very largely by private capital.

The other great event of the eighties and nineties – some thought it greater than the crumbling of the Soviet bloc – was the entry of China and India into the capitalist world. Their dropping of socialist or semi-socialist policies and their opening to the world markets increased their growth, their attractiveness for foreign capital – and showed Russia as a laggard. Its political turbulence, the weakness of its central government, the pervasiveness and much worse the unpredictability of its corruption and crime, the lack of discipline of its workforce and the unenforceability of contract and its laws meant that the capital which flowed into China, India and even into Vietnam stayed away, largely, from Russia. Indeed, Russian capital – some $40 billion since the USSR's collapse – continued to flow out into safer havens throughout the Yeltsin period.

The advanced economies – and the more advanced sectors of the developing economies – were engaged, in the nineties, on complex industrial modernizations. Large corporations were developing rapidly in several directions at once: they were shedding a great deal of labour in favour of technology, or contracted services; they were expanding their sales and/or production to other countries, seeking for lower-cost manufacturing bases; they were concerned to increase the skills and commitment of their core workers, the more so as they became more dependent on their intellectual abilities; and they were seeking alliances with companies with which they had competed for decades. A skein of new relationships within and outside of corporations was created in the decade in which the Soviet Union fell apart and Russia struggled to establish itself. It was a process of which the new country's industrialists and economists were usually only partially aware and which they could not imitate.

That meant that they could not compete. Building cars was no longer simply designing an attractive model and producing it efficiently and reliably – neither of which any Russian enterprise could do. Car production in the nineties had become a matter of fitting production, design and after-sales service network into a global strategy, either through size – like Ford or Nissan – or through alliances. The Russian car plants did not have the size, and the only alliances available were those which – like the Kamaz truck plant – replaced much of the Russian engineering with foreign parts. However, most of the big manufacturers shunned that, and so continued to produce vehicles at, on a quality basis, prices far above those on the world market, in spite of the low cost of the labour embodied in them.

Russian managers and business people were not equipped for the business world – except in Russia, which was a very particular experience. Rosabeth Moss Kantor, the Harvard management expert, called the new lords of world business 'cosmopolitans' – defining them as being 'rich in three intangible assets that translate into pre-eminence and power in a global economy: these are concepts, the best and latest knowledge and ideas; competence, the ability to operate at the highest standards of any place anywhere; and connections, the best relationships which provide access to the resources of other people and organizations round the world.' Almost no one in Russia was a 'cosmopolitan'. Even a man like the head of the Vladimir Tractor Plant, Joseph Bakaleinnik, educated at the Harvard Business School and for long an exotic bloom in Russian industry, was so enmired in trying to save his company that he had no time for the networking and absorbing which a 'cosmopolitan' needed to attain that status. Russian business people tended to be, at best, what Kantor called 'locals' – 'rooted in their communities but open to global thinking and opportunities' – or more often 'isolates – those whose skills are not particularly unique or desirable, whose connections are limited to a small circle in the neighbourhood and whose opportunities are confined to their own communities'.

Russia had pinned its hopes on a rapid transition to the market. Though its market reformers were the best available for the job, their limits were the limits of the country: the wasteland which the Soviet system had established where in other countries, even developing ones, there had been something on which a business culture could be developed. For all their drive and talent, the New Russians could not, in the Yeltsin period, do more than clear the ground and get rich. It was nowhere near enough. The breakthrough was yet to come.

Further, many of the mechanisms and systems which Russian politicians and business people developed – which were adaptations of previous Soviet behaviour as well as ways of coping with the domestic and international market pressures – were contrary to the way in which the world was moving. Anthony Giddens, the British sociologist, had noted that 'globalizing influences tend to break down the formation of monopolies or oligopolies such as are often found within national economies . . . [these] depended in fact on collaborative connections between the state and capital which are now being undermined'. The big multinationals presently depend less on corporatist relations with their 'home' or other states than before; relatively settled domestic market shares are now less important than an intensified global competition with other world businesses. Yet as this process continues and deepens for the multinationals, the Russian companies increased their dependence on the state, as well as the state's dependence on them – walling themselves into an economy with low technical standards, undiscriminating consumers and underdeveloped services.

Russia came into a world which had no steering committee. That world faced a series of possible global or large regional disasters – nuclear wars or accidents; environmental catastrophes; the implosion of much of the African continent; inter-state wars in Asia and the former Soviet Union; intra-state wars or terrorist movements almost everywhere; a limit to growth in the developed capitalist economies giving rise to social unrest. In an age much more knowledgeable than any in the past about the scale of possible breakdown, the world oscillated between an optimism derived from still rising material standards in many (not all) of the richer states and in some of the largest developing countries, and a pessimism based on the fragility of the barriers against disaster or breakdown, particularly in the states which were being left behind.

The leaders among the world states, including the leader, the US, were inclined to passivity. *Realpolitik*, the active shaping of the world according to the interests of the leading states, was out of favour; the power of the powerful had waned. Russia was not given a structure in which to fit, it was requested to have a nice day. In its first period, it could contribute little to a world whose leadership it had left. Its late-twentieth-century time of troubles was not a passing matter; the century which it had dynamized and for a time held in thrall slipped away with other powers, other regions taking its place in the front ranks. Its size, genius and history pointed to a revival; but it needed to discover the resources on which that revival could be based, and that would take time.

PART FIVE

Culture

'We suffer over the past in the present. And as long as we suffer, we are human beings.'

Yevgeny Yevtushenko, 1991

CHAPTER TWENTY-FIVE

'An attempt to be optimistic which failed'

The 'second' Russian revolution – the fall of Soviet communism and its replacement by a continuing search for a national and cultural identity – has brought no great explosion of artistic energy, precisely because it was a collapse and not a revolution. It seems that the task of finding a culture which can explain or comment on the nation and the world, when the nation does not know its place in the world, is presently beyond the powers of its artists – who are condemned, for the moment, to jab and lunge at the maelstrom which surrounds them.

The scale of change in the country calls for a comparison with the events of 1917. But to compare the first with the second revolution is to compare a culture in full flood with one which has exhausted itself. Some of the finest poets of the twentieth century were maturing in the Russian revolutionary period, and in every case their work was deeply marked by it.

The poet Alexander Blok furiously embraced revolution at its inception: in his essay, 'Intelligentsia and Revolution', written in 1918, he called on his fellow intellectuals and artists: 'With all your body, with all your heart, with all your consciousness, listen to the revolution!'

He was not alone in being swayed by the size and scale of contemporary events. In art, Kuzma Petrov-Vodkin marked the third year of the revolution by painting a red Madonna feeding a child, calling it '1918 in Petrograd'. Vladimir Tatlin welcomed the revolution with a monument to the Third International, the medium through which communism was to be consummated as a world movement. Vasily Kandinsky and Casimir Malevich saw in the revolution the realization of their futuristic fantasies. Vladimir Mayakovsky and Vsevolod Meyerhold celebrated the revolution with a production of the former's *Mystery-Bouffe*, a blasphemous inversion of the story of Noah in which the great flood is a metaphor for revolution.

Yet by the thirties, Stalin had strangled the radicalism and diversity of revolutionary culture, smothering it in grandiosity and kitsch. The art of the thirties came to be dominated by order and optimism. Tragedy as a genre was alien, banned. Vsevolod Vishnevsky, one of Stalin's favourite writers, wrote a play which embodied the spirit of the time, called the *Optimistic Tragedy*.

Among the millions of living tragedies were many of the artists who were the first to embrace the revolution and to assist in the creation of the mythology of the Soviet state. Meyerhold, among the most eager of the proponents of revolution, wrote twenty years after it from the cells of the NKVD:

The investigators began to use force on me, a sick 65-year-old man. I was made to lie face down and then beaten on the soles of my feet and my spine with a rubber strap. They sat me on a chair and beat my feet from above with considerable force. For the next few days, when those parts of my legs were covered with extensive internal haemorrhaging, they again beat the red, blue and yellow bruises with the strap . . . I howled and wept from my pain . . . I began to incriminate myself in the hope that this, at least, would lead quickly to the scaffold . . .

It was one of the glories of *glasnost*, that movement of ambiguous openness launched by Mikhail Gorbachev in 1987, that it allowed to be heard these long muffled screams of agony – and gave space and honour once more to the huge trove of suppressed culture of the past seven decades – the revolutionary, anti-revolutionary and dissident writing; the shelved films; the hidden paintings and the testimonies of the repressed.

In these rehabilitations lay the real core of *glasnost*, and a significant part of Mikhail Gorbachev's vast achievement. The second revolution may not have been fecund, but it was immensely generous: it brought back from the literary grave the works of some of the greatest writers of the century, and presented their works once more to the people for whose forebears they had been written. These included Ivan Bunin's *Accursed Days*; Boris Pasternak's *Doctor Zhivago*; Vassily Grossman's *Life and Fate*; Alexander Solzhenitsyn's *Gulag Archipelago*; Yevgeny Zamyatin's *We*; the poetry of Mandelstam, Akhmatova. Novels were published which had lain in the drawer for decades: the most famed was Anatoly Rybakov's *Children of the Arbat*, a sprawling novel of the post-war Stalinist generation.

In the theatre, the director Yuri Lyubimov restaged his anti-régime interpretation of *Boris Godunov*. Films which had lain on the shelves unseen were released in cinemas and shown on television – including Alexander Askoldov's *Commissar*, Andrei Tarkovsky's *Stalker* and *Andrei Rublev*, and most important of all, Tengiz Abuladze's *Repentance*, a surreal satire of dictatorship. These works were shown in pursuit of the Gorbachev goal of socialism with a human face; in fact, they contributed to socialism's rapid destruction by depriving the Communist Party of any moral right to rule. As Ilya Ehrenburg's 1954 novel, *The Thaw*, gave its name to the period of relaxation of terror after Stalin's death in 1953, so Abuladze's film inscribed the theme of repentance into the *glasnost* period – a theme which, however, was too short-lasting to be anything like complete.

Among the works exhumed and republished, or published for the first time in Russia, were the writings of two men who most starkly and uncompromisingly expressed in their work, and in one of the two cases their life, opposition to the tide of repression and mediocrity which Soviet rule had washed in.

Vitaly Grossman was, like Ilya Ehrenburg, both a Jew and a war correspondent (and an honoured one); like Ehrenburg, he saw the liberation of concentration camps and, like him, wrote of them powerfully. Unlike Ehrenburg, he could not let it rest. In *Life and Fate*, written in the late fifties, submitted for publication to some literary ('thick') journals, seized by the KGB in February 1961 and condemned by Mikhail Suslov, the party ideology chief, to 200 years of extinction, the book was smuggled to the West through the good offices of Andrei Sakharov, and published in France in 1980.

It is hard to believe that Grossman thought it could be published in Russia, for it is a book in which Nazism and communism are equated, in which the average Soviet moral character is shown as utterly opportunist, in which the war itself, the sacred and central motif of post-war literature, is seen as a useless sacrifice in the face of equally repugnant régimes – especially repugnant for a Jew, who sees an anti-Nazi war followed by an anti-Semitic crusade launched by Stalin. Grossman pushes his characters into the furthest output of the front line in Stalingrad, into the interrogation cells of the Lubyanka, and into the very gas chamber of an extermination camp, to the moment when the Zyklon B is released – this last a scene which defies continuous reading.

These are some of the moments of this century which art and belief must face: Grossman's desperate embrace of them in his writing was itself a cry against that literature which made it either cloying, or invisible. *Life and Fate*, and the later, shorter novel, *Everything Flows*, lie largely unexplored in their home country, their revelations permitted but not generally absorbed. In a time like the nineties, when the overwhelming mood was to suspend serious investigation of the Soviet system – indeed, to cultivate a selective nostalgia for it – a work which poses the question as to whether or not it was better for the Soviet people to win the war against Nazism could hardly be regarded as a national treasure. Yet it is more than that: it is, as François Furet described it, 'one of the most profound witnesses of our century'.

Alexander Solzhenitsyn has now achieved recognition in his own land, as he had for decades outside of it. He lives as, and will die as, the best-known Russian writer of the twentieth century, an accolade which owes as much to his courage as his prose, which most critics (most of all Russian critics) agree has been clotted and prolix after his first novels. But these first novels – *Cancer Ward, First Circle* and, above all, the first to be published, *A Day in the Life of Ivan Denisovich* – together with his masterwork, *The Gulag Archipelago*, a reconstruction of the terrors of Stalin's time – set those of his generation who read it ablaze because of their steady refusal to blink before both the immensity and the details of his country's and his time's sufferings, a rigour which made the Gulag as unbearable and as morally stunning in parts as was Grossman's epic.

The *Gulag* forced his emigration (following the publication of its first part in Paris in 1973) to Switzerland, and later to the US, where he remained until his return to Russia in 1994. His fame, his works and his longevity (against many odds) has meant that he, alone of the Russian writers of the Soviet period, presents post-Soviet Russia with a series of challenges which it presently is not inclined to take. One of these is the invitation to understand history as a necessary prelude to understanding and reforming the present. Another is to sustain an art of engagement and moral inquiry. And the last, for which he became on his return to Russia more notorious than famous, is his insistence that Russia must be returned to its spiritual roots, or it will perish. He looms over the contemporary period, a voice grown shrill with constant warning, mocked for his eccentric refusal to relinquish the writer's place as prophet.

These were the summits; there were many lesser peaks, such as Rybakov's *Children of the Arbat*, a novel which could not be published when written in the fifties but which achieved a wild success at home and abroad in the late eighties with its descriptions of young lives destroyed by Stalinism – a novel of repression written in a socialist realist style. These and other works flooded out in the late eighties, the one succeeding the other pell mell.

Yet they stimulated, not a new creative spirit, but a kind of literary indigestion. The intelligentsia were unable to digest them; and the wealth of the past masked the fact that little new was being produced in the present. The country was living through its heritage, but was unable to create an art of the new times.

The art of *glasnost* was largely confined to the crafts of journalism and television current affairs. These provided the medium for the testimonies of oppression and marginalization of the generations which had been denied a full public airing, and which turned loose a new generation of journalists on the vast field of official stagnation and corruption. Significantly, the films, plays and novels which achieved a reputation were often documentary in style, such as the film *Is it Easy to be Young?*, by the Latvian Juris Podnieks, and the feature *Little Vera* by Vasily Pichul – a grim tale of a young working-class woman struggling to find a personal liberation while there is still time. In the theatre, kitchen sink dramas in the *Little Vera* mould enjoyed a vogue – with the occasional grand 'renewal of socialism' set-piece, such as Mikhail Shatrov's *Dictatorship of the Conscience*.

'If in the twenties art had huge energy and hope for the future,' says Anatoly Smelyansky, the Moscow Art Theatre's literary director, 'then *perestroika* art was a simulation, an attempt to be optimistic which failed. In 1989 it all died down. People got fed up with the political stuff; life was getting harder; inflation started; people didn't want to see the same hardship in the theatre or on TV as they met in life.'

In the early nineties, cultural life appeared to decouple itself finally from its seventy-year-old subordination to the Communist Party – and, in the eyes of many of the younger writers, artists and film directors, from the hyper-moralism of Russian letters and the stifling duties and guilts of the Russian intellectual as well. For the first time ever, Russian culture was free from political subordination, and Russians were free to read, watch and listen to anything the market would bear. But for many who had put the remnants of their socialist faith and their artistic reputations at the service of Gorbachev, it was experienced as at least in part a loss. The liberation was real but it was quickly followed by a blasé 'so what?' attitude as the economic crisis continued to deepen.

'*Enertainmen*' – as entertainment was Russified – flooded the country. Films largely from the US, unlisted in any film directory, took over the Russian cinemas. As Russia descended economically to the status of a Third World economy, the process was accompanied by an addiction to Mexican soap operas, among which a saga named *The Rich Also Cry* was capable of stopping all activities in offices.

This naturally provoked a reaction: and it increasingly came in the form of nostalgia for Soviet art. This nostalgia was often represented in the West – and by some liberals in Russia itself – as a reactionary, even a Stalinist impulse. But that is to miss the point.

After the brief euphoria, the overwhelming emotion, felt well beyond the ranks of the intelligentsia and well beyond the bounds of Russia, was one of loss. It was a complex kind of loss: it was loss of the secure cultural landmarks: loss of vital parts of the vast and expensive network of theatres, opera houses, cinemas, palaces of culture, general knowledge societies and specialized institutes and colleges; and loss, for the intelligentsia and the artists, of the familiar enemy which had been the Communist Party and of the values which derived from being a culture in semi-opposition.

Artists accustomed to working against the pressure of the system felt lost and confused when it passed. Inna Solovyova, who spent her middle years on the key literary journal *Novy Mir* and later worked as a professor of drama, says: 'The resistance which artists felt from the system benefited them. It is like a river: a river which runs under pressure through mountains is always clean and forceful. A river which spills over makes the ground about it boggy. This is exactly what happened to our culture.' Relatively free writing, she says, was possible about everything except communist ideas. 'We all felt we were living in some sea monster, unsure whether it was alive or dead. We were also unsure as to what to do – break its ribs and get out, or find some way of living more or less comfortably inside it.'

After the terror passed no Soviet art was without some sphere of autonomy, where the practitioners could claw back some space from the ideological controllers. At the same time no one could avoid some submission to the system; the best was ever in danger of being crushed by the mediocre and the faithful. It was a universe of light and dark greys. Artists and intellectuals had reason to be wary of indiscretion: the camps no longer beckoned, but they could suffer stunted careers, lose the opportunity to publish, miss out on foreign trips. At the same time many were members of the Communist Party – which meant that they passed motions, affirmed resolutions and made set speeches in a spirit of paying homage to a necessary, possibly vengeful but generally predictable deity.

The intelligentsia was a very different thing from its pre-revolutionary roots. Russian intellectuals had taught in provincial schools and travelled to remote parts of the country to cure and administer to the peasants. The Soviet intelligentsia had become a large, urban, relatively well-off class of people who had professional skills and often interesting careers in which to deploy them.

They had been given, or took bit by bit, a range of privileges and freedoms unthinkable before the fifties. They read the banned books in the restricted areas of the libraries, the restrictions often being liberally interpreted by sympathetic librarians; they passed samizdat hand-to-hand; they listened to foreign radio broadcasts. The films they watched by Yury Trifonov and Eldar Ryazanov and the songs they heard by Bulat Okudzhava were mildly rebellious, appealing to a gentle humanism which did not directly contradict the precepts of Marxism-Leninism but which only cursorily nodded to it. Jeans, long hair and rock music could not – despite initial efforts to ban them and continuing official disapproval – be kept out, and were thus modified or Sovietized to achieve a compromise between the régime's distrust and the population's desires.

In the natural sciences above all, the senior scientists were able to trade the official favour in which they were held for a freedom of artistic and cultural taste which was practically unlimited. Exhibits by unofficial artists and concerts and readings by the critical singers and poets were held, often, in physics and chemistry institutes, advertised by word of mouth around a circle of professional acquaintances. Andrei Sakharov, who went over to overt and intolerable dissidence, had before been part of this semi-dissident world.

Says Solovyova:

The state of culture in the last years of Brezhnev's rule was excellent. You could do pretty much what you wanted. Of course you had to pay, but you knew what you would have to pay for which freedoms. If you wanted to have money, a free flat, a *dacha* and to travel abroad, you became a *chinovnik* [a minor official, a clerk]. If you wanted to read [the pre-revolutionary religious philosopher] Berdyayev, you could do so in special archives. If you wanted to be a dissident, nobody could stop you, but you had to pay with a prison sentence. If you wrote a letter in support of a dissident you would lose your job.

But these were your own choices. In Stalin's time nothing depended on your will, or indeed your actions. Everything was decided by a stroke of destiny, as in a Greek tragedy. If you are destined to kill your father and marry your mother, you would do it, want to or not. If you were destined to be shot you would be shot.

Comfortable for some, a stimulant to artistic endeavour for a few, the culture was corrosive for many. It was corrosive in two ways. It rubbed away at the self-respect and the sense of responsibility of generations of educated and creative people. And yet at the same time it hollowed out the official and Party beliefs, rendering them hollow set pieces with a dwindling power to move or inspire. When freedom came, the creative generations were unable to rise to it.

CHAPTER TWENTY-SIX

'The sweet aura of the forbidden'

The Soviet universum was quite quickly demonumentalized after Stalin's death. The vast, ornamented towers, put up to awe, ceased to be built. Official painting ceased to be heroic, and became almost intimate. New wave poets, led by Yevgeny Yevtushenko and Andrei Vosnesensky, began to be heard and soon became popular. The 'lieutenants' prose', stories of personal wars, took over from the martial, proletarian heroism. The novel came back from the production front and lurked on the park bench and in the communal flat. Films were rooted in everyday locations and in the comedy and heartaches of quotidian life.

Literature, cramped and directed under Stalin, was avid to explore and also appeared to be allowed to do so. Immediately after Stalin's death *Novy Mir*, one of the leading 'thick' journals of fiction, criticism and comment, published an essay, 'On Sincerity in Literature', which attacked Stalin-era writers for 'varnishing' reality. The writer, Vladimir Pomerantsev, was censured, a later novel he wrote never published and the editor of *Novy Mir*, Alexander Tvardovsky, was fired. But the thaw had begun.

With it began the exploration of themes and dilemmas which was to reach its apotheosis in Gorbachev's time: the attempt, *within* the system, to at once explore its limits, confirm its basic goodness and cleanse it by appealing to its ideals and the necessity of humanism and understanding. It was a period in which, though still unified in structure and theoretically dedicated to the common goal of underpinning communism, literature began to be diverse, basing itself on the different interests within a Soviet society officially declared uniform.

Yuri Trifonov, like Shatrov the scion of a disgraced family, explored in short novels like *The Exchange*, *The Long Goodbye* and *The House on the Embankment* the particular moral universe in which he and his generation lived – where choice on how to live, on where to draw the line on expression and free inquiry, had carried deadly consequences and still determined status, income and even the allocation of housing.

The Exchange, one of the finest of these tales of contemporary urban life, was all about the dilemma of a man pushed by his wife to persuade his dying mother to leave her flat so they can get it – with the high fastidious moralism of the intelligentsia pitted against the ruthless materialism of a new, Stalin-era generation. It is fine because it goes beyond a simple moral dualism to reach into an area in which the attitudes of all are judged wanting, led into grubby moral choice by the harsh facts of life – a pessimism about the human spirit in general and Soviet man in particular which would have been impossible before the mid-fifties and was regarded as deplorable by many of Trifonov's colleagues and by those in power who still wanted a literature of permanent optimism.

But both those who explored these themes – like Ilya Ehrenburg, the most prominent of the Soviet war correspondents, who gave a name to the era in his novel *The Thaw*, published in 1954 – and those who preferred to carry on varnishing shared the same moral universe and paid at least lip service to the perennial task of Russian literature: to find out how to live. These works also showed that Soviet literature had retained something of its old autonomy and traditions, hidden underground throughout the Stalin years. It was this long search for a way of living, always conducted under inauspicious political circumstances, which is now seen by Russian writers old and young to have ended in the meltdown of the late eighties.

The personal, the emotional and the confessional became from the mid-fifties the dominant mode. The 'bards' – as the new poet/singers were called – included Alexander Galich, Vladimir Vysotsky and Bulat Okudzhava. They created a private style, playing their songs to guitar accompaniment to circles of friends in small Moscow kitchens in swirls of cigarette smoke, recording them on domestic tape recorders (in production since the sixties).

These men created a bittersweetness of their times – part kicking against the restraints, part reconciling themselves and their audiences to the inevitability of restraint. Among them, the most important to the Soviet intelligentsia was Okudzhava, who, by the time of his death in June 1997, had imprinted many of his lyrics and his gravelly voice on their genetic code. He was both a symbol and a conscience. Small, sad-eyed and of Georgian background, he was born in Moscow in 1924. His father was a Georgian revolutionary, shot in the thirties. He served at the front in the 1941–45 war, then became a teacher. The beginning of his writing career in 1956 coincided with the Twentieth Congress of the Communist Party, at which Khrushchev denounced Stalin.

His voice was one of the first signs of the thaw. His songs about the war mediated through the eyes of twenty-year-old soldiers differed sharply from the official lyrics of Soviet patriotism. He sang about the Moscow streets, the last trolleybus, an old jacket or François Villon. He used language purged of Sovietisms, rather old-fashioned, almost nineteenth-century. 'My songs,' he said in an interview, 'were a dialogue with people who understood each other with half a hint – a quiet dialogue. I did not have to explain anything to them. They knew exactly what I wanted to say without my saying it. It was as if I was writing for good friends; people liked listening to my songs in the kitchen as if I were a third person there.'

When the Soviet Union collapsed and the intelligentsia began to fall apart as a coherent class, he virtually stopped writing. In 1994, he won the Russian Booker prize – but more as a tribute to his life than to the merits of one of his novels. His concerts were largely sustained by nostalgia.

The bard with the larger name and an audience which included, but went far beyond, the intellectuals was Vladimir Vysotsky. When he died at forty-two as a result of alcohol abuse, his funeral became a national demonstration – unsanctioned, but impossible to stop. In sharp contrast to the velvety songs of the Soviet pop singers, Vysotsky sang about, and often on behalf of, the victims of Stalin's régime, about gangsters and outcasts – all who, for one reason or another, refused to conform. Unlike Okudzhava, he used the harsh language of the streets. His hoarse, rasping voice, synonymous with dissent, pierced the stale air of the Brezhnev years.

He was one of the most extreme examples of the political schizo-phrenia of the period: frequently condemned by the press and the Party, on occasion punished, he was still permitted to grow in popularity, to get rich (he drove a Mercedes), to divorce his Russian wife and marry a French film actress, Marina Vlady, to perform on the stage of the

Taganka and to cut close to the bone. Others cut even closer, especially Galich, a little older than the other two, who took up the cause of the millions repressed by Stalin, intoning in one song – as Solzhenitsyn was to do in *Gulag Archipelago* – the names of the death camps:

> Not as soldiers but as numbers
> We died, yes, we died,
> From Karaganda to Narym,
> All the earth like one abscess,
> Vorkuta, Inta, Magadan.

In rediscovering 'human values', or 'individuality', the writers anticipated the political slogans of *perestroika* and *glasnost* by decades. The poets were particularly important in this, especially the figures of Yevgeny Yevtushenko and Andrei Vosnesensky, both of whom continued working past the Gorbachev period in which they were both very active – though with much less resonance and with an ageing clientèle. Yevtushenko, in his early twenties when he made his debut, handsome, naïve but terribly ambitious, brave and generous but able to calculate the limits of permitted apostasy, was a poet superstar, perhaps the world poet superstar of the sixties, ambassador of a new 'caring' Soviet style which the shrewder politicians promoted and both the stupid and the very shrewd saw as a canker in the system.

Yevtushenko bears more than a passing resemblance to Allen Ginsberg, the American beat poet (though his poetry does not ramble quite as much). In sharp contrast to the writer 'standing alongside other labour groups in the commune', Yevtushenko stood for the artist as a chosen vessel of insight and (personal) truth, a wholly romantic figure as he wrote of himself (and he has written much on himself): 'A hungry insatiability reared me, a craving thirst nursed me.' One of his earliest and still among his most famous poems was 'Zima Junction', written about his Siberian birthplace and his return to it after a few years in just-post-Stalin Moscow. It ends with the town itself bidding goodbye to its son:

> 'Yes, truth is good
> but happiness is better
> but nonetheless without truth there is no happiness.
> Go about the world with a proud head,

with everything facing forward
both heart and eyes
and your face
lashed with wet pine needles,
and on your eyelashes laden
with tears and storms.
Love people
and discriminate among them.
Remember
I've got my eye on you.
But if there's trouble,
come back to me . . .
Go!'
And I went
and I keep on going.

Once these green thoughts of a voracious young poet are let loose in the world, and he is fêted and promoted, scolded but indulged, allowed to gather enough capital abroad to make him practically untouchable at home, the message is clear: the limits of personal choice have been dramatically widened. Henceforth, these limits are increasingly experienced, not as the necessary bulwarks of a Soviet society but as the more and more irksome restraints of an order not set by us, the Soviet people, but by them, the Soviet power. Morality lay in opposing 'them' (up to a point), not in strengthening 'us'.

Those who went beyond the point became dissidents and usually ended up in emigration – to the point where they constituted a separate Russian literature, which no one in Russia believes to contain any works superior to those written by these authors in Russia (with the exception of Vladimir Nabokov, a unique case). The point at which writers and artists transgressed the naturally non-existent line was never wholly definable – why, for example, was the poet Josif Brodsky thrown out and Vysotsky tolerated, when the latter seemed much more socially critical and certainly more dangerously popular than the first? – but on examination appears to have much to do with being in or out of the 'Soviet family'. Vysotsky, Yevtushenko, Shatrov could be bad boys, but usually either made their peace or made it clear they were concerned to make the system tolerable, not fundamentally to oppose or question it. And though they had reputations abroad – especially Yevtushenko – they were *Soviet* reputations, not anti-Soviet ones. Above all, these and other in-system critics did not publish abroad first: the publication of *Doctor Zhivago* abroad after its suppression in the Soviet Union forced Boris Pasternak to renounce the Nobel prize he had been awarded for it (and ensured it was not published in his own country until after his death). Writers like Yuly Daniel and Andrei Sinyavsky were imprisoned together in 1965 following foreign publication, and Vladimir Voinovich and ultimately Alexander Solzhenitsyn used foreign publishers. Josif Brodsky was sent into internal exile in 1964 after organizing a mock trial, then exiled from the country in 1972. A pupil of Akhmatova, he died in 1996, acclaimed as the finest poet of his generation. In 1979, a group of writers led by Vasily Aksyonov and Victor Yerofeev published *Metropol*, a vast journal which included a contribution by the US novelist John Updike, copies of which they lodged abroad. It was suppressed (though without harsh sentences); Aksyonov and Yuz Aleshkovsky, another contributor, emigrated.

Drama was also quick to reflect the new mood after Stalin's death. A play by Leonid Zorin, *Guests*, used Stalin's belief that his doctors were plotting to kill him as a medium for investigating the close connection between a totalitarian system and the power of the secret police as early as 1953. The connection was too close for the authorities, who banned it after two showings (Zorin survived to upset more censors).

Dostoyevsky, absent from the Stalin-era stage, came back within a year after the dictator died. The most famed of the revivals was Georgy Tostanogov's production of *The Idiot* in 1957 in Leningrad, with Innokenty Smoktunovsky as Prince Myshkin. Myshkin, returning from abroad, is made to resemble the hundreds of thousands then coming back from the camps: the production opened a new era in Soviet theatre.

The liberated sixties were embodied in the theatrical world by the studio theatre Sovremennik, which opened in 1956. It was the first to be created by the artists themselves, rather than by Party decree. It brought into the theatre a direct and simple style, reviving the traditions of psychological realism first introduced by Stanislavsky at the beginning of the century. It was a gathering point for the young Turks of the artistic world – not, of course, as a centre for denouncing the Soviet system, but for cleansing the society of Stalin's distortions.

In 1967, the Sovremennik staged a trilogy to mark the fiftieth anniversary of the revolution, which traced the revolutionary movement from the Decembrists to the Bolsheviks. The last play of the trilogy – called *The Bolsheviks* – was written by Mikhail Shatrov. It dealt with the matter of terror and justified means – using the explicit parallel of the French Revolution, a device banned for fifty years. Bureaucrats from the Ministry of Culture had thought the play unsuitable; but Ekaterina Furtseva, the minister of culture of the time, gave the theatre the go-ahead and said it was 'the best party meeting' she had attended.

Shatrov – still writing in the mid-nineties, though rarely performed in Russia – worked for much of his life in at once the most prestigious and the most touchy area for any Soviet artist: the portrayal of Lenin, and of other senior Bolsheviks. He was the nephew of Alexei Rykov, a comrade of Lenin and of Stalin, one of the early Soviet prime ministers, arrested by Stalin in 1937 and shot in 1938. In his earliest years (Shatrov was born in 1932) he lost almost all of his closest relatives to the GULAG. His career, though prestigious and high-profile, was controversial; indeed, some of the themes about which he wished to write from the late fifties were not aired until the late eighties, under the visible patronage of Gorbachev. And not just the themes (others did them in a sacral way and gained by it): it was his wish to approach them, while with the proper respect, with curiosity and with some regard for documentary truth. 'I didn't just want to cleanse and glorify the ideas of the revolution, I wanted to see what happened, to get into all the events and tragedies of that year of 1917.'

At the Taganka theatre, the director Yuri Lyubimov developed a drama which contrasted the purity of the communist revolution with the practice of the Soviet government – an endorsement of the idealistic spirit of Mayakovsky and Blok. In an early sixties staging of *Ten Days that Shook the World*, adapted from John Reed's breathless account of the revolution, the actors were dressed in Bolshevik uniforms, met the audience as it came in and stuck the ticket stubs on the end of their bayonets.

The Taganka was one of the most politically daring theatres. It opened in 1963 with a production of Bertolt Brecht's *The Good Person of Szechuan*, a production which marked the beginning of Lyubimov's poetic theatre. (The production was still showing in Moscow in the nineties.) To contrast with the sentimental and naïve Soviet plays of the time, Lyubimov chose Brecht, and the poetry of Mayakovsky and Yesenin.

Theatre had a flowering in the sixties and seventies: in some ways it was its best time, certainly materially and even artistically. There was censorship, but there were also generous subsidies for the big houses, and a genuine artistic energy. The best directors of the time included Mark Zakharov, Anatoly Efros, Anatoly Vasiliev, Lev Dodin, Pyotr Fomenko and Kama Ginkas – most still working into the mid-nineties.

In film, in the drama and the literature of the time, it is above all the yearning for socialism with a human face – or just the yearnings for a human scale – which comes through much of the work. War films – a staple – were used as a medium for psychological examination and even (impossible before the mid-fifties) an anti-war message, as in Grigory Shukhrai's moving *The Ballad of a Soldier* (1960). The polished films of Eldar Ryazanov epitomize the mood as it developed in the late sixties and seventies: their heroes often bumbling, well-meaning, in danger of being submerged by life but possessed of a human value which comes through, as the feckless economist in *Office Romance* shows when his love for his prim, stern but in the end vulnerable woman boss conquers all. Vladimir Menshov's *Moscow Doesn't Believe in Tears*, made in 1980 but set in the sixties, shows three single young women cleave their separate individual paths through post-Stalinist life. These films, which have lasted, competed with hundreds of filmed editorials from *Pravda* which have mostly not; but they were given wide showings, big budgets and together pulled in very large audiences.

A young and sarcastic critic, Alexander Timofeevsky, sketched out the classic Ryazanov audience as:

middle-aged, middle-class and urban. Engineers and researchers, doctors and instructors – all those usually defined by the term 'technical intelligentsia'. These were the people whom Ryazanov was addressing during the difficult years of the seventies in such films as *Irony of Fate* (1975), *Office Romance* (1978) and *The Garage* (1980). The cultural mythology of this audience is quite extensive, though it rests on the three pillars of Bach, the French Impressionists and Mikhail Bulgakov's *Master and Margarita*. To be wholly honest, we must add that this audience calls any organ piece 'Bach', that their list of French Impressionists begins with Picasso and Modigliani and that Bulgakov's novel was for them a fount of trivial wisdom. In the sixties this audience, poor but proud, exercised properly every day and constantly debated whether skating was a sport or an art.

As elsewhere, the development of something like an artistic civil society forced the leadership's less-than-steely hands. Elite cinema – the kind of film watched by the intellectuals and hailed abroad – was usually not much to the communist leaders' liking; but pressure from the Cinematographers' Union, and from individual prestigious directors, could usually hold off the censor and obtain money. If this was a game, it was a serious one with casualties. Andrei Tarkovsky (who won his first international prize at the Venice festival in 1962 when he was thirty) could make films like *Andrei Rublev, Mirror, Stalker* and *Solaris* with some problems but with eventual success. But *The Commissar* by Alexander Askoldov was shelved for twenty years, breaking the director's career. The big directors, like Sergei Bondarchuk, Sergei Gerasimov and Lev Kulidzhanov (all Heroes of Socialist Labour) did both Russian and Soviet classics on the screen, had great influence on the Soviet leadership and could and did intervene on occasion to protect or promote less acclaimed colleagues. There were parallel powers: GosKino, the state agency, had formal control of the industry; but the big directors and actors – some, like Bondarchuk, combined both roles – could 'open Brezhnev's door with their foot'. Cinema had the advantage of growing up with the Bolsheviks: explicitly conceived of as a medium to the masses (before TV usurped it) it received huge funds, the state establishing two large studios in Moscow and another in Leningrad, together with separate studios in each of the Soviet republics – which meant that republics as tiny as Estonia had cinema industries larger than those of many European states, and the 5 million-strong Georgian republic, with its wealth of artistic talent, could boast a constant and high output of quality films.

In the sixties, the practice of art bifurcated: official art was produced with less enthusiasm and more cynicism: those who wished to explore their talent did so in their own time, occasionally disturbed by the KGB, sometimes excluded from the Union of Artists, never honoured – but allowed to work. The angry outburst by Khrushchev at a 1962 exhibition of 'unofficial art' and the bulldozing of an open-air exhibition in 1974 were both seen as heralding crackdowns; they were, but not of any duration or seriousness compared to the recent past. Nor were they able to do more than temporarily check the general movement towards greater and wider experimentation, deeper disillusionment with and scorn for official diktat and the spread of a bohemian culture among the educated.

Artists developed a bohemian, 'underground' lifestyle which was under more real threat than its Western equivalent – but was liveable. Sergei Barkhin, appointed chief designer at the Bolshoi in the early nineties, lived such a life:

It was not, after 1953, any longer a question of life and death, it was a question of more or less comfortable living. No one could shoot you for not being a socialist realist. It was easy to fool the system – all the institutions were so gigantic, you could slip through the cracks. You could be right [official] in the daytime and left [unofficial] at night. Non-conformist artists felt themselves to be the descendants of the French Impressionists, who were not understood by the rich. They saw their conflict with the Communist Party as the traditional conflict between the artist and bourgeois society. They lived in a bohemian and élitist world. There was the sweet aura of the forbidden in these circles.

A large number of artists made up this movement, most based in or coming to Moscow and Leningrad. Ilya Kabakov (b. 1933), Erik Bulatov (b. 1933) and Ilya Glazunov (b. 1930) were the best known: Kabakov has been the most successful abroad since the fall of communism, Glazunov by far the most successful domestically, to the point where he has almost the title – though certainly no longer among the avant garde – of 'official artist'. Others – both of their generation and younger – include Natalya Nesterova, Tatyana Nazarenko, Mikhail Shvartsman, Vladimir Yankilevski and the poet–painter Dmitri Prigov.

They were thrown together because they were working unofficially, and showed in flats or went out to the country to perform 'happenings'; they sold to a small circle of liberal Soviets (often scientists, given licence to indulge in this) or Westerners. The bundling-together of these men and women was because of their illegal status, but they were of course hugely diverse. Glazunov was and remained the painter of 'Russian nationalist' themes, an obsessive depicter of the cruelty visited upon the country by its rulers and by foreigners, a kitsch Solzhenitsyn on canvas. Shvartsman, with others, found his inspiration in the iconic tradition. Kabakov incorporated text into his pages, an ironic echo of the Stalinist-era propaganda art.

In some art forms, such as music, discipline was hard to enforce by a Party élite largely ignorant of music's development. Composers and artists of worth often preferred to work wholly or in part in the 'underground' than to gain honours and fame within a stifling Soviet framework in which socialist realist norms dictated a tuneful music and a representational art, in order that they would be comprehensible to and inspirational of the masses (at least in the early years, this appears to have been achieved).

The contemporary composers – Schnittke, Denisov (who died in 1996) and the Estonian Arvo Part are the best known – have known greater or lesser degrees of discrimination and official ostracism; their reputations, particularly that of Schnittke, were made in the world before they were made officially in the Soviet Union.

Pop music was more closely monitored and much more politicized. Yet it was popular, after all. The melodic, cheerful and sentimental tunes of such writers as Raymond Pauls – later a Latvian minister of culture in the late eighties – were, when performed by the hugely loved pop star Alla Pugacheva, widely listened to and sung. A red-haired, pre-Madonna, hard-living singer of the Soviet *estrada* (urban popular) tradition, Pugacheva was not so different from many American pop idols of the seventies.

Indeed, one of the more surprising discoveries of the aftermath of the Soviet collapse was how similar trends were in popular culture on both sides of the Iron Curtain. Musical comedies such as *Volga Volga* (1938), *Circus* (1936), *Happy-Go-Lucky Guys* (1934) – all made by Grigory Alexandrov in the midst of the purges – were profoundly Soviet in their optimistic message but were strikingly similar to the European and American musical comedies of the time. These films used music to present a carefree, almost festival atmosphere shorn of any hint of the mass slaughter and privation which accompanied the furious construction to socialism. Isaac Dunayevsky was the principal figure in this – his tunes sung still, his film scores still fresh.

The songs which accompanied people's work and life, which suggested ways in which they could be romantic or patriotic, gay or sentimental, were, after efforts by the revolutionaries to create a new proletarian popular music in the twenties, based on tunes from the folk or *estrada* traditions. Indeed, both folk and *estrada* were Sovietized – an ersatz folk tradition created by more or less talented composers in much the same way as US 'country' songs or Scots 'folk' songs continue to be written and enjoyed. Yevgeny Barankin, a music critic, says of this period: 'This genre was a new thing: it drew from Russia but it was not wholly Russian, it was not Azeri, not Georgian – it was Soviet, a new thing. There were different ways of doing this – it could be patriotic, it could be tender – the words were often rather monotonous but the music was great. One has to say that a lot of the composers and librettists of these "old Russian folk songs" were Jewish.'

It is not just the rosy spectacles of retrospection, or Stalinist kitsch, to see in those early songs and scores a real talent and energy, an energy which lasted some time later than the Stalin era, but which did fade and die. The commissions for the Party became more blatantly hack work, cynically done for money and privilege. The composers, too, had their carrots which kept them, and the system, going: song competitions, for the best song written on Lenin's birthday, the best song for this or that Party gathering. There would be much consulting of the Party calendar. Composers would write songs in honour of the annual conference of the *kolkhozes*, or in honour of the release from prison of the Greek composer Mikis Theodorakis. Such songs were called by the initiated 'fish' – for an unknown reason but perhaps because they so quickly went rotten.

Parallel to the official mass culture there grew an underground rock scene, inspired by the songs of Vysotsky and Galich, neither banned nor officially acknowledged. Rock developed first timidly and imitatively (especially, from around 1964, imitative of the Beatles), but gradually took hold and found a lyrical if not a musical independence.

Imitation was not, initially, despised; on the contrary, the closer the imitation the better. 'The medieval principle prevailed,' says the writer Alexander Sokolyansky. 'The imitation was more important than the original work.' Much more powerful in its appeal – at least to youth – than the bards, the efforts to suppress rock nevertheless put it in the same political camp as they were, or liked to think themselves. The first popular rock singers – Alexander Gradsky, the 'father' of the scene, Andrei Makarevich and his band Mashina Vremeni (Time Machine), Stas Nauman – were themselves from intellectual backgrounds (Nauman was the grandson of Stalin's trade commissar, Anastas Mikoyan. All were more or less tolerated, indeed, promoted. After 1980, when rock passed into a period of very rapid growth, new groups and singers captured the popular mood, and in many cases made closer links with the intelligentsia.

This was especially true of Boris Grebenshchikov, with his band Aquarium, who, while displaying a dramatic, erotic style on stage – homoerotic according to the first outraged Soviet officials who watched the group's debut at a Tblisi concert in 1980 – cultivated the image of a poet, even something of mystic – as well as being, in the immediacy of his lyrics, an heir of Vysotsky. Victor Tsoy, leader of the group Kino, moved in artistic circles in Leningrad; while Konstantin Kitchin, leader of Alisa, staged 'happenings' with stage directors and actors. 'Rock in the eighties,' says Sokolyansky, 'inherited the civic approach of Vysotsky and Galich. Anyone who was content with life was despised by the groups, and was called a "major" [after the major key] – smiling, jolly, smug, bourgeois. That they thought was disgusting.' That view, ironically, was not to survive the collapse of communism – when these groups got their chance to become bourgeois, and mostly took it. Along with almost everyone else who could.

CHAPTER TWENTY-SEVEN

'Is it a Russian playing?'

The nineties was a time of the very rapid decay of the Soviet high art system. The large sums of money spent on it is only one reason, for even had money been available, it alone could not again recreate that interlinked and ideological complex whose products, whatever else they might have been, could only have been Soviet.

In the theatre, the incomparable, emotionally gripping acting style was confined very largely to the classics – Chekhov, Dostoyevsky, Ostrovsky – the best of these presented in studios or rehearsal rooms before deliberately restricted audiences. At the opera, the repertoire was sung (usually) finely, but in ancient sets made for thirty-year-old productions. In avant garde art, the main reference point remained Ilya Kabakov, whose pre-eminence was established in the underground in the seventies and who lived in Paris. Novels and stories became scabrous, sickening, with disjointed plots, the opposite of the linear narratives and nineteenth-century moral purpose of the realist school of the Soviet period. Serious music – that which was produced – was as difficult, hermetic and cultish as anywhere else.

The ballet is popularly thought of as the most 'Russian' of the arts – the one whose identification with the state is a cliché. It has been Russified, then Sovietized to such an extent that the world public, especially that which knows little of ballet, simply assumes that Russia is its capital. That impression, the product of hard work by the Soviet state in taking over and developing the traditions and expertise of a tsarist Imperial ballet promoted as the best in the world, was soon at risk. Indeed, for many ballet lovers and critics, it ended in the nineties.

For the ballet, as for space exploration and the arms race, money had been no object. Once money became worth something, it was finished in its former guise, a guise which preserved and fêted it – in particular the Bolshoi – as a Soviet hothouse, a showcase for visitors and an occasional ambassador for the USSR abroad (nervy affairs, because of defections). Its most famous director, Yuri Grigorovich, ruled the Bolshoi for thirty years from 1964, initially revivifying the repertoire, ultimately unable to innovate further within the restrictions of the canon and finally prised loose from power. He was opposed by many of his leading performers, though not the majority of the staff, who liked a conservative régime. More importantly, he failed to get backing from the Kremlin (which continued to have the last word on the Bolshoi) for his opposition to a contract system of employment, designed in part to cut the huge costs of the theatrical army. The business manager, Vladimir Kokonin, won, and won in a fashion unthinkable in Soviet times. He said in an interview in March 1995: 'People are going to have to start justifying their salaries. We don't want time-serving civil service types.'

In ballet, in opera and in classical music, the companies and orchestras which survive are heavily dependent on such figures as Kokonin, for only by securing foreign tours and the hard currency incomes can their institutions survive and their salaries be more than miserable. This means, in turn, that their repertoire tended to become ossified into the 'favourites'; they played rarely under guest conductors and their tours lasted longer and packed more in than any equivalent Western company would allow. The St Petersburg Philharmonic, a famed orchestra, appeared less than half the year in its home city; one of its two principal conductors, Mariss Jansons, became chief conductor of the Pittsburgh Symphony, the principal guest conductor of the London Philharmonic and had a contract to conduct with the Oslo Philharmonic.

The absence, or only formal presence, of the stars is striking in comparison to the Soviet times. Defections of artists with talent in the most portable and internationally comprehensible of arts – dance, song, musical performance – had been periodic; from Gorbachev's time, it became a flood, as performers realized the relatively huge earnings available on even minor international circuits. The Moscow Conservatoire, until the eighties the best musical school in the world, producing a huge proportion of the century's most gifted pianists and violinists, still had in the nineties an impressive list of professors which included many of these performers; but few gave more than one or two classes a year on the rare occasions they visited Moscow. The result was fewer prizes in the Tchaikovsky and other competitions for the Conservatoire's pupils and, in the complaint of the pianist and Conservatoire professor Nikolai Petrov, 'We are very near the end of what we were most proud of – the Russian style of playing. The professors work so little with their pupils you cannot tell if it is a Russian playing.'

'Near the end': the theme of exhaustion is one which recurs again and again. The great centres were often under the control of one, all-powerful director for many years – Vinogradov for eighteen years at the Maryinsky/Kirov, Grigorovich for thirty at the Bolshoi, and the late Yevgeny Mravinsky for an astonishing fifty years at the St Petersburg Philharmonic (Mravinsky had directed several Shostakovich premières). These régimes were naturally conservative and authoritarian, but they could also create a disciplined, hothouse environment in which talent could be nurtured and at least competence demanded. For many Russians, the conclusion was obvious: capital accumulated in socialist times is now being spent in the capitalist market and, at least in the early days after the Soviet collapse, was not being replaced.

This could take a directly physical form. In 1992, a Russian–American businessman, Tristran Del, began negotiating with the state TV and radio companies for rights to market its enormous archive of recorded classical music, finally succeeding in striking a deal in 1995 which brought in the UK disc marketing company Telstar to issue selections from the 400,000 hours of music – including Shostakovich (playing as well as being performed), Prokofiev and Stravinsky, with performers like Emil Gillels, Sviatoslav Richter and Leonid Rostropovich. The deal was protested, by Nikolai Petrov and the Ministry of Culture, among others. It went through, however; though Del, who said he invested some $5 million, had clearly made a bargain, he was also making available material which might otherwise have been left to decay indefinitely.

The greater exhaustion was that of ideology; and with the exhaustion of the Soviet ideology, it did not seem as if there was an immediately available replacement. The tyranny of the long-lived directors paralleled that of the state; their repertoire was a mixture of preserved classics and approved propagandist works, such as the ballet *Spartacus*, for which Kachaturian wrote the score and Grigorovich did the choreography, which was itself a conventional work, if one using convention and hyper-activity to express the Soviet Union's liberating mission. *Spartacus* is, when danced at full stretch, an astounding event, especially its climax where the hero is raised towards the roof on the tips of spears. But it is regarded by the ballet world as an ageing curiosity. 'Only the Bolshoi could have danced this ballet . . . and only the Bolshoi would have wanted to,' wrote the American writer Luke Jennings. Grigorovich, the central post-war figure in Russian ballet, was initially innovative, and sought to stage *Swan Lake* with its original version, approved by Tchaikovsky, of a tragic ending, to express what the composer called 'the world taken by evil forces', the dominant preoccupation of his later music. Ekaterina Furtseva, the Minister of Culture, demanded that high Soviet art have the required happy ending in which tensions are resolved, and she was obeyed. It was a clear mark of the limits, and though limits preserve as well as constrict, they also aggravate the most talented. Soviet ballet was ferociously conservative, but it was a conservatism which required the strongest of defences, and none was strong enough to stop the escape of some of the finest and the infiltration of much that was subversive. The high Soviet fortress was crumbling, inside and out, by the end.

But as a leading Russian critic, Vadim Gayevsky, put it: 'Killing ballet is not easy. Ballet in Russia is very badly injured but it is not dead yet. As long as there are the amazing schools and as long as there is an interest it will survive. Ballet is an art with a past and a future but with no present.' The notion that socialist artistic capital is now being squandered is a natural thought, but is only another way of noting that Russia is joining the international cultural circuit. That its famous should be trying, by all means, to get rich as well is inevitable, if at times repellent – they have after all been the envious guests on their foreign colleagues' estates and in their palatial apartments for decades. Lacking the old means of coercion over its artists, Russian institutions – and Russian musical society – is now faced with funding the institutions and finding the money with which to attract them. By the mid-nineties, there were some small signs it was doing so: the fees for star artists in Moscow, St Petersburg and other musical cities like Odessa had risen to closer to international levels; the state recording label Melodiya had been broken up, part of it concluding an agreement with the German company BMG to market its archival material, with much larger fees paid to the interpreters.

There may be a benign paradox in this: the collapse of the Soviet musical universe may assist the development of the capitalist one. Orchestras from Russia and other former Soviet republics were pouring on to the world market in the mid-nineties, and by doing so, putting great pressure on the fee structure. It is quite possible a protectionist and élitist music world will put up barriers and keep up their prices. It is also possible that the hungry Easterners will succeed in lowering the price of classical and modern music, and add their weight to the spreading popularity of both.

In *Omon Ra*, a slim novel written by Victor Pelevin in 1992, the eponymous hero muses: 'I realized at once and early on that only weightlessness can give man genuine freedom – which is why all my life I've been bored by all those Western radio voices and those books by various Solzhenitsyns. In my heart, of course, I loathed a state whose silent menace obliged every group of people who came together, even if only for a few seconds, to zealously imitate the vilest and bawdiest individual among them . . .'

There, in two sentences, Pelevin delivers the judgement of his generation (in its early thirties) on both the Soviet state and that of its sternest critics – though is careful to see the second as menacing and the first as merely boring. This careless tossing aside of both totalitarianism and dissidence, of the 'various Solzhenitsyns' along with a 'state [of] silent menace', is a typically bravado-ish gesture which will hopefully cause Pelevin and others much more extreme than he to blush in later life. In the aftermath of the Fall, it seemed an essential pose for writers struggling to cope with a universe whose ruins were made up of *both* good and evil figures, figures who moreover had spent decades calling each other good and evil.

The writers who became known as the 'new' Russian writers in the eighties and nineties were generally not new, not very young and had rejected official communism and official anti-communism while the former was still in business and the latter was still being punished. As they became more securely recognized at home and abroad, and were complimented by a barrage of criticism from the sixties generation who regarded them as an abomination, they became bolder in putting forward their 'manifesto' – which, though never written down as a collective statement, was a set of beliefs and attitudes and preoccupations which does distinguish them from what has gone before – though not so much as they think.

Omon Ra expresses some of it. A finely written and skilful book, its hero – whose name combines the acronym of the Russian special forces and the Egyptian sun god – enrols as a pilot, is recruited as an astronaut, is told by his superiors that his mission will result in the death of him and his fellows – and fulfils it, though the matter of his death is left, literally, in the air. The central dynamic is an interlocking series of lies: that he has no choice but to fulfil the mission for which he has 'volunteered'; that the Soviet space programme is more humane than the American since the former uses unmanned rockets, while actually squads of young men like Omon are sent to their death to further the deception; and that the mission does not go anywhere anyway, being an elaborate charade for television. The KGB colonel who assists in Omon's training tells him: 'We just didn't have the time to defeat the West technologically. But in the battle of ideas you can't stand still for a second. The paradox – another piece of dialectics – is that we support the truth with falsehood because Marxism carries within it an all-conquering truth, and the goal for which you will give your life is in a formal sense, a deception. But . . . the more consciously you perform your feat of heroism, the greater will be the degree of its truth, the greater will be the meaning of your brief and beautiful life.'

Later, in a passage of triumphantly black humour, Pelevin/Omon Ra hears from one of his fellow victim-cosmonauts the story of how, in order to induce a good mood in a visiting Henry Kissinger, the Soviet leadership dresses two other 'volunteers' in bear skins to pose as easy targets. Failing to hit them even at close range, an enraged Kissinger falls upon one 'bear' and wounds it mortally with a knife – and signs an arms control agreement on top of it as it (that is, the man inside the skin) expires. Such marvellous fantasies abound in the novel. The Soviet experience is not so much satirized as represented as wholly controlling and wholly dedicated to the production of lies at once insanely evil and logically fantastic. *Omon Ra* sold modestly in a Russia whose readership was much more attracted to – almost invariably pirated – editions of American thrillers and pornography. Once the officially promoted versions of the classics and of the favoured writers ended, there was a market; and high culture, in the form of contemporary serious novels, found it hard to survive.

Pelevin has been, like most of his contemporaries, indebted to Venedict Yerofeev, a writer who – brought up in an orphanage after his father was imprisoned and his mother ran off in 1938 – led a life of menial jobs and drunkenness while writing, in the late sixties, *Moscow-Petushki*, which became a Soviet underground classic: a complex, parodic work in which the narrator-hero Venichka (diminutive of Venedikt) travels from Moscow to the small town of Petushki while soliloquizing on a world from which all of the standard Soviet virtues are absent. Yerofeev died in 1992, from cancer of the throat.

The 'new' writers owe much to *Moscow-Petushki*, its early indifference to the constraints of both the state and dissidence, its disorienting episodic form, its romantic individualism, its hopelessness. But where it remains for the most part allegorically dense and restrained, many of the newcomers write with an extraordinary violence about the world they have lost, or which they disown. Vladimir Sorokin mixes bestial sex, excrement, disease and amputation – often interwoven with or suddenly erupting into passages of peaceful narrative. Yuz Aleshkovsky, older than most of his 'new' contemporaries and with four years of prison camp in his memory, mixes camp and other obscenities with strong narrative lines drawn from the institutional follies of Soviet life. Yuri Miroslavsky (an exile) writes a kind of expressionless prose of horror, of a universe of matter-of-fact lawless predation: 'The patrolmen caught Katya when she was coming home from a craft club where they taught her how to make green cardigans. They felt her up and decided she was OK, took her back to the station and gang-banged her until blood ran from her mouth. Then they threw her out of the station in a snowdrift, green cardigan and all' (*The Death of Manon*). The rawness of the prose, shocking enough for Western readers, was doubly so for a Sovietized audience whose prose had been decorous and prudish.

In one sense – as Russian critics have noted – these were the first 'social realists'. They presented 'reality' as closely as they could, especially that reality 'socialist realism' (which was in fact socialist idealism) left out. Hence Vladimir Sorokin's famous *Queue*, published in Paris in 1985, is simply a myriad of realistic dialogues in a queue for an unknown commodity available at an indefinite time, yet at the same time achieves the status of an allegory on quotidian Soviet life. Lyudmila Petrushevskaya, one of the best-known (and best) of the 'new writers' (she was born in 1935), has assembled a world of prose and drama in which her characters behave with a consistent vileness – especially the men to the women, as in *Nets and Traps* and *A Girl Like That*. Not only is there no redemption in these tales; there is a grinding-under of the very concept of redemption, a lingering on the arbitrariness and cruelty of fate, an emphasis that nothing better can be expected – the opposite of the Soviet 'bright future' which was still being tacked on to official literature even as the darker was being written and suppressed, or published abroad.

The 'new' writers hated the Soviet Union, had contempt for the sixties generation and only perfunctory respect for the dissidents. Though clearly unable to desist from poking about in the ruins and drains of a society they no longer regarded as 'ours', they tended to disclaim any interest in being part of a tradition, or even literary citizens of any defined country. 'It's wrong to think there's a Russian literature,' says Pelevin. 'There is nowhere Russian literature could come from. We all grew up amid McDonalds, dollars, American cars. What's specifically Russian about it all? The climate perhaps.'

Among the boldest and most prominent of the new writers, a veteran of the *Metropol* affair, is Victor Yerofeev (no relation to Venedict). In essays, interviews and TV appearances, he has drawn a sharp line between the ancient and the modern – or, as he and others would have it, between the Soviet and the post-modern. In a celebrated essay in the *Literary Gazette* he proposed that each of the three 'streams' of literature which had developed after Stalin's death – 'official', 'village prose' and 'liberal' – were in terminal crisis, the first two collapsing into a Russian nationalism made the more bitter on the part of the official writers for the loss of prestige, money and subsidized print-runs, and on the part of the village prose writers by the loss of artistic vigour (with the major exception of Victor Astafiev). As for the liberals and the dissidents, wrote Yerofeev, their literature 'has completed the social mission which literature, alas, was forced to assume during the era of the strong state. But in post-utopian Russia, it's time to return to literature-as-such.' In a later essay, 'Russia's *Fleurs du Mal*', Yerofeev pointed to the decades before the 1917 revolution – Russia's 'silver age' – as one in which some writers raised post-modern themes, by which he meant they disengaged from political and social concerns in the recognition – in the words of Fyodor Sologub's 'Little Demon' – that 'evil has free rein in the human soul . . . a philosophy of hope is superfluous'. This *fin-de-siècle* pose was contrasted to what he called, cuttingly, the 'warmth of goodness' which breathed from the lyrics and the prose of the sixties liberals – Yevtushenko, Okudzhava and even the harder-edged exile writer Vladimir Voinovich. The loss of the Soviet literary hothouse, he acknowledges, was a real one; and through the period, from Yevgeny Zamyatin (*We*) through Bulgakov (*The Master and Margarita*), Boris Pasternak (*Dr Zhivago*) to Alexander Solzhenitsyn, a 'worthy resistance to tyranny' had been carried on. But the loss 'releases the energy that is indispensable for a full journey . . . the new Russian literature flutters out of its mine cage. The intensity with which it experiences freedom, it would seem, underpins its very existence.'

The sixties people thought the opposite. Many of them did not recognize this 'shit' (the most commonly used word) as literature at all. Lev Anensky, among the most prominent of the sixties generation still writing in the mid–nineties, said that 'most modern writers get a kick out of the fact that they buried the sixties liberals and now are dancing on their graves. They get their energy from anger. Only when they kill us completely will they start to appreciate and feel nostalgic about the culture of the past age. We are living corpses, surviving on artificial respiration.' Said Inna Solovyova: 'All the artists want to do today is to yell that everyone is a bastard and everything is shit. I fail to understand the joy and excitement about it.' And the critic Igor Zolotussky: 'Dostoyevsky never showed intercourse; the new writers believe that if they give us pornography they will show us the depths of evil which Dostoyevsky was not capable of plumbing. But they do not show us the depths of evil. They show us the depths of dirt and ugliness.'

The fundamental literary divide carried on into the judgements made on what instantly became – from its founding in 1991 – Russia's richest and most contested literary award, the Russian Booker Prize, worth £10,000, a huge sum in Russian literary circles. The prize – put up by the same corporation which subsidized the most prestigious British literary award – assisted in publicizing, both in Russia and abroad, talents like Mark Kharitonov (winner of the award in 1992), Nikolai Klimontovich (twice nominated) and Alexei Slapovsky (twice nominated). Lev Anensky, the chairman of the Booker jury in 1994, awarded the prize to Okudzhava's novel *The Closed-Down Theatre* on the explicit grounds that Okudzhava's work, an autobiographical account of the fate of his own family reduced from the nomenclatura to prison camps in the late thirties purges, deserved the prize because of his suffering. It was a prize to his clan, the sixties generation clan, the snatching of an award before it was too late and the generation was swamped by the post-modernists and their successors. In 1995, when the jury was again chaired by a sixties man, Stanislav Rassadin, the prize went to the *émigré* (in Germany) Georgy Vladimov, for his short novel *A General and his Army*, a work which tackled among other themes that of the Russians who served on the German side in the Second World War, in the army of General Vlasov. The other two finalists had both reached the shortlist for novels about the GULAG.

All were sixties men with sixties preoccupations. In a very clear expression of the fundamental divide, the always combative daily *Nezavisimaya Gazeta* inaugurated in that year an 'Anti-Booker' prize (which it said would in future years be called the Brothers Karamazov Award) and gave it to a young writer called Alexei Varlamov for his book *The Birth*. The novel dealt with love and the lack of it in a contemporary Russian family, and contains an extended and bitter reference to the shelling of the White House. The woman who is the centre of the novel and who bears a child to a husband she was about to divorce, watches him – who had had some faith in the new Russian government – watching TV as the White House is shelled: '[He was] bewildered and defenceless, and he suddenly grew younger and more stupid . . . it was strange to think that this man was the father of her child.' The meaning of the Anti-Booker award was obvious: the lavish, foreign-sponsored prize went to the sixties people, who had revered the West and were interested in agendas of past decades; a truly Russian award went to a writer who engaged with contemporary life, which foreigners could neither understand nor take part in, even by proxy.

However history may deal with the 'new' writing, there is no doubt the opposition to it is a last, if still powerful, gasp, the kind of unavailing effort to shore up the old world order. It is also a last gasp because Yerofeev is right: the collapse of the Soviet Communist Party killed the *raison d'être* of those who opposed it, both within the system and without. The power of that system is rarely as striking as when one observes the strength and courage of those who openly opposed it, and even more when one recognizes that, for all that, they were enfolded within it, defined by it and left gasping by its passing. By the mid-nineties, the passions which had erupted in the Gorbachev years and which had split the Union of Writers had been replaced by the spitting and hissing of dying arguments.

Alexander Solzhenitsyn survived into the new age. That was unfortunate for his short-term reputation. Alone of the major dissidents – only Sakharov rivalled him in stature and fame, and he was a Westernizer in contrast to Solzhenitsyn's steady Slavophilia – he came back to the country from which he had been expelled in 1974. Josif Brodsky, asked in July 1995 if *he* would return, said flatly: 'I don't think I can. The country in which I grew up doesn't exist any more. You can't walk in the same river twice.' Though he had the same qualms, Solzhenitsyn yielded to the temptation, apparently strong in him, to emulate the later Tolstoy in posing as a moral beacon to his people. Vladimir Voinovich had prefigured the return in an episode in his *Moscow 2042*, when he showed his Solzhenitsyn pastiche, Sim Simych Karavolov, practising his return on a white horse in his North American estates with one of his retainers acting the part of a Soviet soldier:

'Answer me,' said Simych resoundingly. 'Why did you serve the predator authorities? Against whom did you take up arms?'

'Forgive me, Little Father,' said the soldier . . . 'I didn't serve them of my own free will, I was forced by those satans.'

'Will you swear to serve only me from now on and fight steadfastly against the predatory communists and pluralist spongers?'

'Yes, I will, Little Father, I promise to serve you against all your enemies, to defend the borders of Holy Russia from all who hate our people.'

'Kiss the sword!'

Sim Simych does return on a white horse to what becomes his literal kingdom. Solzhenitsyn returned by air to Khabarovsk in the Far East in 1994, then to Moscow via a long train journey, during which – accompanied by BBC film cameras – he consulted with the people. He took an honoured place in Moscow. He had a group of followers and admirers in the media. Most political figures found it advisable to genuflect to his greatness. He addressed the Duma, warning of the decadence of the authorities and the growing impatience of the people. He talked with President Yeltsin on the same themes. And he was given a TV programme on the main state TV channel, every other Monday night after the evening news, on which to give his views – at first through the medium of guests whom he largely ignored, then in the form of a monologue to the camera – a discourse of anguish, complaint, demands and direct warnings. Among other works, mainly written in exile, he published a tract, 'The Russian Question', in which he excoriated most of Russia's past rulers – tsars and Bolsheviks – for betraying her national interest, took a fine tilt at the communists once more, and ended with the warning of racial extinction:

The 'Russian question' at the end of the twentieth century stands unequivo-cal: shall our people *be* or *not be*. The vulgar and insipid wave which seeks to level distinctions between cultures, traditions, nationalities and characters has engulfed the whole planet. And yet how many withstand this onslaught, unwavering and with their head held high! Not we, however . . . If we persist in this way, who knows if in another century the time may come to cross the word 'Russian' out of the dictionary? . . . We must build a moral Russia, or none at all . . . it would not then matter anyway.

Solzhenitsyn had developed his thought, but not substantially changed it, in exile. In his writing were the purest echoes of the late-nineteenth-century Slavophilic writers – a dislike of parliamentary and legalistic forms, a striving for wholeness, a belief that searching for freedom in the external world, while possibly desirable, was strictly subordinate to a search for inner freedom, an elevation of the purifying effects of suffering. He told a Harvard audience in 1978:

A fact which cannot be disputed is the weakening of the human personality in the West while in the East it has become stronger. Six decades for our people and three decades for the people of Eastern Europe; during that time we have been through a spiritual training far in advance of the Western experience. The complex and daily crush of life has produced stronger, deeper and more interesting personalities than those generated by stand-ardized Western wellbeing.

Like all opinions, these 'facts' can and should be disputed, there being arguments on both sides. Nothing which Solzhenitsyn had seen or learned in the nearly two decades since that message was delivered had appeared to change him much: he remained, to the public eye at least, rocklike in his certainties, scornful and abrasive in his disapprovals, showing not a sign of irony or relativism.

He would have done better to follow the Brodsky stratagem. The river in which he stepped for a second time had flowed past him; he became another object at which the hyper-cynical young could tear, and the compromised elders could sneer with relief. His later prose was clotted and 'unreadable'; his earlier work a long time ago; his TV and other performances embarrassingly passionate and long-winded. Even well-wishers were bored. In September 1995, the journalist Konstantin Kedrov, writing in *Izvestiya* and giving full honour to the historic Solzhenitsyn, wrote: 'For many years we were spectators to the Solzhenitsyn political theatre. Now it's quite clear that the new piece hasn't worked. *One Day in the Life of Ivan Denisovich* is worth more than all the days of Solzhenitsyn on TV.' At the same time, in the *New York Review of Books* (October 1995), Tatyana Tolstaya mounted a sarcastic piece of invective (with the minimum of genuflection to the dissident past), stooping to retell rumours that Solzhenitsyn had paid to have his show aired and casting a passing doubt on whether or not his cancer, which formed the subject matter for *Cancer Ward*, was real. He is, she wrote, 'like an elderly pensioner . . . [who] vents the irritation accumulated over a lifetime'; he is a figure of pity: 'I feel rather sorry for him: he tries, he prepares, he believes'; he 'shouts soundlessly, waves his arms about in the dark, tears his hair and flies like an incorporeal spirit in a swirl of electrons through the indifferent ether to beat against my television screen, begging to be let out with his mouldy predictions'.

Shortly after these two articles, the show was killed. A curt message from the new management of Russian Public Television (ORT) mentioned falling ratings. Solzhenitsyn said nothing publicly; his wife talked of communists still in positions of influence who wished to silence him. But this was an old windmill: the new media powers were non-ideological (if ultimately obedient to government), cool – and bored, like Tolstaya. Much of his time since his return had been spent preparing a 24-volume edition of his works, but in December of 1995, Voenizdat, the publisher (formerly the military's publishing house), withdrew from its commitment, citing the government's refusal to buy a set for all 20,000 of the country's libraries. It could not, it said, guarantee sufficient individual buyers to make the project profitable. 'Russia', said *Izvestiya*, 'is not yet ready for such a complex project.'

He had harmed himself. He had given little nourishment, except to the legions of cynics, and the swathes of lesser people than he. His litanies of complaints and moral posturings were futile, he could do nothing by airing them. Most of all he was a spirit of an era past – an era where protest had to be weighed in every scruple, since its punishment was likewise weighed. He survived to an era in which words were both free and cheap . . . and unheeded, in any quarter. His courage had done much to break a system which both his talent and his vanity needed to give him and his work meaning. Without it, his greatness was secure only in the past and the future; in the present, he joined the flow of meaninglessness.

Aphrodite bends over Stalin, caressing his chin, seeming about to incline to whisper in his ear. He sits by massive pillars, a curtain draped about them, a Roman oil lamp burning on a bracket against the wall. The title: *The Appearance of Socialist Realism*. A painting of fleecy clouds in a blue sky is almost blotted out by the huge red letters PRAISE TO THE CPSU'. An empty tin, on whose white label are scribbled numerous signatures, has appearing above its top rim a little notice on a stick reading 'Tin of signatures for the full and unconditional disarmament of America'.

This was Sots Art, a school which flourished from the early seventies underground and abroad to the later eighties when, able to display itself, it died. Its main figures – Erik Bulatov, Dmitri Prigov, Grisha Bruskin, the collaborators Alexander Melamid and Vitaly Komar – were men of the sixties, sometimes younger. Their work, often juxtaposed Western consumer or showbiz symbols with Soviet icons, like Leonid Sokov's *Stalin and Marilyn* or Alexander Kosolapov's *Plan for an Advertisement in Times Square*, showing a huge red poster with the Coca-Cola sign and Lenin's face, and the slogan 'It's the real thing – Lenin'. It was shocking at first, amusing, often with several frames of reference beyond the obvious.

But by the late eighties, each could be his own Sots Artist. The jumble of capitalist and communist, of images once inimical jostling against each other promiscuously, was better seen on the streets and on TV than in galleries. Pushkin, not Times, Square was the epicentre of this – because it was in Pushkin Square that McDonald's developed its first Russian restaurant, the largest in the world. Vice-President General Alexander Rutskoi began a series of articles signalling his distress with economic reform by relating his feelings of despair in seeing Russians queuing in huge numbers for an American hamburger (presumably from the window of his Zil limousine). The writer Anatoly Smelyansky began a booklet on the state of Russian theatre in 1991 by describing the square as a post-modernist hell's kitchen:

Trading goes on above and below ground. Papers from the Baltics, home-made flysheets, hand-printed publications of every possible group and front flash past your eyes. On the wall of the building housing *Moscow News*, appeals are stuck up. A brochure advertised about thirty-seven different kinds of sex, promising instant happiness. And from beneath the ground an age-old Russian accompaniment – harmonica, guitar, blind people, beggars, alcoholics, gypsies. And winding round the square – an endless bending tail of a queue for McDonald's.

No one needed the intercession of the artist to understand what had happened, but the artists had anyway passed on, to a *mélange* of styles of painting, sculpting and 'happening'. The artists of the seventies and eighties worked still into the nineties, but most of the best-known were abroad. Of these, only Ilya Kabakov has attained world fame, and that is considerable. Much of his work, like *This is How we Live*, is 'installations' on Soviet themes. In Moscow, new galleries opened and became fashionable, featuring in the new glossy magazines like *Domovoi*, *Matador* or the Russian *Playboy*. The avant garde took a similar route to the new writers: they cut themselves loose from 'meaningful' art – Sots Art was the last hurrah of that – and took up individualism, mysticism of various kinds, ransacked the silver and earlier ages for inspirations (some of the artists of that era were not publicly shown until the eighties) and sought to amaze, amuse or shock.

Yet – as with the new writers – Soviet themes pulsed through their work still. Ilya Cherkashin conducted a long artistic dialogue with Stalinist art and architecture – painting it, photographing it and cutting up and painting the prints, staging happenings among the statuary in the Moscow metro. Sergei Shutov used the première of the film *Assa* – a post-modernist film about the corruption and sloth of Brezhnev's time – to stage a rock concert, fashion show and installation featuring mock-Stalino-classic pillars rimmed with the limbs of broken dolls. In the nineties, he worked with video and compiled an affectionate, dreamy tribute to the Soviet cinema. A group of artists called *Eti* (These) took off their clothes in Red Square and spelled the world *khui* (prick) with their naked bodies; they achieved their aim of arrest. A performance artist called Alexander Bremmer announced an exhibition, and appeared before the assembled visitors wearing women's stockings on his legs and head screaming, 'Why haven't you included me in this exhibition?' At another extreme, Sergei Barkhin, having survived from the late fifties to the nineties by fitting into the niches left between the institutions of the official world, turned to canvases on which he stuck earth which he brought back from trips round the country, or abroad – as if in an effort to preserve his past and his memory in a vertiginous world.

There was no official style any longer. Art separated into the avant garde (with an audience little larger than that which it had when it was underground), the commercial, which ranged from mainstream artists working largely for corporate buyers and collectors, such as Sergei Volkov, and the new monumentalism of, especially, Moscow, where art was turned to the service of the nation, power and commerce. The Ministry of Culture, a largely liberal institution, had as its slogan 'preserve'. In the arts, it spread its exiguous subsidies round a few artists of the less extreme avant garde in an effort to form a cadre of working professionals who would not go to live abroad and would exhibit.

Like musicians, artists found their society in Moscow and St Petersburg whittled away by defections – though those artists who grew up in the Gorbachev era and after had no compelling reason to leave, other than preference and interest. The system of education remained extensive and strict, the commercial careers opening up in advertising and media expanded greatly, the work of their fellows in the West was freely open to be seen, imitated or surpassed. For older artists, the loss of a system in which their membership of the union gave them a lifetime of guaranteed income, studio space and exhibitions was a real blow; their sons and daughters had to sink or swim by different rules. Quite quickly, the world ceased to be special, and became like the West.

Liberated from censorship but also from the generous state subsidies, the directors and actors who had begun their careers in the fifties and sixties felt lost and disoriented. The old, familiar system of values had vanished: political opposition to the state and the moral guidance of the people were no longer exciting, rewarding or required. Anatoly

Smelyansky, the Moscow Arts Theatre literary director, had a phrase for it: 'With the fall of the super empire, Russian theatre lost its super meaning.'

In that judgement was contained much of what the *glasnost* generation – Russians in their forties and fifties when Gorbachev began his reforms – felt about their drama. Controlled, directed, censored and suppressed, Russian theatre had nevertheless retained and developed a passionate style of acting, a repertoire of Russian classics and foreign imports as well as contemporary dramas and comedies of variable quality – and a range of allusions and a subtle dissidence which were hard to fault but easy to understand if one were part of the wide circle of theatregoers.

The importance of Russian theatre was both political and aesthetic. In a country saturated with lies, it was often perceived as the only public medium in which some truth could be told. Its energy and excitement derived, in part, from its subterranean struggle against the state. *Glasnost* at first increased that excitement, then – when the joy of release and revelation subsided – the theatre's sense of purpose began to dissipate.

Political suppression was only one source of the energy of Russian theatre. The 'supertheatre' tradition goes back to Stanislavsky, the founder of the Moscow Arts Theatre and Russia's greatest director. Stanislavsky sought to create real life on the stage rather than mount an imitation of it – no matter how close. Auditioning an actress, he told her, 'It is generally accepted that our art is one of imitation and representation. Personally I am interested only in the art of re-experiencing. An art which does not represent but generates real feeling and a genuine character.' Theatre thus became more than an entertainment, and was given the same importance as life itself. The tradition had deep religious roots, and gave the Russian theatre an aesthetic and moral energy which sustained it through the years of dictatorship and authoritarianism.

In the first years of *glasnost*, Russian theatre tried hard to maintain its political importance. One of the first *glasnost* performances was mounted by Mark Zakharov, a director whose unfailing sense of theatrical fashion made him the first to sense that times were changing and that daring was in demand.

He chose a play called *The Dictatorship of Conscience* by Mikhail Shatrov. Through the medium of a stage trial and of improvised interviews with members of the audience – including, on one evening, Boris Yeltsin – the ghosts and sins of socialism past were conjured up, and roasted. It was a measure of the radicalism of the production that Pyotr Verkhovensky, the satanic socialist of *The Devils*, was brought to life to illuminate the evils of a creed gone wrong. The main actors stepped down from the stage and held conversations with the audience: censorship, in such circumstances, was impossible. In the end, the play was contained within the bounds of acceptability through the figure of Krupskaya, Lenin's wife, whose letter to future generations was read out: 'If you want to pay a tribute to the memory of the great leader, implement all his ideas in life.'

Zakharov, among whose stagings was that of the burning of his Communist Party card before the TV cameras during the attempted coup of August 1991, was able to make a smooth transition to the new era, and remained a successful director. Shatrov also made a transition: he put aside his typewriter, and became a businessman, chairing a consortium which acquired a large plot of land near the Kremlin for a massive development of hotels, offices and a cultural centre. The patriarch himself came to bless the project in the summer of 1995: Shatrov had retained his ability to set a scene in motion.

The artistic élite had offered its friendship and skill to the new powers-that-be. Several days after the storming of the White House in 1993, Zakharov celebrated his birthday. Pictured on TV with the business and government leaders, the director (fondly referred to by Yeltsin as 'Our Mark') fulfilled Josif Brodsky's prophecy that the real danger for an artist 'is not so much the possibility of persecution on the part of the state, as that of finding oneself mesmerized by the state's features which, whether monstrous or undergoing changes for the better, are always temporary.'

The Dictatorship of Conscience started a fad for 'current affair' plays – *Speak Up* and *The Article* – which came and went rapidly. At the same time, as journals were publishing the suppressed writers and the cinemas and TV were showing prohibited films, so formerly banned productions and plays were revived and staged.

The revival of once-banned productions provided an excitement which was similarly short-lived. In 1988 Yuri Lyubimov, the artistic director of the daring Taganka Theatre, stripped of his Soviet citizenship in 1983, returned to Moscow by private invitation of the actor Nikolai

Gubenko to direct a production of *Boris Godunov*. Lyubimov had staged the play in 1982, at the Taganka, where he was artistic director: he had turned the work into a parable of totalitarianism, by having the actor who played Godunov change into a modern suit, come to the front of the stage, and shout the last words of Pushkin's tragedy about Godunov and the false pretender to the throne, Dmitri: 'Why are you silent? Scream! Long live the Tsar Dmitri Ivanovich.' The demand is supposed to be addressed to a crowd of people; the stage direction reads: 'the people remain silent' − one of Russian history's largest themes. By shouting it to the audience − who of course, in 1982, remained silent − Lyubimov was making the point that (contemporary, suited) rulers and people lived in just as different spheres as they had in Godunov's day. He was exiled for that, and spent six years in Israel.

His return, and his staging of Godunov against the background of the red brick wall he had built across the back of the stage before he went into exile to symbolize his opposition to the system, was greeted with acclamation. But it no longer stunned, as it had in 1982. By 1988, people were not constrained to be silent; indeed, that year was the year of torrents of words in every kind of medium. Lyubimov, caught in the struggles of the past, an 'immigrant' in his own − and at the same time a new − country, he could not repeat his old success at the Taganka. Gubenko, his one-time pupil, fought him for control of the Taganka, and won after a court battle. The vast building, once the cockpit of all that was daring, was rented out for shows, gatherings and conferences.

The theme of loss was repeated in various ways. At the Moscow Children's Theatre, Genrietta Yankovskaya staged an emotional production of *Goodbye America*, a musical based on the children's classic *Mr Twister*, by Samuil Marshak. A man in prison clothes doing a tap-dance appeared from the rear of the stage, which was decorated with hundreds of black prison-camp uniforms. In the middle of the stage stood a red grand piano − a fairy-tale dream in the midst of the GULAG. Young actors in colourful costumes sang cheerful Soviet songs and enacted a Soviet tale of a racist American who comes to Leningrad and is punished by the anti-racist Soviet people.

This carnival of Soviet culture was interrupted by the rock group Nautilus Pompilius singing 'Goodbye America where I will never be. Goodbye forever . . .' It was a farewell to the Russian myth of America, a country of universal happiness, a country which had ceased to exist when the real America had burst into Soviet life.

The commercialization of the Russian theatre started rather strangely – with dark plays. One of the first openly commercial productions was a play by Edward Radzinsky, called *Our Decameron*, put on by the *enfant terrible* director Roman Vityuk at the Yermolova Theatre. The stage was cluttered with Soviet memorabilia – the façade of the Bolshoi Theatre leaning over at a crazy angle, its red curtain decorated with hammers and sickles. A prostitute in pink tights told her story to the accompaniment of Soviet-era hits and new rock songs. Vityuk and Radzinsky were offering a post-Soviet shopping-list of popular topics – prostitutes, the gay subculture, avant garde art, dollars, AIDS. *Our Decameron* was a vivid example that inflation had hit not just the currency, but the culture as well.

The theatres began to open nightclubs and restaurants on their premises. *Bureaux de changes* were opened in their front offices. They abandoned their role as preachers, and went into entertainment. Many churned out cheap and cheerful musicals reminiscent of the forties and fifties style of socialist realism.

The artistic directors who could not or did not wish to make the change hid away from the contemporary reality which their colleagues were attempting to mirror and the growing commercialization which they found distasteful. They drew their inspiration not from life itself, as the theatre of the sixties and seventies had, but from classical literature. In their productions of Gogol, Dostoyevsky, Ostrovsky and Shakespeare, they continued the best traditions of the Russian theatre.

In 1989, Lev Dodin began to plan an epic ten-hour production of Dostoyevsky's *The Devils* as his own revenge on seventy years of communist rule. When it opened in 1992, however, it was marked by an entire lack of any political allusions, surprising an audience which expected precisely that. Where the Shatrov/Zakharov production of *Dictatorship of the Conscience* had plundered the novel to make a political point, Dodin concentrated on what he felt was the essence of the novel – a struggle between God and the Devil for the possession of a human soul. Pyotr Verkhovensky was used, not as the epitome of a demonic Bolshevik, but as a devil of low rank who happened to take the guise of a socialist fanatic. In contrast to the simplistic and too-easy optimism of the first *glasnost* years, Dodin sought to show the omnipresence and omnipotence of evil – never to be vanquished by the mere change in a political system.

In the same spirit, Sergei Zhenovach staged *King Lear,* doing it not as a fable of folly and murderous ambition, but as an almost domestic tragedy of one household which crumbles through pressure from without. He sought to convey the dramatic effects of the world's dislocation – the experience of his audience – in personal, intimate terms. There was no sense of catharsis at the end of Zhenoivach's production, just a nudging pain and the sense of a desolate, orphaned world.

CHAPTER TWENTY-EIGHT

'Everything will be OK'

McDonald's was indeed a potent symbol, for it meant ease and courtesy of service (apart from the queue!), tastiness, clean and bright surroundings and immediate association with Western modernity. No Russian intellectual or vice-president could look at it with equanimity, and neither could do anything about it; the gates had opened, and the culture of which McDonald's was a leading part flowed in. The Russian intellectual establishment joined their Western opposite numbers in sighing over it, but their children and certainly their grandchildren would go to it if they had the money. It was lumped together with pornography, violent films, trashy novels, TV evangelists, Mexican soap operas, Marlboro cigarettes, Scotch whisky, Estée Lauder cosmetics, Snickers bars, Mercedes cars, sensationalist headlines, Nike trainers and sometimes even (nostalgically) rock music by nationalists and the high-minded in an indictment of the materialist values from which the previous society (for all its faults, they might piously add) had preserved them.

They were right. The Soviet Union had been, in the sense they meant, a highly non-materialist society. The share of the gross national product which went to personal consumption and services was, for an urbanized economy, startlingly low. Individual hedonism was further checked by the collective and thus communist-led nature of many leisure activities, especially for the young. By contrast, the readership of newspapers and the 'thick' literary-critical journals was large – despite their (to Western eyes) drabness. And it was because of that (to Eastern eyes) drabness that capitalist materialism was so entrancing; that when Soviet TV showed its traditional Christmas news broadcast from London, Paris and New York – with a commentary which said something like 'Christmas is celebrated in New York, but here on the streets, its poor, unemployed and elderly have no reason to celebrate . . .' –

Soviet viewers sharpened their eyes for the glimpse of the bright shop windows from which they, with the poor, unemployed and elderly of New York, were barred.

Popular culture ceased very rapidly to be controlled and became consumerist. The images of Sots Art went from being daring, to being passé, to being commercials within a decade. By 1994, the most successful TV commercial, for the most successful and rapacious 'pyramid selling' (of shares) scheme, run by MMM (see chapter 16), showed the Golovkovs, a Soviet-style family of industrial worker father, clerical worker mother and two schoolkids in a tiny flat, being catapulted into super-capitalist situations by their luck and judgement in buying MMM shares – these little masterpieces of concision and suggestion being made by the Kazakh film director Tilibayev.

Those who hated it – and many 'hated' it and consumed it at the same time – saw popular culture as a Western intrusion. It was, at first, but only briefly. The MMM commercials were as popular as they were because they showed the Soviet – and post-Soviet – families in charge of their own consumption, and thus masters of their own fate (ironically, since MMM was a scam and many suffered by it). If Soviet industry was slow to produce any products as good as McDonalds, Snickers, Mercedes and Nike, the leaders of its popular culture soon grappled with the new world and – with little foreign assistance or investment, though with much copying – became adept at producing what the consuming Russian wanted.

The main cultural arbiters of the *glasnost* era did not, in the main, last into the new one. The job they had done for Gorbachev was the opposite of the job the new times demanded. Editors like Vitaly Korotich of the weekly *Ogonyok* and Yegor Yakovlev of *Moscow News*, were political appointments. *Glasnost* had a purpose: it was not to allow people free choice, but to mobilize intellectual and general support for a specific leadership style. Though it quickly gathered a momentum which Gorbachev did not seriously attempt to check and which these men and others like them did much to further, its 'ideological cadres' were men with the sixties agenda of a liberalized communism. They came to embrace the market as a concept, but they never had to find out how it worked and did not want to. When the circulations of their magazines turned down they carried on doing the same thing, then left – Korotich to teach in America, Yakovlev to be an unsuccessful chairman of the main state TV company then to found another weekly, for intellectuals, the excellent *Obshchaya Gazeta*.

Television had become the dominant medium even under Brezhnev, and was naturally the dominant one in the new era. Its sixties and seventies fare is judged, by outsiders and contemporary Russians, as meagre. Konstantin Ernst, appointed in 1995 the director of programmes of the re-organized Russian Public Television, or ORT in its Russian acronym – the main channel – considered in 1995 showing a day of programmes broadcast ten years before to remind his viewers what they had been watching in communist times. He then reflected that the other channels would have to follow suit or go off the air for the move to have any effect, since they would never stay with him, even from nostalgia. The news was dully official, with much space given to the formal occasions of the leadership and to achievements of the economy; sport and serious music were given a lot of time, as were stagey discussion programmes. What excitement there was often came from the much more artistically prestigious theatre and cinema. The director Anatoly Efros worked for TV after being fired from the Lenkom Theatre, putting on Bulgakov's *Molière*, while Eldar Ryazanov made films for TV, including one – *Put in a Word for a Poor Hussar* – after it had been turned down by the Film Committee. Films, indeed, were the most popular fare, together with *estrada*, or popular music shows. The judgement of meagreness was made in a much more sated media age. Those who remember television in the US or Western Europe in the fifties, with one or two channels, respectful news and static dramas, will recall children's or variety shows for which they rushed home, or stayed up late. So it was with Soviet TV, which screened good children's programmes drawing on the stock of inventive cartoons made in the USSR or Eastern Europe, presented by figures as popular with children as any other national TV's 'uncles' or 'aunts'. The current affairs coverage was mendacious and wooden, but it did not perturb, as current affairs had done in the West since the sixties. And the treats – big football or hockey games, a foreign or critical film for the intellectuals, a show built round a pop star like Alla Pugacheva or the US 'defector' rock star Dean Reed – were the sweeter for being rare.

Glasnost-era TV (1986–89) is best remembered – sometimes not fondly – for its talk. The discussion programmes, both old-format shows and new ones – such as *Talk Show*, *Before and After Midnight* and *120*

Minutes – were the forums for disclosures, arguments and calls to action. The news was revamped and became exciting, with the selection and ordering of news stories subjected to criteria closer to those used in market economies. Foreigners appeared on it: notably, Prime Minister Margaret Thatcher was given an extended interview with three leading Soviet journalists on prime time, during her visit to the Soviet Union in March–April 1987. Her energetic defence of the nuclear deterrent and disclosure (for such it was to the Soviet Union) that the USSR / Warsaw Pact had a superiority in conventional and chemical weapons and more nuclear warheads than any other single country was broadcast uncut and unchallenged: 'I afterwards regarded [this]', she wrote in her memoirs, 'as proof that my confidence in Mr Gorbachev's basic integrity was not misplaced.'

TV became the medium for popularizing, or at least offering to the masses, the landmark events of the cultural opening. It showed the Georgian anti-Stalinist film *Repentance* in 1988, soon after its general release; it taped and broadcast the *perestroika* plays of Mikhail Shatrov, Alexander Gelman and others; it gave space to the returning dissidents and *émigré* writers, such as Vladimir Bukovsky, Vladimir Voinovich and Vasily Aksyenov; and by express command, it televised large excerpts from the new (1989) Supreme Soviet, and made national stars of its most vociferous deputies – especially, of course, the liberals. Its agenda was that of the sixties generation, who had rehearsed these shows in their kitchens for two decades and now had the heady good fortune to be given space to broadcast them across one-sixth of the world's surface, from the Baltic Sea to the Central Asian deserts. It helped greatly in the construction of a civil, independent society. But because the sixties people depended on Gorbachev, and he found it expedient to shift back to a modified authoritarianism in the latter part of 1990, their agenda was shown to be capable of reverse, if only temporarily, with the appointment of a new head of TV, Leonid Kravchenko, who suppressed the most 'anti-establishment' of the shows.

It was temporary because Gorbachev then swung back again from a desperate authoritarianism to an even more desperate reformism, but also because one of the many unintended consequences of the *glasnost* years had been the creation of a new kind of TV professional – in a sense, the first TV professionals. In the nineties, TV in Russia got down to the task of being like the media of the most developed and many developing societies – market- and consumer-driven, with no particular political project of the kind it had in the Soviet years and under *glasnost*, its values given more by the interaction of its professionals with the consumers than by a Party or by an intellectual class. This is not to say it escaped from state control: with 97 per cent of homes possessing a TV and with viewing figures higher than in most Western countries, this was not a medium to be left to run itself. The state was more massively present, and had to be taken more into account, than in Western countries, and in the 1996 presidential campaign it was tightly controlled and directed. But the state and the politicians now had to strike a deal with TV, rather than simply command it. The formal position of its senior managers was that they wanted balance, fairness, a proper respect for authority and for Russian values, but a broadly liberal view of what constituted the mix of programmes. How far that dispensation would last depended – as anywhere else – on the fortunes of the political marketplace, and on the real marketplace itself.

The beneficiaries of the post-Soviet television scene were, initially, thirty- or forty- or fifty-somethings who had been brought along by the sixty-somethings and quite soon came to the conclusion that the latter were well-meaning but useless. They were tied to Gorbachev, and thus were (or had been) more interested in the success of his political project than in political freedom *per se*. They had no idea of what sold, were fastidious about much popular culture, and they had no money. The post-Soviet people needed both freedom and money.

One reason for the futility of Gorbachev's turn to authoritarianism in 1990 was that he acted in conditions of dual power: Boris Yeltsin was already too powerful to be curbed except by measures more extreme than Gorbachev was prepared to license. When Ostankino ceased to represent the liberal view, Yeltsin managed to get enough funding approved by the Russian parliament whose leader he was to start a Russian TV channel, headed by a supporter, Oleg Poptsov. Many of the liberal journalists at Ostankino went to the new channel or to Leningrad TV (under the political control of the liberal mayor Anatoly Sobchak). Among them was Tatyana Mitkova, who, in January 1991, had read the news that Russian troops had killed civilians in Vilnius with ostentatious tears in her eyes and had been fired by Kravchenko for doing so. She, more than any other single figure, was responsible for a boycott of Ostankino by the liberal intelligentsia.

The Vilnius events, catalytic in many ways, were also a defining moment for one of the two dominant political personalities on the post-Soviet screen, Alexander Nevzorov. Nevzorov had begun his own programme on Leningrad TV in 1987, when he was thirty-one; called *600 Seconds*, it was a rapid-fire documentary programme which specialized in the uncovering of crime and corruption (and thus was initially assumed to be within the liberal consensus of the media). Nevzorov, however, was from the beginning a different type: he wore a black leather jacket and adopted the image of a fearless individualist, a journalistic Rambo fighting for truth and the Russian way. The Russian way began to dominate his programmes: by the time the OMON special forces tried to secure the Vilnius TV tower (some of the most bitter battles across the Soviet Union were to be around TV towers) he had identified himself as a friend of the increasingly fearful Russians outside of the Russian republic, and dedicated a falsified two-part film on Vilnius to the cause of the retention of the Soviet Union. The OMON troops who took part in the event he called *nashi* (ours), the most important personal pronoun in Russian. He lost the remains of his liberal support but garnered so much good opinion from conservative quarters that he was able to beat off a threat to sack him by the liberal management of the station. He later moved to Ostankino, where he produced and presented a programme called *Wild Field* – even more overtly opinionated, and more concerned to shore up falling ratings by the use of revelatory material and sex.

Revelations about sex produced his biggest embarrassment, and appeared to show that the limits of his popularity had been reached. In June 1995, Nevzorov aired a show alleging a widespread lesbian culture at Sablino Prison near St Petersburg: inmates were shown kissing, while Nevzorov described the women – shown in the exercise yard – as 'waiting for the hot night to descend' before falling upon each other. In October, an inmate and former police investigator named Natalya Vorontsova, serving a seven-year sentence for providing a gun to assist in the escape of a murderer whom she was then investigating but whose lover she was, successfully argued before the Information Disputes Chamber that Nevzorov had traduced the prison in general and her in particular. He had, she said, told officials that he was doing a film on embezzlement and had bribed her colleagues with cigarettes to kiss each other for the camera. Saying that the granting of permission for

Vorontsova to appear before the committee was unprecedented, the deputy head of the Interior Ministry's prison service explained that she had been a good investigator and 'stood out' among other criminals. Besides, he added, 'A person's right to privacy has to be protected even if the person is a convict.' A convict's effective rights in even post-Soviet Russia were so small as to make that unlikely to be more than a piety. The affair smelled of an official manoeuvre, and appeared to signify that Nevzorov's role as the spokesman-avenger of the dispossessed Russians was under challenge.

Nevzorov's counterpart on the side of the liberals was Yevgeny Kiselyev, whose career had been in the Ivy League of nineties television. He had been a young journalist on Ostankino, and been one of the team which had made its *Vesti* news section break with its turgid past. When a briefly renewed ice age descended in 1990, he left for Russian TV. Once Ostankino had been returned to liberal hands after the failure of the coup in August 1991, Kiselyev developed and fronted a show called *Itogi* ('Results'), built round his confident screen presence, with reports from around the former Union and the globe, insistent and sometimes scornful interviews of the politically prominent (Kiselyev put it to Andrei Kozyrev, the Russian foreign minister, in October 1995: 'Is it not the case that the rest of the world thinks Russia to be a decrepit nuisance?'). Kiselyev took his show in 1994 to a new station – NTV, funded by the financier Vladimir Gusinsky – where he was given both freedom and, as a director of the channel, a lot of money.

He was the antithesis of Nevzorov. In place of the leather jacket was a smart, conservative double-breasted suit and fashionable tie. His delivery was measured; at times he would grope for a word in the manner of a man dominating a conversation who knows he will not be interrupted. Though he was a much more conscientious journalist than the presenter of *Wild Field*, he made as little secret of his views. The programme was avowedly liberal, and showed its preferences most clearly in coverage of the Chechnya conflict in 1994–95 – where, unfazed by growlings from the nationalists and the Kremlin that the programme betrayed the army, it insistently put the case that the war was a folly whose casualties were citizens of Russia.

Gusinsky's channel was at once a challenge and a stimulus. It challenged the good faith of the post-Soviet administration: could it tolerate so powerful a medium so openly critical of its policies and style? The answer seemed to be that it could, for though Gusinsky received at least one direct warning that he was overstepping the bounds of the state's tolerance, it did not appear to be directly connected with his media activities. In that area, his innovations were bold and accepted: *Itogi* continued to make waves, the quick-fire news was often as sharply critical, and the station began in 1995 a political satire show using puppets in the manner of the British *Spitting Image*. One episode of the show – called *Kukli* ('Puppets') – was held by the prosecutor general, Alexei Ilyushenko, to be disrespectful of the president and the prime minister, since it showed them as a pair of drunken down-and-outs on a Moscow bench. Ilyushenko, however, appeared to be out of touch with his senior colleagues' sense of humour, for Prime Minister Chernomyrdin allowed himself to be photographed, smiling indulgently, next to his puppet while Yeltsin first said Ilyushenko should stop interfering with the media, then replaced him with a man with a liberal pedigree.

The channel was glossy as well as liberal. Its studios were high-tech, its announcers smooth, the films which were a staple fare of its evening entertainment often world-class. It introduced, for the first time, something of the nervy element of ratings and advertising competition into the Russian television scene. Thus the other challenge it posed was to the main state channel, Ostankino, a challenge to which the channel was initially in poor shape to respond.

Ostankino was the inheritor of Soviet TV. Hugely overmanned, with many staff appointed for loyalty or Party service, it had strings of transmitters to maintain across the Soviet Union and a large network of correspondents at home and abroad. But its unparalleled reach was a dream for advertisers: banks, insurance companies, car dealerships and foreign brand names like Coca-Cola, Snickers and BMW poured on to the airwaves from the beginning of the nineties, buying not so much space as programmes, negotiating directly with producers for time on the show in return for which they would sponsor the show itself. Bribery soon became rampant, as the hotter advertisers struggled for the prime time and as criminals became aware that it was an easy way to launder money.

Reform was tried. The station was part (49 per cent) privatized to a consortium of banks, and in 1995 Vladimir Listyev, a veteran of the pioneering current affairs show *Vzglyad*, was appointed to head a renamed body, Russian Public Television (ORT). Listyev decreed a four-month ban on advertising in an attempt to cleanse his stables, and in May 1995, was murdered outside his flat, giving rise to yet another (futile) outpouring of disgust over the ability of assassins to work freely and to a general view that the killing was a revenge for Listiev's putting a finger on a criminal windpipe.

A new team took advertising in-house, shortened the news, encouraged independent production houses from whom they bought programmes, fired Solzhenitsyn and proclaimed that they valued neutrality, balance and objectivity. The firing of Sergei Dorenko, the presenter of a programme called *Versii* ('Versions') – a mildly sacrilegious political show – was of less moment than that of Solzhenitsyn but was more indicative of the station's trend. Challenged on the firing, the channel's general director – a former foreign affairs specialist named Sergei Blagovolin – said: 'He [Dorenko] said many times he followed politicians as he would interesting animals, and didn't see himself as a political figure. I can't agree with that. A political programme on the first channel is a great responsibility.' Dorenko was promptly hired by NTV, all the while saying that ORT had fallen into the hands of its new commercial sponsors, of dubious honesty.

ORT became integrated into the political-financial élite which gathered round Yeltsin in 1995–96. Its deputy chairman was the businessman Boris Berezovsky, who said openly that he was in government to defend the interests of the new capitalist class, and who estimated that the top seven banker-financiers controlled 50 per cent of the Russian economy. Stolichny, Russia's second largest bank, took an ORT stake, as did Gazprom.

At the same time, the first state channel was trying to become the BBC – state-controlled but run by broadcasters, balanced but with a liberal bent. Konstantin Ernst, its programme director – yet another graduate of *Vzglyad* – was in his early thirties when appointed in 1995, had shoulder-length hair, had produced and presented *Matador*, a slick, literate travel programme, and edited a magazine of the same name. He wanted his channel not to reflect, but to improve on life. He wanted it to step back from the political arena and amuse, entertain and explain. Though an intellectual himself – he had been a natural scientist in an academic institute before joining *Vzglyad* in his late twenties – he scorned the Soviet intellectuals' disdain for the masses' taste. He wanted to acquire popular films, develop good native soaps. He was bored by politics, but if he had to have it he wanted to make it interesting.

The ambitions of ORT to become an independent, public service network were in constant tension with the demands of the state and of its new owners – and when the stakes were high, the first ambition lost out – as was made clear during the 1996 presidential elections, during which its record was very poor (see chapter 5).

This movement, away from total to sporadic state control, was mirrored in the press. As recently as 1988, the publication of a letter in the daily *Sovyetskaya Rossiya* from Nina Andreeva, an instructor in Leningrad, calling for a return to socialist principles, had appeared to signal the end of *perestroika* and *glasnost*: the general assumption was that no such letter would have been published had it not been a missive from the leadership.

But by the following year, the press lost its role as bearer of messages from the top and set about trying to explain the world, rather than instruct people on how to see it. More importantly, once the Soviet Union died, it set about trying to sell itself.

It did so with some success: arguably no other institution changed so rapidly and so well. Already in the Gorbachev period, it cast off the formal uniformity of view which various journals were supposed to reflect (though they did, in fact act as the mouthpieces for different factions within the leadership). By 1990, with the aid of the Moscow City Council, a daily called *Nezavisimaya Gazeta* ('The Independent') had appeared, edited by Vitaly Tretyakov, a former deputy editor of the *Moscow News*. After the attempted coup of 1991, Oleg Golembyovsky took over as editor of *Izvestiya*, and changed it into a consistently liberal and brave, if still verbose, newspaper. Vladimir Yakovlev, son of Yegor, started a daily business paper called *Commersant*, initially with the aid of US capital. Artyom Borovik, whose reporting in *Ogonyok* on the Afghan War was one of the magazine's many breakthroughs and prides, became editor of a crime and revelation weekly called *Top Secret*, and he presented a TV show of the same name. Gusinsky launched a bright daily called *Sevodnya* ('Today') in 1993, which took in many refugees from *Nezavisimaya Gazeta* after Tretyakov became too anti-Yeltsin and domineering for his liberal young staff.

These first years of the Moscow press were remarkable. The papers differed greatly among themselves, offering a political and cultural spectrum wider, probably, than any other in the world. The older papers, with the exception of *Izvestiya* and *Trud*, stayed communist or went nationalist; *Pravda*, supported by a Greek millionaire and former communist, became shrilly oppositionist. *Sovyetskaya Rossiya* tended to a right-wing nationalism whose avatar was Alexander Prokhanov of the weekly *Den*, an older Nevzorov with the same taste for melodramatic patriotism. *Komsomolskaya Pravda* and even more *Moskovsky Komsomolets* (former Komsomol dailies) went 'tabloid' while remaining broadsheet in size, publishing scandal, humour and very sharp commentary, using a demotic, even vulgar literary style – a far cry from the stilted, proper Soviet prose. *Nezavisimaya Gazeta* went Tretyakov's way, as he became increasingly gripped with the belief that the Yeltsin government was a rotten one and that Russian national interests had been and were being betrayed for an illusion of Westernism and the reality of corrupt gain. *Izvestiya*, *Commersant* and *Sevodnya* were liberal, in different ways. *Sevodnya* had a lot of young reporters with strong opinions who disagreed openly with each other, engaging in a passionate argument over the nature and conduct of politics in their society, hammering out new positions for themselves as they were driven by events. *Commersant* was always cooler, pioneering the use of explanatory boxes and tables, abstaining from overt judgement on politicians, inventing the phrase 'the New Russians' to describe the new class of the rich – which it defined in the mid-nineties as earning over $2,000 a month.

Early post-Soviet journalistic style was excessively personal, the main news stories of a given day sometimes composed of a ramble flavoured with the journalists' pain, disgust or cynicism. Cynicism, or at best irony, took over as the favoured tone as the self-promotion, cupidity and ignorance of many in the political world became clear to the journalists. Most of them were too young to realize they were little better and their copy was too lightly edited for their own good. The best of them had cut their teeth on the Supreme Soviet, the training ground of Russian political journalism. Many of the most prominent columnists, like Mikhail Berger of *Izvestiya* or Mikhail Leontiev of *Sevodnya*, had been activists in the causes they espoused, and were writing from within this or that circle. Most of the Moscow papers retained the assumption that people had time to read: they ran articles which covered a page, 4–5,000 words of argument and exposition, sometimes flatulent, at times compelling.

Their besetting problems were poverty and old Soviet habits. Poverty meant low pay for journalists, which in turn meant that many were open to being bought by political or commercial interests, especially in the regions. The new rich and the newly powerful routinely bought coverage, including denigration of their opponents and boosting of their characters or projects. Where carrots did not work, sticks were used: after the death of Dmitri Kholodov, a young investigative reporter for *Moskovsky Komsomolets* blown up by a briefcase bomb while investigating corruption in the army, *Izvestiya* ran a front page of some twenty photographs of journalists round the country who had died in similar circumstances. The old Soviet habits were less pernicious but more pervasive, like a clannishness which meant that journalists tended to be captured by one point of view, and a lack of any perceived need to explain in detail, so that press briefings, conferences and trips were disordered, unintelligible except to the initiated or deliberately over-loaded with entertainment and shorn of facts. An example was a liquid tour organized by the company Lukoil of some of its installations in Siberia in February 1995, a tour apparently deliberately structured round cosy, vodka-soaked banquets which acted as havens from the terrible temperatures but which provided nothing in the way of facts about a company then rising to become a major power in the oil world in Russia and abroad.

The activism tended to fade. Politics and journalism separated more and more. Government subsidies, the wealth of proprietors or sponsors and low wages meant circulation wars did not at first play the role they did in the other country with a centralized national press, Britain. The partial collapse of the state distribution system meant that the vast Soviet-era circulations of up to 10 million (25 million for the weekly *Arguments and Facts* (*Argumenty i Fakty*) during its Gorbachev-era peak) were replaced by circulations of a few hundred thousand for *Izvestiya*. The pop papers sold more but the new smart papers like *Commersant* and *Sevodnya* sold a quarter of that. The legacy of the Soviet era lay heavily on the regional papers; even in large cities, like Ekaterinburg or Krasnodar, they were dull or – if taken over by this or that political faction – dully propagandist.

It was the magazines which were the excitement of the mid-nineties. Glossies started coming out in 1993/94. Before then, the first forays into the new magazine market had been Russian versions of *Cosmopol-*

itan, *Vogue* and *Playboy* – the latter edited by an organizer and chronicler of the seventies and eighties rock scene, Artyom Troitsky. A Russian man's magazine *Medved* ('Bear') competed – a gentle version of the breed, with its bear-mate of the month never wearing less than a bra and the editor-in-chief, Igor Maltsev, counselling his readers to help their parents in the garden on Sunday. Ernst at Ostankino put out *Matador*, which was more intellectual but just as interested in fashion, while Stas Nauman, a rock promoter, published a modest journal called *Stas*. Their audience were the newly moneyed young like their editors (or, like Nauman, a grandson of the Stalin-era commissar Anastas Mikoyan, old-moneyed not-so-young). Newly arrived, they wanted to recognize each other and to establish themselves: *Matador* had a photo feature running through it, full-page colour pictures of an individual whose appearance was in some way old style, or trying too hard to be new style, with the slogan underneath: 'This is not a Matador'. *Medved* featured interviews with men who were the Bear of the Month, who had qualities of grittiness, originality, above all individuality, or had the image of having these qualities. They were completely uninterested in politics, except when it was stylish – *Medved* featured the handsome General Alexander Lebed, the mid-nineties moderate nationalist candidate, as a Bear of the Month. Social commentary bored them: *Medved* ran a photo feature of five stylish young men, pricing each article of their (expensive) wardrobes – and put in a picture of an 86-year-old pensioner in their midst, wearing clothes up to twenty years old which he had bought for a few old roubles. The message? Everybody's different, no more.

The best of them all was *Domovoi*, a thick, creamy monthly from the *Commersant* house. *Domovoi* – which means 'House Spirit' – was begun at the end of 1993, when the fever of the Gorbachev and just-post-Soviet years was calming, when talk of civil war and coups were dying away and when the New Russians, spotted by *Commersant*, began to feel they might last. It was then the *kottedzhi* sprang up with the autumn mushrooms about Moscow, St Petersburg and the other cities – big brick houses, fenced in, with picture windows and turrets and bits of gothic and *style moderne*. It was then that the big new hotels and restaurants and health clubs began to shift their clientèles, from foreigners and their Russian contacts or staff to Russians. It was then that consumption became really conspicuous.

Domovoi was aimed at this. Meant mainly, but not exclusively, for women, it was the antithesis of the Soviet-era magazines, like *Rabotnitsa* ('Working Woman') and *Khrestyanka* ('Peasant Woman'), which still sold many more copies than *Domovoi*'s 100,000 two years after its launch. It assumed no profession, but did assume a disposable income (one issue had a feature on personal helicopters). It was a magazine of How to Spend It. The focus was the family – not the family as a haven from Soviet anomie, certainly not the real family where divorce rates were among the highest in the world and the orphanages were overflowing, but the family as a success. The idol was the film director and actor Nikita Mikhalkov, who, already well known for a series of films made since the mid-seventies, went through an extraordinary period of popularity in the mid-nineties after winning an Oscar for his film *Burnt by the Sun*. The popular *Komsomolskaya Pravda* made his fiftieth birthday on 19 October 1995 its lead story, with a photograph showing the Mikhalkov family strolling lovingly out of the sea after a bathe. *Domovoi*'s splashiest item was a selection of pictures from his family album. It was very Russian, but it was Russians as fun-lovers, successes, consumers, not as radicals, ultra-nationalists or criminals. Among its models was the pre-revolutionary *Stolitsa i Usadba* ('Capital and Estate'), an early consumer's magazine for the aristocratic and wealthy of the silver age; but by the time *Domovoi* was established, few of its readers any longer feared they would meet the fate of these forebears.

The new media were sustained by either rich sponsors, or advertising, or both. Advertising established itself firmly from the beginning of the nineties, on TV (state and private), on radio, in newspapers, magazines, on billboards and in the metro. The first efforts – largely by Western companies – to advertise in Soviet newspapers were comic, at least to the Westerners. The editors said they would allow advertising, but reserved the right to dictate the size, position, time of appearance – and content. All the advertiser had to do was to pay. The advertisers were used to being courted, flattered and offered cut-price deals, in short, to being recognized as the foundations of the free press. This was to them an absurdity, a dinner table anecdote. However, they had merely to wait. The decline of subsidies, the spread of a commodity culture largely through imported goods, the explosive growth of Russian banks wishing to create an image, the flourishing of small ads, especially flat rental and purchase, the spread of services, the opening of new restaurants which vied for trade, the activities of the international agencies which established themselves throughout the former Soviet Union, the need for government – especially the privatization agencies – to announce initiatives, contributed to a growth in the advertising market from zero in the late eighties to over $500 million in the mid-nineties.

Advertising reflected and moulded the new contours of Russian society. Like the glossy journals, it was indifferent to profession – the key defining criterion of Soviet society – and concentrated on the ability to spend. This meant that much of the advertising was initially for an élite, who alone had an income which could be disposed on more than food. For the mass, the advertising was more 'brand recognition' than emphasizing why one brand was better than another. The task was to associate Gillette with shaving, Mars with sweetness, Sony with viewing, Xerox with copying. Evidence of success came when, in October 1995, a Moscow paper apologized to Xerox in print for reporting that 'Xeroxes' in a Moscow court did not work. They had been another brand of copiers, but the paper had used the brand name as a synonym for the machine – a common mistake in market economies.

Television commercials, which appeared like much else quite suddenly, worked in curious ways on the Soviet-Russian psyche. Soviet citizens had long been accustomed to taking the news with a very large pinch of salt; at the same time, however, they knew it was official, sanctioned and determined by the Party, usually down to the last detail. When advertising appeared, they made the reasonable assumption that it, too, was sanctioned and official. The advertising for the new Russian banks and finance houses – like the notorious MMM – was thus deemed to have the backing of the state; and when MMM failed, the disillusionment was the greater for the company having been so heavily promoted on public television. The blame was instantly transferred to the state which had 'sanctioned' it.

The commercials annoyed in other ways as well. The brand-recognition advertising was often for commodities which the vast majority could not afford – and often which were not available to anyone. Thus when the charm of the new medium wore off, it became an irritant to add to the others of everyday life.

By 1995, this irritation was so deep that advertising began to have a perverse effect. The heavy political advertising which most of the parties did for the December 1995 Duma elections repelled rather than attracted the audience; the communists, who hardly advertised at all, were the beneficiaries of abstaining from proclaiming their excellence. They also gained from something for which they were not responsible: the showing of old Soviet films and TV series, brought out partly because they were cheap but also because of the nostalgic fondness for them on the part of the viewers. Since the communists were associated with this era, they benefited from the association.

By the 1996 presidential elections, the sophisticated, Western-advised team around President Yeltsin had figured out something of this. Yeltsin's advertisements were oblique, cool, and did not feature the president. Instead, ordinary people were shown coming to the reluctant decision that he was the best of a poor lot. At the same time, he appeared continually on the news bulletins – touring the country, announcing initiatives, meeting foreign leaders, very much in the Soviet style. The old media order had been partially re-established. He was a rock of security in troubled times.

The novelist Victor Yerofeev remarked in an essay that, in the late Soviet period, distinguished writers became split personalities: fighters for communism at their desks in the week, consumers of capitalist luxuries in their *dachas* at the weekends. Those with money or influence in the Soviet Union always found ways to consume (if not so well as in the West), but it was secret, hypocritical. The nineties attacked that, and though many older people never lost the habit of concealing their secret delights and continued to proclaim a bluff just-getting-by egalitarianism, the young tended to another extreme. They wanted to have it and to spend it and to show they were doing so.

The new uninhibited acquisitiveness spelled the death of the old rock scene, which had grown in dissidence and been godfathered by the bards like Vysotsky and Okudzhava. The old scene had been perforce part of the bohemian-intellectual life because of official disapproval amounting, at times, to outright bans and routinely to denial of facilities. When rock music ceased to suffer from any more than the rational dislike of large parts of the population, including intellectuals, which confronted it everywhere, it left its old allies behind and pursued its multiple goals elsewhere. The old scene – called 'unplugged' because the musicians could not use electronic amplifiers in small flats – had been intimate and small-scale. The new stadia with thousands of fans and promise of similar aggregates of earnings rapidly put a wide distance between previous comrades-in-arms. Some of those who were in rock more for the dissidence than the music crossed over to cinema or theatre; some dropped out.

A few tried to perpetuate the underground by different means. A punk movement began in 1990 whose main figure was Yegor Letov and whose most notable group was Civil Defence. Both these and other groups were attracted by the more extreme nationalists, Letov creating a movement called Russian Breakthrough, which sought to put rock at the service of nationalism, but which had a limited appeal. Others took Boris Grebenshchikov's dictum that rock was not music but a way of life, and lived in it: a group called Polite Refusal, a description of their own relationship to contemporary life, developed a complex music composed of free jazz and a new classicism – together with a language of their own and an attitude of disdain for success and for audiences, both of which were, in their case, restricted.

Grebenshchikov himself remained active and popular, and took on some of the appurtenances of, if not a grand old man, at least a middle-aged cultural grandee. He and his group Aquarium toned down their style to a lyrical, even tranquil sound, leaving behind the noisy protest music which had been their trademark. In a long dialogue with Victor Yerofeev printed in *Moskovsky Komsomolets*, he revealed himself as an occasional attender at Esalen, the Northern Californian retreat where the wealthy and the internationally known recharge through meditation, self-communing and various kinds of therapies; Grebensh-chikov had over the course of two years sought to recharge his energy through shamanistic dancing. (In passing, he compared the Russian Black Sea resort city of Sochi unfavourably with Esalen: in the former, he said, men regarded women merely as bodies, in the latter, as human beings.)

Most of the groups embraced the market, and were embraced or repelled in their turn. Nauman went into big-time producing as soon as it was legalized, organizing tours and concerts, running a radio station. Discos and night clubs sprang up everywhere – often gritty and violent in provincial towns, but luxurious in central Moscow, where two of the most fashionable – Pilot and Soho – were owned by Anton Tabakov, son of the actor Oleg Tabakov, who thirty-five years earlier had smashed furniture on the stage of the Central Children's Theatre as a protest against petit-bourgeois corruption of the purity of socialism. The bands came and went relatively rapidly, as elsewhere. Groups like Alisa, Agatha Christie, DDT and Dead Leg either lasted relatively long periods or had a bright flash of success. So fast did the scene move that groups in the nineties garnered some popularity from playing nostalgic music of the eighties. The Beatles still belted out from the pop stations most hours. The old values of bohemianism, dissidence, contempt for money and the middle classes, which the Beatles and the Stones and others of the early heroes and models had themselves at times professed, were largely forgotten. The important thing was not to take oneself seriously; everything was ironic, between inverted commas. In 1995, a recording which mixed excerpts from Mikhail Gorbachev's speeches (read by an impressionist) and a woman's voice pretending sexual ecstasy had a brief success.

How to represent all of this? Film had traditionally been the keenest social critic and commentator in the Soviet Union: Vladimir Menshov, director of *Moscow Does Not Believe in Tears* in 1980, tried to capture some of the new life in a film called *Shirly Mirly* (translated as 'What a Mess'), which was heavily promoted at the 1995 Moscow Film Festival, where foreigners did not like it but Russians did. The critic Kyrill Razlogov explained why when he wrote of it:

The film is a kind of family affair for the initiated, the circle of the initiated is in this case fairly wide, being all of the Soviet people, united not just by history but by the cinema and by common jokes. The initiated will under-stand this film from half a word – something that would have to be explained to foreigners, who even then would not understand it. This is the result of the director's principles – a director who works not, like some, for the Cannes jury, but for Ivanov, Petrov, Sidorov.

Moscow Does Not Believe in Tears was the most popular film of the time: 75 million tickets sold, an Academy Award gained, and at the same time a happy Soviet ending, as the heroine ends up in charge of a factory and married to an honest worker. 'I made this film,' Menshov said then, 'having in view a clean-cut audience, the mass viewer.' It is a hugely energetic film, full of passing allusions, such as a snatch of song from Okudzhava as the heroine walks back to her hostel in the evening, a glimpse of the cinema star Innokenty Smoktunovsky and a vignette of the poet Vosnesensky declaiming in a square, placing the action in the 'liberal' late fifties.

Fifteen years after that success, Menshov could not hope to repeat it. *Shirly Mirly* was energetic and at times very funny; its opening scenes, where a vast diamond is stolen by a fake chief of the general staff in a fake airport is beautifully executed. But the whole film is fake; there are fake Americans, fake blacks, fake Jews – even the diamond turns out to be a fake. Everything is mixed up: a Russian is marrying an American, gypsies are playing in the Conservatoire, Russian crooks are dealing in New York. The shots of Moscow focus on the advertising signs – often in English – for casinos and night clubs. The policemen are comically helpless. All institutions – government, military, intelligentsia, police – are mockingly dismissed. Where *Moscow Does Not Believe in Tears* had Heart with a capital H (and showed that the capital had a heart), *Shirly Mirly* showed a universe already disjointed and meaningless. The acting was, as usual on the Russian stage or screen, outstanding, but it had no core. Even the happy ending – where a planeful of people of all races fly off on a voyage to what appears to be a happy destination – was tacked on, and could have been ironic – which, ironically, the Brezhnev-era happy ending of *Moscow Does Not Believe in Tears* was not.

Another film of 1995, Dmitri Astrakhan's *Everything Will Be OK*, shared some of the fantasy-like quality of Menshov's film, but used fantasy more straightforwardly. *Everything Will Be OK* is a frank fable: a miserable Russian provincial town is transformed by the entrance of a rich businessman and his genius son, who dispense money and love among the film's main characters and make their wildest dreams come true. Astrakhan made the film with a certain purpose: he wanted to show, he said, that 'equal opportunity is a beautiful idea, but it is untrue. It is only natural for a girl to prefer a rich, handsome intelligent boy from a good family to a poor, thick, drinking unimaginative ex-soldier, even if he served honestly in the army and was brought up with unequal opportunities. It may sound anti-humanistic but at least it is true.' Astrakhan's film was popular: it yoked the themes of Western soap opera to the task of making post-Soviet life bearable.

But neither Menshov nor Astrakhan could hope to reach the masses who once flooded into the cinemas. There were no masses left. Cinema attendance plunged after 1991, as the cinemas were taken over by erotic and violent films, aimed at a youth market (which flocked at first, then tired of it), as prices went up, as street crime soared and as TV got more varied. From being a normal outing most weeks, cinema-going became an occasional venture – as elsewhere. People stayed at home to watch videos, sold from street kiosks; cinemas became car showrooms or furniture shops.

This was not what the Soviet directors had wanted when, in 1986 and led by director Elem Klimov, they became the first of the artists to claim the Film-makers' Union to be under their own and not the Party's control, to demand that the state cease censoring their output and that it become self-financing. Their demands drew the perfect response: the first was granted, and censorship retreated then gave up; the second was ignored, and subsidies continued and increased until 1990.

This being the Russian film industry, there *was* talent, though much of it saw salvation and inspiration and money only in the West. A string of 'black' films came out, inspired by Valery Pichul's *Little Vera*, a kind of anti-socialist realist piece starring a luminous actress named Natalya Negoda, whose nude love-making scene, unprecedented in Soviet cinema, ensured its success and her a *Playboy* centrefold. *Intergirl* by Valery Todorovsky and *Taxi Blues* by Pavel Loungin (a French co-production) were shallower pieces, but the second had a similar *succès d'estime* in the West. Todorovsky teamed up with Sergei Livnev, who made a film called *Kicks* in 1992 about a rock and roll star who is also a drug addict, to take over the Gorky Film Studio in Moscow, a virtual gift to them from the state.

The number of films surged in the late eighties and early nineties, from 150–200 to 350–400 – as speculative and criminal money replaced state subsidies, with the new businessmen attracted both by the glamour of the industry and the ease with which they could put dirty money into a film and get clean money out at the other end through receipts. After 1992, the number of films produced in Russia dropped to around 120 (in some of the other republics, none were made) and the state stepped in to pay some 30 per cent of all film production costs, sponsoring 'art' films and prestige projects, like a film of *Anna Karenina*.

The one director who kept, and increased his pre-*glasnost* reputation was Nikita Mikhalkov. He was Soviet aristocracy: the son of a famous children's writer and composer of the Soviet national anthem, brother of Anton Mikhalkov-Konchalovsky, also a famous director (now working largely in the US), a brother-in-law through his first wife of writer Julian Semyenov. Mikhalkov began as an actor, then had an instant success with his early seventies *Slave of Love*; later films, including *Dark Eyes* and *Oblomov*, were also ecstatically received at home and abroad. In 1994, he released *Burnt by the Sun*, a story set in the *dacha* of a Red Army general in the thirties arrested by a young NKVD officer who is a former lover of his wife. Mikhalkov builds up the general and his family (he plays the general, the daughter is played by his real daughter) into a close, loving, upright and sympathetic group, contrasting violently with the world of the NKVD and the serpent-like young man who capitalizes on his friendship with the family to insinuate himself into its midst. The film took the tradition of Russian *dacha* life and transposed it into a Stalinist family, merging – as it were – Chekhov with socialist realism. Mikhalkov had eschewed political themes in the Soviet period; this film, paradoxically, was his most political – an anti-Stalinist statement, somewhat past the fashionable time for such statements in Russia, but so well acted and directed with such style that it won awards at Cannes and Hollywood, which were the forums at which it was directed.

The awards transformed Mikhalkov from being famous to being royalty. Even his father, who had written an anthem which thanked Stalin for the happiness of the people (the line was later excised), was given saintly status, evidently for being his father. Part of the reason lay in the photogeneity of the family; but more lay in its symbolic value as an object of reconciliation. Within it were Soviet values, family values, artistic values, modern values and Russian values; like one of the Stalin-era monumental buildings, all styles were merged together to produce a harmonious whole. *Burnt by the Sun* was not simply an anti-Stalinist film, it was a dissociation of the healthy parts of Russia, and indeed of communism, from Stalinism. Significantly, Mikhalkov's political career was of a piece with the image he presented, and with his art: he joined Sergei Shakhrai's Party of Unity and Reconciliation in 1993, then broke with it to join Victor Chernomyrdin's grouping, Our Home is Russia, being made second to Chernomyrdin himself on its list of candidates for the parliament. Elected, he renounced his seat. Mikhalkov had brilliantly observed the basic rule of a film – continuity. It was that which the Russian nation most desired, and which popular culture strove to give it.

CHAPTER TWENTY-NINE

'The restoration of Russia – that's what art is for'

Continuity is a fitting theme on which to end – for it is precisely what Russia has lacked, and cannot have. Its history has been one of shocking discontinuities and of institutions undeveloped or servile, subservient to the will of rulers who wished to keep society in a permanent state of subjection.

The Soviet experience was the greatest breach with a country's past traditions and culture the world had seen. Political will and coercion which accelerated to reach previously unknown levels of efficiency obliterated or drove deep underground the structures and customs of Russian life – a process symbolized by the renaming of streets, cities and regions, an effort to cancel out the past encapsulated in the old names by their replacement with those of the new masters: Lenin(grad), Stalin(grad), Gorky, Sverdlov(sk), Kalinin(grad).

The end of Soviet power was immeasurably less violent, but the renaming of the parts of the country which had been Sovietized began once more. Leningrad became St Petersburg; Gorky became Nizhny Novgorod; Sverdlovsk became Ekaterinburg. Stalingrad had already been renamed Volgograd, and to change the name of Kaliningrad would have recalled its recent German past – as Königsberg; better to recall the long-serving Soviet president than the birthplace of Kant.

It was a movement which meant well, but which was desperately shallow. It was relatively easily done, but meant no more than that new signs went up on grimy or crumbling Soviet façades. Gorky Street, a central Moscow thoroughfare, was very largely constructed – or reconstructed – in Soviet times: its solid blocks of mansion flats housed many of the country's political and cultural élite. It was renamed Tverskaya Street. At the same time as the new signs went up, the street sprouted a rash of kiosks selling alcohol and cigarettes, acquired several nightclubs, a casino and a pizza parlour in the Intourist Hotel across from what had been Revolution Square.

It seemed as though the Soviet Union had done its job too well. Its collapse meant that Russia had acquired the physical boundaries of a new state before it had the chance to compose itself to express a national culture. It moved from a Soviet state in which nationalism had been cast in an idealized form, merging fraternity with historic destiny, to frenzied efforts, in all of the former Soviet republics, to find a national identity and culture to support the sudden achievement of statehood.

The democrat-radicals, in the ascendant in politics and in the media for the first year or two, attempted to demolish all that was Soviet and communist. In the economy, in the media, in fashion, even in the many English neologisms imported rapidly into the language, the West was elevated to an example and a goal. At the same time, the new authorities, in alliance with the Church and with scholars, tried to reach back to the Russian past in an effort to find a tradition which could arch over the seven Soviet decades and reconnect the nation with its pre-communist roots.

But the Russian identity had been largely lost. A huge social change had taken place under Soviet rule — the urbanization, industrialization and modernization of society — at a tempo much quicker and more brutal than in the West European states. It is still debatable whether or not people became Soviet men or women, but in being called so they had not had to think through what being Russian (or Ukrainian, or Georgian, or Uzbek) meant, in a concrete, rather than an idealized, form. The Russians were particularly cursed in this regard: for where the other peoples could load the blame for their various backwardnesses on Russian/Soviet imperialism — and the leaderships of the Baltic states were particularly adept at this — Russia had the much more demanding task of grappling with the complexity and the consequences both of Russia's imperial stretch, and that of the Soviet Union.

It has not yet done so. The period of largely uncritical enthusiasm for the West, and of undifferentiated contempt for things Soviet, was replaced by 1992 with a growing attachment to the Soviet past, and the merging of a nostalgia for the Soviet era with an equally nostalgic nationalism. This powerful confluence of two apparently antagonistic streams was not so much in competition with pro-Westernism, as caused by its excesses. The attempt to obliterate the past – as the Bolsheviks did, though much more thoroughly and brutally – created a frivolous relationship with history. Soviet communism was a Russian production: it could not be waved away as the creation of a small class of tyrants. The increasingly nationalist mood was less an expression of a new national identity than the expression of a lack of identity. Hence the promiscuous coupling of Stalin and Nicholas II, of Lenin and Christ. Hence the nominally incredible rapprochement between the Russian communists and the Russian nationalists, the embrace by Gennady Zyuganov, the communist leader, of the Orthodox Church. And, seeing Zyuganov's success, Yeltsin's aides moved their leader into the same space to position him for his successful bid for the presidency in 1996: Soviet symbols were used once more, mixed with imperial Russian ones. In the figure of the president the two streams were brought together at the level of image – even as they failed to connect in society.

Both popular and élite culture reflected the confusion. The independent TV station NTV mounted a televised New Year party to bring in 1996, and dressed its presenters in the red scarves of the Pioneers, the communist era youth movement, singing old Soviet songs in a way which was both ironic and nostalgic. In nightclubs like Soho and Pilot the theme was repeated, with Soviet evenings being mounted for the entertainment of the BMW-driving clientèle. In the little GITIS Theatre, a group of young actors put on the thirties play *The Wonderful Fusion*, a musical comedy by Vladimir Kirshon, in conscious nostalgia for the optimistic art of the time – almost as a tribute to a simpler age.

Two men stand as prime examples of successful operators within this promiscuous confusion: an artist and a mayor, both men of great energy who saw in the Russian past an inexhaustible supply of reference points for Russia's future. The first interpreted the past in order to change the future; the second copied it in order to fill a gap in the present.

Ilya Glazunov's art cannot be mistaken, nor does it ask to be passively viewed. Its detractors call it kitsch or pornographic, its supporters an expression of deep sympathy for the individual and his suffering. Of his style, Glazunov has said: 'It is realism in the sense that I understand Dostoyevsky used it, that is, as the interior world of the individual reflected through the truth of the external, objective world, as an expression of the idea of the struggle between good and evil, where the battlefield is the human heart.'

Many of his first pieces of the fifties (he was born in 1930) were men and women expressing a kind of hopeless languor against the background of lowering cityscapes – slightly reminiscent of the US artist Edward Hopper, but less hard-edged. The first exhibitions of these works were closed down by the Artists' Union; indeed, after his first, he was denounced in the pages of *Soviet Culture* by his former professor and exiled to teach drawing in Izhevsk. But he was back in Moscow by the early sixties, painting portraits which were vivid and static at the same time, drawing on mythology for some of his subjects and Russian history for many more. Themes emerge consistently in the seventies: brutal cityscapes, usually of rectangular modern blocks of the kind which were constructed in the heart of Moscow when the slummy, bohemian area of the Old Arbat was torn down; ruined churches, with the crosses on the skeletal domes askew; men guzzling drink or lying sozzled; women painted as if for an erotic magazine, with large firm breasts, curving thighs and wide eyes. He is often accused of anti-Semitism – and the signs are there: Trotsky, always very Jewish-looking, constantly attends on Lenin and in one extraordinary portrait is reproduced as the subject of an anti-Semitic poster, crawling over the walls of the Kremlin; in his painting entitled 'Call of the Devil' one of his full-breasted women sits naked, except for a shawl across her knees with star of David motif repeated on it – a scaly tail curls under her knees; a very Jewish-looking Judas kisses a Slavic Jesus.

In the eighties and nineties, the theme of Russia becomes more and more dominant, until it bursts from each canvas, the painter in his prime pulling ever harder on the painterly equivalent of the *vox humana* stop to leave no mistake as to his purpose. A 1994 canvas, 'Barrier: Humanitarian Aid', shows an old couple standing before the bar of a level-crossing, gazing in stunned misery out of the canvas; a small boy shivers beside them; in her bag, a box of Italian pasta and a Snickers bar; in the old man's pocket, a vodka bottle; behind them, snow and desolation, a ruined church. In the same year, he paints 'The Black-White House' – the Russian parliament as it was after the tanks had bombarded it in October 1993, windows blackened and shot out; behind it, the trademark blood-red sky. And third in that, his sixty-fourth year: 'Russia Awake!', one of the monster canvases, with in the fore-ground a young soldier stripped to the waist holding a Kalashnikov in one hand and a New Testament in the other, his belt buckle reading 'God is With Us'; behind him a young woman in battle fatigues, also with Kalashnikov and a Russian flag in her other hand; a sign saying 'Russians out of Russia' trampled under the soldier's foot; a drunk lying across a chess board on which each piece has a slip saying 'President' on it; a boy playing on a drum decorated with 'Russia for the Russians'; an old woman is bound with thick ropes, a placard around her neck reading 'Trade: Russian for Sale [in English] Inter Price – $1000'. A naked Miss Russia with jutting breasts and a white, red and blue sash; St George slaying the dragon . . . and more.

Even in the Gorbachev time, Glazunov was bestowed with marks of favour: he was made rector of the newly formed Russian Academy of Painting, Sculpture and Architecture, an institution in which his pupils are moulded in his conception of the Russian tradition, turning out works of graphic Glazunov-realism, their themes drawn from the Bible, Russian history and literature and nature. He exhibited beside his prize pupils and staff (including his son Ivan) in St Petersburg, his native city, at the end of 1995. Introduced by an uncharacteristically diffident Mayor Anatoly Sobchak, Glazunov repeated his manifesto: 'There is no nation without a past; and without a memory of the past, there is no future. We all dedicate ourselves to the restoration of Russia – that's what art is for.'

Yuri Luzhkov was the mayor of Moscow, the capital, and thus the advertisement for the country which he thought himself more capable of running than Boris Yeltsin. As he took a tighter and tighter grip on his office, Moscow began to reflect his activism: cranes and scaffolding rose above its grimy buildings. Luzhkov wanted to make his mark. And thus it was the architecture of Moscow which first expressed the new ideas of Russia, or at least, the ideas of Russia which its new rulers, and its new business people, wanted to leave in the minds of the people and the visitors to the capital.

Luzhkov was hyperactive and – especially after he was re-elected in 1996 with over 90 per cent of the Moscow electorate giving him their vote – domineering. He more than any other city or regional boss was uninhibited in his efforts to restore the pre-revolutionary Moscow, renovating street after street of eighteenth- and nineteenth-century housing and leasing it out at Tokyo-level rents to Western and New Russian companies.

But renovation of the remaining mansions was a small part of his ambition. He sought to re-create some of the central, and the sacred, symbols of old Moscow. At the entrance to Red Square, he had rebuilt the Iverskaya Gates, in which a copy of what had been one of Russia's most sacred icons – the Iverskaya Madonna – was set. This madonna had received the prayers of Russian soldiers before they plodded off on their campaigns; the legend was that no icon could be copied, since it became much more than a painting – it became the receptacle of the prayers of the faithful. This consideration did not deter.

Luzhkov's largest project was the rebuilding of the cathedral of Christ the Saviour. This vast church, built over decades and originally meant to celebrate the Russian victory over Napoleon but completed only in 1883, was the largest Orthodox church in the world and was seen as the supreme expression of the imperial glory of Russia. It was able to hold 10,000 worshippers at one time. It was thirty storeys high; twelve great bronze gates led into the centre of the church; its walls, built of 40 million bricks, were over three metres thick. The iconostasis was made with over 400 kilogrammes of gold and the walls were faced with marble from the Altai and from Italy, with granite from Finland.

In 1931 – worship in it having long since ceased – the Party leadership decided to blow it up, to make way for an equally grandiose Palace of the Soviets. It was neither the only nor (as it turned out) the best place to build the structure; but in a city which was to be refashioned to be an image, the symbolism of the replacement of a sacred monument to Russia's imperial grandeur *had* to be replaced by a monument to the triumph of the Soviet ideal – with the figure of Lenin up on the top, gesturing dismissively to a heaven he knew to be empty.

Ryczard Kapuscinski, the Polish writer who lived near the site when he was writing his book *Imperium* about the disappearing Soviet empire, sought to give some notion of the scale of the event:

Stalin orders the largest sacred object in Moscow to be razed. Let us for a moment give free rein to our imagination. It is 1931. Let us imagine that Mussolini, who at that time rules Italy, orders the basilica of St Peter in Rome to be razed. Let us imagine that Paul Doumer, who is at the time President of France, orders the cathedral of Notre Dame in Paris to be razed.

Let us imagine that Poland's Marshal Jozef Pilsudski orders the Jasnogorski monastery in Czestochowa to be razed.

Can we imagine such a thing?

No.

In fact, we can imagine such a thing precisely because the more hideous moments of the twentieth century, many of these associated with Stalin, have both expanded and dulled the imagination to allow it to register precisely that scale of event, and to fit it into a coherent structure. Further, by 1931, the citizens of Moscow were accustomed to the scale on which the Bolsheviks thought, and to their ferocious hatred of religion. Thus, when the cathedral was fenced, and then stripped of its valuables by work gangs, then finally, in December 1931, dynamited into rubble, they dully accepted it, since to do otherwise was to court disaster.

But no Palace of the Soviets could be built, because the marshy ground would not support its weight. The area was left to become overgrown, until an open-air heated swimming pool was constructed in Khruschev's time. Luzhkov conceived his plan to rebuild the cathedral in 1992. The patriarchy instantly blessed the idea, saying it was an act of repentance for seventy years of communism.

The idea was to make a copy of the original, with certain differences such as a huge underground car park beneath it, and eight high-speed, American-built lifts installed to whisk the faithful to the higher levels. It was also poorer than the original in significant ways: 50 kilogrammes of gold had to suffice for the cupola, as against the 400 in the nineteenth-century version – these being donated to the cathedral in fifty 1-kg bars with USSR stamped upon them by the chairman of the Stolichny (Capital) Bank, Alexander Smolensky, who came to the presentation ceremony in his black Cadillac. The church, a monstrous fake, rose slowly to again lower over the Moscow River.

In 1996, as Christ the Saviour neared completion, Luzhkov – dizzy with success – decreed that a statue of Peter the Great rise over Moscow, from a site on an island in the Moscow River. In a no doubt perfectly conscious imitation of the Lenin statue intended for the Palace of Soviets, Peter was to be 60 metres high, standing on a plinth constructed of galleons flying the St Andrew's flag. The sculptor, Zurab Tsereteli, worked in the high classical tradition – a fitting complement to Luzhkov's activity at the time, which was to establish himself as a presidential candidate by — among other manoeuvres — agitating for the return of the Ukrainian province of Crimea to Russia.

In February of 1997, however, a group of artists and intellectuals which had been rousing opposition to the statue won an apparent victory. They forced Luzhkov to scrap the plans for the statue on the proposed site, and to promise to relocate it. They had threatened to organize a referendum on the statue's construction. Luzhkov apparently thought he might lose.

Marat Gelman, a young gallery owner who had organized the protest, said after the mayoral U-turn: 'A new generation has appeared which is strong, self-confident and successful, and sees itself as a real power. Our protest is a sign that this generation has appeared and that we are not just interested in business but in assuming a leadership role in civil society.'

It was an important statement — if true. It showed that, even as the society wallowed this way and that in a search for an exit from its national dilemma, there were forces capable of initiating the national debate Russia needs so that it might make an accommodation — or series of accommodations — with its past. It gave hope that the early efforts to graft a fake future on to a crumbling past could not succeed, that the present had to be constructed out of a new experience, and that traditions had to be absorbed over decades before they could be understood, and superseded. It would be a long haul.

Notes on Sources

I have relied much more on interviews, newspapers both Russian and foreign, research papers, background documents and attendance at events than on books. The best Russian papers were *Izvestiya* for analysis and official positions; *Sevodnya* for news; *Kommersant* for business and the culture of the 'New Russians'; and *Nezavisimaya Gazeta* for polemic. The editors of *Novoe Vremya* turned what had been a KGB-dominated weekly into its opposite – an open and engaged journal of politics. *Express Kronika* continued a tradition of testimony against repression and harrassment, still needed in the New Russia. New magazines, including *Itogi*, were increasingly impressive.

A large number of private or quasi-private think tanks began in the late Gorbachev/Yeltsin periods, producing a mass of analysis, denunciation and polemic. Among the most interesting were the publications of Yegor Gaidar's Institute for the Study of the Economy in Transition; the Institute of Europe, where Sergei Karaganov oversaw a prolific output; the USA-Canada Institute and the political scientists associated with it, especially Andrei Kortunov and Sergei Rogov; the Carnegie Institute's Moscow branch, which mixed American scholars like Michael Faul with Russians like Sergei Markov.

The best of all, from my point of view, was a small think tank set up by three men who had worked with Mikhail Gorbachev before and after his presidency, and who then moved into the new Kremlin orbit on its always considerable liberal wing. These were Igor Bunin, Alexander Salmin and Mark Urnov, who formed the Centre for Political Technologies – its name reflecting their desire that political analysis should move beyond the rehearsal of set positions or the underpinning of prejudice to a reliance on fact, survey and opinion poll. I have used their joint and several publications very much.

The amount of papers and analyses produced by business, academic, journalistic and other sources outside of Russia is a continuous flood, much of which passed me by. Those I grasped from it were the publications of the IMF and the World Bank; brokers' reports, especially those from Morgan Stanley and Morgan Grenfell; and the essays published in the

US journals *Foreign Affairs* and *Foreign Policy*, in the Royal Institute of International Affairs' journal *International Affairs* and in the publications of the International Institute of Strategic Studies, including its periodical *Survey*.

The following is a selective list of books found useful as background for the five parts of the book. I have confined the lists largely – not wholly – to those directly concerned with Russia or the former Soviet Union: I benefited a good deal from books appearing in the first half of the nineties which were grappling with the new world order – or disorder – in a way not directly connected with the Soviet collapse, but heavily influenced by it.

Introduction and Part One: Power

Though my story starts as Gorbachev's leadership ends, the books by him, his aides and about him were indispensable in helping me to 'read into' the period – the more so, since my first-hand reporting of it had been limited.

Mikhail Gorbachev's publications include: *Perestroika*, Collins, London, 1987; *For a Nuclear-Free World*, Novosti, Moscow, 1987; *The August Coup*, HarperCollins, London, 1991; *Gody Trudnyx Reshenii*, Moscow, 1993, *The State of the World*, Harpers, San Francisco, 1995; and *Memoirs*, Orbit, London, 1996.

Books by aides include: *The Challenge; Economics of Perestroika* by Abel Aganbegyan, Hutchinson, London, 1988; *Moving the Mountain* by Abel Aganbegyan, Transworld, London, 1989; *The System* by Georgy Arbatov, Times Books, New York, 1992; *Ten Years that Shook the World* by Valery Boldin, Basic Books, New York, 1994; *Shest Lets Gorbachevym* by Anatoly Chernayev, Moscow, 1993; *Kremlevskaya Khronika* by Andrei Grachev, Eksmo, Moscow, 1994; *V Komande Gorbacheva* by Vadim Medvedev, Bylina, Moscow, 1994; *Chelovek za Spinoi* by Vladimir Medvedev, Moscow, 1993; *The Future Belongs to Freedom* by Eduard Shevardnadze, The Free Press, New York, 1991; *The Second Russian Revolution* by Tatyana Zaslavskaya, I. B. Tauris, 1990.

Books about Gorbachev must begin with Archie Brown's definitive academic study, *The Gorbachev Factor*, Oxford, 1996. Others include: *Gorbachev: Heretic in the Kremlin* by Dusko Doder and Louise Branson, Viking, New York, 1990; *The Gorbachev Phenomenon* by Moshe Lewin, Radius, New York, 1988; *Gorbachev* by Gail Sheehy, Heinemann, London, 1991; and *Gorbatchev: L'URSS, va-t-elle changer?* by Michel Tatu, Le Centurion, Paris, 1987.

On the period, I would pick out two books – both of which go back much further than Gorbachev – which I thought exceptional. One was Ryszard Kapuscinski's *Imperium*, Granta, London, 1994 – an 'encounter' (as he describes it) between a Polish journalist and the Soviet Union in strength and decay. The other is Martin Malia's *The Soviet Tragedy*, Basic Books, New York, 1994, which is as much (as he describes it) 'a commentary on much of twentieth-century intellectual history' as a description of the imperium.

Others, more specifically on the Gorbachev period, include: *The Hard Road to Market* by Roger Boyes, Secker and Warburg, London, 1990; *Soviet Society under Gorbachev* by David Lane, Unwin Hyman, London, 1990; *The Soviet Union under Gorbachev* by Martin McCauley, Macmillan, London, 1987; *Mikhail Gorbachev and the End of the Soviet Power* by John Miller, St Martin's Press, London, 1993; *Glasnost in Action* by Alec Nove, Unwin Hyman, London, 1989; *The Second Russian Revolution* by Angus Roxburgh, BBC Books, London, 1991; *The Age of Delirium* by David Satter, Knopf, New York, 1996.

On the transition period between Gorbachev and Yeltsin, see: *Window of Opportunity* by Graham Allison and Grigory Yavlinsky, Pantheon, New York, 1991; *Goodbye to the USSR* by Steve Crawshaw, Bloomsbury, London, 1992; *The End of Communist Power* by Leslie Holmes, Polity, Cambridge, 1993; *Farewell Perestroika* and *The Disintegration of the Monolith* by Boris Kagarlitsky, Verso, London, 1990 and 1992; *Opening the Soviet System* by George Soros, Weidenfeld and Nicolson, London, 1990; *The Politics of Transition* by Stephen White et al., CUP, Cambridge, 1993; and *The Soviet Transition* by Stephen White et al., Frank Cass, London, 1993.

On the Yeltsin period, the two volumes of autobiography by the Russian president are fascinating – though sometimes rather opaque – reading: *Against the Grain: an Autobiography*, Cape, London, 1990; and *The View from the Kremlin*, HarperCollins, London, 1994.

Other titles include: *Patterns in Post-Soviet Leadership*, ed. Robert Colton and Robert C. Tucker, Westview Press, Boulder, 1995; *The Rise of Russia and the Fall of the Soviet Empire* by John Dunlop, Princeton University Press, 1993; *The Struggle for Russia* by Ruslan Khasbulatov, Routledge, London, 1993; *The New Russia: Troubled Transformation* by Gail Lapidus, Westview Press, Boulder, 1995; *Elections and Political Order in Russia*, ed. Peter Lentini, CEUP, Budapest, 1995; *Modern Tsars and Princes* by Jeremy Lester, Verso, 1995; *The Reincarnation of Russia* by John Lowenhardt, Longman, London, 1995; *The Troubled Birth of Russian Democracy* by Michael McFaul and Sergei Markov, Hoover Institution Press, Stanford, 1993; *Post-Communism: Four Perspectives* by Michael Mandelbaum, Council on Foreign Relations, New

York, 1995; *Russia's Transition to Democracy* by G. D. G. Murrell, Sussex Academic Press, Brighton, 1997; *The Rebirth of Russian Democracy* by Nicolai Petro, Harvard, Cambridge Mass., 1995; *Post-Soviet Puzzles* (four vols.) ed. Klaus Segbers, Nomos Verlag, Baden Baden, 1995; *Moi Golos Budet Vsyo-Taki Uslyshan* by Alexander Shokhin, Nash Dom, Moscow, 1995; *The World After Communism* by Robert Skidelsky, Macmillan, London, 1995; *Politicheskaya Istoriaya Sovremennoi Rossii* by Vladimir Sorgin, Progress Academiya, Moscow, 1994; *How Russia Votes* by Stephen White et al., Chatham House, London, 1997; *Russia 2010* by Daniel Yergin and Thane Gustafson, Random House, New York, 1993; *Chto Takoye Dukhovnoye Naslediye?* by Gennady Zyuganov, Obozrevatel, Moscow, 1996; *Poslednii Brosok Na Yug* by Vladimir Zhirinovsky, Moscow, 1993.

Part Two: State

General reference: *Who's Who in Russia since 1900* by Martin McCauley, Routledge, London, 1997; *Kto est Kto B Roccii i Byvshem SSSR*, Moscow, 1995.

On the constitution: *Comparing Constitutions* by S. E. Finer et al., Clarendon Press, Oxford, 1995; *Striving for Law in a Lawless Land* by Alexander M. Yakovlev, M. E. Sharpe, Armonk, 1996; *Konstitutsiya Rossiskoi Federatsii – Komentarii*, Yuriditskaya Literatura, Moscow, 1994.

On the military: *Red Banner* by Christopher Donnelly, Jane's, London, 1988; *The Kremlin's Agenda* by Mark Galeotti, Jane's, London, 1995; *From Reform to Stability*, MGIMO, Moscow, 1995.

On the secret services: *The State Within the State* by Yevgenia Albats, Farrar, Straus & Giroux, New York, 1994; *A History of the Russian Secret Service* by Richard Deacon, Grafton, London, 1987; *Inside the KGB* by Vladimir Kuzichkin, André Deutsch, London, 1990; *Secret Empire* by Michael Waller, Westview Press, Boulder, 1994.

On crime: *Comrade Criminal* by Stephen Handelman, Michael Joseph, London, 1994; *Inside Yeltsin's Russia* by John Kampfner, London, 1994; *Vory v Zakone* by Georgy Podlesskikh and Andrei Tereshonok, Khudozhestvennaya Literatura, Moscow, 1994; *Crime Without Frontiers* by Clair Sterling, Little, Brown, London 1994; *The Soviet Mafia* by Arkady Vaksberg, Weidenfeld and Nicolson, London, 1991.

On religion: *A Long Walk to Church* by Nathaniel Davis, Westview Press, Boulder, 1995; *Awake to Life!* by Fr Alexander Men, Bowerdean Press, London, 1992; *Christianity for the 21st Century: the Life and Work of Alexander*

Men, ed. Elizabeth Roberts and Ann Shukman, SCM Press, London, 1996.

On the Russian regions: *Russian Nationalism* by Stephen Carter, Pinter, London, 1990; *An Empire's New Clothes* by Bruce Clark, Vintage, London, 1995; *Moscow – Governing the Socialist Metropolis* by Timothy Colton, Harvard University Press, Cambridge Mass., 1996; *Nations and Nationalism* by Ernest Gellner, Blackwell, Oxford, 1992; *Nationalism: Five Roads to Modernity* by Liah Greenfield, Harvard University Press, Cambridge, Mass., 1992; *Nationalism* by Elie Kedourie, Blackwell, Oxford, 1993; *Russia's Politics of Uncertainty* by Mary McAuley, Cambridge University Press, 1997; *Money Sings* by Blair Ruble, Woodrow Wilson Center/Cambridge University Press, 1995; *National Identity* by Anthony D. Smith, Penguin, London, 1991; *The Russian Question* by Alexander Solzhenitsyn, Harvill Press, London, 1995; *The Revenge of the Past* by Ronald Grigor Suny, Stanford University Press, 1993.

Part Three: Economy

The economy of the Soviet Union was a specialized topic under communism – with few able or willing to make sense of scanty and unreliable statistics. Pioneers included Alec Nove, Michael Kaiser and Marshall Goldman – of whom the last two continue to write on Russia and the other post-Soviet republics.

The most useful writing done on the transition were essays in journals and collections, and the material produced by the international financial institutions and large banks. Jeff Sachs, of all Western economists, was most engaged in the first years of reform; Anders Aslund remained so.

Useful books: *Corporate Governance in Transitional Economies* by Masahiko Aoki and Hying-Ki Kim, World Bank, Washington, 1995; *Gorbachev's Struggle for Economic Reform* by Anders Aslund, Pinter, London, 1989; *How Russia Became a Market Economy* by Anders Aslund, Brookings, Washington, 1995; *Socialism Capitalism Transformation* by Leszek Balcerowitz, CEUP, Budapest, 1995; *Kremlin Capitalism* by Joseph R. Blasi et al., Cornell University Press, 1997; *Privatizing Russia* by Maxim Boyko et al., MIT Press, Cambridge, Mass., 1995; *Crisis, Stablisation and Economic Reform* by Michael Bruno, Clarendon Press, Oxford, 1993; *Biznesmeny Rossii: Sorok Istorii Uspekha* by Igor Bunin et al., Moscow, 1994; *What About the Workers?* by Simon Clarke et al., Verso, London, 1993; *The Accidental Proletariat* by Walter D. Connor, Princeton, New Jersey, 1991; *Bear Hunting With the Politburo* by A. Craig Copetas, Simon and Schuster, New York, 1991; *The Privatisation*

Process in Russia, Ukraine and the Baltic States by Roman Frydman et al., CEUP, Budapest, 1993; *Russian Reform, International Money* by Yegor Gaidar and Otto Pohl, MIT Press, Cambridge, Mass., 1995; *Faith and Credit* by Susan George and Fabrizio Sabelli, Penguin, London, 1994; *Lost Opportunity* by Marshall I. Goldman, W.W. Norton, New York, 1994; *What Went Wrong With Perestroika?* by Marshall I. Goldman, W. W. Norton, New York, 1991; *The Success of Russian Economic Reforms* by Brigitte Granville, RIIA, London, 1995; *Post-Communist Societies in Transition: A Social Market Perspective* by John Gray, Social Market Foundation, London, 1994; *Russian Business Relationships in the Wake of Reform* by Noreena Hertz, Macmillan, London, 1997; *Highways and Byways* by Janos Kornai, MIT, Cambridge, Mass., 1995; *Why Doesn't Russian Industry Work?* by Leonid Kosals, I. B. Tauris, London, 1994; *Behind the Factory Walls*, ed. Paul R. Lawrence, Harvard Business School, Cambridge, Mass., 1990; *The Coming Russian Boom* by Richard Layard and John Parker, Free Press, New York, 1996; *Ekonomika i Vlast* by Vladimir Mau, Delo, Moscow, 1995; *China's Rise, Russia's Fall* by Peter Nolan, Macmillan, London, 1995; *Privatisation in Russia* by Alexander Radygin, CRCE, London, 1995; *Why Communist Economies Failed* by Ljubo Sirc, CRCE, London, 1994; *Russia's Stormy Path to Reform* by Robert Skidelsky, SMF, London, 1995; *The New Soviet Labour Market* by Guy Standing, ILO, Geneva, 1991; *Russian Unemployment and Enterprise Restructuring* by Guy Standing, ILO, Geneva, 1996; *Russia and the Challenge of Fiscal Federalism*, ed. Christine I. Wallich, World Bank, Washington, 1994; *Resistance to Change in the Soviet Economic System* by Jan Winiecki, Routledge, London, 1991; *Laissez Faire versus Policy-Led Transformation* by Grigory Yavlinsky, Moscow, 1994.

Part Four: Near and Far

Useful books include: *Windows of Opportunity*, ed. Graham Allison and William Urry, Ballinger, Cambridge, Mass., 1989; *At the Highest Levels* by Michael R. Beschloss and Strobe Talbott, Little, Brown, New York, 1993; *Engaging Russia* by Robert Blackwill, Roderick Braithwaite and Akihiko Tanaka, Trilateral Commission, New York, Paris and Tokyo, 1995; *Nations and Politics in the Soviet Successor States*, ed. Ian Bremmer and Ray Taras, Cambridge University Press, 1993; *The End of the Soviet Empire* by Hélène Carrère d'Encausse, Basic Books, New York, 1993; *The Disintegration of the Soviet Union* by Ben Fowkes, Macmillan, London, 1997; *The Return of the Strong* by Robert Harvey, Macmillan, London, 1995; *Between Marx and*

Muhammad by Dilip Hiro, HarperCollins, London, 1995; *The Clash of Civilizations and the Remaking of the World Order* by Samuel P. Huntingdon, Simon and Schuster, New York, 1996; *Preobrazhenie* by Andre Kozyrev, Mezhdunarodnye Otnosheniya, Moscow, 1995; *Soviet Foreign Policy in a Changing World*, ed. Robbin F. Laird and Erik Hoffman, Aldine, New York, 1986; *The Dawn of Peace in Europe* by Michael Mandelbaum, 20th Century Fund, New York, 1996; *Pandaemonium* by Daniel Patrick Moynihan, Oxford University Press, 1993; *Commonwealth or Empire?* by William E. Odom and Robert Dujarric, Hudson Institute, Indianapolis, 1995; *The War that Never Was* by David Pryce Jones, Weidenfeld and Nicolson, 1995; *Rethinking Russia's National Interest* by Henry Kissinger, CSIS, Washington, 1994; *The Nationalities Question in the Soviet Union*, ed. Graham Smith, Longman, London, 1990; *Tracking Nuclear Proliferation*, ed. Leonard S. Spector et al., Carnegie Endowment, Washington, 1995; *Germany Unified and Europe Transformed* by Philip Zelikow and Condoleeza Ruice, Harvard University Press, Cambridge, Mass., 1995.

Part Five: Culture

Useful books include: *Soviet Dissident Artists* by Renee and Matthew Baigell, Rutgers University Press, New Jersey, 1995; *The Making of Andrei Sakharov* by George Bailey, Allen Lane, the Penguin Press, London, 1989; *Literary Russia* by Anna Benn and Rosamund Bartlett, Macmillan, London, 1997; *The Moscow Art Theatre Letters* by Jean Benedetti, Methuen, London, 1991; *Filosofiya Svobody* by Nikolai Berdayev, Moscow, 1990; *The Icon and the Axe* by James Billington, Vintage, New York, 1970; *Russian Critics on the Cinema of Glasnost*, ed. Michael Brashinsky, Cambridge University Press, 1994; *Art under Stalin* by Matthew Cullerne Bown, Phaidon, Oxford, 1991; *Contemporary Russian Art* by Matthew Cullerne Bown, Phaidon, Oxford, 1989; *To Choose Freedom* by Vladimir Bukovsky, Hoover Institution Press, Stanford, 1987; *After the Future* by Mikhail Epstein, University of Massachussets Press, Amherst, 1995; *Ilya Ehrenburg: Writing, Politics and the Art of Survival* by Anatol Goldberg, Weidenfeld and Nicolson, London, 1984; *Dead Again* by Masha Gessen, Verso, London, 1997; *Totalitarian Art* by Igor Golomstock, Collins Harvill, London, 1990; *The Thinking Reed* by Boris Kagarlitsky, Verso, London, 1988; *Concerning the Spiritual in Art* by Vasily Kandinsky, Dover Publications, New York, 1977; *Sots-Art* by O. V. Kholmogorova, Galart, Moscow, 1994; *The Intellectuals on the Road to Class Power* by George Konrad and Ivan Szelenyi, Harvester Press, Brighton, 1979; *Late Soviet*

Culture, ed. Thomas Lahuisen, Duke University Press, Durham, 1993; *Comrade Rockstar* by Reggie Nadelson, Chatto and Windus, London, 1991; *Russia's Alternative Prose* by Robert Porter, Berg, Oxford, 1994; *Socialist Realism: an Impossible Aesthetic* by Regine Roibin, Stanford University Press, 1992; *Rock Around the Block* by Timothy Ryback, Oxford University Press, 1990; *Russian Studies* by Leonard Schapiro, Collins Harvill, London, 1986; *Is Comrade Bulgakov Dead?* by Anatoly Smeliansky, Methuen, London, 1993; *Solzhenitsyn: a Biography* by Michael Scammel, W.W. Norton, New York, 1984; *The KGB's Literary Archive* by Vitaly Shentalinsky, Harvill Press, London, 1995; *Soviet Russian Literature* by Marc Slonim, Oxford University Press, 1977; *The Oak and the Calf* by Alexander Solzhenitsyn, Harper, New York, 1979; *The Gulag Archipelago* by Alexander Solzhenitsyn, Collins Harvill, London, 1988; *An Arrow in the Wall* by Andrei Voznesensky, Secker and Warburg, London, 1987; *Fatal Half Measures* by Yevgeny Yevtushenko, Little, Brown, Boston, 1991.

A great deal of the New Russian writing can be found in the series *New Russian Writing*, edited by Natasha Perova and Arch Tait, Glas Publishers, Moscow.

Index

ABB 252
advertising 422, 434–6
Aeroflot 122, 267, 268
aerospace industry 266–9
Africa 364
Against the Grain (Yeltsin) 7
Aganbegyan, Abel 209, 220
Agapov, Yuri 301
Agrarian Party 49, 70, 306
Agricultural Industry Bank 286
Akhromeyev, Marshal Sergei 112
Aksyonov, Vasily 392
Aksyuchits, Victor 23, 26
Albats, Yevgenia 135, 136
alcoholism 315
Alekperov, Vagit 275–6
Aleshkovsky, Yuz 406
Alexashenko, Sergei 218, 228
Alexei II 42–3, 158, 161–4, 166, 167, 171
Alfa bank 294
Alfa Capital 290
Alfa-Eco 299
Alfa-Foto 299
Aliev, Geydar 350, 366
Alisa (rock group) 399
Alpha group 288
Ambartsumov, Yevgeny 338
Andropov, Yuri 146, 208, 353
Anensky, Lev 408
Anpilov 76
Anti-Booker award 409
Appearance of Socialist Realism, The (painting) 413

Aquarium (rock band) 399, 437
Arco 276
Ardov, Mikhail 170
arms trade 121–2, 154, 199, 364
army 111–19
   conditions 119
   corruption within 114–16, 130
   decline and retreat 111, 112–13
   during coup 113, 114
   and Gorbachev 111, 112, 118, 119
   gulf between recruits and officers
      118–19
   new military doctrine 124–5
   post-coup re-organization 113–14
   and republics 124
   Soviet era 111–12
   undermanning of and cuts in
      117–18
   and Yeltsin 123
art 380, 413–16
   avant-garde 414–15
   decay of Soviet high in nineties 400
   and Glazunov 296, 361–2, 444–6
   movement towards greater
      experimentation 395–6
   nostalgia for Soviet 384–5
   Sots Art 413–14, 422
   use of Soviet themes in new 415
ASKO 299
Askoldov, Alexander 395
Aslund, Anders 236
Assa (film) 414
assassinations 152, 287–8

Association of Russian Bankers 152, 288
Astrakhan, Dmitri 439
Aven, Pyotr 215, 218, 219, 288
Averintsev, Sergei 162, 344
aviation industry 266–9
Avtovaz 251, 307
Avurkhanov, Uvar 194
Azerbaijan 332, 348, 349–50

Babichev, General Ivan 196–7
Baburin, Sergei 26, 48
Bakaleinnik, Joseph 374
Bakatin, Vadim 134–5, 136–7
Balcerowicz, Leszek 218
Ballad of a Solider, The (film) 394
ballet 400–401, 402–3
Baltics 24, 329, 331, 332, 333, 347–8, 351
bankruptcies 255–6
banks xvi–xvii, 383, 386–95
  assassinations 152, 287–8
  downfall 292–3
  formation of new commercial 286–7
  growth of broking industry 290–91
  growth in prosperity 288–9
  lack of trust of 285–6
  link with organized crime 147, 287–8
  offering of loans to government in return for shares 256, 274, 293–4
  and privatization 150, 241, 257, 282, 289–90
  setting up by companies 301
  Soviet era 286
Barankin, Yevgeny 398
Barannikov, Victor 37, 42, 137–8, 138–9
bards 388–90
Barkashov, Alexander 26–7, 42, 43
Barkhin, Sergei 396, 415
Barnevik, Percy 310

Barsukov, General Mikhail 55, 90, 91, 139
Basayev, Shamil 198
Batanov, Alexander 73
BatteryMarch 260
Belarus 74–5, 125, 214, 329, 341, 345–7, 351
Bendukidze, Kakha 89, 294, 296, 297
Berdyayev, Nikolai xxi, 25
Berezovsky, Boris 89, 303, 307, 429
Berger, Mikhail 219–20
Beria, Lavrenti 132
Billington, James 163–4
Birshtein, Boris 37, 138
Birth, The (Varlamov) 409
birth rates 315
Black Tuesday 58, 59, 235, 237, 292
Blok 379
Bloom, Anthony 163
Blotsky, Oleg 197
Bocherev, Mikhail 217
Boiko, Oleg 61–2, 289, 306, 307
Boldyrev, Yuri 62–3, 116
Bolsheviks, The (play) 393
Bolshoi ballet 401, 402, 403
Bondarchuk, Sergei 395
Booker Prize 408–9
Boris Godunov (play) 381, 418
Borisov, Alexei 169
Borovik, Artyom 430
Borovin, Valentin xxii
Borovoy, Konstantin 122
Bosnia 360
bourgeoisie 249–58
Boyarsky, Vladimir 136
Brakov, Yevgeny 11, 262
Brandwain, Rachmiel 153
Bremmer, Alexander 415
Britain
  miners' strike 318–19
  privatization 245
Brodsky, Josif 391, 410, 417
Bruno, Michael 285
Bryntsalov, Vladimir 81–2

Brzezinski, Zbigniew 365
budget deficit 231, 238
Bukato, Victor 301
Bulatov, Erik 396
Burbulis, Gennady 19, 62, 216, 217, 356
  on market economy 218
  unpopularity 24, 33
  and Yeltsin 4, 12, 102
Burlakov, General Matvei 115, 116, 195
Burnt by the Sun 441
Bush, George 364, 366
business class 3–4, 297–8, 302–10
  attitude and work ethic 304
  cross-holdings 303–4
  family orientated 304–5
  and foreign investment 308–10
  growth of power 302
  political affiliations 47, 84, 89, 306–7
  and power 305

Camdessus, Michel 57–8
car production 374
Caspian Sea 348–9, 366
Castenfeld, Peter 57
Catherine, Empress xxvii
Catholicism 158, 167–8
Caucasus 332–3
Central Bank 58, 59, 60, 234, 236, 286
  conflict with Finance Ministry 284–5, 339
  and Gerashchenko *see* Gerashchenko, Victor
  and Matiukhin 225
  and Paramanova 59, 237, 293
  and republics 227
centrists 27–31, 59, 62–3
charities 318–20
Chechen war 3, 15, 63, 116, 117, 178, 193–202
  attempts at negotiation before invasion 193–4, 199

and constitution 106–7, 108
decision to intervene by Yeltsin 16, 189, 194–6
and democrats 61–2
effect on Russian politics 198–201
fighting by Chechen soldiers 197–8
legitimization of by new military doctrine 124–5
low morale of Russian army 197
media coverage during presidential elections 87
opposition to intervention 65, 196
origin of 193–4
withdrawal 201–2
Chechnya 83, 174, 180, 182
  crime 199
  history 192–3
  vital link in oil chain 199–200
Cheka 132
Cherepkov, Vladimir 187
Cherkashin, Ilya 414
Chernayev, Anatoly 75
Chernenko, Konstantin 174
Chernobyl 346
Chernomyrdin, Victor xxi, 32, 54, 56–8, 71, 196, 223, 277, 316
  allegations of corruption 91
  appointment as prime minister 33, 34, 232
  background 232
  and centrism 59
  character 34, 56
  and Chubais 85
  and economic reform xvi, 57–8, 59, 60, 232–3, 235, 236, 237, 238
  and IMF 57–8
  on Nato xviii
  and 'Our Home is Russia' 63–4, 307
  support for Yeltsin 35, 37
Chevron 349, 366
Children of the Arbat (Rybakov) 383
China 357, 363, 371, 373
Chindyshev, Anatoly 77

Chinese immigrants 363
Christ the Saviour cathedral 158, 170,
   447–8
Christian democrats 22–3
Christopher, Warren 127
Chronicle of Current Events 96
Chubais, Anatoly 35, 55, 59, 91
   character 242
   dismissal 70, 79
   economic policy 215, 218, 219, 238,
      253
   and foreign investment 252
   and presidential elections 84–5
   and privatization 51, 236, 241–2,
      244, 245, 247–9, 250, 253, 256,
      257, 258
   and Yeltsin 58–9
Chukchi 175
Churbanov, Yuri 146
Church Abroad *see* Russian Orthodox
   Church Abroad
Church *see* Orthodox Church
cinema *see* films
CIS (Commonwealth of Independent
   States) 74, 336–8, 347
   creation 14, 99, 336–7
   economic integration 340–41
   problems 337–8
   Russia's relationship with 337–9,
      359, 362, 365
Civic Union 28, 35, 49, 248
Civil Defence 437
civil law 108–9
Clinton, President 51, 364, 365, 366
coal industry 270, 279–81, 312 *see also*
   miners
Commercial Structures Protection
   Bureau 152
commercials, television 422, 435
Commersant 430, 431, 432
Committee on Foreign Investment 252
Commonwealth of Independent States
   see CIS
Communist Party (Russian) *see* RCP

Communist Party of Soviet Union
   (CPSU) 6, 25, 68
communists 338, 436, 444
Communists for Democracy 23, 29
companies
   categories of 263–4
Congress of Peoples' Deputies 11, 21,
   34
   banning of by Yeltsin 34, 41, 42–3,
      97
   see also parliamentary revolt
   conflict with Yeltsin 20, 23–4, 27,
      31–3, 35–6, 40
   early support for Yeltsin 19–20
   opposition to reform 39–40
   struggle for power with presidency
      37–40
Congress of Russian Communities
   64–6, 82
constitution 97, 110
   adoption of 105
   and Chechen war 106–7, 108
   and Constitutional Court 106–8,
      110, 138
   Duma's attempt to amend 106
   features 103–4
   and Gorbachev 98–9
   problems xiv–xv
   referendum vote 104–5
   and republics 104, 106, 182–3,
      183–4
   and Yakovlev 95, 98
   and Yeltsin 47, 51, 99, 102–3,
      105–6, 110
Constitutional Court 106–8, 110, 138
Conventional Forces in Europe treaty
   128, 354, 362
co-operatives 209, 210, 243, 244,
   298–9
corporatism 256
corruption xiv, 47, 142–3, 145
   allegations against Yeltsin's circle
      36–7
   army 114–16, 130

and co-operatives 298
effect of privatization 150–51
and Nazdratenko 186–8
of officials 155–6
in republics 145–6
state enterprises 243
television 428
Cosmos Hotel (Moscow) 254
Cot, Jean-Pierre 13
Council for Foreign and Defence
    Policy 338, 351
coup (1991) xxvii, xxviii–xxix, 13–14,
    99, 113, 114, 116, 133–4, 323
Court see Constitutional Court
Court of Human Rights 200
courts 108–9
credit, issuing of 226–7, 234, 284–5
crime 142–56
    assassinations 152, 287–8
    bombings 147
    as a consequence of new economic
        freedom 149
    and entrepreneurial activity 146–7
    increase in 48, 146–7, 231–2
    on international scale 153–4
    and Nordex 154–5
    organized 143, 145–6, 147–8,
        152–3, 156, 211, 287–8
    and property 148, 150–51
    and protection 151–2
    Soviet era 144–6
    Yeltsin's decree on fighting 105–6,
        109–10
    see also corruption
Crimea 343–4
criminal gangs 144
Croatia 360
CS First Boston 290, 291
Cuba 364
Czechoslovakia 101, 102, 136, 246

Daniel, Yuly 392
death penalty 109
death rates 315

Decree 1,400 41, 42, 97, 103
Del, Tristran 402
Democratic Party 23, 28, 49
democrats 21–2, 38–9, 45, 102
    and Chechen war 61–2
    decline 24
    and parliamentary elections 48,
        49–50
    undermining of 46–8
Den ('Day') 45, 361
Derzhava (State Power) 117
Deuss, John 349
Devils, The 419–20
Dictatorship of Conscience, The (play)
    416, 417, 419
directors see managers
disabled 315–16
discos 437
dissidents 95–8, 391
Doctor Zhivago 392
Dombrowski, Marek 245
Domovoi ('House Spirit') 433–4
Dorenko, Sergei 429
Dostoyevsky 370, 392, 419
Dresner, Richard 85
drugs trade 154
Dubynin, Sergei 58, 237, 277, 288,
    292, 293
Dudayev, General Dzhokar 83, 113,
    191,192–3, 194, 199, 202
Dugin, Alexander 26
Duma 34, 45, 363
    and constitution 106
    elections to see parliamentary
        elections
Dunayevsky, Isaac 397
Duvanov, Gennady 299
Dyachenko, Tatyana 88, 90, 91
Dzerzhinsky, Felix xxii, 132, 134

economic policy 58, 72
    achievement xv–xvi
    appointment and reforms of Gaidar's
        Gang see Gaidar's Gang

economic policy – *cont.*
  attempts at stabilization 236, 238
  change in taxation system 224
  and Chernomyrdin 57–8, 59, 60,
    232–3, 235, 236, 237, 238
  and Chubais 215, 218, 219, 238, 253
  cuts in public expenditure xiv
  differing views on causes of inflation
    224–5, 226, 228, 284
  effect of market reforms on citizens
    60, 212–13, 221
  and Fyodorov 234–5, 236
  and globalization 372–3
  and Gorbachev 208–11, 243
  IMF loans xv–xvi, 45, 57–8,
    59–60, 200, 238
  liberalization of prices 221–2, 231
  Naishul and principles for economic
    reform 240–41
  non-liberalization of energy prices
    222–3, 270
  and privatizaiton *see* privatization
  and republics 234–5
  shock therapy 213–14, 232, 258
  Soviet era xxii, 206–11
  and Yeltsin 5, 18–19, 20, 35, 41, 51,
    52, 217
economy
  collapse at end of 1991 210–11, 220
  crash of rouble 58, 59, 235, 237, 292
Efros, Anatoly 423
Ehrenburg, Ilya 381, 388
Ekaterinburg 147–8, 259
Elchibey, Abulfaz 333
elections *see* parliamentary elections;
    presidential elections
Elishman, Nikolai 161
Elkin, Dmitri 302
energy industry
  and foreign investment 309
  non-liberalization of prices 222–3,
    270
  and privatization 235, 250
  see also gas industry; oil industry

Enterprise Law (1987) 209, 243–4,
    298, 322
enterprises *see* state enterprises
entrepreneurial class 296–302
  bankers 300–301
  characteristics and background
    301–2
  and co-operatives 298–9
  joint ventures with foreign
    companies 299–300
  see also business class
Epicentre 229
Ernst, Konstantin 423, 429–30, 433
Estonia 166, 333, 347, 348
Eti 414
European Union 210, 275, 371
Everything Will be OK 439
Exchange, The (Trifonov) 388

Falcone, Giovanni 152–3
family 318
Favorit 302
Federal Counter-intelligence Service
    139
Federal Security Agency 137
Federation of Independent Trade
    Unions 28–9
Federation of Independent Unions of
    Russia 323
Federation Treaty 177, 181–2, 185,
    194
Filaret 165
Filatov, Sergei 17
films 384, 438–41
  'black' 440
  decline in cinema attendance
    439–40
  glasnost era 381
  musical 397
  numbers produced 440
  Soviet era 394–5
  on television 423
finance 282–95
  currency reforms 285

falling of market 292
and foreigners 291
formation of broking industry
290–91
growth of market 290–92
Soviet 282–4
see also banks
Finance Ministry 60, 234, 283
conflict with Central Bank 284–5,
339
Finer, Samuel 103
First Voucher Fund 254, 290
folk songs 397–8
Foreign and Defence Policy Council
358
Foreign Intelligence Service 139
foreign investment 252–3, 255, 292,
308–10
Foreign Investment Council 308
Foreign Ministry 361
foreign policy
change from pro-Western to power
politics 358–9
and Gorbachev 123, 353–5, 370
G7's attitude towards Russia 356–7
and Kozyrev 355–6, 357, 358–9,
360–61, 362
loss of influence 359–60, 364
opposition to Western policy 357–8
and Primakov 367–8
relations with China 357, 363, 371
stress on CIS 359, 362
under-resourcing of Foreign
Ministry 361
United States policy towards 364–6,
371–2
Yeltsin's idealist-Western policy
xviii, 355–7
Freeh, Louis 153
France 367
Friedman, Mikhail 288
Furtseva, Ekaterina 403
Fyodorov, Boris 34–5, 57, 61, 62, 179
background 233

character 233–4, 339
economic policy 35, 234–5, 236
and Gerashchenko 226, 234, 285
Fyodorov, Svyatoslav 61, 71

Gaidar, Yegor 24, 31, 34, 45, 79, 89,
218, 219, 231, 241
abilities and character 232
appointment as head of economic
reform 18, 216–17
background 214–15
choice of Gerashchenko as chairman
of Central Bank 32, 226
Congress vote against prime
minister appointment 33
criticism of 32
economic reforms 231, 241, 258
on Gorbachev's enterprise law 209
opposition to Chechen war 62
reappointment 41, 236
resignation 17, 57, 229
and Russia's Choice 46, 47, 61, 220,
229, 306
Yeltsin's support for 19
Gaidar's Gang 214–24, 225, 241, 258
background 214–16
coming to power 216–17
criticism of 227–9
economic reforms 218, 220–24,
231, 306
free-market beliefs 217–18, 220–21
and politics 219
and privatization 245
view of inflation 224
Galich, Alexander 388, 390
Gamsakurdia, Zviad 333
gangs, criminal 144
gas industry 270, 277–9
Gayevsky, Vadim 403
Gaz 251, 260
Gazprom 232, 269, 277, 278–9, 287,
290, 303, 307, 429
Gelman, Marat 449
Georgia 125, 331, 332, 338, 350, 362

Gerashchenko, Victor 45, 235–6,
    285–6, 312, 339
    appointed chairman of Central Bank
    32, 226
    background 225
    firing of 58, 292
    and Fyodorov 226, 234, 285
    issuing of credit 226, 237, 284–5
Geremek, Bronislaw 359–60
Germany 357, 367, 371
Giddens, Anthony 375
glasnost 380, 381–3, 416, 417, 422,
    423–4
Glaziev, Sergei 23, 64, 65, 66, 215
Glazunov, Ilya 361–2, 396, 444–6
globalization 372–3, 375
God Forbid 84, 86
Goldman Sachs 252
Golembyovsky, Oleg 430
Golovkov, Sergei 61, 216
Golushko, General Nikolai 138,
    139
Good Person of Szechuan, The (play)
    393–4
Goodbye America (play) 418–19
Gorbachev, Mikhail 4, 12, 177, 364,
    424
    and army 111, 112, 118, 119
    and Church 161
    compared to Yeltsin 6–7
    and constitution 98–9
    and coup xxviii-xxix
    cutting of military budget 120
    downfall 14
    economic policy 208–11, 243
    efforts in introducing law-governed
    state 98–9
    foreign policy 123, 353–5, 370
    and KGB 132–3
    and nationalism 329–30, 334
    and presidential elections 77–8
    relationship with Yeltsin 6–7, 9, 13,
    14, 20
    reliance on patronage 175
    on state enterprises and co-
    operatives 146, 298
    and Volsky 28
Gorbachev, Raisa 354
Gore–Chernomyrdin Commission
    308
Gorky Street 442
Gorton, George 85
Gosbank (Soviet State Bank) 283
GosKino 395
government
    as a clan system 55–6
Govorukhin, Stanislav 23
Grachev, Andrei 134
Grachev, General Pavel 91, 111, 114,
    115, 117, 128
    and Chechen war 194–5
    misappropriation of funds claim
    116
Gradsky, Alexander 398
Graham, Thomas 55–6
Grazhdansky Kontrol (civil control)
    319
Grebenshchikov, Boris 399, 437
Grigorovich, Yuri 401, 402–3
Grigoryants, Sergei 140
Grishin, Victor 8
Gromov, General Boris 117, 196
Grossman, Vitaly 381–2
G7 (Group of Seven) xvi, 356–7, 358,
    367
Gulf War 121
Gurov, Alexander 145
Gusinsky, Vladimir 47, 54, 152, 288,
    301, 306–7, 427, 428, 430

Handelman, Stephen 199
Harris, Ralph 215
Havel, Vaclav 17, 129, 205
Hayden, John 148
health care xiv, 314–16
Honecker, Erich 355
hostage crises 66
housing 316–18

human rights 96−7, 336
Hungary xiv, 101, 102, 215, 246

identity
    losing of Russian under Soviet rule
        443
Idiot, The 392
Ignatenko, Vladimir 187−8
Ignatiev, Andrei 219
Ilarionov, Andrei 219, 233, 311
Iliumzhinov, Kirsan 183
Ilyushenko, Alexei 428
Ilyushin, Sergei 266
Ilyushin, Victor 12
IMF (International Monetary Fund)
        70, 87−8, 224, 227, 340, 356, 363,
        367
    loans xiii-xiv, 200, 238
    negotiations over loan 45, 57−8,
        59−60
Imperial Bank 303
imports 223
India 373
industrialists 222, 306, 338
industry 206, 231
    creation in Soviet Union 259
    crises faced by 265−6
    decline 252
    inability to compete internationally
        373−4
    reorganization 263−4
    self-sufficiency 260
infant mortality 315
inflation 46, 58, 234, 237
    differing views on causes 224−5,
        226, 228, 284
    falling of xiii, 60, 236
Inkombank 303
Institute of Market Reform 215
intelligence services 131−41, 152
    see also KGB
intelligentsia 385, 389
Inter-regional Group of Soviet
    deputies 11−12, 172

Interior Ministry *see* Ministry of
    Interior
International Monetary Fund *see* IMF
Interquadro 299
investment
    cuts in xvi, 262
investment, foreign 252, 255, 291,
        308−10
investment funds 253−5
Ioann, Metropolitan 163, 168
Israel 355
Israeli−Palestine peace process 372
Italy 256−7
Itogi ('Results') 427, 428
Ivankov, Vyacheslav 153−4
Ivanov, Ivan 304
Iverskaya Madonna 447
Izvestiya 31, 32, 86, 105, 430, 432

Jansons, Mariss 401
Japan 354, 355, 356, 358, 371
Jews 167
John Paul II, Pope 167−8
Jordan, Boris 255, 290−292
judicial system 108−9, 110
'Justice and Law' agency 109

Kabakov, Ilya 396, 400, 414
Kadannikov, Victor 70
Kagalovsky, Konstantin 215, 219, 288
Kamaz 251−2
Kandinsky, Vasily 379
Kapuscinski, Ryczard 447
Karaganov, Sergei 129, 357−8
Kashirsky, Anatoly 301
Kazakhstan 125, 146, 341, 347, 348−9
Kazannik, Alexei 11
Kazannikov, Alexei 106
Kazkhalov, Tugar 296
Kazko, Vasily 66
Kedrov, Konstantin 412
KGB 131−41, 237, 309
    history 132−3
    influence on society 141

KGB – *cont.*
 merging of Interior Ministry with
  137–8
 reform of under Bakatin 134–5,
  136–7
 reshaping of under Primakov 368
 role in coup 133–4
Khanin, Grigory 208
Kharitonov, Mark 408
Kharshan, Mikhail 254
Khasbulatov, Ruslan 39, 44, 100
 background 30–31
 conflict with Yeltsin 31, 35, 36, 38,
  41, 42, 192
 as parliamentary chairman 31
Khivelidi, Ivan 298, 299, 300
Khizha, Georgy 226
Khodorkovsky, Mikhail 306
Kholodov, Dmitri 115, 432
Khrushchev, Nikita 83, 160, 342, 343
Kicks 440
King Lear 420
Kino 399
kiosks 223
Kirgizia 206, 340
Kirpichenko, General Vadim 131–2,
  141
Kiselyev, Oleg 296–7, 299, 300
Kiselyev, Yevgeny 87, 427
Kissinger, Henry 365
Kitchin, Konstantin 399
Kivlidi, Ivan 152
Klimontovich, Nikolai 408
Klimov, Andrei 176–7
Klochkov, Igor 323
Kochetkov, Georgy 169
Kohl, Helmut 366, 371
Kokonin, Vladimir 401
Kokoshin, Dr Andrei 114
Kolbin, Gennady 330
Kolesnikov, General Mikhail 114
Komi Oil 251
Komsomolskaya Pravda 86
Kontorovich, Vladimir 208

Kornai, Janos 215
Korotich, Vitaly 422
Korzhakov, General Alexander 15,
  53–4, 55, 89, 90, 91, 139, 413–14
Kovalev, Sergei 17, 95–6, 105,
  200–201
Kozyrev, Andrei 32, 62, 347
 background 355
 foreign policy 355–6, 357, 358–9,
  360–61, 362
Kravchenko, Leonid 424
Kravchuk, Leonid 165, 323, 334, 342,
  343
Kruchina, Nikolai 150
Kryuchkov, Vladimir xxvi, 133, 134
Kuchma, Leonid 366
Kukli ('Puppets') 428
Kulikov, Anatoly 156
Kunadze, Georgy 355
Kunayev, Dinmukhamed 146, 330
Kundera, Milan 359
Kurapaty Wood massacres 346
Kurile Islands 354, 355, 356, 358

labour movement 321–5
Ladygin, General Fyodor 128
Landsbergis, Vytautas 333
Lange, Bend-Peter 86
Latin America 364
Latvia 166, 347, 348
law 95–110
 civil 108–9
 criminal 109–10
 dissidents and search for
  constitutional order 95–8
 see also constitution
Lebed, General Alexander 64, 79, 113,
  345, 372
 appointed national security chief 117
 on army 111
 and Chechen war 65, 196, 201
 on Nato expansion 129
 and presidential elections 82–3, 86,
  90, 119

speech at Congress of Russian
  Communities 65–6
Lenin 159–60
Leninetz electrical plant 260
Leningrad TV 425, 426
Letov, Yegor 437
Lewandowski, Janusz 246
Liberal Democrats 47, 49, 66, 236
Liberman, Yevsei 207
Lieven, Anatole 197–8
Life and Fate (Grossman) 381, 382
Ligachev, Yegor 9, 10
Likhachev, Vasily 185
Lisbon agreement (1992) 125
Lissovilik, Dmitri 150
Listyev, Vladimir 301, 428–9
literature 391–2, 404–10
  Booker Prize 408–9
  exploration of themes after Stalin's
    death 387–8
  glasnost era 380, 381–3
  new Russian writers 404–7, 408
  in nineties 400
  opposition to new writers 408,
    409–10
  see also individual writers
Lithuania 13
Little Vera 383, 440
living standards 46, 313, 320–21
Livshits, Alexander 74
Lobov, Oleg 12, 217
Logovaz 303
Lopukhin, Vladimir 223
Loutchansky, Grigory 154, 155
Lukashenko, Alexander 74, 346
Lukin, Vladimir 62, 357
Lukoil 275–6, 287, 303, 432
Luttwak, Edward 143
Luzhkov, Yuri 5, 55, 151, 306, 307
  power of 189, 446
  and rebuilding of Christ the Saviour
    cathedral 170, 447
  renovation of Moscow 446–7, 448,
    449

and Sevastopol 344
Lyubimov, Yuri 394, 417–18

McCabe and Mrs Miller (film) 142
McDonald's 413, 421
mafia 153, 156, 223
magazines 432–4
Main Guard Directorate 139
Makarevich, Andrei 398
Malevich, Casimir 379
managers 244, 260, 261–2, 302, 324
  growth of incomes 249–50
  and privatization programme 248,
    249–50, 262
  seeking of independence from Party
    242–3
  and unions 324
Margolev, Mikhail 88
Marxism 26
Mashkov, Vladimir 147
Maskhadov, Aslan 201–2
Maslyukov, Yuri 74
Matador 433
Matiukhin, Georgy 225
Mavrodi, Sergei 80, 254
Mayakovsky, Vladimir 379
media
  and parliamentary elections 48
  and presidential elections 86–7
  see also press; television
Medunov, Sergei 145
Medved ('Bear') 433
Melodiya 403–4
Memorial xvi, 319
Men, Father Alexander 168–9
Menatep Bank 257, 294
Menshov, Vladimir 438–9
Menshkov, Yuri 343, 344
Metropol 392
Meyerhold, Vsevolod 379, 380
Middle East xix, 364
Migranyan, Andranik xxvi, 358
Mikhalkov, Nikita 64, 434, 440–41
Mikoyan, Artyom 266

Mikrodin 303
military *see* army
military expenditure
   cuts in 120, 262, 306
military-industrial complex 119–21,
   122–3, 207, 306
miners 12, 279, 280–81, 312, 322, 323
miners' strike (1989) 12, 322
miners' strike (Britain) 318–19
Ministry of Atomic Energy 126
Ministry of Culture 415
Ministry of Defence 116, 126
Ministry of Interior 137–8, 147
Ministry of Security 138, 139
Miroslavsky, Yuri 406
Mitkova, Tatyana 425
Mjavanadze, Vasily 145
MMM 80, 254, 290, 422, 435
Moldova 332, 345, 351
money
   status of in Soviet society 284
   see also finance
Morozov, Pavel xxii-xxiii
mortality age xvii, 315
mortality rates 315
Mosbiznesbank 287, 301
Moscow 189 *see also* Luzhkov, Yuri
Moscow Conservatoire 401–2
Moscow Doesn't Believe in Tears (film)
   394, 438, 439
Moscow News 115
'Moscow Party' 306
Moscow-Petushki (Yerofeev) 406
Moscow 2042 (Voinovich) 410–11
Moskovsky Komsomolets 431
Moslems 167
Moss Kantor, Rosabeth 374
Most group 47, 288, 301, 306
Mravinsky, Yevgeny 402
Murashev, Arkady 23
music 397–9, 402, 436–8
   bards 388–90
   folk tradition 397–8
   in nineties 400

rock 398–9, 436–7
musical comedies 397
My Fatherland 117

Nagorno-Karabakh 22, 333
Naishul, Vitaly 240, 242, 258
National Patriotic Front 73
National Salvation Front 26
nationalism 25, 178, 329–30, 332–4
   see also republics
nationalists 64–5, 338
   opposition to Yeltsin 24–7
Nato 356, 366, 370
   establishment of charter between
      Russia and (1997) 129–30
   expansion xviii, 52, 127–9, 130,
      370–71
Nauman, Stas 398, 433, 437
Nazarbayev, Nursultan 13, 332, 341,
   347
Nazdratenko, Yevgeny 187–8
Nemtsov, Boris 71, 229
Nevzlin, Leonid 306
Nevzorov, Alexander 426–7
New Russians xxiii, 47, 84
Nezavisimaya Gazeta ('The
   Independent') 430, 431
night clubs 437
Nineteenth Party Conference (1988)
   10
Nizhny Novgorod 205–6, 249, 250
nomenclatura 241, 242, 243–4
Nordex 154–5
Norilsk Nikel 257, 294
North Atlantic Co-operation Council
   127
Nosov, Grigory 115–16
Novy Mir 387
NTV 427–8, 444
nuclear weapons 124, 354, 364, 372
   deterioration and insecurity of
      126–7
   Gorbachev and disarmament 123
   and republics 125–6, 344

smuggling 126–7, 154, 156
Nye, Joe 372

Obshchaya Gazeta 423
Ogorodnikov, Alexander 169
oil industry 238, 270–77
    decline in use 272
    dislike of outsiders 274–5, 276–7,
        309
    emergence of new companies 273,
        274, 275
    fall in production 271
    marketization of 272
    price 222, 238, 272–3
    privatization 274
    reduction of state's stake in 274
    reserves around Caspian Sea 348–9
Okudzhava, Bulat 388–9, 436, 438
Omon Ra (Pelevin) 404, 405
Oneximbank 256, 257, 294
opera 400
orchestras 404
Orekhov, Andrei 148–9
Organization for Security and Co-
    operation in Europe (OSCE)
    366
organized crime 143, 145–6, 147–8,
    152–3, 156, 211, 287–8
orphans 316
ORT (Russian Public Television) 307,
    423, 428–30
Orthodox Church 157–71
    and Alexei II 42–3, 158, 161–4,
        166, 167, 171
    anti-Western 158
    and Catholicism 158, 167–8
    and communism 158
    and Father Men 168–9
    and Gorbachev 161
    indifference to 166–7
    relationship with state 158–61,
        169–70, 171
    splits within 159, 164–6
Ostankino 425, 426, 427, 428

Our Decameron (play) 419
'Our Home is Russia' 63–4, 79

Pain, Emil 181, 196, 201
PAKT 187
Pamyat 24, 25
Paramanova, Tatyana 59, 237, 293
Parkhomenko, Sergei 44–5
parliament *see* Congress of Peoples'
    Deputies; Duma
parliamentary elections
    (1993) 48–50, 51, 60, 68, 236
    (1995) 60–61, 62, 63, 64–6, 70, 71,
        296, 297, 436
    (1996) 253
parliamentary revolt (1993) 11, 16, 34,
    42–5, 47–8, 57, 111, 124, 183
Partnership for Peace 127, 363, 371
Party of Russian Unity and Accord 47,
    48, 61
Party of Unions and Industrialists 62
Pasternak, Boris 392
Pauls, Raymond 397
Pavlov, Georgy 150
Pavlov, Valentin xxviii, 210, 285
Pelevin, Victor 404, 406, 407
pensions 314
Peoples' Party of Free Russia 28
perestroika 208, 261, 322
Perestroika (company) 151, 300
Perm Business Club 176
Peter the Great statue 448–9
Petrov, Nikolai 402
Petrov-Vodkin, Kuzma 379
Petrushevskaya, Lyudmila 406–7
Philbro Energy 277
Pimen 161
Piyasheva, Larissa 246
poets 387, 390–91
Poland xiv, 101, 102, 213–14, 218,
    246
Polite Refusal 437
Poltaranin, Mikhail 36
Pomerantsev, Vladimir 387

Ponomaryev, Lev 62
pop music 397, 437–8
Popov, Gavril 24, 189
Poptsov, Oleg 91, 425
Posdnyakov, Yuri 66
poverty 212–13, 221, 311–12
'Power to the People' 261
Pravda 45, 72, 431
presidential elections (1996) 70, 71–91,
    430
  advertising 436
  and business élite 89
  cancellation option 89–90
  and Chubais 84–5
  and Gorbachev 77–8
  and Lebed 82–3, 86, 90, 119
  and media 86–7
  results 90
  sacking of 'war party' 90–91
  and Yavlinsky 63, 78–9, 86, 90
  and Yeltsin 71, 81, 83, 85–6, 87–9,
    90, 436
  and Zhirinovsky 79–81, 82, 86, 90
  and Zyuganov 75–7, 86, 87, 90, 92
press 45, 231, 307–8, 430–32, 434
prices, liberalization of 221–2, 231
Primakov, Yevgeny 136, 139–40,
    367–8
Primorsky Krai 186–8, 189
private property 143–4, 241
privatization 244–53, 256, 262, 290
  and banks 150, 241, 257, 282,
    289–90
  and corruption 150–51
  Chubais's programme for 51, 236,
    241–2, 244, 245, 247–9, 250,
    253, 256, 257, 258
  downfall of programme 250–52
  and foreign investment 252–3
  history of in other countries 245–6
  housing 317
  and managers 248, 249–50, 262
  numbers 248–9
  oil industry 274

in regions and republics 180
resistance to restructuring after xvi–
  xvii, xviii
second phase 150, 241–2, 256, 257
shop auctions 249
Prokhanov, Alexander 361, 431
property
  and crime 148, 150–51
  private 143–4, 241
protection gangs 223
Protestantism 158
Pudsintsev, Boris 140
Pugacheva, Alla 397
punk movement 437
Pushkin Square 414
pyramid selling scheme *see* MMM

Queue (Sorokin) 406–7

radicals 21–2
Rashidov, Sharaf 145–6
Rasputin, Valentin 26, 335
Razlogov, Kyrill 438
RCP (Russian Communist Party) 5,
  102
  banning of by Yeltsin 26
  blunders made 74–5
  economic programme 74
  membership 68
  and parliamentary elections (1993)
    48–9, 68
  programme 68–9
  recovery after banning 68, 72–3,
    324–5, 361
  weakness of not wanting to be in
    power 73–4
  see also Zyuganov, Gennady
realpolitik 375
Red October 294
referendum
  (April 1993) 35, 36, 103, 182
  (Dec 1993 constitution) 104–5
refugees 317–18
regions 186

consequences of parliamentary
revolt on 183
and constitution 184–5
extension of control of local
authorities 179–90
and privatization 180
relationship with Russian state
178–9, 181–2
seeking of protection of economies
179–80
Soviet system 172–3, 174
religion *see* Orthodox Church
Renaissance 292
Repentance (film) 381, 424
republics 19, 125, 173–90
adoption of separate currencies 227,
339, 340
and army 124
boycotting of referendum 182
budgets 179
closing of aid programme to 339–40
and constitution 104, 106, 182–3,
183–4
corruption 145–6
economic policy towards 234–5
'ethnicity' of 175
Federation Treaty 177, 181–2, 184,
194
growth of nationalism 177–8, 180,
332–4
issuing of credit to 226–7
and KGB 136
and nuclear weapons 125–6
and privatization 180
relationship with Russia 329–30,
337–9, 351
relationship with Soviet Union
173–5, 331–2
slackening of control over 175–6
Yeltsin's relationship with 172, 177,
182, 335–6
see also CIS; individual names
Resoin, Andrei 151
Resurrection 28

rock scene 398–9, 436–7
Rodionov, General Igor 92, 113, 117
Rodionov, Pyotr 277
Rodionov, Sergei 152
Rokhlin, General Lev 115
Rosneft 274
Rosvoruzhenie corporation 122
rouble 223, 238, 338
crashing of (Black Tuesday) 58, 59,
235, 237, 292
Rubtsov, Alexander 299–300, 301
Rudolf, Hans-Jorg 290, 292, 294
Rumyantsev, Oleg 100
Russia Our Home 307
Russia's Choice 46, 47, 63, 253
formation 46, 229, 306
parliamentary elections: (1993) 48,
50; (1995) 61, 220
Russian Academy of Painting,
Sculpture and Architecture
446
Russian All Peoples' Union 26
Russian Breakthrough 437
Russian Communist Party *see* RCP-
Russian Foreign Investment Council
308
Russian National Council 26
Russian National Credit Bank 293
Russian National Union 48
Russian Orthodox Church *see*
Orthodox Church
Russian Orthodox Church Abroad
161, 164–5
Russian Peoples' Assembly 26
Russian Public Television *see* ORT
Russian Union of Industrialists and
Entrepreneurs *see* Union of
Industrialists and Entrepreneurs
Russians
adoption of new ways of getting by
xviii–xix
disadvantaged position of 320–21
effect of economic reform 60,
212–13, 221

Rutskoi, General Alexander 5, 117, 413
  allegation of corruption against 36–7
  background and character 29–30
  and Communists for Democracy 23, 29
  and parliamentary revolt 42, 43, 44, 111
  and Yeltsin 29, 30, 38, 42
Ryazanov, Eldar 21, 394, 423
Rybakov, Anatoly 380–81, 383
Rybkin, Ivan 64
Ryzhkov, Nikolai 8, 11, 260–61, 262

Sachs, Jeffrey 236, 290
Sakharov, Andrei 8, 95, 96, 161, 319, 386, 410
Salmin, Alexei 201
Saltykov, Boris 221
Samokhvala, Lydia 73
Satarov, Georgy 63, 89
Schlesinger, James 365
scientists 385
Seabeco 155
Security Ministry *see* Ministry of Security
security services *see* intelligence services
Seliverstov, General Nikolai 115
Serbia 360
Sergeev, Alexei 227–8
Sergei, Patriarch 160, 164
service sector 207, 265, 313
Sevastopol 344
Sevodnya ('Today') 430, 431, 432
Shafarevich, Igor 24, 25
Shakhrai, Sergei 47, 63, 102, 103
Shamiev, Mintimer 177, 185
Shaposhnikov, Marshal Yevgeny 114
shares 290
Shatrov, Mikhail 391, 393, 416
Shebarshin, Leonid 140
Shelest, Pyotr 145

Shevardnadze, Eduard 125, 331, 350, 353, 354
Shirly Mirly ('What a Mess') 438, 439
Shokhin, Alexander 47, 217, 219, 221, 236, 237, 292
shops 205–6
  auction of 249
  privatized 205–6
  socialist 205, 206, 222, 249
Shumate, Joe 85
Shumeiko, Vladimir 32, 36, 48, 226
Shushkevich, Stanislaus 336, 341
Shutov, Sergie 414
Sinyavsky, Andrei 392
Skokov, Yuri 15, 64, 65, 66, 217, 358
Slapovsky, Alexei 408–9
small businesses 265
Smelyansky, Anatoly 383, 414, 416
Smolensky, Alexander 152, 301, 306
Sobchak, Anatoly 15
Sobyanin, Alexander 105
Sochi 145, 146
Social Democratic Party 100
social welfare 314, 318
socialist shops 205, 206, 222, 249
Sokolyansky, Alexander 398, 399
Sokov, Leonid 413
Solikamsk Paper Company 255
Solovyova, Inna 384, 386, 408
Solzhenitsyn, Alexander 7, 92, 382–3, 392
  cutting of television show 412–13, 429
  return to Russia after exile 410–11, 412–13
songs 388–90, 397–8
Sorokin, Vladimir 406–7
Soskovets, Oleg 55, 90, 91, 155, 236, 306
Sots Art 413–14, 422
SotsProf 322–3
South Korea 371
Sovetskaya Rossiya 72, 361
Soviet Union

collapse xiii, xxi, 14, 27
  legacy of xxi–xxiv
  nostalgia for 443, 444
Sovremennik theatre 392–3
Sovyetskaya Rossiya 430, 431
Spartacus (ballet) 402–3
SperBank 286
St Petersburg Philharmonic 401, 402
Stalin, Joseph xix, 160, 259, 315, 380,
  388, 390
Stanislavsky 416
Stankevich, Sergei 27, 338, 357
Starovoitova, Galina 22
Stas (magazine) 433
state enterprises 207, 209, 211, 274
  administration of services to workers
    313–14
  corruption 243
  Gorbachev's laws on 209, 243–4,
    298, 322
  managers of *see* managers
State Privatization Committee 38
Stepashin, Sergei 135, 139
Sterligov, Alexander 26
Stolichny Bank 286–7, 301, 429
Strategic Rocket Forces 126
Strauss, Robert 137, 142
Stroyev, Andrei 151, 300
subsidies 220, 222, 223, 236
Supreme Soviet 20, 32, 35, 36, 100,
  172, 225, 227, 260 *see also*
  Congress of Peoples' Deputies
Surgut Oil and Gas 251, 275

Tabakov, Anton 437
Taganka theatre 393–4, 417–18
Tajikistan 125, 348
Talbott, Strobe 213, 364, 365
Tarasov, Artyom 300
Tarkovsky, Andrei 395
Tatarstan 177, 180, 182, 184–6
  treaty with (1994) 106, 184, 185,
    186, 199
Tatlin, Vladimir 379

taxation xvi, 58, 224
Taxi Blues 440
Tblisi riots (1989) 113
television 423–9, 444
  commercials 422, 435
  glasnost era 423–4
  in nineties 424–5
  and NTV 427–8, 444
  and ORT 307, 423, 428–30
  and presidential elections 86
  and state 425
Ten Days that Shook the World (play)
  393
Ter-Petrosian, Levan 333
Thalwitz, Wilfrid 142
Thatcher, Margaret 21, 245, 366, 424
theatre 416–20, 423
  commercialization of 419
  glasnost era 381, 383, 417
  in nineties 400
  political suppression as source of
    energy 416
  revival of banned plays 418
  in sixties 392–4
Tikhomirov, Captain Alexei 126–7
Tikhon, Patriarch 159, 160
Tikhonov 300
Timofeevsky, Alexander 394–5
Tishkov, Valery 196
Todorovsky, Valery 440
Tokobank 287
Tolstaya, Tatyana 412
Top 152
Top Secret 430
Totskoye 128
trade 363
  with China 363
  liberalization of 223, 231
trade unions 242, 321–4
Transdnestr 345
Travkin, Nikolai 16, 23, 38
Tretyakov, Vitaly 48, 351, 431
Trifonov, Yuri 387–8
Troitsky, Artyom 433

Trska, Dusan 246
Tsereteli, Zurab 448
Tsipko, Alexander 27
Tsoy, Victor 399
Tuleyev, Aman 69
Tumanov, Vladimir 107–8
Tupolev, Andrei 266
Tuva 177

Ukraine 114, 214, 227, 235, 341–5, 351
   Church 165–6
   economy 343
   and nationalism 334, 342
   nuclear weapons 125–6, 344
   relationship with Russia 342–5
   and west 366
unemployment 256, 313
unemployment benefits 314
Uniates 165
Union of Industrialists and Entrepreneurs 28, 147, 228, 248
Union of United Co-operatives 300
unions see trade unions
United Commercial Bank 292
United States
   funding of Russian institutions 308
   joint military exercises with Russia 128
   relationship with Russia 364–6, 371–2
   Yeltsin's emphasis on partnership with 356, 358
Uralmash corporation 259–60, 296
Uzbekistan 366

Vainberg, Lev 299
Valentin, Bishop 164
Varennikov, General Valentin 75, 114
Varlamov, Alexei 409
Vasilyev, Dmitri 24
Vasilyev, Sergei 219, 233, 295
Velichko, General Valery 152
Veness, David 153

Video International 88
Vilnius
   shooting of civilians 425–6
Vishnevsky, Vsevolod 380
Vladimov, Georgy 409
Vladislavlev, Alexander 28
Vlasov, Yuri 134
Voigt, Karsten 129
Voinovich, Vladimir 392, 410–11
Volkogonov, Dmitri 160
Volsky, Arkady 27–9, 32, 59, 62, 228
Vorkuta 46
Vorobyev, General Eduard 196
Vorontsova, Natalya 426–7
Voshchanov, Pavel 73, 344
Vosnesensky, Andrei 387, 390, 439
Vozvrashchenie (Return) 319–20
Vyakhirev, Rem 277, 278
Vysotsky, Vladimir 388, 389–90

wages xvi, 60, 220, 265, 312
Walesa, Lech 127, 128
Warsaw Pact (1955) 112
weaponry 119, 120, 121–2 see also
   arms trade; nuclear weapons
White Nights 277
Witte, Sergei 352
women
   and business 305
Women of Russia 49, 62
workers
   and privatization programme 248
   see also labour movement
workers' clubs 322
Working Russia Party 73, 76
World Bank 224
writers see literature
Wyploscz-Pontbriand survey 263, 264

Xerox 435

Yabloko Party 47, 48, 62–3, 78, 229
Yak production plant 268
Yakobovsky, Dmitri 37

Yakovlev, Alexander (legal scholar) 95, 98

Yakovlev, Alexander (aircraft designer) 266

Yakovlev, Alexander (Gorbachev's aide) xxvii

Yakovlev, Vladimir 430

Yakovlev, Yegor 422

Yakunin, Father Gleb 23, 62, 134, 163

Yakunin, Victor 300–301

Yakutia 182

Yakutia-Sakha 182

Yankovskaya, Genrietta 418

Yasin, Yevgeny 228, 237–8

Yavlinsky, Grigory 28, 217, 228–9
    criticism of Gaidar's Gang 228–9
    policies 63, 229
    and presidential elections 63, 78–9, 86, 90
    and Yabloko Party 47, 62–3, 229

Yazov, General Dmitri xxviii, 111, 112, 114

Yeltsin, Boris xii, 334–5, 425
    achievements 5–6
    and army 123
    ascent to power xxviii-xxix, 3, 4, 11–14
    banning of parliament 34, 41, 42–3, 97
    behaviour in public 53
    character and qualities 3, 4, 9
    and Chechen war 16, 194–6, 201
    and Communist Party 7, 8, 11, 26
    compared to Gorbachev 6–7
    conflict with Congress 20, 23–4, 27, 31–3, 35–6, 40
    and constitution 47, 51, 99, 102–3, 105–6, 110
    on corruption 142–3
    and coup xxviii, 13, 14
    defining of presidency's role 19
    and democrats 38–9
    drinking 4, 11, 17, 20, 36, 52–3
    early political style 8–9, 9–10

    and economic reform 5, 18–19, 20, 35, 41, 51, 52, 217
    foreign policy xx, 355–7, 359, 362
    health 3, 16, 52, 86, 316
    and human rights 96–7
    KGB reform 133, 134, 137
    and Korzhakov 54
    leadership style 3–4, 4–5, 15–16, 17, 19, 21, 52–3, 55
    miners' support for 323
    on Nato expansion 127–8
    opposition to 24–31
    and parliamentary revolt 5, 42–4, 45, 47–8
    political background 7–12
    political philosophy in first term of office 15–16, 18–19
    and populism 10–11, 12, 16
    and presidential elections 71, 81, 83, 85–6, 87–9, 90, 436
    on privatization 246
    public opinion of 72
    relationship with Gorbachev 6–7, 9, 13, 14, 20
    and republics 172, 177, 182, 335–6
    and security services 138–9
    speeches 41, 51–2
    strengths 10
    view of by Western leaders 10, 364
    withdrawals from political life 52, 71

Yeltsin, Naina (wife) 7

Yeltsin, Tatyana see Dyanchenko, Tatyana

Yergorov, Nikolai 196

Yerin, Victor 156

Yerofeev, Venedict 406

Yerofeev, Victor 392, 407–8, 410, 436, 437

Yevtushenko, Yevgeny 377, 387, 390–91, 392

Yugoslavian crisis 360, 372

Yukos 257, 294

Yukunin, Gleb 161

Yushenkov, Sergei 195

Zakharov, Mark 416
Zakharov, Vyacheslav 147
Zaslavskaya, Tatyana 209
Zaverukha, Alexander 236
Zavgayev, Doku 193, 198
Zhenovach, Sergei 420
Zhirinovsky, Vladimir 11, 47, 104,
    361–2
  and parliamentary elections 49
  political style 66–8
  and presidential elections 79–81, 82,
    86, 90
  support of Yeltsin 66
Zhuk, Edward 307
'Zima Junction' (Yevtushenko)
    390–91

Zolotussky, Igor 408
Zorin, Leonid 392
Zorkin, Valery 35, 107, 183
Zosimov, Boris 301
Zyuganov, Gennady 68–70, 72, 73,
    84, 171
  and National Salvation Front
    26
  philosophy 75–6
  presidential elections 75–7, 86, 87,
    90, 92
  qualities and shortfalls 76
  and RCP 49, 68–9, 70
  speech to American Chamber of
    Commerce 67, 68, 69